THE BLACKWELL DICTIONARY OF
COGNITIVE PSYCHOLOGY

THE
BLACKWELL DICTIONARY OF
COGNITIVE
PSYCHOLOGY

Edited by

MICHAEL W. EYSENCK

Advisory editors

ANDREW ELLIS
EARL HUNT
PHILIP JOHNSON-LAIRD

BLACKWELL REFERENCE

First published 1990
First published in USA 1991

Basil Blackwell Ltd
108 Cowley Road, Oxford, OX4 1JF, UK

Basil Blackwell, Inc.
3 Cambridge Center
Cambridge, Massachusetts 02142, USA

British Library Cataloguing in Publication Data

The Blackwell dictionary of cognitive psychology.
1. Cognitive psychology
I. Eysenck, Michael W.   II. Ellis, Andrew   III. Hunt, E.
B. (Earl B)   IV. Johnson-Laird, Philip
153
ISBN 0-631-15682-8

Library of Congress Cataloging-in-Publication Data

The Blackwell dictionary of cognitive psychology/edited by Michael
W. Eysenck; advisory editors, Andrew Ellis, Earl Hunt, Philip Johnson-Laird.
p.   cm.
Includes bibliographical references.
ISBN 0-631-15682-8
1. Cognitive psychology – Dictionaries.   I. Eysenck, Michael W.
II. Ellis, Andrew W.   III. Hunt, Earl B.   IV. Johnson-Laird, P. N.
(Philip Nicholas), 1936–
BF311.B535   1990
153'.03 – dc20   90–34225   CIP

Typeset in 9.5 on 11pt Ehrhardt
by Wyvern Typesetting Ltd
Printed in Great Britain by Butler & Tanner Ltd,
Frome, Somerset

To my daughter Juliet with love

CONTENTS

PREFACE

THIS book had its origins in a pleasant lunch at an Italian restaurant in Belsize Park in north London. Philip Carpenter of Basil Blackwell and I agreed that the time was ripe for a comprehensive dictionary of cognitive psychology. Cognitive psychology has expanded and diversified in several different ways in recent years, and we felt that it would be valuable to attempt to encapsulate this diversity within a single volume. The great majority of books on cognitive psychology present a very limited perspective on the subject, and fail to depict accurately the variety of approaches, methods, and areas of research to be found in contemporary cognitive psychology.

An important reason for producing a dictionary of cognitive psychology is that the information-processing approach of cognitive psychology forms a "paradigm" in the sense used by T. S. Kuhn in his *The structure of scientific revolutions* (1962). According to Kuhn, periods of normal science are characterized by adherence to an overarching theoretical orientation or paradigm to which most scientists adhere. When the deficiencies of a paradigm become very obvious, then there is a period of revolutionary science culminating in the adoption of a new paradigm. Cognitive psychology began to challenge the previous paradigm (Behaviorism) in the mid-1950s, and replaced it as the dominant paradigm some years later. However, it is only relatively recently that the cognitive psychology paradigm became of importance in other areas, such as developmental psychology and social psychology.

Since cognitive psychology is of major importance on both sides of the Atlantic, it seemed appropriate that this dictionary should reflect that state of affairs. This was achieved in part by a judicious choice of contributors, and in part by the selection of the Advisory Editors. At the time the project started, two of the Advisory Editors (Andy Ellis and Phil Johnson-Laird) were working in the United Kingdom and the third one (Buzz Hunt) was working in North America. By the time that the book was finished, the balance had shifted, because Phil Johnson-Laird had moved to the United States.

Many thanks are due to the Advisory Editors for their efforts in the production of this book. Thanks are also due to those who contributed entries to the *Dictionary*. I was very fortunate that so many leading cognitive psychologists were willing to be involved in the project. Thanks are also due to several people at Blackwell, especially Richard Beatty whose patient persistence was invaluable in producing the book on time.

As ever, my wife Christine and our three children (Fleur, Willie, and Juliet) were important sources of support and encouragement during the preparation of this book. The book is dedicated to Juliet, because it is her turn (everyone else in the family having had a book dedicated to them). In any case, it is particularly appropriate that the book should be dedicated to her because of the number of times she climbed on to Daddy's lap and joined enthusiastically in the task of word processing.

MICHAEL W. EYSENCK
Egham, Surrey, March 1990

CONTRIBUTORS

KRISTEN JOAN ANDERSON
Northwestern University

M. D. BARRETT
Royal Holloway and Bedford New College,
University of London

LEE ROY BEACH
University of Arizona

J. GRAHAM BEAUMONT
University College of Swansea

VICKI BRUCE
University of Nottingham

PETER E. BRYANT
University of Oxford

RUTH BYRNE
University of Wales College of Cardiff

DONAL E. CARLSTON
University of Iowa

CHARLES S. CARVER
University of Miami

MICHILENE T. H. CHI
University of Pittsburgh

SVEN-AKE CHRISTIANSON,
University of Stockholm

HERBERT H. CLARK
Stanford University

GILLIAN COHEN
The Open University

ALLAN COLLINS
Northwestern University

STANLEY COREN
University of British Columbia

TOM COX
University of Nottingham

F. I. M. CRAIK
University of Toronto

C. J. DARWIN
University of Sussex

NORMAN F. DIXON
University College London

ERIC EICH
University of British Columbia

J. R. EISER
University of Exeter

ANDREW W. ELLIS
University of York

NOEL ENTWISTLE
University of Edinburgh

K. A. ERICSSON
University of Colorado at Boulder

J. ST. B. T. EVANS
Polytechnic South West

MICHAEL W. EYSENCK
Royal Holloway and Bedford New College,
University of London

RONALD A. FINKE
Texas A & M University

CAROL FOWLER
Dartmouth College and Haskins Laboratories

JOHN P. FRISBY
University of Sheffield

DEDRE GENTNER
Department of Psychology, University of Illinois
at Urbana-Champaign

K. J. GILHOOLY
University of Aberdeen

ROBERT GLASER
University of Pittsburgh

ROBERT GOLDSTONE
University of Michigan

JANE GOODMAN
University of Washington

DANIEL GOPHER
Technion, Israel Institute of Technology

V. H. GREGG
Birkbeck College, University of London

RICHARD J. HAIER
University of California, Irvine

CONTRIBUTORS

DIANE F. HALPERN
California State University, San Bernardino

MARGARET HARRIS
Royal Holloway and Bedford New College,
University of London

MILES HEWSTONE
University of Bristol

M. J. A. HOWE
University of Exeter

G. W. HUMPHREYS
University of Birmingham

G. V. JONES
University of Warwick

MARK T. KEANE
University of Wales College of Cardiff

RONALD T. KELLOGG
University of Missouri at Rolla

BETH KERR
University of Washington

S. M. KOSSLYN
Harvard University

ELIZABETH LOFTUS
University of Washington

J. B. LONG
University College London

COLIN M. MACLEOD
University of Toronto

PETER MCLEOD
University of Oxford

C. NEIL MACRAE
University of Aberdeen

A. S. R. MANSTEAD
University of Manchester

DAVID MARKS
Middlesex Polytechnic

MARYANNE MARTIN
University of Oxford

RICHARD E. MAYER
University of California, Santa Barbara

DOUGLAS L. MEDIN
University of Illinois at Urbana-Champaign

T. R. MILES
University College of North Wales

PETER E. MORRIS
University of Lancaster

T. O. NELSON
University of Washington

KEITH OATLEY
University of Glasgow

DONALD H. OWINGS
University of California at Davis

A. U. PAIVIO
University of Western Ontario

STEPHEN E. PALMER
University of California at Berkeley

A. J. PARKIN
University of Sussex

LAWRENCE M. PARSONS
University of Texas at Austin

PATRICK RABBITT
University of Manchester

D. A. ROSENBAUM
University of Massachusetts at Amherst

D. R. RUTTER
University of Kent at Canterbury

LEE RYAN
University of British Columbia

A. J. SANFORD
University of Glasgow

MICHAEL F. SCHEIER
Carnegie Mellon University

A. M. SLATER
University of Exeter

EDWARD E. SMITH
University of Michigan

CHRISTINE M. TEMPLE
Royal Holloway and Bedford New College,
University of London

STEVEN P. TIPPER
Mount Allison University

ENDEL TULVING
University of Toronto

DOUGLAS VICKERS
University of Adelaide

G. F. WAGSTAFF
University of Liverpool

L. WEISKRANTZ
University of Oxford

J. M. WILDING
Royal Holloway and Bedford New College,
University of London

SPECIAL NOTE

Preparation of the article "self-focus and self-attention" by Charles S. Carver and Michael F. Scheier was facilitated by grants BNS87–06271 and BNS87–17783 from the National Science Foundation.

INTRODUCTION

As little as 15 or 20 years ago, cognitive psychology was rather limited in various ways. Most cognitive psychologists only investigated cognition in normal adult subjects under laboratory conditions. As a consequence, it was frequently pointed out that cognitive psychology had relatively little relevance to real-life issues; in other words, it lacked ecological validity. In contrast, contemporary cognitive psychology is characterized by its diversity. Probably the most important element in that diversity is the number of major approaches that can be identified within the general ambit of cognitive psychology. In addition to traditional experimental cognitive psychology, there are also cognitive neuropsychology and cognitive science or artificial intelligence. Cognitive neuropsychologists argue that the study of cognition in brain-damaged patients can elucidate normal cognitive functioning. Cognitive scientists maintain that the computer metaphor for the human brain is a useful one, and they have devised computational models to clarify our understanding of cognitive processes. It could also be argued that there is a fourth approach which one might term "applied cognitive psychology." However, its methods do not appear to be distinctively different from those of the other approaches.

Diversity is apparent in the range of individuals or groups whose cognitive functioning is assessed. Numerous researchers have considered cognition in young children or the elderly, in various clinical groups (e.g. brain-damaged patients, anxious patients, depressed patients), or in special groups (e.g. eidetikers, *idiots savants*). Diversity is also to be found in terms of the research areas to which cognitive psychology has been applied. Far more than used to be the case, cognitive psychologists are working in the fields of social psychology, developmental psychology, personality psychology, and human factors.

One of the main intentions in producing the *Dictionary* is to provide the reader with the scope and diversity of contemporary cognitive psychology. Inevitably, views will differ as to what does, and does not, form part of cognitive psychology. The approach taken in this book is that the central core of cognitive psychology is primarily concerned with elucidating the processes, structures, and representations involved in human cognition. It is assumed that the human mind should be regarded as an information-processing system. Attention, perception, learning, memory, language, thinking, and problem solving all form part of the cognitive system. As a result of this orientation, most (but not all) of the work carried out within cognitive science and artificial intelligence falls within the scope of the *Dictionary*. The work of those who devise computer programs without considering the potential relevance of those programs to human cognitive functioning is excluded, whereas the work of those who attempt to devise programs that mimic or simulate human cognition is included.

In order to make the boundaries of cognitive psychology as clear as possible, it is useful to consider another example. Some research in applied cognitive psychology (e.g. eyewitness testimony) falls within the scope of the *Dictionary*, but some does not. The acid test is whether or not the research is informative about the detailed functioning of the cognitive system.

There is always a danger with a dictionary like this that the subject may appear to be very fragmented and unorganized. Various steps have been taken in an attempt to prevent this happening and to facilitate the reader's task in finding his or her way around the *Dictionary*. First, there are numerous cross-references, indicated in the text by SMALL CAPITALS, so that the reader can build up a picture of the interconnections between topics within psychology. Second, there are some topics within cognitive psychology (e.g. memory) which are of sufficient importance that there are several entries of relevance to them. What has been done in those cases is to include an entry corresponding to the topic area (e.g. memory); this serves to point the reader toward the entries subsumed under that topic area, and indicates how those entries relate to each other. Third, the general policy has been to entitle each entry in the form that is normally used to describe the topic in question. For example, while one might argue that working memory is a type of memory and should be under the heading "memory, working," the heading actually used is the more familiar and less clumsy "working memory." However, anyone who looks up "memory, working" will find there a cross-reference to "working memory."

It should be noted that several letters of the alphabet – K, O, Q, U, X and Z – did not have any entries falling under them, and so these alphabetical sections do not appear in the book.

The Editor and the Advisory Editors combined forces in order to produce a coherent set of entries that would provide good coverage of the topics which are important in current cognitive psychology. However, it is probably prudent to assume that there will be some omissions. It is to be hoped that the reader will be tolerant of such minor imperfections.

A

absent-mindedness The term used to describe a lack of attentiveness to what is going on. Psychologists tend to study a particular form of absent-mindedness known as "action slips" which involve the performance of actions that were not intended. As the term "absent-mindedness" suggests, attentional failures typically play a major role in producing action slips. However, a detailed analysis of action slips indicates that various other factors are involved.

Since action slips and other forms of absent-mindedness are difficult (though not impossible) to create under laboratory conditions, the usual method of investigating action slips is by asking several people to keep records of their own action slips. Norman (1981) and Reason and Mycielska (1982) carried out diary studies, with the latter investigators collecting a total of 625 action slips from 98 people. While it is possible to assign action slips to different categories, it would be unwarranted to attach much significance to the percentages of action slips falling into the various categories. One reason for this is that the figures are obviously based only on those action slips that were actually detected by those keeping diaries, and so we have no direct knowledge of those slips that were not noticed. Another reason is that the number of times a particular kind of action slip occurs is meaningful only in the context of the number of occasions on which that kind of action slip could potentially have occurred.

It is possible to account for most action slips by drawing a distinction between two modes of control over motor performance (cf. Reason & Mycielska, 1982). A closed-loop or feedback mode of control is used during the early stages of motor learning. This involves a central processor or attentional system utilizing feedback of a visual and proprioceptive nature to provide moment-by-moment control of behavior (*see* ATTENTION; PERCEPTUAL MOTOR COORD-INATION). After prolonged practice, this closed-loop mode of control is more and more abandoned in favor of an open-loop mode of control in which behavior is controlled in a relatively automatic fashion by motor programs or by pre-arranged instruction sequences (*see* AUTOMATIC PROCESSING). In essence, action slips tend to occur when the open-loop mode of control is used at those points in behavior where use of the closed-loop mode of control is necessary for accurate performance.

One of the interesting characteristics of action slips is that they typically occur during the performance of activities which are highly practised and overlearned. This is somewhat surprising, because practice usually produces a substantial improvement in performance and a reduction in the tendency to make errors. Practice permits use of the open-loop mode of control, which has the advantage of freeing attentional resources to engage in other processing activities. However, if the open-loop model of control is used too extensively, then errors will occur.

See also REALITY MONITORING.

BIBLIOGRAPHY

Norman, D. A. (1981). Categorisation of action slips. *Psychological Review, 88,* 1–15.
Reason, J. T., & Mycielska, K. (1982). *Absent minded? The psychology of mental lapses and everyday errors.* Englewood Cliffs, NJ: Prentice-Hall.

MICHAEL W. EYSENCK

acquired dyslexia *See* DYSLEXIAS: ACQUIRED.

aging and cognitive change The attempt to apply the assumptions, methodology, and models of cognitive psychology to the study of old age provides an important test of the extent to which the discipline can illuminate the human condition. A particularly provocative theoretical challenge has been whether and how the functional models for hypothetical "steady state" systems, found in the cognitive psychology of the 1960s and 1970s, but never in nature, can be developed to describe complex patterns of change. These static models were linked to a "modular" neuropsychology (see MODULARITY OF MIND) which assumed that changes in cognitive performance following brain damage were only of theoretical interest if they could be related to anatomically well defined lesions, putatively focal to particular hypothetical cortical mechanisms and implicitly to very tightly definable cognitive functions associated with these areas (see COGNITIVE NEUROPSYCHOLOGY). In this context the study of the aging brain seemed theoretically sterile since it forces attention away from localized and complete extirpation of supposedly "modular" structures with putatively independent and discrete functions and toward the cognitive effects of global and diffuse biochemical, histological, and neurophysiological changes.

The study of cognitive aging also forces us to consider problems which contemporary neuropsychology still prefers to neglect – the extent to which "local" damage can have global effects on cortical function and the interrelationship between the extent to which cognitive skills have been practiced, or memory databases have been developed, and their relative vulnerability to insult or degeneration. In short, the relationship between learning and the plasticity of the neurophysiological substrate on which cognitive processes depend.

Given that even very healthy people obviously do show gross changes in cognitive performance as they grow older, the main questions for cognitive gerontology are few and simple: At what age are the first changes detectable? How quickly do changes then proceed? Do all cognitive skills decline together – perhaps because they are all common outcomes of the same global neuropathological processes – or do different cognitive skills, and so perhaps the separate "modular" brain systems on which they depend, "age" at different rates? (Do we lose all our faculties together, or one at a time, and, if the latter, in what order?) Can we alter the rate, or the pattern, of cognitive change; for example can heroically persistent practice of cognitive skills prevent their decline? Finally there are the existential questions which psychology has alternately muddled and avoided for far too long: What is the *experience* of growing old? How far are individuals conscious of the cognitive changes they suffer, and can they adapt to, or circumvent, them? The present state of cognitive gerontology can be assessed in terms of the extent to which it can give sensible answers to these basic questions.

Cognitive changes in old age are driven by two distinct processes: gradual and, in our present state of knowledge, irreversible degenerative changes in the central nervous system (CNS) (e.g. Rockstein & Sussman, 1979) and the steady accretion, throughout life, of an increasing database of knowledge about the world and an armamentarium of cognitive skills. Considering this latter source of change it is not disingenuous to consider "cognitive aging" as a process which is continuous throughout life and which can only artificially be distinguished from the "developmental processes" of infancy, childhood, and adolescence. Without stretching a metaphor the same can be said of CNS aging. Most of our body cells have a limited lifetime, reproducing themselves by division before dying so that their population is entirely renewed every nine to twelve years. Neurons, in contrast, do not reproduce so that at any age the CNS units we have left are survivors of a much larger number with which we were born. These veterans may continue to grow new dendrites and form new connections with each other throughout their, and our, lifespans. If, as seems probable, changing networks of connections between neurons constitute the biological basis of information storage in the CNS, the fact that our entire corpus of neurons, and so of established connective networks, does not change every decade is an essential design feature providing some stability for memories, information, and skills which we would otherwise have to continually refresh or lose.

The period of maximum neuron loss occurs within the first three years of life and, speculatively, may reflect a process of the establishment and preservation of networks of "useful" connections with loss of units which are not incorporated into such systems. Autopsy data suggest that neuron loss is continuous throughout life so that by age 75 even healthy individuals may have lost up to 10 percent of their young adult brain mass, with temporal and frontal cortex more depleted than other areas. These gross changes are paralleled, perhaps preceded, by changes in individual cells whose bodies and processes begin to incorporate "neurofibrilliary tangles" of lipids, and which may progressively be denuded of their dendritic connections to other units. Surviving units may greatly increase the number of their dendritic processes, speculatively in compensatory attempts to preserve connectivity. Increasing numbers of "senile plaques" mark microscopic areas of neural degeneration. All these histological changes have been observed in young adult brains and, as far as we know, it is the increasing prevalence, rather than the precise nature, of these indicators that characterizes the aging of the brain. It is also likely that even in "normal" aging, specific changes in larger neural structures such as the cholinergic, dopaminergic, and serotinergic neurotransmitter systems which are strongly marked in age-related neurological disorders such as Dementia of the Alzheimer type (DAT) or Parkinson's disease may also occur in "normal" aging. It is still a matter for debate how far these conditions (for example, DAT) reflect step functions of neuropathology, or accelerations of a continuous process toward an inevitable terminal state.

We should not bleakly conclude that intellectual decline may begin even before maturation is completed because it is likely that the gross redundancy of the CNS allows substantial losses of individual units to be tolerated without loss of efficiency, and it is certain that the highest levels of cognitive skills require extremely extended practice, making the passage of time a precondition, rather than a restraint, of attainment. The common-sense idea that a steady decline in absolute capacity is offset by continuous improvements due to learning and practice fits the general pattern of data available. The largest bodies of data come from standardizations of tests of performance IQ and of creativity, and these show measurable declines in average scores between the ages of 25 and 35 years (e.g. Wechsler, 1956). Recent investigations of learning of complex, fast interactive video-games show impairment between 18 and 36 years (e.g. Rabbitt, Banerji, & Szemanski, 1989). Such results are typical of tasks in which novel information has to be processed as rapidly as possible, but strongly contrast with tasks which require unpaced deployment of acquired information, such as vocabulary tests, which may show no loss and even some increase throughout a lifetime of 80 years. Horn (1982) first formalized this contrast as a distinction between "fluid intelligence," associated with maximum information-processing speed, which steadily declines after a peak in the twenties, and "crystallized intelligence" or acquired information and intellectual skills, which may show little age-related loss (see INTELLIGENCE).

This distinction reappears in statistical analyses of lifespan achievements pioneered by H. C. Lehman (e.g. 1957), whose analyses of biographical data suggest that in all professions a relatively early peak is followed by a long slow decline, but that peaks are later and declines less prolonged in disciplines such as history and literature which require the long acquisition and massive deployment of vast bodies of information than in those such as Mathematics which demand the ability to perceive new problems and find entirely original solutions to them. Lehman's conclusions have been criticized and qualified (e.g. by Dennis, 1966; Fox, 1983) but, in general, it seems that the lifetime course of cognitive attainment does represent a shifting balance between continuous loss of "raw" information-processing capacity and problem-solving ability and steady acquisition of information and useful techniques.

Thus the simple question "How fast do cognitive changes proceed once they have begun?" can only be discussed evasively in

3

terms of a shifting balance between individuals' hypothetical initial maximum potentials and their lifetime opportunities and motivation for self-development. It also raises severe methodological problems. Most data on age changes of any kind are "cross-sectional"; that is, mean performance scores for different, samples of individuals in successive age groups. With the possible exception of vocabulary test scores and measures of "crystallized intelligence", all such data show a peak of performance attained in the twenties or early thirties followed by a continuous decline which sharply accelerates in the sixties, seventies, and eighties. A much more laborious alternative is to obtain longitudinal data on the course of aging within rather than between individuals by repeatedly testing them over many years. The logistic difficulty of such comparisons makes such studies rare and, usually, incomplete. However, some authors have found that particular individuals may show little or no change in cognitive function as they age through and beyond their seventies. This has led to an alternative to the "continuous decline" model of aging in which a long plateau of indefinite duration is succeeded by a "terminal drop" in performance, possibly associated with pathologies leading to immanent death; (e.g. Jarvik, 1983). On such assumptions "time backward from death" is a much more interesting index of current cognitive age than "time forwards from birth." It is important to note that it is not at all incompatible that "plateau and drop" age-performance trajectories are often obtained for longitudinal data on individuals while "continuous-decline" trajectories are invariably obtained for cross-sectional data on means of successive age samples. The terminal drop model assumes that while the trajectory for any individual shows a plateau, individuals tend to begin their terminal declines at different ages and that the ratio of "droppers" to "survivors" increases with group mean age. Thus it follows that there will be a continuous decline in mean performance levels for successive groups although the age-performance function for each individual is, in fact, rectangular.

Unfortunately, longitudinal studies do not offer a simple, if arduous, resolution to this problem because they also have their characteristic methodological difficulties. Retrospective reanalyses of published data by Schaie and Labouvie-Vief (1974), among others, have found that longitudinally assessed rates of change may differ between successive generations of individuals who apparently age at different rates. More disturbingly, recent and as yet unpublished very large-scale studies by Flynn and by Raven reveal further difficulties because scores on a wide range of IQ tests obtained from very large samples of young adults, in many different cultures, over the last 50 years seem to show a continuous increase with historical decade. It remains uncertain to what extent this may reflect general medical and social improvements such as in health, hygiene, nutrition, and general education or increasingly widespread specific practice on problems similar to those encountered in IQ tests. In any of these cases it is clear that the original standardization data for older IQ tests is no longer valid for contemporary population samples. This possibility that the performance indices we use as well as the people we test may "age" during the course of longitudinal investigations compounds difficulties of interpretation when large groups of people are, perforce, progressively practiced on the tasks on which they are repeatedly assessed. An important, optimistic conclusion is that the "continuous decline" age-performance functions currently observed may be contrasted with rectangular functions which represent the ideal, obtainable by medical and social advances, both for populations and for individuals.

The next question is whether all cognitive functions change at the same rate, possibly driven by a global change in CNS efficiency, or whether functionally distinct abilities decline at different rates, perhaps determined by idiosyncratic rates of change in the neurophysiological "modules" which support them.

It has been noted that cognitive skills which require the rapid handling of novel information show early and marked declines while those based on the retrieval of learned information or procedures show little change with age. Recent unpublished work by Bryan, Perfect, and Rabbitt suggests that even when information can be accurately retrieved, the speed with which it can be accessed markedly declines as age advances. It seems that age may affect the *accessibility* of information even when its *availability* is apparently unimpaired. Horn (1982) has shown that age changes in performance on tests of "fluid intelligence" show factor commonalities with tests of information-processing rate. Eysenck (1986) and Jensen (1985), among others, make a case for the idea that "g," a single factor of "general intelligence" on which most IQ tests appear to load highly, can be identified as information-processing rate, a performance index common to most laboratory tasks and so, plausibly, a sensitive index of general neural efficiency. Salthouse (1986) suggests that slowing of information-processing rate is the most general and sensitive index of cognitive aging. Experiments by Waugh and Barr (1980) show that slowing of information-processing rate may underlie and determine age differences in learning efficiency, since learning rates of young and older individuals may be equated by allowing the elderly longer study times to compensate for their slower information uptake. These and many other observations seem to support Salthouse's suggestion that a coherent theory of cognitive aging may be predicated on decline in a single general factor of information-processing speed which affects all mental functions.

The attractive idea of a single common factor, which accounts for individual differences in fluid intelligence and for its decline in old age, together with all other aspects of cognitive performance, founders on points of logic rather than of empirical evidence or theoretical plausibility. When we attempt to quantitatively assess human performance, whether by laboratory tasks, intelligence tests, or evaluations of cognitive efficiency in everyday skills, we can only measure how fast or how accurately people do things. As Hick (1952) first pointed out, the index of "information-processing rate" necessarily represents a composite measure, or "equivocation" in which speed and accuracy are jointly taken into account. Thus, *information-processing rate is a performance index logically implicit in all our empirical measurements* rather than, as taken by Eysenck, Jensen, and Salthouse, a privileged index of some functional property of the CNS upon whose relative value theories of intelligence or of cognitive aging can be based. Because nearly all our measures of task performance, including scores on all time-limited intelligence tests, are directly translatable into measures of information-processing rate, it is statistically inevitable rather than functionally important that analyses of between-subject variance across a variety of tasks should yield a single, general factor common to all of them.

Thus, statements that information-processing rate can be considered a single, principal factor in cognitive aging, or in individual differences in intelligence, is bound to be true, but cannot be analytic; i.e. they do not address the question of whether discrete functional "modules," and the skills which they hypothetically support, age at equal or at different rates. Such questions can only usefully be asked by identifying skills which, by studies of focal lesions, have been shown to be associated with particular brain systems and then by carrying out very large-scale investigations to examine the joint regressions, across very large populations, of performance indices for these skills against each other, against chronological age, and against measures of information-processing rate so as to discover to what extent these sets of indices show common, and to what extent idiosyncratic, variance between individuals.

An interesting hypothesis which lends itself to such treatment is that the right cortical hemisphere "ages" faster than the left so that skills such as accurate perception and memory for patterns may decline more rapidly with age than "left hemisphere" skills such as logical computation or linguistic dexterity (*see* HEMISPHERIC LOCALIZATION). While some interesting and well conducted studies seem to support this hypothesis (e.g. Albert, Duffy, & Naeser, 1987), as we have seen, the degree to which cognitive skills survive into old age seems to depend on the extent to which they are based on information and procedures learned over very long periods of time. Our models of the human cognitive system are not yet sufficiently developed to answer important questions about plasticity and its maintenance into old age, i.e. whether identifiable cognitive performances such as "pattern perception" or "language" have been rendered "domain specific" as much by the very extended practice which created them, and which may maintain them in old age, as by the architecture of the particular, anatomically localizable neuronal "modules" which support them. The further question as to whether, and how, practice of a skill may contribute to the continued health and longevity of the particular neural substrate that maintains it also remains obscure. In the present state of knowledge we can only be certain that any regimen which maintains bodily health must benefit the CNS also. As far as we know "jogging one's memory" is probably more effective if undertaken with the feet than by attempts at intellectual athleticism.

A final question is the extent to which individuals are aware of, and can adapt to or learn to circumvent, the cognitive changes which may occur as they grow old. This is of considerable interest in current cognitive theory as a particular instantiation of the general question of how far individuals are consciously aware of their own cognitive processes and how accurately they can monitor and adapt them. The invariable methodology for such investigations is to ask individuals to rate their own ability, or their frequencies of lapses on self-report questionnaires (*see* METACOGNITION). Such studies of changes in self-report with advancing age give remarkably consistent results which highlight some logical problems with this technique. When large populations of older people are interrogated about their memory efficiency, their relative reported frequencies of cognitive lapses, or the frequency with which they mislay their possessions, or their perceived memory deterioration over the last 30 years, the results are remarkably consistent. Individuals' self-reports bear no relation to their IQ test scores, and correlate *negatively* with their ages, so that individuals in their fifties complain of poorer performance than do individuals in their sixties and seventies.

It is, of course, difficult to assess individuals' subjective self-reports against their actual everyday competence, but recent studies have found precisely the same results in comparisons where performance can be objectively assessed – in the case of mild deafness or growing, mild visual handicap. Although, as we would expect, individuals in their fifties show significantly less impairment, their complaints are more frequent and severe. The clue to this paradox is that individuals have no way of making absolute judgements about their own cognitive or, it would seem, sensory abilities. They can only make relative judgements, assessing themselves against companions or colleagues or against the demands of their environments. Individuals in their fifties are usually very much engaged in life and may be unduly self-conscious of their aging in confrontation with taxing demands or able young colleagues. As people grow older their lives and environments change, and may become steadily less demanding. Individuals who maintain homeostasis with their social and work environments receive little feedback which might draw their attention to changes in their capacities. It is pleasant to be able to conclude a commentary on cognitive changes in old age with the reflection that individuals who anxiously perceive deterioration in their cognitive efficiency are probably those who are, as yet, least affected, and have least cause for concern.

See also AGING AND MEMORY.

BIBLIOGRAPHY

Albert, M., Duffy, F., & Naeser, M. (1987). Non-linear changes in memory and cognition with age and their neuropsychological correlates. *Canadian Journal of Psychology*, *41*, 141–57.

Dennis, W. (1966). Creative productivity between the ages of 20 and 80 years. *Journal of Gerontology*, *21*, 1–8.

Eysenck, H. J. (1986). The theory of intelligence and the psychophysiology of cognition. In R. J. Sternberg (Ed.), *Advances in the psychology of human intelligence* (Vol. 3). Hillsdale, NJ: Lawrence Erlbaum.

Fox, M. F. (1983). Publication productivity among scientists. *Social Studies of Science*, *13*, 285–305.

Hick, W. E. (1952). On the rate of gain of information. *Quarterly Journal of Experimental Psychology*, *4*, 11–26.

Horn, J. L. (1982). The aging of human abilities. In B. B. Wolman (Ed.), *Handbook of Developmental Psychology* (pp. 847–70). Englewood Cliffs, NJ: Prentice-Hall.

Jarvik, L. (1983). Age is in – is the wit out? In D. Samuel, S. Aligheri, S. Gershon, V. E. Grimm, & G. Toffant (Eds), *Aging of the brain*. New York: Raven Press.

Jensen, A. R. (1985). The nature of the black–white difference on various psychometric tests: Spearman's hypothesis. *The Behavioral and Brain Sciences, 8*, 193–219.

Lehman, H. C. (1957). The chemist's most creative years. *Science, 127*, 1213–22.

Rabbitt, P. M. A., Banerji, N., & Szemanski, A. (1989). Space Fortress as an IQ test? Predictions of learning and practised performance in a complex interactive video game. *Acta Psychologica, 71*, 243–57.

Rockstein, M., & Sussman, M. (1979). *Biology of aging*. Belmont, Calif.: Wadsworth.

Salthouse, T. (1986). *A cognitive theory of aging*. Berlin: Springer-Verlag.

Schaie, K. W., & Labouvie-Vief, G. (1974). Generational vs ontogenetic components of change in adult cognitive behaviour: A 14 year cross-sequential study. *Developmental Psychology, 10*, 305–20.

Waugh, N. C., & Barr, R. (1980). Memory and mental tempo. In L. W. Poon, J. Cermak, D. Arenberg, & L. Thompson (Eds), *New directions in memory and aging*. Hillsdale, NJ: Lawrence Erlbaum.

Wechsler, D. (1956). *Manual for the Wechsler Adult Intelligence Scale*. New York: Psychological Corporation.

PATRICK RABBITT

aging and memory Most people believe that their ability to learn and remember declines with advancing age, and in general this belief is confirmed by experimental evidence. However, demonstrations of age-related decrements in ability must be treated cautiously for two main sets of reasons: the first is that other factors besides age may be responsible for the observed differences, and the second is that the overall picture of decline masks a more complex pattern in which some types of memory are found to hold up well with age whereas other types decline substantially. In the first category, there is a greater incidence of depression in older people and some memory failures are clearly associated with this condition. Other difficulties of interpretation arise from the usual practice of comparing a young group in their teens and twenties with an older group in their sixties and seventies; the two groups almost always differ in terms of their early educational experiences, and may differ in health, motivation, recent educational experience, and other variables. However, the alternative research strategy of carrying out longitudinal rather than cross-sectional studies is somewhat impracticable, and a reasonable solution may be found in work demonstrating the modifying effects of health, verbal intelligence, activity levels, and the like on the relations between memory and aging.

The second complicating factor is the very different patterns of age-related effects observed on different memory tasks. For example, digit span (the longest string of random digits that a person can reproduce accurately) shows a very slight decline with age, as does memory for world knowledge and for vocabulary. On the other hand, the ability to recall a long set of unrelated words or objects decreases dramatically with increasing age, as does the ability to hold some material in mind while simultaneously carrying out manipulations on the material or while dealing with further incoming material (*see* WORKING MEMORY). Various suggestions have been made to explain such differential patterns. One is that different memory stores exist (e.g. short-term and long-term stores) and that the processes of aging affect the stores differently. An analogous suggestion is that the proposed memory systems of episodic, semantic, and procedural memory are tapped differentially by various memory tasks, and that these systems age at different rates. These and other accounts will be assessed after a review of the evidence.

SHORT-TERM MEMORY

The term "short-term memory" is used here to denote a type of task rather than any special store or system; the tasks in question are those in which the person must hold a small amount of material in mind for a matter of 2–30 sec. (*see* SHORT-TERM MEMORY). As previously mentioned, performance on standard digit span tests declines only slightly from the twenties to the seventies (see Craik, 1977, for a review), although *backward* digit span, and the "alpha span" test devised by Mary Gick and myself do show greater age-related deficits. In the alpha span test, a short list of words is presented and the subject's task is to rearrange the words mentally before reproducing them in alphabetical order. It seems that the requirement to manipulate materials held in mind is associated with poorer performance in older people.

Other traditional short-term memory tasks include the Brown–Peterson paradigm in which subjects are presented with three or four letters or unrelated words to be recalled after a filled retention interval of 0–30 sec. Age differences on this task are again slight, as they are also in the retrieval of the last few items in a list of words presented for free recall (Craik, 1977) (*see* RECENCY EFFECT). Performance levels on the digit span test, the Brown–Peterson task, and in the last-mentioned task of retrieval all depend on the ability to hold a small number of items in mind and reproduce them in the same order. This ability has been described as depending on "primary memory" and shows little change as a function of aging.

It was suggested previously that the requirement to manipulate material held in mind does give rise to age-related decrements. This type of manipulation is inherent in working memory tasks, and indeed other such tasks appear to be vulnerable to the effects of aging. As one example, age differences were found in a task in which subjects were presented with a series of sentences whose truth had to be verified (e.g. "Sparrows build nests in the spring," "An elephant is smaller than a mouse"); then at the end of the series subjects recalled the final word from each sentence ("spring, mouse … etc."). The effects of aging were especially marked when the sentences were grammatically complex (Gick, Craik, & Morris, 1988).

In summary, age differences are typically slight or non-existent in short-term memory tasks requiring verbatim reproduction of the material ("primary memory" tasks), whereas age differences can be substantial when the task requires manipulation and reorganization, or requires a division of attention between holding some items while dealing with further incoming material ("working memory" tasks). However, rather than thinking of these two types of task as involving different stores or mechanisms, it seems preferable to think of a range of tasks requiring active manipulation to a greater or lesser degree.

LONG-TERM MEMORY

When memory proper is considered – that is, memory for events that took place minutes, hours, or years ago – the evidence again shows that age differences are much greater in some circumstances than in others (*see* LONG-TERM MEMORY). It is well established, for example, that performance on recognition tasks (in which the target item is re-presented along with new distractor items) declines only slightly with age, whereas age-related decrements are greater in cued recall tasks, and even greater in free recall tasks in which no explicit cues are provided (Craik, 1977; Salthouse, 1982; Craik & Rabinowitz, 1984) (*see* RECALL; RECOGNITION MEMORY). At first it might seem that the age difference is simply a function of task difficulty, with differences being slighter in the easier recognition task. This does not appear to be the case, however; in an experiment in which recognition was made more difficult than recall by manipulating list lengths and retention intervals, the age decrement remained greater on the recall task (Craik & McDowd, 1987). A straightforward account of this pattern of differences is that older people have particular problems with the *retrieval* of information, and that retrieval problems are greater in recall tasks than in recognition tasks (Burke & Light, 1981). An extension of this idea is that all memory processes, at both encoding and retrieval, depend on a mixture of processes driven by external stimuli and processes initiated from within by the subject. Tasks like recognition memory receive a great deal of support from environmental stimuli, whereas recall tasks receive less environmental support and must therefore rely to a much greater extent on self-initiated mental operations. Craik (1983) suggested that age decrements are found in proportion to the amount of self-initiated processing that particular tasks demand; the point is similar to Hasher and Zacks's (1979) suggestion that age decrements increase as the task becomes more "effortful."

A number of recent studies yield results in line with the notion that age decrements in memory are least when the task receives good environmental support. As one example, Craik and Rabinowitz (1984) describe a study by Waddell and Rogoff in which the investigators presented a set of 30 miniature items (animals, cars, people, etc.) either on a model panorama consisting of roads, fields, and buildings, or in featureless cubicles, the task being to remember the spatial position of each miniature item. The subjects were middle-aged and older women. In the cubicle condition performance levels were 73 percent and 36 percent respectively, but in the more "supportive" panorama condition the levels were 75 percent and 72 percent respectively: that is, the greater amounts of environmental support in the panorama condition were differentially helpful to the older group.

Although the argument is still somewhat speculative (for an alternative account, see Burke & Light, 1981) it therefore seems possible to suggest that age-related differences in memory for specific events are the result of less efficient processing at both encoding and retrieval. At encoding, older people do not form as deep, as distinctive, or as contextually specific representations of episodic events as do their younger counterparts, and at retrieval they are less efficient in reinstating the mental configuration that corresponds to remembering the original event (Craik, 1983). Both types of inefficiency can be overcome, however, by the provision of appropriate environmental support.

Two other sets of observations also fit this general descriptive framework. The first set concerns "prospective memory" or remembering to do things at a future time – to phone a friend in an hour's time or to pick up milk on the way home from work, for example. Such prospective actions often have few environmental reminders associated with them and to that extent are liable to be forgotten. There is emerging evidence that older people are particularly vulnerable to this type of forgetting, although evidence that is both rigorous and "ecologically valid" is difficult to obtain. Anecdotally at least, people report that they are more likely to leave reminders for themselves – letters to mail placed by the door, notes by the telephone – as they get older. The second set of observations concerns so-called implicit memory tasks. Such tasks do not require the subject to recollect the original episode, but merely to carry out some operation like identifying a word flashed very briefly on a computer screen or completing a word presented with some of its letters missing (e.g. _SS_SS_ _). Performance on these tasks is enhanced if the target word (e.g. ASSASSIN) has been studied recently, and such priming effects do not appear to change with age. It is possible to argue that implicit memory tasks require relatively small amounts of self-initiated or effortful processing – the solution is guided or driven by the stimulus array itself – and therefore slight age changes would be expected in light of the previously expressed theoretical framework.

REMOTE MEMORY

One of the stereotypes of aging and memory is that whereas memory for recent events becomes increasingly inefficient with advancing age, memory for the events of one's youth remain clear and easily recallable. This claim is often made by older people themselves, but it is open to a number of criticisms. One is that the early and recent events are rarely comparable in importance to the person in question. Thus, it does not make much sense to compare recent forgetting of what you had for breakfast yesterday with the memory of a salient event (a birthday party, death of a pet) from 70 years ago. A related difficulty is that early personal memories are almost always highly selective, and because they refer to interesting episodes in a person's life they are recounted quite often. Thus, the early memory is not really being retrieved after an interval of 70 years, but is probably a composite "memory" mixing details of the original with details added unconsciously over many retellings of the event. The psychologist Laird Cermak refers to these oft-told tales as "family folk memories"; their accuracy is usually impossible to ascertain.

The results of more objective tests are somewhat mixed. One method is to contrast a questionnaire about public events stretching back several decades. The typical result of such studies is that memory for public events gets progressively poorer as the events recede in time from the present; there is no evidence for particularly good memory of those events that occurred in the person's youth (for a review, see Poon, 1985). On the other hand, studies by Bahrick and his collaborators (see Poon, 1985) have shown very good retention of personally acquired knowledge, such as memory for the names and faces of high school colleagues or memory for the geographical layout of a person's college town, after 50 years and more. More research is required on this interesting but difficult problem (*see* EPISODIC MEMORY).

MEMORY FOR KNOWLEDGE

So far this account of age changes in memory has dealt largely with memory for episodic events. However, everyday memory is as often concerned with memory for factual knowledge, for SEMANTIC MEMORY, and here the picture is more positive. In general, it seems that previously acquired knowledge is retained well by older people, although new knowledge may be more difficult to acquire. Several studies have demonstrated an increase in vocabulary and in general knowledge from youth to middle age, and only slight declines from middle age to older ages (Salthouse, 1982). One crucial factor may be the degree to which the information is *used* by the older person; practice at retrieving specific pieces of knowledge may serve to maintain its accessibility. Studies of expert knowledge in older chess and bridge players by Charness (1981) have shown that the older players retain their skills, although they may respond more slowly and have poorer memory for the specific details of a specific game. However, it would be difficult to argue that all types of semantic memory are immune to the effects of aging given the universal complaint of older people that they have increasing difficulty in remembering proper names.

A further aspect of general knowledge is a person's knowledge of his or her own memory and how to use it effectively. This information is referred to as "metamemory" – for example, which strategies to use, which events will be easy to remember, and which will be difficult (*see* METACOGNITION). It seemed possible that some age changes in memory might be attributable to changes in metamemory, but so far the evidence is that changes in metamemorial knowledge are quite slight. Older people report more reliance on external cues and reminders, but this change in habits is a sensible response to an increase in everyday forgetfulness.

UNDERLYING CAUSES

Given that there are substantial age-related decreases in the ability to remember at least some types of information, what gives rise to these deficits? It is likely that the final answer to this question will involve a complex mixture of biological and psychological factors (Poon, 1985). Several changes in the brain are known to accompany normal aging: there is neuronal loss, and neurons lose their connectivity; there is an increase in senile plaques and in neurofibrillary tangles; there are changes in neurotransmitter and neuroendocrine functions; glucose utilization is less efficient. Any or all of these changes could be associated with cognitive changes, although at present the precise linkages are not well understood. At the psychological level, several researchers have suggested that a decline in "processing resources" accompanies the aging process and is related to a decline in cognitive functioning (Craik, 1983; Salthouse, 1982). These hypothesized processing resources may be linked to neuronal glucose metabolism. At a more practical level, it now seems clear that continued active involvement in social and intellectual pursuits plays a positive role in maintaining memory and other cognitive functions in the elderly.

See also REALITY MONITORING.

BIBLIOGRAPHY

Burke, D. M., & Light, L. L. (1981). Memory and aging: The role of retrieval processes. *Psychological Bulletin, 90,* 513–46.

Charness, N. (1981). Aging and skilled problem solving. *Journal of Experimental Psychology: General, 110,* 21–38.

Craik, F. I. M. (1977). Age differences in human memory. In J. E. Birren & K. W. Schaie (Eds), *Handbook of the psychology of aging* (pp. 384–420). New York: Van Nostrand Reinhold.

——. (1983). On the transfer of information from temporary to permanent memory. *Philosophical Transactions of the Royal Society of London, Series B, 302,* 341–59.

Craik, F. I. M., & McDowd, J. M. (1987). Age differences in recall and recognition. *Journal of Experimental Psychology: Learning, Memory, and Cognition, 13,* 474–9.

Craik, F. I. M., & Rabinowitz, J. C. (1984). Age differences in the acquisition and use of verbal information: A tutorial review. In H. Bouma & D. G. Bouwhuis (Eds), *Attention and performance* (pp. 471–99). Hillsdale, NJ: Lawrence Erlbaum Associates.

Gick, M. L., Craik, F. I. M., & Morris, R. G. (1988). Task complexity and age differences in working memory. *Memory and Cognition, 16,* 353–61.

Hasher, L., & Zacks, R. T. (1979). Automatic and effortful processes in memory. *Journal of Experimental Psychology: General, 108,* 356–88.

Poon, L. W. (1985). Differences in human memory with aging: Nature, causes, and clinical implications. In J. E. Birren & K. W. Schaie (Eds), *Handbook of the psychology of aging* (2nd edn) (pp. 427–62). New York: Van Nostrand Reinhold.

Salthouse, T. A. (1982). *Adult cognition: An experimental psychology of human aging.* New York: Springer-Verlag.

F. I. M. CRAIK

agnosia Agnosia is a relatively rare clinical disorder, reflecting the failure by a patient (typically following a brain lesion) to recognize commonly occurring objects. It is a recognition rather than a naming disorder. Unlike anomic patients, who have problems in finding the appropriate names for objects, agnosic patients fail to show any recognition for objects they cannot name – for instance, they cannot describe or pantomime the object's use. Agnosic problems can be specific to objects presented in just one sensory modality – such as a failure to recognize only visually presented objects, or felt objects, or a failure only to recognize objects from their associated sounds. In each of these instances, it is important that the patients can be shown to have adequate sensory discrimination (e.g. visual acuity, tactile sensation, and hearing respectively) – so that agnosia reflects a recognition failure in the presence of intact sensation.

The first, and still influential, theoretical discussion of agnosia (specifically, visual agnosia) was provided by the German neurologist Lissauer in 1890. Lissauer made a distinction between an apperception process, concerned with generating a stable perceptual representation of a stimulus, and an association process, concerned with linking the perceptual representation with stored knowledge about the object's function and associations. According to this distinction, agnosia could result from an impairment of either the apperception or the association process – with apperceptive and associative agnosic patients being distinguished according to whether the patients show good performance on tests of perceptual processing, along with impaired recognition. For instance, in the visual modality, patients may be asked to copy the objects they fail to recognize, to match the same object seen from two different views, or even to decide whether an object has a familiar structure (i.e. to judge whether they have seen the object before). Some patients can do well on all these tests – and yet still fail to recognize the object's function. This is consistent with the patient having a problem in associating perceptual information with stored knowledge of the object's function (e.g. Riddoch & Humphreys, 1987a). It further indicates that rich perceptual descriptions of stimuli can be derived without feedback based on functional and other forms of associative knowledge – since such patients fail to access functional knowledge and yet they can copy objects, match them across different views, and so on.

Other patients can fail on different aspects of the perceptual tests. Some have problems in copying (not linked to a motor disorder), others in matching objects seen in different viewpoints, and so forth. This suggests that we may need to distinguish different kinds of "apperceptive" problem in different patients (Humphreys & Riddoch, 1987a). In vision, a problem in early edge coding could result in poor copying, while a problem in integrating depth and surface information could produce problems in matching objects in different views (*see* PERCEPTION). Yet other problems may be linked to the grouping processes that normally organize the world into coherent perceptual objects – coding parts of a scene as belonging to a single object if the parts are visually similar, and so forth (so that we may fail to identify an animal whose coat is similar in color or texture to the background undergrowth) (*see* GESTALT PRINCIPLES OF PERCEPTUAL ORGANIZATION). Patients with impaired grouping procedures may tend to segment objects into separate parts, seeing each part as a distinct object (for examples, see Humphreys & Riddoch, 1987b). Distinctions between different types of apperceptive problem are also possible in other modalities, although the most detailed work has been carried out on visual agnosic patients. In general, studies of such patients provide a rich source of evidence for understanding the usually hidden processes underlying normal object recognition.

In some instances, patients can have especial problems recognizing particular types or categories of object – such as animals, fruits, and vegetables, or inanimate objects (e.g. Warrington & McCarthy, 1987; Silveri & Gainotti, 1988). For some patients the category-specific problems seem to reflect the close visual similarity between the objects within particular categories – with objects from natural biological categories presenting the greatest problems, perhaps due to the similarity of the exemplars within many of these categories (Riddoch & Humphreys, 1987b). However, patients with specific problems with other types of object (such as indoor objects) may have difficulties because of damage to the knowledge associated with the particular objects. These patients may be important for guiding theories concerned with the nature of the functional and associative knowledge mediating object recognition.

BIBLIOGRAPHY

Humphreys, G. W., & Riddoch, M. J. (1987a). The fractionation of visual agnosia. In G. W. Humphreys & M. J. Riddoch (Eds), *Visual object processing: A cognitive neuropsychological approach* (pp. 281–306). London: Lawrence Erlbaum Associates.

——. (1987b). *To see but not to see: A case study of visual agnosia.* London: Lawrence Erlbaum Associates.

Lissauer, H. (1890). Ein Fall von Seelenblindheit nebst einem Beitrage zur Theorie derselben. *Archiv für Psychiatrie und Nervenkrankheiten, 21,* 222–70.

Riddoch, M. J., & Humphreys, G. W. (1987a). Visual object processing in optic aphasia: A case of semantic access agnosia. *Cognitive Neuropsychology, 4,* 131–86.

——. (1987b). A case of integrative visual agnosia. *Brain, 110,* 1431–62.

Silveri, M. C., & Gainotti, G. (1988). Interaction between vision and language in category-specific semantic impairment. *Cognitive Neuropsychology, 5,* 677–710.

Warrington, E. K., & McCarthy, R. (1987). Categories of knowledge: Further fractionation and an attempted integration. *Brain, 110,* 1273–96.

G. W. HUMPHREYS

amnesia A general term covering any form of temporary or permanent memory loss. Amnesia can be divided broadly into psychogenic or functional states and organic states (Parkin, 1987). In psychogenic states, loss of memory has a psychiatric origin. In most cases the memory loss is related to an extremely negative life event such as bereavement. The most extreme and rare form is fugue, in which patients forget who they are and may even adopt a new identity. More common are selective hysterical amnesias in which people lose the ability to remember traumatic events; combat amnesia and amnesia for violent crime are the most commonly observed examples of this. Explanation of these disorders is difficult.

It has been suggested that some hysterical amnesia is caused by emotional state dependency but in many cases an explanation based on a theory of repression seems the only course (*see* FORGETTING). In the case of amnesia for crime, the issue is further complicated because many violent crimes are committed under conditions of extreme intoxication resulting in consolidation failure, and there is the added problem of malingering.

Multiple personality is another and controversial form of psychogenic amnesia. Here the patient adopts a number of different personalities each of which denies conscious knowledge of the other. These personalities can often be used as an alternative way of relating negative life experiences without involving the normal self.

In organic amnesia the loss of memory is attributed to some form of brain dysfunction. Some forms of amnesia are transient in that the patient's memory returns to normal after a period of time. Post-traumatic amnesia following head injury and transient global amnesia (thought to be caused by temporary cerebro-vascular disruption) are the most common causes of temporary organic amnesia. Epileptic seizures and electro-convulsive therapy also cause temporary amnesic states.

Permanent organic amnesia arises from a wide number of different causes including head injury, strokes, aneurysms, tumors, metabolic deficiencies, and malnutrition (Kapur, 1988). The irreversible nature of brain damage means that the patient's memory never returns to normal. This form of amnesia is often referred to as the amnesic syndrome because all patients suffering from it have certain unifying features, which are: intact immediate apprehension of information, normal or near normal intelligence, and intact language abilities. Amnesic patients are also known to have intact procedural memory (*see* DECLARATIVE AND PROCEDURAL KNOWLEDGE). This term is rather imprecise but can be used to describe the memory processes underlying the acquisition of skills and other forms of knowledge that are not directly accessible to consciousness.

Patients with the amnesic syndrome have two major deficits: a severe anterograde amnesia which prevents them from acquiring any new knowledge, and retrograde amnesia, whereby the patient is unable to remember events and knowledge learned at a time prior to the brain injury that caused the amnesia. An interesting feature of retrograde amnesia is that it demonstrates a temporal gradient: memories formed early in life are more likely to survive than those formed during a later period.

Despite its wide variety of causes, organic amnesia, whether temporary or permanent, is caused by disruption to either one or two specific regions of the brain: a structure in the medial temporal lobe of the cortex known as the hippocampus and nuclei in the midline of the diencephalon, most notably the mamillary bodies. Diencephalic damage is most commonly found in Korsakoff's Syndrome – a result of brain damage due mainly to chronic alcoholism. Temporal lobe amnesia has more widespread origins including encephalitis, head injury, and stroke.

Patients with the amnesic syndrome have been studied intensively. The fact that some aspects of their memory remain intact while others are badly affected provides important information about the organization of memory. Preserved immediate apprehension supports the widely held distinction between short- and long-term storage processes. Intact procedural learning indicates the separate existence of a memory system concerned with the representation of skills and related abilities although there is considerable doubt about whether there is a single procedural memory system.

Psychologists are less agreed on how to describe the deficit in amnesia. Some (e.g. Tulving, 1985) believe that amnesics have a selective loss of EPISODIC MEMORY with preserved SEMANTIC MEMORY. However, others argue that this division is inconsistent with the evidence (e.g. Squire, 1987). In retrograde amnesia, for example, it has been shown that patients' general knowledge about the world is as disrupted as their ability to remember specific events. This has led Squire (1987) to propose that the amnesic deficit is best described as one of declarative memory (*see* DECLARATIVE AND PROCEDURAL KNOWLEDGE). A third approach has been to define the amnesic deficit in terms of the characteristics of tasks on which they succeed or fail. Schacter (1987) has suggested that amnesics are poor on all tasks which require reference to a specific past experience – a function which he calls explicit memory. In contrast, amnesics perform quite well on tasks that do not require reference to a specific point in the past. This form of memory is known as implicit memory and it has become the focus of much interest in recent amnesia research (*see* IMPLICIT AND EXPLICIT MEMORY; LONG-TERM MEMORY).

There have been many attempts to explain human amnesia but as yet there is little progress or agreement among workers. However, one theory gaining reasonable support argues that amnesia represents a deficit in the encoding of contextual information (Mayes, 1988). According to this theory amnesic patients are unable to encode those features of new events that are essential if those events are to be recalled at a subsequent point in time. In contrast, amnesic patients perform quite well on learning tasks which do not require the encoding of contextual information. One problem, however, is that the evidence supporting this theory derives almost exclusively from patients with Korsakoff's Syndrome. There is evidence that this may represent only one form of amnesia and that amnesia arising from temporal lobe pathology may have a different origin (Parkin, 1987). This issue is in turn complicated by the discovery that certain features of amnesic learning performance arise from frontal lobe deficits that are unrelated to primary amnesia.

See also CONNECTIONIST MODELS OF MEMORY; HYPNOSIS; SHORT-TERM MEMORY.

BIBLIOGRAPHY

Kapur, N. (1988). *Memory disorders in clinical practice*. London: Butterworths.

Mayes, A. R. (1988). *Human organic memory disorders*. Cambridge: Cambridge University Press.

Parkin, A. J. (1987). *Memory and amnesia: An introduction*. Oxford: Basil Blackwell.

Schachter, D. L. (1987). Implicit memory: History and current status. *Journal of Experimental Psychology: Learning, Memory, and Cognition, 13*, 501–18.

Squire, L. R. (1987). *Memory and brain*. Oxford: Oxford University Press.

Tulving, E. (1985). Memory and consciousness. *Canadian Psychology, 25*, 1–12.

A. J. PARKIN

analogies Analogies are partial similarities, typically between rather different situations, that support further INFERENCES. More specifically, analogy has been described as a kind of similarity in which the same relational structure holds in different domains (Gentner, 1983). A good example is Rutherford's analogy between the atom and the solar system. We begin with the knowledge that the sun is *more massive than* the planet and *attracts* the planet, and that these two relations *cause* the planet to *revolve around* the sun. The analogy tells us that, given the correct object correspondences, a common relational structure will emerge. Indeed, if we map sun to nucleus and planet to electron and carry across the relational structure, we discover that the nucleus is *more massive than* the electron, that it *attracts* the electron, and that these *cause* the electron to *revolve around* the nucleus.

Psychologists study analogies for several reasons. First, analogies are important in learning. They are often used in explaining scientific concepts, such as the hydrogen atom, heat, or electricity. Once learned, they can serve as MENTAL MODELS for understanding the new domain (Gentner & Gentner, 1983). Second, analogy is important in PROBLEM SOLVING (see, for example, Gick & Holyoak, 1980). Gick and Holyoak gave subjects Duncker's radiation problem: how can one cure an inoperable tumor when enough radiation to kill the tumor would also kill the surrounding flesh? The solution is to converge on the tumor with several weak beams of radiation. Normally, only about 10 percent of the subjects discover this solution. If given a prior analogous story in which soldiers converged on a fort, however, three times as many subjects (about 30 percent) produced the correct answer, apparently transferring the convergence solution to the radiation problem. A final reason to study analogy and similarity is that they seem to underlie many other cognitive processes. Indeed, recent exemplar-based theories of conceptual structure in psychology and case-based reasoning models in artificial intelligence suggest that much of human reasoning and categorization is based on implicit or explicit analogies between the current situation and prior situations.

PSYCHOLOGICAL APPROACHES TO ANALOGY

Although simple four-term analogies have long been used in intelligence testing, detailed modeling of the analogy process began fairly recently. Rumelhart and Abrahamson (1973), using a multidimensional space representation of knowledge, modeled analogy as a mapping from one subspace to another. They found that subjects given analogies like "Horse is to zebra as dog is to ——?" would choose the answer (e.g. fox) whose position relative to dog was the same as that of zebra relative to horse. Sternberg (1977) measured solution times to solve such four-term analogies as a way of studying component processes – encoding, inference, mapping, application, and response – and individual differences in their use.

Current approaches continue to treat analogy as a mapping. However, they generally use complex domain representations, such as PROPOSITIONAL REPRESENTATIONS or SCHEMATA. Gentner (1983) defines analogy as a "structure-mapping": a mapping of knowledge from one domain (the base) into another (the target), which conveys that a system of relations that holds among the base objects also holds among the target objects. Given such a match, any additional predicates that belong to the base system may be imported into the target as candidate inferences. Another prominent approach to analogy is Holyoak's (1985) pragmatic account. Holyoak defines analogy as similarity with respect to a goal, and suggests that, while structural mapping processes occur, they are oriented toward attainment of goal states.

COMPUTATIONAL APPROACHES TO ANALOGY

Artificial intelligence research on analogy has suggested computational principles applicable to human processing (e.g. Carbonell, 1981; Winston, 1982). Some current programs are explicitly intended as cognitive simulations of human analogical processing. Thus, for example, given two potential analogs, the Structure-Mapping Engine (SME) of Falkenhainer, Forbus, and Gentner (1986, 1989/90) first finds local matches, and then combines these into the maximal structurally consistent mapping and draws candidate inferences that should follow from the match. Connectionist-style simulations (*see* CONNECTIONIST MODELS OF MEMORY) have been developed, and M. H. Burstein's (1983) CARL simulates the use of multiple analogies to model a new domain (*see* ARTIFICIAL INTELLIGENCE).

CURRENT ISSUES IN ANALOGICAL RESEARCH

One set of current issues concerns the mapping process: How are the predicates that enter into an analogy selected, and what determines which matches are crucial and which can be ignored? How do contextual factors, such as the current goal state, interact with the intrinsic match in knowledge structures?

A second important question is how potential analogies are accessed in long-term memory (*see* LONG-TERM MEMORY). People often fail to access potentially useful analogs. In Gick and Holyoak's research, as discussed above, 30 percent of the subjects given the fortress convergence story spontaneously used it to solve the Duncker radiation problem. However, if they were told to use the story, between 70 and 80 percent could solve the problem. Ross (1984) demonstrated that, although people in a problem-solving task are often reminded of prior problems, these remindings are often based on surface similarity (e.g. between objects and story lines) rather than on structural similarities between the solution principles. Gentner and Landers (1985) tested a large set of stories and found that surface similarity was the best predictor of memory access, while similarity in relational structure was the best predictor of ratings of inferential soundness. However, Novick (1988) suggests that experts in mathematics are superior to novices both in making use of structurally similar prior mathematics problems and in resisting misleading surface similarities. Given the importance of analogy in transfer, working out the determinants of analogical access is an important research problem.

CONCLUSION

Analogy is a particularly interesting cognitive mechanism, in that it can serve to import a complex system of interrelated knowledge from one domain to another. Recent research has advanced our knowledge of how people align representational structures and compute further inferences over them. The study of analogy leads us to deeper insight into the role of similarity in human thought.

See also REDUCTIONISM.

BIBLIOGRAPHY

Burstein, M. H. (1983). A model of learning by incremental analogical reasoning and debugging. *Proceedings of the National Conference on Artificial Intelligence* (pp. 45–8). Los Altos, Calif.: Morgan Kaufmann.

Carbonell, J. G. (1981). A computational model of analogical problem solving. In A. Drinan (Ed.), *Proceedings of the Seventh International Joint Conference on Artificial Intelligence* (pp. 147–52). Los Altos, Calif.: Morgan Kaufmann.

Falkenhainer, B., Forbus, K. D., & Gentner, D. (1986). The structure-mapping engine. *Proceedings of the Fifth National Conference on Artificial Intelligence* (pp. 272–7). Los Altos, Calif.: Morgan Kaufmann.

——. (1989/90). The structure-mapping engine: Algorithm and examples. *Artificial Intelligence, 41,* 1–63.

Gentner, D. (1983). Structure-mapping: A theoretical framework for analogy. *Cognitive Science, 7,* 155–70.

Genter, D., & Genter, D. R. (1983). Flowing waters or teeming crowds: Mental models of electricity. In D. Gentner & A. L. Stevens (Eds.). *Mental models* (pp. 99–129). Hillsdale, NJ: Erlbaum.

Genter, D., & Landers, R. (1985). Analogical reminding: A good match is hard to find. In *Proceedings of the International Conference on Systems, Man, and Cybernetics* (pp. 607–13). New York: IEEE.

Gick, M. L., & Holyoak, K. J. (1980). Analogical problem solving. *Cognitive Psychology, 12,* 306–55.

Holyoak, K. J. (1985). The pragmatics of analogical transfer. In G. H. Bower (Ed.), *The psychology of learning and motivation* (Vol. 19, pp. 59–87). New York: Academic Press.

Novick, L. R. (1988). Analogical transfer, problem similarity, and expertise. *Journal of Experimental Psychology: Learning, Memory, and Cognition, 14* 510–20.

Ross, B. H. (1984). Remindings and their effects in learning a cognitive skill. *Cognitive Psychology, 16,* 371–416.

Rumelhart, D. E., & Abrahamson, A. A. (1973). A model for analogical reasoning. *Cognitive Psychology, 5,* 1–28.

Sternberg, R. J. (1977). Component processes in analogical reasoning. *Psychological Review, 84,* 353–78.

Winston, P. H. (1982). Learning new principles from precedents and exercises. *Artificial Intelligence, 19,* 321–50.

DEDRE GENTNER

anaphora In connected discourse, entities and events may be referred to more than once; after an initial mention, subsequent references are described as anaphoric, meaning referring back. Anaphors can take many forms. They may be pronouns. Thus, with the sentence "When John came home he threw his hat on the floor," "he" is an anaphor of John. Since "he" and "John" denote the same individual, they are said to be coreferential expressions. The following also illustrates an anaphor: "Mary bought a Porsche so John had to buy one too." Here "one" and "Porsche" do not refer to the same individual, and so they are not coreferential; rather, they simply share the same sense. Apart from noun phrase anaphora, there is also verb anaphora, which has received rather less attention. For example: "Mary put roses in her garden and so did John." In this case, "did" stands for "put roses in his garden." Some other cases are discussed below.

Anaphora is one of the devices which causes a text to hold together or cohere (*see* LANGUAGE COMPREHENSION), and has received much attention from cognitive psychologists (see, for example, Garnham, 1987). It is clearly central to comprehension to keep a clear representation of which things are which in memory, and of which expressions refer to which objects, hence the psychological interest in the pervasive phenomenon of anaphora. For the psychologist, the problem is to establish how anaphora is realized in processing terms. With the sentence "Max dropped the vase and he cried," some process must establish how it is established that "he" is "Max" (how the reference is "resolved"). In this case, it may be that a match is made between "he" (male, singular) and Max (male and singular too). It has been proposed that pronouns initiate a search in immediate memory for items which have a matching semantic description (see Sanford and Garrod, 1981; Sanford, 1985).

CONSTRAINTS ON PRONOMINAL INTERPRETATION

As with many other aspects of language comprehension, pronominal anaphora often requires the integration of quite elaborate information in order to receive an interpretation. One of these factors is (mundane) world knowledge. Consider "Jack gave Jim the money because he was hard up." In order to recognize that he = Jim, the processor must use the knowledge that hard up people do not give money, but are ideally recipients of it. By contrast, the following is more clearly ambiguous, since world knowledge does not help: "Harry met Bill and he was angry." However, even here there is a weak bias toward the subject of the sentence.

There are purely syntactic constraints which influence pronoun interpretation as well, as illustrated by the following examples:
– Before he went to the library, John put on his jacket.
– He went into the library, before John put on his jacket.
In only the first case is "he" coreferential with "John." The precise nature of these sorts of constraint are still the subject of debate in linguistics, although some headway has been made (see Reinhart, 1983). But clearly, under some conditions, syntactic constraints may preclude certain otherwise possible interpretations. In the vast majority of cases, however, syntax alone is not enough to determine reference. For the psychologist and cognitive scientist alike, the interest is in solving the problem of how various constraints come together to enable an appropriate resolution to be made.

The fact that pronoun resolution can result from evidence coming from many sources means that under the right circumstances, resolutions can be made even in the face of conflicting cues, as in: "If the books are too technical, don't get your knickers in a twist. Leave them in the library and go for a walk." In this example, some processes show a preference for the resolution "they = your knickers," but the dominant interpretation, based on plausibility and the expected intention of the speaker, is that "they = the books." Such examples are often funny, having the status of howlers, but more often we would simply judge them as examples of poor style (called "strained anaphora"). Indeed, it is the case in conversation that anaphora is often strained to the point where the listener has to ask the speaker to state explicitly what the intended referent of a pronoun actually was!

ANAPHORS AND MEMORY STATES

Not all anaphors are pronouns, of course. A simple case of noun-phrase anaphora is when a previously used noun phrase is repeated. This is usually reserved for situations when the entity has not been referred to for some time, so that it has to be reintroduced into the focus of attention, or when it would be ambiguous to use a pronoun. However, the use of repeat expressions is governed by some restrictions. For instance, the first time an entity is mentioned, it may be introduced using either a definite description (e.g. the waiter) or an indefinite description (a waiter). On subsequent occasions, however, it is normal to use the definite form. This is because the definite requires a unique entity, while the indefinite implies one of a set. It is perhaps this tendency to treat indefinites as introducing something new which can make an anaphoric use so powerful, as in: "John was left overnight in the dungeon. In the morning, they collected a gibbering wreck."

A more complex way of referring back to something than by a simple noun phrase is to use a restricted relative clause, for example "the waiter at the Ritz." This is a very informative form of description, and can be used by the processor to accurately identify an individual mentioned long ago in the text. Sanford and Garrod (1981) argue that pronouns are used to identify individuals which are currently in the focus of attention, and that fuller noun phrases are typically used to reintroduce individuals into focus. This is consistent with the observation that pronouns tend to be used to refer to main characters in narratives, while repeat noun phrases are used for less prominent characters (e.g. Marslen-Wilson, Levy, & Tyler, 1982). In this way, the forms of description used in anaphoric expressions can be thought of as different types of cues controlling access to memory.

Since the process of language understanding involves the mapping discourse into background knowledge of situations (see LANGUAGE COMPREHENSION), some forms of referring expressions can be used to access individuals which are only implied by a text – for instance, "John went to a restaurant. The waiter was an old friend of his." In this case, we can use the expression "The waiter" because waiters are what one expects to find at restaurants. Sanford and Garrod present evidence to show that this type of reference is handled rapidly and easily. In contrast, normally in written text, a pronoun will not be used to refer to something not explicitly mentioned. Thus, the following sounds strange: "John sailed to Ireland. It sank without trace." Yet the same thing with a full noun phrase is acceptable: "John sailed to Ireland. The boat sank without trace." Thus, it can be argued that pronouns are useful for referring to things mentioned explicitly, and less useful for implied entities which require a different kind of memory operation for their recovery.

A further type of anaphor is the epithet: use of a new type of description to refer to the same individual. Sometimes these rely upon

mundane general knowledge to be understood: "Mrs Thatcher worked all night. The premier planned to change the cabinet." This requires retrieving the fact that Mrs Thatcher is premier (at the time of writing). A slightly more colorful example is: "John came home late last night. The idiot forgot he was getting married today." It is clear that there is more to the epithet than simple coreference. They are informative too. From a processing point of view, they require pragmatic inference based on the presumed intention of the writer (see LANGUAGE, PRAGMATICS OF), and the use of mundane knowledge for their interpretation. They await psychological investigation (but see Bosch, 1988).

See also AUTOMATIC PROCESSING.

BIBLIOGRAPHY

Bosch, P. (1988). Representing and accessing focussed referents. Language and cognitive processes, 3, 207–31.

Garnham, A. (1987). Understanding anaphora. In A. W. Ellis (Ed.), Progress in the psychology of language (Vol. 3). London: Lawrence Erlbaum Associates.

Marslen-Wilson, W. D., Levy, E., & Tyler, L. K. (1982). Producing interpretable discourse: The establishment and maintenance of reference. In R. J. Jarvella and W. Klein (Eds), Speech, place and action. Chichester: John Wiley.

Reinhart, T. (1983). Anaphora and semantic interpretation. London: Croom Helm.

Sanford, A. J. (1985). Cognition and cognitive psychology. London: Lawrence Erlbaum Associates.

——, and Garrod, S. C. (1981). Understanding written language. Chichester: John Wiley.

A. J. SANFORD

animal communication Two parallel lines of study in animal communication have recently converged upon the conclusion that social exchanges among animals are not nearly as "mechanical" as they were previously thought to be. One of these lines has discovered the involvement of cognitive systems through empirical studies of communication. The other has accounted for such complexity by applying the theory of evolution through natural selection.

Detailed empirical studies of animal communication uncovered the following three general classes of complexity.

(1) The discovery that animal reactions to signals were variable rather than stereotyped led Smith (1965) to emphasize the importance of context. Animals enrich the information extractable from a signal with that available from other concurrent inputs, and with the perceiver's memory of past experiences with that signal. Male white-throated sparrows, for example, are not strongly responsive to the sound of a familiar neighbor's song when it comes from the neighbor's territory. In contrast, strong aggressive action ensues when that song originates from outside the neighbor's home area (Falls & Brooks, 1975).

(2) Some animal signals are now known to afford quite specific information, in some ways like the nouns that humans use to label specific objects in their environment (see CONCEPTS). California ground squirrels and vervet monkeys, for example, use distinct calls for the different categories of mammalian, avian, and reptilian predators that threaten them (Owings & Hennessy, 1984; Seyfarth, Cheney, and Marler, 1980).

(3) The repertoires of communicative actions available to animals are larger than initially estimated. Systematic quantitative studies have demonstrated that what were originally thought to be signals are actually classes of signals. The "coo" call of Japanese macaque monkeys, for example, proved on further scrutiny to be a class of at least seven structurally different vocalizations, used in different social situations (Green, 1975). Furthermore, an animal's communicative potential has been found to depend on more than simply the size of its signal repertoire. The patterning of signals offers an additional means of participating in communication, loosely analogous to the patterning of words into sentences (see SPEECH PRODUCTION). Territorial male red-winged blackbirds, for example, call almost continually; their vocal reaction to predatory disturbances involves not the emission of a call, but a change in the structure of the call emitted repeatedly (Beletsky, Higgins, & Orians, 1986).

Darwin's theory of natural selection helps to account for the evolution of such complexity. According to evolutionary theory, communicating individuals should pursue their own self-interested social goals in two ways: (1) by emitting signals to manage the behavior of others, and (2) by extracting the information needed to make adaptive decisions, rather than relying only on that derivable from signals (Owings & Hennessy, 1984). Where the interests of signaler and perceiver conflict, signals may be used manipulatively, e.g. to misguide perceivers. The use of the "meral spread" display by mantis shrimp illustrates this point; residents use this signal to threaten intruders with attack even while they are shedding their hard exoskeletons and are thus unable to use their smashing appendages effectively. Such practices should increase pressure on perceivers for the use of such tactics as probing and extraction of contextual information, to "see through" such misleading behavior by signalers. Rather than simply accepting threats from residents, for example, some intruding mantis shrimps probe home crevices with their heavily armored tails, thereby forcing a context in which a resident's failure to attack divulges the vulnerable state of molt (Caldwell, 1986). Such perceiver tactics should, in turn, select for new strategies by the signaler, resulting in a co-evolutionary spiral analogous to the "arms races" that persist between competing nations (Krebs & Dawkins, 1984).

Biologists have recently proposed that past research may have been biased toward the study of conspicuous signals, whose elaborate form may be peculiar to situations of conflict. Such exaggeration may be necessary where discord occurs, to overcome the "resistance" or "skepticism" of perceivers (Krebs & Dawkins, 1984). In contrast, when the interests of signaler and perceiver are compatible, signals should be subtly structured rather than elaborate, both because no resistance needs to be overcome, and as a defense against detection by "unintended" perceivers such as predators. Pygmy marmosets, for example, stay in contact with group members by calling to each other while foraging in the forest. Charles Snowdon has shown that these "contact trills" become less audible and more difficult for predators to pinpoint when individuals are closest to each other. With high compatibility of interests one might also predict that signals would provide precise guidance to perceivers, not mislead them (e.g. the case described above of ground squirrels emitting specific warnings to offspring). Thus, animals may have even larger repertoires than suggested above, since they include previously unnoticed sets of subtle but specific signals. In turn, the evolution of even more sophisticated information-extraction systems would be stimulated by the demands on perceivers to base specific decisions on such subtlety.

See also LANGUAGE ACQUISITION.

BIBLIOGRAPHY
Beletsky, L. D., Higgins, B. J., & Orians, G. H. (1986). Communication by changing signals: Call switching in red-winged blackbirds. *Behavioral Ecology and Sociobiology, 18,* 221–9.
Caldwell, R. L. (1986). The deceptive use of reputation by stomatopods. In R. W. Mitchell & N. S. Thompson (Eds), *Deception: Perspectives on human and nonhuman deceit* (pp. 129–45). Albany: SUNY Press.
Falls, J. B., & Brooks, R. J. (1975). Individual recognition by song in white-throated sparrows. II. Effects of location. *Canadian Journal of Zoology, 53,* 1412–20.
Green, S. (1975). Communication by a graded system in Japanese monkeys. In L. Rosenblum (Ed.), *Primate behavior* (Vol. 4) (pp. 1–102). New York: Academic Press.
Krebs, J. R., & Dawkins, R. (1984). Animal signals: Mind-reading and manipulation. In J. R. Krebs & N. B. Davies (Eds), *Behavioural ecology: An evolutionary approach* (pp. 380–402). Sunderland: Sinauer Associates.
Owings, D. H., & Hennessy, D. F. (1984). The importance of variation in sciurid visual and vocal communication. In J. O. Murie & G. R. Michener (Eds), *The biology of ground-dwelling squirrels* (pp. 169–200). Lincoln: University of Nebraska Press.
Seyfarth, R. M., Cheney, D. L., & Marler, P. (1980). Vervet monkey alarm calls: Semantic communication in a free-ranging primate. *Animal Behaviour, 28,* 1070–94.
Smith, W. J. (1965). Message, meaning, and context in ethology. *American Naturalist, 99,* 405–9.

DONALD H. OWINGS

aphasia The term "aphasia" refers here to the partial or complete loss of spoken language following brain injury. It can be distinguished from impaired language acquisition in children ("developmental dysphasia") and from impaired processing of written language (*see* DYSLEXIAS: ACQUIRED). Aphasia is of interest to the cognitive psychologist if it is studied from the viewpoint of COGNITIVE NEUROPSYCHOLOGY, an approach which assumes that we can learn about the organization of language in the normal, intact brain from studying the patterns of impaired and preserved performance that can be seen following brain injury.

The broad separation of language processes from other forms of cognitive activity can be deduced from the existence of patients who have suffered extreme loss of language capabilities yet retain other cognitive abilities. For example, nonverbal intelligence may be preserved in severely aphasic patients (Allport, 1983), as may nonverbal artistic skills (Gardner, 1982), suggesting that the cognitive processes which sustain those abilities are separate from the processes which sustain spoken language, and hence can be separately impaired.

Aphasia is not a single condition, but comes in many different forms. Cognitive neuropsychologists tend to use much finer classifications, and pay more attention to differences between patients, than has often been the case in aphasia research. Patients may be studied intensively as single cases, with close attention being paid to the aspects of language which are preserved, as well as those which are impaired. Hypotheses regarding the nature of the underlying cognitive impairment are tested experimentally using the procedures of cognitive psychology. It is not possible to discuss all the known forms of language disorder: the emphasis here will be on illustrating the approach with some selected examples.

Anomic patients experience difficulty in "word retrieval," for example when trying to name objects. Among anomics, one can distinguish patients in whom the primary impairment is to the semantic representations which encode the meanings of words from patients whose semantic understanding of word meanings is intact but who experience difficulties in retrieving the spoken forms of words from some form of internal lexical store. The patients with semantic deficits may have more difficulties with some semantic categories than with others. They may make semantic errors in naming (e.g. calling a "lion" a "tiger"), and have problems making fine discriminations in word comprehension which mirror their naming difficulties (e.g. they may accept "tiger" as the correct name for a lion). Patients with purely retrieval deficits can show intact comprehension of words they cannot retrieve in production, and their ability to remember a word may be related to its frequency of usage. This latter form of anomia might be interpreted as a grossly exaggerated form of the TIP-OF-THE-TONGUE PHENOMENON seen in normal subjects.

Word retrieval difficulties often occur in combination with other language problems, but of more interest to the cognitive neuropsychologist is the fact that they *can* occur in relatively pure form in patients who have little or no difficulty with such things as the formulation of grammatical sentence structures. There are, in contrast, other patients in whom grammatical problems are paramount, but again cognitive neuropsychological analysis reveals finer distinctions among patients. In some patients the underlying deficit is one of converting an intact grasp of causal relations between objects and actions into the linguistic form of a sentence with a subject, a verb, an object, and so on. In other patients the core problem lies in the use of "function words" such as "the," "on," and "to," and grammatical inflections such as the plural "-s" and the past tense "-ed." This problem is referred to as *agrammatism*.

Many aphasic patients experience difficulties with speech perception. These problems are occasionally seen in pure form in patients with pure word deafness. These patients are unable to perceive speech accurately yet can perceive nonspeech sounds like telephones ringing or dogs barking. Their speech output remains intact, as does their reading comprehension. The patients perceive some speech sounds, particularly vowel sounds, reasonably well. They benefit from slowed speech, from semantic cues about the words they are trying to identify, and from being able to see the speaker's lip movements. The core problem appears to lie in an inability to make the very fine acoustic discriminations that are necessary if one is to distinguish between speech sounds such as "p" and "b," or "g" and "k." Slowing the speech helps with such discriminations, as do lip movements, and semantic cues help the patient identify words from the degraded input that their perceptual processes provide.

A condition like pure word deafness is of considerable interest to cognitive neuropsychologists though it is rare in pure form. Like most forms of aphasia it is most often seen following injury to the left hemisphere of the brain (in right-handed individuals). There are, however, forms of language disorder which may occur following injury to the right hemisphere. Patients who have suffered right hemisphere damage may be unable to impart emotional tone of voice to their speech. They may also tend to adopt literal rather than metaphorical interpretations of phrases like "Don't cry over spilt milk" and may be unable to appreciate verbal humor. The latter observations suggest that certain high-level aspects of language comprehension draw upon cognitive capabilities which are not exclusive to verbal processing, and for which an intact right hemisphere is necessary.

Although the scientific study of aphasia is over 100 years old, specifically cognitive neuropsychological work is much more recent. One hope is that an approach which focuses on identifying the nature of the cognitive deficit(s) underlying a patient's impaired performance may lead to better targeted and more effective remedial procedures. At the time of writing, the prospects of those hopes being realized look good (Howard & Hatfield, 1987).

BIBLIOGRAPHY

Allport, D. A. (1983). Language and cognition.

In R. Harris (Ed.), *Approaches to language* (pp. 61–94). Oxford: Pergamon Press.

Caplan, D. (1987). *Neurolinguistics and linguistic aphasiology*. Cambridge: Cambridge University Press.

Ellis, A. W., & Young, A. W. (1982). *Human cognitive neuropsychology*. London: Lawrence Erlbaum Associates.

Gardner, H. (1982). Artistry following damage to the human brain. In A. W. Ellis (Ed.), *Normality and pathology in cognitive functions* (pp. 299–323). London: Academic Press.

Howard, D., & Hatfield, F. M. (1987). *Aphasia therapy: Historical and contemporary issues*. London: Lawrence Erlbaum Associates.

ANDREW W. ELLIS

articulatory loop *See* WORKING MEMORY.

artificial intelligence Artificial intelligence is concerned with the attempt to develop complex computer programs that will be capable of performing difficult cognitive tasks. Some of those who work in artificial intelligence are relatively unconcerned as to whether the programs they devise mimic human cognitive functioning, whereas others have the explicit goal of simulating human cognition on the computer. Sanford (1985) has described the appropriate relationship between computer programs of cognition and human cognition:

Although the design of ... programs and the study of the principles behind intelligent programs is a study in its own right, it has fairly obvious implications for the study of mind. It is difficult to write programs which mimic essentially human activities without at the same time studying how humans do things, and it is foolhardy to devise theories of human cognition without considering the computational implementation of the theory.

(Sanford, 1985, p. 6)

There is a substantial amount of overlap between artificial intelligence and COGNITIVE SCIENCE. Definitions of the two terms vary, but it is probably generally accepted that cognitive science is a rather general term referring to an interdisciplinary approach which incorporates cognitive psychology, artificial intelligence, and aspects of neurophysiology.

The artificial intelligence approach has been applied to several different areas within cognitive psychology. These areas include perception, memory, imagery, and thinking and problem solving (*see* CONNECTIONIST MODELS OF MEMORY; IMAGERY, COMPUTATIONAL THEORY OF; PERCEPTION, COMPUTATIONAL THEORY OF; PROBLEM SOLVING).

It is difficult at present to make any definitive statement about the long-term impact of artificial intelligence on cognitive psychology, as work within artificial intelligence is still developing rapidly. As Boden (1988, p. 260) has pointed out, "The space of computational possibilities has hardly been entered, never mind fully explored or satisfactorily mapped.... It is too early, therefore, to predict the success of the computational approach in general."

Even at this stage, however, it is possible to identify some advantages of the artificial intelligence approach to cognition. One such advantage concerns the extent to which the processes involved in performing a cognitive task are spelled out. Many cognitive psychologists have relied heavily in their theoretical work on verbal statements of the processes, and have omitted to specify adequately crucial aspects of what is involved. In contrast, computer programing requires that every process be specified in detail. A case in point is Marr's (1982) computational work in visual perception. His computer simulations of some of the early stages in visual processing revealed that previous theoretical assumptions about the role of feature detectors were substantial oversimplifications.

Another clear advantage of the artificial intelligence approach is that its focus tends to be highly theoretical. Whereas many cognitive psychologists are mainly concerned with obtaining empirical data from human subjects performing cognitive tasks, those working in artificial intelligence have suceeded in producing rather general theoretical orientations having wide applicability. For example, as is discussed by Eysenck and Keane (1990), computer models based on semantic networks, production systems, and connectionist networks have all emerged from artificial intelligence (*see* CONNECTIONIST MODELS OF MEMORY).

In terms of the disadvantages of the artificial intelligence approach, there has been much controversy about the ultimate similarity between human cognitive functioning and computer functioning. It is certainly true that there are aspects to most computer programs which are there because of the particular programing language being used or because of the characteristics of the computer. It has been argued (Palmer & Kimchi, 1986) that cognitive theories can be decomposed through a number of levels (e.g. flowchart) until eventually one arrives at a written program. In most cases, there will be a point in the decomposition above which what is assumed is psychologically reasonable but below which it is not.

Some of the major differences between brains and computers were spelled out in the following terms by Churchland (1989, p. 100): "The brain seems to be a computer with a radically different style. For example, the brain changes as it learns, it appears to store and process information in the same places.... Most obviously, the brain is a parallel machine, in which many interactions occur at the same time in many different channels." This contrasts with most computer functioning, which involves serial processing and relatively few interactions. It is true that connectionist models with their parallel distributed processing and with their modifiable connections provide a somewhat closer approximation to brain functioning, but even such models do not correspond well to human brain functioning.

Another difference between brain functioning and computer functioning was identified by Boden (1988). She pointed out that human cognition is often affected by several different motivational and emotional influences at the same time. This can be contrasted with the "single-minded nature of virtually all current computer programs" (p. 262).

A final problem with the artificial intelligence approach was discussed by Norman (1980). He noted that human cognition

involves interactions between the cognitive system (which he referred to as the Pure Cognitive System) and the biological system (which he referred to as the Regulatory System). Much of the activity within the Pure Cognitive System occurs in response to the demands of the Regulatory System. In contrast, most work in artificial intelligence focuses almost exclusively on the Pure Cognitive System at the expense of the Regulatory System.

See also ANALOGIES.

BIBLIOGRAPHY

Boden, M. (1988). *Computer models of mind.* Cambridge: Cambridge University Press.
Churchland, P. S. (1989). From Descartes to neural networks. *Scientific American*, July, 100.
Eysenck, M. W., & Keane, M. T. (1990). *Cognitive psychology: A student's handbook.* London: Lawrence Erlbaum Associates Ltd.
Marr, D. (1982). *Vision: A computational investigation into the human representation and processing of visual information.* San Francisco: W. H. Freeman.
Norman, D. A. (1980). Twelve issues for cognitive science. *Cognitive Science, 4*, 1–32.
Palmer, S. E., & Kimchi, R. (1986). The information processing approach to cognition. In T. Knapp & L. C. Robertson (Eds), *Approaches to cognition: Contrasts and controversies.* Hillsdale, NJ: Lawrence Erlbaum Associates Ltd.
Sanford, A. J. (1985). *Cognition and cognitive psychology.* London: Lawrence Erlbaum Associates Ltd.

MICHAEL W. EYSENCK

attention

PHENOMENOLOGY, HISTORY, AND
SCIENTIFIC PERSPECTIVE

The word attention is widely used in our daily language as it serves as a topic of study and scientific debate in experimental psychology. It therefore seems appropriate to begin our review of the study of attention in psychology with two brief quotations from William James's book *The principles of psychology* (1890) (*see* JAMES, WILLIAM). These quotations underline the linkage between the two regimes of usage, while also dating the scientific interest in the concept to the early days of experimental psychology.

> Every one knows what attention is. It is the taking possession by the mind, in a clear and vivid form of one out of what seem several simultaneously possible objects or trains of thought. Focalization, concentration of consciousness are of its essence. It implies withdrawal from some things in order to deal effectively with others, and is a condition which has a real opposite in the confused, dazed, scatter-brained state which in French is called DISTRACTION and ZERSTREUTHEIT in German.
>
> (pp. 403-4)

When discussing the nature of the attended events William James was careful to observe that:

> The number of things we may attend to is altogether indefinite, depending on the power of the individual intellect, on the form of the apprehension, and on what things are. When apprehended conceptually as a connected system, their number may be large. But however numerous the things, they can only be known in a single pulse of consciousness for which they form one complex "object", so that properly speaking there is before the mind at no time a plurality of IDEAS, properly so called.
>
> (p. 405)

Equal weights are given in James's thinking to external and internal objects of attention (see SELF-FOCUS AND SELF-ATTENTION). Objects can be external stimuli such as pictures and tunes or internal events such as specific trains of thought and attempts to retrieve information from memory. There is no unique, fixed, correspondence between stimuli, their properties, and attention objects. Experience, strategy, and individual capabilities may influence the connection between elementary stimulus units, thereby affecting the ways they combine to create a single complex attention object. In this observation William James anticipated by many years the contemporary distinctions between isolated items and chunks of information in working memory, grouping principles and integrality of dimensions in perception, and the development of organized memory and response schemas through practice and training. Each of these larger, many elements units, can constitute a single object of attention (see CHUNKING; WORKING MEMORY).

There are other effects of attention. In James's words, the immediate effects of attention "are to make us (a) perceive, (b) conceive, (c) distinguish, (d) remember better than otherwise we could" (p. 424). Six decades later, in his famous series of experiments on the "cocktail party phenomena," Cherry (1957) describes the perceived clarity and intensity, for a person standing in one corner of the room, of a conversation taking place at another remote corner, but is of high interest to him. This is the "work" of focused attention that seems to attenuate and override the physically much louder vocalizations of his own discussion partner and other surrounding parties. Embedded in the claim for such focalization, clarity, and increased processing efficiency is the idea of involved mental effort. This will in later models be argued to be an important determinant of the limits of attention.

Last but not least is the linkage between attention and consciousness. In the thinking of James and his contemporaries, the two concepts were closely linked. Attention determines the content of consciousness, and consciousness, through activation of interest and intent, is the main, though not the sole, guide of attention. Although attention may be "captured" involuntarily by salient features of the environment, in most instances it is directed by conscious intentions (see CONSCIOUSNESS).

The above quotations that describe so vividly one of the basic experiences of which every human is well aware seem also to encapsulate the main observations, topics for research, theoretical concerns, and debates which have motivated a century of scientific study of the concept. Setting out from the basic axiom that the human mind is limited and hence at any one moment only a limited set of the plurality of stimuli available or imposed on the organism can be attended to and processed, experimental psychologists rolled up their sleeves to study attention processes.

How does selective attention operate? What portion of the information can be attended to? Is the control of attention voluntary or involuntary? What is the relationship between attention and consciousness? What is the influence of attention on the focused, relevant information, and what happens to the unattended, irrelevant information? What happens when attention is divided between several concurrent goals; can we do two things at once? What is the nature of attention limitations and the sources of scarcity? What happens when a person is required to maintain attention and concentration for long durations? Is attention a single unified entity, or are there many types of attention (e.g. visual, auditory, motor)? This is a representative list of the main issues with which research has been concerned over the years.

Taken together, the study of attention has come to encompass all manifestations of behavior that involve the active influence of the human mind (which in contemporary terminology is often termed the human processing and response system) on the perception and transformation of stimuli from the outside world, and on the preparation and conduct of response. Aspects of the situation that without training are processed automatically, cannot be selectively ignored even with training, and cannot be shown to interfere with other concurrent processing activities, are termed preattentive and excluded from the study of attention. An example is the perception of the color of an object when the task is only to identify its shape. Preattentive processes have been argued to provide a preliminary organization to perception by a process of grouping and segmentation. The objects of perception are defined at that stage, and subsequent processes operate on these objects.

The study of attention has had its ups and downs as a focal topic of investigation. It was central in the three decades between 1890 and 1920, when psychology was most interested in the study of consciousness and mental activity, and when INTROSPECTION was the main methodological tool. The interest declined and almost disappeared during the following three decades (1920–50), that were dominated by Behaviorism and Gestalt psychology. These schools of thought were more interested in the influence on perception and overt behavior of external stimulus properties and sophisticated conditioning methods.

During the following three decades (1950–80), the pendulum had swung again, with cognition and attention having moved to the center of interest in experimental psychology. Our present knowledge and models are mostly based on the voluminous work conducted during these years. Since the beginning of the 1980s we have been witnessing the start of yet another shift of interest in attention studies. With the advance of computer technology and artificial intelligence, on the one hand, and of physiological research on the other, there is a growing interest in computational models of brain and behavior, that are mostly driven by the objective properties, probabilities, and time functions of stimulus and response. Attention processes, though not disposed of, are superfluous for these models. Thus, the pendulum swings again (see ARTIFICIAL INTELLIGENCE).

THE STUDY OF ATTENTION

The interests, findings and models in the study of attention over the last three decades are best represented in the 13 volumes on *Attention and performance* published biannually since 1967. They present the papers and discussions from the meetings of the International Association for the Study of Attention and Performance, which was established in 1966 in The Netherlands. The following is a brief summary of paradigms and major topics of study and debate.

EXPERIMENTAL PARADIGMS

Experimental paradigms in the study of attention may be categorized along several leading dimensions.

Time One dimension is time, distinguishing between studies concentrating on the short term, immediate effects of attention on performance, and studies interested in long duration tasks of sustained attention. The first and the larger group is interested in the micro analysis of single or short-term processing cycles, such as the ability to focus attention on, and process information from, one of several distracting elements, or divide attention between two concurrently performed tasks. Sustained attention studies concentrate on the long-term time function of attention, lapses and cycles of attention, and the ability to maintain vigilance and alertness over long periods of time. Typical examples are radar observers and prolonged shifts of air traffic controllers. These studies are closely linked to the research on diurnal cycles of arousal and physiological activity, and examine the effects of such variables as sleep deprivation and background noise.

Type of task Experimental tasks can be generally classified into the filter paradigm and the selective set paradigm (Kahneman & Triesman, 1984). In the filter paradigm, the subject is exposed simultaneously to relevant and irrelevant stimuli. The relevant stimuli control a relatively complex process of response selection and execution. The property that differentiates the relevant from the irrelevant stimuli is different from the property that determines the response. An example is the shadowing of a string of words presented through one speaker while ignoring concurrent strings presented through another speaker. The main measure of performance is accuracy. In the selective set paradigm the subject is prepared for particular stimuli and is instructed to indicate by a speeded response the detection or recognition of those stimuli. Thus, the subject chooses which of several possible stimuli to anticipate or search for rather than which of several actual stimuli to analyze. An example may be a designation of a small set of letters, the existence of which should then be detected in brief exposures of arrays comprising both relevant and irrelevant letters.

Attention assignment The main distinction is between performance of tasks under *focused* or *divided* attention instructions. Tasks of focused or selective attention are used to study the resistance to distraction and to establish

the locus beyond which relevant stimuli are treated differentially. Divided attention tasks are used to assess the limits of performance and the extent to which different concurrent tasks can be performed or combined without loss (*see* DUAL-TASK PERFORMANCE).

Stimulus and response characteristics There are large variations in the selection of stimuli and responses and in the choice of variables along which they are manipulated. These are usually reflecting the specific domain of interest of the researcher. Tasks may vary in the modality of presentation, physical properties, semantic attributes, and type of responses. This variability is an important contributor to the identification of communalities and differences in functions of attention.

SELECTIVE ATTENTION AND THE
NATURE OF ATTENTION LIMITATION

Where is attention limited? One of the major topics for study and modeling was the locus of selective attention: the mechanisms, processes, and stages at which selection operates. Models have differed in their emphasis on early versus late selection. Early selection models maintain that the main problem facing the organism is the richness and complexity of information presented to the senses at any one time, which may confuse and overload high-level processing mechanisms. The mind is limited on the processing side. Using preattentive physical features such as spatial location, auditory pitch, and color, selective attention is likened to a filter which attenuates and excludes irrelevant information from further analysis of meaning, or storage in long-term memory. Most noted of the early selection models was the "filter model" proposed by Broadbent (1958). A wide variety of experiments, mostly employing the "filter paradigm," showed evidence in support of early selection. Thus, for example, subjects required to listen and repeat verbal information presented to one ear were unable to report the content or language of irrelevant messages presented simultaneously to the other ear, though they could identify the pitch and gender of the speaking voice. Similar findings were reported for other modalities.

Late selection models have contested the assertions of early filtering by designing experiments and tasks that demonstrated high-level analysis of all simultaneous information, both relevant and irrelevant. According to these approaches, the bottleneck and confusion are on the response selection side, resulting from the multitude of conflicting response tendencies that are instigated at any one time. Selective attention serves to magnify the relevant response tendency and inhibit competing responses. Supportive experiments primarily followed the "selective set" paradigm: they showed, for instance, that subjects can search effectively for relevant letters, or identify them in tachitoscopic presentations, in stimulus arrays containing both relevant and irrelevant letters. This is even if all stimuli are of the same modality and type, thus precluding the operation of perceptual filters.

Recent discussions have concluded that the human is modular, and the locus of selection is strategic and task dependent rather than fixed. It is adapted to the features of the situation and the nature of the required response. It can hence be early, late, or both.

How is capacity limited? What is the nature of attention limitations, and what are the sources of failures to process and attend? Models differ in their emphasis on structural versus capacity limitations. Structural models postulate that processing mechanisms and operations operate in an all-or-none fashion. Attention controls the scheduling and access of competing tasks to the limited mechanisms. Problems also arise when the inputs, throughputs, or outputs of competing tasks are hard to distinguish, so that the scheduler is confused.

Capacity, or resource approaches, emphasize the intensive costs of mental operations. The human processing system is conceptualized as an ensemble of limited capacity mechanisms – processing resources which can be allocated in various shares to the performance of tasks. A mechanism can serve several tasks simultaneously if their joint demands do not exceed its available capacity. This approach has been termed "energetic" because it is concerned with task demands, mental effort, and notions of scarcity in energy and space of mental operations, as sources of attention failure. Scarcity of resources has a central position in capacity models, while the only scarce resource in structural models is time. By their nature capacity models are more interested in short- and long-term modulations of the physiological mechanisms of arousal. They also emphasize a detailed study of mental effort. These interests constitute a first step toward building a bridge, that has hitherto been missing, between the study of the microstructure of attention and models of performing long duration sustained attention tasks. In these tasks, arousal, motivation, and voluntary effort play a major role.

At present, there seems to be sufficient experimental evidence to support the effects of both structural and capacity factors on performance. However, there is still an ongoing debate as to which model accounts for larger portions of the phenomena and performance variability.

ATTENTION CONTROL

Attention mechanisms and attention control appear to play a major role in the performance of new and changing situations and in the acquisition of new skills. When the situation remains constant and experience is accumulated, consistent modes of processing and response emerge. Behavior becomes more automatic and attention demands are reduced. Contemporary research has shown that efficient control of attention in complex situations is a skill that can be trained and improved. Humans have limited knowledge on the efficiency of their efforts. They can be trained to develop better attention allocation policies, and strategies of coping with concurrent complex demands.

INDIVIDUAL DIFFERENCES

Consistent individual differences in basic attention capabilities have been reported by several researchers. The main dimensions of differences were in the ability to switch attention rapidly upon request, and in attention flexibility. These differences were used to construct tests of selective attention which have been found to predict success in flight training, differentiate between high- and low-ability pilots, and predict accident proneness of bus drivers.

ATTENTION AND WORKLOAD

Attention theory and attention mechanisms are the building blocks for the study of mental workload, which is of major concern to engineering psychology. The complexity and high number of information sources in modern engineering systems impose high processing and decision demands on the human operators and push them to their limits. Interest in the study of attention is thus as strong in the applied domain as it is in basic research.

See also ATTENTION, INHIBITORY PROCESSES IN; AUDITORY PERCEPTION.

BIBLIOGRAPHY

Attention and performance Volumes 1–13, 1967–89. Vols 1–4 published by North-Holland, Amsterdam; Vol 5 by Academic Press, New York. Vols 6–13 by Lawrence Erlbaum, New York.

Broadbent, D. E. (1958). Perception and communication. London: Pergamon Press.

Cherry, E. C. (1957). On human communication: A review, a summary and a criticism. Cambridge, Mass.: MIT Press.

James, W. (1890). The principles of psychology. New York: Holt.

Kahneman, D. (1973). Attention and effort. Englewood Cliffs, NJ: Prentice-Hall.

— —, & Triesman, A. (1984). Changing views of attention and automaticity. In R. Parasuraman & D. R. Davis (Eds), Varieties of attention. Orlando, Fla.: Academic Press.

DANIEL GOPHER

attention, inhibitory processes in Complex perceptual–motor interactions require mechanisms of selective attention, the ability to prevent processing of the many irrelevant external and internal stimuli that are available. For example, a hawk swoops down on a flock of pigeons. For its attack to succeed, action has to be directed to only one of the many available objects of prey.

For many theories of attention, the emphasis has been upon excitatory processes, where information to which the organism attends receives further processing beyond that of initial perceptual analysis (see ATTENTION). Although various filter mechanisms have been suggested as the means by which irrelevant information is blocked, the possibility of underlying inhibitory processes has not been fully explored. Indeed, Wilhelm Wundt, the founder of the first psychology laboratory, was already aware of such a bias when he noted:

> The basic phenomenon of all intellectual achievement is the so-called concentration of attention. It is understandable that in the appraisal of this phenomenon we attach importance first and therefore too exclusively to its positive side, to the grasping and clarification of certain presentations. But for the physiological appraisal it is clear that it is the negative side, the inhibition of the inflow of all other disturbing excitations … which is more important.
>
> (Wundt, 1874, 4th edn, p. 481)

Models proposed over the last decade have begun to redress this imbalance in their increased emphasis of inhibitory components. Here we can examine two such models.

The first model describes attention as resembling the beam of a spotlight which can be directed toward particular objects in different environmental locations, enabling more detailed processing. For efficient examination of a visual environment, it is important that attention does not continually return to recently attended locations. Recent research has suggested that inhibitory processes prevent this "return of attention." Thus, when attention is automatically oriented to a change in the environment (for example, by a peripheral box brightening) and is then redirected to a different spatial location, the detection of a target stimulus within the box that recently attracted attention is impaired. It is proposed that detection of the target requires attention, and that attention is actively inhibited from returning to the target.

Further investigations have provided support for such an inhibitory process. This process is not the result of motor inhibition, as the effect occurs after response to the stimulus; it cannot be accounted for by peripheral masking, as inhibition has a relatively long time-course; and inhibition occurs in an environmental rather than a retinal coordinate system. These results confirm that the coherent movement of attention around the spatial environment is achieved by actively inhibiting those locations previously examined.

A second model has also used inhibitory processes to explain other facets of attention, such as how we are able to ignore competing information. Substantial research has demonstrated that in many situations people analyze the meaning of objects that are irrelevant to their current behavior. Furthermore, these studies show that the presence of irrelevant distractors can interfere with responses to a relevant object. Yet experimental subjects can be remarkably accurate, rarely making inappropriate responses to objects that are irrelevant to the ongoing task. It is proposed that such selection is achieved by inhibiting the internal representations of distractor objects.

Empirical support for such a claim has been obtained from priming studies (see PRIMING). It was predicted that if the internal representations of ignored objects are actively inhibited, the subsequent processing of an object requiring the same internal representation should be impaired: a form of "negative priming." If, for example, a subject is presented with two drawings (a green table and red guitar) and told to name the red one, the internal representations activated by the green table are inhibited. On a subsequent trial, when a table has to be identified response times are increased, presumably because the second presentation of table needs to access those representations of table inhibited earlier during selection of the red object.

Such inhibition does not appear to be tied to the specific visual properties of the ignored stimulus, as it transfers between pictures and words representing the same object: that is, ignoring the picture of a dog slows the response to the subsequent word "dog." Nor is the inhibition located in the motor system, as it transfers between manual (key press) and verbal identification responses. It therefore appears that inhibition of conflicting irrelevant stimuli is confined to a central locus of processing between perception and action, common

to a variety of different perceptual inputs and response outputs.

Approaches other than those utilized by cognitive psychologists have also begun to provide evidence for inhibitory processes in attention. Electrical recordings have been undertaken of the action potentials of cells in prestriate and inferior temporal cortex of the macaque monkey, areas known to be concerned with visual object recognition. The response of these cells to a visual stimulus appeared to be severely attenuated when the stimulus was ignored. The inhibition of neuronal responses when a stimulus was ignored may be the primary mechanism of selection in these cortical regions. Such a result perhaps provides both an initial glimpse of the neurophysiological mechanisms underlying inhibitory processes in attention, and the direction future studies may take.

These descriptions of inhibitory processes in attention have been motivated by the observation that opposing mechanisms of excitation and inhibition appear to be ubiquitous in the nervous system. In each model, excitation processes are also described, and they are responsible for the early stages of information processing, whereas the inhibitory processes are a crucial mechanism for subsequent conscious strategic processing, such as responding to one stimulus rather than another. It is still unclear what relationship, if any, there is between these various inhibitory processes. For example, it is unknown whether the inhibition that prevents attention from returning to a recently investigated location, and the inhibition that prevents attention from orienting to irrelevant objects, have the same underlying mechanism.

Further knowledge concerning the inhibitory processes of attention will be gained within the tradition of human experimental psychology. For a unified theory of attention, however, other levels of analysis will be required. For example, computational models are necessary to formalize and test the inhibitory processes described, and our increasing knowledge of the neurophysiology of the brain should provide a foundation for models proposed by cognitive psychologists.

See also STROOP EFFECT.

BIBLIOGRAPHY

Maylor, E. A., & Hockey, R. (1985). Inhibitory components of externally controlled covert orienting in visual space. *Journal of Experimental Psychology, Human Perception and Performance*, III, 777–87.

Moran, J., & Desimone, R. (1985). Selective attention gates visual processing in the extra-striate cortex. *Science*, 229, 782–4.

Neill, W. T. (1977). Inhibition and facilitation processes in selective attention. *Journal of Experimental Psychology: Human Perception and Performance*, 3, 444–50.

Posner, M. I., & Cohen, Y. A. (1984). Components of visual orienting. In H. Bouma & Bouwhuis (Eds), *Attention and performance X*. Hillsdale, NJ: Lawrence Earlbaum Associates.

Tipper, S. P., MacQueen, G. M., & Brehaut, J. C. (1988). Negative priming between response modalities: Evidence for the central locus of inhibition in selective attention. *Perception and Psychophysics*, 43, 45–52.

STEVEN P. TIPPER

attitudes According to Rosenberg and Hovland (1960), attitudes are "predispositions to respond to some class of stimuli with certain classes of responses" (p. 3). They further proposed that the three major types of response are cognitive, affective, and behavioral. It is thus feasible to argue that attitudes basically consist of cognitive, affective, and behavioral components. The study of attitudes has been a central concern of social psychologists since the beginnings of the discipline. In 1935 Gordon Allport referred to "attitude" as "the keystone in the edifice of American social psychology" (p. 798), and it has retained this central status during most of the intervening decades. There are three key reasons for this focus on attitudes. First, attitudes are widely assumed to influence behavior. Thus, knowing someone's attitude toward something or someone should enable one to predict how that person will behave when confronted with the attitude object. Furthermore, effecting a change in this person's attitudes should result in corresponding behavioral change. Second, it has been assumed by some attitude theorists that attitudes serve important psychological functions for the individual. A third reason for the considerable research effort directed at attitudes is that reliable methods for the assessment of attitudes were devised relatively early in the history of psychology, the best known early example being Thurstone's (1928) paper entitled "Attitudes can be measured."

Despite the important role played by attitude research in the history of social psychology, there has never been complete consensus among attitude theorists regarding the most appropriate way to define and conceptualize attitudes. Three approaches to this issue serve to illustrate the diversity of conceptualizations. The term "attitude" was originally used in everyday speech to refer exclusively to a physical state, such as the posture of a person depicted in a painting, and of course is still used in this sense. This emphasis on bodily orientation has been reflected in one of the psychological approaches to attitude, which treats it as a mental or internalized "readiness for action" or "predisposition to respond." In modern psychology this view has its echoes. A second approach to the conceptualization of attitudes is one which emphasizes their affective character. The essentially affective nature of attitudes is often used by commentators to distinguish attitude from belief. Thus, Petty and Cacioppo (1981) note the "widespread agreement among social psychologists that the term *attitude* should be used to refer to a general and enduring positive or negative feeling about some person, object, or issue" (p. 7), whereas the term "belief" "is reserved for the information that a person has about other people, objects, and issues" (p. 7). A third approach to the conceptualization of attitudes is one that emphasizes their cognitive basis. Here, the argument is that attitudes are founded on beliefs, and this is illustrated in the so-called expectancy-value model of attitude. As explained by Ajzen (1988), this model holds that the formation of beliefs leads to the development of attitudes consistent with those beliefs:

> Generally speaking, we form beliefs about an object by associating it with certain

attributes.... Since the attributes that come to be linked to the object are already evaluated positively or negatively, we automatically and simultaneously acquire an attitude toward the object

(p. 32)

In more formal terms, the expectancy-value model holds that attitudes reflect the subjective probability (or expectancy) that the object has certain attributes, weighted by the subjective value of each attribute. Thus, if beliefs are regarded as "information," attitudes can be viewed as having an informational basis.

Each of the three approaches outlined emphasizes a particular facet of attitude: behavioral, affective, or cognitive. One further conceptualization of attitudes embraces all three facets. Early Greek philosophers divided all human experience into knowing, feeling, and acting, and this trichotomy has been applied more specifically to attitudes. The best known version of this tripartite approach is the one advanced by Rosenberg and Hovland (1960), which was referred to above. Rosenberg and Hovland's approach is a hierarchical model in which cognition, affect, and behavior are first-order factors, and attitude is a single second-order factor. The question of whether attitude is best conceptualized as a single entity or as multidimensional therefore depends to a large extent on the level of analysis at which one is working. At the level of specific responses to an attitude object, the distinctions between the three components are useful; however, all these responses share an evaluative character and it is this that makes them attitudinal in nature.

Empirical research findings are broadly consistent with this tripartite, hierarchical model of attitudes. To date the most compelling evidence in favor of this model comes from research reported by Breckler (1984). He found that when subjects' attitudes to snakes were assessed by measures intended to assess the cognitive, affective, and behavioral components of these attitudes, a three-factor solution provided a significantly better fit than a one-factor solution, confirming the discriminant validity of the three components proposed in the tripartite model. At the same

time, there was considerable overlap between the factors, consistent with the view that these three factors can reasonably be regarded as different facets of a single, higher-order construct.

Attitude measurement invariably depends on verbal responses to questionnaire items. Although the technique advocated by Thurstone (1928) broke new ground, it is relatively cumbersome and present-day attitude researchers typically use more recent techniques. Construction of a so-called Likert scale (Likert, 1932) is a three-stage process. The researcher first assembles a large number of opinion statements that are relevant to the issue in question. Each statement should express a basically positive or negative orientation to the issue. Thus, if the researcher wanted to develop a Likert scale measuring attitudes to abortion, he or she should begin by assembling statements such as "Each mother should have the right to terminate her own pregnancy if she so wishes" (pro-abortion) and "Human life is sacred from the moment of conception" (anti-abortion). Ideally, the "pro" and "anti" statements would be equally balanced. In the next stage, these statements are rated by a large sample of people drawn from the same population as those who will participate in the main phase of the research. These people are asked to indicate the extent to which they personally agree or disagree with each statement by selecting one of five response options: strongly disagree, disagree, neither disagree nor agree, agree, or strongly agree. The final stage involves "item analysis": first, the responses to each statement are assigned a numerical code (e.g. 1 to 5, being careful to reverse the scoring for negatively keyed items), and then the correlations between responses to individual items and the sum of the responses to all items are examined. Since the aim is to produce a set of statements which together assess an underlying evaluative orientation toward the issue in question, statements that yield poor item–whole correlations are discarded. The final Likert scale typically consists of between 10 and 25 statements. Alternative attitude scaling techniques include the semantic differential and scalogram analysis. Detailed treatment of measurement techniques is beyond the scope of the present entry, and interested readers are referred to Dawes and Smith (1985) for a comprehensive overview of verbal assessment procedures, and to Cacioppo and Tassinary (1989) for arguments in favor of psychophysiological assessment procedures.

The attitude–behavior relationship has attracted a good deal of research attention, primarily as a result of Wicker's (1969) paper reviewing empirical research on the degree to which attitudes to some issue correlated with behavior directed at that issue. Wicker was led to conclude that "taken as a whole, these studies suggest that it is considerably more likely that attitudes will be unrelated or only slightly related to overt behaviors than that attitudes will be closely related to actions" (p. 65). Subsequent research has shown that Wicker's conclusion was far too pessimistic. Fishbein and Ajzen (1975), for example, have developed a compelling argument to the effect that attitudes only correlate with behaviors when the two constructs are measured at the same level of specificity. They note that behaviors can be regarded as having four elements: (1) action (i.e. what is done); (2) target (i.e. the person or object at which the action is directed); (3) context (i.e. the physical setting in which the action is performed); and (4) time (i.e. the time at which the action is performed). In Fishbein and Ajzen's view, attitudes will not be predictive of behaviors unless they are measured at the same level of generality or specificity as the behavioral measure. This was the problem in the majority of the studies reviewed by Wicker (1969): researchers were taking very general, abstract measures of attitude (e.g. of racial prejudice), and then examining the relationship between such measures and a very specific index of behavior (e.g. how the respondent behaved toward a particular black person on a particular occasion). When the two constructs are measured at corresponding levels of specificity, reasonably high correlations are observed. Davidson and Jaccard (1979), for example, examined the relationships between attitudinal measures and a fairly specific behavioral measure, namely whether or not the respondent used oral contraceptives over a

two-year period. Attitudes were assessed at the beginning of the two-year study period, and behavior at the end of that period. Correlations of the different attitudinal measures with the behavioral measure were as follows: attitude to birth control, $r = 0.08$; attitude toward oral contraceptives, $r = 0.32$; attitude to using oral contraceptives, $r = 0.53$; attitude to using oral contraceptives during the next two years, $r = 0.57$.

As Fishbein and Ajzen's analysis would lead one to expect, the attitudinal measure that corresponded most closely with the behavioral measure with regard to action, target, context, and time was the most successful predictor. It follows that if one wants to use a general measure of attitude, one should use an equally general behavioral measure. This will necessarily entail sampling across actions, targets, contexts, and times. Just such a study was conducted by Weigel and Newman (1976). They assessed general attitudes to environmental issues and a broad range of behavioral criteria. The composite behavioral index correlated strongly ($r = 0.62$) with the attitudinal measure, although there was considerable variability in the strength of relationship between attitudes and any single behavioral measure. Fishbein and Ajzen (1975) and Ajzen and Fishbein (1980) have also developed a more general model of the relationship between attitudes and behavior, which they call the "theory of reasoned action." The essence of the model is that behavior is seen as being determined by intentions, which in turn are shaped by attitudes to behavior (i.e. the individual's evaluation of the goodness or badness of performing the action in question) and by subjective norms (i.e. the individual's perception of the extent to which significant others would like him or her to perform the action). There is a good deal of empirical support for this theory (for a summary, see Ajzen, 1988); however, a limitation of the theory of reasoned action is that it applies only to those behaviors which are predominantly volitional in nature. This limitation has been addressed by Ajzen (e.g. Ajzen, 1988) in his more recent "theory of planned behavior," which adds the construct of perceived control to the explanatory framework offered by the theory of reasoned action.

A second approach to the attitude–behavior relationship is one that emphasizes the role played by the accessibility of attitudes in memory. Accessibility is thought to be a function of the strength of the association between the attitude object and an evaluative response, and is defined operationally in terms of reaction time. The shorter the latency to make an evaluative response to the attitude object, the more accessible the attitude is said to be. If an attitude is highly accessible, it should be relatively easy to retrieve from memory when the individual is confronted with the attitude object. In this way, attitudes high in accessibility should play a stronger role in determining behavior toward the attitude object, as compared with less accessible attitudes. Thus, responses to attitudinal measures and overt behaviors should be guided by the same evaluative reaction to the attitude object, in the case of accessible attitudes, thereby enhancing attitude–behavior consistency. There is a good deal of evidence that indirectly supports this argument and also some more directly supportive evidence.

Attitude change is another topic that has been a focus of much research. The three primary ways in which attitudes can be changed are through (1) direct experience of the attitude object; (2) persuasive communications; and (3) induced behavior change. The effects of direct experience begin with mere exposure to the attitude object. Repeated exposure to a novel stimulus can in itself enhance an individual's attitude to that stimulus. Although experimental support for this proposition is quite consistent (see Harrison, 1977), there is still some uncertainty about how this effect is mediated. Harrison (1977) has advanced an explanation couched in terms of response competition, the essence of which is that a novel stimulus evokes some competition between alternative response tendencies; that this response competition is subjectively unpleasant; and that repeated exposure to the stimulus reduces the response competition and thereby enhances liking of the stimulus. Although there is some empirical support for this explanation it cannot account for findings showing that repeated exposure to a stimulus can enhance liking even when the

subject is unaware of having been exposed to the stimulus (because it has been presented subliminally, or to the non-attended ear in a dichotic listening task). Another way in which direct experience of the attitude object can change attitudes is through classical conditioning. There is a good deal of evidence showing that attitude objects encountered in positive contexts are evaluated more positively than those encountered in negative contexts. This effect is usually explained in terms of classical conditioning principles.

As regards the effects of persuasive communications on attitudes, they are widely regarded as depending on two kinds of factor: reception and acceptance. Reception simply refers to the degree to which the individual attends to and comprehends the communication. Attention is likely to vary as a function of the perceived utility of the communication and the attentional capacity of the recipient, while comprehension is likely to vary as a function of the recipient's intelligence. Much research attention is currently being devoted to the determinants of message *acceptance*, largely as a result of Petty and Cacioppo's (1986) elaboration likelihood model. "Elaboration" is the term used by Petty and Cacioppo to refer to the extent to which the recipient of a persuasive communication thinks about relevant issues or arguments contained in the message. Lasting attitude change depends on such elaboration. The direction of such attitude change depends on the nature of the thoughts evoked by the message. If recipients find the arguments contained in the message to be compelling, the communication should elicit favorable cognitive responses – for example, they may rehearse and memorize the arguments. This should result in persuasion. However, if the arguments are perceived by recipients as weak, the communication may well elicit unfavorable cognitive responses – for example, they may generate counterarguments of their own. This should result in a "boomerang" effect, i.e. change in the opposite direction to that advocated. Cognitive elaboration of message content represents the so-called "central route" to attitude change. Less enduring attitude change can be brought about via the "peripheral route," which

33

includes all those factors and processes that create attitude change without the recipient engaging in issue-relevant thinking. Examples would be associating an advertised product with intrinsically valued attributes, such as health, wealth, or sexual attractiveness; or associating an advocated position with someone regarded as powerful or high in expertise. The elaboration likelihood model predicts that these techniques will be ineffective in changing attitudes on issues about which the recipients already have a good deal of information, or in which they are keenly interested, since they will tend to focus on the issue-relevant information in the message and to ignore the peripheral cues (such as who is delivering the message). However, such techniques can evoke attitude change where recipients lack information about the issue or are not highly involved, although the resulting change will be temporary unless the message is repeated. There is a good deal of experimental support for this model (see Petty & Cacioppo, 1986).

With regard to the third main way in which attitudes can be changed, the notion that induced behavior change (or "forced compliance") can bring about attitude change was first suggested by L. Festinger in the original statement of COGNITIVE DISSONANCE theory. This theory is founded on the assumption that the awareness of inconsistency between cognitions creates an aversive, tension-like state ("cognitive dissonance") that the individual is motivated to reduce. It follows that if someone is persuaded (e.g. by financial incentives) to behave in a manner that runs counter to his or her attitudes, he or she should experience cognitive dissonance. The amount of dissonance associated with the knowledge that one has behaved in a certain way is said to increase as a function of the number and importance of the cognitions that are dissonant with the behavioral cognition, and to decrease as a function of the number and importance of the cognitions that are consonant (or consistent) with the behavioral cognition. Clearly, when someone engages in counter-attitudinal behavior, awareness that the behavior runs counter to attitudes constitutes a dissonant cognition (the importance of which will vary depending on the attitude involved). If the behavior has been performed for financial incentive, the incentive constitutes a consonant cognition. Thus, the smaller the incentive, the greater will be the amount of dissonance experienced. To reduce dissonance, the individual is expected to change his or her original attitude, making it more consistent with the behavior. This, indeed, is what researchers have found. In this way incentive-induced behavior change can result in attitude change, and the amount of change that results is *inversely* related to the size of the incentive that evoked the behavior change. Although this theoretical account of the processes responsible for attitude change resulting from induced behavior change has been challenged by others, most commentators now accept that the dissonance explanation is correct under the following conditions: (a) when the behavior is clearly inconsistent with a firmly held prior attitude; (b) when the individual believes that he or she freely engaged in the counter-attitudinal behavior; (c) when the behavior is believed by the individual to lead to negatively valued consequences.

See also PERSON PERCEPTION; SOCIAL COGNITION.

BIBLIOGRAPHY

Ajzen, I. (1988). *Attitudes, personality, and behaviour*. Milton Keynes: Open University Press.

——, & Fishbein, M. (1980). *Understanding attitudes and predicting social behavior*. Englewood Cliffs, NJ: Prentice-Hall.

Allport, G. W. (1935). Attitudes. In C. Murchison (Ed.), *A handbook of social psychology* (pp. 798–844). Worcester, Mass.: Clark University Press.

Breckler, S. J. (1984). Empirical validation of affect, behavior, and cognition as distinct components of attitude. *Journal of Personality and Social Psychology, 47,* 1191–205.

Cacioppo, J. T., & Tassinary, J. G. (1989). The concept of attitudes: A psychophysiological analysis. In H. L. Wagner & A. S. R. Manstead (Eds), *Handbook of social psychophysiology* (pp. 307–44). Chichester: Wiley.

Davidson, A. R., & Jaccard, J. J. (1979). Variables that moderate the attitude–behavior relation: Results of a longitudinal survey. *Journal of Personality and Social Psychology*, *37*, 1364–76.

Dawes, R. M., & Smith, T. L. (1985). Attitude and opinion measurement. In G. Lindzey & E. Aronson (Eds), *Handbook of social psychology* (3rd edn) (pp. 509–66). New York: Random House.

Harrison, A. A. (1977). Mere exposure. In L. Berkowitz (Ed.), *Advances in experimental social psychology* (pp. 39–83). New York: Academic Press.

Likert, R. A. (1932). A technique for the measurement of attitudes. *Archives of Psychology*, *140*, 1–55.

Petty, R. E., & Cacioppo, J. T. (1981). *Attitudes and persuasion: Classic and contemporary approaches*. Dubuque, Iowa.: Wm. C. Brown.

——. (1986). The Elaboration Likelihood Model of persuasion. In L. Berkowitz (Ed.), *Advances in experimental social psychology* (pp. 123–205). New York: Academic Press.

Rosenberg, M. J., & Hovland, C. I. (1960). Cognitive, affective, and behavioral components of attitude. In M. J. Rosenberg, C. I. Hovland, W. J. McGuire, R. P. Abelson, & J. W. Brehm (Eds), *Attitude organization and change: An analysis of consistency among attitude components* (pp. 1–14). New Haven, Conn.: Yale University Press.

Thurstone, L. L. (1928). Attitudes can be measured. *American Journal of Sociology*, *33*, 529–44.

Weigel, R. H., & Newman, L. S. (1976). Increasing attitude–behavior correspondence by broadening the scope of the behavioral measure. *Journal of Personality and Social Psychology*, *33*, 793–802.

Wicker, A. W. (1969). Attitudes versus actions: The relationship of verbal and overt responses to attitude objects. *Journal of Social Issues*, *25*, 41–78.

A. S. R. MANSTEAD

auditory perception Humans and other animals can use sound to perceive the location and nature of vibrating and sound-reflecting objects in their environment. Our conscious experience of sound consists of a number of different attributes: we are aware of sounds generated by familiar objects and events (footsteps, coughs, car horns) which may be recognizable as produced by a particular object or person; we are also aware of the direction from which the sound comes and of the environment in which the sound has been produced (someone speaking in a reverberant church or in an acoustically dead living-room). We may be aware of many different sounds at the same time, yet generally each keeps its own identity in the presence of others. The study of auditory perception helps us to understand the mechanisms that give rise to these apparently effortless percepts.

To help understand the complexity of the problem faced by the brain, imagine that you are looking at the pattern of waves entering a harbor, and that you have to decide *solely on the basis of those waves* what events are happening out at sea. Waves from different events are mixed together, and the nature of the waves will have changed as they travel across the sea and around obstacles to reach the harbor.

FREQUENCY ANALYSIS

For sound to be perceivable, pressure changes in the air must be converted to neural impulses. A very simple way to do this is to allow movement sensitive hairs to feel the vibrations of a membrane – like a cat's whiskers touching a drum-skin. This method could give a crude indication of the presence of sound, but because of the limited information that can be transmitted down individual nerve fibers it would be of little use for distinguishing between complex sounds. How evolution improves on this method depends on the sounds that are important to the animal. If sounds of a particular frequency are especially significant, the animal might tune the drum to that frequency. Such tuning has the tremendous advantage that irrelevant sounds are filtered out. A frog trying to hear its potential mate's croak against the sound of a waterfall will be much more successful if it can tune out as much of the noise of the waterfall as possible. Adult frogs have resonators in their amphibian papillae which resonate to the frequency of the male's croak. Immature females do not; ignorant of what they are missing, they give the grown-ups a clear run.

Mating success among higher animals

requires a less specialized approach to sound. Generalizing from the amphibian resonator, our ears can resonate to any frequency within a range between about 20 Hz and 20,000 Hz. Different places along the basilar membrane in the inner ear resonate to different frequencies. Hair cells respond to the membrane's movement and the firing rate and temporal firing pattern of the auditory nerves connected to these cells present the brain with a frequency analysis of the incoming sound.

A major recent discovery is that the basilar membrane in the healthy ear shows extremely sharp tuning with filter slopes of many hundreds of decibels/octave (Sellick, Patuzzi, & Johnstone, 1982). The mechanism responsible for this remarkable tuning is not known, but it can be damaged easily by mechanical trauma, anoxia, or certain drugs. The mechanism may require positive feedback and appears to involve active elements in the outer hair cells. These active processes lead to sound being emitted from the ear either spontaneously or in response to sound (Kemp, 1978). Paradoxically, while the healthy ear responds to sound in a non-linear way (producing distortion tones that were first described by the violinist Tartini in 1754), the damaged ear has a more linear response. But along with the increased linearity, the sensorineurally damaged ear is less sensitive, less sharply tuned, and has a more limited dynamic range. As a consequence, the sensori-neurally deaf patient finds it more difficult to hear quiet sounds, to separate sounds from a background of noise or of other sounds, and cannot tolerate loud sounds. Many of these symptoms are a consequence of damage to the outer hair cells.

While the outer hair cells are responsible for sharpening the tuning of the basilar membrane (and perhaps also for adjusting its mechanics through efferent fibers), the basic transduction from mechanical movement of the basilar membrane to nerve impulses is performed by the inner hair cells. Inner hair cells along the length of the membrane respond to its vibration by making their voltage less negative (depolarizing) as the "hairs" (stereocilia) are bent in one direction. The depolarization leads to neurotransmitter release which in turn increases the probability that an auditory nerve fiber connected to that cell will fire. More intense sounds cause a greater voltage change in the hair cell and a greater firing rate in the connected auditory nerve fiber.

A limit on how rapidly a hair cell can change voltage has an important influence on the temporal pattern of firing in the auditory nerve. For low-frequency tones, the hair cell's voltage change can follow the individual cycles of the waveform causing auditory nerve fibers to fire predominantly during one half of the tone's cycle (*phase-locking*). Phase-locking allows the brain to determine the frequency of the tone from the pattern of time intervals between neural firings (*timing mechanism*) as well as from the relative rate of firing of different nerve fibers (*rate mechanism*). For high-frequency pure tones the inner hair cells cannot change voltage fast enough, and so the nerve's firing pattern cannot reflect their frequency. Consequently, the frequency of tones above about 4000 Hz in man can only be coded by a place mechanism. However, for high-frequency complex sounds the auditory nerve can phase-lock to relatively slow changes in amplitude of the sound's envelope. This ability is important in localizing complex sounds, and for coding the fundamental frequency (giving pitch) of the high-frequency part of speech and music.

A very large body of psycho-acoustic data can be quite well explained by a simple approximation to the mechanisms described so far: incoming sound is filtered through a bank of (linear) band-pass filters, rectified and smoothed; detection processes inspect the output of individual channels from this filter bank (Moore, 1989).

However, an interesting recent development in basic psycho-acoustics has been the discovery that some very simple detection tasks cannot be explained by mechanisms which only inspect single auditory channels. Green's profile analysis (1983) and Hall and Haggard's co-modulation masking release (Hall, Haggard, & Fernandes, 1984) are examples where detectability is influenced by what is happening in auditory filters other than those receiving the tone that is to be detected.

Apart from making sounds more detectable, the fact that the ear codes sound by a frequency analysis helps in recognizing a sound's properties such as its position, pitch, and timbre.

LOCALIZATION

By comparing the intensity and time of arrival (or phase) of sounds at the two ears, we can estimate a sound's azimuth (direction in the horizontal plane). Intensity differences are caused by the head casting an acoustic shadow. This shadow is darker for high-frequency sounds (a 20 dB difference between the ears for a 10 kHz sound to one side) than for low (6 dB at 500 Hz). If the ear did not separate different frequencies, intensity difference would be a more ambiguous cue. Differences in time of arrival and phase of low-frequency sounds and of complex high-frequency sounds can be used to help localization because of the ability of the auditory nerve to phase-lock to changes in amplitude. Neurophysiological evidence and models based on human psycho-acoustic data (Stern & Colburn, 1978) agree that the brain treats intensity differences and timing differences as separate cues, estimating direction for each frequency according to each cue separately, and then combining the direction estimates. Owls have different brain nuclei for performing these separate functions (Konishi, Sullivan, & Takahashi, 1985). Our remarkable sensitivity to interaural time differences may arise through a delay-line mechanism described by Jeffress in 1948.

A sound's elevation (direction in the vertical plane) is coded by changes in a sound's timbre that occur through its interaction with the external ear (or pinna). High-frequency sounds (above about 4000 Hz) reflect off the structures of the outer ear causing some frequencies to be amplified and others attenuated, depending on the direction from which the sound has come. If a sound lasts long enough for the listener to make head movements during it, localization (particularly in azimuth) is improved.

We can also estimate a sound's distance; this is easier if the sound is familiar. Distant sounds are quieter, more reverberant, and more lacking in high frequencies than are close sounds. If the sound is unfamiliar we can be misled. A sound interpreted as coming from the street outside will change its character when one realizes that it is coming from inside the room.

Localization within rooms is complicated by echoes. Echoes have a spectrum similar to the original sound, but will come from different directions. The ear exploits the principle that a straight line is the shortest distance between two points, by giving more weight in localization to the first sound to arrive than to subsequent ones (the Precedence Effect). It has come directly and so indicates the correct direction.

PITCH

The pitch of a sound is important in SPEECH PERCEPTION and in the perception of music. Pitch is the attribute of sound that gives melodies; it contributes to the intonation of speech. The pitch of a pure tone is closely related to its frequency (although it also depends on intensity and the state of the listener's ears). The mechanisms underlying our perception of the pitch of complex tones have been intensively studied for over a hundred years. A complex tone consists of harmonics of the fundamental. Thus, when the oboe plays an "A" to the orchestra at a fundamental of 440 Hz, the sound it produces will have harmonics at whole-number multiples of that frequency (440, 880, 1320, 1760, and so on). Any instrument playing the same note will also produce harmonics in that same series; different instruments vary in the relative intensity of each harmonic, as well as in the detailed way in which the note starts and stops.

The ear can separate the first ten or so harmonics of a complex tone, estimating their frequencies through a combination of place and timing mechanisms. It is clear that these low-numbered harmonics are the dominant ones in determining the musical pitch of a note. They are also generally the loudest both in music and in speech. Goldstein's (Gerson & Goldstein, 1978) widely accepted theory of pitch proposes that the brain finds the best fitting series of consecutive harmonics to the frequencies that the ear has resolved.

However, it is also clear that we can hear a pitch with only high-numbered harmonics, which are not resolved. The pitch is musically more vague; but we can still tell whether it is increasing or decreasing even though we can no longer tell whether it has gone up, say, a major or minor third. The most likely explanation for our ability to hear pitch from unresolved harmonics was originally proposed by Schouten in 1948. It exploits the mechanism of phase-locking to the envelope of a complex sound described above. Unresolved harmonics beat at the frequency of the fundamental and this beating captures the phase-locking of the auditory nerve. The pitch percept from envelope timing cues is exploited in cochlear implants for very deaf patients, which stimulate the ear with a train of electrical impulses at the voice pitch. Patients with no usable peripheral frequency resolution can often hear the pitch of the voice with such a device (Rosen & Fourcin, 1986).

TIMBRE

What aspects of sound code the difference between two different instruments playing a note on the same pitch? The most obvious difference is that different instruments have different amounts of energy at the different harmonic frequencies. Clarinets, for example, are weak in the even-numbered harmonics. But the characteristic sounds of different musical instruments can only be approximated very crudely by synthesizing steady-state sounds that reproduce the relative amplitudes of the harmonics. Much more important is the nature of the attack and the decay of the note and the presence or absence of vibrato during the main body of the note. Some improvement towards a life-like sound can be obtained by giving a note the appropriate overall amplitude contour (so that a piano note rises abruptly and then decays more slowly). But to get sounds that are indistinguishable from the real thing, much more complex dynamic information must be provided. The individual harmonics must start, stop, and change in amplitude at different times and rates. The ear appears to be extremely sensitive to such dynamic aspects of timbre.

AUDITORY GROUPING AND ATTENTION

Sounds from many different simultaneous sources add together at the ear, yet we generally perceive separate sources and can attend selectively to one of them (see ATTENTION). Sounds that come from different *directions* are likely to be from separate sources (although one could be an echo). Selective attention experiments in the 1950s (see Broadbent, 1958) demonstrated that it was easier to listen to one voice among two or more when it came from a different direction. Selection on the basis of interaural time differences could be made by choosing one of the rows of second-order cells in Jeffress's cross-correlation model of localization.

Direction is not the whole story. We can still organize sound into separate apparent sources when it comes over a single loudspeaker. The principles that help us to achieve this organization follow similar principles to those devised by the Gestalt psychologists for grouping visual stimuli (see GESTALT PRINCIPLES OF PERCEPTUAL ORGANIZATION). They are exploited implicitly by composers (see review by McAdams & Bregman, 1979). For instance, a single sequence of notes can break into two perceived melodic lines if one set of notes is in a different frequency range (Bregman & Campbell, 1971) or has a different timbre (Wessel, 1978, cited in Pierce, 1983, p. 191) from the other. This effect is common in baroque writing for recorder or violin and is called "implied polyphony." Similarly, a tune and its accompaniment may appear from the combination of two quite different parts when, say, alternate notes of the two parts lie close together. This effect is exploited in Tchaikovsky's Pathetique Symphony where the notes of the melody at the beginning of the last movement alternate between the first and second violins (see Deutsch, 1982). These examples illustrate grouping by frequency proximity. Other principles of grouping include common fate, where, for example, a common onset time of frequency components indicates a common source (Bregman & Pinker, 1978). Common harmonic structure or common amplitude modulation helps to separate two simultaneous periodic sounds such as vowels (Scheffers, 1983).

See also PATTERN PERCEPTION.

BIBLIOGRAPHY

Bregman, A. S., & Campbell, J. (1971). Primary auditory stream segregation and perceptual order in sequences of tones. *Journal of Experimental Psychology, 89*, 244–9.

Bregman, A. S., & Pinker, S. (1978). Auditory streaming and the building of timbre. *Canadian Journal of Psychology, 32*, 19–31.

Broadbent, D. E. (1958). *Perception and communication*. London: Pergamon.

Deutsch, D. (1982). (Ed.) *The psychology of music.* New York: Academic Press.

Gerson, A., & Goldstein, J. L. (1978). Evidence for a general template in central optimum processing for pitch of complex tones. *Journal of the Acoustical Society of America, 63*, 498–510.

Green, D. M. (1983). Profile analysis. *American Psychologist, 38*, 133–42.

Hall, J. W., Haggard, M. P., & Fernandes, M. A. (1984). Detection in noise by spectrotemporal pattern analysis. *Journal of the Acoustical Society of America, 76*, 50–6.

Jeffress, L. A. (1948). A place theory of sound localization. *Journal of Comparative and Physiological Psychology, 41*, 35–9.

Kemp, D. T. (1978). Stimulated acoustic emissions from within the human auditory system. *Journal of the Acoustical Society of America, 64*, 1386–91.

Konishi, M., Sullivan, W. E., & Takahashi, T. (1985). The owl's cochlear nuclei process different sound localisation cues. *Journal of the Acoustical Society of America, 78*, 360–4.

McAdams, S., & Bregman, A. S. (1979). Hearing musical streams. *Computer Music Journal, 3*, 26–43, 60; reprinted in C. Roads & J. Strawn (Eds), *Foundations of computer music*, MIT Press, 1985.

Moore, B. C. J. (1989). *An introduction to the psychology of hearing* (Third edition). London: Academic Press.

Pierce, J. R. (1983). *The science of musical sound.* New York: Freeman.

Rosen, S., & Fourcin, A. (1986). Frequency selectivity and the perception of speech. In B. C. J. Moore (Ed.), *Frequency selectivity in hearing*. London: Academic Press.

Scheffers, M. T. M. (1983). Sifting vowels: Auditory pitch analysis and sound segregation. Doctoral dissertation: Groningen University.

Sellick, P. M., Patuzzi, R., & Johnstone, B. M. (1982). Measurement of basilar membrane motion in the guinea pig cochlea using the Mossbauer technique. *Journal of the Acoustical Society of America, 72*, 131–41.

Stern, M., & Colbourn, H. S. (1978). Theory of binaural interaction based on auditory nerve data. *Journal of the Acoustical Society of America, 64*, 127.

C. J. DARWIN

automatic processing An automatic process can be defined as any mental operation that occurs without the need for conscious initiation. Alternative terms for such processes are preconscious or preattentive. Many experimental demonstrations of automatic processes exist. The most well known is the STROOP EFFECT – the finding that naming the ink color of a word will be impaired if the carrier word is incongruent with the color response, e.g. green written in red. This effect is extremely robust and cannot be avoided by any voluntary strategy except squinting which, by defocusing, reduces the salience of carrier word information.

There have been a number of attempts to produce frameworks within which to understand the nature of automatic processing. Posner and Snyder (1975) proposed a two-process theory of attention. Presentation of a stimulus is first assumed to make direct automatic contact with its internal representation including its semantics (thus accounting for inability to suppress knowing the meaning of a familiar word). This automatic stage is assumed to be fast acting and results in the activation of representations associated with the target. This associative activation provides the basis for facilitation in the processing of subsequent related stimuli. The second stage of processing is dependent on conscious effort, is slower acting, and can generate expectancies based on prior stimulus analysis. Conscious processing therefore provides a basis for perceptual facilitation if expectancies are confirmed, and perceptual inhibition if not.

The existence of these two processes was elegantly demonstrated by Neely (1977). Subjects were required to carry out lexical decisions to target words that were preceded by PRIMING stimuli. He demonstrated that rapid sequential presentation of natural associations (e.g. bird → robin) facilitated lexical decision but no inhibition occurred with unrelated sequences. However, subjects were also told to expect certain arbitrary pairings of stimuli (e.g. "body" will always be followed by a word describing part of a building). These pairings produced no facilitation or inhibition with rapid sequential presentation but, with increasing intervals between prime and target, both facilitatory and inhibitory effects emerged. One further finding was that natural associations which subjects were told not to expect (e.g. "body" → "arm") produced facilitation with short interstimulus intervals and inhibition with larger intervals. Neely's experiment therefore illustrated the existence of both fast-acting automatic processes which gradually receded as slower conscious processing of the stimulus took over.

An alternative perspective on automatic processes is provided by Hasher and Zacks (1979). They proposed that automatic mental processes had a number of specific properties that distinguished them from conscious effortful processes. These properties were: age invariance, insensitivity to training procedures, individual differences, strategy manipulations, unaffected by secondary demands on attention. Hasher and Zacks proposed that certain dimensions of experience were automatically committed to memory. They provided evidence that both spatial memory and memory for item frequency occurrence met the criteria of automaticity. However, subsequent research, notably by Naveh-Benjamin (1988), has cast doubt on these claims.

Parkin and Russo (1990) have shown that Hasher and Zack's criteria may be meaningful when applied to the distinction that is drawn between implicit and explicit memory (*see* IMPLICIT AND EXPLICIT MEMORY). They report data indicating that implicit memory tasks including picture completion and fragment completion appear to be unaffected by secondary processing tasks during learning and show evidence of age invariance.

A third approach to automatic processes derives from the work of Schneider and Shiffrin (1977). These authors distinguished automatic processes from controlled processes using a visual search paradigm. Subjects are given a target number and then required to scan a series of visual displays for that target. Two factors are varied – the number of items in each display and whether the nontargets in the displays are drawn from the same (numbers) or a different (letters) category to the target. Subjects performed much better in the different-category condition and were unaffected by the number of nontargets in each display. In contrast, the same category condition produced poorer levels of performance and systematically slower responses as the number of nontargets in each display increased. The investigators argued that subjects in the different-category condition were well practised at detecting numbers in arrays of letters such that the process had become automatic – rather in the same way that our eyes seem drawn automatically to a familiar face in a crowd. The same-category condition, however, was not well practiced and required a conscious directed search of each frame to identify a target.

Further experiments have shown that tasks that seem initially to be carried out using conscious effort gradually become automatic with practice. These findings provide a basis for understanding the acquisition of skills which, in the early stages of learning, require a good deal of conscious effort to perform them. Learning to read, for example, is thought to be crucially dependent on the development of automatic word decoding skills. The concept of automaticity has also been implicated in our attempts to explain the resolution of ambiguity and anaphoric reference. In the former case automatic processes are thought to make available both meanings of an ambiguous word with conscious, contextually directed processing, resolving which meaning is processed further. With ANAPHORA, it is thought that all possible antecedents are activated automatically and the choice of referent then made consciously.

The extent to which mental operations can be assimilated into automatic processes is a key determinant of an organism's cognitive flexibility. By removing the need to expend conscious effort on routine mental operations the organism is free to explore new and possibly more complex forms of mental operation.

See also DECLARATIVE AND PROCEDURAL KNOWLEDGE; EXPERTISE; POSNER, MICHAEL.

BIBLIOGRAPHY

Hasher, L., & Zacks, R. T. (1979). Automatic and effortful processes in memory. *Journal of Experimental Psychology: General, 108*, 356–88.

Naveh-Benjamin, M. (1988). Recognition memory of spatial location information: Another failure to support automaticity. *Memory & Cognition, 16*, 437–45.

Neely, J. H. (1977). Semantic priming and retrieval from lexical memory: The role of inhibitionless spreading activation and limited capacity attention. *Journal of Experimental Psychology: General, 106*, 226–54.

Parkin, A. J., & Russo, R. (1990). Implicit and explicit memory and the automatic/effortful distinction. *European Journal of Cognitive Psychology, 2*, 71–80.

Posner, M. I., & Snyder, C. R. R. (1975). Attention and cognitive control. In R. L. Solso (Ed.), *Information processing and cognition: The Loyola Symposium*. Hillsdale, NJ: Lawrence Earlbaum.

Schneider, W., & Shiffrin, R. M. (1977). Controlled and automatic human information processing: I Detection, search, and attention. *Psychological Review, 84*, 1–66.

A. J. PARKIN

B

Bartlett, Sir Frederic FRS (1886–1969).
First professor of Psychology at the University
of Cambridge, Sir Frederic Bartlett was a
leading figure in the development of British
psychology and the author of a number of
books, including *Psychology and the soldier*
(1927) and *The problem of noise* (1934).
However, within cognitive psychology, Bartlett's lasting influence comes from his work
Remembering: An experimental and social study,
published in 1932.

Bartlett took the view that experimental
psychology should relate to the real world – a
fact reflected in the assistance he gave to the
Ministry of Defence during both world wars.
In *Remembering*, Bartlett advanced the view
that much of the experimental work concerned
with human memory lacked validity because
the experiments were unrealistic. At the time
memory research was dominated by the empirical methods originating from Ebbinghaus in
the nineteenth century. Ebbinghaus stressed
the importance of using meaningless material
such as nonsense syllables in memory experiments – the argument being that greater
experimental rigor could be obtained because
subjects could not bring pre-existing knowledge to bear on the learning task.

Bartlett argued that these methods were
unlikely to discover anything significant about
memory. He proposed that the basis of human
learning was an "effort after meaning" and
that to exclude it from investigation was to
miss the essence of human memory.

In *Remembering*, Bartlett describes a number
of experiments investigating how people remember meaningful material. Most well known
is "The War of the Ghosts" experiment in
which he examined subjects' successive recall
of a Red Indian folk story. The most striking
aspect of the data was that subjects introduced
aspects of their own knowledge about the
world so as to make the story more coherent
from their own point of view.

To account for these results Bartlett introduced the term schema. Originated by the
neurologist Head, the term schema was used
to describe the internal body image that
enables us, for example, to know the relative
position of our limbs and their relation to
other features of the environment. Bartlett
extended the idea by suggesting that we also
have internal SCHEMATA dealing with our
knowledge of how the world is. When remembering he believed that these schema were
brought into play as a means of aiding
retrieval. Schema could take many forms. At
one level schema reflecting the subject's
attitude to the whole story could influence the
manner in which it was recalled. At a more
specific level a schema might result in a distortion or transformation of detail more consistent with the subject's view of the world.

Because of methodological shortcomings
associated with tasks such as successive recall,
and the difficulty of devising specific theories,
Bartlett's arguments had little impact on
memory research. However, in 1978, Neisser
revived the objections first raised by Bartlett
and there has since been a growing interest in
studying memory outside the laboratory.
Bartlett's views on schema are also reflected in
recent developments in cognitive psychology,
most notably Schank and Abelson's (1977)
concept of scripts (*see* COGNITIVE SCIENCE;
SCHEMATA).

See also CONCEPT LEARNING; PERCEPTUAL
MOTOR COORDINATION.

BIBLIOGRAPHY

Bartlett, F. C. (1932). *Remembering: An
experimental and social study*. Cambridge: Cambridge University Press.

Neisser, U. (1978). Memory: What are the
important questions. In M. M. Gruneberg,
P. E. Morris, and R. N. Sykes (Eds), *Practical
aspects of memory*. London: Academic Press.

Schank, R. C., & Abelson, R. P. (1977). *Scripts,*

plans, goals and understanding. Hillsdale, NJ: Erlbaum Associates.

A. J. PARKIN

Bayes' law Bayes' law is a theorem of probability theory resulting from the definitions of conditional probability and additivity. For two elements, H and D, $P(H \cap D) = P(H|D)\, P(D) = P(D|H)\, P(H)$, which means that, $P(H|D) = [P(D|H)/P(D)]\, P(H)$, which is Bayes' law. The relevance of the law to the study of cognition stems from its interpretation as a prescriptive model for the revision of the prior probability, $P(H)$, about the truth of a hypothesis, H, in light of observed data, D, in order to arrive at a posterior probability, $P(H|D)$. The informativeness of the data is the likelihood ratio, the ratio of the unconditional probability that the data would be observed under any circumstances to the conditional probability that the data would be observed if H were true, $P(D|H)/P(D)$. Under specific conditions (see below), subjective uncertainty, stated in probability form, is admissible as a probability. In this case the probabilities are called personal probabilities or subjective probabilities.

To see how Bayes' law operates, suppose a physician's patient were to exhibit a particular symptom, D, and the physician were interested in the probability that the patient had disease H. Bayes' law prescribes that the physician begin with his or her subjective prior probability that a presenting patient would have the disease, $SP(H)$, which might be the base rate of the disease. This subjective probability should then be multiplied by the likelihood ratio: the subjective probability of the symptom occurring were disease H responsible, $SP(D|H)$, divided by the subjective probability of the symptom occurring were H or any other disease responsible, $SP(D)$. The product of the prior probability and the likelihood ratio would be the subjective posterior probability, $SP(H|D)$, that the patient has disease H given that he or she exhibits symptom D.

Psychologists who study decision behavior are particularly interested in the properties of uncertainty stated as subjective probabilities because, together with utilities, they determine the subjective worth of gambles. Gambles have been widely regarded as the appropriate metaphor for all risky decision alternatives. The subjective worth of a gamble is its subjective expected utility,

$$SEU = \sum_{i=1}^{n} SP_i(U_i),$$

where the subjective expected utility, SEU, is the product sum of the utility, U_i, of each of the n outcomes of the gamble and the associated subjective probability, SP_i, of each of those outcomes occurring.

Savage (1954) showed that (personal) subjective probabilities are admissible as "real" probabilities when they are coherent, i.e. when they conform to the constraints of probability theory. Beginning with studies by Ward Edwards and his colleagues, the research agenda throughout the 1960s and much of the 1970s was to examine the degree to which untrained subjects' subjective probabilities are coherent. A large part of this research centered on whether the revision of subjective probabilities conforms to Bayes' law.

The earliest and most noteworthy finding of the Bayesian research was that revisions of subjective probabilities are conservative: that is, data appear to have less impact on subjective probabilities than would be prescribed by Bayes' law. Subsequent research showed that subjects' revisions also are influenced by factors that are irrelevant to Bayes' law and to probability theory. Among these are the order in which the data are observed (primacy effects), the amount of data observed (sample size effects), familiarity with the data generating process, the way in which the data are displayed, and the response mode employed.

Interest in the Bayesian paradigm has declined, but the research left an important legacy. On the one hand, conservatism and the apparent fragility of subjective probabilities, their vulnerability to extraneous factors, have led to methods for making the task of assessing them easier. These methods require the decision maker to make assessments only for simple (as opposed to compound) events, and then a computer programed with Bayes' law is used to perform the revisions. Such methods have become common in applied decision analysis and computerized schemes for decision aiding. On the other hand, the conservatism finding has prompted extensive examination of the coherence of subjective probabilities in other than revision tasks. This research, widely known as the "heuristics and biases" research, has had a major impact on descriptive theories of decision making as well as fueling an ongoing controversy about the nature and adequacy of human REASONING (e.g. Kahneman, Slovic, & Tversky, 1982).

See also INFERENCES; STATISTICAL INFERENCE.

BIBLIOGRAPHY

Beach, L. R., Christensen-Szalanski, J. J. J., & Barnes, V. E. (1987). Assessing human judgment: Has it been done, can it be done, should it be done? In G. Wright & P. Ayton (Eds), *Judgmental forecasting* (pp. 49–62). London: Wiley.

Kahneman, D., Slovic, P., & Tversky, A. (1982). *Judgment under uncertainty: Heuristics and biases.* New York: Cambridge University Press.

Peterson, C. R., & Beach, L. R. (1967). Man as an intuitive statistician. *Psychological Bulletin, 68,* 29–46.

Phillips, L. D., & Edwards, W. (1966). Conservatism in a simple probability inference task. *Journal of Experimental Psychology, 72,* 346–54.

Savage, L. J. (1954). *The foundations of statistics.* New York: Wiley.

Slovic, P., Fischhoff, B., & Lichtenstein, S. (1977). Behavioral decision theory. *Annual Review of Psychology, 28,* 1–39.

LEE ROY BEACH

blindsight The term is used in the broadest sense to refer to residual vision in the absence of primary visual (striate) cortex, especially in primates. As portions of the optic nerve terminate in a number of targets in the brain in parallel to the direct projection of the retina (via the thalamus) to striate cortex, it is not surprising that some visual function can still be demonstrated in animals. Thus, monkeys without striate cortex can locate objects in space, can discriminate different orientations of patterns, can detect relatively fine gratings and thus have a measurable visual acuity, although none of these capacities is quite up to normal levels.

In the narrowest sense, however, the term refers to the visual discriminations that are still possible in human subjects with damage to the visual cortex who, nevertheless, are not aware of any experience of "seeing" the stimuli they are discriminating. It was first coined by the authors of a report of one such patient (Weiskrantz, Warrington, Sanders, & Marshall, 1974). Typically, damage to visual cortex in human subjects through disease, tumor, accident, and so on produces regions of apparent absolute blindness in those regions of the visual fields that correspond by classical mapping procedures to the cortex that is damaged. In some subjects, however, good visual discrimination can be demonstrated in these "blind" regions of the field if the subjects are tested in the same way that is necessary with animals, i.e. by forced choice discrimination or by reaching to the stimuli. Blindsight subjects insist that they are not aware of the stimuli and are only "guessing", but nevertheless can perform some discriminations quite well (*see* INTROSPECTION). The first report of such a visual capacity appears to be the study of Pöppel, Held, and Frost (1973) showing that some subjects can move their eyes to the position of a stimulus previously presented in the "blind" field. With some highly salient stimuli and for some subjects, an intermediate state of awareness is reported, such as a "gut feeling" that something is in the blind region.

Because it is virtually impossible for damage to striate cortex in humans not to be accompanied by damage to neighboring cortical association regions, and because such lesions also can produce specific "modular" visual defects, it is to be expected that qualitative differences in the profiles of residual visual capacities among human subjects with field defects will be the rule. To date, some human subjects have reported to have some, but not necessarily all, of the following visual discriminative capacities without acknowledged awareness of the discriminative stimuli: location in space either by reaching or by eye movements to the position of the previously exposed stimulus, discrimination of orientation of a grating in the frontal plane, discrimination of presence and direction of movement, closure of stimuli presented simultaneously to the intact and blind fields (but not to either alone), match/mismatch of stimuli in the good and blind fields, good field/blind field summation or inhibition of reactions times to stimuli presented to both fields (for reviews, cf. Weiskrantz, 1986, 1989). Evidence of color discrimination has been more ambiguous, but recently good evidence for such a capacity has also been published (Stoerig, 1987; Stoerig & Cowey, 1989). It is clear that more capacities remain to be examined, and it seems likely that this list will be expanded in future research, as well as a definition of capacities that may be impossible (for example, perhaps, form). Methodology is also advancing to enable blindsight patients' visual capacities to be assessed without requiring guessing responses, either by measuring the effects of stimuli placed in the blind field upon the perception of concurrent stimuli in the intact field, or by using reactions of the autonomic system to visual stimuli presented in the blind field.

The phenomena entailed by the narrow usage of the term has been the subject of vigorous discussions in the literature regarding their interpretation and possible artefacts (Campion, Latto, & Smith, 1983). Suggestions have been ventilated that the phenomena are caused indirectly by diffusion of light into the intact field, or that subjects' altered response criteria are critically involved, or that there may be residual striate cortex within the lesion site. The last possibility cannot be ruled out empirically because no patients have yet come to post mortem, although the reports of blindsight capacity in hemispherectomized patients make it extremely unlikely to be a general explanation (Perenin & Jeannerod, 1978; Ptito, Lassonde, Lepore, & Ptito, 1987). Strong counter-evidence has been provided against the other two possibilities (cf. Stoerig, Hubner, & Pöppel, 1985; Weiskrantz, 1986; Stoerig, 1987).

Quite aside from the linking together of the animal and human evidence, and allowing inferences to be drawn concerning the role of the non-striate pathways, the phenomenon of discrimination without awareness has also been of interest to philosophers of perception and consciousness (Searle, 1979; Natsoulas, 1982; Churchland, 1986). Also, within cognitive neuropsychology it appears that there are a number of other domains in which "implicit" processing can take place even though subjects have lost or are disconnected from their "explicit" knowledge of them, e.g. in AMNESIA, APHASIA, neglect, and dyslexia (cf. Schacter, McAndrews, & Moscovitch, 1988) (see DYSLEXIAS: ACQUIRED). Similar dissociations have also been explored in normal subjects (cf. Tulving, 1983) (see IMPLICIT AND EXPLICIT MEMORY).

BIBLIOGRAPHY

Campion, J., Latto, R., & Smith, Y. M. (1983). Is blindsight an effect of scattered light, spared cortex, and near-threshold vision? *Behavioural Brain Science, 6*, 423–48.

Churchland, P. S. (1986). *Neurophilosophy*. Cambridge, Mass.: MIT Press.

Natsoulas, R. (1982). Conscious perception and the paradox of "blind sight." In G. Underwood (Ed.), *Aspects of consciousness*. New York: Academic Press.

Perenin, M. T., & Jeannerod, M. (1978). Visual function within the hemianopic field following early cerebral hemidecortication in man. I. Spatial localization. *Neuropsychologia, 16*, 1–13.

Pöppel, E., Held, R., & Frost, D. (1973). Residual visual function after brain wounds involving the central visual pathways in man. *Nature, 243*, 295–6.

Ptito, A., Lassonde, M., Lepore, F., & Ptito, M. (1987). Visual discrimination in hemispherectomized patients. *Neuropsychologia, 25*, 869–79.

Schachter, D. L., McAndrews, M. P., & Moscovitch, M. (1988). Access to consciousness: Dissociations between implicit and explicit knowledge in neuropsychological syndromes. In L. Weiskrantz (Ed.), *Thought without language* (pp. 242–78). Oxford: Oxford University Press.

Searle, J. R. (1979). The intentionality of intention and action. *Inquiry, 22*, 253–80.

Stoerig, P. (1987). Chromaticity and achromaticity: Evidence of a functional differentiation in visual field defects. *Brain, 110*, 869–86.

Stoerig, P., & Cowey, A. (1989). Wavelength sensitivity in blindsight. *Nature, 342,* 916–18.

— —, Hubner, M., & Pöppel, E. (1985). Signal detection analysis of residual vision in a field defect due to a post-geniculate lesion. *Neuropsychologia, 23,* 589–99.

Tulving, E. (1983). *Elements of episodic memory* (pp. 100–20). Oxford: Oxford University Press.

Weiskrantz, L. (1986). *Blindsight. A case study and implications.* Oxford: Oxford University Press.

— —. (1989). Blindsight. In F. Boller and J. Grafman (Eds), *Handbook of neuropsychology* (Vol. 2) (pp. 375–85). Amsterdam: Elsevier.

— —, Warrington, E. K., Sanders, M. D., & Marshall, J. (1974). Visual capacity in the hemianopic field following a restricted occipital ablation. *Brain, 97,* 709–28.

L. WEISKRANTZ

body image This expression denotes an abstract internal representation of spatial and physical-mechanical properties of one's body (including muscle, skeleton, organs, and so on). It is based on some combination of past and current information from proprioceptive, kinesthetic, muscular, articular, postural, tactile, cutaneous, vestibular, equilibrium, visual, and auditory senses, as well as from our sense of physical effort and from contact with objects and among our body parts.

We likely possess more than one representation of our body and at least some are essential to the organization of all action and much perception. Representations of the body and of its configuration are formed interactively. Thus, the apparent position of some parts affects the represented shape of others (Lackner, 1988).

A body schema can participate in higher cognitive functions and at least some body images are cerebrally lateralized (some in parietal areas). Thus, each hemisphere can judge whether a visual stimulus is a right or left hand if it is the contralateral hand but not if it is the ipsilateral hand (Parsons & Gabrieli, 1990) (*see* HEMISPHERIC LOCALIZATION). This left–right task is performed by imagining movements of one's limbs, and results show that the limbs are represented as connected (not disjoint) with accurate ranges of joint motion. The latter information is embedded in processes underlying the mental simulation of one's action and is not directly accessible to consciousness (Parsons, 1987).

We have a remarkable ability to remember body positions accurately and for a long period of time, but we overestimate to varying degrees many of the linear distances of our body (e.g. on the head, forearm, waist), while underestimating other distances (e.g. on the foot) (Shontz, 1969).

The form of the representation of one's body image is unknown. It may be hierarchically nested sets of cylindrical primitives with spatial relations between movable parts encoded as allowable angles of rotation between pairs of connected shape primitives and angles described with respect to coordinate systems centered on the subpart and on the part (Marr & Vaina, 1982). The body has also been modeled in neural and semantic networks (Hinton, 1984; Korein, 1985), often as a tree of rigid segments connected by joints, with each segment a node and each joint an arc connecting two nodes. Others propose processes and representations are integrated in a single mechanism (Head, 1920).

Emotive, intentional, and semantic factors also likely influence body images.

BIBLIOGRAPHY

Head, H. (1920). *Studies in neurology* (Vol. 2). London: Oxford University Press.

Hinton, G. E. (1984). Parallel computations for controlling an arm. *Journal of Motor Behavior, 16,* 171–94.

Korein, J. U. (1985). *A geometric investigation of reach.* Cambridge, Mass.: MIT Press.

Lackner, J. R. (1988). Some proprioceptive influences of the perceptual representation of body shape and orientation. *Brain, III,* 281–97.

Marr, D., & Vaina, L. (1982). Representation and recognition of movements of shapes. *Proceedings of the Royal Society of London B, 214,* 501–24.

Parsons, L. M. (1987). Imagined spatial transformation of one's hands and feet. *Cognitive Psychology, 19,* 178–241.

— —, & Gabrieli, J. D. E. (1990). Each cerebral hemisphere can discriminate, and imagine actions of, the contralateral but not ipsilateral hand. *Society for Neuroscience Abstracts.*

Shontz, F. C. (1969). *Perceptual and cognitive aspects of body experience*. New York: Academic Press.

LAWRENCE M. PARSONS

bottom-up processing See DATA-DRIVEN AND CONCEPTUALLY DRIVEN PROCESSES.

Broadbent, Donald Eric, FRS, CBE (*b.* 6 May 1926). British psychologist. Donald Broadbent is one of the key figures in the development of cognitive psychology. His book *Perception and communication*, which was published in 1958, served in many ways to set the agenda for the subsequent direction taken by cognitive psychology (*see* COGNITIVE PSYCHOLOGY, HISTORY OF). In that seminal book, he argued persuasively that one can understand such apparently diverse phenomena as PERCEPTION, ATTENTION, and SHORT-TERM MEMORY by putting forward a theory in which information flows through a cognitive system. In other words, instead of considering all of these phenomena in isolation from each other, it is preferable to treat them as interdependent ingredients in a single cognitive system.

Some of the ideas to be found in Broadbent (1958) represent extensions of earlier theories of communications systems (e.g. Shannon & Weaver, 1949). However, Broadbent (1958) was the first psychologist to propose a systematic and detailed account of the cognitive system viewed as consisting of a set of separate but interacting components. This general approach is still influential and continues to be endorsed by cognitive psychologists, cognitive scientists, and cognitive neuropsychologists (*see* COGNITIVE NEUROPSYCHOLOGY; COGNITIVE SCIENCE).

At the more specific level, Broadbent (1958) made particularly major contributions to our theoretical understanding of attention and short-term memory. There had, of course, been previous theories of both attention and short-term memory (e.g. James, 1890 – see JAMES, WILLIAM). However, Broadbent's (1958) theoretical contributions provided the impetus for a substantial reawakening of interest in these, and other, topics. For example, he addressed the issue of the fate of unattended information both theoretically and empirically, and his pioneering work set the stage for subsequent theories of attention (e.g. Treisman, 1964).

Broadbent subsequently developed and extended his theoretical views in various ways (e.g. Broadbent, 1971). For example, he greatly increased our theoretical understanding of the relationship between stress and cognitive functioning. In addition, he modified his theoretical views on attention in light of the new research which had been carried out in response to his earlier book. During the 1980s, he and his colleagues carried out much innovative research concerned with some of the factors associated with cognitive failure. Broadbent's Cognitive Failures Questionnaire (Broadbent, Cooper, Fitzgerald, & Parkes, 1982) was the main measure of cognitive failure that was used. Among the important findings that emerged was the suggestion that there is a general factor of cognitive failure.

In sum, Broadbent is the most influential of all British cognitive psychologists. Apart from the outstanding contribution he has made at the theoretical level within academic psychology, he also has the rare ability to carry out practically important applied research having a genuine theoretical focus.

BIBLIOGRAPHY

Broadbent, D. E. (1958). *Perception and communication*. Oxford: Pergamon.
——. (1971). *Decision and stress*. London: Academic Press.
——, Cooper, P. F., Fitzgerald, P., & Parkes, K. R. (1982). The cognitive failures questionnaire (CFQ) and its correlates. *British Journal of Clinical Psychology*, *21*, 1–16.
James, W. (1890). *Principles of psychology*. New York: Holt.
Shannon, C. E., & Weaver, W. (1949). *The mathematical theory of communication*. Urbana, Ill.: University of Illinois Press.
Treisman, A. M. (1964). Verbal cues, language, and meaning in selective attention. *American Journal of Psychology*, *77*, 206–19.

MICHAEL W. EYSENCK

C

cascade processing The term refers to the notion that "later" stages of processing can be set into operation prior to the completion of processing of earlier stages (McClelland, 1979). A complex task can be broken down into a number of distinct stages, which, put together, enable the complete task to be performed. In addition, many of these stages can be sequentially ordered, in the sense that "early" stages must begin before "later stages." For instance, before we can retrieve the meaning of a written word, we may first need to encode the letters or the overall shape of the word; we may then need to match the encoded information with our "internal lexicon" (the store for all the known words in our vocabulary; see DUAL-ROUTE MODEL OF READING); and we may finally retrieve the meaning associated with the particular word. We cannot retrieve the meaning without first going through the earlier "encoding" and "matching" stages. Information processing models of cognitive performance typically assume that processing is based on a series of such component stages.

A *discrete* processing model is one in which information is passed from one stage to another only after processing at the earlier stage is completed (see Sternberg, 1969). To continue with our example of written word recognition, a discrete stage model would hold that the encoding stage would have to be complete (e.g. all the letters in the word would need to be identified) before the word could be matched against the internal lexicon. Similarly, a complete match with a lexical entry would need to be found before any of the word's meaning could be retrieved. Within such a model, the total time taken to perform a task would be the sum of the time taken to complete each of the component stages (including response preparation and execution). If we carry out a manipulation that lengthens a particular processing stage, then the overall time taken to perform the task will increase by the extra time required by the affected stage. Thus, if we increase the number of letters in a word, so lengthening the time taken at the encoding stage, the overall time taken to retrieve the word's meaning increases by extra encoding time. If we now manipulate a second variable that affects a different processing stage – such as the frequency of occurrence of the word within the internal lexicon – the overall time taken increases by the *sum of the extra time taken at each processing stage*: that is, if the two manipulations affect different processing stages, they will produce an *additive* overall effect on task performance. Discrete stage models of this general type have held a long sway over experimental investigations of information processing, and they provide a ready way in which to understand the effects of different variables on the performance of a given task.

In contrast to such discrete stage models, cascade models assume the existence of cascade processing (see McClelland, 1979). For instance, a word may be matched against a lexical entry before all of its letters have been identified; similarly, partial lexical matches may enable some of the word's meaning to be retrieved before a complete match is established. A system operating in cascade can be thought of as entertaining sets of hypotheses about stimuli, that are confirmed or disconfirmed as more stimulus information is gathered.

The way in which different variables affect a system operating in cascade is considerably more complex than the way in which variables affect a discrete processing system. Within a cascade system, for instance, it is possible for variables affecting different processing stages to produce an interactive effect on task performance (e.g. slowing down a first process, such as letter encoding, could in turn slow the rate of a later process, such as lexical matching). Consequently, it can become difficult to provide experimental tests of such models, and experimenters need to study how performance changes across a range of manipulations – instead of looking at the effects of (for instance) just two variables on performance (see McClelland, 1979).

Cascade models of performance have gained in popularity since the advent of "connectionist" models of information processing, many of which operate in a cascade manner (*see* CONNECTIONIST MODELS OF MEMORY). An early example of this was McClelland and Rumelhart's (1981) interactive activation model of word recognition, and similar arguments have been made concerning speech recognition (e.g. Elman & McClelland, 1984), speech production (Stemberger, 1984), and picture naming (Humphreys, Riddoch, & Quinlan, 1988). Cascade operations are also important for the way in which such models can learn relations between stimuli and responses (e.g. Rumelhart, Hinton, & Williams, 1986).

Tests of whether human information processing is best conceptualized in terms of a discrete or a cascade processing model have to date produced mixed results. Studies of choice reaction time performance suggest that a range of models may be appropriate, depending on the particular task, the subject's state of expertise, and so on (e.g. Meyer, Osman, Irwin, & Yantis, 1988). Further, information may be transmitted between some processing stages in cascade but in a discrete manner between others. An important task for future research is to try and define the circumstances under which processing operates in different ways, since we need to answer this basic question in order to generate accurate models of human performance.

BIBLIOGRAPHY

Elman, J. L., & McClelland, J. L. (1984). The interactive activation model of speech perception. In N. Lass (Ed.), *Language and speech*. New York: Academic Press.

Humphreys, G. W., Riddoch, M. J., & Quinlan, P. T. (1988). Cascade processes in picture identification. *Cognitive Neuropsychology*, 5, 67–103.

McClelland, J. L. (1979). On the time relations of mental processes: An examination of systems of processes in cascade. *Psychological Review*, 86, 287–330.

— —, & Rumelhart, D. E. (1981). An interactive activation model of context effects in letter perception: Part I. An account of basic findings. *Psychological Review*, 88, 375–407.

Meyer, D. E., Osman, A. M., Irwin, D. E., & Yantis, S. (1988). Modern mental chronometry. *Biological Psychology*, 26, 3–67.

Rumelhart, D. E., Hinton, G. E., & Williams, R. J. (1986). Learning internal representations by error propagation. In D. E. Rumelhart & J. L. McClelland (Eds), *Parallel distributed processing: Explorations in the microstructure of cognition* (Vol. 1): *Foundations*. Cambridge, Mass.: MIT Press.

Stemberger, J. P. (1984). Structural errors in normal and agrammatic speech. *Cognitive Neuropsychology*, 1, 281–313.

Sternberg, S. (1969). The discovery of processing stages: Extensions of Donders' method. In W. G. Koster (Ed.), *Attention and performance II*. Amsterdam: North Holland.

G. W. HUMPHREYS

chunking The concept of "chunking" refers to the notion that some of the limitations of short-term memory can be overcome by grouping or chunking of information into larger units. The information-processing view of memory and cognition was given a major boost by George Miller's (1956) influential article entitled "The magical number seven, plus or minus two." One of the ideas put forward by Miller was the notion that people "stretch the informational bottleneck" imposed by a limited-capacity short-term memory system by grouping items and then using some special symbol to represent the group (*see* SHORT-TERM MEMORY). At the time of recall the original items are reconstructed from the series of remembered symbols. As an example, the number sequence

7 4 7 2 4 6 2 1 2 1 9 4 5

is too long for most people to repeat back without error, but if the items are grouped and each group given a meaningful label – 747 (type of aircraft), 246 (ascending even num-

49

bers), 212 (boiling point of water), 1945 (end of the Second World War) – the sequence can easily be recalled. Miller termed each recoded group a "chunk" and proposed that the immediate memory span, measured in chunks, is relatively constant ("seven, plus or minus two") for different types of material.

What is the appropriate unit of measurement for chunks, and is it really true that the number of chunks we can repeat back remains constant despite differences in the items and in the symbols that represent each group? Miller suggested that if a person can repeat back five words, it is "intuitively clear" that the units are words rather than phonemes or syllables; but can the units be larger than single words? Simon (1974) found that he could not recall the following series of words after one quick reading: "Lincoln, milky, criminal, differential, address, way, lawyer, calculus, Gettysburg", but also found that when he arranged the words into meaningful groups – "Lincoln's Gettysburg address, Milky way, Criminal lawyer, Differential calculus" – he had no trouble remembering all nine words. Simon proposed that the capacity of short-term memory is approximately five chunks, but that as the number of words and syllables per chunk increases, there is a slight decrease in the number of chunks that can be recalled.

It is obvious that the ability to group items into meaningful chunks depends strongly upon previous learning. It therefore follows that short-term (or "primary") memory cannot totally precede long-term memory in the information-processing system. Either pre-formed chunks must be retrieved from long-term memory, or new relations must be constructed on the basis of existing knowledge (see LONG-TERM MEMORY). As a further point, it seems likely that the number of chunks that a person can remember does not increase dramatically from childhood to adulthood; rather, the amount of information per chunk increases as knowledge increases. The flow of information between the short-term and long-term memory systems is clearly two-way; new chunks formed in short-term memory contribute to the organization of the permanent memory system.

A final dramatic illustration of the power of chunking is provided by Ericsson, Chase, and Faloon (1980). After massive amounts of practice, their subject increased his digit span from 8 or 9 to approximately 80 digits. He was able to do this by training himself to recode digit strings into dates, birthdays, and running times (he was a keen amateur runner) such as 3.57, "excellent time for 1 mile." Interestingly, the subject's memory span for *letters* remained at 6 or 7; the increase in span represents the specific skill of recoding meaningless strings of digits into highly organized semantic structures.

See also SHORT-TERM MEMORY, RETRIEVAL FROM.

BIBLIOGRAPHY

Ericsson, K. A., Chase, W. G., & Faloon, S. (1980). Acquisition of a memory skill. *Science*, *208*, 1181–2.

Miller, G. A. (1956). The magical number seven, plus or minus two: Some limits on our capacity for processing information. *Psychological Review*, *63*, 81–97.

Simon, H. A. (1974). How big is a chunk? *Science*, *183*, 482–8.

F. I. M. CRAIK

clinical psychology *See* COGNITIVE THERAPY; EMOTION; MOOD DISORDERS AND COGNITION.

cognition, distributed *See* DISTRIBUTED COGNITION.

cognition, social *See* SOCIAL COGNITION.

cognition and mood disorders *See* MOOD DISORDERS AND COGNITION.

cognition and personality *See* PERSONALITY AND COGNITION.

cognition and positron emission tomography *See* POSITRON EMISSION TOMOGRAPHY AND COGNITION.

cognitive change *See* AGING AND COGNITIVE CHANGE.

cognitive development This term refers to the changes which occur to a person's cognitive structures, abilities, and processes during the course of that person's life-span. The cognitive changes which occur during adult aging are dealt with elsewhere in this volume (*see* AGING AND COGNITIVE CHANGE; AGING AND MEMORY); the present entry will focus instead on the cognitive changes which occur during childhood.

PIAGET'S STAGE THEORY OF
COGNITIVE DEVELOPMENT

The most comprehensive theory of children's cognitive development to have been proposed is that put forward by Piaget (e.g. Piaget & Inhelder, 1969) (*see* PIAGET, JEAN). Piaget interpreted cognitive development as consisting of the development of logical competence. He argued that the development of this competence proceeds through a sequence of four major stages (sensori-motor, preoperational, concrete operational, and formal operational). Piaget proposed that, within any given stage, cognitive performance is not task specific but is homogeneous and structurally equivalent across a range of different tasks, with transitions from one stage to the next being marked by relatively abrupt but generalized qualitative changes in cognitive structures and performance.

However, more recent studies have cast some doubt upon Piaget's account of cognitive development. In particular, it has been found that children's cognitive performance is not homogeneous in the manner proposed by Piaget; instead, performance can vary considerably as a function of changes in task materials and administrative procedures. For example, children's performance on visual perspective-taking tasks varies as a function of the stimulus array which is used; performance on conservation tasks varies depending upon whether the child is asked to produce either a single judgement or two judgements in close succession; performance on drawing tasks varies as a function of the wording of the verbal instructions which are given to the child; and performance on transitive inference tasks varies depending upon whether or not the child is given the opportunity to memorize the premises properly. Furthermore, on all of these different tasks, it has been discovered that young children are capable of functioning at a level which Piaget claims is possible only at a later age, as long as the appropriate task materials and procedures are employed.

TASK ANALYSIS

This finding, that children's performance varies as a function of task factors, implies that much greater attention needs to be paid to these factors if an adequate account is to be given of children's cognitive development. Task analysis also helps to elucidate the range of cognitive faculties and abilities which the child requires in order to perform successfully on any given task.

Piaget's classification task can be used to illustrate this point. In this task, the child is shown a set of flowers, some of which are primroses, and is asked the question "Are there more flowers, or more primroses?" (The original aim of this task was to test whether the child can conserve the quantity of the superordinate class when comparing it with the quantity of the subordinate class.) It should be noted that, in order to answer the question correctly, the child must be able to: (a) comprehend the syntax, semantics, and pragmatics of the question which is being asked; (b) store the question's intent in memory, at least for the duration of the execution of the task; (c) perceptually discriminate the primroses from the other flowers; (d) assign the discriminated primroses to the category that was designated by the word "primroses" in the question; (e) quantify the number of primroses; (f) hold the number of primroses in working memory; (g) assign all of the objects in the array to the category that was designated by the word "flowers" in the question; (h) quantify the number of flowers; (i) hold the number of flowers in working memory; (j) compare the two numbers which are stored in working memory; (k) apply an appropriate decision rule (such as "Choose the larger number unless both numbers are equal");

(l) encode the output of that decision rule in a linguistic format for verbal production.

In short, for a child to succeed on this kind of problem, he or she must possess sufficient linguistic knowledge, adequate perceptual abilities, a large enough working memory, basic cognitive processes (such as storage and retrieval), suitable decision rules, and sufficient real-world knowledge (such as natural object categories). And notice that failure on this task could be due to a failure of any one of these subcomponents (and need not be due to a failure to conserve the quantity of the superordinate class). Thus, task analysis implies that cognitive development should be construed not merely as the acquisition of an abstract logical competence (as Piaget proposed) but as the acquisition and development of language, perception, working memory, cognitive processes, decision rules, and real-world knowledge. LANGUAGE ACQUISITION and PERCEPTUAL DEVELOPMENT are dealt with elsewhere in this volume; consequently, the remainder of this essay will focus upon the other four topics in this list.

WORKING MEMORY

It is known from use of the digit-span task (which entails asking children to listen to a sequence of numbers, and then to repeat them immediately back to the tester) that children's working memory improves considerably as they get older: 3-year-olds only have a digit span of two items, 5-year-olds have a span of four items, 12-year-olds have a span of six or seven items, while students have a span of about eight items (see WORKING MEMORY). Pascual-Leone (1970) has interpreted this increase as reflecting an increase in the size of the child's "central computing space M." According to Pascual-Leone, M space is divisible into two components, e and k: e is the space which is necessary for storing the task instructions, and for scanning the perceptual array; k is the space which is available for storing information while executing the task. It is hypothesized that the size of e remains constant during development, while the size of k increases with age; hence older children are able to handle tasks that require more information to be stored than younger children.

An alternative point of view has been advocated by Case (1985). He also argues that the child's total processing space is divisible into two components: operating space (which is that space which is devoted to executing current cognitive operations) and short-term storage space (which is where the products of previous operations are stored). Unlike Pascual-Leone, though, Case argues that total processing space remains constant through development. Instead, what changes with age is the child's operational efficiency; that is, cognitive operations are executed more efficiently as the child gets older. Consequently, the operating space nees to occupy less of the total processing space with increasing age; as a result, more of that total space becomes available for use as short-term storage space.

Case (1985) presents strong evidence to support the notion that operational speed increases with age. In addition, there is good evidence that the acquisition and practice of mnemonic strategies such as rehearsal produce substantial improvements in children's short-term memory performance. However, it should be noted that the conclusion that operational efficiency improves with age does not rule out the possibility that total working memory space also increases with age, and that the superior performance of older children is a consequence of both increased capacity and superior efficiency.

COGNITIVE PROCESSES

Basic cognitive processes such as storage and retrieval are already functional at birth. This conclusion is supported by the fact that neonates exhibit habituation; that is, if a neonate is repeatedly presented with the same stimulus, he or she will spend progressively less time looking at it, and if a different stimulus is then shown, attention will recover (see PERCEPTUAL DEVELOPMENT). Notice that for habituation to occur, the neonate must have stored the initial stimulus, and must be retrieving it and comparing it with the current stimulus on each subsequent presentation. When there is a match between the previous and the present stimulus, habituation occurs; when there is a noticeable discrepancy between the two stimuli, dishabituation occurs. Thus, these types of basic cognitive processes are present from the very outset of infancy, and are probably inherent in the cognitive system itself.

However, this is not to say that basic cognitive processes do not exhibit any changes during the course of development. As we have already seen, Case (1985) presents evidence which suggests that efficiency and speed of execution improve with age. Such improvements could be caused either by biological maturation (e.g. through the increased myelinization of neurones, which would improve neural conductivity – see Case, 1985) or by practice and experience.

DECISION RULES

The acquisition and development of decision rules in children have been studied extensively by Siegler (e.g. 1976), who proposes that cognitive development in some problem-solving domains can be explained entirely in terms of the progressive acquisition of increasingly powerful decision rules. This proposal can be explained most clearly by reference to the balance-scale task, which Siegler (1976) has investigated in detail. The apparatus for this task consists of a balance scale, which has four positions to which variable numbers of weights can be attached on either side of the fulcrum; the arm of the balance tips either left or right or remains horizontal, depending upon the precise arrangement of weights on either side of the fulcrum. On any particular trial, the arm of the balance is locked into a horizontal position, an arrangement of weights is placed on both sides on the fulcrum, and the child is asked to predict how the balance will behave when the lock is released.

Siegler postulates that performance on this task can be based upon one of four different decision rules. Rule I takes into account only the number of weights on each side of the fulcrum: if they are the same, the balance will remain horizontal; if they differ, the side with the greater number of weights will descend. Rule II also relies exclusively on weight if the two sides have different numbers of weights; however, if the numbers of weights are equal, then the distances of the weights from the fulcrum on each side are also taken into

account. Rule III considers both weight and distance, and solves the problem correctly if one or both are equal; however, if one side has more weights but the other side has its weights further from the fulcrum, then the child is reduced to guessing. Rule IV involves the calculation of torque (weight $\times$ distance) for each side, and predicting that the side with the greater torque will descend.

By presenting a child with a range of different problems, and by examining the pattern of correct and incorrect answers which are given across this range of problems, it is possible to work out whether or not the child is following one of these four rules and, if so, which particular rule is being followed. Using this procedure, Siegler (1976) found that 90 percent of 5- to 17-year-olds perform in accordance with just one of the four decision rules, and that there is a trend toward the use of the more complex rules with age. In addition, Siegler found that children's explanations of how they make their decisions is consistent with the rule which is postulated on the basis of their actual performance.

Siegler's rule assessment approach has since been applied to a wide variety of different problem domains (e.g. the projection of shadows, probability, conservation of liquid, and the Tower of Hanoi), and it has been found that the cognitive-developmental changes which occur on all of these different problems can be explained in terms of a progression through a sequence of increasingly powerful decision rules.

REAL-WORLD KNOWLEDGE

During the course of their development, children acquire a vast range of real-world knowledge, including knowledge of objects, events, relations, people, social institutions, and so on. Children's knowledge of objects and events constitutes two areas that have received particular attention from developmental psychologists; the present discussion will be limited to these.

KNOWLEDGE OF EVENTS

Nelson (1986) is the most influential theorist to have examined children's event knowledge. She argues that, during the course of their

53

development, children acquire and elaborate mental representations of entire events. These event representations (ERs) have four main characteristics. First, they specify sequences of acts that are linked together temporally (and possibly causally as well) which are appropriate to particular contexts (e.g. a meal-time ER might specify the acts of "sitting," "being served," "eating," and so on). Second, ERs specify the people who are involved in the constituent acts, and the roles which these people occupy in those acts. Third, ERs specify the objects which may be involved in the constituent acts. Finally, ERs may contain slots which can be variably filled by different people or objects, in which case they also specify the range of alternative slot-fillers for each particular slot.

This theoretical formulation has generated a variety of studies. In one study, for example, Nelson (1978) examined 4- to 5-year-old children's descriptions of the events which occur when eating at home, at a McDonalds, and at a daycare centre. These descriptions contained a regular temporal sequencing of the constituent acts, and they included mentions of both obligatory and optional elements. In another study, Gruendel (1980) studied ERs in children aged between 4 and 8 years of age. This study revealed that as the children got older, they included more optional alternative elements and paths in their event descriptions, indicating that development entails the incorporation of greater complexity and flexibility into ERs.

Studies investigating children's memory for stories have shown that children's ERs can influence their recall of information. Nelson and Gruendel (1981), for example, presented 4- to 5-year-old children with stories that followed a familiar sequence of acts, which the children then had to recall. In some of these stories, one act was presented in the wrong temporal position. During recall, this act was either omitted or put back into its proper position in the sequence. This suggests that the children's recall was being influenced by their ERs, which provided them with normative information about correct temporal sequencing.

Finally, it has been found that even 1-year-old children have already acquired some ERs. This conclusion emerges from studies which have investigated the very early linguistic productions of 1-year-old children (see, for example, Barrett, 1983, 1986). These studies reveal that many early words are produced only in the context of highly specific events. This type of early word use can be explained in terms of the children having mapped these words on to ERs, and consequently confining their use of these words to situations in which those represented events occur (see Barrett, 1989).

KNOWLEDGE OF OBJECTS

The main influence upon the study of children's knowledge of objects has been Rosch's prototype theory (see CONCEPTS). This theory postulates that an object category is represented mentally by means of a prototype, which is a specification of the most typical and clearest example of the kind of object which is included within the category. Actual objects are then included within that category if they share attributes with the prototype. Depending upon how many attributes are shared with the prototype, the object will be a more or less typical member of the category. Because category membership is determined by the number of attributes which are shared with the prototype, and because more typical category members share many attributes with the prototype while less typical members share fewer attributes with the prototype, this theory predicts that the degree of typicality exhibited by a category member will influence the cognitive processing of that object. In addition, the theory predicts that while typical category members (which all share many attributes with the prototype) should have many attributes in common with each other, atypical category members (which each have relatively few attributes in common with the prototype) need not have any attributes in common with each other. Thus, categories should display a family resemblance structure (rather than a structure defined by a set of necesary and sufficient features).

A variety of studies has been conducted with children in order to test the first of these two predictions (that children's cognitive processing of objects is influenced by their degree of typicality). These studies have produced strong support for this prediction. Mervis and Pani (1980), for example, found that it is easier for 5-year-old children to acquire a new category from exposure to a typical category exemplar (which bears a high degree of resemblance to the prototype) than from exposure to an atypical category exemplar. Similarly, Kuczaj (1982) found that when 2-year-old children are asked to select an object (e.g. "a ball") from an array of objects, they initially select highly typical exemplars, and only subsequently go on to choose less typical exemplars if they are asked to select further category members.

The second prediction, that children's object categories should display a family resemblance structure, has also been confirmed in several studies. Barrett (1982), for example, has shown that the full range of objects to which a 1- to 2-year-old child refers by means of an object name does not necessarily display any common attributes which are shared by all of the category members; however, all of the objects within the category have at least one attribute in common with one of the child's initial referents (the prototype) for that object name. Similarly, Kuczaj (1983), in a detailed scrutiny of the range of real and possible objects that 2- to 5-year-old children are prepared to include within the category "airplane," found that these objects are not linked together by a set of necessary and sufficient attributes; instead, this category displays a family resemblance structure.

CONSTRAINTS ON COGNITIVE DEVELOPMENT

Finally, it should be noted here that, in recent years, several authors have proposed that the course of cognitive development is held within particular bounds by a set of very specific constraints. It is argued by these authors that children sometimes master enormously complex cognitive domains with such apparent ease that their progress must be facilitated by constraints which eliminate, right from the outset, many of the potential errors which these children might otherwise make. To give a specific example drawn from the domain of word

learning, Markman and Hutchinson (1984) point out that, when an adult directs a child's attention to a particular object (e.g. a black dog) and utters a word (e.g. "dog"), there is an indefinite range of conclusions which the child could in principle draw from this event (for example, that "dog" is the name for dogs in general, that "dog" is the proper name of this particular dog, that "dog" means "black," that "dog" means "four-legged," and so on). However, Markman and Hutchinson argue that children only consider the one correct conclusion (that "dog" is the name for dogs in general), the reason for this being that they are limited by a taxonomic constraint which restricts them to the assumption that words must refer to categories of similar objects. Other constraints which have been proposed in the domain of word learning are the natural category constraint, which leads children to assume that individual words must refer to either objects or events but not both, the principle of contrast, which leads children to assume that all words must contrast in meaning, and the principle of mutual exclusivity, which leads children to assume that each object has one and only one name. In addition, some authors (e.g. Markman & Hutchinson, 1984) suggest that these constraints may not be learnt by the child during the course of development, but might be innate.

However, Nelson (1988) has drawn attention to several problems with this approach to cognitive development. For example, she raises the question of whether these proposed constraints actually constrain the child, or whether they represent instead just the processing biases and strategies of the child. True constraints should be manifested as all-or-none behavior; biases and strategies would be manifested instead merely as statistical trends. In fact, the evidence indicates the presence of trends rather than all-or-none behavior; that is, all of the proposed constraints are actually violated with considerable frequency by children during the course of their development. Also, Nelson points out that if these constraints are to be of maximum benefit to the child, they ought to be operative very early in development when the child requires the maximum assistance. However, the evidence

55

suggests that these proposed constraints only become operative after the child's development has already commenced by other means, a finding which is more consistent with the view that these constraints are merely processing biases or strategies which are acquired during the course of development.

Nevertheless, the issue of constraints raises some crucial questions about the nature of children's cognitive development, questions about the extent to which the child's cognitive development proceeds via domain-specific processing or via the application of more general cognitive processes, and the extent to which there may be specific innate inputs to children's cognitive development. These questions are currently the focus of much debate by developmental psychologists.

See also MODULARITY OF MIND.

BIBLIOGRAPHY

Barrett, M. D. (1982). Distinguishing between prototypes: The early acquisition of the meanings of object names. In S. A. Kuczaj (Ed.), *Language development* (Vol. I): *Syntax and semantics*. Hillsdale, NJ: Erlbaum.

——. (1983). The early acquisition and development of the meanings of action-related words. In Th. B. Seiler & W. Wannenmacher (Eds), *Concept development and the development of word meaning*. Berlin: Springer-Verlag.

——. (1986). Early semantic representations and early word usage. In S. A. Kuczaj & M. D. Barrett (Eds), *The development of word meaning*. New York: Springer-Verlag.

——. (1989). Early language development. In A. Slater & G. Bremner (Eds), *Infant development*. London: Erlbaum.

Case, R. (1985). *Intellectual development: Birth to adulthood*. Orlando, Fla: Academic Press.

Gruendel, J. (1980). Scripts and stories: A study of children's event narratives. Unpublished doctoral dissertation: Yale University.

Kuczaj, S. A. (1982). Young children's overextension of object words in comprehension and/or production: Support for a prototype theory of early object word meaning. *First Language, 3,* 93–105.

——. (1983). On the acquisition of the notion of types of flying objects: Support for prototype-based theories of word meaning development. In D. Rogers & J. Sloboda (Eds), *The acquisi-*

tion of symbolic skills. New York: Plenum Press.

Markman, E. M., & Hutchinson, J. (1984). Children's sensitivity to constraints on word meaning: Taxonomic versus thematic relations. *Cognitive Psychology, 16,* 1–27.

Mervis, C., & Pani, J. (1980). Acquisition of basic object categories. *Cognitive Psychology, 12,* 496–522.

Nelson, K. (1978). How children represent knowledge of their world in and out of language: A preliminary report. In R. Siegler (Ed.), *Children's thinking: What develops?* Hillsdale, NJ: Erlbaum.

——. (1986). *Event knowledge: Structure and function in development*. Hillsdale, NJ: Erlbaum.

——. (1988). Constraints on word learning? *Cognitive Development, 3,* 221–46.

——, & Gruendel, J. (1981). Generalized event representations: Basic building blocks of cognitive development. In M. Lamb & A. Brown (Eds), *Advances in developmental psychology* (Vol. 1). Hillsdale, NJ: Erlbaum.

Pascual-Leone, J. (1970). A mathematical model for the transition rule in Piaget's developmental stages. *Acta Psychologica, 32,* 301–45.

Piaget, J., & Inhelder, B. (1969). *The psychology of the child*. London: Routledge and Kegan Paul.

Siegler, R. (1976). Three aspects of cognitive development. *Cognitive Psychology, 8,* 481–520.

M. D. BARRETT

cognitive disorders *See* ABSENT-MINDEDNESS; AGNOSIA; AMNESIA; APHASIA; COGNITIVE NEUROPSYCHOLOGY; COGNITIVE THERAPY; *IDIOTS SAVANTS*.

cognitive dissonance As originally proposed by Festinger (1957), cognitive dissonance theory deals with the consequences for behavior and attitude change of a person experiencing a sense of inconsistency or contradiction ("dissonance") between two or more cognitions (*see* ATTITUDES). Dissonance is conceived of as a noxious state that motivates cognitive change aimed at eliminating or reducing such inconsistency. Where cognitive dissonance theory differs most from other attitude theories that incorporate notions of cognitive consistency is in its concern with cognitions related to behavioral decisions. Thus, the main issue addressed in cognitive dissonance research has been that of how people deal with thoughts or information implying that they have made a wrong decision. In terms of the theory, dissonance arises in this context from a person holding the belief "I performed action A" at the same time as the belief "Action A was inconsistent with my attitude." Since it is typically less easy to deny a previous action than to find justification for it, dissonance may be resolved by changing the latter belief to "Action A was consistent with my attitude" or at least "Action A was excusable."

A large number of experiments have examined this hypothesis by using a procedure termed "induced" or "forced compliance." The idea is to induce subjects to perform an action assumed to be inconsistent with their prior attitudes, and then observe any shift in their attitudes following their action. Thus, Festinger and Carlsmith (1959) had subjects perform a boring task and then inform another person apparently waiting to perform this same task that it was enjoyable. Where subjects were offered only a small reward for giving this misinformation, they gave higher ratings of their own enjoyment of the task than did others who had been offered a large reward. The interpretation is that the former group resolved dissonance by bringing their previous attitudes into line with their subsequent behavior. For the latter group, the high reward may have led them to regard their behavior as more excusable, or simply have provided a compensation for the unpleasantness of the experienced inconsistency, thereby reducing its motivational force. Whatever the interpretation, the prediction is that *lesser* rewards produce *greater* attitude change within this paradigm. A parallel prediction is that attitudes will be held more strongly when associated with more rather than less costly commitment, as in the case of members of a cult prophesying the end of the world who persisted with their proselytizing even after the day of doom had safely passed (Festinger, Riecken, & Schachter, 1956).

These predictions only hold, however, under certain limiting conditions, the most important of which is that subjects should see their decision as having been freely made. Under conditions of free choice, one finds greater attitude change (in the direction of reduced inconsistency with behavior) with lesser rewards; under conditions of low choice, greater rewards produce greater change (Linder, Cooper, & Jones, 1967).

Subsequent research has questioned Festinger's assumption of dissonance as a noxious motivational state, produced by inconsistency and removed (typically) by attitude change. Bem (1967) has argued that subjects' reports of their own attitudes are not derived from any such motivational processes, but are merely self-descriptions of behavior that take into account situational factors such as incentives and constraints on free choice, and are no different in principle from the descriptions that might be offered by another person observing their behavior. An observer would infer a closer match between a person's attitudes and behavior if the behavior were performed for a small rather than large reward. Objections of a different kind have been raised by Nuttin (1975) who proposes that, in forced compliance studies, dissonance is *produced* by inequitably low rewards rather than *reduced* by high rewards.

There appears to be a renewal of sympathy for Festinger's theory in contemporary attitude research, helped particularly by evidence that procedures designed to influence dissonance produce changes in physiological arousal, and that arousal that cannot be attributed to some other cause (e.g. a drug) can lead to attitude change (Cooper, Zanna, & Taves, 1978). The idea of dissonance as a state of tension or unpleasant arousal is therefore quite plausible. On the other hand, there is less support for the idea that what produces such tension is merely the experience of an inconsistency between different cognitions. According to Cooper and Fazio (1984), dissonance should be thought of more as an emotional reaction to the knowledge that one has been responsible for an action that has produced unwanted consequences. Cognitions that reduce this sense of responsibility (e.g. that one acted under compulsion, or that the consequences could not have been anticipated) will reduce the extent

57

to which one "feels bad" about one's behavior, and hence the motivation to re-examine one's beliefs. However, this "feeling bad" depends on the consequences of one's behavior rather than on the holding of contradictory beliefs.

BIBLIOGRAPHY

Bem, D. J. (1967). Self-perception: An alternative interpretation of cognitive dissonance phenomena. *Psychological Review*, *74*, 183–200.

Cooper, J., & Fazio, R. H. (1984). A new look at dissonance theory. In L. Berkowitz (Ed.), *Advances in experimental social psychology* (Vol. 17). New York: Academic Press.

Cooper, J., Zanna, M. P., & Taves, P. A. (1978). Arousal as a necessary condition for attitude change following compliance. *Journal of Personality and Social Psychology*, *36*, 1101–6.

Festinger, L. (1957). *A theory of cognitive dissonance*. Evanston, Ill.: Row, Peterson.

— —, & Carlsmith, J. M. (1959). Cognitive consequences of forced compliance. *Journal of Abnormal and Social Psychology*, *58*, 203–10.

Festinger, L., Riecken, H., & Schachter, S. (1956). *When prophecy fails*. Minneapolis: University of Minnesota Press.

Linder, D. E., Cooper, J., & Jones, E. E. (1967). Decision freedom as a determinant of the role of incentive magnitude in attitude change. *Journal of Personality and Social Psychology*, *6*, 245–54.

Nuttin, J. M., Jr (1975). *The illusion of attitude change: Towards a response contagion theory of persuasion*. London: Academic Press.

J. R. EISER

cognitive maps A cognitive map is a mental representation of some area of one's environment. It might be a representation of the layout of the interior of one's house, one's neighborhood, or even one's country or the world. It is sometimes useful to speak of cognitive maps because people can use their mental representations of their environment in ways similar to their use of maps. Thus, for example, in a well known environment, people can plan their routes in advance, take short cuts, and, in general, move around in a sensible and economical way. However, the term cognitive map is potentially misleading. It is very unlikely that the processes which allow us to navigate around familiar environments employ any of the same processes as are involved when we navigate with a real map.

When we move to a new town we begin to acquire spatial knowledge about our environment as we move around and develop memories of the routes that we have followed. Landmarks within the town help us to interlink these routes so that we gradually develop the ability to represent our environment two-dimensionally. We begin to know how the separate routes are interrelated and the ways in which one would take short cuts between them (Appleyard, 1976; Evans, Marrero, & Butler, 1981). Despite the success with which people familiar with a location can navigate around it, there is considerable research that suggests that the mental representations that they use are not as exact as those to be found on Ordnance Survey maps. Byrne (1979), for example, found that long-term residents in a town give longer estimates for routes within the town center and for those routes with many changes in direction. He argued that the number of landmarks and turns contributed to the judgement of distance. He also found that when people were asked to draw the angles with which roads joined, they tended to draw them as meeting at right angles even though this could involve an error of 30°.

The tendency to think of roads as meeting at right angles, found by Byrne, may reflect a general tendency for mental representations of the environment to be simplified into north, south, east, west alignments. When asked which is the further west, Bristol or Edinburgh, most British people say Bristol since they know that Bristol is on the west coast while Edinburgh is on the east coast. Most people's mental representations of the British Isles ignore the fact that Scotland leans to the west of England so that Edinburgh is, in fact, west of Bristol (Moar, 1979; Tversky, 1981). Similarly, Stevens and Coupe (1978) found that Americans make, on average, an error of 67° when asked to indicate the direction of Reno, Nevada, from San Diego, California. California appears to be imagined as stretching north-south with Nevada to the east. In reality, California lies in a north-west to south-east angle so that Reno is north-north-west of San Diego.

BIBLIOGRAPHY

Appleyard, D. A. (1976). *Planning a pluralistic city*. Cambridge, Mass.: MIT Press.

Byrne, R. (1979). Memory for urban geography. *Quarterly Journal of Experimental Psychology, 31*, 147–54.

Evans, G. W., Marrero, D. G., & Butler, P. A. (1981). Environmental learning and cognitive mapping. *Environment and Behaviour, 13*, 83–104.

Moar, I. (1979). The internal geometry of cognitive maps. Unpublished doctoral dissertation: Cambridge University.

Stevens, A., & Coupe, P. (1978). Distortions in judged spatial relations. *Cognitive Psychology, 10*, 422–37.

Tversky, B. (1981). Distortions in memory for maps. *Cognitive Psychology, 13*, 407–33.

PETER E. MORRIS

cognitive neuropsychology Cognitive neuropsychology studies the effects of brain injury on such things as language, memory, perception, and attention. Most of the research is done with adult subjects who have suffered a cerebral vascular accident (cva or stroke), tumor, missile wound, or other form of brain injury, but work is also done on developmental disorders such as developmental dyslexia (*see* DYSLEXIA, DEVELOPMENTAL).

Cognitive neuropsychology has two main aims (Ellis & Young, 1988). The first aim is to explain the patterns of impaired and intact performance seen in brain-injured patients in terms of damage to one or more of the components of a theory or model of normal cognitive functioning. Thus, a cognitive neuropsychologist interested in reading would study patients with acquired dyslexia (*see* DYSLEXIAS: ACQUIRED) (impaired reading following brain injury), and would seek to explain the different patterns of reading breakdown in terms of damage to different components of an information-processing model of skilled reading. Similarly, a cognitive neuropsychologist interested in APHASIA or AMNESIA would endeavor to explain the different patterns of language and memory breakdown in terms of impairment to different components of a psychological theory of language processing or learning

and memory respectively. To the extent that one can speak in cognitive neuropsychology of "localizing" the deficit in a given patient, that localization is within an information-processing model of cognitive processes and takes the form of saying that the patient has suffered damage to the direct visual procedure for word recognition, syntactic processes, episodic long-term memory, or whatever. This does not mean, though, that cognitive neuropsychologists are necessarily disinterested in which brain structures mediate which aspects of cognition (*see* MODULARITY OF MIND).

The second aim of cognitive neuropsychology is to draw conclusions about the nature and organization of normal, intact cognitive processes from the patterns of impaired and intact capabilities seen in brain-injured patients. In other words, cognitive neuropsychologists assert that studying neurological patients is a valuable alternative or adjunct to carrying out experiments on normal subjects where the objective is to understand how the normal mind works. Thus, it is common in cognitive neuropsychological papers to see claims to the effect that it would not be possible to observe a particular pattern, or set of patterns, of impaired and preserved cognitive performance following brain injury unless the cognitive system in the normal, intact brain were organized in a particular way.

Modern day cognitive neuropsychology bears quite a close resemblance to work done in the late nineteenth and early twentieth century by neurologists and aphasiologists such as Wernicke, Lichtheim, Charcot, and the young Sigmund Freud (see Arbib, Caplan, & Marshall, 1982; Morton, 1984). In recent times, cognitive neuropsychology was revived in the late 1960s. The work of Marshall and Newcombe at the Radcliffe Infirmary, Oxford, and Shallice and Warrington at the National Hospital for Nervous Diseases, London, was particularly influential in convincing the world that cognitive neuropsychology is a worthwhile enterprise. Shallice and Warrington (1970) studied a patient whose pattern of preserved and intact abilities could, they maintained, be explained if one argued that he had suffered damage to his auditory-verbal short-term memory, while other forms of short-term memory and access to long-term memory were preserved. The patient had a very reduced digit span and performed badly on all tests of short-term memory involving letters, digits, or words, yet his immediate recall of nonverbal material (e.g. shapes or sounds) was intact, as was his ability to commit lists of words to long-term memory. Marshall and Newcombe (1973) described three different forms of acquired dyslexia, and argued that their occurrence was compatible with some models of reading but not others.

Much of the strength of cognitive neuropsychology derives from the fact that many of its practitioners entered the area after training as experimental cognitive psychologists. This means that cognitive neuropsychological studies employ the same experimental paradigms, and analyze their data using the same statistical methods, as are seen in mainstream cognitive psychology. Indeed, many cognitive neuropsychologists alternate between case-studies of neurological patients and laboratory experiments with normal subjects, arguing that some questions about how the mind works are best answered by case-studies while other questions are best answered by laboratory experiments.

Traditional neuropsychology studied groups of patients considered to belong to the same "syndrome" group (e.g. "Broca's aphasia" or "Wernicke's aphasia"), usually comparing the group's performance with that of either another patient group or normal subjects without brain injuries. The widespread belief among cognitive neuropsychologists is that the conventional syndrome groups are too broad, encompassing patients who differ one from another in theoretically important ways. The trend in cognitive neuropsychology has been to carry out intensive investigations of single cases, or at least to pay close attention to individual differences between patients.

Like all approaches in psychology, cognitive neuropsychology rests on a set of assumptions (Caramazza, 1984; Shallice, 1988). It is assumed, for example, that the mind is composed of a large number of semi-independent processing components or *modules* which are separately represented in the brain and are therefore capable of separate impairment (*see* MODULARITY OF MIND). It is also assumed that the pattern of impaired and intact performance seen in a patient, including the pattern of errors, will provide a reasonably transparent guide to the nature of the underlying deficit. Finally, it is commonly assumed that although modules may be lost through brain injury, new modules are not developed in the mature brain.

Any assumption can, of course, be wrong, but one of the attractions of cognitive neuropsychology is that its assumptions are to some extent different from those upon which conventional cognitive psychology rests. Where research in the two approaches converges upon the same conclusion regarding an aspect of the mind's structure and function, one can be doubly confident in the validity of that conclusion.

See also HEMISPHERIC LOCALIZATION; PERCEPTUAL MOTOR COORDINATION.

BIBLIOGRAPHY

Arbib, M. A., Caplan, D., & Marshall, J. C. (1982). Neurolinguistics in historical perspective. In M. A. Arbib, J. C. Marshall, & D. Caplan (Eds), *Neural models of language processes*. New York: Academic Press.

Caramazza, A. (1984). The logic of neuropsychological research and the problem of patient classification. *Brain and Language, 21*, 9–20.

Ellis, A. W., & Young, A. W. (1988). *Human cognitive neuropsychology*. London: Lawrence Erlbaum Associates.

Marshall, J. C., & Newcombe, F. (1973). Patterns of paralexia: A psycholinguistic approach. *Journal of Psycholinguistic Research, 2*, 175–99.

Morton, J. (1984). Brain-based and non-brain-based models of language. In D. Caplan, A. R. Lecours, & A. Smith (Eds), *Biological perspectives on language*. Cambridge, Mass.: MIT Press.

Shallice, T. (1988). *From neuropsychology to mental structure*. Cambridge: Cambridge University Press.

——, & Warrington, E. K. (1970). Independent functioning of verbal memory stores: A neuropsychological study. *Quarterly Journal of Experimental Psychology, 35A*, 111–38.

ANDREW W. ELLIS

cognitive psychology Cognitive psychology is concerned with information processing, and includes a variety of processes such as attention, perception, learning, and memory; it is also concerned with the structures and representations involved in cognition. The greatest difference between the approach adopted by cognitive psychologists and that followed by the Behaviorists is that cognitive psychologists are interested in identifying in detail what happens between stimulus and response (*see* COGNITIVE PSYCHOLOGY, HISTORY OF). Some of the major ingredients of the information-processing approach to cognition were spelled out clearly by Lachman, Lachman, and Butterfield (1979). In essence, it is assumed that the mind can be regarded as a general-purpose, symbol-processing system, and that these symbols are transformed into other symbols as a result of being acted on by different processes. These processes require time to be carried out, so that reaction-time data can provide a useful source of information. The mind has structural and resource limitations, and so should be thought of as a limited-capacity processor.

It is generally accepted that the human mind is an information-processing system, and the same is true of computers. A key issue is the extent to which these two kinds of information-processing systems resemble each other (*see* ARTIFICIAL INTELLIGENCE; COGNITIVE SCIENCE). Some psychologists have had no doubts about the answer. For example, according to Simon (1980, p. 45), "It might have been necessary a decade ago to argue for the commonality of the information processes that are employed by such disparate systems as computers and human nervous systems. The evidence for that commonality is now overwhelming." The consensual view is probably that there are, indeed, striking similarities between computers and human minds, but there are also substantial differences.

One of the most significant developments within cognitive psychology in recent years has been a proliferation of the number of different approaches to human cognition. As Eysenck and Keane (1990) pointed out, it is possible to identify at least three major categories of psychologists whose main interest is in cognition:

experimental cognitive psychologists; cognitive scientists; and cognitive neuropsychologists. Experimental cognitive psychologists concentrate on empirical research into cognition on normal subjects. Cognitive scientists develop computational models, and attach great significance to the computer as a metaphor for human cognition. Cognitive neuropsychologists investigate cognition in brain-damaged patients, and claim that the study of such patients can provide valuable insights into normal cognitive functioning (*see* COGNITIVE NEUROPSYCHOLOGY).

Another major development within cognitive psychology has involved the application of the paradigms and theories of cognitive psychology to several different areas of study. For example, explicitly cognitive approaches have been adopted in social and developmental psychology (*see* COGNITIVE DEVELOPMENT; SOCIAL COGNITION), as well as in occupational and clinical psychology (*see* COGNITIVE THERAPY; HUMAN FACTORS; MOOD DISORDERS AND COGNITION).

BIBLIOGRAPHY

Eysenck, M. W., & Keane, M. T. (1990). *Cognitive psychology: A student's handbook.* London: Lawrence Erlbaum Associates Ltd.

Lachman, R., Lachman, J. L., & Butterfield, E. C. (1979). *Cognitive psychology and information processing.* Hillsdale, NJ: Lawrence Erlbaum Associates Ltd.

Simon, H. A. (1980). Cognitive science: The newest science of the artificial. *Cognitive Science, 4,* 33–46.

MICHAEL W. EYSENCK

cognitive psychology, history of The evolution of cognitive psychology during the second half of the twentieth century can usefully be discussed in the context of the dominant approach which preceded it, i.e. Behaviorism. In the early years of this century, John Watson argued that the way to make psychology a legitimate experimental and scientific discipline was by focusing only on observable entities (*see* INTROSPECTION). This meant that the emphasis was very firmly on the relationship between observable stimuli and observable responses. As part of the Behaviorist approach, there was a reluctance to introduce hypothetical mental constructs into theoretical psychology.

The emergence of Behaviorism occurred to some extent because Watson and other Behaviorists wanted psychology to emulate the more established sciences such as physics and chemistry. It was argued by logical positivists such as Carnap, for example, that theoretical constructs in any science are meaningful only to the extent that they can be observed. In addition, scientific theories can only be justified by appealing to observed facts. The views of the logical positivists led some of the leading Behaviorists (e.g. B. F. Skinner) to argue that physics and chemistry had been more successful than psychology because physicists and chemists had adhered more firmly than psychologists to those characteristics of good science advocated by the logical positivists.

Behaviorism was extremely influential for a long time, especially in the United States of America. However, even there it gradually lost its appeal, particularly during the 1950s and thereafter. There were basically two reasons why this happened. First, Behaviorism never produced detailed or adequate accounts of complex cognitive functioning. It was possible (although probably erroneous) to explain many phenomena in conditioning in terms of associations between stimuli or between stimuli and responses, but it made little or no sense to attempt to account for our knowledge of a complex system such as language in stimulus–response terms (see GRAMMAR; LANGUAGE COMPREHENSION). Precisely the same was true of attempts by Behaviorists to account for cognitive activities such as CREATIVITY and PROBLEM SOLVING.

Second, philosophers of science during the twentieth century increasingly challenged traditional views of the scientific enterprise. Popper (e.g. 1972), for example, attacked the notion that scientific observation possesses objectivity. He claimed instead that scientific observations are based very much on preconceived ideas and theories. He used to make this point when lecturing by instructing the members of the audience that they should observe, to which their response was typically, "Observe what?" In other words, observation does not proceed in a vacuum, but is influenced strongly by what we are looking for.

Traditional views of science were challenged most strongly by Feyerabend (1975). He argued that there are remarkably few rules which actually constrain the activities of scientists. In practice, the only rule which is followed extensively is "anything goes." Science differs more from non-science than Feyerabend admitted, but there is no doubt that his views and those of many other philosophers of science had a liberating effect on psychology. If the hard sciences such as physics and chemistry did not follow very strict rules, then there was no need for psychology to do so either. This meant that the way was open for the rigidities and limitations of Behaviorism to be discarded in favor of more flexible approaches, of which cognitive psychology soon established itself as the main one.

It is extremely difficult to identify the starting point for a major academic discipline such as cognitive psychology. One of the issues is that one needs to distinguish between early work which has clear affinities with contemporary cognitive psychology but which nevertheless had minimal impact on the development of cognitive psychology, and work which actually played a part in the emergence of cognitive psychology. A very clear example of work falling into the former category is the research carried out by neuropsychologists toward the end of the nineteenth century (see Ellis & Young, 1988). They endeavored to account for language impairments in brain-damaged patients by postulating damage to specific language-processing components of the brain, and they also tried to locate the parts of the brain in which these components were to be found. In spite of the fact that their work has strong relevance to that branch of contemporary cognitive psychology known as COGNITIVE NEURO-PSYCHOLOGY, the research and theory of the nineteenth-century neuropsychologists had practically no impact on the emergence of cognitive psychology in the 1950s.

There is general agreement that the ideas of

William James (1890) were extremely influential in the development of cognitive psychology (see JAMES, WILLIAM). He was primarily a theorist, but many of his ideas on ATTENTION and on MEMORY still seem acceptable today. For example, he distinguished between "primary memory," which he regarded as forming the psychological present, and "secondary memory," which he defined as the psychological past. Cognitive psychologists such as Atkinson and Shiffrin (1968) proposed a very similar distinction between SHORT-TERM MEMORY and LONG-TERM MEMORY.

Another important influence on cognitive psychology was the work of BARTLETT (SIR FREDERIC) (1932). As early as the First World War, he began investigating memory in a relatively naturalistic way by considering how well stories could be remembered at different retention intervals. Of particular importance was his theoretical approach to memory. He argued that what is remembered is determined in part by the SCHEMATA (= organized knowledge) which are possessed by those reading a story. Bartlett's (1932) schema theory had little impact on memory research during the 1940s and 1950s, but became the focus of considerable interest to cognitive psychologists during the 1960s and thereafter.

Some of the other important antecedents of contemporary cognitive psychology are to be found within Behaviorism itself. Tolman (1932) was one of the leading Behaviorists, but his research led him to modify Behaviorism in various ways that made it resemble cognitive psychology more closely. Hull and other researchers had argued in strict Behaviorist terms that rats learned to run through mazes by associating the maze stimuli with specific responses, including particular muscle movements. Tolman (1932) became convinced that maze running in the rat involved much more than these simple stimulus–response connections. He discovered that rats who had initially been trained to run through a maze were remarkably good at swimming through the maze when it was flooded with water, in spite of the fact that the muscle movements involved were quite different to those that had allegedly been acquired. This led Tolman to argue that a rat

running through a maze several times gradually builds up a 'cognitive map'; this is an internal representation (see COGNITIVE MAPS) of the maze which permits the rat to run or to swim through the maze depending on the prevailing circumstances. What is significant here is that Tolman discovered that learning in the rat could be understood only by considering internal processes and structures.

The advent of the digital computer as a metaphor for the human cognitive system played an important role in the development of cognitive psychology (see ANALOGIES). Psychologists have historically shown a strong tendency to make use of recent technological developments as metaphors for major aspects of human functioning. This can be seen very clearly in the case of theoretical attempts to describe memory (Roediger, 1980). The ancient Greeks likened the functioning of the memory system to wax tablets and avaries. Over the centuries, these metaphors were replaced by others involving switchboards, gramophones, tape-recorders, libraries, conveyor belts, and underground maps. In the case of the digital computer, it was argued that there are important similarities between its functioning and that of the human mind. According to Simon (1980, p. 45), "It might have been necessary a decade ago to argue for the commonality of the information processes that are employed by such disparate systems as computers and human nervous systems. The evidence for that commonality is now overwhelming."

Gardner (1985) has charted the development of cognitive psychology. He argued justifiably that 1956 was a crucial year. There was a meeting held at the Massachusetts Institute of Technology in that year at which George Miller talked about the magic number seven in short-term memory, Newell and Simon discussed their computational model known as the General Problem Solver, and Noam Chomsky presented a paper on his theory of language. During the same year, there was the well-known Dartmouth Conference, which was attended by Chomsky, McCarthy, Miller, Minsky, Newell, and Simon. It has often been argued that this conference saw the birth of ARTIFICIAL INTELLIGENCE. The same year also saw the publication of the first book in which concept formation was investigated from a cognitive-psychological viewpoint (Bruner, Goodnow, & Austin, 1956).

Cognitive psychology during the 1960s and 1970s was strongly influenced by the seminal theorizing of BROADBENT (1958). In essence, it was accepted that there are important relationships among the phenomena of attention, perception, short-term memory, and long-term memory. All of them could be understood by assuming that information flows through a complex cognitive system consisting of many interdependent processes. Within this theoretical framework, stimulus processing proceeds through a relatively invariant sequence of stages from modality-specific stores to its ultimate destination in long-term memory.

One of the best attempts to characterize the dominant information-processing framework in cognitive psychology was that of Lachman, Lachman, and Butterfield (1979). This framework incorporates a number of assumptions. One assumption was that the mind can be regarded as a general-purpose, symbol-processing system. Another assumption was that the goal of cognitive psychology is to identify the symbolic processes and representations which are involved in performance on all cognitive tasks. A further assumption was that the mind is a limited-capacity processor which has limitations of both structural and resource kinds.

This general framework still seems to be reasonable. However, one of the major weaknesses with this approach as it was usually implemented in the 1960s and 1970s was that the emphasis tended to be on data-driven rather than on conceptually driven processes (see DATA-DRIVEN AND CONCEPTUALLY DRIVEN PROCESSES). In other words, the ways in which stimulus processing is modified as a function of the individual's past experience and expectations were ignored. It was often assumed that processing occurs in a serial fashion (i.e. one process is completed before the next process starts). While strictly serial processing probably occurs on certain tasks, it is now recognized that the assumption that processing is always serial is invalid. Alterna-tive views which acknowledge that processes frequently overlap and interact with each other have become increasingly popular in recent years (see CASCADE PROCESSING).

Another major limitation of the research in cognitive psychology of the 1960s and 1970s was that it was mostly carried out in laboratory conditions and addressed academic rather than applied questions. In other words, cognitive psychology lacked what is generally termed ECOLOGICAL VALIDITY, meaning relevance to real-life problems and issues. The position has changed considerably in recent years. For example, there has been an enormous increase in research on language, and language is, of course, of central importance in real life. Key applied issues such as EYEWITNESS TESTIMONY have been investigated in great detail. In addition, and perhaps most noticeably, there has been a dramatic rise in the amount of research within cognitive psychology which is concerned with examining the cognitive performance of numerous special groups within society (e.g. brain-damaged patients; mood-disordered patients) (see COGNITIVE NEUROPSYCHOLOGY; MOOD DISORDERS AND COGNITION).

If one considers the current position of cognitive psychology, then it is apparent that cognitive psychologists differ considerably among themselves in terms of their aims and their approaches. Indeed, it is probably correct to claim that the most obvious difference between contemporary cognitive psychology and the cognitive psychology of ten or twenty years ago lies in its diversity. Cognitive psychologists are to be found within social psychology (see SOCIAL COGNITION), developmental psychology (see COGNITIVE DEVELOPMENT; PIAGET, JEAN), and personality psychology (see PERSONALITY AND COGNITION). Perhaps most surprisingly of all, cognitive psychologists have even begun to attack the citadel of Behaviorism, i.e. conditioning phenomena. For example, it is increasingly recognized that conditioning depends on information processing, and that it involves the selection of relevant information and its integration with stored information about relevant past experiences and events (Alloy & Tabachnik, 1984).

Eysenck and Keane (1990) argued that it is possible to divide cognitive psychologists into at least three major groups. First, there are the experimental cognitive psychologists, who follow the traditional cognitive-psychological approach of focusing on data collection and theory construction. Second, there are cognitive scientists, who develop computational models, and who argue that the computer provides a good metaphor for human cognition. Cognitive scientists differ among themselves in terms of their assessment of the value of traditional experimentation (*see* COGNITIVE SCIENCE). Third, there are cognitive neuropsychologists (*see* COGNITIVE NEUROPSYCHOLOGY). They are interested in the patterns of cognitive impairment shown by brain-damaged patients in part because they believe that the study of brain-damaged patients can be informative about the processes involved in normal human cognition. In essence, their claim is that several processing modules or components are involved in cognition. Since different patients have different modules impaired, it should in principle be possible to identify most (or even all) of the modules involved in cognition by detailed investigation of brain-damaged patients.

There are arguments for identifying a fourth group of cognitive psychologists who might be called applied cognitive psychologists. It is certainly true that applied cognitive psychologists differ from other cognitive psychologists in terms of what they investigate and the methods they employ. However, it is much less clear that applied cognitive psychologists and other cognitive psychologists differ systematically in terms of their theoretical preconceptions and orientations, and it is for this reason that it seems unnecessary to extend the categorization scheme beyond the three groupings discussed above.

Of course, there are many cognitive psychologists who do not fit neatly into any of the above categories. For example, there are many cognitive psychologists in the United Kingdom who sometimes behave like experimental cognitive psychologists but at other times like cognitive neuropsychologists. As a consequence, the distinctions between the three categories of cognitive psychologists cannot be regarded as absolute. However, Eysenck and Keane (1990) argued that there are very many cognitive psychologists who fall squarely into one or other of the categories, and so the categorization scheme is of value.

The various categories of cognitive psychologists differ in terms of their adherence to empiricist and rationalist perspectives. Experimental cognitive psychologists and cognitive neuropsychologists tend to be empiricists, in that they assume that the way to understand human behavior is via observation and experimentation. In contrast, cognitive scientists tend to be rationalists – that is to say, they believe that the construction of formal systems resembling those to be found in mathematics is the appropriate way to proceed. Of course, there are many cognitive psychologists who adopt a compromise position which is neither entirely empiricist nor completely rationalist.

The recent history of cognitive psychology has not indicated that one of the approaches (i.e. experimental cognitive psychology, cognitive science, cognitive neuropsychology) is intrinsically superior to the others. Each of the approaches is of value in its own right, and what is of particular importance is the attempt to demonstrate that all three approaches produce *converging evidence*. In other words, it is possible to have more confidence that a theory is on the right lines when it is supported by all three approaches than when it is supported by only one or two. That means that in future there is likely to be an expansion and development of the three approaches rather than an abandonment of any of them.

In sum, the history of cognitive psychology indicates that cognitive psychology has become increasingly influential and diverse over the years. At one time, cognitive psychology was rather narrowly focused on laboratory phenomena. However, the methods and theoretical perspectives of cognitive psychology have now permeated nearly every area of psychology. Thomas Kuhn has argued famously that a scientific discipline is generally dominated by a particular theoretical orientation which he called a "paradigm." There are strong arguments for supposing that the information-processing approach of cognitive psychology constitutes such a paradigm.

BIBLIOGRAPHY

Alloy, L. B., & Tabachnik, N. (1984). Assessment of covariation by humans and animals: The joint influence of prior expectations and current situational information. *Psychological Review, 91*, 112–49.

Atkinson, R. C., & Shiffrin, R. M. (1968). Human memory: A proposed system and its control processes. In K. W. Spence and J. T. Spence (Eds), *The psychology of learning and motivation* (Vol. 2). London: Academic Press.

Bartlett, F. C. (1932). *Remembering: A study in experimental and social psychology.* Cambridge: Cambridge University Press.

Broadbent, D. E. (1958). *Perception and communication.* Oxford: Pergamon.

Bruner, J. S., Goodnow, J. J., & Austin, G. A. (1956). *A study of thinking.* New York: Wiley.

Ellis, A. W., & Young, A. W. (1988). *Human cognitive neuropsychology.* London: Lawrence Erlbaum Associates Ltd.

Eysenck, M. W., & Keane, M. T. (in press). *Cognitive psychology: A student's handbook.* London: Lawrence Erlbaum Associates Ltd.

Feyerabend, P. (1975). *Against method: Outline of an anarchist theory of knowledge.* London: New Left Books.

Gardner, H. (1985). *The mind's new science.* New York: Basic Books.

James, W. (1890). *Principles of psychology.* New York: Holt.

Lachman, R., Lachman, J. L., & Butterfield, E. C. (1979). *Cognitive psychology and information processing.* Hillsdale, NJ: Lawrence Erlbaum Associates Ltd.

Popper, K. R. (1972). *Objective knowledge.* Oxford: Oxford University Press.

Roediger, H. L. (1980). Memory metaphors in cognitive psychology. *Memory & Cognition, 8*, 231–46.

Simon, H. A. (1980). Cognitive science: The newest science of the artificial. *Cognitive Science, 4*, 33–46.

Tolman, E. C. (1932). *Purposive behavior in animals and men.* New York: Appleton-Century-Crofts.

MICHAEL W. EYSENCK

cognitive science Cognitive science refers to the interdisciplinary study of the acquisition and use of knowledge. It includes as contributing disciplines: artificial intelligence, psychology, linguistics, philosophy, anthropology, neuroscience, and education. As one might surmise from this list, the cognitive-science movement is far-reaching and diverse, containing within it several viewpoints.

GENERAL ASPECTS OF COGNITIVE SCIENCE

Cognitive science grew out of three developments: (1) the invention of computers and the attempts to design programs that could do the kinds of tasks that humans do; (2) the development of information-processing psychology, where the goal was to specify the internal processing involved in perception, language, memory, and thought; and (3) the development of the theory of generative grammar and related offshoots in linguistics. Cognitive science was a synthesis concerned with the kinds of knowledge that underlie human cognition, the details of human cognitive processing, and the computational modeling of those processes (*see* ARTIFICIAL INTELLIGENCE; PERCEPTION, COMPUTATIONAL THEORY OF).

With regard to the overall architecture of an intelligent system, the traditional view has been inherited from von Neumann. Roughly, sets of symbols are moved about from one memory store to another, and are processed by explicit rules applied in sequence. In recent times, this "symbol-system view" has been best articulated by Newell and Simon (e.g. 1972); their emphasis has been on the components of the human information-processing system, particularly working memory and long-term memory, and how information is stored and used in these memories to solve problems.

The major challenge to the rule-based symbolic architecture is a "connectionist architecture," sometimes called a "parallel distributed processing system" (e.g. Rumelhart, McClelland, & the PDP Research Group, 1986) (*see* CONNECTIONIST MODELS OF MEMORY). Connectionists disavow that intelligent processes consist of the sequential application of explicit rules. Instead, they posit a large number of simple processing units, operating in parallel, where each unit sends excitatory and/or inhibitory signals to other units. In some cases, the units stand for possible hypotheses about the state of the world; in other cases, the units stand for goals and actions. In all cases, information processing takes place through the interactions of a large number of units.

A variety of methodologies has evolved in cognitive science. One methodology that is linked to AI is "protocol analysis" (e.g. Newell & Simon, 1972). In it, subjects are asked to think aloud while they solve a problem or do a task. Subsequent analysis attempts to specify the knowledge and processes needed to generate such protocols. A "computational model" is then usually constructed that replicates the problem-solving process manifest in the protocol. Other common methodologies are borrowed from experimental psychology, including memory studies and reaction-time analyses. Still other methodologies come from other disciplines, including, for example, discourse analysis (linguistics), dissociations caused by brain damage (see COGNITIVE NEUROPSYCHOLOGY), and the kind of formal analyses characteristic of philosophy.

TOPIC AREAS IN COGNITIVE SCIENCE

Cognitive science can also be defined in terms of its topic areas. Research has centered on five major areas that are addressed below: knowledge representation, language, learning, thinking, and perception.

Knowledge representation One of the earliest formalisms for representing knowledge about objects or concepts was the "discrimination net". A discrimination net is a tree structure; each branch point of the tree discriminates one set of objects or concepts from another on the basis of some feature, and the final leaves of the tree represent the objects or concepts themselves. To illustrate: knowledge about animals might be represented by a tree that contains separate branches for birds, mammals, and so on, where the branch from birds contains subsequent branches for songbirds, birds of prey, and so on, and the leaves emanating from songbird included species like bluejays, orioles, and so on. Such a discrimination net may be used in categorizing a novel animal by determining the values of the animal that correspond to the branch points in the

tree, e.g. "It's feathered and flying, so it's a bird, it's small and sings so it's a songbird, etc."

Quillian (1968) introduced a "semantic network" as a formalism for representing concepts. In a semantic network, a concept is represented by a set of properties, which in turn consists of pointers to other concepts. The properties are made up on attribute–value pairs, so that an oriole might be represented by the pairs: superset=bird, color=orange, location=Eastern United States. Any amount of information can be represented in this format. Along with this representation, Quillian proposed "spreading activation" (or "marker passing") as a means for searching a semantic network. When asked, for example, "Does an oriole have skin?," the concepts corresponding to oriole and skin are activated, and the activation from both sources spreads through the network; when the activation from both sources intersects, a possible answer to the question has been found. A semantic network goes beyond a discrimination net in that it permits different kinds of relations, (or links), which are differentially labeled and which are critical in using the network to answer questions. These ideas inspired a host of models in both artificial intelligence and cognitive psychology (see SEMANTIC MEMORY).

Semantic networks evolved into even more structured representations. Minsky (1975) extended the idea of a concept-in-a-semantic-network into the notion of a large organized data structure, or "frame," embedded in a "frame system." Each frame contains "slots," which accept only certain input values, and frequently have "default values" to use if there are no input values. The frame for a bird, for example, has slots for shape, size, and color, which can be instantiated by any particular bird that one happens across. Similarly, the frame for a bedroom has a slot for a bed, which can be instantiated by any object playing the role of a bed, and also has as a default value the prototypical bed. Frames are essentially models of parts of the world; to understand input information is to determine which frame, or configuration of frames, best fits it. An important variation on the idea of frame is the notion of a "script," which is a representation for a stereotypical action sequence like "going to a restaurant" (*see* SCHEMATA). Scripts contain defaults not only for the specific actions likely to be encountered in such a sequence, but also for the actors and props that are likely to figure in such a situation (Schank & Abelson, 1977).

Another important formalism for representing knowledge is a "production system" (Newell & Simon, 1972). Knowledge is represented as condition–action pairs called "production rules" (e.g. "If an animal has a long neck and brown blotches, then infer it is a giraffe"). A production system operates roughly as follows: if the current state satisfies one of the rules, the rule fires, which changes the current state, so that either a new rule fires or the system stops (*see* PRODUCTION SYSTEMS).

One final representational approach in the symbolic tradition, a mental model, specifies the domain-specific knowledge needed to understand a dynamic system or natural physical phenomenon, specifically the knowledge needed to qualitatively simulate the system or phenomenon (*see* MENTAL MODELS). The key idea is that one can decompose a complex system (a door buzzer, for example) into a set of component models (switches, coils, and the like), whose characterization is independent of the particular system in which they are embedded (e.g. de Kleer & Brown, 1983). Then, to construct a qualitative simulation of the system, one must know two things: (1) the topology of connections between the various components (that is, what is connected to what), and (2) the incremental input–output functions of the various components (that is, if a particular input to a component goes up, what happens to the output).

The connectionist tradition has not focused on knowledge representation, because all knowledge is assumed to be represented in the same way – a neural-like network of nodes.

Language Though psycholinguistic research is covered elsewhere in this dictionary, it has been a central research focus in cognitive science. We choose one topic from each of the three major divisions in language: syntax,

semantics, and pragmatics (*see* ANAPHORA; APHASIA; GRAMMAR; LANGUAGE, PRAGMATICS OF; LANGUAGE ACQUISITION; LANGUAGE COMPREHENSION; SPEECH PERCEPTION; SPEECH PRODUCTION).

Cognitive-science research on syntax often focuses on how a language understander parses a sentence into syntactic units like noun phrases and verb phrases. Such a parse is frequently a prerequisite for understanding the sentence's meaning. Parsing is complicated by the fact that at numerous points during the process, more than one analysis is possible. Consider the sentence, "The French bottle smells." When the parser reaches the word "bottle," it has to decide whether this word should be grouped with the preceeding two to form the noun phrase "The French bottle," or whether "bottle" is the start of the verb phrase "bottle smell." A critical question is whether the human language parser considers both parses simultaneously, or instead commits itself to one analysis and then backtracks to the other only if needed. Other foci of interest are the extent to which linguistic constraints can be used to expedite parsing (e.g. Berwick & Weinberg, 1984), and whether syntactic analysis can be done solely by a connectionist architecture (e.g. Rumelhart, McClelland, & the PDP Research Group, 1986).

Research on semantics has emphasized the decomposition of words into more primitive meaning units. Thus, the verb "kill" can be composed into "cause to die," while "give" can be decomposed into "transfer of possession." One virtue of "semantic decomposition" is that it makes it clear why some verbs are related to one another (they share some components). What remains controversial, however, is whether the semantic decomposition of a word is a necessary step in understanding the word. Some experiments have found evidence for this link between decomposition and understanding, but others have not (*see* SEMANTIC MEMORY).

Work in pragmatics has been dominated by the "ordinary language" philosophers. Particularly important is Grice's (1975) analysis of implicit rules of conversation. According to Grice, participants in a conversation adhere to a "cooperation principle," which means, among other things, that the speaker tries to make his or her contribution relevant to the aims of the ongoing conversation. When a speaker violates this "relevancy criterion," a listener assumes that the communication is still cooperative, and draws inferences that will make the speaker's utterance relevant. To illustrate, suppose a host says to a guest, "Do you want some coffee?," and the guest replies, "Coffee would keep me awake." The direct meaning of the guest's reply is irrelevant to the host's question; but the host makes it relevant by using knowledge that generally people do not want to be kept awake, which leads to the inference that the indirect meaning of the guest's response is "No" (*see* LANGUAGE, PRAGMATICS OF).

Learning Research on learning in cognitive science involves both machine learning and human learning. There are three traditions in machine learning: similarity-based learning, explanation-based learning, and neural-net learning. Similarity-based learning is concerned with the question of how a system that is presented multiple exemplars of a concept and multiple non-exemplars can induce a rule that distinguishes exemplars from non-exemplars. Explanation-based learning induces a concept-membership rule from only a single exemplar by using detailed knowledge about the domain. Perhaps the most important strand of research in neural-net learning grew out of earlier work on learning in perception systems, in particular the "delta rule." The delta rule assumes there is training or feedback with respect to what the output should be from each node in a neural (or connectionist) net. If the expected output for a node is greater than the actual output, then the rule increases the weight of any inputs to the node that were acting to increase its output (and decreases the weight of inputs acting to decrease the output). Similarly, if the expected output for a node is less than the actual output, the rule decreases the weight of any input to the node that acts to increase its output.

Most cognitive-science research on human learning has focused on learning procedures. There are three competing "architectures" for such learning. Brown and VanLehn (1980) postulate that learning occurs only at "impasses." They looked extensively at human errors in subtraction and found that when students are doing a problem that their subtraction procedure cannot handle, they reach an impasse. At that point they invoke one of the repair (or problem solving) procedures to deal with the impasse. This repair may lead to constructing a correct procedure, but more often it leads to constructing an incorrect procedure.

Anderson (e.g. 1983) developed a three-stage model of procedural learning within his ACT ("Adaptive Control of Thought") theory. The theory uses semantic networks to represent "declarative knowledge" ("knowing that"), and PRODUCTION SYSTEMS to represent "procedural knowledge" ("knowing how"). In the first, or interpretative stage of procedural learning, people use declarative knowledge to solve problems, much like a computer program is used as data by a computer-language interpreter. The second stage is the knowledge compilation stage; declarative knowledge is converted into procedural knowledge, and productions that occur repeatedly are composed by joining together pairs of productions and proceduralized by instantiating variables. The third stage, tuning, involves refining this procedural knowledge by means such as generalization and discrimination (*see* DECLARATIVE AND PROCEDURAL KNOWLEDGE).

Laird, Newell, and Rosenbloom (e.g. 1987) have recently proposed a new architecture for human learning that is implemented as a computer model, called SOAR. It is a problem-solving system built on production rules. When it encounters an impasse in problem solving, it sets up a subgoal to deal with that impasse. If it succeeds, it stores the solution as an operator that it uses when the same impasse occurs again. Like Brown and VanLehn's theory, the system learns at impasses, but in the context of a general problem-solving system.

Thinking Cognitive-science research on thinking has centered on problem solving. Almost any cognitive activity can be construed as an instance of problem solving, but the kinds of situations labeled "problem solving" typically require putting together novel sequence of processes to achieve some difficult goal. Such situations include mathematical puzzles, games like chess, and scientific problems.

Newell and Simon (1972) view problem solving as a search through a "problem space." The space consists of "states" with paths between them. The initial givens in a problem (e.g. the opening board position in chess) constitute an "initial state"; the solution of the problem (e.g. the taking of the opponent's king in chess) constitutes the "goal state"; all possible states of the problem constitute the other states in the problem space; and transitions between states constitute permissible "operators." Problem solving consists of searching through the space for a path or sequence of operators that takes one from the initial state to the goal state.

Almost inevitably the problem space is sufficiently large that blind search is useless (thousands if not millions of paths would have to be checked). The problem solver therefore needs to employ some kind of "heuristic search." Newell and Simon (e.g. 1972) have proposed a number of such "heuristic strategies," the best known of which is "means–ends analysis" (*see* PROBLEM SOLVING).

Perception Most cognitive-science research on perception has centered on visual processing and imagery. Some of the leading work has been inspired by Marr (e.g. Marr & Poggio, 1979). This research concerns the early stages of perception, and constructs computational models of how the visual system uses retinal information (points of varying brightness) to construct two-dimensional and then "two-and-a half-dimensional" descriptions of input objects. (Their two-and-a-half-dimensional sketch represents what is in front of what, but omits three-dimensional aspects of the objects.) (*See* PERCEPTION, COMPUTATIONAL THEORY OF.)

Other researchers have concentrated on the later stages of perception, in particular on matching input descriptions (like those mentioned above) to stored representations of objects. Some of the most seminal work has

dealt with simple perceptual objects, namely letters and words. In the McClelland and Rumelhart (1981) model, for example, matching is implemented via a connectionist network using top-down and bottom-up activation and inhibition processes, operating over separate levels for features (i.e. line segments at different orientations), letters, and words. The model explains a host of empirical findings, and has fostered the development of connectionist models in general.

The basic idea guiding imagery research is that imaging is like perceiving. For example, studies of mental rotation have found that the time people need to decide that two forms are identical increases regularly with the rotational difference between the forms. This result suggests that people are "mentally rotating" one of the forms to "see" if it coincides with the other. But the idea that imaging is like seeing has proved controversial. Pylyshyn (1981), for example, argues that imagery consists of nothing more than the use of general thought processes to simulate physical or perceptual events, based on tacit knowledge of how physical events unfold. For example, "mental rotation" occurs because people are *thinking* (as opposed to *imagining*) in real time about the course of a physical rotation; they know implicitly the time needed to physically rotate an object, and they wait the corresponding amount of time before indicating their response. The debate about imagery continues, and has led proponents of imagery to turn to neuropsychology and the study of brain-damaged patients for evidence that imagery and perception are mediated by the same brain structures (*see* IMAGERY, COMPUTATIONAL THEORY OF; IMAGERY AND PERCEPTION).

See also MODULARITY OF MIND.

BIBLIOGRAPHY

Anderson, J. R. (1983). A spreading activation theory of memory. *Journal of Verbal Learning and Verbal Behavior*, 22, 261–95.

Berwick, R., & Weinberg, A. (1984). *The grammatical basis of linguistics performance: Language use and acquisition.* Cambridge, Mass.: Bradford/MIT Press.

Brown, J. S., & VanLehn, K. (1980). Repair

theory: A generative theory of bugs in procedural skills. *Cognitive Science, 4,* 379–426.

de Kleer, J., & Brown, J. S. (1983). Assumptions and ambiguities in mechanistic mental models. In D. Gentner & A. L. Stevens (Eds), *Mental models* (pp. 155–90). Hillsdale, NJ: Erlbaum.

Grice, H. P. (1975). Logic and conversation. In P. Cole & J. L. Morgan (Eds), *Syntax and semantics* (Vol. 3): *Speech acts*. New York: Seminar Press.

Laird, J. E., Newell, A., & Rosenbloom, P. S. (1987). Soar: An architecture for general intelligence. *Artificial Intelligence, 33*(1), 1–64.

McClelland, J. L., & Rumelhart, D. E. (1981). An interactive activation model of context affects in letter perception: Part 1. An account of basic findings. *Psychological Review, 88,* 375–407.

Marr, D., & Poggio, T. (1979). A computational theory of human stereo vision. *Proceedings of the Royal Society of London, Series B, 204,* 301–28.

Minsky, M. (1975). A framework for representing knowledge. In P. H. Winston (Ed.), *The psychology of computer vision* (pp. 211–77). New York: McGraw-Hill.

Newell, A., & Simon, H. A. (1972). *Human problem solving*. Englewood Cliffs, N.J.: Prentice-Hall.

Pylyshyn, Z. (1981). The imagery debate: Analogue media versus tacit knowledge. *Psychological Review, 88,* 16–45.

Quillian, M. R. (1968). Semantic memory. In M. Minsky (Ed.), *Semantic information processing*. Cambridge, Mass.: MIT Press.

Rumelhart, D. E., McClelland, J. L., & the PDP Research Group (1986). *Parallel distributed processing: Explorations in the microstructure of cognition* (Vol. 1): *Foundations*. Cambridge, Mass.: Bradford/MIT Press.

Schank, R. C., & Abelson, R. P. (1977). *Scripts, plans, goals, and understanding*. Hillsdale, NJ: Erlbaum Press.

ALLAN COLLINS AND EDWARD E. SMITH

cognitive therapy An increasingly important approach to therapy, especially with mood-disordered patients, is based upon the notion that treatment can usefully focus on producing changes in patients' cognitive systems. Major cognitive therapists such as Beck (1976), Ellis (1962), and Meichenbaum (1977) all agree that patients suffering from the main mood disorders of anxiety and depression have unduly negative and self-defeating thoughts about themselves and their circumstances, and that producing major positive changes in these thought patterns can lead to recovery (*see* MOOD DISORDERS AND COGNITION).

Historically, the views of Ellis (1962) are important, because he was one of the first therapists to propose a systematic, explicitly cognitive approach to therapy. According to his approach, unhappiness occurs as the result of a three-point sequence. Point A is the occurrence of some unpleasant event (e.g. rejection by a valued other), point B is the cognitive reaction to that unpleasant occurrence (e.g. "I must be worthless to be rejected in this way"), and point C is a state of great anxiety or depression. In other words, anxiety or depression does not occur as a direct result of unpleasant events; instead, it occurs because of the irrational thoughts that are triggered off by the occurrence of unpleasant events.

The rational-emotional therapy developed by Ellis (1962) involves eliminating the irrational and self-defeating thoughts which all of us experience some of the time, and replacing them with more rational and positive thoughts. As Ellis (1962) expressed it, "If he [i.e. the individual] wants to be minimally disturbable and maximally sane, he'd better substitute for all his absolutistic *It's terrible's* two other words which he does not parrot or give lip-service to but which he incisively thinks through and accepts – namely, 'Too bad!' or 'Tough shit'!"

The approach to cognitive therapy adopted by Meichenbaum (1977) focuses on the patient's internal dialog, and in particular on the negative or unhelpful things which he or she says to him- or herself when problems are encountered. These negative thoughts need to be replaced by more adaptive self-talk, in which the patient actively attempts to cope with the situation by talking to him- or herself about the appropriate actions required to achieve the immediate goals. This form of self-talk makes it easier to succeed, and can have the further beneficial effect of leading to positive changes in the information stored in memory.

Beck (e.g. Beck & Clark, 1988) has proposed a somewhat more complex theoretical framework as the basis for cognitive therapy. He argues that there are important differences between the thought processes involved in anxiety and in depression. Anxious individuals have a heightened sense of vulnerability, and are concerned about physical and/or psychological threats. In addition, their negative appraisals of people and situations tend to be rather specific, and their thoughts focus on possible negative events in the future. In contrast, depressed individuals are concerned primarily about loss, and they have negative attitudes toward themselves, the world, and the future. Their negative thoughts tend to be more pervasive and global than those of anxious patients, and are often focused on past events.

In Beck's cognitive therapy, the first step is to make the patient aware of his or her negative and irrational thoughts. When this has been achieved, the therapist endeavors to challenge these negative thoughts, often by presenting the patient with new and incompatible information. This can involve presenting the patient's problem in a different way, by suggesting different strategies of handling the patient's current problems, or by re-analyzing the patient's previous difficulties.

There have been several attempts to assess the efficacy of cognitive therapy as a form of treatment (see Brewin, 1988). While there are many complexities in assessing recovery, equating groups receiving different forms of therapy in terms of severity, and so on, the evidence generally suggests that cognitive therapy is at least as effective as most other forms of therapy, and possibly more effective. However, even if this evidence is taken at face value, there are two major interpretative problems. First, most forms of cognitive therapy involve a mixture of several different ingredients. For example, cognitive therapy typically makes use of encouragement and persuasion, various different techniques for altering irrational thought patterns, and assignments designed to alter behavior in key situations. As a consequence, it is usually extremely difficult to know which particular ingredient or ingredients are responsible for any recovery which is observed.

Second, behavioral treatments (sometimes known as 'behavior therapy') have sometimes been contrasted with cognitive therapy. However, while it is true that the emphasis in such treatments is more on changing behavior than on changing thinking and other aspects of the cognitive system, the distinction is relative rather than absolute. For example, as Brewin (1988) points out, behavioral treatments usually begin by offering the patient encouragement and a detailed rationale for the proposed treatment. Such ingredients in behavioral treatments closely resemble some of the ingredients incorporated into cognitive therapy. It is a matter of current controversy as to the precise relationship between behavior and cognitive therapy. Some cognitive therapists (e.g. Meichenbaum, 1977) would go so far as to claim that most behavior therapy is effective because it produces beneficial effects on cognitive functioning, in spite of the assertion by many behavior therapists that they are interested only in changing behavior rather than cognition. What is certainly becoming increasingly clear is that the similarities between behavior therapy and cognitive therapy are greater than used to be believed, and that cognitive interpretations of the effectiveness of behavior therapy are often at least as plausible as the traditional interpretations based on conditioning principles.

See also EMOTION; SUBLIMINAL PERCEPTION.

BIBLIOGRAPHY

Beck, A. T. (1976). *Cognitive therapy of the emotional disorders*. New York: New American Library.
——, & Clark, D. A. (1988). Anxiety and depression: An information processing perspective. *Anxiety Research*, 1, 23–36.
Brewin, C. R. (1988). *Cognitive foundations of clinical psychology*. London: Lawrence Erlbaum Associates Ltd.
Ellis, A. (1962). *Reason and emotion in psychotherapy*. Secaucus, NJ: The Citadel Press.
Meichenbaum, D. (1977). *Cognitive-behavior modification*. New York: Plenum.

MICHAEL W. EYSENCK

communication, animal *See* ANIMAL COMMUNICATION.

communication, nonverbal *See* NONVERBAL COMMUNICATION.

computational theory of imagery *See* IMAGERY, COMPUTATIONAL THEORY OF.

computational theory of perception *See* PERCEPTION, COMPUTATIONAL THEORY OF.

concept learning The concept is considered by many to be the basic structure in cognition which enables us to classify and interpret the information that we have about the world in which we live (*see* CONCEPTS). For this reason, the notion of the concept has played a major role in both philosophical and psychological theories of human thinking. However, in neither discipline have authors managed to achieve a consensus on how a concept should be defined, with a clear division between those who emphasize a system of classification by well defined taxonomic categories, and those who propose that concepts are based upon prototypes or fuzzy-set membership (see Cohen & Murphy, 1984). Psychological theories of concept learning have also been divided between a Behaviorist approach based upon conditioning principles and a cognitive approach couched in terms of inductive inference and hypothesis testing.

CLASSICAL STUDIES

The traditional definition of a concept in psychology is that of a category which divides some domain into positive and negative instances, i.e. items which do or do not "belong" to the category. Such concepts can be defined by a rule. Thus, for example, one of the earliest reported psychological experiments in this area, conducted by the Behaviorist Hull (1920), involved presenting subjects with Chinese characters which the subjects were required to classify into two categories. The concept was actually based upon the presence or absence of a common radical element in the pictograms displayed. After a number of trials with feedback the subjects were able to classify stimuli correctly but were unable to describe or draw the feature upon which the concept was based (*see* INTROSPECTION). The suggestion that we may learn concepts through our experience with the world without having a conscious, or at least verbalizable, representation of the rule is supported in a number of modern studies of concept or rule learning (e.g. Berry & Broadbent, 1984).

Learning a concept necessarily involves the processes of generalization and abstraction, so it is not sufficient to show simply that subjects can learn to discriminate the set of stimuli with which they are trained. Simple concepts can often be discovered by subjects and stated verbally, but where this is not possible, as in the Hull study, it is necessary to use a transfer test to show that the knowledge acquired can be used to classify a new set of stimuli to which the same rule applies. Transfer tests of a more complex kind have also featured in some neo-Behaviorist research designed to show the importance of language in human concept learning. Kendler & Kendler (1962), for example, showed that preverbal children, like animals in discrimination learning experiments, will transfer learning more successfully on tasks involving a "non-reversal shift," whereas children who have acquired language perform better on "reversal shifts." Suppose, for example, that the task involved red and green figures which could be either triangular or circular in shape and which are to be classified into categories A and B. If the initial rule were red-A and green-B then a reversal shift would be to a rule green-A and red-B, and a non-reversal shift to a rule square-A and triangle-B. The reversal shift can only be easier because the task is learned in two stages: first, the relevant dimension (color) is learned, and then the appropriate responses are attached. With one stage learning, the non-reversal shift is easier because only two of the four stimuli require new responses to be learned. The Kendlers believed that language provided the basis for "mediated" or two-stage learning.

The cognitive approach to concept learning

– or concept identification, as cognitive theorists sometimes prefer – dates from the classic study of Bruner, Goodnow, & Austin (1956). They reported a series of laboratory experiments involving arbitrary sets of instances defined across several dimensions (shape, color, number of figures, and so on). Hence, rules could be defined both conjunctively ("blue circles," "two red figures," and so on) or disjunctively ("Either green or square"). Bruner et al. used two main paradigms for training concepts, which they described as selection and reception. In the selection method, subjects were required to select stimuli and ask the experimenter to give their classification, hence encouraging active strategies of hypothesis testing. In the reception method, they were instead provided with a sequence of stimuli determined by the experimenter, asked to guess the classification and then given feedback of correctness.

The theoretical analysis offered by Bruner et al. was in terms of the hypothesis-testing strategies adopted by their subjects. With conjunctive concept learning, for example, they proposed that some subjects used "wholist" and others "partist" approaches. The former group would form a hypothesis based upon a whole instance and then attempt to eliminate irrelevant dimensions, whereas the latter would form a particular hypothesis based upon one or two dimensions, and then revise it when they encountered contradictory evidence. Bruner et al. showed that the effectiveness of these alternative strategies depended upon the experimental conditions set for the tasks. They also showed that disjunctive concepts are extremely difficult to learn, because the optimal strategy requires subjects to focus on negative rather than positive instances and because members of disjunctive concepts need not share common instances. The special difficulty of disjunctives has subsequently been demonstrated in deductive-reasoning tasks, with comparable conclusions, and evidence from a variety of sources supports the view that negative information causes special difficulty in problem solving (*see* REASONING).

Following Bruner et al., a large number of concept learning experiments have been reported which investigate hypothesis-testing strategies using "simple" concepts. These are concepts where a number of binary dimensions are used to compose the instances and where only one dimension is relevant. The structure of this task is sufficiently simple as to have encouraged the development of mathematical models to describe learning in terms of Markov chains, which entail discontinuous transitions between discrete states of learning. One such model (Bower & Trabasso, 1964) includes the assumption that subjects hold a current hypothesis until such time as they discover evidence against it. Direct evidence in support of this assumption was provided by Levine (1966) using an ingenious "blank trials" technique. This involved presentation of a series of non-reinforced trials with a combination of features which allowed the experimenter to infer whether or not a consistent hypothesis was being used throughout.

SEMANTIC APPROACHES TO CONCEPT LEARNING

While some research continues in the classical tradition to the current day, a number of psychologists have questioned the value of the orthodox concept-learning experiment on the grounds of artificiality, both with regard to the use of meaningless, arbitrary problem content and the use of well defined categories to define concepts. A number of developments in cognitive psychology have led to a greater interest in the nature of how people's real-world knowledge is stored and organized. One such development is the field of semantic memory in which the organization of knowledge is studied, as distinct from memory of particular episodes. A number of models have been developed involving networks of propositions, some of which involve hierarchically organized concepts based on taxonomies (e.g. Collins & Quillian, 1969). One of the experimental paradigms methods used in this field is that of sentence verification tasks in which subjects have to decide as quickly as possible whether or not a statement is true. For example, Collins and Quillian showed that subjects take longer to verify a sentence such as "Robins have feathers" than "Robins eat worms," which they explain on the grounds that the information conveyed by the former statement, for reasons of cognitive economy, is stored with the generic concept of birds at a superordinate level in the hierarchy (*see* SEMANTIC MEMORY).

Semantic theorists have, however, also challenged the notion of concepts as well defined, set inclusive categories and proposed instead that concept memberships may be ill-defined, variable, or fuzzy. An important concept here is that of the "prototype," emphasized particularly in the writings of Eleanor Rosch (*see* CONCEPTS). The idea here is that a natural concept is defined by a typical example, so that category members may be more or less typical. Thus, for example, a robin is a very typical bird since it shares many features with the prototype, whereas an ostrich is atypical. In categorization tasks, where subjects have to identify the category of either a verbal description or a picture of an object as quickly as possible, it has been shown that items rated as more typical can be more quickly classified. In practice, prototype theories are difficult to distinguish from models which define concepts in terms of the relative likelihood of a set of identifying features (for a discussion of fuzzy concept theories see Smith & Medin, 1981).

A broader notion in the semantic organization of human conceptual knowledge is that of the "schema" (*see* SCHEMATA). The term has been used in various ways by psychologists from Bartlett (1932) onwards, but generally involves the notion that new information is assimilated into broad conceptual frameworks which evolve through our experience of real-world domains (*see* BARTLETT, SIR FREDERIC). Bartlett, for example, demonstrated that long-term recollections of stories were influenced and structurally altered by assimilation into schemata reflecting the cultural and social learning of the subjects. An important modern treatment of the notion of schema is provided by Rumelhart (1980), who argues that schemata exist at many different levels of abstraction, contain variables whose values may be fitted in a particular application, and include their own procedures for testing goodness-of-fit. He discusses an example of a purchaser schema which people might apply when buying an item (be it a new car or a pair of jeans). Such a schema would have variables such as purchaser, vendor, merchandise, and so on, and include some general procedures for action, such as shopping around for the best price, bargaining, and so on.

The notion that a schema may include procedural as well as conceptual knowledge has some powerful implications for human reasoning and discussion of a number of recent relevant studies is provided by Holland, Holyoak, Nisbett, and Thargard (1986). For example, it has been proposed that the induction of schemata may mediate transfer of problem solving and analogical reasoning, and the notion of pragmatic reasoning schemata has been applied to deductive reasoning research, with the suggestion that subjects may solve otherwise very difficult logical problems when the content and context encourage the elicitation and application of appropriate schemata learned through real-life situations. Recent theoretical developments in the semantic approach to concept learning also include the proposal that concepts and schemata may be described as emergent properties of parallel distributed processing (PDP) networks (Rumelhart, Smolensky, McClelland, & Hinton, 1986) and that induction of concepts, schemata, and mental models is based upon rules arranged in default hierarchies (Holland et al., 1986).

RULE LEARNING AND CONFIRMATION BIAS

So far, we have seen how a debate between Behaviorist and cognitive theorists about the process of concept learning in arbitrary experimental tasks has been displaced, to a large extent, by theory and experimentation concerned with the organization of real-world knowledge. However, it should also be recognized that a number of relevant experiments have been conducted upon inductive reasoning and rule learning which fall outside of the rather narrow traditions of work in the concept-learning paradigms. Of particular interest is a set of studies using a task devised by the British psychologist, Peter Wason, which purports to demonstrate that subjects manifest a "confirmation bias" when attempting to test hypotheses in rule discovery tasks. A detailed review of experiments in this area is provided by Evans (1989, ch. 3) (*see* REASONING).

The 2-4-6 problem, introduced by Wason (1960), has some similarities to the Bruner et al. selection paradigm, in that subjects have responsibility for choosing exemplars to be classified by the experimenter. However, Wason's subjects were required to generate their own examples from a potentially infinite set of "triples," each consisting of a sequence of three integer numbers. They were given "2 4 6" as an initial – and deliberately misleading – example. The actual rule was "any ascending sequence" but the example invited subjects to form more specific hypotheses, such as "ascending with equal intervals." It was found that subjects would test many examples which were consistent with their hypothesis, e.g. 10 20 30, 12 14 16, and so on, but rarely asked about an instance which was inconsistent, e.g. 10 11 15. The consequence was that many subjects failed to discover any triples which were inconsistent with their hypotheses and hence became convinced of its correctness.

Wason and a number of other authors conducting similar experiments have asserted that the behavior of these subjects reflects a confirmation bias, and have further suggested that since such experiments constitute laboratory analogs of scientific reasoning, then there may be serious real-life consequences. It has also been suggested that this bias may be resistant to education since a number of studies have failed to improve reasoning by presentation of detailed instruction on the importance of attempting to falsify particular hypotheses and the need to consider alternatives. Confirmation bias in rule-learning experiments has also been linked to evidence in social psychology that people have a strong tendency to maintain existing beliefs about the world and are apparently adept at avoiding disconfirmatory evidence.

A number of psychologists have, however, questioned the relevance of such studies to real-life reasoning and have even questioned whether a "confirmation bias" has been demonstrated at all. One argument is that subjects only think of testing positive examples

of their hypotheses and are not aware that this strategy cannot lead to falsification on the 2-4-6 task and others of similar construction. Scientific theories are, of course, frequently tested under conditions where a positive prediction can lead to disconfirmation. For example, Newtonian mechanical principles yield highly inaccurate predictions about the motion of particles accelerated close to the speed of light.

CONCLUSIONS

It is evident that we perceive and understand the world by use of concepts and categories, and equally apparent that the use of inductive thought processes involved in the discovery of general rules, and the formation of schemas, must play a central role in cognition. It is rather less clear, however, that classical studies of concept and rule learning in the laboratory have contributed greatly to our understanding of inductive reasoning due to rather artificial constraints in the experimental tasks used and the implicit definitions of a "concept" which they carry. The picture of rational hypothesis testing emerging from more recent studies in the classical paradigm is also challenged by the confirmation bias literature in which problems of slightly different construction are used to investigate inductive reasoning.

The development of semantic theoretical approaches to the understanding of human conceptual knowledge, including prototype and schema theories, is clearly to be welcomed. However, it must also be said that research in this line has so far yielded rather limited understanding of the mechanisms of learning and induction that underlie the acquisition of such knowledge.

BIBLIOGRAPHY

Bartlett, F. C. (1932). *Remembering*. Cambridge: Cambridge University Press.

Berry, D. C., & Broadbent, D. E. (1984). On the relationship between task performance and associated verbalizable knowledge. *Quarterly Journal of Experimental Psychology, 36A*, 209–31.

Bower, G. H., & Trabasso, T. R. (1964). Concept identification. In R. C. Atkinson (Ed.),

Studies in mathematical psychology (pp. 32–94). Stanford: Stanford University Press.

Bruner, J. S., Goodnow, J. J., & Austin, G. A. (1956). *A study of thinking.* New York: Wiley.

Cohen, B., & Murphy, G. L. (1984). Models of concepts. *Cognitive Science, 8,* 27–58.

Collins, A. M., & Quillian, M. R. (1969). Retrieval time from semantic memory. *Journal of Verbal Learning and Verbal Behavior, 8,* 240–7.

Evans, J. St. B. T. (1989). *Bias in human reasoning: Causes and consequences.* Hove and London: Erlbaum.

Holland, J. H., Holyoak, K. J., Nisbett, R. E., & Thagard, P. R. (1986). *Induction: Processes of inference, learning and discovery.* Cambridge, Mass.: MIT Press.

Hull, C. L. (1920). Quantitative aspects of the evolution of concepts. *Psychological Monographs, 28* (Whole Number 123).

Kendler, H. H., & Kendler, T. S. (1962). Vertical and horizontal processes in problem solving. *Psychological Review, 69,* 1–16.

Levine, M. (1966). Hypothesis behaviour by humans during discrimination learning. *Journal of Experimental Psychology, 71,* 331–8.

Rumelhart, D. E. (1980). Schemata: The building blocks of cognition. In R. J. Spiro, B. C. Bruce, & W. F. Brewer (Eds), *Theoretical issues in reading comprehension.* Hillsdale, NJ: Erlbaum.

——, Smolensky, P., McClelland, J. L., & Hinton, G. E. (1986). Schemata and sequential thought processes in PDP models. In J. M. McClelland & D. Rumelhart (Eds), *Parallel distributed processing: Explorations in the microstructure of cognition* (Vol. 2): *Psychological and biological models.* Cambridge, Mass.: MIT Press.

Smith, E. E., & Medin, D. L. (1981). *Categories and concepts.* Cambridge, Mass.: Harvard University Press.

Wason, P. C. (1960). On the failure to eliminate hypotheses in a conceptual task. *Quarterly Journal of Experimental Psychology, 12,* 129–40.

J. ST. B. T. EVANS

concepts

WHAT IS A CONCEPT?

Definition A concept is a mental representation or idea that includes a description of important properties of a class or term. Concepts refer to categories, a category being a partitioning to which a certain assertion or assertions apply. Whenever a category includes two or more members, then classification involves treating multiple entities as in some way equivalent. An alternative contrast between categories and concepts, which we specifically wish to disavow, suggests that categories are classes of entities that are objectively in the real world and that concepts are mental descriptions of them. We believe that this distinction is misleading because concepts need not have real-world counterparts (e.g. unicorns), because the set of potential real-world categories is indefinitely large, and because people may impose rather than discover structure in the world. Concepts need some sort of anchoring, but we do not think it must take the form of apprehending pre-existing, organism-independent, real-world categories.

Our definition of concept is necessarily vague because the question of just what constitutes "important properties" is a matter of considerable debate. Concept representations are variously thought to be comprised of essential attributes, defining properties, properties that are only characteristic, or theories concerning origin, function, or relationship to other concepts. Shortly we will turn to that debate but first we review some distinctions associated with concepts and their constituents, and address the question of what functions concepts serve (*see* SEMANTIC MEMORY).

Some distinctions and terminology The "intension" of a concept includes both criteria for determining category membership and properties that specify the concept's relation to other concepts. For example, part of the intension of "boy" includes the properties "young" and "male," and these properties underlie the relation of boy to other concepts such as "girl," "man," and "colt." The "extension" of a concept is a set of entities referred to by the concept. Some theorists draw a further distinction between the "core" and the "identification procedure" for a concept. The core of a concept consists of its essential attributes or definition, whereas the identification procedure is the method for recognizing instances of a concept. A key aspect of this distinction is that the properties associated with the identification procedure may be different from those associated with the core. Thus, for example, one might use hair length, clothing, and gait to identify some person as a woman, but none of these properties need be part of the core of the concept "woman."

"Features" are aspects or properties of things that facilitate comparisons and *explain* similarity. For example, a boy is like a colt in that they share being young and male. Features also help instantiate goals – for a person on a diet "number of calories" is an important property to know. Properties may differ in their abstractness (e.g. blond, male, honest), and a difference at one level (six feet six inches versus six feet nine inches in height) may be a similarity at a higher level (they are both tall).

"Relations" show how parts/features of a concept are connected to create structure. Connections may be spatial (the eyes are above the beak), temporal (nest building precedes egg laying), causal (hormones cause secondary sexual characteristics such as body coloring), functional (heart for pumping blood), or derived from a theory (some biological theories relate singing behavior to mate selection).

Conceptual functions Concepts serve multiple functions. We describe seven.

(1) *Classification.* The classification function involves determining that a particular instance is an instance of a concept or that one particular concept is a subset of another (e.g. that robins are birds). Other functions presuppose the classification function.

(2) *Understanding and explanation.* Classification allows intelligent systems to parse their experience into meaningful chunks and to construct an interpretation of it. A major facet of this understanding is bringing old knowledge to bear on the current situation. If a person recognizes an animal as a "rattlesnake," for example, he or she will interpret their situation as dangerous. Concepts also support the explanation of relationships among entities. For example, the concept "introvert" might help to explain why some person did not attend a party.

(3) *Prediction.* In the example of the rattlesnake just described one may also access knowledge that might allow one to make predictions concerning the future. One might, for instance, predict that sudden movements might cause the rattlesnake to strike and on the basis of this prediction one might slowly back away from the snake to avoid being bitten.

(4) *Reasoning.* Concepts and conceptual structure support reasoning. One does not need to store every fact and possibility if one can derive knowledge from the information that is stored. From the knowledge that all animals breathe, that birds are animals, and that flamingos are birds, one may reason that flamingos breathe. Concepts support not only logical inferences but also plausible reasoning. From "doctor" one might infer (fallibly) "large salary, long and irregular work hours," and so on (*see* INFERENCES; REASONING).

(5) *Communication.* To the extent that people share knowledge and index it in terms of the same categories, they will be able to communicate with each other. Communication allows learning on the basis of indirect experience. If a friend tells us how she avoided danger in a confrontation with a rattlesnake, we may be able to profit from her experience should a similar situation arise for us.

(6) *Conceptual combination.* Concepts can act as building blocks of higher order concepts. From the concepts "paper" and "bee" one might construct the combined concept "paper bee" (presumably a bee made of paper). Combining concepts allows for the expression of totally novel concepts and the creative envisioning of future states of affairs.

(7) *Production of instances.* People can start with a concept description, and from this description, retrieve or derive instances of the concept. While fixing a device, a person may formulate a need for a "long, pointed metal object"; old tools (e.g. screwdriver) will be retrieved or new tools (e.g. bent wire hanger) will be devised to fit the description.

One reason for emphasizing multiple functions is that theories of classification and concept representation often embody implicit assumptions concerning the purpose of classification. Some theories focus on some functions to the neglect of others, and keeping the various functions in mind is a useful strategy for evaluating competing theories.

WHAT IS THE STRUCTURE OF CONCEPTS?

The most active ground for research and theorizing about concepts is involved with determining the structure of concepts. Four theories concerning conceptual structure have received attention.

The classical view The classical view has had a profound historical impact on psychology and linguistics. On this view, concepts are structured around defining features – features that are singly necessary and jointly sufficient to define the concept. The category "even number" has a classical definition provided by the feature "evenly divisible by two"; this definition acts as a fixed criterion for evaluating whether an object belongs to the concept. According to the pure form of the classical view, *all* concepts are like "even number" in being organized around defining features.

(1) *Strengths.* The classical view captures people's intuition (first expounded by Plato) that concepts have defining and organizing "essences." Representing concepts by lists of defining features results in a structure that is highly concise, and may seem to capture the critical aspects of the concept.

(2) *Weaknesses.* A number of criticisms have been leveled at the classical view. The most damaging criticisms include:

(a) Failure to specify defining features. Ludwig Wittgenstein argued that common concepts such as "chair" and "game" have no defining features. Rather, the instances of these concepts are connected by "family resemblances" – features characteristic of "chairs" and "games" but not necessary or sufficient.

(b) Typicality effects. An extremely robust finding is that not all instances of a concept are equally good examples of the concept. For example, a robin is judged to be a better example of the concept "bird" than is a penguin. This is incompatible with the classical view's claim that the only features represented in a concept are those possessed by all of the concept's instances.

(c) Unclear cases. There is a multitude of cases where it is not clear whether an item belongs to a concept or not (e.g. are radios furniture?). Unclear membership is problematic for the classical view's claim that a fixed definition determines whether an example belongs to a particular concept.

The prototype view The prototype view developed out of dissatisfaction with the classical view. Its central claim is that concepts are organized around a prototype or best example that summarizes the most common or typical features among a concept's instances. The similarity between an item and a concept's prototype determines whether, and how well, the item belongs in the concept.

(1) *Strengths.* The prototype view manages to solve many of the problems which plagued the classical view. The inability of people to give defining features for their concepts is no longer a problem; prototypes are based on characteristic, not defining, features (Rosch & Mervis, 1975). Similarly, the presence of typicality effects or unclear cases is predicted by the prototype view. The more similar an item is to the concept's prototype, the more typical it will be of the concept; if an item is far (but not too far) from the prototype, then it may be unclear as to whether it belongs in the concept. Finally, the prototype view leads to promising models for conceptual combination (Smith & Osherson, 1988).

The prototype view also provides an account of different levels of concepts. For artefacts (e.g. chair) and other taxonomic categories there are hierarchies of concepts, with subordinate concepts at the lowest level ("German shepherd"), basic-level concepts at the intermediate level ("dog"), and superordinate concepts at the highest level ("mammal"). Basic-level concepts appear to be psychologically privileged. They are, for example, the first to be learned, are the natural level at which objects are named, show cross-cultural consistency, provide the most new information, and are the highest level in which the instances all share the same parts, overall shape, and function (see Rosch, Mervis, Gray, Johnson, & Boyes-Braem, 1976). According to the prototype view the basic level is the highest level where examples of a category share many properties with each other and tend not to share properties with members of contrasting categories.

(2) *Weaknesses.*
(a) Does not preserve enough item information. The prototype view assumes that concept representations consist of central tendencies (means or modes). These representations discard too much information to be viable theories of human concepts. In addition to central tendency, people are sensitive to the number of instances that make up a concept, the variability of features, the correlations between features, and the particular instances used (for a review, see Oden, 1987).
(b) Does not address context effects. How well an item belongs to a concept depends upon the context in which it is presented. For example, a harmonica is typical of "musical instrument" in the context of a campfire, but is not typical in the context of a concert hall. The prototype view cannot account for context effects unless a separate prototype for each context is posited.
(c) Concept coherence is not explained. The prototype view does not distinguish between coherent and incoherent concepts in that there are no grounds for calling one concept more structured than another as long as a central tendency can be extracted (Murphy & Medin, 1985). Moreover, some concepts derive their coherence from ideal properties, not central tendencies. Barsalou (1985), for example, has shown that the concept "diet foods" is organized around the ideal property "zero calories"; and that typicality is based on similarity to this ideal rather than similarity to an average.

The exemplar view Unlike the earlier views, the exemplar view does not create a summary description to represent concepts. Concepts are represented by the individual instances (or exemplars) that constitute it. To decide whether an item belongs to a concept, the item is compared with the concept's exemplars. If the item is similar to the exemplars then it will be placed in the concept (e.g. Brooks, 1978).

(1) *Strengths.*
(a) Conservation of information. Exemplar models would seem to discard no information. Most exemplar models assume that generalization occurs at the time of retrieval and, therefore, that people do not have distinct access to each example. In practice, however, exemplar models tend to preserve more information than do prototype models. In general, human induction appears to be conservative in the sense of preserving information and exemplar models have fared better than prototype models in describing this conservatism.
(b) Context sensitivity. Exemplar models are naturally sensitive to and consistent with context effects. Ad hoc or goal-derived categories such as "things to take on a camping trip" may not be prestored but rather created by retrieving potential examples.

(2) *Weaknesses.*
(a) Generalizations are not formed during learning. Although exemplar models allow generalizations to be computed at the time of retrieval, there is evidence that humans form generalizations or abstractions during learning that cannot be computed at retrieval (see Oden, 1987).
(b) Coherence is not explained. Items are placed in the concept with the exemplars they are most similar to, but the exemplar view does not explain how the concepts are created in the first place. The exemplar view cannot account for concepts such as "diet foods" being organized around ideals such as "zero calories." As previously suggested, concepts are important for constructing explanations/interpretations of events. The only explanation of an event that an exemplar model can produce is: "Because it is similar to an old exemplar" – a very limited form of explanation.

Concepts as theory dependent To explain the coherence of concepts, several researchers (e.g. Carey, 1985; Murphy & Medin, 1985; Keil, 1987) have suggested that concepts are based on knowledge and world theories that constrain the construction and organization of concepts. Susan Carey (1985) and Frank Keil (1987) have shown that children's biological theories influence their patterns of induction at a very early age. Classification decisions may be based on running the inference process in reverse. We may induce that a man is drunken because we see him jump into a pool fully clothed. If so, it is probably not because the feature "jumps into pools, clothed" is listed with the concept "drunk." Rather, it is because part of our concept of "drunk" involves a theory of impaired judgement that serves to explain the man's behavior.

People's theories determine the features that will be important for a concept. The exemplar and prototype views did not constrain the features or relations that are important for a concept; the knowledge-guided view of concepts claims that a feature or relation is important for a concept to the extent that it fits into the theories concerning the concept.

It has been suggested that concepts are sometimes organized around idealized models or theories and not typical features. Lakoff (1987) argues that lexical concepts are often ensembles of separate models. The concept "mother" includes the following models: "woman who raised child," "woman who is responsible for the child's genetic information," and "woman who is married to child's father." Lakoff reasons that typicality effects (X is a better example of "mother" than Y) are due to the number of models that X and Y satisfy, and not the existence of a prototypical mother. The cognitive models underlying concepts themselves are well defined; it is only when they are applied to the real world that "fuzziness" enters in.

(1) *Strengths.*
(a) Coherence. The idea that concepts are organized around theories provides a good account of coherence. Both intra- and inter-conceptual structure can be tied to the role that concepts play in a theoretical structure. Theories themselves are anchored and coherent to the extent to which the predictions derived from them receive support in the world.
(b) Structure and knowledge. Theory-based categorizing gives proper emphasis to inter-property relations and structure. The general point is that there is more to conceptual structure than listing features or pooling examples. Theory-based categorization is also knowledge-driven and follows parallels to work on scripts and frames (*see* SCHEMATA; MENTAL MODELS).

(2) *Weaknesses.*
(a) Lack of constraints. If theory-based categorization is to address questions of coherence in a deep sense, then we need to have constraints on theories. If a theory can take any form, and dictate any categories, we will have simply substituted the term "theory" for "concept" in the question of why we have the concepts we have and not others. The fact that theories should make predictions that are generally correct is not, by itself, a tight enough constraint.
(b) Neglect of similarity. One can argue that the theory-based approach downplays the role of similarity in cognition too much. For example, hypotheses concerning causes and effects appear to be biased toward expecting causes and effects to *resemble each other* or to be of *similar* magnitude.

ONGOING PROBLEMS AND ISSUES

Our brief review should have conveyed the fact that psychological theorizing concerning categories and conceptual structure has not achieved anything approximating a stable consensus. This situation is simultaneously a source of discomfort and excitement. We close with a summary of some of the problems and issues that continue to make the study of concepts dynamic.

Observation versus theory as a basis of concepts
Although it appears that concepts are often organized by theories, similarity relations are also important. Although it is clear that theories of similarity will need to go beyond independent features to capture structure, the proper integration of empirical and theory-guided induction is anything but clear. One

approach to integration is referred to by Medin and Ortony (1989) as psychological essentialism. They suggest that people have a tendency to assume that concepts have essences and that the identifying (superficial) features of concepts are linked to the deeper, essential properties of the concepts. On this account people may use similarity heuristically because things that are superficially similar are often similar in more fundamental ways.

Structure and similarity We need a theory of similarity that is compatible with our understanding of conceptual structure. Instead of independent features all at the same level of abstractness, an adequate theory of similarity will need features linked by relations at multiple levels. On this view, features may differ not only in their salience but in their centrality. For example, the property "curved" may be equally true of both bananas and boomerangs but more central for boomerangs because of the important structure/function relation.

Concept stability We tend to think of concepts as well established mental entities. Barsalou (1989) and others, however, have found marked instability in people's definitions of concepts, classification judgements, and typicality ratings. These are a challenging set of observations for theorists who think of concepts as quite stable. At the very least we need better theories for how people access and use their conceptual knowledge if we are to address questions concerning stability.

Types of concepts It may turn out that questions about conceptual structure hinge on the types of concepts being considered. For example, natural kinds ("whale," "grass") may support more inductive inferences than do artefacts. Keil (1979) has suggested that concepts are organized in terms of ontological knowledge. Ontological concepts can be thought of as a tree of distinctions that become more specific as the tree descends. The first ontological distinction is between abstract ideas and concrete objects; lower on the "concrete" object branch is the animate/inanimate distinction; and so on. The tree implies con-straints on predictions or inferences, and Keil argues that children's conceptual development obeys these implied ontological constraints. For example, a child should not ever think that people and rocks can sleep without also thinking that animals can sleep, because animals are between people and rocks on the ontological tree.

Numerous other distinctions are potentially important. To give but one example, Gentner (1982) has argued that verbs differ from nouns in a number of ways, the most distinctive of which is that verbs are more relationally defined.

Representation and non-explicit tokening Fodor, Pylyshyn, and others have argued for a representational theory of mind where concepts are tokens or symbols of mental language (e.g. Fodor and Pylyshyn, 1988). In contrast, connectionist or parallel distributed processing models suggest that concepts are represented dynamically in terms of a (distributed) pattern of activation where no such explicit tokens exist. On this account, prototypes are an emergent property of activation. These contrasting views are currently being hotly debated. Although it is too early to draw any definitive conclusions, connectionist models face serious challenges with respect to addressing relations, structure, and multiple levels of features (*see* CONNECTIONIST MODELS OF MEMORY).

SUMMARY

It is tempting to suggest that the various theories of concepts are all partially correct. Given that concepts serve multiple functions, perhaps different forms of representation will be especially suitable for only a subset of these functions. However, there is a big difference between a list of ingredients and a recipe, and we still lack integrated theories that assume multiple forms of representation.

BIBLIOGRAPHY

Barsalou, L. W. (1985). Ideals, central tendency, and frequency of instantiation as determinants of graded structure in categories. *Journal of Experimental Psychology: Learning, Memory and Cognition*, II, 629–54.

——. (1989). Intraconcept similarity and its implications for interconcept similarity. In S. Vosniadoy & A. Ortony (Eds), *Similarity and analogical reasoning* (pp. 76–121). Cambridge: Cambridge University Press.

Brooks, L. R. (1978). Nonanalytic concept formation and memory for instances. In E. Rosch & B. B. Lloyd (Eds), *Cognition and categorization* (pp. 169–215). Hillsdale, NJ: Erlbaum Associates.

Carey, S. (1985). *Conceptual change in childhood.* Cambridge, Mass.: Massachusetts Institute of Technology Press.

Fodor, J. A., & Pylyshyn, Z. W. (1988). Connectionism and cognitive architecture: A critical analysis. *Cognition, 28,* 3–71.

Gentner, D. (1982). Why nouns are learned before verbs: Linguistic relativity versus natural partitioning. In S. Kuczaj (Ed.), *Language development: Language, cognition and culture* (pp. 301–34). Hillsdale, NJ: Erlbaum Associates.

Keil, F. C. (1979). *Semantic and conceptual development: An ontological perspective.* Cambridge, Mass.: Harvard University Press.

——. (1987). Conceptual development and category structure. In U. Neisser (Ed.), *Concepts and conceptual development: Ecological and intellectual factors in categorization* (pp. 175–200). Cambridge: Cambridge University Press.

Lakoff, G. (1987). *Women, fire, and dangerous things: What categories tell us about the nature of thought.* Chicago: University of Chicago Press.

Medin, D. L., & Ortony, A. (1989). Psychological essentialism. In S. Vosniadou & A. Ortony (Eds), *Similarity and analogical reasoning* (pp. 179–95). Cambridge: Cambridge University Press.

Murphy, G. L., & Medin, D. L. (1985). The role of theories in conceptual coherence. *Psychological Review, 92,* 289–316.

Oden, G. C. (1987). Concept, knowledge, and thought. In M. R. Rosenzweig & L. W. Porter (Eds), *Annual Review of Psychology, 38,* 203–27.

Rosch, E., & Mervis, C. G. (1975). Family resemblances: Studies in the internal structure of categories. *Cognitive Psychology, 7,* 573–605.

Rosch, E., Mervis, C. G., Gray, W. D., Johnson, D. M., & Boyes-Braem, P. (1976). Basic objects in natural categories. *Cognitive Psychology, 8,* 382–439.

Smith, E. E., & Osherson, D. N. (1988). Compositionality and typicality. In S. Schifter & S. Steele (Eds), *Cognition and representation* (pp. 37–52). Boulder, Colo.: Westview Press.

DOUGLAS L. MEDIN AND
ROBERT L. GOLDSTONE

conceptually driven processes *See* DATA-DRIVEN AND CONCEPTUALLY DRIVEN PROCESSES.

connectionist models of memory Connectionist networks, neural networks, or parallel distributed processing models characterize concepts as distributed patterns of activation in a network; they also differ from conventional computational models in that the networks are modifiable as a function of experience, i.e. they exhibit learning. Connectionist networks typically consist of numerous interconnected elementary units or nodes. These units influence each other by means of excitatory and inhibitory activation.

According to the connectionist or parallel distributed processing model proposed by McClelland (1981), information about people, events, and objects is stored in several interconnected units rather than in a single location. The strengths of the connections among these units increase as a function of learning. Subsequent retrieval of information about a particular person, event, or object involves gaining access to one or more of the relevant units, followed by a spread of activation to other relevant units.

There are some theoretical advantages in assuming that information is distributed in this fashion rather than concentrated in complex memory traces. For example, it permits the retrieval system to function efficiently under most circumstances, even if one of the relevant units is damaged. The reason for this is that the levels of activation in the undamaged units will typically be sufficient to ensure that the correct concept is activated.

One of the general characteristics of connectionist or parallel distributed networks is that they provide an explanation of the fact that we seem to possess both episodic or autobiographical memories and semantic, or knowledge-based, memories (*see* EPISODIC

MEMORY; SEMANTIC MEMORY). For example, we have information about several chairs that we are familiar with, and we also have knowledge of the general concept of "chair." According to McClelland and Rumelhart (1986a), the stimulus word "chair" leads to activation of several units referring to specific chairs, and an averaging process indicates the typical features of chairs in general.

Theories based on connectionist networks are also of use in accounting for some aspects of AMNESIA. The basic assumption (McClelland & Rumelhart, 1986b) is that each learning experience produces a more modest increase in the connection strengths of relevant units for amnesic patients than for people with normal ability to learn and remember. As a consequence, amnesic patients should find it extremely difficult to remember the idiosyncratic features of situations. However, their memory for the common features of situations should be much better, because connection strengths for repeated information should increase with each repetition. These predictions are supported by much of the evidence.

In sum, connectionist network models show the promise of providing a useful way of conceptualizing human memory. The theoretical assumption that processing within the memory system occurs in parallel is certainly more in accord with what we know of the human brain than the alternative assumption that processing is serial (see ARTIFICIAL INTELLIGENCE). However, it appears unlikely that the detailed functioning of the brain corresponds at all closely to that assumed by connectionist theorists.

See also COGNITIVE SCIENCE; CONCEPTS; PATTERN PERCEPTION.

BIBLIOGRAPHY

McClelland, J. L. (1981). Retrieving general and specific information from stored knowledge of specifis. *Proceedings of the Third Annual Meeting of the Cognitive Science Society,* 170–2.

— —, & Rumelhart, D. E. (1986a). A distributed model of human learning and memory. In D. E. Rumelhart, J. L. McClelland, & the PDP Research Group (Eds), *Parallel distributed processing* (Vol. 2): *Psychological and biological models.* Cambridge, Mass.: MIT Press.

McClelland, J. L., & Rumelhart, D. E. (1986b). Amnesia and distributed memory. In D. E. Rumelhart, J. L. McClelland, & the PDP Research Group (Eds), *Parallel distributed processing* (Vol. 2): *Psychological and biological models.* Cambridge, Mass.: MIT Press.

MICHAEL W. EYSENCK

consciousness The term refers to awareness of our own mental processes (or of the products of such processes); this awareness can be made manifest by introspective reports, in which an individual provides information about his or her mental experience (*see* INTROSPECTION).

There has been a considerable amount of controversy over the centuries concerning the value to psychology of assessing the contents of consciousness by means of introspective evidence. On the one hand, Aristotle claimed that the only way to study thinking was by introspection. On the other hand, Galton (1883) argued that the position of consciousness "appears to be that of a helpless spectator of but a minute fraction of automatic brain work." The Behaviorists agreed with Galton that psychologists should not concern themselves with consciousness and introspection.

It has been argued (Tulving, 1989) that most cognitive psychologists in recent years have subscribed to the doctrine of concordance of cognition, behavior, and experience. According to this doctrine:

> ... there exists a close and general, even if not perfect, agreement between what people know, how they behave, and what they experience. Thus, conscious awareness is required for, and therefore accompanies, the acquisition of knowledge, or its retrieval from the memory store; retrieved knowledge *guides* behaviour, and when this happens, people are aware of the relation between the knowledge and the behaviour.
> (Tulving, 1989, p. 8)

This doctrine of concordance implies that conscious experience generally provides reasonably valid evidence which is consistent with an individual's cognition and behavior. In fact, however, there is increasing evidence that the doctrine of concordance is wrong (*see* AMNESIA; BLINDSIGHT; IMPLICIT AND EXPLICIT MEMORY; SUBLIMINAL PERCEPTION). For example, amnesic patients frequently provide behavioral evidence indicating long-term retention of previous learning in spite of the fact that they have no conscious recollection of any learning having taken place. The implication is that conscious awareness can be considerably less informative about cognitive functioning than is usually thought to be the case. There is much evidence from normal individuals for substantial amounts of information processing below the level of conscious awareness. For example, prolonged practice at a task can lead to rapid and efficient performance without conscious awareness of the processes involved (*see* AUTOMATIC PROCESSING).

An even stronger attack on the validity of conscious awareness was mounted by Nisbett and Wilson (1977). They argued that people are generally unaware of the processes that influence their behavior, and they supported their argument by means of experimental evidence. Subjects in one experiment were asked to choose the best pairs of stockings from five highly similar pairs placed in a horizontal display. Since most of the subjects chose the right-most pair of stockings, their decision was clearly affected by relative spatial position. However, in their introspective reports the subjects did not explain their decision by referring to spatial position. Even when they were asked explicitly if spatial position had influenced their decision, they denied it emphatically.

Of course, Nisbett and Wilson (1977) admitted that people's introspective reports about the reasons why they have behaved in a particular way are sometimes accurate. However, they argued that an individual's introspections about the factors influencing his or her behavior are typically no more accurate than the guesses about those factors made by other people. The implication is that conscious awareness does not provide access to useful information about one's own cognitive system which is denied to other people.

The position advocated by Nisbett and Wilson (1977) is too extreme. A more fruitful approach is to attempt to distinguish between those situations in which introspective reports of conscious experience are valid and those in which they are not. For example, introspective reports are more likely to be valid when they refer to current conscious experience than when they are obtained retrospectively (Ericsson & Simon, 1980). They are also more likely to be valid when a subject describes what he or she is currently attending to than when a subject is asked to interpret a situation or to explain his or her behavior.

Close examination of the experimental evidence produced by Nisbett and Wilson (1977) reveals that they consistently obtained introspective evidence under conditions which were not conducive to valid reports of conscious experience. More specifically, their subjects were typically asked to provide retrospective interpretations relating to information which had not been the central focus of attention.

In sum, it is often important for cognitive psychologists to obtain evidence about the contents of consciousness. In some cases (e.g. the work on problem solving by Newell and Simon, 1972), conscious experience provides valid information about the processes and products involved in cognitive task performance. In other cases (e.g. subliminal perception), the fact that there is a discrepancy between conscious experience and behavioral evidence is of theoretical significance.

See also HYPNOSIS; MENTAL MODELS.

BIBLIOGRAPHY

Ericsson, K. A., & Simon, H. A. (1980). Verbal reports as data. *Psychological Review, 87,* 215–51.

Galton, F. (1883). *Inquiries into human faculty and its development.* London: Macmillan.

Newell, A., & Simon, H. A. (1972). *Human problem solving.* Englewood Cliffs, NJ: Prentice-Hall.

Nisbett, R. E., & Wilson, T. D. (1977). Telling more than we can know: Verbal reports on mental processes. *Psychological Review, 84,* 231–59.

Tulving, E. (1989). Memory: Performance, knowledge, and experience. *European Journal of Cognitive Psychology, 1,* 3–26.

MICHAEL W. EYSENCK

constructivist theories of perception
According to the constructivist approach, perception depends not only on the presented stimulus but also on internal hypotheses, expectations, and stored knowledge. Thus, perception can be regarded as an inferential process which is much influenced by conceptually driven or top-down processes (*see* DATA-DRIVEN AND CONCEPTUALLY DRIVEN PROCESSES). It follows from this theoretical position that perception should be relatively prone to errors, since the inferences made on the basis of the sensory input may be mistaken (Neisser, 1967; Gregory, 1980).

There is very strong evidence that perception can be influenced by conceptually driven processes initiated by contextual information. For example, it has been found that the identification rate for objects presented very briefly was much higher when the preceding context was appropriate than when it was inappropriate or than when there was no preceding context (Palmer, 1975).

One of the major predictions that follows from the constructivist position is that perceptual errors will occur if a situation is created in which stored knowledge leads to the formation of erroneous hypotheses. This prediction has been confirmed in research using the Ames distorted room (Ittelson & Cantril, 1954). This room has a very unusual shape (i.e. it deviates substantially from being rectangular, and one corner of the wall opposite to the viewing point is much further away from the observer than the other corner). In spite of its shape, it is so constructed that it produces the same retinal image as a conventional room. The illusion that the room is of normal rectangular shape is so powerful that someone walking backward and forward along the rear wall appears to grow and shrink.

Gregory (1980) has argued that the constructivist approach can explain many of the well-known two-dimensional VISUAL ILLUSIONS (e.g. the Müller-Lyer). In essence, he claimed that knowledge based on perceiving three-dimensional objects is applied inappropriately to the perception of these two-dimensional figures, and this is what causes the classic illusions. There is some support for this theory, but it cannot account for all of the

relevant findings (see Eysenck and Keane, 1990).

The major weakness of the constructivist approach is that it does not provide an adequate account of the fact that perception is typically accurate. In general terms, conceptually driven processes have their greatest influence on perception when stimuli are presented very briefly. Under normal circumstances, the stimulus usually provides sufficient information for veridical perception.

BIBLIOGRAPHY

Eysenck, M. W., & Keane, M. T. (1990). *Cognitive psychology: A student's handbook*. London: Lawrence Erlbaum Associates Ltd.

Gregory, R. L. (1980). Perceptions as hypotheses. *Philosophical Transactions of the Royal Society of London, Series B, 290*, 181–97.

Ittelson, W. H., & Cantril, H. (1954). *Perception: A transactional approach*. New York: Doubleday.

Neisser, U. (1967). *Cognitive psychology*. New York: Appleton-Century-Crofts.

Palmer, S. E. (1975). The effects of contextual scenes on the identification of objects. *Memory & Cognition, 3*, 519–26.

MICHAEL W. EYSENCK

coping *See* STRESS, ADAPTATION TO.

creativity "Creativity" refers to the ability to produce unusual, high-quality solutions to problems. It has often been argued that there are significant aspects of human intelligence which are not adequately assessed by intelligence tests (*see* INTELLIGENCE; LEARNING STYLES). Guilford (1961), for example, drew a distinction between convergent thinking, which is required by most intelligence tests, and divergent thinking, which is not. Convergent thinking refers to thinking of a deductive kind in which there is a single appropriate answer, whereas divergent thinking involves non-logical processes and novel situations in which there may be several relevant answers. For example, divergent thinking can be assessed by asking people to think of as many different uses of a brick as possible. Divergent thinking, or the ability to think of diverse valuable alternatives to a novel situation, forms a major part of which is often known as creativity.

Creativity is notoriously difficult to investigate in the laboratory. Many tests of divergent thinking or creativity are basically measuring originality rather than creativity. That is to say, they assess the tendency to produce unusual solutions to a problem, but do not evaluate satisfactorily the quality and usefulness of those solutions. There is no convincing evidence that any currently available test provides a suitable measure of creativity.

From the perspective of cognitive psychology, one of the major issues of interest is to attempt to establish as far as possible the processes involved in creativity. Wallas (1926) was one of the first theorists to propose a sequence of stages in the creative process. He argued that there is an initial stage of "preparation," during which information is gathered. This is followed by the stage of "incubation," in which the problem is put aside, and then by "illumination," in which there is a crucial insight into the solution of the problem. The fourth and final stage is that of "verification," in which there is careful checking of the proposed solution.

Anecdotal reports of the creative process in several famous creative individuals from the arts and sciences often indicate that insights occur despite an absence of focusing on the problem beforehand. This suggests that Wallas (1926) was right to postulate a stage of incubation. However, it has proved rather difficult to establish the phenomenon of incubation under laboratory conditions.

A more empirically based approach was proposed by Sternberg and Davidson (1983). In essence, they argued that there are at least three different ways in which insight or illumination can occur. First, there is selective encoding, which involves identifying that information which is relevant from the total available information. Second, there is selective combination, which involves knowing how to put together the relevant pieces of information. Third, there is selective comparison. This involves relating information in the current problem to relevant information acquired previously (e.g. problem solving by analogy).

In sum, creativity is an important aspect of intelligence, but one which has proved difficult to measure. There are indications that several different processes can be involved in creativity, and therefore that there are various subcategories of creativity.

See also PROBLEM SOLVING.

BIBLIOGRAPHY

Guilford, J. P. (1961). Factorial angles of psychology. *Psychological Review, 68,* 1–10.
Sternberg, R. J., & Davidson, J. E. (1983). Insight in the gifted. *Educational Psychologist, 18,* 52–8.
Wallas, G. (1926). *The art of thought.* London: Jonathan Cape.

MICHAEL W. EYSENCK

D

data-driven and conceptually driven processing This distinction refers to the flow of control in information processing. Data-driven processing is initiated, guided, and determined by stimulus information coming in from the outside world and currently being received by the sense organs. Conceptually driven processing is guided by information already stored in memory; that is, by the prior knowledge and concepts acquired from previous experience. This distinction is often characterized as bottom-up and top-down processing, terms which originated from computer science (Norman & Rumelhart, 1975).

In bottom-up processing the sequence starts with low-level analysis of the physical features of the sensory input and builds upwards toward the final interpretation. Top-down processing begins with higher level processes that generate expectations and hypotheses relating to the interpretation and evaluation of the input. In this case, the processing sequence begins at the highest level and works downward. Many cognitive activities, such as memory, perception, and language understanding, can involve both data-driven and concept-driven processing, but the role of each type of processing is often controversial. Some theories stress the primacy and importance of data-driven processing; other theories give much greater prominence to conceptually driven processing. In many cases, however, it is recognized that the two kinds of processing operate in combination, working simultaneously and interactively.

In theories of perception the distinction has been applied to the processes involved in object recognition. Feature detection models emphasize the role of bottom-up processing. According to those models, the visual system incorporates innate specialized feature detector cells. Hierarchies of feature detectors are arranged so that the output of cells at one level feeds upwards to the next level. Objects such as letters of the alphabet are recognized by the specific combination of lines and loops identified by the feature detectors. Gibson's theory of direct perception (1979) (*see* DIRECT PERCEPTION) also emphasizes data-driven processing. In his view, the optic array (the complex pattern of light reflected from the surfaces of objects in the visual scene), and the dynamic changes in this pattern that occur with movement, provide stimulus information that is sufficiently rich for objects to be directly recognized without drawing on previously acquired conceptual information.

These bottom-up models contrast with top-down models of perception which are also known as constructivist or inferential models. According to these models, perception is influenced by expectations that derive from past experience and from the current context. Recognition is the product of inferences based on knowledge about how the world is organized which supplement the sense data (*see* FORM PERCEPTION; PATTERN PERCEPTION). It can readily be demonstrated that, when stimulus information is distorted, ambiguous, or incomplete, conceptually driven mechanisms operate to normalize the distortion, to select an interpretation of what is ambiguous and to fill in missing elements. People can recognize handwritten words when the letters are grossly ill-formed or nonexistent, or objects that are upside-down or partly obscured. According to top-down constructivist models, expectations are generated by the context and hypotheses are tested. If the context suggests that the distorted letter is likely to be an A or the obscured object is a cup, the stimulus information is evaluated for goodness-of-fit to stored knowledge about As or cups. The most striking aspect of human perception is its robust ability to function effectively with stimulus information that is faulty or inadequate, and purely data-driven models have difficulty in accounting for this.

Models such as Neisser's (1967) analysis-by-synthesis model incorporate both data-driven and conceptually driven processing working interactively, with the relative contribution of each type of processing being flexibly determined by the quality of the stimulus information and the availability of contextual information. In the analysis-by-synthesis model the initial stage of data-driven analysis is followed by a stage in which an internal representation is synthesized. The synthesis is based on the information derived from the initial analysis together with conceptually driven hypotheses derived from prior knowledge. This representation is then matched against the input. If there is a match, the stimulus is recognized; if a mismatch occurs, the cycle is repeated and alternative representations are synthesized until a match is found.

Interactive models of this general kind have been developed to account for language processing. Language understanding involves several levels of analysis. Low-level processes of physical analysis extract the visual features of written material or acoustic cues from spoken inputs; higher level processes carry out syntactic and semantic analysis. Prior knowledge of spelling patterns and phonological constraints, knowledge of grammatical rules, knowledge of the context and experience of the world allow the reader or listener to generate expectations. In reading and speech perception data-driven and concept-driven processes interact (see LANGUAGE COMPREHENSION; READING DEVELOPMENT; SPEECH PERCEPTION).

The contribution of top-down processing varies with the availability of contextual information and with the quality of the stimulus information. When context is available, recognition of expected letters or expected words is primed; missing fragments can be filled in; and ambiguous or degraded inputs can be interpreted. Top-down processing offers short cuts so that a message can be understood without having to be completely analyzed. However, the evidence suggests that a skilled reader dealing with clear print can rely on bottom-up processing which is automatic and effortless (Perfetti and Roth, 1981). Spoken language is generally of much poorer quality than written language and top-down processing plays a greater part in speech comprehension. Words spoken out of context can be difficult to recognize.

The distinction between data-driven and conceptually driven processing overlaps with other distinctions between different types of cognitive processing. Data-driven processes can also be characterized as parallel, automatic, unconscious, and relatively unaffected by capacity limitations (see AUTOMATIC PROCESSING). Concept-driven processing, by contrast, is serial; it requires conscious control; and it draws on limited capacity resources. This distinction has been useful in that it has clarified models and theories by forcing them to specify the nature, sequence, and scope of operations more precisely. It exemplifies the way in which computer science can influence cognitive psychology. In building artificial intelligence systems, computer scientists are forced to confront questions about the sequence of operations and the amount and type of knowledge that has to be built in for the system to function (see COGNITIVE SCIENCE). Their solutions have provided useful evidence of the relative power of data-driven and conceptually driven processes and indicated how these might operate in human cognition.

See also IMPLICIT AND EXPLICIT MEMORY.

BIBLIOGRAPHY

Gibson, J. J. (1979). *The ecological approach to visual perception*. Boston, Mass.: Houghton-Mifflin.

Neisser, U. (1967). *Cognitive psychology*. New York: Appleton-Century-Crofts.

Norman, D. A., & Rumelhart, D. (1975). *Exploration in cognition*. San Francisco: Freeman.

Perfetti, C. A., & Roth, S. F. (1981). Some of the interactive processes in reading and their role in reading skills. In A. Lesgold & C. Perfetti (Eds), *Interactive processes in reading*. Hillsdale, NJ: Erlbaum.

GILLIAN COHEN

decision making and judgement In decision tasks the goal is to make as good a choice as possible between a set of alternatives. Except in the simplest cases there is a requirement on the decision maker to form judgements of the values of the possible outcomes of alternative choices and of the probabilities of those outcomes occurring. Finally, judgements of value and probability need to be combined to make the final choice.

Decision problems can be characterized on the following dimensions: *risky vs riskless*; *single-attribute vs multi-attribute*, and *single-stage vs multi-stage*. In a risky decision there is some uncertainty about the outcome of the choices available. Deciding which horse to bet on in a race or which color to back at roulette are good examples of risky decisions. Choosing between T-shirts in a store is essentially an example of riskless decision making in that "what you see is what you get." Choosing between objects that differ only on a single attribute (e.g. two quantities of money) is simple enough but most choices are between multi-attribute objects, such as houses, word-processing packages, or cars. Such choices require assessment of the relevant attributes and a strategy for integrating information about the attributes into an overall judgement about each object, so that the overall judgements can be compared and a final decision reached. In multi-stage decision problems each choice leads to another set of choices and so on. For example, should one go out or stay home? If the decision is to go out, should one go to the theatre, the cinema, or a restaurant? If the decision is to go to the cinema, which movie should one go to? Real-life decisions are typically risky, multi-attribute, and multi-stage. Research on decision making has generally tackled simplified forms of decision problem and it is hoped to build up to real-life complexities from simpler laboratory versions.

Studies of decision making can be divided into normative and empirical. Normative studies are aimed at deriving recommendations for optimal or rational decision making. Such studies have a long history in mathematics and economics. Empirical studies seek to aid our understanding of the mental processes involved when humans make decisions whether those decisions are optimal or not. However, the two approaches are linked.

From the psychological point of view, normative models provided starting points for empirical research by suggesting questions, such as: To what extent do people approximate to normative models? Can normative models be transformed into empirical models that will fit behavioral data? Recent research has drawn more on notions of cognitive economy and use of heuristics in decision making and less on idealized normative models.

NORMATIVE APPROACHES TO RISKY DECISION MAKING

The basic idea of the normative approach to decision making is that the decision maker should choose so that a measure of *expected value* is maximized. For example, if one bets \$10 that a fair coin will land heads up when tossed, the expected value of that bet is $0.5 \times 10 - 0.5 \times 10 = 0$, because if the gamble is repeated then half of the trials would yield a gain of 10 and the other half of the trials would yield a loss of 10, giving an overall mathematical expectation or mean outcome of 0. Again, suppose at a racetrack you are offered odds of 2:1 on a horse which you know has a 0.8 probability of winning. Then the expected value of betting \$100 would be $0.8 \times 200 - 0.2 \times 100 = +140$. If your aim is to maximize expected value, the bet should be made, since not betting in those imaginary circumstances would have an expected value of zero.

To make use of expected value analysis in decision making you must know the objective probabilities involved and judge the value of money to be a linear function of objective money amount. In practice, objective probabilities are not always known. In such cases, a modified version of the expected value approach can be followed in which objective probabilities are replaced by *subjective probabilities* that represent the decision maker's degree of belief in the possible outcomes. The normative model is then one of subjectively expected value maximization. Factors affecting the subjective assessment of probabilities will be discussed in a later section of this essay.

From an empirical point of view, the

assumption that subjective value is linearly related to money amounts is also questionable. For example, the subjective value or utility of a fixed amount of money appears to depend on how much money the individual already has. Intuitively, it seems clear that the utility of an extra dollar is less for a billionaire than for a pauper. If utility were linear with money value then rational people would not take out insurance or buy lottery tickets since in both cases the purchaser must be expected to lose (or else insurance companies and lotteries would collapse). Since buying insurance or even lottery tickets are not, intuitively, irrational acts, it is plausible to suppose that the assumption of a linear relationship between money value and utility may be mistaken. In view of such considerations, over 200 years ago, Bernoulli argued that a fixed increment of cash wealth results in ever decreasing increments to utility as the basic cash wealth increases; that is, there is a law of diminishing marginal utility.

Further information about the shape of the function relating utility to money value comes from studies by Kahneman and Tversky (1984) on the phenomena of "loss aversion," "risk aversion" in the area of gains, and "risk seeking" in the area of losses. Most respondents were found to refuse to bet $10 on the toss of a coin unless they stood to win at least $30 (expected value of such a wager = $10). This indicates loss aversion, i.e. that a loss of $x is more aversive than a gain of $x is attractive. Kahneman and Tversky also found that most subjects displayed risk aversion in that they would prefer $800 for certain as against a 0.85 chance of $1000, despite the expected value of the gamble being greater than the value of the sure thing. Risk seeking in the area of losses was demonstrated by subjects' strong preference for a 0.85 chance of losing $1000 over a certain loss of $800. The phenomenon of risk seeking in the area of losses has been upheld in other studies also, for example Slovic, Fischhoff, and Lichtenstein, 1982.

The results and observations regarding risky choices involving money are well fitted by a utility function which is concave in the area of gains and convex in the area of losses, with a steeper slope for losses than gains. Given a utility function and some means of estimating subjective probabilities it can be argued, normatively, that the rational policy is to choose so as to maximize "subjectively expected utility." If rational behavior is to be forthcoming then two principles or axioms must hold. These are the axioms of "invariance" and "dominance." Invariance requires that an individual's preference between two options should not be affected by how the options are described; while dominance states that if option A is at least as good as option B in all respects and better than B in at least one respect then A should be preferred to B. Tversky and Kahneman (1981) found that subjects could be readily induced to violate the invariance principle. If exactly the same public-health programs were described in terms of "lives saved" then one option was chosen overwhelmingly, but if the descriptions were in terms of "lives lost" then the other option was typically chosen. The majority choice in the "lives saved" description is a "risk averse" choice, as is typical in the area of gains. The preferred choice in the "lives lost" description is a "risk seeking" choice commonly found in the domain of losses. Similarly, Kahneman and Tversky have shown violations of the dominance principle brought about by risk aversive and risk-seeking tendencies. Thus, depending how subjects "frame" a choice problem, as involving choices between gains or between losses, violations of basic principles of rationality can be observed. These results are in line with findings from studies of deductive and inductive REASONING which have cast doubt on the notion that people are completely rational processors of information.

MULTI-ATTRIBUTE CHOICES

Deciding between multi-attribute objects could be very demanding if the precepts of normative multi-attribute utility theory (MAUT) were followed. On this approach, the decision maker should identify relevant dimensions, decide how to weight the dimensions, obtain a total utility for each object by summing its weighted dimensions values and choose the object with the highest weighted total (Wright, 1984). Given working-memory limitations, MAUT seems unlikely as a descriptive theory and more plausible alternatives are provided by Tversky's (1972) "Elimination-by-Aspects" (EBA) theory and Simon's (1978) "satisficing" theory (see WORKING MEMORY).

With the EBA strategy the chooser first selects an attribute and eliminates all options that do not meet a criterion set for that attribute. For example, in house purchasing, cost will probably have a ceiling value. All properties above the cost ceiling can be ruled out without considering their other attributes. Next, a second attribute is used and all items not meeting the criterion value on the second attribute are ruled out. This elimination process continues until only one option remains and is thus chosen. EBA is clearly less demanding than MAUT; however, it is not an optimal approach and the final choice made can vary depending on the order of elimination adopted.

In the satisficing approach, rather than attempting to maximize utility, a minimum acceptable level is set and the first option encountered which meets the minimum is chosen. This seems especially plausible when options are not simultaneously available but rather arise sequentially. The housing market provides a good real-life example of such a situation. If the initial satisficing level has been set too high, Simon (1976) suggests that the level is adjusted in the light of the average values in the market so that more realistic levels are arrived at.

Payne (1976) experimentally investigated multi-attribute choice strategies by tracking information selection during the decision process in an apartment-selection task. Subjects were presented with cards each of which carried information about one aspect of one apartment. The cards were laid out face down in an Apartment-by-Attribute array so that subjects could readily obtain information apartment by apartment, attribute by attribute, or in some mixed pattern. From the patterns of information selection it emerged that no one of the models outlined above held throughout. Initially, subjects used techniques such as satisficing and EBA to reduce the

choice set and then analyzed the remaining few options more thoroughly as proposed by MAUT. These results indicate that subjects are compromising between minimizing cognitive load (through use of EBA or satisficing) and maximizing utility (through use of MAUT).

JUDGEMENTS OF PROBABILITY

Since the judged probability of events is critical in decision making, considerable research has been directed at unraveling the processes underlying such judgements. Tversky and Kahneman have proposed two major heuristics, "availability" and "representativeness," which can help (by reducing cognitive load) and hinder (by leading to inaccuracies).

Judgements of probability often seem to be made on the basis of how available relevant examples are in long-term memory. Thus, Tversky and Kahneman (1983) found that when subjects were asked to rate the frequency of words ending "ing" and ending with "n" in the second last position, "ing" words were rated as more frequent. This judgement matches the ease of producing words matching the requirements of an "ing" ending as against the requirement of having "n" in second-last position. Note that these judgements based on availability violate a fundamental law of probability, known as the "extension rule," which states that if the extension of a set, A, includes the extension of a set, B, then the probability of A must be greater than or equal to the probability of B. The set of words with "n" in second-last position includes the set of "ing"-ending words and so the typical judgement of probability of these examples is clearly fallacious.

Use of availability to judge frequency or probability does of course work some of the time since frequency affects availability. However, since availability is also affected by recency and emotional impact, availability is not always a valid guide to objective frequency or probability.

According to Tversky and Kahneman's (1983) second heuristic of representativeness, representative instances of a category tend to be judged more probable than unrepresentative instances. This heuristic has been implicated in a particular form of error dubbed the "conjunction fallacy." In the classic example of this fallacy, subjects are given a personality sketch of an imaginary person ("Linda") who is described as a former student activist, single, very bright, and a philosophy graduate. Subjects are then invited to say how probable they think it is that Linda is a bank teller, is a feminist, or a feminist bank teller. There is a very marked tendency for subjects to say that Linda is much more likely to be a feminist bank teller than a bank teller. These judgements of probability match judgements of how representative Linda is of the categories. However, the typical response clearly violates the extension rule, since the set of bank tellers includes the set of feminist bank tellers. The conjunction fallacy is a very robust finding and has been replicated under many variations of the task. For example, Tversky and Kahneman (1983) found that medically trained subjects judged the conjunction of an unusual and a common symptom as more likely than the unusual symptom.

Overall, then, it seems clear that human decision makers depart from the complete rationality of normative theory and rely on a variety of heuristics to reduce cognitive load at the expense of optimal decision making.

See also INFERENCES; PROBLEM SOLVING; SOCIAL COGNITION.

BIBLIOGRAPHY

Kahneman, D., & Tversky, A. (1984). Choices, values and frames. *American Psychologist, 39,* 341–50.

Payne, J. (1976). Task complexity and contingent processing in decision making: An information search and protocol analysis. *Organizational Behavior and Human Performance,* 16, 366–87.

Simon, H. A. (1976). Motivational and emotional controls of cognition. *Psychological Review,* 74, 29–39.

— —. (1978). Rationality as process and product of thought. *American Economic Association,* 68, 1–16.

Slovic, P., Fischhoff, B., & Lichtenstein, S. (1982). Response mode, framing, and information processing effects is risk assessment. In R. Hogarth (Ed.), *New directions for methodology of social and behavioral science:*
Question framing and response consistency. San Francisco: Jossey-Bass.

Tversky, A. (1972). Elimination by aspects: a theory of choice. *Psychological Review, 79,* 281–99.

— —, & Kahneman, D. (1981). The framing of decisions and the psychology of choice. *Science, 211,* 453–8.

— —. (1983). Extensional versus intuitive reasoning: The conjunction fallacy in probability judgment. *Psychological Review, 90,* 293–315.

Wright, G. (1984). *Behavioural decision theory.* Harmondsworth: Penguin Books.

K. J. GILHOOLY

declarative and procedural knowledge Declarative knowledge can be defined as knowledge to which an individual has conscious access and which can therefore be stated directly, either verbally or by some other means. Procedural knowledge is knowledge to which the individual has no conscious access and, as such, its presence can only be demonstrated indirectly through some form of action.

The distinction between declarative and procedural knowledge parallels that within philosophy between "knowing how" and "knowing that." The latter distinction also acknowledges that some dimensions of our knowledge are not open to conscious inspection whereas others are. Riding a bicycle, for example, is something that most of us "know" how to do, but if asked to explain how we do it our account would be very superficial (e.g. "I push, start pedaling, and somehow I stay upright"). In contrast, we can give a detailed description of the structure of a bicycle and explain its mechanisms (e.g. we know that a bicycle has a chain and it is this that transfers the force applied to the pedals back to the driving wheel).

Declarative knowledge, by its very nature, is flexible. It can be used in many different situations and accessed in many different ways. Procedural knowledge is inflexible in that it is tied to one particular situation. Our declarative knowledge about bicycles, for example, can be used to explain how they work or provide the basis for drawing a picture of one. Procedural knowledge about how to ride a bicycle is, by contrast, only of use when we want to go cycling.

Because it is open to conscious inspection, declarative knowledge can easily be modified by both new experiences and internal thought processes. Procedural knowledge cannot be affected in this way and for this reason it is far less vulnerable to change. We are constantly surprised by our ability to perform skills that we have not used for years – a phenomenon that reflects the robust nature of procedural knowledge. In contrast, abilities dependent on declarative knowledge (e.g. knowledge of history, geography) will deteriorate if not used due to the influence of other conscious mental operations which will overwrite and distort existing knowledge with time.

Declarative and procedural knowledge form the basis of Anderson's (1987) theory of skill learning known as ACT* ("Adaptive Control of Thought") (see COGNITIVE SCIENCE; PRODUCTION SYSTEMS). The basic idea of this theory is that in the acquisition of any skill an individual will rely initially on declarative knowledge but, with practice, transfer performance of that skill to procedural memory. A good example of this is learning to type. Initially novices will depend on declarative knowledge of the keyboard layout in order to direct their fingers to the correct keys. With practice, however, the need to think about where their fingers go becomes gradually reduced to a point where conscious direction via declarative knowledge is no longer necessary. At this point the typing skill has become procedural in nature. This can be demonstrated by asking an experienced typist to state where individual letters are on a keyboard. Rather than state the answer directly, the typist will first make hand movements and infer the place of the letters from the finger positions. The lack of direct conscious access to procedural knowledge is further emphasized by experiments which have shown that attempts to verbalize highly developed skills while performing them result in much poorer performance.

One of the important features of the transfer of performance from declarative to procedurally based knowledge is that it reduces the amount of conscious processing effort required in performance of that skill. This is why, when we first learn to drive, we find it hard to carry on a conversation at the same time because we need to remember the position of the clutch, where the indicator stalk is, and so on. However, as we progress, the various routines of driving become established procedures which, in turn, free our thought processes for other activities. Seen in this way procedural knowledge can be thought of as a form of automatic processing (see AUTOMATIC PROCESSING).

The distinction between declarative and procedural knowledge has gained considerable impetus from studies of patients with the amnesic syndrome (see AMNESIA). It is now an accepted feature of the amnesic syndrome that existing procedural knowledge is preserved. One well-known patient, an accomplished musician, lost most of his memory for both personal events and general knowledge of music but completely retained the procedural skills of playing the piano and conducting. Other similar examples are described by Parkin (1987). Moreover, it is now well established that amnesic patients can acquire new procedural memories. The famous amnesic patient HM was able to learn a number of different motor skills as rapidly as normal even though he had no declarative knowledge about the tasks or of having done them before. Cohen and Squire (1980) demonstrated the development of procedural memory in amnesics, this time within the perceptual domain. They presented amnesics with word triples printed back-to-front and asked them to read them out as quickly as possible. The ability of the patients to perform this task increased dramatically across test sessions even though, at a declarative level, the subjects had little knowledge of the task.

Some writers have argued that the distinction between procedural and declarative knowledge provides an adequate framework for describing the nature of the amnesic syndrome. As we have seen, existing procedural knowledge appears preserved and can also be added to. However, evidence is also accumulating which suggests that certain forms of declarative knowledge can be acquired in amnesic patients. Wood, Brown, and Felton (1989) report an amnesic child who, despite remaining classically amnesic (e.g. zero delayed recall of a short story), nonetheless progressed satisfactorily through high school and graduated. Similarly, there are reports of a densely amnesic woman who was able to learn French at the same rate as a normal person. Both these examples indicate the acquisition of declarative knowledge within an amnesic state and they cast doubt on the value of the procedural/declarative distinction as a means of fully accounting for the pattern of memory breakdown in amnesia (Parkin, 1990). Nevertheless the distinction appears to provide some genuine insights into the representation of knowledge and provides a plausible basis for understanding many aspects of skill acquisition.

See also IMPLICIT AND EXPLICIT MEMORY; MEMORY SYSTEMS.

BIBLIOGRAPHY

Anderson, J. R. (1987). Skill acquisition: Compilation of weak method problem solutions. *Psychological Review*, 94, 192–210.

Cohen, N. J., & Squire, L. R. (1980). Preserved learning and retention of pattern analysing skill in amnesia: Dissociation of knowing how and knowing that. *Science*, 210, 207–10.

Parkin, A. J. (1987). *Memory and amnesia: An introduction*. Oxford: Basil Blackwell.

——. (1990). Recent advances in the neuropsychology of memory. In J. Weinmann & J. Hunter (Eds), *Memory: Abnormal and clinical perspectives*. London: Harwood.

Wood, F. B., Brown, I. S., & Felton, R. H. (1989). Long-term follow-up of a childhood amnesic syndrome. *Brain & Cognition*, 10, 76–86.

A. J. PARKIN

development, cognitive *See* COGNITIVE DEVELOPMENT.

development, memory *See* MEMORY DEVELOPMENT.

development, perceptual *See* PERCEPTUAL DEVELOPMENT.

development, reading *See* READING DEVELOPMENT.

developmental dyslexia *See* DYSLEXIA: DEVELOPMENTAL.

developmental psychology *See* COGNITIVE DEVELOPMENT; DYSLEXIA: DEVELOPMENTAL; MEMORY DEVELOPMENT; PERCEPTUAL DEVELOPMENT; PIAGET, JEAN; READING DEVELOPMENT.

direct perception The theory of direct visual perception was developed by J. J. Gibson over a period of more than 35 years (Gibson, 1950, 1966, 1979); according to this theory, all of the information needed to perceive the environment is available in the optic array in the form of invariants. In its mature form, the main outlines of the theory were as follows.

The flux of light, termed the "ambient optic array," reaching the visual sense organs of a perceiving animal is richly structured by the nature of the environment and by the movements of the animal. As objects move and as the animal moves, so some aspects of the array change, while others remain constant. Hence, the optic array is made up of "variants" and "invariants." The latter are held to be components which are sufficient in themselves to specify one or other aspects of the environment, such as the spatial layout of surfaces. By "sufficient" is meant that the structure of the environment can be recovered *directly* (hence the name of the theory) from invariants without recourse to memory and inferential processes.

The latter have been postulated as essential by *indirect* theories of perception, such as those developed within the empiricist tradition of perceptual theorizing (*see* VISUAL ILLUSIONS). The starting point of indirect theories is the claim that sensory data are so impoverished as to be in themselves an unreliable and ambiguous basis for perception, and therefore useful only when interpreted in the light of various forms of knowledge about the world. This contrasts sharply with the assumptions of Gibson's direct theory which holds that it is the task of the science of "ecological optics" to discover the mappings from the environment to invariants in the optic array. In doing so, respect should be paid to the *mutuality* between an animal and its environment: the animal is finely tuned to its ecological niche, and that niche can be said to "specify" the kind of animal which can inhabit it successfully. This approach leads to an analysis of what the environment "affords" the animal. These are entities such as a ground plane suitable for supporting locomotion, food, water, shelter, fire, tools, and so on. Such things are termed "affordances." The theory makes the bold claim that even though affordances are to do with the meanings and values of things for the animal, and as such include higher order concepts such as throwable, graspable, knottable, nutritious, and so on, they are directly perceivable from invariants in the optic array.

Whereas orthodox indirect theories hold that such complex perceptions are built up

> by first discriminating the qualities of objects and then learning the combinations of qualities that specify them, [for the theory of direct perception] it is the other way round. The affordance of an object is what the infant begins by noticing. The meaning is noticed before the substance and surface, the colour and form, are seen as such. An affordance is an invariant combination of variables, [or sometimes] an invariant combination of invariants.
>
> (Gibson, 1979, pp. 134 and 140)

Once an invariant has been discovered in the optic array, it is the task of the psychologist to find out, using psychophysical experiments and/or field observations, whether it is indeed used by the animal of interest. In such tests, emphasis should be given to the importance of perception for guiding the animal's actions within its environment, such as its locomotion, prey capture, predator avoidance, mailing letters, and so on. If an animal is found to use an invariant, then it does so via mechanisms which "pick up" the invariant in the ambient optic array by "resonating" to it directly. For Gibson, perception is thus emphatically not a matter of "unconscious inference" relying on knowledge of the world to interpret inadequate input data, as Helmholtz and others working in the empiricist and constructivist traditions of perceptual theorizing have always maintained. The use of the term "direct" emphasizes this distinctive claim of the theory.

Apart from Gibson's own writings, an enthusiastic exposition of the theory can be found in Michaels and Carello (1981). Sympathetic but critical textbook reviews are given by Bruce and Green (1985) and Gordon (1989). A valuable research monograph arising from the Gibsonian tradition but whose critical stance clarifies many issues is that of Cutting (1986). An influential critique that is mandatory reading for anyone deeply interested in the theory is provided by Ullman (1980), a paper which is itself the target of numerous commentaries in the issue of the journal in which it appeared (those mentioned here are cited under the Ullman reference).

Some comments on the theory are as follows.

(a) The above outline of the theory is deceptively simple. Detailed analyses show that it is by no means a straightforward matter to explicate exactly what is to be understood by "direct" perception. Ullman (1980) noted eleven different interpretations of this label, as fine an example as could be wished of Bartlettian "effort after meaning" in the psychological literature. This confusion can be generously interpreted:

> Gibson was a pioneer, and like all pioneers he oversimplified and disregarded pieces of evidence to accentuate his principal proposition: that visual perception is primarily a function of the structure of the ambient array and not of (acquired) knowledge.
>
> (Prazdny: see Ullman, 1980, p. 395)

The alternative view is that if Gibson had been clearer in his thinking about direct perception then a great deal of time and paper would have been saved. The struggle that many have felt in trying to do justice to Gibson is well brought out by Hinton's remarks:

... how could someone who says so many sensible things about perception maintain that perception is direct and does not involve computation? Either Gibson is being very silly or there is a deep misunderstanding about what it means for perception to be direct.

(Ullman, 1980, p. 387)

Hinton then went on to offer his own suggestion on how the confusion might be clarified. Even Koenderink (1986, p. 161; see also Ullman, 1980, p. 390), an ardent but not uncritical admirer of Gibson (see below), believes that the case for or against the "curious notion" of direct visual perception "gets more argument than it deserves."

Ullman's own stance in the debate is to regard ecological optics as a separate matter from direct visual perception (a conclusion shared by Koenderink, Marr, and many others), because even if the optic array is rich in information, inferential processes may conceivably be involved within a visual perception process utilizing that information. Ullman goes on to argue that for a stimulus–percept relation within a visual perception process to be called direct, it should not be possible to decompose that relation into more elementary constituents. He believes this criterion most clearly discriminates the direct formulation from all others; quite simply, if more elementary constituents are involved then the theory must be in some sense "indirect":

If it is acknowledged that the main concern of a theory of perception is to explain the perceptual 'information pickup' in terms of constructs internal to the perceiver (such as internal processes, computations, representations, and the like), then the direct visual perception formulation no longer holds.

(Ullman, 1980, p. 411)

Ullman believes that a further weakness in Gibson's theorizing is neglect of analysis at what Marr called the algorithm level (see PERCEPTION, COMPUTATIONAL THEORY OF). Marr concluded that it is much harder to understand how invariants can be utilized than

Gibson seemed to imagine. Marr sought to do so by specifying processes operating to create sequences of representations culminating in useful descriptions of the environment. On the other hand, while agreeing with Ullman that the study of internal representations (anathema to Gibsonians) and their functional properties is a crucial step toward understanding perceptual events, Grossberg (see Ullman, 1980, p. 385) nevertheless regards Gibson's use of the concept of resonance akin to his own use of this notion in designing neural networks. On the other hand, resonance is not a concept central to all neural net models and, despite the current explosion of renewed interest in the field, it would be premature in the current state of knowledge to conclude that neural net models will inevitably come down on Gibson's side. For example, considerable interest is presently being shown in multiple level nets, with each level representing a different form of information in a processing hierarchy. Here we have networks of networks, whose component nets implement multiple intervening representations in a clearly *in*direct manner. The somewhat similar hierarchies of neural systems found in the primate visual system, from retina through striate cortex to temporal cortex, also seem most readily consistent with indirect perceptual mechanisms. The controversy continues.

(b) Invariants have not proved easy to find. One discussed by Gibson (1950) and elaborated by Sedgewick (see Cutting, 1986) is the "horizon ratio": because the line from the eye to the horizon is effectively parallel to the ground plane, a point on an object that intersects the line of sight to the horizon is one eye height above that plane. Other invariants are the "cross ratios" (Gibson, 1950; Cutting, 1986): they specify that ratios of the separations of four collinear points are preserved when projected on to any straight line through a point not collinear with those four points. Perhaps the best known candidates for invariants arising from Gibson's work, in that they are mentioned in almost all introductory textbooks on visual perception, are "texture density gradients." These are higher order structures in the optic array which depend on the fact that the visual angle subtended by a physical object is inversely proportional to its distance from the observer. This means that the more distant elements of a (stochastically) uniformly textured surface project smaller visual angles than do nearer elements on that surface. However, texture gradients cannot strictly be called invariants in that they change with the observer's own movements (Cutting, 1986).

Analyses of the information in texture density gradients show that it is useful to distinguish two components: a gradient due to compression (foreshortening) and a gradient due to perspective (distance). Cutting and Millard (see Cutting, 1986) demonstrated that the compression gradient is based upon the assumption that textures lie flat and it accounted for almost all the variance in their studies of the perception of curved surfaces by the human visual system. The perspective gradient, on the other hand, relies upon an assumption about the uniform absolute sizes of objects and it accounted for most of the variance in their studies of the perception of flat surfaces. Stevens (1984) has challenged the legitimacy of inferring from psychophysical results such as these that the human visual system contains processes directly sensitive to texture gradients, offering an alternative interpretation (see also Cutting & Millard's reply which follows Stevens's paper). This debate highlights the general difficulty, not specific to Gibsonian ways of thinking, of inferring mechanisms from psychophysical experiments. Computational studies have an easier time, being synthetic and therefore completely in control, in principle, of the processes being studied. Such studies have explored the effectiveness of each of the two components of texture density gradients discussed above (e.g. Blake & Marinos, 1990), an example of productive work on the nature of the information available in the optic array, perhaps stimulated in part by Gibson's ecological optics but cast within a computational framework that has no use for his notion of direct information pickup. Indeed, whether it would be possible in principle to design "direct pickup" mechanisms for extracting the information in texture gradients identified by these studies is far from obvious.

In the search for invariants it is important to remember that invariants are sources of information that correspond to object properties, they are not the object properties themselves (see, for example, Cutting, 1986, p. 70). There is an ever-present danger here, to which Cutting believes Gibson sometimes succumbed in his discussion of affordances, of falling into tautological statements and the delusion that one has said something useful: to claim that we perceive a flat surface because it is flat, or "catness" because the object is a cat, is to add nothing to our understanding of how we perceive these object properties. Also, it needs to be borne in mind that several different invariants may be available to specify the same object property, a consideration which has led Cutting to prefer the notion of direc*ted* perception.

(c) Gibson is widely respected for the emphasis he gave to the richness of the information reaching the observer in the ambient optic array. While many antecedent sources (including Helmholtz: see Cutting, 1986) can be found claiming that both object motion and observer movement convey a great deal about scene structure, Gibson was the first to give pre-eminence to this source of information. In examining the nature of optic flow and what it might convey about the environment and about the movements of the animal, he came to reject the value of laboratory studies of simple static stimuli on the grounds that the latter were quite uncharacteristic of the normal situation confronting the perceiving animal. Inevitably, therefore, Gibson argued, they give a wholly false impression of the richness of the information actually available for perception. He used the same ground for rejecting the constructivist's use of illusions as a valuable source of information about mechanisms of visual perceptions (*see* VISUAL ILLUSIONS). It also led him to reject the retinal image (for him an impoverished static snapshot quite uncharacteristic of the true input for vision) as a useful starting point for theories of perception in favor of the ambient optic array, a dynamically changing and richly structured source of information.

Koenderink (1986, p. 161), whose mathematical expertise in the analysis of optic flow provides him with a particularly good vantage point, regards Gibson's work on optic flow as showing

> the intuitive sense of a real genius for what is important about a problem. Although he made quite a few slips it seems fair to say that he pointed out about everything that seems worthwhile to study in the subject and that modern developments generally follow in his footsteps.

Those developments, which depend upon a mathematical training which Gibson lacked, show how the optic flow vector field can be decomposed into the "differential invariants" of "divergence," "curl (rotation)" and "deformation." Each of these quantities can signal a useful aspect of the environment or of the observer's motion with respect to it. For example, if the divergence component is positive (expanding flow field) then this signals movement of the observer towards a surface or vice versa. Lee has shown how "time to collision" can be computed from this component: his analyses of the wing-folding of diving gannets just prior to their entry into the sea in terms of their possible use of the divergence invariant is a classic within the Gibsonian tradition (see Bruce & Green, 1985). Koenderink and his colleagues (particularly van Doorn and Rogers) have pursued the idea that deformation invariants of the optic flow and disparity vector fields, perhaps extracted using orientationally-tuned mechanisms (Koenderink, 1986), are used by the human visual system to recover surface slant, with promising but not unambiguous results. More recently, Rogers and Cagnello (1989) have explored the same kind of analysis of the binocular disparity vector field for the recovery of surface slant and curvature, and report evidence consistent with the notion that the deformation component is extracted using orientationally tuned mechanisms, as suggested by Koenderink (1986) for the case of optic flow.

Gibson's promotion of ecological optics is generally acknowledged to have provided a valuable corrective to constructivist approaches that have too readily assumed that sensory information is extremely impov-erished. On the other hand, discovering invariants in the optic array has not proved an easy matter, particularly for complex object properties such as "nutritious," "hard," and so on. Just as problematic is the business of demonstrating whether any given invariant is in fact used by a given animal. Also, it seems fair to say that those subscribing to the theory of direct perception, in the sense of "direct pickup" of information by "resonating" perceptual mechanisms, are few in number. Computational approaches have brought to the fore both the difficulties of extracting invariants, possible methods for so doing, and the usefulness of treating the task involved as an information-processing one incorporating many intermediate stages before the goal is attained of constructing useful representations making explicit scene and object properties. Viewed in this way, that is, taking up Gibson's insights in ecological optics but leaving aside his "curious notion" of direct perception, it is possible to agree with the views of Johansson, von Hofsten, and Jannson (see Ullman, 1980, p. 388):

> In general, we have found a strong tendency toward convergence in the theories of perception today. The differences between theories are now more a question of aspects of focus, and less a matter of contradictory statements as to the points at issue.

See also DATA-DRIVEN AND CONCEPTUALLY DRIVEN PROCESSES; PERCEPTUAL DEVELOPMENT.

BIBLIOGRAPHY

Blake, A., & Marinos, C. (1990). Shape from texture: estimation, isotropy and moments. *Journal of Artificial Intelligence* (in press).

Bruce, V., & Green, P. M. (1985). *Visual perception physiology, psychology and ecology*. London: Lawrence Erlbaum Associates.

Cutting, J. E. (1986). *Perception with an eye for motion*. Cambridge, Mass.: MIT Press.

Gibson, J. J. (1950). *The perception of the visual world*. Boston: Houghton Mifflin.

——. (1966) *The senses considered as perceptual systems*. Boston: Houghton Mifflin.

——. (1979). *The ecological approach to visual perception*. Boston: Houghton Mifflin. (Republished in 1986: Hillsdale, NJ: Lawrence Erlbaum Associates.)

Gordon, I. E. (1989). *Theories of visual perception.* Chichester: John Wiley.

Koenderink, J. J. (1986). Optic flow. *Vision Research*, 26(1), 161–80.

Michaels, C. F., & Carello, C. (1981). *Direct perception.* Englewood Cliffs, NJ: Prentice-Hall.

Stevens, K. A. (1984). On gradients and texture "gradients." *Journal of Experimental Psychology*, 113(2), 217–20.

Ullman, S. (1980). Against direct perception. *The Behavioral and Brain Sciences, 3*, 373–415.
JOHN P. FRISBY

discrimination reaction time A fundamental capacity of any organism is the ability to detect differences between aspects of the environment with respect to some objectively measurable dimension, such as brightness, length, or weight. Human discriminative performance has usually been studied by instructing an observer to compare a stimulus of variable magnitude v along some particular dimension with a second stimulus of constant or standard magnitude s, and to indicate, by pressing one of two keys, whether the variable appears to be greater or less than the standard with respect to the dimension in question. For example, observers may be asked to compare pairs of vertical lines, presented simultaneously on a computer display, and to press one of two keys, according to whether the line on the right (in this case the variable) appears longer or shorter than the standard line on the left. The time elapsing between the presentation of the stimulus and the pressing of the key is the discrimination reaction time.

Whatever the precise form of the experiment, research on human discriminative performance has focused on three dependent variables: the relative frequency with which the observer makes each alternative response, the time the response takes, and the degree of confidence associated with it. Attention has also been concentrated on the effects of manipulating three independent variables. The first – ostensibly objective – variable is that of discriminability, usually measured by the effective physical difference $(v-s)$ between

the value of the variable v and that of some actual or inferred standard s. The second – more subjective – variable is that of response bias (or the comparative readiness of the observer to make each alternative response), and the third is the observer's degree of caution (or the overall carefulness with which judgements are made). Most theories of the discriminative process can be construed as attempts to account for the correlated changes in response frequency, time, and confidence which accompany variation in one or more of these independent variables. Before looking briefly at these theories, it is useful to summarize some of the main empirical findings (for more complete treatments, see Vickers, 1979, 1980).

EFFECTS OF VARIATIONS IN DISCRIMINABILITY

In general, as the objective stimulus difference $(v-s)$ is steadily reduced, so the proportion of errors made by an observer undergoes a smooth increase, the mean time taken to respond also increases, and the average confidence rating associated which the judgement decreases. The continuous nature of these changes has been interpreted as evidence for the operation of internal "noise" or random neural disturbance, which has a progressively greater effect on the representation of stimuli as the objective difference between them is made smaller.

Even if the stimulus difference is varied unpredictably from one presentation to the next, both response time and the proportion of errors remain inversely related to the size of the difference, while confidence ratings retain a direct relationship. It has been argued that this is inconsistent with the notion that the observer bases each judgement on a sample of the sensory representation which is fixed in size. It suggests instead that the observer continues to sample from the sensory representation until a certain critical level of evidence in favor of one or the other alternative has been reached.

EFFECTS OF VARIATIONS IN CAUTION

At the same time, experiments in which the relative emphasis on speed or accuracy has been varied have shown that observers are capable of controlling the overall caution within which responses are made (irrespective of which alternative is chosen). That is, there is a tradeoff between speed and accuracy, in which observers may choose to make more accurate and more confident responses, but at the expense of taking more time.

EFFECTS OF VARIATIONS IN BIAS

A second subjective variable which has been investigated is that of response bias, where the observer appears to exhibit some preference for making one response rather than another in a way which does not depend on the stimulus information available on a particular presentation. Vickers (1985) has presented data which suggest that a simple unitary concept of response bias is inadequate to account for the changes in response frequency, time, and confidence observed when observers: (a) are told to exercise unequal caution with the two responses; (b) are informed clearly that the two responses alternatives are not equally likely; or (c) are presented without warning with a series of stimuli for which one response is objectively appropriate on a greater number of occasions than the other. Instead, Vickers argues, it may be necessary to distinguish between: (1) the relative caution or carefulness with which the two responses are made; (2) differences in the observer's estimate of the likelihood of the two responses; and (c) shifts in a subjective referent or standard, with respect to which evidence is classified by the decision mechanism as favoring one response rather than the other.

THEORIES OF DISCRIMINATION

Theories of the discrimination process usually assume that information is sampled at a steady rate from the sensory representation of the two stimuli. This stream of information is classified with respect to an internal referent, or standard, and the evidence so classified is accrued until a critical level or response threshold is reached in favor of one response. When the stimulus difference is very small, and the stream of evidence is about equally balanced, the chances of an error are high, it

takes longer to reach the response threshold, and confidence is low. By increasing the thresholds for both responses, judgements may be made with greater accuracy and confidence, although it takes longer for the evidence to reach the higher response threshold. The observer may also choose to adopt unequal thresholds for the two responses, making one response more carefully and slowly than the other. When the observer expects one response to be more likely than the other, he or she may bias the process of accumulating evidence by starting it at a point closer to the threshold for the response deemed more likely. Finally, when the observer has no access to information or instructions explicitly favoring one response, but when the series of stimulus presentations is objectively biased, it may be assumed that this produces compensatory shifts in the position of the internal referent, or standard, with reference to which the sampled information is classified.

Differences of opinion exist among theorists concerning whether the stream of information is sampled continuously or discretely, concerning the precise nature of the response threshold, and concerning whether or not evidence is accumulated quite independently for the alternative responses, or whether there there is some interaction between them. Critical evaluations of the main theoretical formulations may be found in Townsend and Ashby (1983), Vickers and Smith (1985), Luce (1986), and Smith and Vickers (1988, 1989).

BIBLIOGRAPHY

Luce, R. D. (1986). *Response times*. New York: Oxford University Press.

Smith, P. L., & Vickers, D. (1988). The accumulator model of two-choice discrimination. *Journal of Mathematical Psychology, 32*, 135–68.

——. (1989). Modeling evidence accumulation with partial loss in expanded judgment. *Journal of Experimental Psychology: Human Perception and Performance, 15*, 797–815.

Townsend, J. T., & Ashby, F. G. (1983). *The stochastic modeling of elementary psychological processes*. Cambridge: Cambridge University Press.

Vickers, D. (1979). *Decision processes in visual perception*. London: Academic Press.

——. (1980). Discrimination. In A. T. Welford (Ed.), *Reaction times* (pp. 25–72). London: Academic Press.

——. (1985). Antagonistic influences on performance change in detection and discrimination tasks. In G. d'Ydewalle (Ed.), *Cognition, information processing, and motivation: Proceedings of the XXIII International Congress of Psychology* (Vol. 3) (pp. 79–115). Amsterdam: North-Holland.

——, & Smith, P. L. (1985). Accumulator and random walk models of psychophysical discrimination: A counter-evaluation. *Perception, 14*, 471–97.

DOUGLAS VICKERS

distributed cognition This is a term used by Hutchins (1987) in arguing that for many purposes cognition is shared among several agents, and that without this some goals could not be achieved. Civilization, society, technology ... these are not the achievements of individuals but of cooperation among and elaboration by groups of people. Even the simplest household article, and all but the wildest landscapes, testify to division of labor, the distribution of agency. One person provides raw materials for another's manufacture or elaboration. Even in conflict we cooperate, as small groups, large corporations, or nations.

Until recently, in cognitive psychology there has tended to be a concentration on the structures and uses of knowledge in the individual mind. This can be contrasted with distributed cognition, in which the cognitive process is shared among a number of people. In a court of law, for instance two people take the roles of prosecution and defense. A third person or set of people make the judgments. We conceive justice as a goal that cannot always be achieved, but which is more easily approached by such distributed cognition than by the individualized cognition of the witch hunt. Science, too, is a matter of distributed cognition, not just of clever individuals. Each of us is able to stand on the shoulders of those who have gone before, and while one person puts forward a hypothesis, someone else sees what is wrong with it, yet others find syntheses and provide wider contexts.

We may thus describe distributed cognition as several agents sharing cognitive resources of symbolic knowledge, plans, and goals, to accomplish something that one agent could not achieve alone. We may distinguish this from parallel distributed processing, in which subcognitive processes are distributed within a single agent (*see* CONNECTIONIST MODELS OF MEMORY).

FOUR PIECES OF RESEARCH ON THE PSYCHOLOGY OF DISTRIBUTED COGNITION

Hutchins (1987) has shown how a large US Navy ship is navigated in confined waters by a group of seven people, cooperating closely to perform the whole task. One person plots and updates the ship's position on a chart. Two people take compass bearings on landmarks designated by him in order to determine the position of the ship from the intersection of bearings. One person is time keeper and communicates by a phone circuit with the bearing takers. One person keeps the deck log, writing down changes of the ships heading, speed, and other events of consequence. One person reads and reports the depth of the water. One steers on the direction of the conning officer. The system is the enactment by these seven people of a single plan, to achieve top-level goals that are given by the conning officer.

The mental model for the plan and computations over it are externalized in the chart and operations with a special navigational ruler that allows courses and bearings to be drawn on to it (*see* MENTAL MODELS). Agents perform parts of the plan, updating pieces of knowledge, and as in an object oriented programing language, passing messages between them. For cognitive scientists these messages are of interest because they are easily accessible, and arguably are comparable to messages passing among modules of an individual cognitive system. Hutchins has also shown how the system works to induct new members of the team, rotating them through the various roles. Because of this each member has an understanding of the nature of the communications arising from each role. This allows ambiguities in messages to be recognized and errors to be corrected.

A second line of work is on conceptual understanding reached through interaction, as in an investigation by Miyake (1986) of how two heads might be better than one. Miyake studied pairs of people interacting to try and understand how a sewing machine works. One member of each pair claimed to understand the mechanism to some extent. As a result of the interaction this knowledge was challenged, and fuller understanding had to be approached iteratively by examining the machine, and conversing about it. She describes four levels of understanding, each progressively deeper, each emerging in the interaction as the resolution of a paradox or contradiction. For instance, if the needle carrying the upper thread just goes in and out, and the lower thread is wound round a bobbin, how does this lower thread get hooked round the upper one beneath the cloth without either thread having, apparently, a free end? Other research, including some on children's conceptual understandings, indicates that interactions in which two people each have partial but different knowledge typically result in both improving their understandings as they discuss the problem.

Hutchins's and Miyake's studies are respectively of distributed agency in planned action and in conceptual understanding. A third line of research is on how one or more people act in relation to a quasi-intelligent machine. Suchman (1987) has studied two people cooperating to work a photocopier which has an expert help system. She argues that the kind of analysis that COGNITIVE SCIENCE would tend to give is of knowledge and a set of procedural rules for its use. The assumption is that human operators will become skilled at knowing how to act as auxiliary agents to do what the machine cannot do in each of its procedures, load documents, press a button for some option, refill the paper tray, and so on. As she found however, actual users understand their roles differently. They conceive their task as that of accomplishing their goal of copying this or that document by picking up information they need about the state of the machine, and of solving problems as they arise. Suchman points out that there is a difference between the conception of an engineering designer of users as passive agents subordinated to a technical plan or procedure, and the users' conception of themselves as active agents discovering how to accomplish what they want to do as they go along. This difference is emphasized in cognitive theory: according to such theory planned action means that a plan tree is constructed, stored, and then executed. The role of users would then be to learn the designer's plan, and execute their part of it. Suchman puts forward an alternative account, which she describes as "situated action." People know, though often not exactly, what they want to achieve, and typically any plan they have is not an exact recipe but a resource for productive interaction with the local environment. Nor do they have an exact mental model by which a plan could be constructed in order to be stored. Instead, they interpret each event as it occurs in the context of the situation from which it arises, in order to decide the next step in approaching an objective. Often these events are ambiguous to them, and therefore call for creative problem solving in the course of action. This general approach applies both to actions with physical objects and interactions with other people.

A fourth avenue of exploration is more specifically applied, a social equivalent of the study of HUMAN–COMPUTER INTERACTION. The question is how information technology might assist people in working on a shared project, or on shared materials. The term that has arisen here is "computer supported cooperative work" (see Grief, 1988). A well known project in this area is Co-Lab, described in Greif's book, in which two to six people in a special room each have a workstation linked by an ethernet that supports a distributed database. Each participant can see a large display where, for instance, text appears. The question for designers is what kind of software support should be provided, so that all the participants can work on it cooperatively to add, transpose, and delete material.

SOCIAL PSYCHOLOGY AND THE CONCEPT OF ROLE

Whereas the cognitive theory of goals and plans has until recently concentrated on a single actor, we may now ask how people cooperate to achieve joint goals, and we may call this joint planning. The concerns of distributed cognition clearly overlap with those of social psychology, but the focus of cognitive theory has been largely on planning, action, and mutual understanding. It is thus somewhat different from concerns of traditional social psychology with attitudes, attributions, and motivations. One key concept, however, is a common one – that of role. Its development in social psychology and sociology gives invaluable pointers to cognitive psychologists.

"Role" is a term that has slipped so easily from the social sciences into common speech that it now seems barely technical. It implies that social actors as individuals are to some extent interchangeable. What allows this interchangeability is that roles in employment, negotiation, and even close relationships are patterns with outline scripts that are partly independent of the player. A script can be elaborated. It is a schema or frame in which rules indicate how one part of an interaction should be conducted in relation to the other. Roles can be slipped into by anyone with certain attributes who can follow the rules, and give plausible performances of the parts afforded.

Two metaphors inform the idea of role: the theatrical performance, from which the idea of role is directly taken, and the game, which provides scripts for players who use its rules to give structure to their interactions.

The theatre, from ancient times and in many societies, has been a place where consequences of human action could be modeled and explored. In classical Greek tragedy, the protagonist stands for everyone, implying universality of the predicaments enacted. The actors are masked, which implies both attributes that are not directly visible, and presentation of a particular face to the world. The protagonist's actions are commented upon by society, represented by the chorus. He or she suffers powerful emotions in a world which it is impossible to understand fully in advance, but in which she or he must nevertheless act and take responsibility for actions. Here then is modeled one of the fundamental problems for a psychology of distributed cognition: how we can act and interact with very incomplete, and often inaccurate, mental models of the domains of our actions.

Games are models of certain recurring types of interaction in society, and demand abilities of motor skill or problem solving that are too difficult or risky for real life. In a game it is possible to form mental models by which the world of the game may be almost completely understood, by strictly limiting the domain and the rules that apply. Chess is thus a digitized, limited, and safe version of medieval battles with nobles as the cavalry able to dash about in an exciting way, and proletarian foot soldiers able only to plod slowly and liable to be killed easily. The player can perform feats of reasoning in a limited universe, which would be quite impossible in the ordinary world. *Monopoly* is an allegorical re-enactment of commercial competition and the accumulation of wealth, preferably by putting other people out of business, which would be crass in real commerce, and where the only unknowns are the random generator of dice, and limited negotiations with other players. Tennis requires skills of motor coordination and prediction of the other's actions that would be hard to acquire if being beaten meant being maimed, as when fighting with swords.

Rules, conceived in this kind of way are of course very close to the kinds of rules that form the basis of cognitive modeling. This is seen clearly when we start playing a game. We pass through what Goffman (1961) calls a semi-permeable membrane, into the microworld afforded by the rules of the particular game, to take up the role of a player. We become black who moves second at chess, the top hat and whatever chances the dice provide in *Monopoly*, or the server in tennis. Real life is only different, continues Goffman, in that the rules are usually not so simple or so codified, but semi-permeable membranes are there just the same. They provide a setting for what Goffman calls focused interactions, face-to-face encounters subject to certain customs and in which there is an agreed subject of attention. When we enter a shop we become a customer. The focused issue is whether or not to buy something, and we are subject to the conventions of this situation. When we get married we pass through another membrane into a new state with different customs and conventions than the single state.

Another aspect is the actor's personal engagement in roles. As an actor, one can become caught up in a role, experiencing what occurs in it as happening to oneself, and indeed shaping one's selfhood. To be a player merely implies generating legal moves conforming to the rules of the game. It allows us to go through certain motions. To be a participant means to engage oneself in the role afforded. Only as a participant could one have fun in a game. Only then could one be excited by a plan for attacking on the queen's side, delighted to be able to start putting up hotels on one's property, or anxious to avoid serving yet another double fault.

The rules of the game allow a world of meaning to be built. In Goffman's words:

A matrix of possible events and a cast of roles through whose enactment the events occur constitute together a field for fateful dramatic action, a plane of being, an engine of meaning, a world in itself.

(Goffman, 1961, p. 26)

PURPOSEFUL CONVERSATION AS MUTUAL PLANNING

Conversation offers perhaps the most informative example of mutual planning, typically with two roles which may be similar. Each person acts with certain common goals which may be renegotiated as the conversation proceeds. Rules of the kind described by Grice (1975) tend to be followed: people must say about the right amount for the purpose in hand, be truthful, be relevant, and be clear. These maxims obtain within the membrane of the conversation. There is continuous ad hoc improvisation in conversation, an example of situated interaction as described by Suchman. Grice's maxims are the outline rules for the conduct of this improvised interaction.

Improvisation is unlike a technical plan, in which there is a clear goal and perhaps diagrams or instruction manuals. We do not know exactly what will occur in a conversation, and we do not even plan each utterance exactly before speaking. We may not know what we think until we hear what we have said.

As often occurs in cognitive science, one of the most informative ways of gaining theoretical leverage on a phenomenon is computational modeling. One of the few computational explorations of the interaction of two cognitive systems is that of Power (1979). Power simulated two robots, John and Mary, on either side of a door with a bolt. This world is very simple, consisting of only four objects, each of which can be in one of two positions: the robots themselves can be in or out, the door may be open or shut, and the bolt may be up or down. The robots can each have a goal, a specific state of the world. If their goals agree they can cooperate to achieve that state. A robot can attempt just three actions: "Push" is an attempt to change the position of the door; "move" is an attempt of a robot to change position; and "slide" is an attempt to change the position of the bolt. There are laws of nature: for instance, if a robot moves, it changes position if the door is open. When it slides, the bolt changes position, if the robot is in.

The point of the program is to explore what is needed cognitively for two agents to cooperate to achieve something that neither can achieve alone. Recognizable conversation arises naturally out of such cooperations. Although they build a planning tree which looks familiar to cognitive scientists, this work augments previous computational work on planning in that the action includes responses to events which for one or other robot are unexpected.

A run of the program may start from a particular state of the world, with each robot either knowing or being ignorant of certain laws of nature, and with beliefs that may be true or false. A robot will change a belief if a more complex belief is offered by the other, or if it acts and something unexpected happens. The program is started by setting up initial conditions, beliefs, and so on, and giving one or both robots a goal.

Here is a brief excerpt from a sample run of Power's program, after about a dozen exchanges. John is out and has been given the goal of being in. He believes that if he moves nothing happens. The bolt on the inside is down, securing the door. Mary is in and is able to operate it, but whereas John can directly perceive the state of the world, Mary is blind. Also, she does not have a goal to start with, so she accepts the one suggested by John, having nothing else to do. The conversation continues, formulating and checking subgoals and plans, and passing knowledge back and forth.

Mary: I suggest that we get the door open and then you move.

[John does not respond to this suggestion, but seemingly interrupts.]

John: Mary.
Mary: Yes.
John: I want to explain something.
Mary: Go ahead.
John: If you move, nothing happens.
Mary: I disagree.
If you move when the door is open, you change position.
John: I see.
Mary: I suggest that we get the door open and then you move.

Mary has accepted John's goal, and they have discussed some pieces of plan and belief related to it. The first utterance of Mary in this excerpt is a proposal about a plan. She begins an exchange, but John does not complete it. Instead, he interrupts and takes the initiative. He has checked Mary's plan against his model of the world, and found that it would not advance toward the agreed goal. He calls her attention, and she completes the exchange with an acknowledgement. John next asks if he may tell her something about a piece of knowledge he has. She agrees. His next move is to give her this piece of world knowledge, that if he moves, nothing happens. Mary then makes two utterances in succession, the first being a disagreement with John's explanation of the law of nature, completing the exchange he started with his explanation. Then she takes the initiative, sug-

gesting a revision. The rule here is that the robots will substitute more complex laws of nature for simpler ones, and John therefore changes his belief. Mary next re-suggests the plan she offered previously, which had been forgotten at John's interruption.

It has been implicit in cognitive science that private thinking is the primary activity to be understood, and that speaking is a secondary activity that one does when wanting to affect the other's cognitive system. The alternative is that the social is more primary, and that private cogitation is an internalization of public discourse. However this may be, it is clear that to analyze conversation we need both kinds of thinking, private and public, and Power's program provides both.

An informal idea of how the program works is as follows. When they are given goals, the robots think privately, trying to formulate plans to achieve the goals. When one of them, say John, reaches a point at which he wants something from the other, perhaps information or help with something he cannot do himself, he contacts Mary, by calling her name. This causes both to stop their private thoughts, and conduct a conversation. When this conversation is over they return to their private thoughts, but now with changes having been made to their minds, so if John had wanted to know something he now either knows it or knows that Mary does not know it.

When a robot is thinking publicly, that is to say conversing, it takes part in what Power calls conversational procedures which are like exchanges in Wittgenstein's (1958) language games. Power has programed seven kinds of conversational procedure, including asking for help in achieving a goal, arranging for one of the other conversational procedures, asking for information, explaining a law of nature. A conversation, then, is made up of procedures for two players in which each takes a different role. Conversation involves getting procedures like these loaded in both minds, and using them to agree goals, and then to construct and enact a plan.

In these exchanges, the robots undertake two kinds of activity. First, they build planning trees; then they enact the plans as they go along whenever they can. Each robot constructs a copy of the shared planning tree. Joint planning trees are similar to the single agent's tree but with two modifications: some goals can be joint, and the actions at terminal nodes can be conducted by either agent, depending in an ad hoc way on the history of negotiations and the local state of the world. So in this example, after Mary has agreed to it, the topmost goal is shared: to get John in. As for terminal nodes, whereas John will do the action move, Mary will slide the bolt. Each robot also develops and updates a model of the physical world, though these can be incomplete. In this example John can keep his model of the world up to date by direct perception, though there are laws of nature that he needs instruction on. Mary, being blind, needs to update her model of the world by asking John questions. In addition each develops a partial model of the other. For instance, before the excerpt given here Mary has learned that John could move. Models are updated either by information from the other, or changes in the state of the world following an action.

Here again, in this ARTIFICIAL INTELLI-GENCE approach, the conclusion from the study of cognition distributed among two agents is that augmentations are needed to current cognitive theory. These augmentations include the idea that, rather than cognitive agents simply having a goal and trying to change the world to match the goal, goals can be shared. Utterances are then not typically acts upon the other's cognitive system to change it, but moves in a game-like sequence to achieve those aspects of the goals that have been jointly agreed. Second, conversation and action can begin when very little of the way ahead can be seen. According to Power, purposeful conversation is itself the process of planning, and proceeds not by reasoning within fully articulated models but by proposal and repair.

In the areas of planning theory, of the growth of understanding, of the nature of our interactions with quasi-intelligent machines, and of naturally occurring conversation, the study of distributed cognition is providing fundamental challenges to cognitive theory, and an important kind of new data. Principles that have been central to cognitive science, such as that of the stored plan and of the well articulated model of the world being necessary for any action, are being revised and extended.

BIBLIOGRAPHY

Goffman, E. (1961). *Encounters: Two studies in the sociology of interaction*. Indianapolis, Ind.: Bobbs-Merrill.

Grief, I. (1988). *Computer supported cooperative work: A book of readings*. San Mateo, Calif.: Morgan Kaufman.

Grice, H. P. (1975). Logic and conversation. In P. Cole & J. L. Morgan (Eds), *Syntax and semantics 3: Speech acts*. New York: Academic Press.

Hutchins, E. (1987). Learning to navigate in context. Paper presented at workshop on context, cognition and activity, Stenugsund, Sweden.

Miyake, N. (1986). Constructive interaction and the iterative process of understanding. *Cognitive Science*, 10, 151–77.

Power, R. (1979). The organisation of purposeful dialogues. *Linguistics*, 17, 107–52.

Suchman, L. A. (1987). *Plans and situated action: The problem of human–machine communication*. Cambridge: Cambridge University Press.

Wittgenstein, L. (1958). *Philosophical investigations*. Oxford: Blackwell.

KEITH OATLEY

dual-code theory of imagery According to the dual-code theory (DCT), cognition consists of the activity of two interconnected but functionally independent subsystems: (1) a nonverbal imagery system which is specialized for dealing with information concerning objects and events; and (2) a verbal system which is specialized for perception and generation of speech and visual linguistic symbols, which can also be experienced as images (e.g. of speech sounds, letters, manual signs of the deaf). Various properties of imagery entail many scientific puzzles that some cognitive psychologists are trying to solve, usually within the framework of a general theory of cognition. Dual coding is such a theory.

THE GENERAL THEORY

DCT consists of a series of assumptions and hypotheses about the origins, structural

DUAL-CODE THEORY OF IMAGERY

properties, and functional characteristics of cognitive representational (symbolic) systems. The theory is empirically based in that the representational systems are assumed to be experientially determined and to retain the modality-specific properties of the sensori-motor experiences from which they are derived. Moreover, the structural and functional properties of the systems are inferred from observational data rather than by analogy with computers, as in some other contemporary approaches to imagery.

SYMBOLIC VERSUS SENSORI-MOTOR SYSTEMS

The DCT assumption is that the verbal–nonverbal symbolic distinction is orthogonal to the sensori-motor systems. The general point is that both symbolic systems are composed of modality-specific sensori-motor representational units and processes that operate on them. The assumption further implies that symbolic and sensory modalities are functionally independent. Neuropsychological and other data consistent with that assumption are reviewed in Paivio (1986, chap. 12) (*see* HEMISPHERIC LOCALIZATION).

REPRESENTATIONAL UNITS OF THE SYSTEMS: IMAGENS AND LOGOGENS

Our ability to generate conscious images of objects means that we must have representations for those objects in long-term memory. The term "imagen" (short for image generator) is a convenient label for those underlying representations. Theoretically, we have a multiplicity of specific imagens for any given class of objects and their parts. Thus, imagens vary hierarchically in size, permitting us to generate, for example, images of an eye, a face, a person, and so on. It is convenient similarly to refer to the representational units of the verbal system as logogens ("word generators," a concept introduced by the British psychologist John Morton), which in DCT correspond to integrated verbal units of any size, including words.

STRUCTURAL INTERCONNECTIONS AND PROCESSING LEVELS

Another set of assumptions pertains to structural interconnections that link representations to each other and to the external world, and processes that operate over those connections to activate imagens and logogens. The theory distinguishes between *representational*, *referential*, and *associative* connections and activating processes. In representational processing, familiar objects and words activate imagens and logogens relatively directly. Referential processes operate over connections between imagens and logogens, enabling us to generate images to the names of referent objects and to name or describe such objects. Associative processes operate within systems, permitting imagens to activate other imagens and logogens to activate other logogens. The multiplicity of interconnections between units implies that activation of particular representations must be probabilistic and optional, with the selection being based on the relative availability of different imagens and logogens, the strength of connecting pathways, and contextual cues that bias processing activity.

The different kinds of interconnections and processing levels are defined and measured by specific operational procedures. For example, referential processing is operationalized by ratings or direct reaction time (RT) measures of how easy it is to image to words or name objects (e.g. see Paivio, Clark, Digdon, & Bons, 1989).

ORGANIZATIONAL AND TRANSFORMATIONAL PROCESSES

Other processing assumptions focus on the organization and transformation of imaginal and verbal information. According to DCT, the information in visual images is organized synchronously, so that different parts of an imaged object or familiar scene are simultaneously available for further processing. However, the amount of information that can be accessed and processed in parallel is limited, much as it is in visual perception, where an entire scene may be available all at once but visual attention is focused at a fixation point and the scene must be scanned to access detailed information in different locations. Mental images seem to require such scanning as well. The principal defining operation for synchronous organization is the demonstration that processing is free from sequential constraints. In contrast, linguistic information is organized sequentially and processing is sequentially constrained, so that it is easier, for example, to spell words, recite the alphabet, or recite a poem forward than backward (Paivio, 1986, chap. 9).

Mental transformations also are constrained by the structural properties of the representations. Thus, visual images can be transformed on any spatial or sensory dimension: imaged objects can be rotated, altered in size or shape, changed in color, and so on (*see* IMAGERY, COMPUTATIONAL THEORY OF; IMAGERY AND PERCEPTION). Verbal transformations, on the other hand, are imposed on a sequential frame, permitting us to change the order of words or insert new words into the sequence.

ADAPTIVE FUNCTIONS OF THE SYMBOLIC SYSTEMS

Another set of assumptions has to do with the adaptive functions of imagery and verbal processes, which entail more or less complex applications of their structural properties and processing capacities. These functions can be classified into three general types, namely evaluative, mnemonic, and motivational. The evaluative functions refer to the use of imagery or language to estimate the absolute or relative, quantitative or qualitative properties (size, weight, color, shape, pleasantness, and so on) of absent objects and situations (see Paivio, 1986, chap. 9). Mnemonic functions refer to the stategic or automatic use of imagery and language as memory aids (see Paivio, 1986, chap. 8). Motivational functions refer to the use of imagery and language to aid in goal-directed behavior, promote positive affect and relaxation, and so on (e.g. see Paivio, 1985).

INDIVIDUAL DIFFERENCES IN IMAGERY AND VERBAL PROCESSES

The DCT approach also deals with individual differences in imagery in terms of the general assumptions of the theory (Paivio, 1986, chap. 6). Thus, the relevant conceptual analyses and data bear on the verbal–nonverbal symbolic distinction, the orthogonal relation between symbolic and sensory systems, the different structural and processing levels, and the various adaptive functions served by the two systems. Here, I touch on a few of the salient points. The results of factor-analytic studies of cognitive abilities are generally consistent with the nonverbal–verbal distinction in that tests of the two classes of abilities load on separate factors. More relevant for present purposes, the separation has also appeared in studies that were specifically designed to measure aspects of imagery and verbal processes. One of these was on responses to an individual difference questionnaire (IDQ) designed to measure imagery habits and skills (Paivio & Harshman, 1983). Another pertinent example is our research (Paivio et al., 1989) on referential processing abilities using RT measures to determine how quickly individuals can generate images to the names of objects and name pictures of those objects. Individual differences in the ability to transform or manipulate images have long been studied using various measures of spatial ability, and these proved to be predictive of performance in other tasks such as mental comparisons of objects from memory (see Paivio, 1986, chap. 9). Individual differences in vividness of experienced imagery have been extensively studied using questionnaires patterned after Galton's original breakfast-table questionnaire (e.g. see Finke, 1980; Denis, 1988).

To summarize the scientific status of the dual-coding approach to imagery, all of the assumptions of DCT are supported by at least some empirical evidence, and some have firm support. The evidence comes from behavioral effects of relevant stimulus attributes (e.g. imagery value of words, pictures versus words), experimental procedures (e.g. instructions to image, modality-specific interference between imagery and perception), and individual differences (e.g. in imagery abilities and habits). It also comes from neuropsychological data (e.g. hemispheric differences in verbal and nonverbal processing, different locations within hemispheres for processing different sensory modalities of imagery and language, and so on.) New evidence from these sources will confirm or challenge the theory and lead to whatever modifications may be necessary to accommodate the facts.

BIBLIOGRAPHY

Denis, D. (1988). Imagery and prose processing. In M. Denis, J. Engelkamp, & J. T. E. Richardson (Eds), *Cognitive and neuropsychological approaches to mental imagery*. Amsterdam: Martinus Nijhoff.

Finke, R. A. (1980). Levels of equivalence in imagery and perception. *Psychological Review*, *87*, 113–32.

Paivio, A. (1985). Cognitive and motivational functions of imagery in human performance. *Canadian Journal of Applied Sport Sciences*, *10*, 22 S–28 S.

——. (1986). *Mental representations: A dual-coding approach*. New York: Oxford University Press.

——, & Harshman, R. A. (1983). Factor analysis of a questionnaire on imagery and verbal habits and skills. *Canadian Journal of Psychology*, *37*, 461–83.

Paivio, A., Clark, J. M., Digdon, N., & Bons, T. (1989) Referential processing: Correlates of naming pictures and imaging to words. *Memory & Cognition*, *17*, 163–74.

A. U. PAIVIO

dual-route model of reading According to the dual-route model of reading, there exist separate lexical and non-lexical routes to reading words out loud, and these routes can operate independently of one another. Words can be read out loud by means of different procedures, that mediate the transcription of print into sound. For instance, we can read aloud words that contain unique correspondences between the printed letters and their sounds (such as "yacht," since no other word in English shares the correspondence between –acht and the sound "ot"). In such cases, the transcription between spelling and sound depends on the specific association between the word (yacht) and its sound (yot). Such word-specific associations are said to comprise a *lexical route* in reading, since they depend on our recognizing the stimulus as a known word within our internal dictionary or lexicon – the store for all the words in our vocabulary. However, other stimuli may be read aloud using spelling-to-sound correspondences smaller than the whole word. For instance, we can read aloud nonwords such as "vip," even though we have never seen such items before and so there cannot be any direct association between the spelling of the whole string and its sound. Nonwords must be read aloud using some other process. One suggestion is that nonwords are read aloud using a *non-lexical* process, perhaps operating by means of "grapheme to phoneme conversion." The term grapheme here refers to the letter(s) that comprise a single phoneme in speech; thus the letters *ph* are a grapheme when they correspond to the phoneme /f/. The sound of the whole nonword could be built up serially by converting each grapheme into its most frequently corresponding phoneme, and then by blending the sounds together (Coltheart, 1985). This second process is termed non-lexical because it does not depend on word-specific associations between spellings and sounds. Such a non-lexical process enables us to pronounce new words, before they become part of our vocabulary (*see* READING DEVELOPMENT).

An early dual-route model of reading was proposed by Coltheart (1978) . In this model, the non-lexical route was characterized as containing only the most frequent correspondences between particular graphemes and phonemes. Thus, the nonword "acht" would be pronounced /ætʃt/ (rhyme with matched) because the most frequent phonemes corresponding to the graphemes *a*, *ch*, and *t* are /æ/, /tʃ/ and /t/. This means that the non-lexical route will provide an incorrect translation of irregular words that have unusual spelling-to-sound correspondences. "Yacht" would be translated into /yætʃt/ (rhyming with "matched"). This assumption captures several results in the word recognition literature, particularly the finding that, in normal English readers, irregular words are named more slowly than regular words (e.g. Coltheart, 1978). According to dual-route theory, this result occurs because regular words (containing the most frequent grapheme–phoneme correspondences) are translated correctly via either route, while irregular words can only be pronounced via the lexical route. Dual-route theory also provides a useful account of how word recognition breaks down following brain damage (*see* DYSLEXIAS: ACQUIRED). For instance, the term "phonological dyslexia" is applied to patients who can read words relatively well but are very poor at reading nonwords (e.g. Funnell, 1983). Such patients seem to be reading lexically, but are severely impaired at reading non-lexically. In contrast, "surface dyslexic" patients are impaired at reading irregular words but can be relatively good at reading regular words and nonwords (e.g. Coltheart, Masterson, Masterson, Byng, Prior, & Riddoch, 1983). In surface dyslexia, reading via the lexical route seems impaired, and non-lexical reading relatively intact.

More recently, several criticisms of dual-route theory have been raised. For instance, non-lexical processes do not seem to operate in an all-or-none fashion. Differences in naming time arise between words that have very irregular spelling–sound correspondences (such as "yacht") and those having irregular but nevertheless quite frequent spelling–sound correspondences (e.g. "love," which should be pronounced "loav" using English spelling-to-sound rules) (Glushko, 1979). This suggests that grapheme–phoneme rules operate probabilistically (so that irregular but relatively frequently correspondences have a non-negligible probability of occurring). Also, the pronunciations assigned to nonwords (read non-lexically) can be biased by the prior reading of irregular words (read lexically). Thus, having just read the irregular word "wolf" we are quite likely to assign the irregular pronunciation to a nonword such as "solf" (as in "sulf"). This suggests that lexical and non-lexical processes can interact. Such results have led to the generation of more complex models of word recognition and naming, where non-lexical processes are viewed as probabilistic, and influenced by ongoing lexical processes (e.g. Patterson & Morton, 1985). Some researchers have even abandoned the dual-route account, and maintain that there are no qualitative differences between the processing of words and nonwords (see Humphreys & Evett, 1985). It remains to be seen how such models explain the dissociations between the reading of words and nonwords found in some dyslexic patients, which are well accounted for by dual-route theory (see Patterson, Seidenberg, & McClelland, 1989).

BIBLIOGRAPHY

Coltheart, M. (1978). Lexical access in simple reading tasks. In G. Underwood (Ed.), *Strategies of information processing*. London: Academic Press.

——. (1985). The cognitive neuropsychology of reading. In M. I. Posner & O. S. M. Marin (Eds), *Attention and performance XI*. London: Erlbaum.

——, Masterson, J., Byng, S., Prior, M., & Riddoch, M. J. (1983). Surface dyslexia. *Quarterly Journal of Experimental Psychology, 34A,* 469–96.

Funnell, E. (1983). Phonological processes in reading: New evidence from acquired dyslexia. *British Journal of Psychology, 74,* 159–80.

Glushko, R. J. (1979). The organisation and activation of orthographic knowledge in reading aloud. *Journal of Experimental Psychology: Human Perception and Performance, 5,* 674–91.

Humphreys, G. W., & Evett, L. J. (1985). Are there independent lexical and nonlexical routes in word processing? An evaluation of the dual route theory of reading. *The Behavioral and Brain Sciences, 8,* 689–740.

Patterson, K. E., & Morton, J. (1985). From orthography to phonology: An attempt at an old interpretation. In K. E. Patterson, J. C. Marshall, & M. Coltheart (Eds), *Surface dyslexia: Neuropsychological and cognitive studies of phonological reading*. London: Erlbaum.

Patterson, K. E., Seidenberg, M. S., & McClelland, J. C. (1989). Connections and disconnections: Acquired dyslexia is a computational model of reading processes. In R. G. M. Morris (Ed.), *Parallel distributed processing: Implications for psychology and neuroscience*. Oxford: Oxford University Press.

G. W. HUMPHREYS

dual-task performance

RATIONALE AND SCOPE

Dual-task is an experimental paradigm in which subjects are asked to perform two concurrent tasks under different performance instructions. For example, a person may be asked to use a hand controller to track the movement of a graphic element on a computer screen, while simultaneously responding to auditory messages presented through head-phones; or he or she may be required to monitor the appearance of target words in two strings of words, each presented through a separate speaker located in a different corner of a room, or instructed to search for target letters in random-letter arrays presented tachistoscopically, while also performing a mental arithmetic task.

Dual-task is one of the more prevalent research paradigms employed in cognitive psychology to study the processing and response limitations of the human organism (*see* ATTENTION). It has been a key tool in the investigation of such topics as attention limitations, workload, the architecture of the human processing system, voluntary control of attention, coordination of activities, and individual differences in basic attention capabilities. (For major reviews and discussion see Kahneman, 1973; Navon and Gopher, 1979; Wickens, 1980; Gopher and Donchin, 1986; O'Donnell and Eggemeier, 1986).

The main appeal of the dual-task paradigm for studying these questions appears to be in the ability to resolve or circumvent, at least in part, some of the difficult methodological and theoretical handicaps that are enforced on the study of cognition, by its dependence on indirect, external observations, in its effort to model the internal structure the "Black Box" of the mind, labeled the "Human Processing System." Put differently, the dual-task paradigm represents an attempt to compensate for the inability to decompose, identify, and provide clear descriptions and measures of the components, processes and demands which comprise a single experimental task; a task with which subjects are presented and required to cope.

In psychological research, "Task" is a generic term employed in a rather loose and fuzzy manner, to characterize an "entity" which encompasses all elements of the stimulus, response, and experimental instructions that are given by the experimenter to the

subject and utilized by him or her, to achieve a specified goal, or pursue an intention. Goals and intentions can thus be conceived as the binders that tie all elements together, delineate task boundaries, and set its territory in a given situation. They are the common reference, distinguishing one task from all others that can be constructed in the same situation and may even include the same ingredients. In a given situation, task elements comprise features of the environment, the performer, and the performance instructions.

Elements of *the environment* include such things as the modality, type, quality, and presentation rate of stimulus, as well as the mode, type, and complexity of the required response and the general conditions within which a task is performed. As regards *subject parameters*, examples of performer-related task elements are: availability and completeness of memory codes, availability of relevant performance repertoire, stimulus–response compatibility, level of practice, or elementary capabilities such as finger dexterity and motor coordination. The set of *performance instructions* details the type and expected level of performance on a task, as well as the relative importance of different aspects of behavior (e.g. speed–accuracy trade-off).

It is clear from this short discussion that the overall nature of each task is a joint product of many external and internal variables and the interaction between them. Thus, a systematic decomposition and evaluation of the contribution of elements and their interaction is a difficult mission, which is further complicated by the fact that some of the variables involved are hypothetical constructs or internal properties of the black box (e.g. memory representations), that are not amenable to direct observation.

Another factor that complicates matters is the existing conceptual distinction between "task structure" and "task demands." While the term structure is used to identify the elements that are incorporated into the task, task demands specify the operations that are performed upon them by the human processing system in the service of the goal. The distinction is between having the knowledge of numbers and arithmetic operations, which is part of the task structure, and the actual execution of multiplication exercises, which represents task demands. The notion is that tasks impose demands on the human processing system which is required to cope with them.

Although conceptually the distinction may be clear, in practice there are serious difficulties in drawing the line between structure and demands when the performance of a task is examined. For example, availability of memory codes is assumed to be a property of the task, while operations upon these codes are part of the demands. But how can the influence of the two be distinguished when a failure of performance is observed? Where does one draw the line?

One escape route from the problem, adopted by earlier schools of thought in psychology, was to exclude internal variables and processes altogether and base the definition of tasks only on observable properties and experimental instructions. This was the solution proposed by Behaviorism and by early proponents of Information Theory applications to psychology (see COGNITIVE PSYCHOLOGY, HISTORY OF). The revival of cognitive psychology in the second half of the century stems to a large extent from the criticism of this approach and advocating the equal contribution to performance of internal, top-down, concept-driven processes and data-driven, bottom-up processes (see DATA-DRIVEN AND CONCEPTUALLY DRIVEN PROCESSES). Hence, given that internal entities and operations are integral composites of an experimental task, alternatives solutions should be sought, to help task decomposition and measurement.

The dual-task paradigm is an attempt to find a way out. Instead of trying to solve the problems of isolating and assessing the components of a single task, one creates another focal point, a second entity, which clearly represents a different task. This manipulation is much easier to perform. It changes the focus of observations and analysis and gives the researcher additional power. In a single-task experiment, a researcher has to rely on a single stimulus configuration and a single set of response measures, at any instance of observation. In the dual-task situation, the investigator has two clear sets that he or she can contrast and pit against each other, to uncover their internal structure and the properties of the underlying driving system. The conduct of experiments is much facilitated because the experimenter is free to select and manipulate one task while maintaining the other intact. Experimental freedom is also increased by the improved ability to manipulate attention and emphasis among two distinct task configurations. The two concurrent tasks serve as reference and anchor points to each other. As practice shows, the work of science in general, and in the behavioral sciences in particular, seems to progress better if it is conducted on a comparative rather than on an absolute basis.

To conclude, when compared with single-task designs, the dual-task paradigm appears to have provided cognitive psychology with a better tool for the study of the composition of single tasks, and the underlying dimensions of the human processing and response system.

VARIETIES OF DUAL-TASK RESEARCH

Although all research employing the dual-task paradigm has been generally concerned with the properties of the central processor and the mapping rules of task characteristics to task demands, researchers have focused on different aspects of the question. These differences led to several versions of dual-task designs. The following paragraphs review major classes of designs and the theoretical questions that prompted them.

Attention control – the ability to focus and divide attention Research concerned with the ability of human subjects to control, focus, and divide their attention at will was the first to employ systematically the dual-task paradigm as an experimental tool. The fundamental issue was the nature of attention capacity. Is it a unitary quantity which is deployed, in an all-or-none fashion, to the performance of tasks, or can it be divided in shares among concurrently performed tasks? There were two major derivatives of this central issue. One was the question of whether attention to tasks operates sequentially or in parallel: namely, does concurrent performance entail parallel processing or rapid switching? If parallel, are there extra costs of coordination? If sequential, what are the durations and costs of switching? A second question was the properties and characteristics of a task that can constitute an "Attention Channel," defined as a string of information that can be focused upon voluntarily, to the exclusion of all other strings present in the situation. Dual-task design configurations developed to study these issues were of two general types, focused attention and divided attention.

In the focused-attention design, subjects are instructed to concentrate on one of several possible information sources in the environment and ignore all others. The experimenter may vary the nature and characteristics of the irrelevant or the focused-upon information, and test the ability of subjects to focus attention and resist interference. For example, in a dichotic listening task, two strings of words may be presented simultaneously, at a fast rate through headphones to the two ears, such that each ear is presented with a different string. Subjects may be instructed to listen and respond only to the messages presented to one ear and ignore the other. Despite the fact that in this design, the subject is asked to respond only to a single string of words, and thus can be argued to perform a single task, it is included in the dual-task paradigm because the irrelevant information is not a by-product or randomly selected. It is carefully engineered to create alternative distracting tasks, which may compete on subject's attention and probe the limits of voluntary attention.

In divided-attention tasks, subjects are required to divide attention among concurrent tasks. Although in principle the theory ventures to cover and be relevant to situations comprising multiple concurrent tasks, practical considerations have limited research to dual-task situations. In a typical design, subjects may be instructed to divide attention between two strings of words presented dichotically (see above), perform a manual tracking task together with a letter classification task, both presented visually on the computer screen, or perform mental arithmetic while reading a book aloud.

Taken together the research results were unable to provide general or conclusive answers to the questions that were raised. It became increasingly clear that the processing system is versatile and task properties are difficult to define and are amenable to tradeoffs. Hence, performance strategies adopted by subjects depend on the type and composition of the tasks involved. This realization has led researchers to try and identify patterns of interaction under dual-task conditions, and typify classes of processing resources that can be competed for.

The nature of processing resources – patterns of interference in dual-task performance Research work in this category has been set to test the idea that at any moment the human system possesses a finite amount of processing facilities, which are also labeled resources. Tasks impose differential demands on these resources according to their characteristics, and compete with each other to the extent that they tap the same resources and their joint demand exceed the available resources amount. The theoretical focus of the work is on the attempt to uncover the nature of processing resources and the principles that map task profiles on to resource demands.

The empirical examination of these questions is based on the interpretation of interference patterns and the lack of interference among concurrently performed tasks. Researchers contrast different combinations of tasks under dual-task conditions, and explore the effects of different difficulty manipulations of one task or both, on their level of performance. The selection of tasks and manipulations reflects the researcher's theory on the nature of the processing system. Typical studies may pair a memory task with a manual-control task, each presented visually or auditorily; or explore combinations that contrast encoding processes or response selection requirements. Others may study a task based on verbal processing paired with another based on spatial analysis, and so on.

A common experiment may include several dual-task pairs and several difficulty manipulations. Lack of interference is as informative as the existence of interference, because it is interpreted to indicate independence of demand profiles. The most interesting studies are those that obtain differential patterns of interference: that is, they are able to demonstrate within the same experiment that some tasks interfere with each other, but are differentially sensitive to pairing with other tasks. For instance, when paired tasks A and B are mutually interfering, tasks B and C are also interfering, but A and C are performed concurrently with no interference. A detailed discussion of the theoretical interpretation of such a pattern of results is beyond the scope of this essay: suffice to say that findings of this type have led researchers to propose distinctions between the demand characteristics of perceptual, mediational, and response execution processes, between verbal and spatial demands, or to isolate the pronounced influence of working-memory involvement.

Measurement of mental workload – the secondary task methodology This category of dual-task research has been developed in the applied environment, when HUMAN FACTORS specialists and design engineers were tasked to evaluate the mental load imposed on human operators when interacting with engineering systems, such as flying an aeroplane or driving a car. The objective was to provide an estimate of task load and the performer's spare capacity that is free to perform additional requirements. Although the theoretical foundations and initial concerns of this work were not different from those that were discussed in the first two categories, it was developed for many years in relative detachment. Consequently, the terms, methods, and experimental designs that have been developed are somewhat different and deserve separate consideration.

The focus on the measurement of task load and spare capacity has led to the development of the secondary task technique, which is a special variant of the dual-task paradigm. In this technique, performance levels on one task serve as a measure of the performer's spare capacity, and by inference an estimate of the load of another task with which it is paired. Since it is not possible to obtain direct measures of load from the performance of the (single) primary task of interest, and the remaining capacity is also unknown, the idea is

to load the situation by adding a second, concurrent secondary task. The added task is assumed to create an overload and exhaust operator capacity. Subject's ability to perform the secondary task is hence postulated to index his or her spare capacity and to be complementary to the load imposed by the primary task itself.

Early work in this category searched for a single secondary task that can serve as a common standard ruler for all tasks. This approach is consistent with the unitary model of attention (as reflected in the first category of tasks discussed in this subsection). With the accumulated evidence on the multiple nature of the human processing and response limitations (see previous category) the focus has changed to the development of a standard battery of secondary tasks.

Experimentation with the secondary-task technique also turned attention back to another aspect of the dual-task paradigm that was in focus in the early works, but neglected in later years, viz. voluntary control on attention and the ability to assign priorities to tasks. For a successful application of the secondary-task technique, it is mandatory that subjects will protect performance of the primary task at all times, so that all scarcity and shortage of resources will show up only in secondary task performance. If performance of both tasks is affected, interpretation in terms of load and spare capacity is hampered, if not made entirely impossible. Yet performance decrements on both tasks are a frequent finding. Is it because subjects are unable to protect the primary task, or because their commitment is not strong enough? It should be recognized that the introduction of a secondary task creates ambiguity and double-bind communication. On the one hand subjects are instructed to secure primary-task performance; on the other hand they are encouraged to respond to the secondary task if "spare capacity" is available. But what is the meaning of such instruction? The mere presence of the secondary task is tempting. It is clear that one is much better off if one can respond to both tasks. The ambiguous priority instructions embedded in the secondary-task technique, have underlined the importance of attention allocation policy in the interpretation of dual-task performance.

Assessing the combined effect of task characteristics and allocation policy – the POC methodology Performance Operating Characteristics (POC) is the most recent and elaborated paradigm of dual-task research. A POC is a curve depicting all possible dual-task performance combinations arising from splitting a common and limited pool of resources. Given the structure of the tasks and the capabilities of the processing system, some levels of joint performance are possible while others are not. A POC depicts the set of all dual-task combinations that are obtained when a performer operates at full capacity but adopts different attention allocation policies that change the relative priority of the concurrently performed tasks. The term "full capacity" is used to refer only to those processing facilities competed for by the tasks. The overlap in task demands may be partial and some resources may be relevant to the performance of one task only.

In essence the POC methodology is an elaboration of the secondary-task technique, but rather than enforcing a single priority condition, attention policy is manipulated systematically. On different trials, subjects are requested to assign different priorities to the concurrently performed tasks. Hence, the POC is a performance tradeoff function that describes the improvement of performance on one task due to added resources from lowering the standard of performance on the other task with which it is time shared. It is easy to observe that different task pairs will produce different POCs, and when the difficulty of one task is manipulated, a new POC should be created for every level of difficulty. Hence, for every pair of concurrently performed tasks it is possible to construct a famility of POCs describing the change of performance tradeoffs as a result of manipulations of differing difficulty.

The POC methodology is a powerful paradigm that enables improved experimental design and more comprehensive investigation of the issues that have stimulated the construction of the paradigms described in the three categories previously discussed. Most important, it appears to allow a better examination of the interaction between task structure and the human control of processing resources. How many different allocation policies can a person adopt at will? What is the relative efficiency of different policies? How do they affect the tradeoff between tasks? How much of the policy making and its consequences is conscious? Attempts to answer these questions are on their way, and are crucial for a better understanding of the structure, functions, and limits of the human processing system. Dual-task research and the development of the POC methodology in particular are important vehicles for addressing these questions.

BIBLIOGRAPHY

Gopher, D., & Donchin, E. (1986). Workload: An examination of the concept. In K. Boff, L. Kaufman, & J. Thomas (Eds), *Handbook of perception and human performance* (Vol. 2). New York: John Wiley.

Kahneman, D. (1973). *Attention and effort* (chaps 7–10). Englewood Cliffs, NJ: Prentice-Hall.

Navon, D., & Gopher, D. (1979). On the economy of the human processing system. *Psychological Review, 86,* 214–55.

O'Donnell, R., & Eggemeier, T. (1986). Workload assessment methodology. In K. Boff, L. Kaufman, & J. Thomas (Eds), *Handbook of perception and human performance* (Vol. 2). New York: John Wiley.

Wickens, C. D. (1980). The structure of processing resources. In R. Nickerson (Ed.), *Attention and performance VIII* (pp. 239–57). Hillsdale, NJ: Lawrence Erlbaum.

DANIEL GOPHER

dyslexia: developmental When used in the strict sense this term refers to those difficulties with written and spoken language which are believed to be the result of anomalies of development. It can therefore usefully be contrasted with acquired dyslexia (*see* DYSLEXIAS: ACQUIRED), where, as a result of stroke or injury, existing language skills have become lost. An indication of some of the similarities and differences between the two conditions will be found in Ellis (1984). In what follows the words "dyslexia" and "dyslexic" will be used to refer to developmental dyslexia only; looser senses of the word, in which it is used to mean simply "difficulty with reading," are confusing and therefore best avoided. Reading problems which are of ocular or oculo-motor origin are beyond the scope of the present discussion.

MEDICAL BACKGROUND

As early as the 1870s the German neurologist, A. Kussmaul, described certain brain damaged patients as suffering from "word blindness" and "word deafness." Such patients appeared to have special difficulty in identifying written or spoken words despite normal eyesight and hearing. In the 1890s two British doctors, W. Pringle Morgan and J. Hinshelwood – the first a general practitioner, the second an eye surgeon – suggested that there could be a form of word blindness which was congenital. Hinshelwood noted that the condition sometimes ran in families and that it was more common in boys than in girls; later research has shown him to be right on both these points (Critchley, 1970). He also made some suggestions for remediation which are largely in line with current practice.

In the 1920s the issues were taken up in North America, mainly through the influence of the neurologist, S. T. Orton. On Orton's view an important characteristic of those affected was the twisting round of symbols ("strephosymbolia"). This took the form either of "static reversals," which involve the reading or writing of the mirror image of the correct symbol, for instance *b* for *d*, and "kinetic reversals," when the letters of a word are seemingly written in reverse order, as in "tworrom" for "tomorrow." Orton's theory was that in some cases the "engrams" (traces) which entered the two halves of the brain as mirror images were not properly "elided." This kind of "local sign" theory, as the Gestalt psychologists would have called it, is highly questionable; and it is arguable that the writing of "tworrom" for "tomorrow" is simply the result of a general uncertainty over letter order and does not necessarily indicate a progression from right to left. Whatever the force of this criticism the important part played by

Orton in calling attention to the phenomena of dyslexia is not in dispute.

In the 1940s and 1950s the same issues were discussed in the Scandinavian countries, notably by B. Hallgren and K. Hermann; and since that time interest has grown in many different parts of the world. (For an account of these early developments see in particular Critchley, 1970; and for some further details, Thomson, 1984.)

More recently, after post mortem examination of a small number of dyslexic brains, Galaburda, Corsiglia, Rosen, and Sherman (1987) have indicated not only that there are ectopias (intrusions of cells from one layer to another) but that there is symmetry of the temporal plana of the two cerebral hemispheres, in contrast with the more common asymmetry.

> Indirect evidence suggests that asymmetry of the planum results from the greater pruning down of one of the sides during later fetal life and infancy.... The exuberant growth of the otherwise smaller side in the symmetrical cases might produce complex qualitative alterations in the functional properties of the system.
>
> (Galaburda et al., 1987, p. 867)

It is not impossible, therefore, that the special talents sometimes displayed by dyslexics in art, architecture, and constructional tasks are no accident but are the result of unusual organization in one of the two hemispheres, more commonly the right.

Other developments on the biological side include investigation of possible genetic factors by means of twin studies, use of blood flow techniques for comparing the activities of the two hemispheres, and chromosomal studies, from which an abnormality in chromosome 15 is suspected. (For a brief review of the evidence in these areas see Vellutino, 1987.)

DYSLEXIA AS A SYNDROME

It has been argued by Critchley (1970) that "specific developmental dyslexia" constitutes an identifiable syndrome – a pattern of symptoms the elements of which form a meaningful whole. Although the extent to which the phenomena of dyslexia are homogeneous is still a matter of dispute, Critchley's view is supported in that many of those who have experienced difficulty in learning to read and spell (where this is not due to lack of intelligence or opportunity) are likely, outside normal limits, to display other weaknesses – uncertainty over left and right and over times and dates, confusion between *b* and *d*, difficulty in learning arithmetical tables, problems with the recall of auditorily and visually presented digits, slowness at picture and color naming, and some degree of struggle when disconnected items, such as the months of the year, have to be recalled in sequence (Miles, 1983; Thomson, 1984).

Typical cases of dyslexia in this sense are not difficult to pick out clinically, though in contexts where a precise definition is needed researchers are confronted (as they are in other areas) with the problem of where exactly to draw boundaries. This difficulty is not limited, of course, to those who regard dyslexia as a syndrome.

A logical consequence of the "syndrome" view is that, at least in principle, there must be criteria for distinguishing those poor readers and spellers who manifest the syndrome from those who do not. In much research the criterion used has simply been underachievement: in other words, a person is dyslexic if he or she is *discrepantly* weak at reading or spelling in comparison with other skills, in particular those that can be assessed by traditional intelligence tests. If the "syndrome" view is correct, however, this criterion is inadequate, at least if underachieving children can be found who do not display the typical dyslexic signs. As a result of a survey of over 12,000 ten-year-olds an attempt has been made to distinguish "dyslexic underachievers" from "non-dyslexic underachievers" (for sources see Miles, 1989); and if in future research this distinction turns out to be of value the case for the "syndrome" view will be strengthened. A rough estimate from this survey suggests that the number of ten-year-olds who were significantly handicapped by dyslexia was between 2 and 4 percent.

DYSLEXIA AS A DIFFICULTY AT THE PHONOLOGICAL LEVEL

There are good reasons for supposing that the difficulties of dyslexics show themselves only or mainly when incoming stimuli have to be *named*. Now the kind of naming which occurs earliest in life, except in the case of the congenitally deaf, involves the representation of the thing named by means of speech sounds. The dyslexic's difficulty in naming can therefore be described as a difficulty at the phonological level, phonology being the study of sounds in so far as they convey meaning.

If this view is correct, then differences between dyslexics and controls can be expected at the pre-reading level; and this has in fact been shown to be the case. Thus, there is evidence from a variety of sources that dyslexics are late in the acquisition of oral language (Miles, 1989). In addition it has been found that when non-readers aged four and five were required to pick the "odd one out" from a list of four orally presented words, for instance the word with a different middle sound in the list "nod, red, fed, bed," there was a high correlation between weakness at this task and later reading difficulty. An account of the research in question, along with references to two earlier articles published in *Nature*, will be found in Bryant and Bradley (1985). This research will also be discussed under the Remediation subheading, below.

It is perhaps helpful in this connection to think of each individual as possessing an internal "lexicon" (or dictionary) in which entries are gradually built up – first for spoken words and later for written words and other symbolic material (including mathematical symbols, the ampersand, punctuation marks, and so on). Using this model one might say that dyslexics require more "exposures" before a particular lexical entry is established and that even when this has happened retrieval of the entry takes extra time. This account makes sense not only of dyslexics' weakness at associating spoken words with their written representation but of their weak immediate memory for any nameable material (since a lesser amount can be verbalized per unit of time). Vellutino (1987, p. 20) expresses the position as follows:

"Along with other researchers ... we have been finding that dyslexia is a subtle language deficiency." He then speaks of "inability to represent and access the sound of a word in order to help remember the word" and "inability to break words into component sounds." In contrast, the ability to make good use of already existing lexical entries is unimpaired; and this makes sense of the fact that some dyslexics are extremely creative, while many have obtained high scores on "similarities" and "reasoning" items in traditional intelligence tests (Miles, 1983).

The above account carries two further predictions, namely (1) that tasks will be found in which dyslexics perform less efficiently not only than chronological-age matched controls but than reading-age or spelling-age matched controls, and (2) that tasks will be found in which even adequately reading and successful dyslexic adults will be at a disadvantage. In experiments which called for rapid processing of symbolic material both these predictions held up (Miles, 1989).

It also follows that if naming and non-naming tasks are compared, the differences between dyslexics and controls will be found to be more marked in the former. This has been confirmed in some research by N. C. Ellis (for references see Snowling, 1987; Miles, 1989). Ellis found that dyslexics were no slower than age-matched controls in responding "same" or "different" when pairs of upper-case letters were presented ("visual match" condition) but consistently took longer time than controls if one member of the pair was upper case and the other lower case ("name match" condition). This result is, of course, strong evidence against the view that dyslexics are weak at visual tasks per se.

In all research in this area it is important to allow for stages of development. According to the model offered by Uta Frith, a child cannot satisfactorily move on to the spelling of irregular words such as "yacht" or "pint" ("orthographic stage") without having passed through the "alphabetic" stage which involves awareness of normal letter-sound correspondences (see SPELLING). Now it is this kind of "paired associate learning" which the typical dyslexic finds very hard to achieve, and

the result is that many of them come to use wholly inappropriate spelling strategies at a later age. (For references and an account of some of the research based on Frith's model see Snowling, 1987.)

On the issue of whether there are distinctive subtypes of dyslexia there may have been argument at cross purposes. If "dyslexia" simply means "poor reading" it is not in dispute that people can be poor readers for many different reasons. Among those, however, whose reading and language difficulties are the sequelae of weakness at the phonological level, the evidence for distinctive subtypes is unconvincing; in particular the distinction between those with "auditory" and those with "visual" weaknesses has been called into question by many researchers (see, for instance, Miles, 1983; Liberman, 1985). There have also been attempts at subtyping on the basis of the different syndromes of acquired dyslexia, but no very convincing conclusions have so far emerged from this approach. The relationship, if any, between dyslexia and unusual handedness also remains a matter of controversy.

REMEDIATION

Some of the disputes as to what is the "best" way of teaching beginners to read and spell have been unproductive (see READING DEVELOPMENT). In the case of dyslexics, however, there are two points which do not seem open to dispute. The first is that one cannot rely on their "picking up" reading and spelling without special help; the second is that targets need to be set which take account of their distinctive problems. Thus, even if it is true that adequate readers can save time if they are encouraged to "skim" rather than study each word in detail, it does not follow that "saving time" is a suitable objective for those beginner readers who are struggling. In their case greater accuracy is clearly more important; and if they attempt to read at speed, as any experienced teacher knows, they will almost certainly be reduced to wild guessing. In addition, it is hard to see how "skimming" can contribute to accurate spelling, which is surely an essential element in literacy. Where there is controversy, therefore, it is important in the first place to define objectives; and, given that children need both to read and to spell, there is clearly a good case for choosing techniques which help both.

For several decades experienced teachers of dyslexics have insisted that the correspondences between spoken sounds and written letters should be taught systematically and that the approach needs to be "multisensory": that is to say, the pupil needs to listen carefully, to look carefully, and to pay attention both to the mouth movements used in speaking the word and to the hand movements used in writing it. Although these techniques evolved in advance of the research evidence cited above, there is clearly a remarkable concordance in this area between practice and theory. Thus, given that dyslexics do not easily pass through the "alphabetic" stage of development (see above) this is of itself a good reason for teaching them sound–letter correspondences. Moreover, the work of Bryant and Bradley (1985) gives at least some support to the view that training in categorization of sounds can lead to improvement at reading and spelling, particularly if each sound is represented by a plastic letter of the alphabet. An ingenious feature of the design of their experiments was that the children in question performed better at reading and spelling not only than a control group who received no training but better than a further control group who were trained to classify not by sound but by meaning, for example to group "hen" and "pig" together as farm animals. Further support for multisensory teaching will be found in the experiments of Hulme (1981).

A similar approach has been adopted by Liberman and her colleagues at the Haskins Laboratories, Connecticut. There is abundant evidence from their research that dyslexia is basically a language problem rather than an "auditory" or "visual" problem as such.

To make best use of an alphabetic orthography, the reader, whether he is skilled or a beginner, had best go beyond visual shape to apprehend the internal structure of the word. The skilled reader does it quite automatically, and beginners, though it may be difficult for them, should, in my view, be

given instruction directed toward that goal from the very beginning.

(Liberman, 1985, p. 101)

Although the evidence is not conclusive there is reason to think that the problems of dyslexia tend to be less pronounced in those languages where there is a large amount of regularity between speech sounds and their representation by letters, Spanish and Italian, for instance, rather than English or Danish. Also, where syllables are represented pictorially, as in the Japanese kanji script, there is some evidence that dyslexics are less at a disadvantage (Thomson, 1984, pp. 115–18). The whole area, however, is one which requires further research; indeed, it is not impossible that the incidence of dyslexia may be different among different races.

Finally, to return to languages which use an alphabetic script, it may be helpful to bear in mind the view of Gibson (1968), who has argued that when different senses are stimulated, for instance vision, hearing, and touch, there can be equivalent "stimulus information." "Information about the world can be obtained with any perceptual system alone or with any combination of systems working together" (p. 55). If this is correct it is not surprising that stimulation via a *combination* of the different senses should both contribute to the establishing of lexical entries and lead to more accurate recall and more secure temporal ordering. Overall, there is good reason for believing that the use of multisensory methods is not just a "fad" (of which there have been all too many in the educational world over the years) but is supported by systematic research.

See also MODULARITY OF MIND.

BIBLIOGRAPHY

Bryant, P. E., & Bradley, L. (1985). *Children's reading problems*. Oxford: Blackwell.

Critchley, M. (1970). *The dyslexic child*. London: Heinemann.

Ellis, A. W. (1984). *Reading, writing, and dyslexia: A cognitive analysis*. London: Lawrence Erlbaum Associates.

Galaburda, A. M., Corsiglia, J., Rosen, G. D., & Sherman, G. F. (1987). Planum temporale asymmetry: Reappraisal since Geschwind and Levitsky. *Neuropsychologia*, 25(6), 853–68.

Gibson, J. J. (1968). *The senses considered as perceptual systems*. London: Allen & Unwin.

Hulme, C. (1981). *Reading retardation and multi-sensory teaching*. London: Routledge & Kegan Paul.

Liberman, I. Y. (1985). Should modality preferences determine the nature of instruction for children with reading disabilities? In F. H. Duffy and N. Geschwind (Eds), *Dyslexia: A neuroscientific approach to clinical evaluation* (pp. 93–103). Boston: Little Brown & Co.

Miles, T. R. (1983). *Dyslexia: The pattern of difficulties*. Oxford: Blackwell.

——. (1989). The work of the dyslexia group at Bangor. *The Psychologist*, in press.

Snowling, M. E. (1987). *Dyslexia: A cognitive developmental perspective*. Oxford: Blackwell.

Thomson, M. E. (1984). *Developmental dyslexia*. London: Edward Arnold.

Vellutino, F. R. (1987). Dyslexia. *Scientific American*, 256(3), 20–7.

T. R. MILES

dyslexias: acquired The term "acquired dyslexia" refers to a disorder of reading occurring in a previously literate adult as a consequence of brain injury. It should be distinguished from developmental dyslexia seen in children with unexpected reading problems (*see* DYSLEXIA: DEVELOPMENTAL).

Acquired dyslexia is of interest to the cognitive psychologist if it is studied from the standpoint of COGNITIVE NEUROPSYCHOLOGY; that is, from a standpoint which seeks to explain the patterns of impaired and intact reading performance in brain-injured patients in terms of damage to components of a theory of normal, skilled reading. To the extent that the theory of normal reading can account for the observed pattern, that theory receives corroborative support, just as if it had successfully predicted the result of a laboratory experiment using skilled readers as subjects. To the extent that the theory is unable to explain the acquired dyslexic pattern, the theory stands in need of modification.

Modern interest in the acquired dyslexias stems in large measure from the seminal work of Marshall and Newcombe (1973). They dis-tinguished three forms of acquired dyslexia (visual dyslexia, surface dyslexia, and deep dyslexia) and sought to explain them in terms of contemporary models of visual word recognition. They also reviewed historical cases from the neuropsychological literature and attempted to show how they could be assimilated to the same schema.

Subsequent work has shown that reading is a complex skill which draws upon numerous cognitive subsystems which are capable of being impaired independently of one another, giving rise to a substantial number of different patterns of acquired dyslexia. It is still the case, however, that those patterns can be accounted for reasonably well by models of skilled reading. The list of acquired dyslexias discussed here will not be exhaustive (see Ellis & Young, 1988; Shallice, 1988).

Shallice and Warrington (1980) proposed a useful subdivision of the acquired dyslexias into peripheral and central dyslexias. Patients with peripheral dyslexias have impairments affecting the visual perception of letters or letter strings. The forms of peripheral acquired dyslexia that will be considered here are neglect dyslexia, attentional dyslexia, and letter-by-letter reading. Patients with central dyslexias have intact perceptions of words but have problems in processing their meanings and/or accessing and producing their spoken forms. Central acquired dyslexias usually (but perhaps not invariably) occur in the context of more general language impairments. They include phonological dyslexia, surface dyslexia, and deep dyslexia.

Most acquired dyslexias follow damage to the left cerebral hemisphere (of right-handed adults). An exception to this rule is neglect dyslexia – a variety of peripheral acquired dyslexia which typically follows damage to the *right* cerebral hemisphere. When trying to read a passage of text, patients with neglect dyslexia often fail to read the initial (leftmost) words on each line. When attempting single words they will make errors on the initial letters of words, which may be omitted (e.g. misreading "lever" as "ever") or replaced by different letters (e.g. misreading "log" as "dog," or "yellow" as "pillow"). Neglect dyslexics tend to replace rather than delete initial letters, even when deleting the initial letters leaves a real word. Thus, they will misread "plate" as "slate" or "crate" rather than as "late" or "ate." The error word is usually of the same length as the target word the patient is trying to read. This pattern could arise if neglect dyslexics encode the presence and position of all the letters in a word, but cannot reliably encode the identity of the first one or two letters. They would then be attempting to read "plate" on the basis of a representation something like –late, knowing that *l* is not the first letter, but not knowing what precedes it. Hence, they would be more likely to guess "slate" or "crate" than "late" or "ate."

Patients with attentional dyslexia can read individual words reasonably well, but have great difficulty naming the letters within a word. They also make errors when faced with more than a single word – errors which involve transposing letters out of one word into another. Thus, an attentional dyslexic asked to read "win" and "fed" might read them as "fin" and "fed." In general, letters move from one word to the corresponding position in another word. Similar errors can be induced in normal readers if groups of words are presented very briefly. When a single word is seen, letters can be identified and their positions correctly encoded, and that is sufficient to identify the word, but when more than one word is present, those letters belonging together as part of the same word must be grouped together by virtue of their common position in space. That perceptual grouping process seems to be impaired in attentional dyslexia.

Some peripheral acquired dyslexic patients are only able to read words by painstakingly identifying the letters serially from left to right. This form of peripheral dyslexia is known as letter-by-letter reading. In some but not all patients, letters are named as they are identified. Because words are being identified letter-by-letter, the longer a word is, the more time the patient takes to read it. Normal readers can identify the component letters of familiar words more or less simultaneously and in parallel, but that capacity for simultaneous letter identification is clearly impaired in letter-by-letter readers who seem

to be reduced to a single-letter perceptual "window." Letter-by-letter reading with correct, if labored, word identification only appears to occur in patients in whom the capacity to spell is preserved. One theory proposes that access to the normal reading system has been completely blocked by the brain injury such patients have suffered, and that they read instead by an abnormal, reverse use of preserved spelling processes.

In order to understand the central dyslexias, we must make a distinction between two ways of accessing the meaning of a word from its printed form (*see* DUAL-ROUTE MODEL OF READING). The first method involves the direct visual recognition of a letter string as a familiar word. The second, phonic method is applied by skilled readers when they are trying to read an unfamiliar word or an invented nonword like "ploon"). It involves breaking a word down into its component letter or letter groups and converting those letters into sounds. A word which is unfamiliar in its written form may be familiar in its spoken form, and may be capable of being recognized via this phonic method. Words which resist the phonic method are irregularly spelled words like "yacht" or "colonel." The only way to read these successfully is the direct visual recognition of the letter string as familiar. Thus, we can assess the intactness of direct visual recognition by testing reading of irregularly spelled words, while phonic reading can be assessed by asking patients to read invented nonwords (strings of letters which we can be confident a patient has not seen before).

Although the cognitive processes responsible for direct and phonic word recognition may not be totally separate, evidence for a degree of separation comes from central dyslexias which impair one method of reading while leaving the other broadly intact. Patients with phonological dyslexia can still employ the direct visual method of word recognition but are severely impaired at using the phonic method. That is, they are still able to read familiar words, but cannot read unfamiliar words or invented nonwords. Faced with a nonword, the best they can do in many cases is to "read" it as a similar-looking familiar word, for example reading "cobe" as "comb," or "ploon" as "spoon." The fact that phonological dyslexics can repeat nonwords spoken by an examiner shows that the problem is not one of articulating unfamiliar strings of sounds: rather, the problem seems to lie in the mapping of letters and letter groups on to sounds. The fact that familiar-word recognition can survive such damage suggests that phonic reading processes are not involved in the processing of familiar words by skilled readers. This conclusion is reinforced by studies of aphasic patients who demonstrate intact comprehension of written words whose sound forms they cannot retrieve correctly. For example, when a patient studied by Ellis, Miller, and Sin (1983) was asked to read words aloud and then define their meanings, he read "grief" as "preevd," adding "one is sad," and read "chaos" as "kwost," adding "people all muddled up ... out of order." He showed good understanding of the meanings of written words on a range of tasks despite being unable on many occasions to pronounce the words correctly.

The converse pattern of preserved phonic reading with impaired direct visual recognition of familiar words is seen in a condition (or rather, as we shall see, a collection of conditions) known as surface dyslexia (Patterson, Marshall, & Coltheart, 1985). Surface dyslexic patients have in common the fact that they read once-familiar words, especially irregular words, as if they were unfamiliar. That is, they sound out words which they would have recognized directly as wholes before their brain injuries. The result is that irregular words are read aloud as they would be if their spellings were regular. For example, a surface dyslexic patient may read "colonel" as "kollonell," "come" as "kome," or "plough" as "ploff." As a result, the meaning of the irregular word will not be understood, or will be misunderstood if the sound form which the patient derives phonically is that of a different word. Thus, the patient who reads "come" as "kome" may think that the word is "comb." Words which have regular spellings are words which can be read successfully using the phonic method, so the hallmark of the surface dyslexic is poor reading of irregular words ("yacht," "biscuit") in the context of reasonably good reading of regular words ("boat," "cake") and nonwords ("loat," "fiskit").

Although this pattern holds for all surface dyslexics, and indicates that phonic reading is preserved while direct visual reading is impaired, further testing reveals that the precise nature of the impairment to direct visual reading differs from patient to patient. The recognition of familiar words as whole units involves at least three stages beyond identifying the component letters of the word. Knowing that a letter string forms a familiar word must involve matching that string to representations in memory. Models of the reading process refer to the internal store in which familiar words are stored as letter strings by various titles, including the visual input logogen system, the orthographic lexicon, or (the term we shall use) the visual input lexicon. Whatever name one gives it, it is clear that brain injury which damages that store, or affects access to it, will mean that the patient can no longer recognize familiar words by the direct visual method. If the phonic method has survived the brain injury, then the patient will be surface dyslexic. Patient JC described by Marshall and Newcombe (1973) appears to match this predicted form of surface dyslexia fairly well. He was surface dyslexic but showed good comprehension of spoken words (as one would predict if the problem was confined to visual memories of words). In addition to reading irregular words phonically he also made straightforwardly visual errors (e.g. misreading "apron" as "open" and "direction" as "decision"), which may denote an impairment of the visual input lexicon itself.

If the entry for a word in the visual input lexicon can be successfully accessed, then the next stage in direct visual reading is to access the word's meaning in some form of SEMANTIC MEMORY system. Damage to that system should also affect direct visual reading and lead to surface dyslexia if phonic reading processes survive. Patients with senile dementia suffer impaired semantic memory, affecting their understanding of the meanings of words, and in the evolution of the disease may pass through a phase in which their reading is surface dyslexic. Unlike the previous variety of surface dyslexia, their comprehension of spoken words is affected in the same way as their comprehension of written words.

When the direct method is working properly, then the stage beyond recognizing the word at the visual input lexicon and accessing its meaning in the semantic system is retrieving the word's sound form from a further memory store – the phonological lexicon or speech output lexicon. Impairment at that level means that the patient can recognize words as familiar, and knows their meanings, but cannot remember their pronunciations. If the phonic route remains it may be used to assemble a pronunciation, but will be unsuccessful in the case of irregular words. A patient manifesting this third variety of surface dyslexia was described by Kay and Patterson (1985).

A final form of central acquired dyslexia which has received a great deal of attention is deep dyslexia (Coltheart, Patterson, & Marshall, 1980). The most dramatic symptom of deep dyslexia is the semantic error, where a patient will misread one word as another word similar in meaning. Thus, a deep dyslexic patient might misread "tandem" as "cycle," "cost" as "money," "deed" as "solicitors," "decay" as "rubbish," or "city" as "town." Patients who make such errors also show a number of other associated features. Like phonological dyslexics they are very poor at reading nonwords. This denotes an impairment of the phonic reading method, which could be a necessary condition for the occurrence of semantic errors (because a patient who could sound words out phonically would know that "cost" was not "money" simply on the grounds that the letter c is never pronounced m).

As well as semantic errors, deep dyslexics also make visual errors such as misreading "signal" as "single" or "charter" as "garters." They are more successful at reading concrete, imageable nouns like "butter" or "windmill" than abstract nouns like "grief" or "wish." Faced with an abstract noun, their response is often to make a semantic or visual error in which the response word is more concrete than the original target word. A particularly striking type of error occurs when a deep dyslexic patient produces a combination of a visual and a semantic error. One patient, for example, read "favour" as "taste," presumably by first misidentifying "favour" as "flavour" (a visual error), then commuting "flavour" into "taste" (a semantic error). Similar visual-then-semantic errors convert "pivot" into "airplane" (via "pilot") and "sympathy" into "orchestra" (via "symphony").

Theoretical accounts of deep dyslexia fall into two categories. One school takes the same approach to deep dyslexia as to all the other forms of acquired dyslexia by seeking to explain it in terms of damage to components of the normal reading system. It is accepted that no single locus of impairment could explain all the features of deep dyslexia, and that several separate impairments would need to be posited. These would include impairments to the semantic system and the phonic route from print to sound. An alternative school of thought asserts that what we see in deep dyslexia is not the workings of a damaged normal reading system based in the left hemisphere of the brain, but is the expression of a secondary reading system based in the right cerebral hemisphere. Proponents of this "right-hemisphere hypothesis" of deep dyslexia point to the fact that the isolated right hemispheres of so-called "split-brain" patients (see HEMISPHERIC LOCALIZATION) are unable to read phonically and may make semantic errors in tasks such as pointing to the picture that matches a written word (e.g. shown the word "orange" they might point to a picture of an apple rather than a picture of an orange). Although this explanation of deep dyslexia may turn out to be correct, questions such as why the right-hemisphere reading system develops at all, whether it develops in everyone or just in some people, and what role (if any) it plays in normal reading remain unanswered.

There is much more to be learned about acquired disorders of reading. New forms of acquired dyslexia continue to be reported, and new facts about known forms continue to emerge. As noted above, the list of types discussed here is by no means exhaustive. Some cognitive neuropsychologists would dispute the notion of types of acquired dyslexia, pointing to theoretically significant individual differences between patients assigned to the same group. The important point is that as well as explaining data from normal subjects performing laboratory tasks, theories in cognitive psychology should be able to give a principled account of the patterns of performance which can be seen after brain injury (and those that cannot).

BIBLIOGRAPHY

Coltheart, M., Patterson, K. E., & Marshall, J. C. (Eds) (1980). *Deep dyslexia*. London: Routledge & Kegan Paul.

Ellis, A. W. (1984). *Reading, writing and dyslexia: A cognitive analysis*. London: Lawrence Erlbaum Associates.

— —, & Young, A. W. (1988). *Human cognitive neuropsychology*. London: Lawrence Erlbaum Associates.

Ellis, A. W., Miller, D., & Sin, G. (1983). Wernicke's aphasia and normal language processing: A case study in cognitive neuropsychology. *Cognition, 15*, 111–44.

Kay, J., & Patterson, K. E. (1985). Routes to meaning in surface dyslexia. In K. E. Patterson, J. C. Marshall, & M. Coltheart (Eds), *Surface dyslexia: Neuropsychological and cognitive studies of phonological reading*. London: Lawrence Erlbaum Associates.

Marshall, J. C., & Newcombe, F. (1973). Patterns of paralexia: A psycholinguistic approach. *Journal of Psycholinguistic Research, 2*, 175–99.

Patterson, K. E., Marshall, J. C., & Coltheart, M. (Eds) (1985). *Surface dyslexia: Neuropsychological and cognitive studies of phonological reading*. London: Lawrence Erlbaum Associates.

Shallice, T. (1988). *From neuropsychology to mental structure*. Cambridge: Cambridge University Press.

— —, & Warrington, E. K. (1980). Single and multiple component central dyslexic syndromes. In M. Coltheart, K. E. Patterson, & J. C. Marshall (Eds), *Deep dyslexia*. London: Routledge & Kegan Paul.

ANDREW W. ELLIS

E

echoic store In information-processing models of perception and memory the echoic store is postulated to hold sound in a relatively unprocessed state for a short time in order to provide a temporally extended window as input to subsequent categorization mechanisms. It is analogous to the ICONIC STORE in vision.

The sounds that we recognize as instances of particular categories, such as phonemes in speech, are often extended in time, involving the integration of perceptual cues that occur at different times. Our ability to integrate these cues provides a strong a priori case for a pre-categorical auditory memory, which maintains an analog representation of sound over a temporal window of at least a few tenths of a second.

The experimental evidence cited for echoic memory is very diverse, and may reflect more than one type of store. An early demonstration of memory for sound that could not be due to the use of verbal categorical labels was by Guttman and Julesz (1963). They repeatedly cycled identical sections of white noise, and showed that listeners could distinguish such repeating noise from normal random noise when the repeating section was up to about 1 sec. long. Although verbal labels are clearly useless in this task, it is likely that occasional peaks of energy at particular frequencies provide a way of making the distinction without having to remember all the information in 1 sec. of white noise.

Rather different approaches appear in the selective attention literature. Treisman (1964) asked subjects to shadow the message to one ear while ignoring the message to the other, which was in fact either a leading or a lagging version of the shadowed ear's message. If the unattended ear lagged, subjects spontaneously noticed that fact at up to about 4 or 5 sec. lag (depending on the material) but when the unattended ear led they failed at about 1.25

sec. independent of the type of material. The difference could be due to categorical versus pre-categorical memories, but it is not clear whether unattended channels are phonetically categorized. A similar criticism can be made of experiments by Darwin, Turvey, and Crowder (1972) who performed an auditory equivalent of the Sperling partial report procedure used to study the iconic store, and obtained an estimate of the store's decay time of between 2 and 4 sec.

A technique that explicitly controls for verbal labels was used by Howell and Darwin (1977). They measured subjects' reaction times for indicating whether two sounds were phonetically the same. Reaction times to sounds that were also acoustically identical were faster than to those that were phonetically identical but acoustically slightly different, provided that the interval between the sounds was less than about 800 millisec. The reaction time difference here cannot be due to different phonetic labels, but requires subjects to remember the detailed acoustic structure of the sound.

A popular technique for measuring "Pre-Categorical Acoustic Storage" (PAS) during the 1970s was introduced by Crowder and Morton (1969). In serial digit recall, the final one or two items in a list are recalled better when the lists are heard than when they are (only) seen. This modality-specific recency effect is abolished by the presentation of an auditory verbal suffix that need not be recalled. The results of numerous experiments on this suffix effect were interpreted as indicating the presence of an auditory memory that decayed and could be overwritten. However, the validity of this paradigm is seriously questioned by the findings that lip-read (but not heard) digits give a clear recency effect and that cross-modal suffix effects can be obtained between heard and lip-read digits (Spoehr & Corrin, 1978; Campbell & Dodd,

1980). A specifically auditory memory is not necessary for the interpretation of recency and suffix effects.

BIBLIOGRAPHY

Campbell, R., & Dodd, B.(1980). Hearing by eye. *Quarterly Journal of Experimental Psychology*, 32, 85–99.

Crowder, R. A., & Morton, J. (1969). Precategorical acoustic storage (PAS). *Perception and Psychophysics*, 5, 365–73.

Darwin, C. J., Turvey, M. T., & Crowder, R. G. (1972). An auditory analogue of the Sperling partial report procedure: Evidence for brief auditory storage. *Cognitive Psychology*, 3, 255–67.

Darwin, C. J., & Baddeley, A. D. (1974). Acoustic memory and the perception of speech. *Cognitive Psychology*, 6, 41–60.

Guttmann, N., & Julesz, B. (1963). Lower limits of periodicity analysis. *Journal of the Acoustical Society of America*, 35, 610 (A).

Howell, P., & Darwin, C. J. (1977). Some properties of auditory memory for rapid formant transitions. *Memory & Cognition*, 5, 700–8.

Spoehr, K. T., & Corrin, W. J. (1978). The stimulus suffix effect as a memory coding phenomenon. *Memory & Cognition*, 6, 583–9.

Treisman, A. M. (1964). Monitoring and storage of irrelevant messages in selective attention. *Journal of Verbal Learning and Verbal Behaviour*, 3, 449–59.

C. J. DARWIN

ecological validity Ecological validity is an attribute of research which applies to naturally occurring behavior in the real world. Neisser (1976) argued that traditional general-principles research based on formal experiments has little or no relevance to everyday behavior outside the laboratory, i.e. that it lacked ecological validity. Cognitive psychologists should, in his view, aim for ecological validity by making "a greater effort to understand cognition as it occurs in the ordinary environment and in the context of natural purposeful activity" (Neisser, 1976, p. 7).

Many examples can be cited of research which is demonstrably lacking in ecological validity. Studies of learning which have focused on the behavior of rats in mazes have little application to the learning abilities of rats in their familiar natural habitat, where purposeful behavior patterns can develop over time, guided by accumulating experience. In studies of perception many experiments were concerned with the perception of highly artificial patterns or static two-dimensional objects shown without any surrounding context. Gibson (1979) argued that perception of these impoverished stimuli is unrepresentative of perception in the natural environment where the three-dimensional visual scene comprises a far richer and more complex configuration of cues including dynamic and textural information (*see* DIRECT PERCEPTION). Neisser (1978) was particularly critical of the lack of ecological validity in memory research, claiming that it had failed to answer any important questions and was mostly trivial and worthless. General-principles research has tended to base theories on the performance of subjects learning lists of unrelated words or nonsense syllables. In such studies variables such as spacing and timing are rigidly controlled, but variables such as motivation or past experience, which are of paramount importance for memory in everyday life, are ignored or eliminated. Traditional verbal learning studies have, as Neisser pointed out, failed to shed light on how people remember such things as faces, music, appointments, shopping lists, or what they were taught at school.

Neisser's views have produced a major shift of approach with changes in aims and methods as well as in the kind of topics that are studied. Ecologically valid research is functional rather than theoretical. It aims to describe and explain how and why cognitive abilities develop and operate, rather than to deduce the general principles that govern cognitive mechanisms. Instead of being concerned with nonsense syllables, syllogisms, or rows of dots, ecologically valid research addresses real-life problems about, for example, the credibility of child witnesses (*see* EYEWITNESS TESTIMONY) or memory for medical advice. Studying natural situations like these means studying the whole context of the event, not just a few selected aspects. It means studying individual differences so that results apply to different kinds of people, not just to some "average" person. It means taking account of variations in the habits and strategies that people choose to employ rather than assuming that a task is always performed in the same way. And it means studying the development of cognitive abilities over a lifetime rather than sampling a half hour of performance in the laboratory (*see* AGING AND COGNITIVE CHANGE). Currently, the trend in cognitive psychology is to opt for a combination of formal experimental general principles methods and natural ecologically valid research. Ideally, the two approaches can work in tandem, complementing and reinforcing each other.

BIBLIOGRAPHY

Gibson, J. J. (1979). *The ecological approach to visual perception.* Boston: Houghton-Mifflin.

Neisser, U. (1976). *Cognition and reality.* San Francisco: Freeman.

——. (1978). Memory: What are the important questions? In M. M. Gruneberg, P. Morris, & R. N. Sykes (Eds), *Practical aspects of memory.* New York: Academic Press.

GILLIAN COHEN

eidetic imagery Leask, Haber, and Haber (1969) define the eidetic image as "a visual image representing a previously scanned stimulus, persisting for up to several minutes, and phenomenologically in front of the eyes" (p. 25). How detailed are such images, are they distinct from other forms of imagery, and how common are they? (*See* IMAGERY AND PERCEPTION.) Current interest in eidetic imagery is due largely to R. N. Haber, who has followed the methodological tradition established by Jaensch and the Marburg school early this century. In Jaensch's method subjects carefully inspect a picture for up to 40 seconds, then gaze at a plain grey screen and report what they experience. Some subjects, mainly children, report an image of the picture "*on* the surface" for periods ranging from a few seconds to a minute or more.

Such eidetic (from the Greek *eidos*, "that which is seen") images are distinguished from after-images by their occurrence even when eye movements are made during stimulus exposure, by their stability when eye movements are made during report, their durability, and their positive colors. According to Haber (1979), eidetic images may also be distinguished from nonvisual forms of memory representation by their continuity with the stimulus, their phenomenological projection on to a surface in space, and subjects' use of the present tense when describing them. According to such criteria about 8 percent of children aged from 7 to 12 years, and about 0.1 percent of adults, are eidetic. The low incidence and the apparent lack of any relationship between eidetic and cognitive abilities suggest that eidetic imagery has no necessary role in normal development. Also, as Haber (1979) concluded, there is no convincing relationship between eidetic imagery and neurological impairment, as some accounts suppose.

The phenomenological criteria for identifying eidetic imagery described above are open to criticisms, such as their proneness to demand characteristics, especially with children. Recall of detail from complex visual displays and superimposition of separate images to form a composite image provide *objective* criteria. Examples of eidetikers on these criteria are the three children discovered by Allport (1924), who, despite having no knowledge of German, could spell *Gartenwirthschaft* forwards and backwards after seeing it in a picture, and Stromeyer and Psotka's (1970) subject who could combine images of two random dot stereograms. But such individuals are rare and most eidetikers classified on phenomenological criteria cannot be distinguished from non-eidetikers on objective criteria. As Haber (1979) notes, this situation seems to leave only the phenomenological aspects of eidetic imagery, with all the attendant methodological and inferential problems, as the basis for exploring eidetic imagery in all but a very few exceptional subjects.

Several authors, including Ahsen (1977) and Marks and McKellar (1982), believe that Haber's conceptualization of eidetic imagery is too narrow. Ahsen believes typographical imagery, which has continuity with the stimulus, and structural imagery, which has no such continuity, should be included in the single concept of eidetic imagery. Given that so much of the evidence concerning eidetic imagery is of a subjective nature it is not surprising that even classification of the phenomena remains a problem.

BIBLIOGRAPHY

Ahsen, A. (1977). Eidetics: an overview. *Journal of Mental Imagery*, *1*, 5–38.

Allport, G. W. (1924). Eidetic imagery. *British Journal of Psychology*, *15*, 100–20.

Haber, R. N. (1979). Twenty years of haunting eidetic imagery: where's the ghost? *The Behavioral and Brain Sciences*, *2*, 583–629.

Leask, J., Haber, R. N., & Haber, R. B. (1969). Eidetic imagery in children: II. Longitudinal and experimental results. *Psychonomic Monograph Supplements*, *3*, 25–48.

Marks, D., & McKellar, P. (1982). The nature and function of eidetic imagery. *Journal of Mental Imagery*, *6*, 1–28.

Stromeyer, C. F., & Psotka, J. (1970). The detailed texture of eidetic images. *Nature*, *225*, 347–9.

VERNON H. GREGG

emotion The term "emotion" denotes various enjoyable or distressing mental states. There has been a tendency to think of emotions as biological and of little interest for cognitive analyses. Indeed, they have even been somewhat neglected in psychology generally. The study of emotions has, however, come to be of considerable importance for cognitive psychology and there is a growing body of evidence and theory about the attributes and functions of these states.

HISTORY OF CONCEPTS OF EMOTION IN PSYCHOLOGY

The reason emotions have previously been neglected in human psychology is no doubt due to the tradition in which they have been seen as enemies of reason. This view was held by Plato, who thought that they were like drugs that distort rationality. This distrust was continued by the Stoics who argued that emotions were diseases of the soul.

Modern investigations of emotions began with Darwin, whose work continued this line of thinking. After writing the *Origin of species*, in which humans were scarcely mentioned, he devoted much of his time to collecting evidence for human evolution. He found similarities of emotional expression between humans and other animals, and between adults and children. He observed that these expressions occurred whether or not they were of the least use. He was therefore able to argue that when they occur in adult humans, they are echoes of evolutionary history, and of the history of our development from childhood. They are behavioral vestiges, no longer necessarily functional, rather like the small bones at the base of our spine which are anatomical remnants of tails that our ancestors once had.

Following Darwin, JAMES (WILLIAM) argued that emotions are perceptions of bodily happenings, and Walter B. Cannon argued that they are upwellings of impulses from lower, non-rational parts of the brain. Such proposals constituted the mainstream of psychological theorizing about emotions.

Influential though this tradition has been, there has also been another tradition of thought about emotions in the history of Western psychological ideas. It started with Aristotle, who argued that emotions are based on cognitive judgements; and he gave componential analyses of emotion terms. So, for instance, he analyzed anger as a state caused by a belief that one has been insulted. It is directed at the perpetrator, and it is diminished by an apology or remedy. It does not occur if one is treated justly. This program of analyzing the meaning of emotion terms was continued by Spinoza.

In this cognitive tradition, the work which marks the modern starting point is that of Frédéric Paulhan, who in 1887 argued that emotions occur when there is an interruption of an ongoing activity or tendency. An emotion then produces mental disturbance which entirely occupies conscious attention. This has become known as the conflict theory because emotions are seen as arising either with conflicts between a goal and an unexpected outcome, or when one goal conflicts with another.

EMOTIONS IN THE EARLY DAYS OF COGNITIVE PSYCHOLOGY

From around 1960 cognitive psychologists began to realize that, in computation, interruptions of one process by another are needed where resources are limited and where there are multiple goals. Systems must allow interruptions and establish goal priorities. These issues are coextensive with those of emotions in humans. Such arguments implied that we can take steps toward understanding emotions by considering the design of cognitive systems, and by analyzing emotions in terms of theories of action.

During the 1960s, also, Schachter and Singer (1962) published a paper which is the most influential recent research on emotions. They gave injections of adrenalin which produced arousal. If their subjects had no other explanation for the arousal produced by the adrenalin, they attributed it to the social context in which it occurred. So arousal in a context of light-hearted social interaction was experienced as happiness, and where frustrating and intrusive things were going on it was experienced as anger. An emotion, according to this idea, has two components, a non-cognitive, undifferentiated arousal – not very different from the kind of input postulated by James and Cannon – together with a cognitive attribution of the cause of the arousal. At one stroke Schachter and Singer united the biological, cognitive, and social-psychological traditions. They also gave a theoretical basis for understanding psychosomatic interactions which has still not been much improved upon.

The implications of Schachter and Singer's theory of misattributing the causes of arousal have been only partly supported empirically, but their idea has provided foundations for cognitive theory (see Mandler, 1984). When an event interrupts an ongoing plan, arousal occurs. The evaluation of the event gives rise to the emotion and prompts the next phase of action.

Current cognitive-psychological interest in emotions is in three main areas: cognitive theories of emotions as evaluations of circumstances, interactions of emotions with memory and thinking, and linguistic analyses of inferences that can be made about emotions.

COGNITIVE THEORIES AND EVIDENCE OF EMOTIONS AS EVALUATIONS

Since the 1960s there has been growing interest in theories of emotions as evaluations of events. The most comprehensive review of empirical evidence in this area, together with a scholarly discussion of the kind of cognitive theory that can account for it, is Frijda's (1986) book.

Frijda's type of theory now has rather general agreement. It is that we can think of emotions as occurring when events are evaluated in relation to a person's important goals – concerns, as he calls them. An emotion is a process that typically starts with an eliciting event. This is perceived and coded, and it is then appraised in relation to concerns. Its significance is assessed in terms of priorities and what can be done about it. Readiness for action occurs, which may be accompanied by physiological changes such as increasing the heart rate. According to Frijda, then, readiness is the core of an emotion. It may issue in actual actions, including emotional expressions.

Emotions differ in the kinds of appraisals and evaluations that are made. For example, if an event occurs that frustrates an important goal, and you judge that it was deliberately caused by someone who had no right to do it, and that you might be able to obtain some redress – then you are likely to feel anger. But if you judge that the event was an accident, or if it is impossible to do anything about it, then anger is less likely.

Of course, this is close to the kind of analysis that Aristotle gave. What has happened recently is that there is now substantial empirical evidence drawn from a range of psychological methods, in different cultures, on adults and children, that emotions do indeed occur like this.

It is now accepted that, despite Schachter and Singer's use of adrenalin to cause arousal, emotions are psychological. Whereas physical exposure of a person to a cold atmosphere has reliable bodily effects of making that person feel cold and shiver, emotions do not occur purely as a result of physical events. They typically occur because of evaluations of events in relation to a person's individual concerns and expectations. For instance, the same physical pattern of pressure of a hand on the skin could elicit a feeling of happiness, of anger, or of disgust, depending on who was doing the touching and how its recipient evaluated it.

A variation on this type of cognitive theory, which relates more closely to issues raised by Darwin, is due to Oatley and Johnson-Laird (1987) who argue that in mammalian life there is a small number of basic types of evaluation of event in relation to goals. These evaluations produce a set of basic emotions, corresponding to (a) happiness, (b) sadness, (c) anger, (d) fear, and (e) disgust. These five types of emotion occur when there is: (a) achievement of subgoals, (b) loss of a goal, (c) frustration of a plan or goal by another person, (d) conflict of goals including conflict with a self-preservation goal, and (e) perception that something is noxious or toxic.

These emotions depend on each of our goals being monitored whether they are contributing to an ongoing plan or not. From the monitoring processes simple signals are sent out whenever progress toward any significant goal changes substantially, for better or worse. These signals have no propositional structure, but each tends to set the cognitive system into a mode which, during evolution, has been selected as appropriate to whatever juncture (of types a to e) has been detected. There may be more than five of these general modes. Determining the number will depend on physiological and cross-cultural evidence.

The different modes are not equivalent to the general arousal postulated by Schachter and Singer. Rather, happiness, sadness, anger, fear, and disgust are physiologically distinguishable, as shown by Ekman, Levenson, and Friesen (1983). However, as with Schachter's theory, Oatley and Johnson-Laird postulate that the non-propositional part of the emotion is typically accompanied by propositional information about what caused it, about whom it concerns, and so on. This theory, moreover, resolves the difficulty of most conflict theories in explaining happiness. Happiness occurs when subgoals in a sequence of actions are being achieved, with problems that arise being solved from available resources, and when other goals do not conflict or distract.

Emotions are not just vestiges. They maintain their importance in human cognition because action is typically influenced by many simultaneous goals. Human action takes place without perfect mental models of the world, and often involves coordination with other people. Since, therefore, the world is not entirely predictable, and since conflicting goals cannot always be reconciled either within ourselves or between people, our action can hardly ever be perfectly rational. So to argue that emotions are irrational, as Plato did, misses an important point: rational solutions to problems of human action are only occasionally possible. Emotions function to help manage the vicissitudes of action in a world that can only be very imperfectly known. We detect junctures at which the unexpected happens or when progress toward any of our goals changes significantly. At such points emotions make the system ready in a certain kind of way, prompting us towards the next phase of action, and communicating nonverbally to others nearby. Thus, if a subgoal is achieved, we move happily towards the next phase of action. If some danger is detected, the current plan is interrupted, checks are made anxiously on what had been done, the environment is scanned, escape or other actions to gain safety are prepared. As Oatley and Johnson-Laird put it, the function of emotions is to communicate these changes in readiness to ourselves and to others.

Emotions have evolved, according to this argument, because achieving subgoals, suffering losses, detecting conflicts of goals, and so on recur frequently in the life of mammals. Each of these general junctures is recognizable, and it has been cognitively efficient for a general readiness appropriate to each of these junctures to be available, so that it can be invoked along with the default plans and interpersonal communications that are stored in association with it. These default plans are either those that have proved successful in evolution and have been genetically transmitted, or they are habits acquired in individual development.

If we were to analyze each individual

circumstance of subgoal achievement, loss, goal conflict, and so on only by thinking about it, we would take too long, and would be too prone to errors. We would often not have the necessary evidence for good solutions. Emotions as automatic evaluations of recurring classes of basic evaluations, each prompting an appropriate readiness to act, has proved advantageous in evolution, not because emotions offer perfect solutions – there is often no perfect solution in such circumstances. They have been selected, presumably, because on average the genetically stored programs and individually acquired habits have been more successful than other kinds of solution.

We humans are not ants, biological machines emitting fixed action patterns in response to particular stimuli. Nor are we gods who have complete knowledge of the consequences of all actions and power to control all outcomes. We are somewhere in between. For us there is a substantial problem: we have imperfect mental models and limited resources, although our own plans do have some of the effects we aim for. We need, therefore, a means for managing those junctures in which all has not gone quite as expected. For such beings, readiness and default plans must be invoked quickly and without thinking, to prompt the next phase of action when a change of evaluation has occurred. Then, where something has gone wrong, the readiness to act must be followed by longer-lasting mental preoccupation in which we can concentrate on some cognitive reprograming. These are indeed the properties of emotions, which are part of the biological-cognitive solution to these problems of goal and plan management.

INTERACTIONS OF EMOTIONS WITH MEMORY AND THINKING

A second area of active cognitive interest is in the effects that emotions have on memory and other psychological functions. Bower's (e.g. 1981) work has been influential: he and his colleagues did a series of experiments in which happy or sad moods were induced by hypnosis (*see* FORGETTING). When recalling a list in the same mood as that in which they had learned it, subjects recalled more words than when in the opposite mood (*see* STATE-DEPENDENT MEMORY).

Effects of mood have now been found using methods other than hypnosis, and there is now a wide range of evidence on this issue, collected in many different types of experiment. Mood affects attention, problem solving, imagery, free associations, social perceptions, and response to stories. And as well as memory for laboratory tasks, autobiographical events are affected by mood. Remembered events that are congruent with mood during recall come selectively to mind.

These results have aroused clinical interest, since it has been shown that mood-congruent ideas come to the minds of patients with clinical depression or anxiety. So when patients are sad or anxious, sad or anxious thoughts come to their minds, and these then reinforce their distressed moods (*see* MOODS DISORDERS AND COGNITION). Cognitive therapists, therefore, have become interested in cutting into this self-reinforcing cycle of dysphoria (*see* COGNITIVE THERAPY). Cognitive therapists also share the Platonic distrust of emotions: their favored way of cutting into the cycles of depression and anxiety is a version of the ancient Stoic idea that thinking about things in certain ways can minimize emotions. Again, there have been modern additions to this classical idea: there is now convincing evidence that cognitive therapy is more effective than other forms of therapy, including drugs, for alleviating depression, and that it has effects of a magnitude comparable to drugs for anxiety states.

ANALYSES OF THE LANGUAGE OF EMOTIONS

The third area in which there has been considerable recent research has been in the language of emotions. Two kinds of work have recently become important. First, there has been continuation of the work begun by Aristotle on componential analyses of emotion terms.

Emotions are mental states to be distinguished from states that are not primarily mental, like pain or sleepiness. Many terms imply knowledge of emotions, embedded in folk theories that support the semantics of ordinary language (see Johnson-Laird, 1988). Thus, in English, many emotion terms, perhaps the majority, indicate both a kind of emotion and indicate that something elicited it or that it has effects. So to use the term "happy" means merely that I have a particular kind of emotion. But to use the term "glad" indicates that I also know that something caused my happiness. To say correctly that someone is jealous refers to a basic feeling of anger or disgust, and also to a complex social situation involving the possibility of losing a loved person to another, and to the kinds of actions that might occur.

Other research has implicated the idea of scripts, sequences of events occurring in a predictable order (*see* SCHEMATA). Since the emotion process runs through a sequence of cognitive events, some researchers have proposed that it has properties of a script. The argument is that terms such as happiness, anger, anxiety, and so on may refer to this general script, in a prototypical way. Any given emotion term may thus be thought of as indicating a more or less good exemplar of a prototypical emotion. This type of proposal is at variance with componential analyses, and the question of how best to understand emotion terms is controversial.

Terms for emotions occur in all languages so far studied, though some languages have only a few such terms, and some have no generic term for "emotion." Not all cultures perceive emotions primarily as subjective experiences (see Lutz, 1988). Some focus on their interpersonal effects, and languages reflect these differences. Interpersonal issues are present also, although perhaps less obviously, in European and American culture. If the meaning of emotion terms is concerned with semantics and the meaning of individual experiences, these interpersonal effects can be thought of as concerned with pragmatics and on effects on others communicated by facial and other expressions. So, for instance, sadness tends to prompt others to help. Anger is directed toward someone with an intention of redress and is often the opening phase of renegotiation in a relationship.

Because meanings and interpersonal implications of emotions are important to humans, they are crucial for any understanding of narrative (see, for example, Lehnert & Vine, 1987). Narratives of many kinds tend to turn around incidents in which emotions occur – often an emotion brings an episode to a close, and is followed by a new episode. Emotion words are informationally rich, and it is possible to make inferences about story characters, particularly about their goals and plans, from the emotions that the storyteller describes. Thus, for computational understanding of narratives, these kinds of inferences must be available. They must be made from goals and plans to the likely emotions of characters in the narrative, and also from emotion terms to implications for goals and plans. For these reasons, understanding the semantics and pragmatics of emotions will be necessary for computational understanding of narrative.

CONCLUSION

From a state in which understanding emotions seemed to have little part to play in cognitive psychology, research on emotions has become important, as is appropriate to the role of these states in managing problems of acting in the ordinary world with multiple goals and imperfect knowledge.

BIBLIOGRAPHY

Bower, G. H. (1981). Mood and memory. *American Psychologist, 36,* 129–48.

Ekman, P., Levenson, R. W., & Friesen, W. V. (1983). Autonomic nervous activity distinguishes among emotions. *Science, 221,* 1208–10.

Frijda, N. H. (1986). *The emotions.* Cambridge: Cambridge University Press.

Johnson-Laird, P. N. (1988). *The computer and the mind: An introduction to cognitive science.* Cambridge, Mass.: Harvard University Press; and London: Fontana.

Lehnert, W., & Vine, E. W. (1987). The role of affect in narrative structure. *Cognition and Emotion, 1,* 299–322; reprinted in Oatley, K. (Ed.), *Cognitive science and the understanding of emotions.* Hillsdale, NJ: Erlbaum, 1988.

Lutz, C. (1988). Ethnographic perspectives on the emotion lexicon. In V. Hamilton, G. H. Bower, & N. H. Frijda (Eds), *Cognitive perspec-*

tives on emotion and motivation. The Hague: Nijhoff.

Mandler, G. (1984). *Mind and body: Psychology of emotions and stress*. New York: Norton.

Oatley, K., & Johnson-Laird, P. N. (1987). Towards a cognitive theory of emotions. *Cognition and Emotion*, *1*, 29–50.

Schachter, S., & Singer, J. E. (1962). Cognitive, social and physiological determinants of emotional state. *Psychological Review*, *63*, 379–99.

KEITH OATLEY

encoding operations in memory This phrase denotes cognitive activities that accompany the perception of a to-be-remembered item or event, thereby influencing the properties of the resulting memory trace.

A major empirical problem in laboratory research on memory has always been that of the identification of variables and factors that influence the "goodness" of memory performance, and the measurement of their effects. A major theoretical problem has concerned the determination of the relations between these variables and factors on the one hand, and the hypothetical component processes of learning and memory on the other. The conceptualization of an act of remembering as consisting of three successive processing stages – encoding, storage, and retrieval – has guided this theoretical enterprise in the recent past (*see* MEMORY). Thus, memory phenomena can be identified as "encoding effects," "storage effects," or "retrieval effects." When other variables are held constant in an experiment, and only the nature of retrieval cues is varied, the observed differences in memory performance can be classified as reflecting retrieval effects. When encoding and retrieval conditions are held constant, and the length and activities of the interval between encoding and retrieval are varied, the observed differences can be said to reflect storage effects. When the experimental manipulations performed at encoding produce differences in subsequent memory performance, we speak of encoding effects.

It is well known that variables such as study time, the number of repetitions, and the intention to learn facilitate subsequent perform-ance. In the early days of the study of learning and memory, theorists even talked about corresponding "laws," such as the law of frequency and the law of recency. More recently, however, other important determinants of the goodness of encoding have been identified. The major concept in this later work is that of the encoding operation. Many findings have been reported in the literature that attest to the important role that encoding operations play in memory. Much of this work is subsumed under the concept of LEVELS OF PROCESSING.

In experimental situations, different kinds of encoding operations are induced by instructions, by manipulating the context of the to-be-remembered items, through orienting tasks, or combinations of these. Variations in encoding operations lead to differences in recall or recognition (*see* RECALL; RECOGNITION MEMORY). Thus, for example, experimental subjects can be asked to classify words, at the time of study, as belonging or not belonging to a particular category, versus just copying the words. Regardless of whether the subjects know that their retention of the words is going to be tested, they recall a larger proportion of classified words than copied words. Thus, classification is a more effective encoding operation than copying. Similarly, making judgements about the pleasantness of words is a more effective encoding operation than making judgements about the presence or absence of certain letters in the words. Instructions to subjects designed to induce particular encoding operations may also lead to more effective encoding, and hence to enhanced recall or recognition, than do general instructions to "learn" the words.

Large differences in both recall and recognition, attributable to different encoding operations, have been found in many experiments (e.g. Hyde & Jenkins, 1969; Craik & Tulving, 1975). In these experiments, all other conditions are held constant, and only the encoding operations are varied. For example, subjects may be asked to make judgements about a given word's appearance (e.g. "Is it typed in lower-case letters?"), its sound (e.g. "Does it rhyme with 'park'?"), or its meaning (e.g. "Is it a kind of vehicle?"). Subjects would respond to each question either affirmatively or negatively.

The results of such experiments show that both recall and recognition of the studied items vary with the type of encoding operation and response category at the time of study. Semantic judgements are more effective than phonemic judgements which in turn are more effective than graphemic ones; also for the first two kinds of judgements, encoding questions requiring affirmative responses are more effective than those requiring negative ones. The superiority of semantic encoding is regularly found in most situations. But the fact that recognition is higher for semantic questions answered affirmatively than for those answered negatively suggests that semantic encoding operations can be further analyzed into differentially effective classes.

Such further analysis shows that different kinds of semantic encoding operations can also vary in effectiveness. In one experiment, for example (Mathews, 1977), people were presented with word triplets (e.g. "lion," "whale," "mammal"; or "lion," "whale," "circus"; or "lion," "whale," "metal") and were asked to judge whether both, one, or none of the first *two* words were semantically related to the third. All subjects were subsequently given one of the two first words from the triplet as a cue (e.g. "lion") and asked to recall the other one (here, "whale"). The results showed that the probability of such cued recall varied greatly – over a range of 0.10 to 0.68 – with the number of semantic relations in the study triplet.

The effects of many different encoding operations have been reliably documented in the literature, using such standard measures of memory performance as free recall and recognition. It is generally assumed that encoding operations play an important role in memory even when they are not specifically manipulated, and even when the rememberer is not consciously aware of how any particular event has been encoded. It is also known that the exact effects of any encoding operation depend on the nature of retrieval information available to the learner at the time of retrieval. These effects are subsumed under the rubric of the ENCODING SPECIFICITY PRINCIPLE.

BIBLIOGRAPHY

Craik, F. I. M., & Tulving, E. (1975). Depth of processing and the retention of words in episodic memory. *Journal of Experimental Psychology: General, 104*, 268–94.

Hyde, T. S., & Jenkins, J. J. (1969). Differential effects of incidental tasks on the organization of recall of a list of highly associated words. *Journal of Experimental Psychology, 82*, 472–81.

Mathews, R. C. (1977). Semantic judgments as encoding operations: The effects of attention to particular semantic categories on the usefulness of interitem relations in recall. *Journal of Experimental Psychology: Human Learning and Memory, 3*, 160–73.

ENDEL TULVING

encoding specificity principle A general statement regarding the relation between encoding and retrieval conditions necessary for the remembering of an item or event: the effectiveness of encoding operations depends on retrieval cues, and the potency of the cues varies with encoding operations.

How well a person remembers an event or a fact depends on two critical factors: (1) the initial encoding operations and the resulting memory trace, and (2) the subsequent retrieval environment or retrieval cues (*see* ENCODING OPERATIONS IN MEMORY; FORGETTING; RECALL; RECOGNITION MEMORY). The encoding specificity principle is a general theoretical statement regarding the relation of these two determinants of remembering. It holds that the specific encoding operations performed on what is perceived determine what is stored in memory, and what is stored determines what retrieval cues are effective in providing access to what is stored (Tulving & Thomson, 1973, p. 369).

It has been known for a long time that the recall and recognition of items of presented information depend greatly on the *properties* of these items in the "permanent memory store," properties such as meaningfulness, concreteness, imaginability, and general familiarity. Another important class of determinants of memorability has also been known for a long time, namely conditions of learning and retention. It comprises variables such as the intention to learn on the part of the learner, the frequency and recency of presentation of the to-be-remembered material, the length of the retention interval, and the amount of proactive and retroactive interference present in the situation (*see* PROACTIVE INTERFERENCE; RETROACTIVE INTERFERENCE). Finally, it is commonplace that memory performance may vary greatly with the conditions of retrieval, defined by variables such as the presence or absence of retrieval cues and their character-istics. A good deal of experimental evidence has been accumulated since Hermann Ebbinghaus in support of all of these ideas.

More recent research, however, has shown that it is quite possible to hold constant all of these "classical" learning and retention vari-ables, and still observe large differences in how well the studied material is recalled or recognized. Such differences in memory per-formance come about as a consequence of dif-ferences in the *relation* between the encoding operations performed at study and the cues available at retrieval. Thus, how effective a given encoding operation is depends on the nature of the cues given to the rememberer later on. Conversely, the effectiveness of a cue depends on the nature of encoding operations performed earlier, at the time of study.

Consider two illustrative experimental facts. First, it can be readily shown that a strong semantic association exists between the words "king" and "queen." But whether or not "king" as a cue word facilitates recall of the previously studied target word "queen" depends greatly on the specific encoding operations performed on the word "queen" at the time of study. For instance, if the subject sees the target word "queen" as a member of a pair of words, such as "lady"–"queen," and encodes "queen" in relation to "lady," the presentation of the cue word "king" at time of retrieval does not facilitate recall of "queen" when compared with recall in the absence of any specific cues. Second, when a person has heard a sentence such as "The man tuned the piano," the cue "nice sound" is quite effective in helping him to recall "piano" whereas the cue "something heavy" helps little. Con-versely, when the originally heard sentence is "The men lifted the piano," "something

heavy" is an excellent cue whereas "nice sound" is not (Barclay, Bransford, Franks, McCarrell, & Nitsch, 1974). This interaction between encoding and retrieval conditions occurs despite the fact that in the learner's semantic memory the "piano" that can be tuned and the "piano" that can be lifted are believed to be represented by the same code (*see* SEMANTIC MEMORY).

These kinds of experimental facts – show-ing that the specific form of encoding affects the potency of cues, and that the potency of cues depends on the specific encoding opera-tions performed on the item at time of study – are subsumed under the general concept of the encoding specificity principle.

A particularly striking manifestation of the encoding specificity principle is given by the fact that under certain conditions people can-not identify previously seen words as such, although they can produce the same words when the retrieval cues previously associated with the words are provided. Relevant research is known under the rubric of "recog-nition failure of recallable words" (Tulving & Thomson, 1973; Flexser & Tulving, 1978). It has also been shown (Nilsson, Law, & Tulv-ing, 1987) that even unique names of famous people – such as George Washington, Sig-mund Freud, and Florence Nightingale – exhibit recognition failure. Subjects do not recognize some of these names as those they had seen in a previously presented list, but they can recall them in response to the de-scriptive phrases that had accompanied the to-be-remembered names at study (e.g. "He was the first of a long line, but the only one on horseback" – George Washington). Thus, under special conditions the typical superiority of recognition over recall can be reversed: recall can succeed where recognition fails (*see* RECALL; RECOGNITION MEMORY). Such a reversal can be explained in terms of the encoding specificity principle.

Although initially the encoding specificity principle was assumed to hold only for EPI-SODIC MEMORY tasks (Tulving & Thomson, 1973), subsequent research has suggested that it also characterizes the relation between what is stored and what can be retrieved from semantic memory. The domain of research on encoding specificity has also been referred to as research on "encoding/retrieval interactions." An early version of the same general idea that is represented by encoding specificity was known as the "principle of reinstatement of stimulating conditions." It held that retrieval succeeds to the extent that stimulating conditions present at study are reinstated at the time of attempted retrieval (Hollingworth, 1928). An idea essentially identical with encoding specificity has been proposed and is known under the label of "transfer appropriate processing" (Morris, Bransford, & Franks, 1977). Like encoding specificity, it emphasizes the importance of active processing and processes at study and test, rather than stimulating conditions.

BIBLIOGRAPHY

Barclay, J. R., Bransford, J. D., Franks, J. J., McCarrell, N. S., & Nitsch, K. (1974). Comprehension and semantic flexibility. *Journal of Verbal Learning and Verbal Behavior, 13,* 471–81.

Flexser, A. J., & Tulving, E. (1978). Retrieval independence in recognition and recall. *Psychological Review, 85,* 153–71.

Hollingworth, H. L. (1928). *Psychology: Its facts and principles.* New York: Appleton.

Morris, C. D., Bransford, J. D., & Franks, J. J. (1977). Levels of processing versus transfer appropriate processing. *Journal of Verbal Learning and Verbal Behavior, 16,* 519–34.

Nilsson, L.-G., Law, J., & Tulving, E. (1987). Recognition failure of recallable unique names: Evidence for an empirical law of memory and learning. *Journal of Experimental Psychology: Learning, Memory, and Cognition, 14,* 266–77.

Tulving, E., & Thomson, D. M. (1973). Encoding specificity and retrieval processes in episodic memory. *Psychological Review, 80,* 352–73.

ENDEL TULVING

episodic memory The kind of memory that renders possible the conscious recollection of personal happenings and events dated in the rememberer's past. The concept has undergone considerable changes since its introduction (Tulving, 1972) and is now used in different senses by different writers and in different contexts. Two principal senses of the term are discussed here.

The first one, almost universally accepted now, is that of episodic memory as a type of memory performance. Episodic memory in this sense refers to the acquisition of symbolically representable information on one occasion and its reproduction on a subsequent occasion. The prototypical laboratory experiment, in which subjects are exposed to a collection of verbal items and then tested for their knowledge of some aspect of what they perceived, can be regarded an episodic memory experiment in this first sense of the term: the subjects' recollection of miniature laboratory events from their personal past is the object of interest.

In an episodic memory experiment, the subject is given a task consisting of two parts: (1) she or he observes or studies a set of materials presented by the experimenter, and (2) takes a test for her or his knowledge of the studied material. A large number of different test questions has been used, including the following: (1) What were the items in the study set or list? (free recall task). (2) In what order were they presented? (serial recall, or serial reproduction, task). (3) What item appeared together with Item X? (paired-associate task). (4) What item in the study list was the name of a four-legged animal? (cued recall task). (5) Did Item X appear in the study set? (yes/no recognition task). (6) Which of these two items, X or Y, appeared in the study set? (two-alternative forced choice recognition). (7) Which of these two items, X or Y, appeared earlier in the study list? (relative recency judgement) (*see* RECALL; RECOGNITION MEMORY). Each of these questions is designed to elicit the subject's recollection of an event that the subject has personally observed or witnessed. Each question, therefore, can be paraphrased in these terms; for example: Which items do *you* remember *seeing* in the list? Do *you* remember *hearing* Word X in the list? Which of these two items, X or Y, did *you encounter* earlier in the list? – hence the designation of these tasks as episodic memory tasks.

In the first sense, much of the research on verbal learning and memory that has been carried out in psychological laboratories since Hermann Ebbinghaus could be classified as research on episodic memory. Different measures of memory performance in this kind of research – such as free recall, cued recall, and recognition – can be regarded as measures of episodic memory. They reflect the extent to which the learner has retained the information that was presented during a particular study episode. As a result of many decades of research, the effect of many variables on episodic recall and recognition is now known. Major determinants of the accuracy of reproduction of materials studied in episodic memory experiments include ENCODING OPERATIONS IN MEMORY and relations between encoding and retrieval conditions subsumed under the ENCODING SPECIFICITY PRINCIPLE. An explanation of the findings and phenomena of episodic memory in terms of underlying psychological processes has been the major objective of many cognitive theories of memory.

Only a small part of human memory is episodic. Most of the knowledge that people learn, retain, and make use of in the course of their daily lives has to do with things other than the recollection of particular personal events. The ability to comprehend and speak one or more languages, to read, to write, to recognize objects in the environment, to know their properties and function, to know how to classify these objects into categories according to criteria such as their nature or value, the ability to answer questions about geography or history, the ability to appreciate literature or art, to understand problems of economy and politics, and a myriad other skills and knowledges, have developed through learning and depend on memory. But they do not entail the remembering of particular occasions from one's past. They represent capabilities other than episodic memory.

The second sense of the term "episodic memory" is that of a hypothetical memory system that differs from two other major hypothetical memory systems, SEMANTIC MEMORY and procedural memory (see DECLARATIVE AND PROCEDURAL KNOWLEDGE; MEMORY SYSTEMS). According to the hypothesis, the ability of the individual to *remember* personally

experienced past events – that is, to become consciously aware again of a previous experience – is possible only by virtue of an intact brain system specialized for that purpose. The retrieval of a great variety of general information about the world, including some purely factual information about one's own past, can be accomplished by the semantic memory system alone, but such retrieval, according to the current hypothesis, differs from episodic remembering in terms of the brain mechanisms that subserve it, in terms of operating principles, and in terms of the qualitative nature of the accompanying conscious experience.

The postulation of episodic memory as a separable memory system is part of the enterprise of the *classification* of natural phenomena of memory; it does not imply any hypotheses concerning the processes underlying such phenomena in the specified domain. The evidence in support of such a separable system is still fragmentary, and the whole issue is being widely debated. The principal observations of interest have been provided by the study of brain-damaged patients suffering from AMNESIA. It has been observed that amnesic patients are capable of acquiring and retaining *some* new general factual information even though they are completely incapable of remembering the learning episodes or any other recent happenings in their lives. For instance, even the world's best known and most thoroughly studied amnesic patient HM (q.v.) can perform quite adequately in an episodic (in the first sense of the term) picture recognition task, displaying a forgetting rate indistinguishable from that of normal control subjects, provided that he is given a great deal of study time (Freed, Corkin, & Cohen, 1987). But no amount of "study time" will enable him to remember that he participated in such a recognition experiment. Such a dissociation between the ability to identify recently seen pictures and the ability to remember equally recent personal happenings can be seen as supportive of the hypothesis of a distinct episodic memory system.

Another kind of evidence is that of "source amnesia": amnesic patients can recall recently learned facts as well as normal people can, if the retention intervals for the two groups are appropriately adjusted, but they cannot recollect the learning episode as such nearly as well as normal subjects do (Shimamura & Squire, 1987).

Although the two senses of episodic memory – type of memory performance and type of memory system – are related, they cannot be equated. On the one hand, an individual's ability to reproduce material presented in an episodic memory task, such as the recall of a list of words, obviously depends on his or her episodic memory system. On the other hand, however, evidence now exists that even people without functioning episodic systems, such as HM and other densely amnesic patients, can perform at higher than chance levels in episodic memory tasks. Moreover, there are good reasons to believe that the performance of normal subjects, too, on episodic memory tasks depends not only on their episodic memory system, but also on some other system. For instance, many students of memory now accept the idea that episodic (in the first sense) *recognition* of previously studied items involves two different sets of processes, one of which can be hypothetically identified with episodic retrieval of information about the study episode, and the other with processes that seem to be related to those underlying implicit memory (Mandler, 1980) (*see* IMPLICIT AND EXPLICIT MEMORY).

BIBLIOGRAPHY

Freed, D. M., Corkin, S., & Cohen, N. J. (1987). Forgetting in H. M.: A second look. *Neuropsychologia, 25*, 461–71.
Mandler, G. (1980). Recognizing: The judgment of previous occurrence. *Psychological Review, 87*, 252–71.
Shimamura, A. P., & Squire, L. R. (1987). A neuropsychological study of fact learning and source amnesia. *Journal of Experimental Psychology: Learning, Memory, and Cognition, 13*, 464–74.
Tulving, E. (1972). Episodic and semantic memory. In E. Tulving & W. Donaldson (Eds), *Organization of memory* (pp. 381–403). New York: Academic Press.

ENDEL TULVING

ergonomics *See* HUMAN FACTORS.

expertise Attempts to develop a scientific account of the nature of expertise have recently produced an integrated body of results. In the late 1960s and early 1970s, efforts to describe and simulate complex reasoning in cognitive science and ARTIFICIAL INTELLIGENCE research demonstrated that models of the well defined rule systems of symbolic logic or chess and powerful heuristics or general problem-solving processes did not capture the speed and insightfulness of human experts' performance. Simulations of chess playing, which were key in this work, showed that a machine with a knowledge base of chess rules, search heuristics, and a nearly unlimited capability to search for the best moves was slow and ineffective by comparison to a proficient chessplayer. Studies of grand masters' performances indicated that their strategies depended on knowledge of an array of patterns more diverse than even they realized and that this knowledge somehow yielded rapid perception of the ramifications of a chess board's layout (Chase & Simon, 1973; de Groot, 1978) (*see* PATTERN PERCEPTION).

As research on other forms of performance, particularly in semantic information processing and symbolic integration tasks, sharpened the sense that the apparently intuitive understanding displayed in expertise rests on extensive specialized knowledge, cognitive science and artificial intelligence became increasingly occupied with exploring knowledge's role in problem solving (Feigenbaum, 1989). It became clear that the fundamental problem in accounting for expert performance was representing specific structured knowledge rather than the domain-independent heuristics that interact with it. This shift from a generalized power-based to a knowledge-based paradigm encouraged the design of knowledge engineering approaches; major empirical efforts were redirected to assay competence through sophisticated task analyses. Studies of experts' PROBLEM SOLVING, in domains ranging from physics, medical diagnosis, computer programing, skilled memory, and mental calculation, to taxi driving and typing, produced, in less than two decades, generalizable findings that permit characterization of expertise along well defined lines (Chi, Glaser, & Farr, 1988).

STRUCTURED, PRINCIPLED KNOWLEDGE

As competence is attained, elements of knowledge become well integrated, so that proficient individuals store coherent chunks of information in memory (*see* CHUNKING). Through experience, newer elements are linked to established knowledge structures so that the expert rapidly retrieves meaningful patterns in working through problems. Where well articulated principles or laws obtain, say in physics or geometry, the influence of organized knowledge on thinking is readily apparent. Experts perceive a problem as exemplifying an underlying principle that subsumes the problem's givens or surface features. Asked to sort problems in terms of the information needed to solve them, the experienced physicist groups those involving Newton's second law or the conservation of energy, whereas the novice represents them as spring problems or inclined plane problems, categories that refer to objects in the problems but that require different principles for solution (Chi, Feltovich, & Glaser, 1981).

PROCEDURALIZED KNOWLEDGE

With experience and practice in their domains, the experts' declarative or propositional knowledge becomes bound to conditions of applicability and procedures for use (*see* DECLARATIVE AND PROCEDURAL KNOWLEDGE). Indeed, although experts and novices may be equally competent at recalling a principle, a rule, or a specialized vocabulary, novices seldom recognize where such knowledge applies and what procedures to use in implementing it. In this sense, the experts' knowledge has become functional and compiled in a condition-action form (Anderson, 1983); knowing what and knowing how are usually simultaneous events, as the findings

from the physics problem classification task suggest.

SKILLED MEMORY

Evidence suggests that experts and novices have similar memory storage and retrieval capacities. At first glance, therefore, the sheer extent of the knowledge entailed in expertise might seem an impediment to quick thinking. In expert performance, however, the large domain-specific knowledge base is drawn upon in a skilled manner that reduces the role of memory search and general cognitive processing. Through extensive practice in their domains, experts develop capacity to use long-term memory in a way that resembles short-term memory use (*see* LONG-TERM MEMORY; SHORT-TERM MEMORY, RETRIEVAL FROM): because their knowledge is stored in conditionalized procedural form, experts' encoding processes circumvent the usual limits of short-term memory and their retrieval processes sharply to reduce the time-consuming search typical of long-term memory use (Chase & Ericsson, 1982).

AUTOMATICITY

Experts' swift, accurate performance is the result not only of skilled memory, but another benefit of practice as well: automaticity in accomplishing certain aspects of a task. In the development of proficiency with attention-demanding complex tasks, some component skills must become automatic, so that conscious processing capacity can be devoted to reasoning and decision making with minimal interference in the overall performance (Shiffrin & Schneider, 1977) (*see* AUTOMATIC PROCESSING). Expert readers, for example, automatically decode the phonetic units in which words and sentences appear, so conscious processing capacity is available for comprehending meaning and for reflective thought. Studies of the development of skill in radiologists and air traffic controllers are even more illuminating; proficient performance requires intense concentration on pattern interpretation, as well as automaticity with certain perceptual tasks.

EFFECTIVE PROBLEM REPRESENTATION

Although experts' performances are marked by a speed that their access to knowledge and their automaticity with certain task components afford, they often spend extended time in initial analysis of a problem. In this phase, experts qualitatively assess the nature of the problem, building a mental model (*see* MENTAL MODELS) or representation from which they can make inferences and add constraints to reduce the problem space. By contrast, novices plunge immediately into applying equations or otherwise getting on with the job (Chi, Glaser, & Farr, 1988).

The utility of initial representation in adding constraints to a problem can be seen clearly in domains like history or political science, where well articulated principles or laws do not obtain. In the absence of principles that imply direct paths to solution, elaborations of the problem situation can focus and frame the problem and thereby delineate approaches to solutions.

STRONG SELF-REGULATORY SKILLS

Through their extensive experience, experts develop a critical set of self-regulatory or metacognitive skills, which control their performances (*see* METACOGNITION). As they become informed and accomplished thinkers in their fields, they learn to monitor their problem solving by predicting the difficulty of problems, allocating time appropriately, noting their errors or failures to comprehend, and checking questionable solutions (Larkin, McDermott, Simon, & Simon, 1980). It is likely that, when confronted with novel problems or problems in domains where their knowledge is slight, their facility with these metacognitive skills gives experts an edge. They may reason by envisioning analogies to familiar situations (*see* ANALOGIES), by considering extreme cases of a problem's essential features, or by decomposing a problem into a structured set of subproblems. This use of general reasoning skills identifies potential links with experts' structured knowledge.

The understanding of expertise that has emerged since the early 1970s has allowed the

design of artificial intelligence systems that can diagnose and prescribe the best antibiotic for treating infectious diseases, test pulmonary functions, or select areas for geological exploration with an effectiveness that resembles that of human experts. Awareness that structured knowledge has a pervasive influence on tacit aspects of performance has driven research that now guides the simulation of massive knowledge bases and of their efficient use (Duda & Shortliffe, 1983). The hypothesis proffered two decades ago that structured knowledge is the source of power in expert thinking is now a central principle in cognitive science and artificial intelligence; it shapes decisions about empirical and theoretical research on cognition, as well as about prospects for intelligent computer systems.

As deeper understanding of human mental capabilities is achieved, analyses of the competences involved in expertise and models of expert performance will have important implications for new theories of learning. Detailed accounts have yet to appear of the interplay, over extended periods of learning and experience, between increasing levels of knowledge-derived competence and effective use of the processes and heuristics of "general" intelligence. But the body of results and new research techniques that have emerged can provide the basis for study of the changes in performance that a mature cognitive science must explain.

BIBLIOGRAPHY

Anderson, J. R. (1983). *The architecture of cognition*. Cambridge, Mass.: Harvard University Press.

Chase, W. G., & Ericsson, K. A. (1982). Skill and working memory. In G. Bower (Ed.), *The psychology of learning and motivation* (Vol. 16). Hillsdale, NJ: Erlbaum.

Chase, W. G. & Simon, H. A. (1973). Perception in chess. *Cognitive Psychology, 4,* 55–81.

Chi, M. T. H., Feltovich, P. J., & Glaser, R. (1981). Categorization and representation of physics problems by experts and novices. *Cognitive Science, 5,* 121–5.

Chi, M. T. H., Glaser, R., & Farr, M. (Eds) (1988). *The nature of expertise*. Hillsdale, NJ: Erlbaum.

deGroot, A. D. (1978). *Thought and choice in chess* (2nd edn). The Hague: Mouton. (Originally published 1965)

Duda, R. O., & Shortliffe, E. H. (1983). Expert systems research. *Science, 220*, 261–8.

Feigenbaum, E. A. (1989). What hath Simon wrought? In D. Klahr & K. Kotovsky (Eds), *Complex information processing: The impact of Herbert A. Simon* (pp. 165–82). Hillsdale, NJ: Erlbaum.

Larkin, J. H., McDermott, J., Simon, D. P., & Simon, H. A. (1980). Models of competence in solving physics problems. *Cognitive Science, 4*, 317–45.

Shiffrin, R. M., & Schneider, W. (1977). Controlled and automatic human information processing: II. Perceptual learning, automatic attending, and a general theory. *Psychological Review, 84*, 127–90.

ROBERT GLASER

explicit memory *See* IMPLICIT AND EXPLICIT MEMORY.

eyewitness testimony Eyewitness psychology studies factors that influence the accuracy and completeness of an eyewitness account. Research on human perception, memory, and suggestibility, as it pertains to eyewitness ability, generally shows that people do not passively record and store information from the environment. Rather, perceiving and remembering are constructive processes. When a person experiences and then tries to remember a past event, a complex interaction occurs, involving the witness's psychological characteristics, the type of event, and the specific context in which the witness is asked to remember the event. Even though it is understood that the witness's ultimate memory results from this interaction, the theoretical analyses of memory for an event typically divide the memory process into three stages: encoding, storage, and retrieval (*see* MEMORY). People are selective about what they pay attention to in the first place, and they are selective about what they store in memory. Moreover, they differ in the extent to which they are susceptible to suggestions. Numerous factors are present at each of these stages that affect the accuracy and completeness of an eyewitness account. Much psychological research on eyewitness testimony is aimed at discovering and illuminating those factors (Loftus, 1979; Wells & Loftus, 1984).

FACTORS INFLUENCING ENCODING

Psychological studies on factors that influence the encoding stage – that is, the initial perception of an event – have shown that witnesses are more accurate under the following circumstances: (a) when exposure time is longer rather than shorter; (b) when witnesses are not undergoing extreme stress or fright; (c) when witnesses are generally free from biased expectations; (d) when witnesses are young adults rather than children; (e) when witnesses are instructed at the outset to report salient aspects of an event rather than peripheral details; and (f) when no weapon, such as a gun or a knife, is displayed to the witness.

Some variables influence eyewitness performance in more complicated ways. The sex of a witness has a complex effect: women tend to be more accurate about items that they are generally interested in, for example clothing, while men are more accurate about the make and model of automobiles, things typically of interest to them. Furthermore, prior training can teach a witness to notice certain kinds of details, but it does not seem to enhance their memory for the faces of strangers or for information that was not specially noted. We also know that subjects recognize faces of their own race better than faces of other races (e.g. white subjects are superior at recognizing white versus black faces, while the reverse is true for black subjects) (*see* FACE RECOGNITION).

On some issues there remains some controversy: Are elderly witnesses invariably less accurate than young adults? How susceptible to suggestion are children's memories? Which personality characteristics are associated with good memory? How does the complexity of an event influence its subsequent recollection? How well are details of emotional events remembered as compared to details from neutral events? Past research has shown that the details of violent events are not remembered as well as details of less violent events.

However, more recent research has shown a complex interaction: certain central details from violent events can be better retained than those from nonviolent events, while peripheral details in a violent event are less well retained (Christianson & Loftus, 1987).

FACTORS INFLUENCING STORAGE

At the storage stage, new factors come into play. One of these is the period of time that elapses between encoding and retrieval of the memory for the event. The more typical result supports original research by Hermann Ebbinghaus, showing a decline in accuracy as the retention interval lengthens (*see* FORGET-TING). But what is important about the reten-tion interval is not the mere passage of time, but what goes on during that interval. After an event takes place, people think about it, talk about it, overhear conversations about it, may be asked leading questions by an investigator, or may be asked to identify photographs. All these activities can introduce new information to the witness. A number of studies have shown that information learned by witnesses subsequent to observing an event is very likely to distort the witness's memory of the event. Typically, this research is designed to present misleading information – that is, to suggest the existence of an object that was not present in the original event. The overall pattern of results shows that subjects exposed to mis-leading post-event information were more likely to later remember having seen the non-existent object than subjects who were not exposed to misleading information. Thus, people pick up information, whether it is true or false, and integrate it into their recollection. Once the new information is integrated, the eyewitness has difficulty recalling the source of the new information (Wells & Loftus, 1984; but see also McCloskey & Zaragoza [1985] for a different perspective). Confusion about the source of information is often at the root of errors of unconscious transference, when information learned at one time or in one con-text is associated with or substituted for infor-mation acquired in another context.

Suggestive influences are, of course, com-plex factors. We know, for example, that dis-cussions about an event, or overhearing conversations between other witnesses, can have both positive and negative effects, depending upon whether the post-event infor-mation is false or true. Furthermore, the ability of the witness to resist misleading suggestions varies with the source of the suggestion.

FACTORS INFLUENCING RETRIEVAL

Witnesses to complex events retrieve infor-mation from memory in numerous ways. Sometimes witnesses are asked open-ended questions, sometimes they are asked specific, closed-ended questions, or they are presented with objects, photographs, or an in-person lineup for purposes of identification. There is substantial agreement that eyewitness reports can be biased or distorted at the retrieval stage. For example, small changes in question wording can result in dramatically different answers. Thus, the way information is elicited from a witness is critical. Another source of error is the use of biasing words in a question (e.g. "Did the cars smash into each other?" versus "Did the cars hit each other?"), which can contaminate a witness's recollection (Lof-tus, 1979). Furthermore, lax instructions given to witnesses (e.g. "Don't worry about mistakes") result in more errors than do strict instructions (e.g. "Be careful of mistakes"). Similarly, lineup procedures in which eye-witnesses are led to believe that the target is present, or in which eyewitnesses infer that they must choose one of the individuals, tend to produce a higher number of false alarms – responses in which the eyewitness falsely claims to recognize one of the faces – than lineup procedures in which there is no sugges-tion that the target is present or that the eye-witness must make a choice (Malpass & Devine, 1981).

A large body of research has shown that witnesses produce the most accurate and complete accounts when they first engage in free recall in their own words, and then answer specific questions to fill in gaps in recollection. Several studies on context effects have shown that a witness's ability to remem-ber the event is enhanced if the context in which the witness viewed the initial event is reinstated at the time of retrieval (*see* STATE-

DEPENDENT MEMORY). Unfortunately, in real life, the context of recollection is typically very different from the context in which the witness viewed the initial event and thus diminishes the accuracy of recall. One other source of influence during retrieval is the person who is asking the questions. Research indicates that high-status interviewers (e.g. a police chief) obtain more information from witnesses than do low-status interviewers.

A surprising result from eyewitness research is the finding that there is little or no reliable relationship between the confidence of an eyewitness account and the accuracy of that account – this is especially true under poor viewing conditions (Wells & Murray, 1984; Brigham, 1988).

In sum, research on eyewitness testimony has demonstrated that the encoding, storage, and retrieval processes are susceptible to the influences of different factors. The retrieval stage provides maximal opportunity to use psychological research findings to recommend changes in procedure to enhance the accuracy of recollection. Vigorous research activity is under way to develop methods of enhancing witness recollection. Research on the distinction between implicit and explicit memory tasks may reveal new parameters about what people encode, store, and retrieve from memory. All eyewitness research helps us to evaluate the quality of eyewitness testimony. The implications of the research are that testimony based on memory involving few of the known problematic factors is more trustworthy than testimony based on memory involving many problematic factors (Loftus & Doyle, 1987).

See also REALITY MONITORING.

BIBLIOGRAPHY

Brigham, J. M. (1988). Is witness confidence helpful in judging eyewitness accuracy? In M. M. Gruneberg, P. E. Morris, & R. N. Sykes (Eds), *Practical aspects of memory: Current research and issues* (pp. 77–82). Chichester, UK: Wiley.

Ceci, S., Toglia, M., & Ross, D. (1987). *Children's eyewitness memory*. New York: Springer-Verlag.

Christianson, S.-Å., & Loftus, E. F. (1987). Memory for traumatic events. *Applied Cognitive Psychology*, 1, 225–39.

Loftus, E. F. (1979). *Eyewitness testimony*. Cambridge, Mass.: Harvard University Press.

——, & Doyle, J. M. (1987). *Eyewitness testimony: Civil and criminal*. New York: Kluwer Law Book Publishers.

McCloskey, M., & Zaragoza, M. (1985). Misleading postevent information and memory for events: Arguments and evidence against memory impairment hypotheses. *Journal of Experimental Psychology: General*, 114, 3–18.

Malpass, R. S., & Devine, P. G. (1981). Eyewitness identification: Lineup instructions and the absence of the offender. *Journal of Applied Psychology*, 66(4), 482–9.

Wells, G. L., & Loftus, E. F. (Eds) (1984). *Eyewitness testimony: Psychological perspectives*. New York: Cambridge University Press.

Wells, G. L., & Murray, D. M. (1984). Eyewitness confidence. In G. L. Wells & E. F. Loftus (Eds), *Eyewitness testimony: Psychological perspectives* (pp. 155–70). New York: Cambridge University Press.

SVEN-ÅKE CHRISTIANSON, JANE GOODMAN,
AND ELIZABETH F. LOFTUS

F

face recognition The term relates to an area of research concerned with the processes involved in the recognition or identification of facial stimuli. Research on this topic has increased rapidly in recent years and can be described under three main headings.

MEMORY FOR UNFAMILIAR FACES

This is usually studied by presenting one or several target faces for study, and then later examining how accurately subjects can recognize these targets, using either a "forced choice" procedure (in which subjects must select one target from a set containing one or more distractors), or a "yes–no" procedure (where subjects respond to each individual target or distractor face shown). Compared with recognition memory for other, homogeneous classes of stimuli (such as houses), recognition memory for faces is generally rather accurate. However, performance is reduced if views of faces are changed between study and test, or if the appearances of the faces are altered through disguise. Recognition memory for faces is sensitive to exposure duration, encoding instructions, contextual change, and, though less consistently, delay. Recognition of own-race faces is generally superior to recognition of faces from another race. Recognition of faces is disproportionately affected by inversion, compared with recognition of other stimuli, though other materials differentiated primarily through subtle changes in configuration may be similarly affected in expert subjects.

In contrast to generally accurate performance in laboratory tasks of recognizing faces, eyewitness identification is notoriously fallible and yet often forms an important component of legal testimony (*see* EYEWITNESS TESTIMONY). Many of the factors known to reduce face recognition accuracy in the laboratory may be operative in the witnessing situation. Conduct and composition of identi-

fication parades may also contribute to inaccuracies. Psychologists are increasingly involved in the development of new tools for probing eyewitness memory for faces, which may involve elements of recall as well as recognition. Shepherd (1986), for example, describes a computer system to present witnesses with a limited set of mug-shots to examine, based on their initial verbal descriptions, which reduces interference from searching through a file of many hundreds of such faces. The efficacy of reconstructive kits such as Identikit and Photofit has been evaluated and it has been found that such kits deliver rather poor likenesses. Psychologists are involved in the design of new systems and in training police operators to use these systems.

RECOGNITION OF FAMILIAR FACES (FRIENDS AND CELEBRITIES)

This has been studied using speeded recognition and classification tasks similar to those used in the study of word and object recognition. Much use has been made in recent years of the "face familiarity" decision task, analogous to the lexical decision task used in reading research. Recognition of faces as familiar is faster than categorizing faces in terms of their occupation which is in turn faster than naming faces or making decisions that require access to names. Recognition of a face's familiarity can be speeded by prior exposure to the face (repetition or identity priming) or by preceding the to-be-recognized face with that of a closely associated face (semantic or associative priming) (*see* PRIMING). Naming of faces suffers interference from irrelevant, to-be-ignored names, particularly if these are names from the same occupational category. Categorizing faces into occupational categories is not, however, affected by the presence of irrelevant names. Such findings have been used to support a three-stage sequential model of familiar face recognition (e.g. see Bruce & Young, 1986). In this model, "structural codes" stored for familiar faces within "face recognition units" allow the recognition of known faces from any viewpoint. Face recognition units may be primed by earlier presentation or by momentary expectations. Perceptual recognition of a face as familiar (within the face recognition units) then leads to access of semantic information about the personal identity of the person, stored at the "person identity nodes." Access of the person identity nodes may in turn lead to access of the person's name.

Effects of distinctiveness may help provide the key to the nature of the "structural codes." Famous or personally familiar faces which have been rated as distinctive in appearance are recognized as familiar more quickly than those rated as typical in appearance. When the task is changed to one of deciding whether each item is a face or a jumbled face, then distinctive faces are classified more slowly (Valentine & Bruce, 1986). These findings support a theory in which a face may be represented in terms of its deviation from a facial "prototype" – a theory lent support by observations of caricature. Such effects may emerge more naturally from instance-based models of memory than from abstractive models (see CONNECTIONIST MODELS OF MEMORY).

Identification of familiar faces is sometimes impaired as a result of brain damage, a condition termed "prosopagnosia." Although impaired face recognition is often associated with other visual agnosias, sometimes the condition appears in relatively isolated form. Some prosopagnosics show implicit recognition of faces they cannot recognize explicitly. Young, de Haan, and Hellawell (1988), for example, found that their patient's speed of classifying names as familiar was increased if they were preceded by faces of closely associated people – even though the patient was unable to recognize these faces. Some prosopagnosics are able to recognize expressions of faces, showing a dissociation between the identification of faces and the processing of emotional expressions, a distinction also supported by experiments with normal subjects.

PROCESSING FACE PATTERNS

The methods used involve asking subjects to make simple decisions (often "same–different") to faces whose structure may be varied systematically by altering or displacing different features, or by spatial freqency filtering. Such experiments have shown that faces are processed as *configurations* of interacting features, not just as collections of isolated features (*see* PATTERN PERCEPTION). Relatively low spatial frequencies provide sufficient information to support simple classification as male or female, old or young, and so on, but higher spatial frequencies become important for more subtle discrimination between faces. Such research may also help elucidate the nature of structural descriptions which individuate faces, though Bruce (1988) has argued that the field would benefit from a proper understanding of the face as a three-dimensional surface rather than as a two-dimensional pattern.

FURTHER READING

Detailed reviews are to be found in the collections edited by Davies, Ellis, and Shepherd (1981); Ellis, Jeeves, Newcombe, and Young (1986); Young and Ellis (1989), and in the recent monograph by Bruce (1988).

See also PERCEPTUAL DEVELOPMENT.

BIBLIOGRAPHY

Bruce, V. (1988). *Recognising faces*. London: Lawrence Erlbaum Associates.
––, & Young, A. (1986). Understanding face recognition. *British Journal of Psychology, 77,* 305–27.
Davies, G., Ellis, H., & Shepherd, J. (1981). *Perceiving and remembering faces*. London: Academic Press.
Ellis, H. D., Jeeves, M. A., Newcombe, F., & Young, A. (1986). *Aspects of face processing*. Dordrecht: Martinus Nijhoff.
Shepherd, J. W. (1986). An interactive computer system for retrieving faces. In H. D. Ellis, M. A. Jeeves, F. Newcombe, & A. Young (Eds), *Aspects of face processing*. Dordrecht: Martinus Nijhoff.
Valentine, T., & Bruce, V. (1986). The effects of distinctiveness in recognising and classifying faces. *Perception, 15,* 525–35.

Young, A. W., & Ellis, H. D. (1989). *Handbook of research on face processing.* Amsterdam: North Holland.

Young, A. W., de Haan, E. H. F., & Hellawell, D. (1988). Cross-domain semantic priming in normal subjects and a prosopagnosic patient. *Quarterly Journal of Experimental Psychology,* 40A, 561–80.

VICKI BRUCE

forgetting The term denotes lowered memory performance following learning. The dynamics of human forgetting were first investigated by the nineteenth-century psychologist Hermann Ebbinghaus. He taught himself lists of nonsense syllables and then measured how long it took him to relearn the lists after different periods of time. He demonstrated that human forgetting shows a nonlinear function with most forgetting occurring very soon after learning.

More recent research has shown that a good deal of human forgetting does take the same pattern as that observed by Ebbinghaus. One recent demonstration shows, somewhat alarmingly, that recall of cardiopulmonary resuscitation technique declines to 15 percent of original learning in one year (see Baddeley, 1989). But there are many notable exceptions to this. Some motor skills, such as riding a bicycle or driving, exhibit remarkably little forgetting and knowledge of foreign languages declines little across the years. Another complicating factor is that the rate of forgetting may be different depending on how one measures memory. Older people, for example, appear to forget much more rapidly than younger people when tested for free recall but these differences are greatly reduced or eliminated if recognition testing is used. This might indicate that recall and recognition are to some extent different processes and that only the latter is affected by aging. Alternatively, recognition may be a less sensitive procedure in that less information needs to be encoded to enable a recognition response to be made (see AGING AND MEMORY).

Studies of amnesia provide additional demonstrations of how the rate of forgetting is determined by the nature of the retention test (see AMNESIA). Many studies have shown that people with amnesia have extremely poor recall and recognition even when tested a few minutes after initial learning. However, it has now been shown that this forgetting is not total and that, with the right kind of test, amnesic patients can exhibit quite good memory. One technique first involves showing patients unusual words like "pendulum." When asked to recall these words subsequently, they are unable to do so. However, when shown a fragment of the word (e.g. __e__du____m /) they were more likely to give the correct answer than for an equivalent fragment in which the solution was not one of the words on the original list. Thus, when considering how much someone forgets about a learning experience one must take into account the form of memory being assessed (see IMPLICIT AND EXPLICIT MEMORY).

Within experimental psychology two of the most prominent explanations of forgetting are decay and interference. Decay theory can be traced back to E. L. Thorndike's "Law of Disuse" in which he claimed that a memory would decay as a function of the time it was not used. However, in an influential paper, McGeoch (1932) pointed out that explanations of forgetting based on elapsed time were no explanation at all. What was needed was an account of what happened during that time in order to cause forgetting.

McGeoch's criticism gave rise to the only systematic attempt to construct a general theory of forgetting – interference theory (see PROACTIVE INTERFERENCE; RETROACTIVE INTERFERENCE). The basic idea was that forgetting arose from the interaction between old and new learning processes. Interference theory was founded on the associationist view of learning first proposed by philosophers such as John Stuart Mill. At the outset they viewed human memory as a *tabula rasa* (a blank slate) upon which all memories were built up from the association of ideas. This view was adopted by the Behaviorists and translated into the terminology of associations between stimulus and response.

According to the theory, forgetting was thought to arise when two associations competed with each other. Central to this approach was the distinction between proactive and retroactive interference. Proactive interference arises when an existing association prevents a new response being learnt to a particular stimulus. Retroactive interference represents the converse in that learning a new association serves to weaken an existing association.

The most commonly used experimental technique was paired associate learning in which the subject had to learn associations between arbitrarily paired words or nonsense syllables. A typical interference manipulation would be to learn the association A→B followed by a new list requiring the subject to learn A→C. Proactive interference could be measured by examining the ease with which A→C was learned compared with a control in which nothing preceded A→C learning. Retroactive interference could be examined by asking subjects to recall A→B after they had learned A→C compared with a condition involving no prior learning.

Interference theory generated a number of robust phenomena and paired associate learning is still widely used today although mainly in neuropsychological assessment. Interference theory itself failed in that it was unable to account for forgetting even within the artificial confines of the verbal learning laboratory. It also suffered because it lacked ECOLOGICAL VALIDITY. There are some instances of real-life forgetting that can be conceived of in terms of paired associate learning. In Italy, for example, one must learn that "C" on a tap means hot ("caldo") whereas in Britain it means "cold." However, such examples are not commonplace and the bulk of human forgetting experience does not fit readily into a simple associationist framework.

Within modern memory research there is no successor to interference theory and the study of forgetting has receded quite dramatically. Most modern work has concentrated on the various factors that govern the extent to which an individual forgets at any particular point in time. Central to this approach is the distinction between forgetting caused by storage failure and forgetting caused by retrieval failure. In the former case forgetting is thought to occur because the storage system has failed to retain the memory. The idea that forgetting could arise like this makes intuitive sense but it is very difficult to demonstrate unequivocally. The problem is that forgetting can also be caused by retrieval failure. Here the information is in memory but the retrieval process is faulty for some reason, resulting in a failure to remember. Because forgetting can arise in this way it is difficult to be sure that a person failing to remember does so because of storage failure.

For this reason psychologists have been most interested in demonstrating the various ways in which forgetting can be determined by various factors operating at the time of retrieval. Central to this is the work of Tulving and Thomson (1973) who argued that remembering information depends critically on presenting the correct cues at retrieval. In their experiments subjects learned word pairs such as "glue–chair" – note here that there is only a weak associative link between the two words. They were then given the word "table" and asked to free associate. This very frequently led to subjects giving "chair" as a response but, surprisingly, when asked if it was a word they had been asked to learn they said no. However, when given the weak associate "glue" they showed a very good level of recall for "chair." From this type of finding Tulving and his colleagues developed the theory of cue-dependent forgetting in which the extent of forgetting is partly determined by the overlap between the information originally learned and the information provided as a retrieval cue. "Glue" is therefore more effective than "table" because it was "glue" that was associated with "chair" at the time of learning.

Cue-dependent forgetting and its associated theory of retrieval, encoding specificity, stress the importance that context plays in determining how well we remember (see ENCODING SPECIFICITY PRINCIPLE). Thus, our failure to recognize a friend encountered in an unusual set of circumstances occurs because our knowledge of that person is linked to a specific set of circumstances which, when present, make it easier for us to identify him or her. Context is a pervasive term in cognitive psychology but one that is often ill defined. Within memory research Baddeley (1982) has distinguished between intrinsic and extrinsic context when considering how contextual factors determine how well we remember. His idea assumes that in any learning situation there is target information and incidental background information that bears no direct relevance to what has to be learned. When learning a face, for example, the fact that a person is wearing glasses is part of the intrinsic context but the fact that they are standing in a field constitutes extrinsic context.

Experimental work on context effects and forgetting is most interesting when one considers the possible effects of extrinsic context. Demonstrations that changes in intrinsic context affect memory are less valuable because they merely tell us that making changes in target information between learning and test, e.g. removing the glasses from our hypothetical person in the field, reduces our ability to recognize them. From a theoretical and practical point of view it is much more valuable to discover whether extrinsic context influences memory because, from a subjective viewpoint, we are unaware that such influences exist.

The most common form of extrinsic context thought to cause significant forgetting is the environment in which learning takes place. Early studies claimed, for example, that students produced better examination results when tested in their classroom than when tested somewhere else – the implication being that the classroom somehow provided a cue for retrieval. However, attempts to replicate these findings have been inconsistent. More drastic changes of environmental context do, however, reduce memory performance. Godden and Baddeley (1975) showed that information learned underwater was recalled better when the subjects remained submerged than when they returned to dry land. More recently Smith (1979) has shown that subjects remember more successfully if they are tested in the same room in which they learnt, but that this effect is abolished if subjects moved to a different room recall the original room before attempting recall of what they learned. This type of finding has been extended to eye-witnessing where it has been shown that witnesses who recollect the environment in which a crime took place show superior recall of the crime itself (see EYEWITNESS TESTIMONY).

A related phenomenon concerns the extent to which our physiological status can affect how well we remember. The term state-dependent learning refers to a phenomenon in which an individual shows less forgetting if learning and retrieval occur when the person is in the same physiological state than in a different state. There have been a number of demonstrations of state-dependent learning involving alcohol, marijuana, and other psychoactive agents such as benzodiazepines. However, there have been almost as many failures to show state-dependency in human learning. This controversy was resolved by Eich (1980), who pointed out that most of the studies showing positive evidence of state dependency used a free recall measure whereas those that failed to do so used recognition or some form of cueing. This suggests that state-dependent effects are most influential when subjects are left to their own devices when trying to remember (see STATE-DEPENDENT MEMORY).

Over the years a number of theories have proposed that emotional factors can lead to forgetting. Most influential perhaps is Freud's theory of repression in which knowledge considered injurious to the ego could be kept out of mind. Evidence for these repressed memories could be gained indirectly by observing an individual's Freudian slips – slips of the tongue or pen which revealed unconscious knowledge and desires. The uncovering of repressed memories was central to the Freudian method of psychoanalysis and there is little doubt that repression is an important concept when interpreting certain forms of mental disturbance. It is much more difficult to go along with Freud's view that repression plays an important role in everyday forgetting. Indeed, attempts to validate repression as a significant factor in normal forgetting have been a complete failure (Parkin, Lewinsohn, & Folkard, 1982).

More general emotional factors have been thought to play an important role in how well we remember things (*see* EMOTION). One early view was the hedonic selectivity or Pollyanna hypothesis which asserts that human beings are naturally optimistic and will tend to remember information with pleasant emotional connotations more readily than unpleasant information. Unfortunately the experiments demonstrating this hypothesis were methodologically unsound in that one could not be sure that unpleasant memories were less well remembered or whether people were just less willing to report unpleasant memories when they came to mind.

An alternative view about emotion and memory has been put forward by Bower (1981) who has argued that mood congruency between learning and retrieval is the critical factor. According to this theory a memory will be retrieved more easily if the person once again experiences the mood state that was present during the original learning episode. Bower and his colleagues presented a number of findings showing that subjects in hypnotically induced mood states remembered more information congruent with their mood state, i.e. "sad" subjects remembered more sad aspects of a passage, but that these effects did not occur when mood was induced only at retrieval. Bower thus argued that mood state was an influential factor during initial learning and that its reinstatement was a powerful influence over retrieval (*see* STATE-DEPENDENT MEMORY).

Unfortunately, there have been problems replicating some of Bower's key findings but the importance of mood state as a cause of forgetting is unambiguously demonstrated in studies of depressed people. In a series of studies Teasdale (1983) and his colleagues have shown that depressed patients take much longer to recall pleasant experiences than normal people. Furthermore, they have found that the relative accessibility of pleasant and unpleasant memories varies with the level of the patient's depression. More recently it has also been shown that depressed people are far less able to remember specific experiences when cued with pleasant as opposed to unpleasant cue words (*see* MOOD DISORDERS AND COGNITION).

One extreme account of forgetting is that it

arises entirely from retrieval failure, the argument being that our brain contains a complete record of experience and that all difficulties reflect problems of accessibility. This idea stems from the remarkable experiments of the neurosurgeon Wilder Penfield. His operative procedures often involved stimulating the temporal cortex of conscious patients. He noted that stimulated patients would tend to relate memory experiences and that these experiences were often extremely trivial. From these observations he leapt to the conclusion that he had located the stream of consciousness in which all experience was recorded and that forgetting was entirely due to retrieval failure. We have seen above that various types of retrieval failure can account for a good deal of forgetting but we cannot go along with Penfield's more extreme conclusion. Loftus and Loftus (1980) have shown that Penfield's observations were not accurate and in fact offer little support for his conclusions.

Most experimental psychologists reject Penfield's view but his ideas are still surprisingly popular with other psychologists. In particular, psychologists who claim that hypnosis can aid memory often cite Penfield's work as supporting evidence. However, studies of HYPNOSIS and memory show conclusively that it does not alleviate forgetting (Parkin, 1987).

See also RECALL; REHEARSAL; SENTENCE PROCESSING.

BIBLIOGRAPHY

Baddeley, A. D. (1982). Domains of recollection. *Psychological Review*, *89*, 708–29.

— —. (1990). *Human memory: theory and practice.* London: Erlbaum.

Bower, G. H. (1981). Mood and memory. *American Psychologist*, *36*, 129–48.

Eich, J. E. (1980). The cue-dependent nature of state-dependent retrieval. *Memory and Cognition*, *8*, 7–73.

Godden, D., & Baddeley, A. D. (1975). Context-dependent memory in two natural environments. *British Journal of Psychology*, *66*, 325–31.

Loftus, E. F., & Loftus, G. R. (1980). On the permanence of stored information in the human brain. *American Psychologist*, *35*, 409–20.

McGeoch, J. A. (1932). Forgetting and the law of disuse. *Psychological Review, 39*, 352–70.

Parkin, A. J. (1987). *Memory and amnesia: An introduction.* Oxford: Basil Blackwell.

––, Lewinsohn, J., & Folkard, S. (1982). The influence of emotion on immediate and delayed recall: Levinger and Clark reconsidered. *British Journal of Psychology, 73*, 389–93.

Smith, S. M. (1979). Remembering in and out of context. *Journal of Experimental Psychology: Human Learning and Memory, 5*, 460–71.

Teasdale, J. D. (1983). Affect and accessibility. *Philosophical Transactions of the Royal Society, London, B, 302*, 403–12.

Tulving, E., & Thomson, D. M. (1973). Encoding specificity and retrieval processes in episodic memory. *Psychological Review, 80*, 352–73.

A. J. PARKIN

form perception A basic question in vision research concerns how we perceive three-dimensional forms from the two-dimensional images that fall on our eyes, i.e. form perception. The most common answer to this question is that three-dimensional perceptions are constructed, by embellishing the original two-dimensional (retinal) images with depth information. Two-dimensional images contain many optical correlates to depth, including linear perspective (parallel lines converge towards the horizon), motion parallax (near objects move faster than far objects as the observer moves), occlusion (near objects occlude far objects), and texture gradients (the grain of the surface texture on an object is larger at nearer distances). Depth can thus be coded from the values taken by these optical correlates in two-dimensional images. Further, the two-dimensional image from each eye can be combined to generate an additional cue to depth, namely "stereopsis." Stereopsis refers to the process of integrating the two-dimensional descriptions from the left and right eyes. For objects within arm's reach, the images in the two eyes differ slightly. When the images from the two eyes are integrated, these "binocular disparities" are used to code the relative depths of the objects (Julesz, 1971). By embellishing the two-dimensional descriptions of visual patterns with information about the relative depths of the surfaces of the patterns, the visual system may generate a description of a three-dimensional form.

Perhaps the clearest framework for understanding form perception was given by Marr (1982). Marr argued that form perception involved a number of distinct substages. The first stage is concerned with coding what Marr termed a "Primal Sketch," where the presence and orientations of bars and edges in the two-dimensional image are coded. The Primal Sketch essentially provides an edge-map of visually presented objects, coded in two-dimensional space. Following the construction of the Primal Sketch, Marr argues that a $2\frac{1}{2}$D sketch is created by integrating outputs from the Primal Sketch with depth information. The $2\frac{1}{2}$D sketch thus provides a description not only of the visual pattern created by the object on the retina, but also a description of the relative depths of the surfaces of the object in three-dimensional space. It is termed a $2\frac{1}{2}$D and not a 3D description because the $2\frac{1}{2}$D sketch does not represent full three-dimensional knowledge about the properties of the object, such as the properties of a surface that may be hidden in the image (so it is not a full 3D description), but it does represent surface depths explicitly (so it is not a two-dimensional description).

Marr also argued that processes such as stereopsis can only contribute to the perception of three-dimensional forms because of the constraints of the natural world. The natural world is made up of objects with three-dimensional volumes. This means that there are certain constraints on the two-dimensional images falling on the left and right eyes. For instance, the depths of the surfaces of the objects will by and large change continuously, except where the edges of the object occur. Further, any one point in the combined image from the two eyes can only correspond to one depth in the world. By assuming these constraints, the visual system is able to solve the problem of matching the images from the two eyes, which would otherwise be extremely difficult. The construction of three-dimensional form representations by the visual system is not an arbitrary solution to a difficult problem, but a natural solution constrained by the nature of the world we inhabit. In particular, form descriptions are necessary in order for us to reach and navigate around objects, which would be impossible on the basis of two-dimensional pattern representations alone.

As suggested by Marr, there is evidence that three-dimensional representations of form are coded after two-dimensional descriptions of shapes. For instance, if we are exposed to objects for a very brief duration, we tend to perceive them as being flatter than they really are (Epstein & Hatfield, 1978) – presumably because we code the two-dimensional pattern prior to the three-dimensional form.

However, representations such as the $2\frac{1}{2}$D sketch retain some properties in common with two-dimensional pattern representations (such as the Primal Sketch), in that the representations change every time the observer moves to a new viewing position (or an object moves relative to the viewer). This is because both pattern and depth information is coded relative to a specific viewpoint. Although such viewpoint-specific form representations support actions such as reaching, they are relatively uneconomical vehicles of form *recognition*, simply because we would need to store representations of all possible objects from all possible viewpoints to ensure that we could match any given input with our stored knowledge of the object – such matching presumably being required to generate a learned response to an object.

How might form recognition be achieved when objects are seen under radically different views? Various solutions to this problem have been proposed (for a review, see Humphreys & Quinlan 1987). One possibility is that we store more than one representation of a given object, but that these multiple representations are confined to the most common positions under which the object is encountered. Recognition is achieved by finding the best match between a viewpoint-specific form representation and the multiple stored descriptions (*see* PATTERN PERCEPTION).

An alternative is that we attempt to transform the viewpoint-specific form represen-tation so that a match can be achieved with a limited number of stored representations that exist for any object. For instance, the form representation may be rotated or magnified so that it matches the stored description (e.g. Shepard & Metzler, 1971); or the visual system may attempt to construct a form representation that is not viewpoint-specific. Marr and Nishihara (1978) suggested that an object-centered rather than a viewer-centered form representation may be constructed by coding the parts of an object relative to some constant reference frame – such as the main axis in the object. Thus, for example, the main axis of the standing human body is the axis of symmetry and elongation that runs vertically through the head, torso, and legs. The "parts" of the body (e.g. the legs and arms) stay relatively constant with respect to this axis irrespective of whether the body is standing or lying down. Once the orientation of the axis has been coded, the same description of the parts relative to the axis can be derived even when the viewpoint changes – allowing the object to be matched to a single stored representation even when the object is seen from an unusual viewpoint. Since the parts are coded relative to a reference frame based on the object (rather than the viewpoint), the resulting description can be termed "object-centered."

There is evidence for both internal transformation processes and for the coding of object-centered descriptions being used to recognize forms seen from unusual views. Internal transformation processes seem particularly useful when we need to code the "handedness" of an object – that is, whether the object is pointing left or right (Hinton & Parsons, 1981). The handedness of objects does not seem to be efficiently coded during object recognition – at first glance we may fail to notice whether a car points left or right, as we simply recognize the car – and special processes (such as mental transformation) may be needed to code handedness explicitly, especially when the object is in an unusual position (e.g. if the car is upside down). When people are simply asked to recognize objects (and not judge their handedness), then evidence for object-centered representations emerges.

Thus, for instance, it tends to be easier to recognize objects whose main axis is visible than objects whose main axis is shortened when seen at the particular viewpoint (Humphreys & Riddoch, 1984), and form recognition is affected by placing the form in a surrounding context that biases the axis used as a perceptual reference frame (Palmer, 1985). Overall, the data indicate that there is considerable flexibility in the processes mediating form perception in humans – with the processes involved affected by our experience with a particular stimulus (e.g. whether or not it is commonly encountered in a particular view), its geometrical characteristics (e.g. the presence of an axis of symmetry or elongation), and the task (e.g. handedness judgement or not) (see Humphreys & Quinlan, 1987).

However, the standard argument, that three-dimensional form perception is derived from two-dimensional pattern perception, is not accepted in all quarters. Recent work using visual search procedures, for instance, suggests that three-dimensional features are detected directly, without their initial coding in two-dimensional space. In visual search studies, subjects search for a target against varying numbers of distractor items. When the target has a distinguishing feature relative to the distractors, the target appears to "pop out," and there are few effects of the number of distractors on performance (e.g. Treisman, 1988). "Pop out" can be achieved when targets differ only in terms of their apparent three-dimensional structures (Enns, 1989), consistent with three-dimensional features being directly detected.

In sum, it seems likely that certain visual features are directly interpreted in three-dimensional terms (e.g. two receding lines, generating linear perspective), though representations of complete objects may require the integration of three-dimensional depth information with two-dimensional pattern descriptions – to generate three-dimensional form perception.

BIBLIOGRAPHY

Enns, J. (1989). Three-dimensional features that pop out in visual search. In D. Brody (Ed.), *The First International Conference on Visual Search*. London: Taylor Francis.

Epstein, W., & Hatfield, G. (1978). Functional equivalence of masking and cue reduction in perception of shape at a slant. *Perception & Psychophysics, 23*, 137–44.

Hinton, G. E., & Parsons, L. M. (1981). Frames of reference and mental imagery. In J. Long & A. D. Baddeley (Eds), *Attention and performance, IX*. Hillsdale, NJ: Lawrence Erlbaum Associates.

Humphreys, G. W., & Quinlan, P. T. (1987). Normal and pathological processes in visual object constancy. In G. W. Humphreys & M. J. Riddoch (Eds), *Visual object processing: A cognitive neuropsychological approach*. London: Lawrence Erlbaum Associates.

Humphreys, G. W., & Riddoch, M. J. (1984). Routes to object constancy: Implications from neurological impairments of object constancy. *Quarterly Journal of Experimental Psychology, 36A*, 385–415.

Julesz, B. (1971). *Foundations of cyclopean perception*. Chicago: University of Chicago Press.

Marr, D. (1982). *Vision*. San Francisco: W. H. Freeman.

——, & Nishihara, K. (1978). Representation and recognition of the spatial organisation of three-dimensional objects. *Proceedings of the Royal Society, London, B, 200*, 269–94.

Palmer, S. E. (1985). The role of symmetry in shape perception. *Acta Psychologica, 59*, 67–90.

Shepard, R. N., & Metzler, J. (1971). Mental rotation of three-dimensional objects. *Science, 191*, 952–4.

Treisman, A. (1988). Features and objects: The fourteenth Bartlett Memorial Lecture. *Quarterly Journal of Experimental Psychology, 40A*, 201–38.

G. W. HUMPHREYS

G

Gestalt principles of perceptual organization Gestalt psychologists demonstrated and explored the importance of perceptual organization: the ways in which various parts of a complex sensory stimulus relate to each other perceptually and the factors that systematically influence these relations. Prior to this work, perceptual theory was dominated by the assumptions of atomism and associationism: complex percepts were thought to be constructed from "atoms" of elementary color sensations (as registered by retinal receptors) with associations due to contiguity in space and time holding them together. Gestalt theorists rejected both assumptions, proposing instead that perception was holistic and intrinsically organized by the nature of the underlying brain processes.

The fundamental problem of perceptual organization was first discussed by Max Wertheimer (1923), one of the founders of the Gestalt movement. He asked the important question of "what goes with what" in visual perception: why is it that people do not see a visual scene as a chaotic juxtaposition of different colors that fall on retinal receptors, but rather as an organized entity in which there are regions, surfaces, and objects coherently arranged in space? (*see* FORM PERCEPTION).

Wertheimer studied perceptual organization by constructing visual arrays of simple geometrical elements and varying a single factor, if possible, to determine its effect on perceived grouping. The factors that he identified are called "the laws of grouping" (or sometimes "the laws of perceptual organization"). Several of the most important ones are illustrated in Figures 1–4. Figure 1, for example, demonstrates the law of "proximity": when just the spacing of otherwise identical circles is varied, the closest ones are grouped together. Figures 2 and 3 illustrate the law of "similarity": all else being equal, the most similar elements (in color or size, for these examples) are grouped together. Another important factor is what Wertheimer called "common fate": all else being equal, elements that move in the same way will be grouped together (Figure 4). Note that common fate is actually a special case of similarity (due to motion) and that even proximity can be viewed as grouping by similarity (in position). Other examples of factors that affect grouping are continuity, connectedness, closure, and symmetry.

Wertheimer's laws of organization are *ceteris paribus* rules: *all else being equal*, elements (or figural parts) will be grouped together perceptually if they are more closely related by the factor specified. An important weakness of this formulation becomes evident if one tries

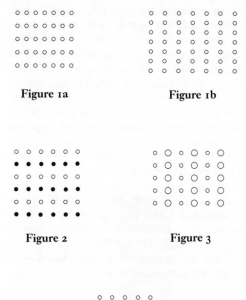

Figure 1a   Figure 1b

Figure 2   Figure 3

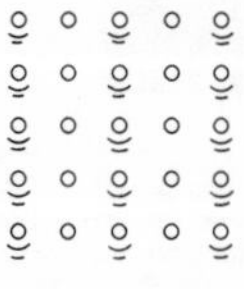

Figure 4

to apply the laws to more complex cases in which several factors vary in opposition to one another. The laws may allow one to say *a posteriori* which factor dominates in a given situation, but there is no way to predict the outcome in advance. Indeed, nobody has yet succeeded in formulating a general theory of grouping that overcomes this problem.

Although Wertheimer's laws of grouping are sometimes taken to be synonymous with "Gestalt principles of organization," there are many further organizational aspects of perception that the Gestaltists identified in the perception of visual scenes and that are properly considered to fall within this topic. Among the most important is the figure/ground relation first discussed by Edgar Rubin (1921). As illustrated in Figure 5, either of the two regions can be perceived as the "figure," resulting in either the perception of the sharp, claw-like protrusions of the black figure or of the curved, finger-like protrusions of the white object. Because the boundary is perceived as "belonging" to the figural region, the figure seems "thing-like" and has a definite shape. The other region is then seen as a shapeless "background" that extends behind the contours of the figure.

Gestaltists identified several factors that bias the visual system toward selecting certain kinds of regions as figures. Among the

strongest is the factor of "surroundedness," in which the surrounded region is usually perceived as figure. Other factors that influence figural selection include size, symmetry, and convexity, in which the smaller, symmetrical, and/or more convex region tends to be seen as the figure. This analysis of figure/ground organization suffers from the same general defect as the laws of grouping: it simply does not apply to cases in which factors conflict.

Another important aspect of perceptual organization as studied by Gestalt psychologists is the relationship between perceptual objects and a frame of reference relative to which their properties are defined. A compelling example is provided by the perception of orientation in a tilted room. An observer inside the room soon begins to perceive the room as upright and their own bodies as tilted in the opposite direction. This is because their visual system erroneously takes the surrounding room to define gravitational vertical. A similar effect occurs in motion perception in a phenomenon called "induced motion." If a stationary dot is surrounded by a rectangular frame that moves slowly (below threshold) in an otherwise dark field, observers almost invariably perceive the frame to be stationary and the dot to be moving in the direction opposite to the actual motion of the frame (Duncker, 1929). These experiments demonstrate that the visual system seems to prefer using larger surrounding objects to define the upright, stationary frame of reference, while the orientation and motion of smaller enclosed objects are defined relative to the larger ones. In the case of induced motion, this tendency produces an illusion.

Further issues of perceptual organization arise from the relations among two or more figural regions. Most people see a triangle behind a partly transparent square in Figure 6, for example, but the actual stimulus contains three homogeneously shaded regions, none of which is either triangular or square. With some effort this stimulus can be seen as the mosaic organization of the three irregular regions that are actually present, but when the color and spatial relations among the regions are consistent with an interpretation of

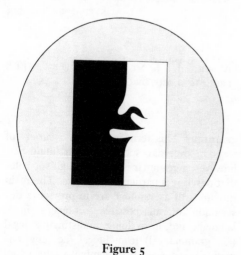

Figure 5

Figure 6   **Figure 7**

"transparency," the perceptual system clearly prefers the latter organization (Metelli, 1974). A closely related phenomenon, called "completion," arises in Figure 7, which is normally seen as a triangle behind an opaque square. Even though only part of the triangle is actually present in the stimulus, one perceives it as whole because its contours are perceptually extended beneath the occluding circle (Kanizsa, 1979). The visual system apparently "prefers" the interpretation of a partly occluded complete square to that of a fully visible incomplete square.

Although the above examples do not exhaust the types of organizational relations investigated by Gestalt psychologists, they are a representative set that provide a good feel for the Gestalt contribution (for a more compre-
⸱hensive recent review of this topic, see Pomerantz & Kubovy, 1986). It is important to notice that all of these examples involve, in one way or another, the notion of perceptual *preference*: one organization is "preferred" to the alternatives because of the factors that Gestalt psychologists identified. Gestalt theorists tried to account for these preferences in their "principle of pragnanz" (sometimes called "the minimum principle"): the percept will be as "good" as the stimulus conditions allow in the sense that it will have the *simplest* possible organization. Unfortunately, the Gestaltists did not provide a rigorous definition of pragnanz, and so this principle ultimately fails to explain their findings adequately. Later theorists have attempted to ground this concept in more objective analyses, such as the proposals that simple organizations correspond to low information content, economy of symbolic representation, and/or minimal transformational distance. Others have followed Helmholtz's lead in

ascribing these preferences to the operation of a bias toward *likely* situations rather than *simple* ones (e.g. Pomerantz & Kubovy, 1986). Still, it is correct to say that the problems of perceptual organization identified by the Gestaltists have not been solved to this day.

See also PERSON PERCEPTION.

BIBLIOGRAPHY

Duncker, K. (1929). Über induzierte Bewegung. *Psychologische Forschung, 12*, 180–259. (Condensed translation published as: Induced motion. In W. D. Ellis (Ed.), *A sourcebook of Gestalt psychology.* New York: Harcourt, Brace, 1938)

Kanizsa, G. (1979). *Organization in vision.* New York: Praeger.

Metelli, F. (1974). The perception of transparency. *Scientific American, 230*(4), 90–8.

Pomerantz, J. R., & Kubovy, M. (1986). Theoretical approaches to perceptual organization. In K. R. Boff, L. Kaufman, & J. P. Thomas (Eds), *Handbook of perception and human performance* (Vol. II): *Cognitive processes and performance.* New York: Wiley.

Rubin, E. (1921). *Visuell Wahrgenommene Figuren.* Glydendalske.

Wertheimer, M. (1923). Untersuchungen zur Lehre von der Gestalt, II. *Psychologische Forschung, 4*, 301–50. (Condensed translation published as: Laws of organization in perceptual forms. In W. D. Ellis (Ed.), *A sourcebook of Gestalt psychology.* New York: Harcourt, Brace, 1938)

STEPHEN E. PALMER

Gibson, J. J. *See* DIRECT PERCEPTION; PERCEPTUAL MOTOR COORDINATION.

grammar This term is used in a variety of ways in everyday speech; within linguistics, however, a grammar is a set of linguistic rules that describe a particular language. The main functions of a grammar are to provide a description of all possible sentences in a language and, in so doing, to distinguish legal (i.e. grammatical) from illegal (i.e. ungrammatical) sentences. For example, a satisfactory grammar of English should be able to explain why sentences (1) and (2) are grammatical – that is, they are considered to be acceptable by speakers of English – and sentence (3) is ungrammatical:

(1) Matthew is certain to leave.
(2) Matthew is likely to leave.
(3) *Matthew is probable to leave.

Grammars contain information about the structure of words and the structure of sentences. Words are not, however, the smallest unit of linguistic description and grammars often refer to morphemes instead. In order to understand what is meant by a morpheme, consider the contrast between "boy" and "boys" and between "carry" and "carrying" and "carried." In the first example, the singular and plural forms of "boy" share a common element called the "stem" morpheme. The singular form consists only of the stem morpheme, whereas the plural form consists of the stem "boy" + the plural "s" morpheme. Similarly, in the second example, the simple present tense of "carry" consists only of a stem morpheme, whereas the other two forms of the verb are formed by adding the "ing" and "ed" morphemes respectively.

Part of the task of a grammar is to provide information about the meaning of individual words. This is usually done by specifying the meaning of individual stem morphemes in lexical entries; and by providing information about the morphemes that can be added to particular stems together with a description of the meaning changes that these additions bring about.

There is considerable disagreement about the best way to specify lexical entries and morphological rules, but the description of sentence structure – syntax – has proved to be even more controversial. For many linguists, syntax is at the core of any grammar and it is in syntactic descriptions that the differences between different grammatical theories become most apparent.

During the 1960s and 1970s the most dominant syntactic theory was transformational grammar. This first version of this was "phrase structure grammar" (PSG) which was set out in Chomsky's *Syntactic structures*

(1957). PSG was a constituent structure grammar. Sentences were subdivided into their constituents and each constituent was then subdivided until no further division was possible. In *Syntactic structures* the rules for such subdivision were expressed by using expressions of the form:

S → NP + VP	(Sentence can be subdivided into Noun Phrase + Verb Phrase)
NP → Det + N	Noun Phrase can be subdivided into Determiner + Noun)
VP → V + NP	(Verb Phrase can be subdivided into Verb + Noun Phrase).

The information about sentence structure that is yielded by rules of this kind can be represented either by using brackets to separate the various sentence constituents or by a "tree structure." For example, the phrase structure of sentence (4)

(4) The cat drank the milk.

can be represented by the tree structure shown in Figure 1.

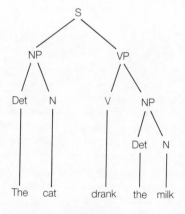

Figure 1

In addition to phrase structure rules, the grammar of *Syntactic structures* also used "transformational rules" which could be applied to simple sentence structures in order to produce complex sentences such as negatives and passives. The transformational rules attempted to explain the relationship between sentences such as (4), (5) and (6).

(5) Did the cat drink the milk?
(6) Which cat drank the milk?

Since *Syntactic structures*, Chomsky has produced other grammars in an attempt to use fewer and fewer rules to account for a greater number of syntactic phenomena. In *Aspects of the theory of syntax* (Chomsky, 1965), he attempted to take greater account of sentence meaning as well as sentence structure; and in his *Theory of government and binding* (Chomsky, 1982), he used syntactic rules which were much more abstract and which could be used to describe languages other than English.

Chomsky's grammars have had a great influence on psychological research into language processing (see Garnham, 1985) but more recently, other approaches such as Generalized Phrase Structure Grammar (Gazdar, 1982) have attracted the interest of researchers who are attempting model parsing – the ability to compute the syntactic structure of a sentence – both in humans and in machines (*see* ARTIFICIAL INTELLIGENCE; LANGUAGE COMPREHENSION).

See also LANGUAGE ACQUISITION.

BIBLIOGRAPHY

Brown, K. (1984). *Linguistics today*. London: Fontana.

Chomsky, N. (1957). *Syntactic structures*. The Hague: Mouton.

——. (1965). *Aspects of the theory of syntax*. Cambridge, Mass.: MIT Press.

——. (1982). *Some concepts and consequences of the theory of government and binding*. Cambridge, Mass.: MIT Press.

Garnham, A. (1985). *Psycholinguistics: Central topics*. London: Methuen.

Gazdar, G. J. M. (1982). Phrase structure grammar. In G. K. Pullum & P. Jacobsen (Eds), *The nature of syntactic representation*. Dordrecht: Reidel.

Lyons, J. (1977). *Chomsky*. London: Fontana.

Radford, A. (1981). *Transformational syntax*. Cambridge: Cambridge University Press.

MARGARET HARRIS

H

hemispheric localization The hypothesis that, in humans, the two hemispheres of the cerebral cortex differ in the psychological functions which they support is given the term hemispheric localization or lateralization. The relative functional organization of the two hemispheres, and the localization of particular functions to one or the other hemisphere, have constituted the leading topic of research in neuropsychology for the last three decades.

Evidence that the two hemispheres of the human brain differ in their functional cognitive organization comes from three sources: from the observation of patients with brain injury or disease (clinical neuropsychology); from the particular study of the "split-brain" patients who have undergone cerebral commissurotomy; and from the study of normal subjects in the laboratory (experimental neuropsychology).

Clinical neuropsychology has a long history extending back into the last century. It consists essentially of the study of the functional deficits to be observed in those with damage to the central nervous system. The existence of large populations of previously healthy subjects receiving relatively discrete injuries associated with missile wounds during the First and Second World Wars was a particular stimulus to the field. Recent advances have been encouraged by the introduction of modern brain-imaging techniques which can greatly assist in the accurate description of the anatomical localization of the injury (*see* POSITRON EMISSION TOMOGRAPHY AND COGNITION). However, despite improvements in the technology, the logic of the investigation remains the same: the correlation of pathology assessed in terms of anatomical location with the functional psychological disorders which result from the pathology.

The findings of clinical neuropsychology, which have an application in the assessment and rehabilitation of patients in addition to their scientific importance, clearly show that to a certain degree functions can be localized to areas of the cortex. Even if this localization cannot, because of the nature of the organization of the brain, be exact there are undoubtedly functional differences among the various regions of the cortex and particularly between the equivalent homolateral regions in the left and right cerebral hemispheres. The most obvious of these is the representation of speech and language functions in the left hemisphere. Damage to the appropriate regions of the left hemisphere almost invariably produces APHASIA, while damage to homologous areas on the right rarely produces this effect, at least in right-handed subjects.

The study of split-brain patients from about 1960 onward was a powerful stimulus to the field. These patients, as a treatment for intractible epilepsy, have had severed the commissures which provide direct neural links between the cortex of the left and right hemisphere. Although these patients show a surprising lack of effects upon their everyday activities, under controlled laboratory conditions it is possible to show that the two isolated cerebral hemispheres have an ability to perceive, to remember, and to learn, quite independently of the other. It has also been possible to demonstrate lateral specialization in these patients, which essentially supports the clinical evidence.

Modern experimental neuropsychology relies principally upon two techniques which have been classic tasks in experimental psychology, and which were used in the split-brain research: divided visual field presentation and dichotic listening. In each of these techniques, one in the visual and one in the auditory modality, the stimuli to be presented are lateralized to the left or right of the sensory field of the subject. As a result, because of the projection of the sensory systems to the cortex, the stimuli will initially arrive at the contralateral cerebral hemisphere. It is possible to record the speed or accuracy of response in a task which involves these stimuli and infer hemispheric lateralization from differences which are a function of which hemisphere receives the stimulus. There is a very extensive literature of studies of normal human subjects which have employed these tasks. In recent years, these studies have been supplemented by others using a range of more specialized techniques which have included electrophysiological measures (electroencephalogram and evoked potentials), measurement of cerebral blood flow, the observation of lateral eye movements, and other physiological techniques.

The findings of these studies are broadly in accord with the clinical literature and suggest that there are functional and organizational differences between the hemispheres. While there is extensive evidence for performance differences associated with lateralized presentation, the degree to which these differences can be attributed to structural neuropsychological factors, as opposed to internal attentional and cognitive processes, is still a matter of considerable debate. The importance of certain methodological details, including in particular the characteristics of the stimulus display, in generating artefactual asymmetries is also a continuing concern in the literature.

Whatever the nature of the processes underlying hemispheric localization, it is clear that this localization is only relative. That is, with the possible exception of speech, no function is absolutely localized to one or the other hemisphere: the differences which are observed are a matter of preference or degree of ability. Early conceptions considered that the nature of the stimuli as "verbal" or "figural" were important in determining the hemispheric localization. However, it has been possible to show that manipulating the cognitive demands of the tasks, while holding the stimuli constant, can generate differential hemispheric localization. As a consequence, interest has shifted to the cognitive nature of the task, with an emphasis on the characteristics of the processing undertaken. Certain contemporary theories invoke LEVELS OF PROCESSING, while others concentrate upon modes of processing or the contribution of specific component processes. Some recent research has suggested that certain of the asymmetries observed may relate to the internal representation of the lateral arrangement of the sensory world, rather than to specific lateral neural projections to the cortex.

Although the details of the hemisphere localization which may be observed remain unclear, it is reasonable to conclude on current evidence that there are performance asymmetries which relate to hemispheric localization and that these arise in part from the relatively peripheral stages of lateralized sensory projection into the brain and lateralized output systems controlling response, and in part from central cognitive processes which differ in character and organization between the hemispheres. The central processing asymmetries rely, at least in part, upon asymmetries in the cerebral representation of speech and language.

The concept of cerebral lateralization has had a wider influence in cognitive psychology, partly by emphasizing the general relevance of neuropsychological evidence in constructing models of cognitive function (see COGNITIVE NEUROPSYCHOLOGY), and partly through a specific contribution to cognitive neuropsychological models in such areas as reading, spelling, language function, and object recognition (see READING DEVELOPMENT; SPELLING).

See also AGING AND COGNITIVE CHANGE; DYSLEXIAS: ACQUIRED; LEARNING STYLES; POSNER, MICHAEL.

BIBLIOGRAPHY

Beaumont, J. G. (1983). *Introduction to neuropsychology*. Oxford: Blackwell Scientific.
— —. (Ed.) (1982). *Divided visual field studies of cerebral organisation*. London: Academic Press.
Bradshaw, J. L., & Nettleton, N. C. (1983). *Human cerebral asymmetry*. Englewood Cliffs, NJ: Prentice-Hall.
Bryden, M. P. (1982). *Laterality: Functional asymmetry in the intact brain*. New York: Academic Press.
Corballis, M. C. (1983). *Human laterality*. New York: Academic Press.
Hannay, H. J. (Ed.) (1986). *Experimental tech-*

niques in human neuropsychology. New York: Oxford University Press.

Heilman, K. M., & Valenstein, E. (Eds) (1985). Clinical neuropsychology (2nd edn). New York: Oxford University Press.

Hugdahl, K. (Ed.) (1988). Handbook of dichotic listening: Theory, methods and research. Chichester: Wiley.

Kolb, B., & Whishaw, I. Q. (1983). Fundamentals of human neuropsychology (2nd edn). San Francisco: Freeman.

J. GRAHAM BEAUMONT

human–computer interaction The area of human–computer interaction is concerned with how computers are used, and with ways of facilitating interactions between people and computers. If cognitive science is the study of the representation and use of knowledge in acting, seeing, thinking, conversing, and so on, one of its applications is cognitive engineering: applying this science to the design of information technology (see the chapter entitled "Cognitive engineering" by Norman, in Norman & Draper, 1986) (see COGNITIVE SCIENCE). With the development of cognitive engineering based on computers we might imagine that retrieving information, sending it to another person, organizing it in a document, analyzing it, making calculations based on it, and so forth, should all become much easier than with a technology based on paper. Indeed, the computer seems to promise us as much.

But as we know, except for professionals, for the intrepid, and for the eager schoolchildren who gather round computer counters in electrical stores, computers still seem to many people somewhat frightening, better left alone. The new understandings of the applied cognitive psychology of human–computer interaction are attempts to allow more people to approach computers with confidence – to allow us all to use them easily and pleasurably, just as now a high proportion of people are able to use the technologies of reading, writing, and paper. (These understandings should be distinguished from the sociological studies of the impact of computers on various groups in society – see, for example, Turkle (1984) –

though the psychological and sociological studies are highly relevant to each other.)

Though in theory computers allow us to do many things that were previously either impossible, or impossibly tedious, a large investment of time and effort is usually needed to get on speaking terms with computers. Many of us think that even with such an investment we would not manage interactions with computers very well. With a few exceptions one has to learn exotic languages, read manuals of forbidding size, perform complex rituals, and stare at messages which are seemingly as arcane as Egyptian hieroglyphs.

The situation can be compared with automobile ownership at the turn of this century. If one could afford an automobile, one also needed either to employ, or to be oneself, a skilled mechanic to make use of it. Now that has changed. We accept that a certain amount of time is spent learning to drive. This time is substantial, though small compared with the amount needed to read, or play a musical instrument. But when one has learned, one can now expect to be able to get into a car of any kind, anywhere, switch it on, drive it away, and not worry about what might be going on under the bonnet.

What has happened is that by a combination of engineering to make cars reliable, the gradual evolution of controls that offer easily intuitive actions, some standardization and some attention to road layouts, signposts, and maps, we do not have to be expert mechanics or navigators to use cars. We just use them effectively to go where we want to go. What originally had to be compiled into the mind of the skilled chauffeur is now compiled into the engineering design and ergonomic layout of controls of the car, and into the environment of roads and road signs, to prompt users with what they need to know in order to get where they want to.

The challenge for human–computer interaction is to bring computers to a comparable state, where we can simply turn them on and use them for the goals we desire. The aim is to leave our minds free to concentrate on the activity for which we are using the computer, not on idiosyncrasies of computer software. Understandings in cognitive science have grown to the point where the new subject of cognitive engineering is indeed emerging as the design of systems of this kind.

TWO KINDS OF INTERACTION AND A COGNITIVE THEORY

If we take an ordinary small home computer, two modes of interaction are now emerging which move us toward the goal of the easily usable system.

Direct manipulation The first is called direct manipulation. It is based on the idea that the computer and its input devices are like a tool and that the computer allows us to accomplish actions directly on objects of the kind in which we are interested. The idea of direct manipulation interfaces and the methods for achieving them are perhaps the first substantial result of cognitive engineering (see, for example, Schneiderman, 1987). The concept of direct manipulation helps also to distinguish the subject of human–computer interaction from ergonomics, which tends to concentrate on matters such as what height work surfaces should be, what levels of lighting are optimal for given tasks, how control levers should be designed for easy manipulation, the limits of human abilities in reading displays, and so forth (*see* HUMAN FACTORS).

Direct manipulation can be illustrated in the activity for which many people now use small computers, word processing. Let us imagine that if one wants to write something, that one could enter "Writing World" where the objects and activities of writing are easily available in an intuitive way. In Writing World we can think about what we are writing without distraction, compose text, check spellings and grammar, change the order of passages, browse through a document when making changes, sort and keep documents for easy access, send off a document to someone, and so on. We do not want to think about the operating system of the computer, and we will probably not want to have learned a specific set of computer commands and skills to do the operations of composing, altering, transposing, printing, or storing the information. In other words we do not want to be operating in "Computer World" – we would like the work-

ings of the computer to be of as little concern to us as the timing of the ignition system when we are driving a car.

An apt metaphor is that of the theatre, as described by Laurel (in Norman & Draper, 1986). Laurel explains that in theatrical presentations a world is simulated, and we enter into it to engage ourselves in the dramas that unfold. Similarly, as she points out, in computer arcade games, such as space invaders, we are invited into imaginary worlds. The computer supplies a passable simulation of a world which is without some of the constraints of the ordinary world. So, comparably, in Writing World, some of the less useful properties of paper can be suspended; that once paper is written on, corrections make a mess and that reordering of passages is difficult.

The currently preferred solution is largely based on research on an experimental computer interface called the Xerox Star (Smith, Irby, Verplanck, & Hurslem, 1982). It is commercially embodied in the Apple Macintosh range of computers, and their imitators. So successful is this type of interface that it promises to become the standard. In work stations, computers of the next size up to personal computers, so called "windows," are now standard and derive from this same idea.

A window is an area on the screen within which one kind of computational activity can be displayed or manipulated; for instance, results of a particular program running can be displayed. In another window, perhaps beside it on the screen, another activity can take place, perhaps editing the program, or indeed doing something quite unrelated. Windows can be moved anywhere on the screen, opened or closed, and have their size adjusted by directly pointing to parts of them with an arrow that can be moved about the screen by a device called a mouse. As the mouse is moved on the desk with one hand, it moves the arrow on the screen. So to change the size of a window one points at a corner with the arrow, and one can drag the corner, directly, until the window is of the required size.

For word processing, direct manipulation interfaces offer writers environments in which they can act, apparently directly, to do things concerned with writing. Part of this simulated world is a desk top. On it folders and documents can be placed, and opened. The mouse can be used to move any of these about, just as one might move a document on a real desk. It can also be used to open a folder, to find a place in a document, and so on, much as one might do with real paper. Then, if one wishes to write something, one can do it on a page, that appears on the screen, much as does paper in a typewriter. Now, however, the advantages multiply. One can alter what one has written at will, and each alteration produces something better, not an intermediate product that will have to be retyped. So if one wants to move a paragraph, for example, one merely points to the passage, then to a menu to indicate that the passage is to be cut out, and then to the place where one wants it to go.

The development of this system involved a great deal of research including behavioral experiments to evaluate the interaction (see, for example, Roberts & Moran, 1983). In general, design of interfaces and the interactions they support go through an iterative series of prototypes which have to be debugged and developed by trying them out with users. Thus, successful design is likely to depend more and more on the psychological measurement of user's performance, adapting methods such as think-aloud protocols, structured incident diaries, checklists, questionnaires, semi-structured interviews, and experimental measures of performance variables such as learning time and errors. Moreover, it is clear that when computerized equipment is installed in work settings, it is not just how the computers work that must be considered, but the whole context of personal and organizational structure that must be reconsidered. This, once again, depends on being able to evaluate the actual user's interactions with the equipment (see, for example, Clegg et al. 1988).

With interfaces of the Star or Macintosh kind, the advantages of word processing appear in something approaching a developed form. One need not learn special word processing languages so that one can utter legal computer commands with the correct syntax. In this simulated world, composition is done by typing and alteration by pointing. The effects of such operations appear directly, and the revised text remains in a pristine state. Once one has made the relatively small investment of learning to type, and put in about an hour's exploration of the facilities of the system, nearly all the operations of writing are actually quicker, easier, and more pleasurable than they are with paper. One can concentrate on thinking about what one is writing, not on incidentals of the devices used to mediate the process.

Direct manipulation interfaces use the simulation capacities of the computer to create worlds, such as that of the desktop, which allow us to transpose pre-existing mental models, such as those about desks and folders. It also improves the properties of paper to produce a new super-paper, writeable-on in any type font, automatically searchable, and instantly correctable.

Of course, word processing was a substantial advance even without Macintosh-like interfaces. With less advanced word-processing packages that were based on computer operating systems like CP/M and MS-DOS, users typically had to compile into their minds a vocabulary of computer commands. They had to supplement the shortcomings of the computer with acquired skills. The objective of human–computer interface engineering is to eliminate the need for people to help out the computer designers. Instead, with the perspective of user-centered design, designers develop systems that allow people to do what they wish, using computational power to simulate the kinds of worlds in which they might want to act.

A cognitive theory of action On what kinds of cognitive science are practices of designing direct manipulation interfaces based? It is probably best to think of this in terms of the theory of planning and action. A version of this is by Norman (in Norman & Draper [1986] and extended to devices other than computers by Norman, 1988).

The theory is that actions are based on a goal to accomplish something. From a goal we form an intention to achieve it in a particular way. From this we create a plan made up of ordered actions. But whereas goals and intentions are psychological, actions must be made on the physical world, taking account of the characteristics of physical things, for instance of the properties of paper, or computers. Inevitably there is a gap between the psychological intention and the physical action. Norman (in Norman & Draper, 1986), in fact, identifies two gaps: he calls them the gulf of execution and the gulf of interpretation. The first is crossed by knowing what physical things must be done to accomplish psychological intentions. The second is crossed by knowing how to interpret the physical state of the system to monitor progress towards accomplishing an intention.

In interactions with computers designers have until recently assumed that these gulfs will, as described above, be crossed by human skills. But with direct manipulation interfaces they are narrowed by drawing on computational power, aiming to bring actions and effects closer to existing human intentions and intuitions. As well as interfaces for writing, other examples are spreadsheets that create an Accountancy World, in which one can see directly on accounting tables, effects such as making an alteration at one place, and the repercussions of this occurring automatically wherever in the table they might apply; databases in which one can discover what species a plant or bird might be by indicating features of a specimen one has; statistical packages in which one can look at graphs to see effects of this or that transformation of the data; learning environments for physics in which one can change the force of gravity or friction and explore its effects on the interactions of moving bodies.

Conversational interfaces The second kind of interaction that has been developed can be called conversational. It is necessary because there is a snag with direct manipulation. It is that if someone using such a device does not know what kinds of things can be done with it, it is not clear what should happen next. How do we deal with those frequent occasions in using computers, when we do not know what we might want to know?

In this situation the direct manipulation interface is not always much help. Instead, we want to enter into a conversation of some kind, from which it might emerge, for instance, that there is a facility for inserting pictures in a piece of writing, and a suggestion about how to go about it.

At present, implementations of conversational interfaces are in a much less advanced state than direct manipulation interfaces. They tend to take the form of menus, including so-called pop-up or pull-down menus arranged around the side of a window in which direct manipulation can occur. Menus may be accompanied by so-called dialog boxes in which there appear on the screen displays rather like small questionnaires: "Do you want to do this or that? Indicate by pointing."

Such devices are conversational in the crude sense that user and computer take turns. The user asks the computer to display options. It does this, and the user's next turn is limited to choosing among them.

This does not address the question of how a computer might answer users' questions in general, questions like: "Now I'm stuck. What do I do next?" or "How do I do such and such?" Surveys have been conducted where users have a choice of sources of information: i.e. manuals, lecture notes, on-line help facilities, colleagues, or skilled advisors. Most users, most of the time, even when they are skilled, prefer to go to a human for a conversation about a problem, rather than to turn to printed paper or on-line help sources. Cognitive engineering has not proceeded far enough to allow the possibility of the kinds of conversation with a computer that users have with other human beings, even only partly knowledgeable ones when they need some new piece of knowledge, or do not know quite what they need to know.

The reasons for this are complex and only partly to do with progress in computational understanding of utterances in natural language. One problem can be illustrated as follows. What a user wants when he or she gets stuck is to find the next piece of plan that will move toward accomplishing a goal, to cross the gulf of execution. A user of a word processing system might want to know how to accomplish the minor goal of joining two paragraphs which have blank lines between them. This is a real example of a difficulty experienced by someone learning word processing from Mack, Lewis, and Carroll (1983), who have used think-aloud protocols to discover the range of difficulties that new users have with word processing.

One reason this user will be frustrated in finding what he or she wants from even the best manuals or on-line help systems is that access to the information needed will not be indexed under any such goal as "joined up text" or "paragraphs merged together." It will be indexed under an action, in this case "deletion." But the translation from goals to actions that would accomplish them was the problem in the first place. To merge paragraphs the user must delete a character (carriage return) that is unlikely to be visible on the screen. This operation is not similar to anything one could do with an ordinary typewriter, and hence one's mental model of typewriting does not transpose. But a more experienced user can recognize the goal of "joined up text," know what kind of plan must be assembled to accomplish it, and hence help easily in a conversational enquiry.

We need to imagine, therefore, not just creating simulated worlds on which the user can act, but also understanding sufficiently well the properties of joint planning in conversation, that we can provide computational conversation partners at those junctures when users get stuck.

Here the theory of planning by single agents must be extended – to a theory of purposeful conversation in constructing joint plans. A joint plan is a plan with more than one agent, cooperating to achieve a goal which one agent could not accomplish alone. So the user has some goals, and perhaps asks for and receives information from the computational conversation partner about what it could do to help. Constrained by some of the maxims of human conversation, the computer would say something relevant, at an appropriate level to the topic, giving an appropriate quantity of information, not either enigmatic telegraphic messages, or pages of text for the user to search through. Possible bases for joint planning are described in this volume under DISTRIBUTED COGNITION.

SOME IMPLICATIONS FOR GENERAL COGNITIVE THEORY

It would be most helpful for human–computer interaction if cognitive theory based on improved ideas of planning could inform design of both direct manipulation interfaces and conversational interfaces.

What might such a theory look like? It is traditional in cognitive science to think of knowledge as either procedural or declarative (*see* DECLARATIVE AND PROCEDURAL KNOWLEDGE). The distinction is natural where a stored procedure (plan) computes over stored data structures without much reference to the outside world. Much human activity does not resemble this, however, but is organized around what Draper (in Norman & Draper, 1986) calls "information flow," in which information is picked up from the world in the course of action.

The difference is not merely one of feedback: people often decide what to do on the basis of information flow, and embark on action expecting to find out how to succeed as they go along, as if acting on faith rather than knowledge. For instance, in setting out to find an office in an unfamiliar building we expect to succeed even though we do not know the room numbering system. We have neither a mental model adequate to finding the room without search, nor a procedure guaranteed to find it. Observing new users of such interfaces indicates that their behavior similarly is of this kind, and is guided from moment to moment by what they take to be clues. This can also be characteristic of experienced users.

It has been found that even experienced users of direct manipulation systems recall little of the contents of the displays and menus they use, even though these have mediated their successful performance. The necessary information is picked up, used, and discarded, but not learned. This has implications for decreasing learning times for new systems, since not having to learn commands even for skilled performance makes for fast acquisition, and for writing manuals, since there is no need to teach what need not be learned.

The development of cognitive theory relevant to human–computer interaction thus continues analyses of the sources of knowledge that support cognitive skills, e.g. studies of mental models, incidental learning, and depth of processing. It differs from these approaches because modern interfaces have forced us to realize that many of the ways in which humans prefer to act depend not only on internalized knowledge, but also on information left in the world, used as external memory to be consulted via perception, and as steps of partly completed plans which will be able to prompt the next step.

Conversation has some similar properties acting by means of information flow. We set out on conversations not knowing exactly what will occur, and without having a definite plan of what will happen. We are guided continuously by cues, and reach goals that we could formulate only very vaguely at the outset.

No general theory yet exists that shows how and why collaborations of users and machines can be successful. But a perspective that seeks to augment traditional cognitive theories of planning with processes of information flow and cooperative agency is prompted by studying human–computer interaction. It promises also to have important theoretical consequences for cognitive science more generally.

See also LANGUAGE COMPREHENSION.

BIBLIOGRAPHY

Clegg, C. et al. (1988). *People and computers: How to evaluate your company's new technology.* Chichester: Ellis Horwood.

Mack, R. L., Lewis, C. H., & Carroll, J. M. (1983). Learning to use word processors: Problems and prospects. *ACM Transactions on Office Systems, 1,* 254–71.

Norman, D. A. (1988). *The psychology of everyday things.* New York: Basic Books.

——, & Draper, S. W. (1986). *User centered system design.* Hillsdale, NJ: Erlbaum.

Roberts, T. L., & Moran, T. P. (1983). The evaluation of text editors: Methodology and empirical results. *Communications of the ACM, 26,* 265–83.

Schneiderman, B. (1987). Direct manipulation: A step beyond programming languages. In R. M. Baeker & W. S. Buxton (Eds), *Readings in human–computer interaction: A multidisciplin-ary approach.* Los Altos, Calif.: Morgan Kaufman.

Smith, D. C., Irby, C., Verplanck, W., & Hurslem, E. (1982). Designing the Star user interface. *Byte, 7,* 242–82.

Turkle, S. (1984). *The second self: Computers and the human spirit.* New York: Simon & Schuster.

KEITH OATLEY

human factors

BACKGROUND

The "human factors" discipline seeks to optimize the relationship between people and their work. It is complementary to machine factors which is concerned to optimize the relationship between machines and their work. Since people and machines together form work systems, both types of optimization are required to ensure the effectiveness with which human and machine together perform work (Dowell & Long, 1989). Consider the case of a postal worker sorting letters into destination categories on the basis of numerical codes entered into an electro-mechanical sorting device by means of a 0–9 matrix keypad. Effective sorting in terms of correctness and speed would require the optimal design of the coding scheme and the layout of the keys on the pad (human factors) and the optimal design of key and sorting device mechanisms (machine factors).

Human factors is an emergent discipline with its own scope – that is, people interacting with machines to perform work, its own practice – that is, the design of the interactions for effectiveness, and its own knowledge – that is, design guidelines derived from human-science research. Human factors, thus, has a research activity – acquiring discipline knowledge – and an operational activity – applying discipline knowledge. Human factors is often closely associated with the superordinate disciplines of engineering – reflecting its concern with efficiency and productivity, and medicine – reflecting its concerns with comfort and mental and physical well-being. Human factors is considered to be synonymous with ergonomics, although human factors is more pervasive in North America, perhaps with a more psychological and engineering emphasis, while ergonomics is more pervasive in Europe, perhaps with a more physiological and medical emphasis.

In what follows, the psychological aspects, and in particular the cognitive psychological aspects, of human factors knowledge, practice, and scope are emphasized. However, the role of psychology predates the recent "cognitive revival" and the latter should be viewed in the context of a psychology which has always included cognition. In turn, psychology should be viewed within the wider context of human factors.

HISTORY AND ORIGINS

Human factors as a craft has existed since the very beginnings of work and its design – witness the construction of Roman roads, the Egyptian pyramids, and the great Chinese wall. The craft has changed with the evolution of notions of work and its design (from medieval to modern). It has also changed with the advent of new technologies (the manual and mechanical tools of the cottage industry and the steam-powered machines of the Industrial Revolution – Brown, 1979).

Further, attempts have been made to systematize work and its design based on studies of the "time and motion" of work – particularly the physical behavior of the worker (Barnes, 1937); its "scientific management" (Taylor, 1911), and the importance of "morale" for its workgroups (Urwick & Brech, 1948). However, human factors as a self-confessed discipline originated with the inadequate performance of new technologies such as radar and sonar produced during the Second World War (Murrell, 1965). Their design included machine factors but apparently not human factors. For example, the sonar and radar operators were unable to sustain the high levels of vigilance required over time to ensure the correct identification of enemy targets. Human scientists attempted to improve operator performance by the application of psychology and its methods (including rest pauses, knowledge of results, drugs, etc. – Mackworth, 1950) (*see* ATTENTION).

DEVELOPMENT

Following the Second World War, human factors has developed as a discipline. Professional societies have been formed. Research into work and work design has been conducted by universities and research institutes. And human factors practice in designing work has been introduced into industry as well as extended by the military.

Human factors has been developed throughout North America and Europe. Its development underwent two important phases. The first, or "classical" phase, laid emphasis on the use of scientific knowledge and methods in the evaluation and redesign of machines and equipment difficult, or even impossible to use for their purpose (Shackel, 1974). The second, or "systems" phase, laid emphasis on the development of methods for integrating human factors knowledge and guidelines into initial machine and system design and development (Singleton, 1974). The development of technology over the same period from electro-mechanical (as in process control, for example oil refineries) to electronic (as in narrow-band communication, for example telephones), has required commensurate development of the knowledge base of human factors, including psychology, and its application in practice.

Human factors continues to gain in recognition as an emergent discipline. The recognition comes partly from an economic climate which emphasizes the productive efficiency of work and the importance of competition. The recognition also comes from the attempt of human factors to meet the challenge of information technology. The increased computerization of work has required the research and development of support for the design of computers which are easy to learn and safe to use (*see* HUMAN–COMPUTER INTERACTION). The decreased emphasis on physical work and the increased emphasis on information-based or knowledge-intensive work has given rise to cognitive human factors (or cognitive ergonomics) with an associated emphasis on cognitive psychology (see below).

The human factors discipline currently possesses three different conceptions – each with its own knowledge and practice, but the same general problem of designing human interactions with machines for effective work (Long & Dowell, 1989). Craft practice of "trial-and-error" design is supported by the rules of thumb of successful designers. Applied science practice of "specification and implementation" is supported by guidelines based on science which explains human behavior. Engineering practice of "specification then implementation" is supported by principles based on engineering theories which prescribe effective performance. Current human factors practice consists of craft and applied science. Since the craft discipline of human factors is implicit in good practice, and since human factors engineering principles (which guarantee performance) are as yet undeveloped, the perspective adopted in what follows is that of human factors as applied (human) science, and in particular as applied (cognitive) psychology.

SCIENCE SUPPORT

Human sciences provide support for human factors design practice. Human sciences include both the biological and the psychological. Support takes the form of guidelines for design or redesign. Individual sciences have a scope, knowledge, and topics of current research. These aspects will be considered next with respect to the sciences of physiology, biomechanics, psychology, and sociology as they support human factors design practice. Where appropriate, illustrations of knowledge which might support practice will be provided from the problem of designing a code and a keypad for sorting letters (cited earlier).

The scope of physiology is physical behavior as mediated by the respiratory and the cardio-vascular systems. These provide energy to the human body and control its temperature. Physiological models of behavior are typically self-regulatory servo-systems. Physiological effects on behavior are determined by diet quality, fitness, training, oxygen costs of work, etc. Energy demands of a letter sorter keypad operator would be expected to be low. But, were such a sedentary task to be unrelieved by others, and ones involving more physical activity, problems of

understimulation and underfitness might be expected to result. Current topics of research include energy expenditure (in mining, forestry, etc.), optimal climates (heating, ventilation, etc.), and protective clothing (against both heat and cold).

The scope of biomechanics is also physical behavior, but as mediated by the linked segments of the body (including bones and muscles). These support behavior by the exertion of forces as in sitting, lifting, etc. Biomechanical models are typically based on principles of springs and levers expressing torques about an angle. Factors affecting behavior include fatigue, posture, and size of the workers. Biomechanical aspects of the letter sorter's coding task would include force characteristics of the keys, seating posture, dimensions of the work station, etc. Current research topics include dynamic anthropometrics (that is, work involving bending, reaching, etc.) and injuries caused by repetitive strain.

The scope of psychology is mental behavior as mediated by the mind and the brain. Traditionally, mental behavior is considered to have three aspects: cognition, supporting the acquisition and use of knowledge; conation, supporting actions, motivation, and will; and affect, supporting feelings and emotions. Psychological models of mental behavior, as they relate to work in the context of human factors, are typically information-processing models of cognition. They embody the physical limits on mental behavior as set by light and sound quantity, sleep loss, sensory deprivation, etc. They also accommodate psychological factors affecting mental behavior, including color and brightness of physical objects, patterns of events, semantics of language, levels of skill, etc. Cognitive psychological aspects of the letter sorter's coding task would include: the coding scheme, relating letter addresses to letter destinations, both with respect to its learning and retention; the layout of the keypad, especially with regard to other layouts experienced by sorters – for example, the calculator top line 789, etc. versus the telephone top line 123, etc.; and the planning and control of coding behavior, especially with regard to the anticipation of events and the overlapping of behaviors. Current research addresses the topics of visual search (and inspection), instructions, memory load, communication, etc.

The scope of sociology (including occupational psychology, social studies, etc.) is the social and organizational relations between people and groups. The scope includes group organization, communicaton, social values, control, etc. People and groups are modeled as autonomous but collaborative actors or agents. Limits on human social behavior are set by isolation and crowding. Social factors affecting behavior include team or group structure, leadership type and style, lines of communication, quality of life, communication, etc. Social aspects of the letter sorter's coding task might include: whether coding was an individual or team task; communicative distance between coders; status relations between workers; etc. Current research topics address the issues of role playing, selection, training, organizational stress, effect of shift work regimes, etc.

This completes the characterization of some of the sciences providing support for the human factors practice of design and redesign. Although analytic decomposition of the differing scopes of science (into biomechanics, psychology, etc.) facilitates the acquisition of knowledge, it makes resynthesis for the purpose of human factors design more difficult. First, scientific knowledge must be expressed prescriptively with respect to design (usually as guidelines). Second, it must be applied to the context in which work is carried out. The work situation is conceptualized next.

WORK

Work takes place in and originates with organizations which usually intersect some social need with technology (mining, publishing, etc.). As indicated earlier, the basic work system consists of a worker and a machine. Together, they effect work in the domain of application of the work system. Work is expressed as the change in attribute state of objects in the domain (air passengers safely transported, quality books published, etc.). Work systems may have one or many operators, one or many machines, and be related to other work systems (in a typing pool, an air traffic control room, etc.). Workers and machines exhibit behaviors which interact to perform the work of the system. How well the work is performed is expressed as performance, in terms of the quality of the work, and the costs to the user and the machine of carrying out the behaviors necessary to achieve it.

The human factors design problem can be expressed in terms of optimizing human behaviors, such that when they interact with machine and environmental behaviors, desired performance of work is achieved. Human interaction occurs by means of sensors (eyes and ears), processes (understanding, reasoning), and effectors (hands, feet, voice). Machine interaction occurs by means of displays (dials, screens), processes (conveying, mixing), and controls (knobs, keyboards). Environment involves the climatic conditions (light, temperature) which may affect both human and machine behaviors. In what follows, a brief illustration is provided of how guidelines, derived from science, can be applied to human factors design problems conceptualized in the terms expressed here. Given the focus of this volume, interest is restricted to (cognitive) psychology applications.

Displays represent machine and work states to support control. Criteria for their operation include speed, accuracy, etc. Displays may be qualitative – on/off; quantitative – a dial; or representational – a map. Constraints on displays include the function and range of values to be represented, and their meaning. Guidelines for design would be that scale dimensions on a dial should trade operational speed (few divisions) for accuracy (many divisions), and that diagrammatic representations support the effective expression of relations (spatial, safety). In the case of the letter sorter's keypad, feedback should be provided on the code number or the destination keyed. This would help ensure correct coding, and so the quality of the work performed. Controls enable a machine to be put in a desired state and so control work. Criteria for their design include speed, force, range, etc. Many types of control exist – knobs, levers, switches, which can be operated by hand, foot, head, etc. Constraints on controls include function, range of values, meaning, etc. Guidelines for design would be that switching controls should be accompanied by a directional arrow, and that precision of control requires large rather than small controls. In the case of the letter sorter's keypad, it would be necessary to ensure compatibility between the layout and other layouts experienced by workers.

Guidelines also exist which relate displays to controls, since the spatial and other relations between them affect workers' ability to carry out procedures and infer the need for action. For example, people's expectations (population stereotypes) and previous training should be taken into account in a design. A clockwise movement of a control knob would be expected by most people to move a display pointer up (not down), or to the right (not to the left). Likewise, the frequency, functions, and sequence of use of controls and their associated display representations should be compatibly related for ease of learning and of use. In the case of the letter sorters keypad, the key controls should be clearly labeled.

Work-space layout supports the interaction between human and machine in the interests of desired performance. Criteria for design include comfort, safety, operational speed, etc. Of particular importance is the easy access of information either from the machine or working environment. Work spaces may be for individual (office) or groups (assembly line). The letter sorter's work space should afford a clear view of the letters and the keypad.

Environmental conditions limit worker behaviors. Conditions include light, sound, temperature, vibration, etc. Criteria for design would be comfort, operational speed, safety, etc. Constraints would include limits and desired ranges for the particular conditions. Guidelines would be to avoid glare and flicker from lighting; if possible to insulate unacceptable levels of sound at source, or if not to insulate the operator (by screen or ear protectors); and to vary ambient working temperatures as a function of the energic requirements of the tasks being performed. In the case of the letter sorter's environment, light, sound, and temperature levels would

need to be appropriate to support the achievement of desired performance.

Guidelines such as those cited have contributed to the design and redesign of work by human factors specialists in a number of different domains of work: light and heavy manufacture (shoes, cars, etc.) of "natural" production (coal, oil, gas, etc.); passenger and cargo transport; leisure and business activities (both public and private); mental and physical care, involving nurses, doctors, and hospital/health administrators; and weapon and defense developments. In all these areas, specific design solutions to human factors design problems could be cited which are supported by guidelines whose origins are in cognitive psychology (the design of nuclear power station control rooms, the redesign of underground systems, the design of tanks, etc.).

COGNITIVE HUMAN FACTORS

The revival of cognition in psychology as "cognitive psychology," with its emphasis on internal representations and their transformation in higher mental processes, such as REASONING, LANGUAGE COMPREHENSION, imaging, etc. has been reflected in human factors by the development of cognitive human factors (or cognitive ergonomics – Long, 1987). The development constitutes an attempt to meet the challenge of the novel machine factors exhibited by the behavior of computers, the new information technology. The computer is the most sophisticated tool-machine so far invented, and its pervasive introduction into the domain of work has resulted in the requirement to extend human factors knowledge and practice.

The extension is needed to accommodate complex computer behaviors supported by novel representation of application domains (wire frame modeling of engineering artefacts, such as an oil rig); tasks (navigation procedures involved in searching a bibliographic database); and users (embedded models of student competence in computer-aided learning systems). Accommodation is achieved by developing user models of the behaviors, which both describe and explain, and can be used to support design. The extension is also required to support an understanding of user behaviors based on mental structures reflected in representations and processes associated with the application domain (air-traffic controllers' image of airspace); the task (reasoning concerning constraint satisfaction in design); and the computer (acquisition of a mental model to support an understanding of its behaviors). The guidelines prescribing the relatively simple cognitive relations between "knobs and dials" are now being replaced by guidelines prescribing complex cognitive relations between computer and human representations.

Extension of human factors knowledge, design guidelines, and practice has been achieved by broadening its concerns to include linguistics and psycholinguistics (for command language syntax, for natural language interfaces); ARTIFICIAL INTELLIGENCE (for symbolic planning and reasoning techniques); computing (for algorithms, for example, to complete obscured images); and newly developing aspects of cognitive psychology (for document/text structures, for mental models, for event and semantic memory). Cognitive human factors constitutes the single most important trend in human factors at this time.

In conclusion, human factors continues to advance and to develop as an emergent discipline. It continues to shape its knowledge base, and in particular that of cognitive psychology, as a function of the work to be performed, and the people and machine technologies available to support the performance of effective work.

BIBLIOGRAPHY

Barnes, R. M. (1937). *Motion and time study*. New York: Wiley.
Brown, J. A. C. (1979). *Social psychology of industry*. Harmondsworth: Penguin.
Dowell, J., & Long, J. B. (1989). Towards a conception for an engineering discipline of human factors. *Ergonomics, 32*, 1513–35.
Long, J. B. (1987). Cognitive ergonomics and human–computer interaction. In P. Warr (Ed.), *Psychology at work* (pp. 73–95). Harmondsworth: Penguin.
——, & Dowell, J. (1989). Conceptions of the discipline of HCI: Craft, applied science and engineering. In A. Sutcliffe & L. Macaulay (Eds), *People and computers*. Cambridge: Cambridge University Press.
Mackworth, N. H. (1950). *Researches in the measurement of human performance*. MRC Special Report Series No. 268, HM Stationery Office.
Murrell, K. F. H. (1965). *Ergonomics – man in his working environment*. London: Chapman and Hall.
Shackel, B. (Ed.) (1974). *Applied ergonomics handbook*. Guildford, Surrey: IPC.
Singleton, W. T. (1974). *Man–machine systems*. Harmondsworth: Penguin.
Taylor, F. W. (1911). *Principles of scientific management*. New York: Harper Bros.
Urwick, L., & Brech, E. (1948). *Making of scientific management* (Vol. 3): *The Hawthorne investigations*. London: Management Publications Trust.

J. B. LONG

humor There are many reasons why people find something humorous, which are reflected in the large number of quite different theories of humor. For instance, humor is often related to aggression, with a negative action happening to someone else forming the basis of the humor. This is especially obvious in the case of jokes made at the expense of disliked minority, ethnic, or religious groups.

Even in jokes having an aggressive theme, however, there often exists the additional ingredient of incongruity or surprise. To the cognitive psychologist, the theoretical approaches emphasizing the notion that much humor stems from the resolution of incongruity are particularly interesting (see Nerhardt, 1976). In other words, the comprehension and appreciation of humor involve a biphasic sequence of incongruity and resolution.

Consider the following W. C. Fields joke: "Do you believe in clubs for young people?" "Only when kindness fails." There is an apparent incongruity between the question and the answer, because there is a natural initial tendency to interpret the homograph "clubs" in the sense of "social groups." The joke is understood only when the alternative interpretation (i.e. "large sticks") is accessed.

Shultz (1974) asked subjects to indicate the

order in which they processed the different elements in jokes. The typical order was as follows: first, the incorrect interpretation of the ambiguous element was detected ("clubs" meaning "social groups"); second, the element of the incongruity was processed ("only when kindness fails"); and third, the hidden meaning of the ambiguous element was perceived ("clubs" meaning "large sticks"). The contextual information in the joke biases the initial interpretation of the ambiguity, and only the subsequent detection of incongruity leads to a reinterpretation that makes sense of all of the information in the joke.

The incongruity–resolution theory of humor explains the fact that a joke or a cartoon previously encountered usually seems much less funny on subsequent exposure. Since one generally remembers the resolution of the incongruity, there is no longer any "double take" or incongruity resolution; thus, the main ingredient in humor is now missing.

Although most cognitive psychologists have not extended their theorizing to humor, much humor clearly has an important cognitive aspect. In particular, the reasons why verbal jokes are found amusing can be understood in terms of the comprehension processes involved (see LANGUAGE COMPREHENSION).

BIBLIOGRAPHY

Nerhardt, G. (1976). Incongruity and funniness: Towards a new descriptive model. In T. Chapman & H. C. Foot (Eds), *Humour and laughter: Theory, research and applications* (pp. 237–45). London: Wiley.
Shultz, T. R. (1974). Order and processing in humour appreciation. *Canadian Journal of Psychology, 28*, 409–20.

M. W. EYSENCK

hypnosis Hypnotic-induction procedures typically involve suggestions for sleep and relaxation and instructions for eye fixation to produce hypnosis, which may represent an altered state of consciousness. A "deepening" of hypnosis may be facilitated by the use of imagery to divorce the individual from influences external to the hypnotic process. Standardized tests, which may include motor items such as arm levitation, and cognitive items such as hallucinating a buzzing insect or post-hypnotic suggestions, effectively discriminate between individuals and show hypnotic susceptibility to be a reasonably stable characteristic.

Although most commentators trace the origins of hypnosis to the eighteenth-century proponents of "animal magnetism," such as Franz Anton Mesmer (1734–1815), the word "hypnosis" was reputedly coined in the 1840s by a Scottish physician, James Braid (1795–1860). Braid believed that the "magnetized" individual was in a sleep-like state, so he derived the word "hypnosis" from the Greek "hypnos," meaning "to sleep" (Sheehan & Perry, 1976). After the magnetic theory was discredited by the Royal Commission of Inquiry appointed in France in 1784, the Portuguese priest di Faria, Bernard in France, and Braid in England all contributed to the increasing recognition that magnetic phenomena were of mental, not physical, origin. Bernheim (1837–1919) did much to establish the view that hypnotic phenomena result from increased suggestibility.

At the risk of over-simplification, modern theories of hypnosis may be classified as *state* or *non-state* (see Sheehan & Perry, 1976). Spanos (e.g. 1986) has conceptualized the distinction as one between theories which maintain that hypnosis brings into play special processes and those which believe that the processes involved in hypnotic phenomena are those which operate in other situations. Supporters of the traditional state-approach to hypnosis usually assume that the deeper the state of the hypnotized subject, the more likely he or she is to respond to suggestions.

Although state theorists vary greatly in the claims they make for hypnosis, they seem to agree that hypnotized individuals can exhibit some unusual and remarkable phenomena. These include: involuntary actions (including automatic writing), distortions of memory (including amnesia), hallucinations, and insensitivity to both clinical and experimentally induced pain. Such phenomena are of considerable interest to cognitive psychologists because, if valid, they would appear to have fundamental implications for our understanding of CONSCIOUSNESS and perceptual processes.

Possibly the most widely acclaimed state theories are those which maintain that in hypnosis the experience of effect is dissociated from consciousness (e.g. Hilgard, 1986). According to Hilgard's neo-dissociation theory, the cognitive system has a central control which directs subsystems and communication between them. Hypnotic phenomena are accounted for by dissociation or separation of one part of the system from the remainder by "amnesic barriers." Hilgard argues that these systems are not all conscious at the same time, but that they can be brought into or removed from consciousness through hypnotic suggestion. Thus, the hypnotized subject can, for instance, write or move an arm without being aware of it (because the actions are dissociated from awareness), be amnesic for items which are actually available at another level or in another "part" of the mind, and experience little or no pain in response to a noxious stimulus, even though the pain is actually felt at another level not represented in consciousness.

Barber (1969) has been the most vociferous critic of state theories. He showed that hypnotic procedures are not necessary to achieve responses to suggestions such as arm levitation and selective amnesia. They can be achieved to a similar extent with instructions to become imaginatively involved, or think along with the suggestions. Furthermore, state theorists have traditionally found their strongest support in evidence that hypnotized subjects can exceed the physical and mental abilities of unhypnotized subjects. However, when proper controls (such as simulating and task-motivating instructions favored by Orne, 1959) are employed, it is difficult to find unqualified support for such claims. Hypnotic analgesia, which is often taken as the strongest evidence for special hypnotic effects, is well documented, but distraction, anxiety reduction, and the use of imagery can be effective in the absence of hypnosis (see Wagstaff, 1981). Any memory enhancement associated with hypnosis in forensic investigations can possibly be accounted for by processes not peculiar to hypnosis such as reminiscence, relaxation, or "talking back" the subject to the mental context of the episode (*see* ENCODING SPECIFICITY PRINCIPLE).

"Non-state" theorists argue that hypnotic phenomena can best be described and explained in terms of concepts and processes from mainstream social and cognitive psychology such as attitudes, expectations, conformity, imagination, beliefs, and relaxation (Spanos & Chaves, 1989; Wagstaff, 1981). The induction procedure provides the context for both subject and hypnotist to play the roles they believe appropriate. Non-state theorists do not argue that all hypnotic behaviors are "faked" (though some may be); rather, they claim that the full range of hypnotic phenomena, including reports of involuntary actions, amnesia, hallucinations, and the control of pain (including surgical pain) can be readily and more parsimoniously accounted for without reference to a special hypnotic process or altered state of consciousness. For example, post-hypnotic amnesia can be explained in terms of self-generated distraction from retrieval cues. Although the *distraction* is deliberate, subjects are able to interpret the *forgetting* as effortless.

A large amount of experimental work has been carried out in an attempt to decide between the state and non-state theoretical positions. Most of this research has involved comparing hypnotic subjects (that is, subjects given a hypnotic induction procedure) with various control groups set up to test alternative non-state explanations. For example, control subjects may be instructed to simulate or fake hypnosis, or to try hard to imagine various effects (Sheehan & Perry, 1976). The evidence remains unclear. Orne (1959) has long maintained that hypnotically susceptible subjects can be distinguished in a number of meaningful ways. In one such demonstration, Orne instructed hypnotic and simulating subjects to describe a real object behind an imagined person. Hypnotic subjects usually do so: it is possible to accept the presence of the person and that the object is visible. This *trance logic* usually escapes the simulator who insists the object cannot be seen.

In general terms, experimental research has failed to isolate any definitive, unique physiological correlate of a hypnotic state, and there is little support for the view that hypnotic suggestions enable individuals to transcend normal motivated performance on cognitive and motor tasks. Nevertheless, other proposed features of the hypnotic state such as the reporting of hallucinations, disorganization of recall in partial amnesia, and the alleged appearance of multiple levels of control, especially in pain reports, remain highly contentious. Considerable debate also surrounds the stability of hypnotic responding. While state theorists tend to claim that hypnotic susceptibility is a stable trait, some non-state theorists claim that hypnotic susceptibility can be modified if subjects are taught appropriate attitudes, expectations, and cognitive strategies.

The basic state versus non-state controversy remains unresolved. However, one important result of this research has been a tendency by both sides of this debate to perceive the hypnotic subject more as an active cognizing agent rather than as a passive automaton under the power of the hypnotist (e.g. Wagstaff, 1986).

BIBLIOGRAPHY

Barber, T. X. (1969). *Hypnosis: A scientific approach*. New York: Van Nostrand.

Hilgard, E. R. (1986). *Divided consciousness: Multiple controls in human thought and action*. New York: Wiley-Interscience.

Orne, M. T. (1959). The nature of hypnosis: Artifact and essence. *Journal of Abnormal and Social Psychology, 58*, 277–99.

Sheehan, P. W., & Perry, C. W. (1976). *Methodologies of hypnosis: A critical appraisal of contemporary paradigms of hypnosis*. New York: Wiley.

Spanos, N. P. (1986). Hypnotic behavior: A social psychological interpretation of amnesia, analgesia, and "Trance Logic." *Behavior and Brain Sciences, 9*, 449–502.

— —, & Chaves, J. F. (Eds) (1989). *Hypnosis: The cognitive-behavioral perspective*. New York: Prometheus.

Wagstaff, G. F. (1981). *Hypnosis, compliance and belief*. Brighton: Harvester; New York: St Martin's Press.

— —. (1986). Hypnosis as compliance and belief: A socio-cognitive view. In P. L. N. Naish (Ed.), *What is hypnosis?* Milton Keynes: Open University Press.

V. H. GREGG and G. F. WAGSTAFF

I

iconic store This is a high capacity, short-lived visual memory located early in the processing of visual information, and is analogous to the ECHOIC STORE in auditory memory. Current interest in iconic memory began with experiments by Sperling (1960) in which subjects were presented with visual arrays of random letters (e.g. three rows of four) for brief periods (typically 50 millisec.). They were required to report either as many letters as possible in the correct locations (*whole* report) or the items from only one row cued after the display had terminated (*partial* report). Whole report was no more than four or five items. In contrast, partial report with no cue delay was almost perfect but declined steadily with increasing cue delays of up to about 500 millisec. The superiority of partial over whole report suggests there is more information available about the array immediately after stimulus offset than can usually be reported, but it is lost after about half a second. This conclusion is consistent with subjects' reports of a persisting visible trace. Other studies have shown that color and size are effective for cueing partial report, and that information persistence is affected by the visual characteristics of pre- and post-exposure fields (jumbled letter fragments especially disrupt persistence). An important early finding was that categorical cues (e.g. report only letters from a display of letters and digits) do not yield partial report superiority.

The findings described above suggest the existence of a *visible*, precategorical memory of high capacity but brief duration. This may serve the function of holding information while it is passed further into the processing system. But it is difficult to maintain a simple, sequential model of visual memory, in which partial report superiority and the phenomenologically visible persistence are attributed to a single source. Coltheart (1983) argues that it is necessary to distinguish at least two forms of visual persistence – namely, visible persistence and visual information persistence. Visible persistence – the subjective impression that the terminated stimulus is physically present – can be assessed by direct methods such as judgements of stimulus-–stimulus continuity and is influenced by both stimulus intensity and duration. The partial report superiority is not so influenced and seems best attributed to some other form of persistence, i.e. visual information persistence.

Other problems for a unitary account of visual persistence arise in the partial dissociation between location and identity errors: when errors are made in partial report they tend to be location errors rather than the report of visually similar letters not included in the display (Townsend, 1973). Also, there is evidence now for partial report superiority with categorical cues (e.g. Merikle 1980). One way of coping with such findings is to assume a memory containing a visual (but not visible) analog of the display lasting up to about 300 millisec., as shown by visual masking effects: the partial report superiority is assumed to arise in a parallel, nonvisual memory containing both spatial coordinates and identity codes with spatial information being lost faster than identity information (Mewhort, Marchetti, Gurnsey, & Campbell, 1984).

BIBLIOGRAPHY

Coltheart, M. (1983). Iconic memory. *Philosophical Transactions of the Royal Society, B, 302*, 283–94.
Merikle, P. M. (1980). Selection from visual persistence by perceptual groups and category membership. *Journal of Experimental Psychology: General, 109*, 279–95.
Mewhort, D. J. K., Marchetti, F. M., Gurnsey, R., & Campbell, A. J. (1984). Information persistence: a dual-buffer model for initial visual processing. In H. Bouma & D. C. Bouwhuis

(Eds), *Attention and performance, X.* Hillsdale, NJ: Lawrence Erlbaum Associates.

Sperling, G. (1960). The information available in brief visual exposures. *Psychological Monographs, 74* (whole no. 498).

Townsend, V. M. (1973). Loss of spatial and identity information following a tachistoscopic exposure. *Journal of Experimental Psychology, 98,* 113–18.

VERNON H. GREGG

idiots savants This expression has been applied to a heterogeneous body of individuals who have two attributes in common: first, they are mentally retarded; second, they perform one or more intellectual skills at a much higher level than would be expected from a knowledge of their general level of intellectual competence. Some *idiots savants* are also autistic. The majority are solitary and withdrawn people, lacking social skills.

Most of the skills acquired by *idiots savants* are ones that can only be learned by a person who – unlike many mentally handicapped individuals – is able to concentrate for long periods and give sustained attention to a particular task. Some of the feats are essentially ones of memory. An *idiot savant* may remember large amounts of information concerning, say, timetable information, population statistics, names, dates, or detailed knowledge of some other kind (for reviews, see Hill, 1978; Howe, 1989a). Memory is also an important element in other skills possessed by *idiots savants*. For instance, some *idiots savants* demonstrate considerable ability at solving mental arithmetic problems. Also, a substantial number of published case histories describe *idiots savants* who have acquired the skill of "calendar calculating." Such a person, if told a specified calendar date in the past or the future, is able to state the day of the week on which that date falls. Virtually all the *idiots savants* who perform this feat are self-taught, and the methods they have acquired for solving calendar-date problems vary considerably. However, in each case the individual is able to draw upon a substantial body of remembered knowledge about particular dates (Howe & Smith, 1988).

Some *idiots savants* have highly impressive musical skills, sometimes accompanied by extensive knowledge of music and musicians. In a few instances a person's musical activities may demonstrate qualities of spontaneity and emotional expressiveness, and an ability to improvise, as well as knowledgeability and technical expertise, although the same individual's non-musical capabilities are highly restricted. Outside music, the person is rigid and unemotional, and lacks even the basic skills and elementary general knowledge that a normal young child possesses (see, for example, Viscott, 1970).

A few mentally retarded people display impressive artistic skills. In rare cases (for instance, Selfe, 1977) child *idiots savants* have possessed an ability to produce representational drawings that would be totally impossible for a normal child of the same age. It is possible that this extraordinary skill depends upon mental activities that would normally be directed toward processing and attending to the meanings of perceived objects being exclusively engaged in processing information concerning structural or non-meaningful attributes, such as physical dimensions.

The fact that mentally retarded *idiots savants* can perform intellectually demanding feats although their general intelligence is invariably very low presents something of a paradox (Howe, 1989a, 1989b). It appears that, at least in these individuals, particular abilities can be to a considerable extent independent of a person's measured INTELLIGENCE.

BIBLIOGRAPHY

Hill, A. L. (1978). Savants: mentally retarded individuals with special skills. In N. R. Ellis (Ed.), *International review of research in mental retardation* (Vol. 9) (pp. 277–99). New York: Academic Press.

Howe, M. J. A. (1988). Memory in mentally retarded "idiots savants." In M. M. Gruneberg, P. Morris, & R. N. Sykes (Eds), *Practical aspects of memory: Current research and issues* (Vol. 2) (pp. 267–73). Chichester: Wiley.

——. (1989a). *Fragments of genius: The strange feats of idiots savants.* London: Routledge.

——. (1989b). Cognitive processes in "idiots savants." In A. M. Colman & G. Beaumont

(Eds), *Psychology Survey 7* (pp. 194–210). Leicester: British Psychological Society.

— —, & Smith, J. (1988). Calendar calculating in "idiots savants": how do they do it? *British Journal of Psychology, 79,* 371–86.

Selfe, L. (1977). *Nadia: A case of extraordinary drawing ability in an autistic child.* London: Academic Press.

Viscott, D. S. (1970). A musical idiot savant. *Psychiatry, 33,* 494–515.

MICHAEL J. A. HOWE

illusions, visual *See* VISUAL ILLUSIONS.

imagery, computational theory of Computational theories of imagery attempt to account for how information is stored and processed when one uses imagery; such theories focus on the brain activities involved in imagery rather than on the conscious experience of imagery itself. Mental imagery has been recognized as an important facet of cognition at least since the time of Aristotle. However, it has had a checkered role in psychological theorizing, and has proven to be a particularly thorny topic for scientific study. One of the major difficulties in theorizing about imagery has been its elusiveness. Mental images are not actual images; they are not drawn on any tangible canvas or viewed by actual eyes. It has been difficult to conceptualize what an image is, which has repeatedly put the very concept in jeopardy in theories of mental activity. Indeed, difficulties in studying imagery were in large part responsible for the Behaviorists' swing away from studying mental activity of any sort (*see* COGNITIVE PSYCHOLOGY, HISTORY OF).

With the advent of computers has come a new vocabulary for conceptualizing mental events, the vocabulary of computation. This new set of constructs has allowed theories of imagery to be specified much more precisely than was heretofore possible. These clearer characterizations of the construct have in turn led to empirical studies that have revealed important properties about imagery. This article outlines the computational approach to theorizing and studying imagery (*see* COGNITIVE SCIENCE).

Imagery is usually accompanied by the experience of "seeing with the mind's eye," "hearing with the mind's ear," and so on. This experience is a hallmark that specific types of activities are taking place in the brain. However, computational theories, and experiments designed to address such theories, attempt to characterize the nature of the brain activity, not the accompanying experience itself.

COMPUTATION

Computation theories of imagery specify the computations used in mental imagery. This conception of computation is much broader than adding, subtracting, and other manipulations of numbers. Alphabetizing a list, determining whether two names are the same, and locating edges of a picture can all be performed by computations. A computation is an informationally interpretable, systematic mapping of input to output. That is, given that an input can be interpreted as standing for something, a computation converts that input to a particular output that stands for something else; the particular computation specifies the relation between the interpretations of the input and the output. For example, if the input were "2, 2," and these marks were interpreted as standing for two digits, the output should be "4" if the computation adds, "0" if it subtracts, and "1100" if the first number indicates how many 1's should be printed and the second number indicates how many 0's should be printed thereafter. Similarly, if the input were "dog," the output should be "cat" if the computation produces the most common associate, "pet" if it produces the most common role, and so on. The critical feature of all of these cases is that the input and output have interpretations and that there is a systematic connection between the two.

Computations can be understood at multiple levels of coarseness. One can specify a computation purely in terms of what it does (the relation between the input and the output), independently of how the mapping is actually performed. For example, multiplication can be performed in any number of ways (e.g. adding one number to itself the number of times specified by the other number, converting the numbers to logarithms and adding the exponents, finding the numbers in the rows and columns of a lookup table, and so on). One can specify the operation without worrying about the particular method used to carry it out. Marr (1982) distinguished between the "computation," which specifies *what* is done, and the "algorithm," which specifies *how* it is done. The algorithm specifies the step-by-step process whereby a computation is carried out (*see* PERCEPTION, COMPUTATIONAL THEORY OF).

Unfortunately, this distinction between what and how is not very clear. For example, addition can be part of the method used to multiply two numbers, but it also can be regarded as a computation in its own right. Similarly, if we look at how a correlation coefficient is computed, in this context multiplication is part of the algorithm. Thus, what corresponds to a part of an algorithm at one level can be taken as computation in its own right at another. The key point, then, is that computation can be understood at multiple levels of coarseness. At very coarse levels, the algorithm will specify only a few, relatively complex steps; at finer levels, the algorithm will specify relatively many, relatively simple steps.

In short, computational theories specify the computations that result in a given stimulus leading to the production of a given behavior. Computational theories of imagery focus on the system of computations that involves mental images. Mental images are a particular kind of representation, which are produced by some computations and serve as the input to yet other computations.

REPRESENTATION

The idea of representation lies at the heart of computational theories. Many computations involve associating specific information with a specific input. In order to accomplish such associations, previously acquired information must be stored and used. For example, if asked to name common pets, "dog" and "cat" will invariably be reported. We were not born knowing this information; it was learned, stored, and then retrieved when the person was queried.

Different ways of storing information make different information explicit. For example, storing information about quantities in terms of arabic numerals makes explicit powers of ten, whereas storing information about quantities in terms of Roman numerals does not. And depending on what information is made explicit by a representation, a given computation will be more or less easily performed. For example, if one stores amounts using Roman numerals, multiplication is a very different kettle of fish than if one stores amounts using arabic numerals. The kinds of operations that are necessary to perform a computation depend in large part on how the input is represented and on how previously acquired information is represented (*see also* PERCEPTION, COMPUTATIONAL THEORY OF).

All computational theories of imagery, then, specify two kinds of things: the types of representations of information used, and the ways in which these representations are processed to carry out specific computations. Theories typically posit many different computations, which form images, combine them in new ways, transform them in various ways, and so on. These computations are often posited to be accomplished by dedicated "modules" (or subsystems) (*see* MODULARITY OF MIND), each of which accepts some type of input and produces the requisite output. All of these computations are tailored to mesh with the kinds of representations that are posited for imagery.

CANDIDATE REPRESENTATIONS FOR IMAGERY

Thus, an essential feature of any computational theory of imagery is specification of the type of representation(s) assumed to underlie imagery. Because many computational theories have been developed to guide the construction of computer simulation models (computer programs that actually perform the computations), computational theories often have been quite precise and detailed in specifying the nature of the representation.

Two general classes of computational theories of imagery have been developed to date. These classes are characterized by differences in the way images are represented.

One class posits that imagery relies on representations of the same sort used in language; these are called PROPOSITIONAL REPRESENTATIONS. The other class of theories posits that imagery in part relies on a distinct type of representation, unlike those used in language; this type of representation is called a "depictive representation."

The two types of representation can be specified rather precisely, and this degree of rigor of definition is an important prelude to attempting to distinguish empirically between the two. That is, unless we have a clear distinction between the two types of representation, it is difficult to know how to perform experiments to discover which type is actually used in imagery.

Propositional representations are language-like, in that they assert properties of objects or entities. However, propositional representations are not sentences in a natural language. For example, the notation "on(ball, box)" might be used to express a proposition that asserts that a ball is on a box. Propositional representations can be characterized in the following way. The basic elements are symbols, which can stand for relations (e.g. "on," "likes," "gives"), objects, properties, logical conditions (e.g. if, all, and, or), and so on. These elements are combined according to rules; the rules specify that a "well formed" representation must include at least one relation. The relations themselves have requirements on the number and types of other symbols that must be specified. For example, "on" requires two entities; "on(ball)" does not assert anything and is an ill-formed fragment.

Propositional representations are unambiguous, unlike sentences in natural languages. Thus, for example, different symbols would be used to indicate the rectangular container and fisticuffs. Furthermore, these representations can represent classes (e.g. boxes in general) and they are amodal; the same representation can arise from multiple different sensory modalities.

All propositional theories have in common the idea that an image corresponds to a description (for examples of such theories, see reviews in Kosslyn, 1980; Pylyshyn, 1973; Pinker, 1985). The description specifies the spatial arrangement of parts of the imaged object. When one manipulates an imaged object, for example by imagining it rotating, the process that performs this computation alters the description. For example, the image of the letter A might be represented by a description such as "One diagonal line slanted up to the right, that meets at the top another diagonal line slanted to the left; a short horizontal line connects the two midway down." If the letter were to be imaged on its side, the description would be altered to something like, "One diagonal line slanted down to the right, that meets at the right side another diagonal line that is slanted up to the right; the two are connected midway to the left by a short vertical line."

Depictive representations differ in almost every respect from propositional ones. The basic elements are not symbols that fall into different form classes. Rather, the basic element is a point. The rules of combination are similarly unstructured: points need only be placed in spatial juxtaposition. Furthermore, depictions convey meaning via a process of a nonarbitrary mapping between parts of the representation and parts of the represented object: not only must each part of the representation correspond to part of the object (as seen from a single point of view), but also the distances between the parts of the representation must correspond to the actual (projections of) distances between the represented parts themselves.

Thus, depictions are inherently spatial; they correspond to patterns in a functional space. An array in a computer can serve as a functional space, given that cells have geometric relations to one another (e.g. they are next to, above, or below, left or right of one another, and so on; see Kosslyn, 1983). Thus, depictions make explicit the shape of empty space in a pattern (e.g. a depiction of an upper-case letter a will make explicit the shape of the enclosed region), which would require additional computation to infer if a propositional description were used. Similarly, one cannot represent a shape using a depiction without necessarily also specifying an orientation and size. In contrast, a propositional representation need not necessarily specify either spatial property.

179

All depictive computational theories of imagery have in common the idea that images correspond to patterns in a functionally spatial short-term memory structure (for reviews of such theories, see Kosslyn, 1980; Pinker & Kosslyn, 1983; Pinker, 1985) (*see* SHORT-TERM MEMORY). Such images are posited to be generated on the basis of information stored in long-term memory (which typically is thought also to include propositional information; see, for example, Kosslyn, 1980). According to these theories, the spatial pattern is processed by computations that interpret patterns as representing objects or parts or that alter the pattern. For example, the letter *A* would be represented by a pattern of lines; when rotated, the actual spatial arrangement of the pattern would be altered.

DISTINGUISHING BETWEEN THE THEORIES

The critical differences between the two types of representations hinge on the way spatial/geometric properties are represented. In depictive theories, space is used to represent spatial properties, whereas in propositional theories spatial properties are described in the same way as would any other type of information. The experiments that were designed to implicate depictive representations all attempted to show that image representations are functionally spatial; that parts of the object are represented such that their interpart distances are preserved in a functional space.

One class of such experiments, for example, used mental scanning as a kind of "tape measure." That is, the time to shift attention across an imaged object was measured. It was reasoned that if images are depictive, then more time should be required to scan greater distances across an imaged object. And in fact, numerous experiments have demonstrated that more time is required to shift attention greater distances across an object. Many experiments of this type were conducted to demonstrate that images have spatial properties, including size, direction, and orientation (for reviews see Kosslyn, 1980, 1990; Shepard and Cooper, 1982; Finke & Shepard, 1987).

The demonstration that spatial properties affect the time to use imagery did not succeed in implicating depictive representations in imagery. Indeed, Anderson (1978) went so far as to provide a mathematical proof that behavioral data will in principle never allow one to decide between the two classes of theories. Consider an example of the problem. Depictive theories account for the increase in time to scan across imaged objects by positing a depictive image representation with an incremental scan process operating over it. Propositional theories can account for the result simply by tailoring a list that describes properties of the object, which is then scanned down an item at a time. If the list preserves the spatial arrangement of the parts, then more time will be required to scan farther "distances." Propositional theories can posit more complex networks of descriptions that can mimic the two- or three-dimensional properties of objects.

A *structure/process trade-off* occurs when one theory mimics another by positing a different representation, and then compensates for that difference by positing a different process. In the case of scanning, the differences in depictive and propositional representations were compensated for by different types of scanning. In both cases, the end-result is the same: more time is required to scan farther distances over represented objects. This structure/process trade-off can always be done.

Anderson (1978) pointed out that structure/process trade-offs are only possible if one sticks solely to behavioral data. If one has some other grounds for fixing the properties of the representations or processes, such fast and loose theorizing will not be possible. And in fact, there is good reason to suspect that computational theories of imagery will be distinguished among by examining the actual brain events that occur during imagery.

Farah (1988) reviewed a host of evidence that parts of the brain used in visual perception are also active during visual mental imagery. These results in and of themselves do not serve to distinguish between the classes of theories. There are plenty of propositional theories of visual perception (e.g. Winston, 1975; Marr, 1982), and it is possible that both imagery and perception rely solely on propositional representations (indeed, this claim is made by all propositional theories of imagery).

More to the point, it is now known that there are many topographically mapped areas of cortex in primate brains. These areas are typically retinotopically organized: they preserve the basic two-dimensional spatial layout of the retina (but with greater area typically being allocated to the fovea). Patterns of activity in these areas are depictive representations. There is evidence suggesting that the visual areas of the human brain are structured in a way that corresponds to the monkey brain (e.g. Levine, 1982; Fox et al, 1986). If so, then some of the areas that are active during imagery are topographically mapped, and hence the patterns of activity within the areas are depictive representations. If it can be shown that visual mental imagery cannot occur unless these areas are intact, then we will have conclusive evidence that imagery relies on depictive representations. If the type of representation underlying imagery can be ascertained, this will place very strong constraints on theories of the computations that produce and use these representations.

Computational theories have produced numerous hypotheses regarding the subsystems that carry out specific computations, and there should be dramatic progress in understanding these components once the basic nature of the image representation is determined.

See also DUAL-CODE THEORY OF IMAGERY; IMAGERY AND PERCEPTION.

BIBLIOGRAPHY

Anderson, J. R. (1978). Arguments concerning representations for mental imagery. *Psychological Review*, *85*, 249–77.

Farah, M. J. (1988). Is visual imagery really visual? Overlooked evidence from neuropsychology. *Psychological Review*, *95*, 307–17.

Finke, R. A., & Shepard, R. N. (1987). Visual functions of mental imagery. In K. R. Boff, L. Kaufman, & J. P. Thomas (Eds), *Handbook of perception and human performance* (pp. 31-1–37-55). New York: Wiley-Interscience.

Fox, P. T., Mintun, M. A., Raichle, M. E., Miezin, F. M., Allman, J. M., & Van Essen, D. C. (1986). Mapping human visual cortex with positron emission tomography. *Nature*, *323*, 806–9.

Kosslyn, S. M. (1980). *Image and mind*. Cambridge, Mass.: Harvard University Press.

——. (1983). *Ghosts in the mind's machine*. New York: W. W. Norton.

——. (1990). Mental imagery. In D. N. Osherson, S. M. Kosslyn, & J. M. Hollerbach (Eds), *Visual cognition and action: An invitation to cognitive science* (Vol. 2). Cambridge, Mass.: MIT Press.

Levine, D. N. (1982). Visual agnosia in monkey and man. In D. J. Ingle, M. A. Goodale, & R. J. W. Mansfield (Eds), *Analysis of visual behavior* (pp. 629–70). Cambridge, Mass.: MIT Press.

Marr, D. (1982). *Vision*. San Francisco, Calif.: W. H. Freeman.

Pinker, S. (1985). Visual cognition: An introduction. In S. Pinker (Ed.), *Visual cognition* (pp. 1–63). Cambridge, Mass.: MIT Press.

——, & Kosslyn, S. M. (1983). Theories of mental imagery. In A. A. Sheikh (Ed.), *Imagery: Current theory, research, and application* (pp. 43–71). New York: Wiley.

Pylyshyn, Z. W. (1973). What the mind's eye tells the mind's brain. *Psychological Bulletin*, *80*, 1–24.

Shepard, R. N., & Cooper, L. A. (1982). *Mental images and their transformations*. Cambridge, Mass.: MIT Press.

Winston, P. H. (ed.). (1975). *The psychology of computer vision*. New York: McGraw-Hill.

S. M. KOSSLYN

imagery, dual-code theory of *See* DUAL-CODE THEORY OF IMAGERY.

imagery, eidetic *See* EIDETIC IMAGERY.

imagery and perception Recent scientific studies on mental imagery have greatly increased our understanding of the relation between imagery and PERCEPTION. These studies have helped to identify the spatial, perceptual, and transformational properties of images, how imagery interacts with perception, and how visual discoveries can be made using imagery.

SCANNING MENTAL IMAGES

The spatial structure of mental images has been explored using the technique of mental image scanning (*see* IMAGERY, COMPUTATIONAL THEORY OF). Kosslyn, Ball, and Reiser (1978) reported that the time it takes to imagine scanning between locations on imagined maps is proportional to the actual distances between the locations. A similar relation between scanning distance and response time has also been shown for distances among imagined objects in three-dimensional space. Such findings suggest that mental image scanning corresponds to the actual scanning of perceived objects and their features.

Mental image scanning enables people to judge, from memory, whether an object lies in a particular direction with respect to a new, unexpected location. In such cases, image scanning is used spontaneously; people report imagining that they are scanning from one location to the other along the indicated direction. This implies that image scanning is not merely an artefact of instructions to deliberately simulate an actual physical scan. Rather, mental images appear to represent the true spatial properties of objects and their configurations.

DISTRIBUTION OF SPATIAL ATTENTION

Another way in which imagery resembles perception concerns the manner in which attention is distributed within an imagined or presented pattern. Using a probe-detection task with real and imagined block letters, Podgorny and Shepard (1978) found that reaction times to verify that the probe is presented on some part of the letters varies with probe location in the same way in imagery and perception conditions. In particular, reaction times are most rapid, in each case, when the probe falls on the intersection of bar-shaped segments of the patterns, and as the overall compactness of the patterns increases.

MENTAL IMAGE ACUITY

Imagery also resembles perception with regard to constraints on resolution for fine visual details. Kosslyn (1975) reported that the time it takes to locate features of imagined objects increases as the features decrease in size. This finding could not be explained in terms of the association strength between the features and the object; large, poorly associated features can be detected more quickly than small, highly associated features (*see* SEMANTIC MEMORY).

As in perception, the visual field in imagery appears to be restricted, because images will "overflow" when the image is formed at too large a size. Direct comparisons between the visual fields in imagery and perception reveal a close correspondence between the two; the fields are the same shape, and increase in size in the same way as the features of the object or pattern become easier to distinguish. Criticisms of studies on image acuity, however, have suggested that experimenter bias may be responsible for at least some of these findings.

IMAGERY AFTER-EFFECTS

There is some evidence that imagery can lead to the adaptation of certain types of feature analyzing mechanisms in the visual system. Finke and Schmidt (1977) reported that orientation-specific color after-effects could be induced when bar gratings were visualized in association with actual colors presented during the adaptation procedures. These after-effects were not obtained, however, when colors were visualized in association with actual bar gratings, suggesting that there are limits on the extent to which imagery might involve the visual system.

Subsequent findings have raised questions about whether imagery can actually lead to the adaptation of visual mechanisms sensitive to bar gratings. There are important differences between orientation-specific color after-effects obtained using real and imagined gratings, and there have been failures to obtain imagery-induced after-effects using testing procedures that reliably reveal the perceptual after-effects. Moreover, prior visualization of a bar grating fails to produce orientation-specific changes in sensitivity in a subsequent grating detection task. Taken together, these findings suggest that imagery probably does not involve the activation of visual mechanisms responsible for the early processing of color and feature information.

VISUAL-MOTOR ADAPTATION

Visualizing errors of movement can lead to adaptive changes in visual-motor coordination that correspond to changes resulting when errors are actually observed. Finke (1979) reported that prism adaptation could be achieved by simply visualizing the same kinds of errors that prisms normally create. Imagery adaptation procedures also result in visual-motor after-effects resembling those following actual prism adaptation (*see* PERCEPTUAL MOTOR COORDINATION).

IMAGE FACILITATION OF PERCEPTUAL PROCESSES

Imagining a pattern can facilitate the detection or identification of the pattern. Farah (1985) reported that letters can be detected more easily when the letter is concurrently visualized in the correct location. Similarly, a tone can be recognized more accurately when exactly the same tone is imagined. This type of facilitation may result from the PRIMING of perceptual pathways during imagination.

Imagery can also facilitate perception by providing helpful visual contexts. Objects can be detected more quickly when people imagine visual scenes that are semantically compatible with the objects. Line length discriminations can be made more rapidly and accurately when a helpful surrounding pattern is mentally superimposed over the lines. This facilitation resembles that obtained using actual context patterns.

INTERFERENCE BETWEEN IMAGERY AND PERCEPTION

Under certain conditions imagery can also interfere with perception. Segal and Fusella (1970) found that the detection of faint visual and auditory stimuli is impaired whenever images are formed in the same sensory modality. Images can also function as pattern "masks," interfering with detection of the pattern. Whether imagery facilitates or interferes with perception probably depends on a number of factors, such as the intensity of the stimuli, the type of perceptual judgement, and

the extent to which the imagined and presented object correspond.

Perception can also interfere with visualization. Brooks (1968) showed that performance on difficult imagery tasks, such as identifying the shape of successive corners of block letters, worsens when the responses are given by pointing to visually presented characters, compared to giving the responses verbally. These interference effects, however, are due mainly to the spatial properties of images, rather than to their visual characteristics.

REALITY MONITORING

Imagery and perception can sometimes be confused when one attempts to reall whether or not an event actually occurred. These errors in REALITY MONITORING increase the more frequently the event is imagined, and the more easily the images are formed. In general, reality monitoring depends on the perceptual qualities of the memory, the context of the memory, and the amount of cognitive effort used in establishing the memory (Johnson & Raye, 1981).

MENTAL ROTATION

A considerable number of studies have shown that imagined rotations of objects correspond in many respects to actual rotations. Shepard and Metzler (1971) found that imagined rotations are used to verify the equivalence of shape between three-dimensional objects that, in perspective drawings, are depicted as being rotated with respect to each other. The imagined rotations are performed at a constant rate, regardless of whether the rotations occur in the picture plane or in depth. In each case, the response times are proportional to the angular separation distances.

Subsequent studies on mental rotation have shown that the imagined rotations are holistic – that is, performed on images of the entire object or pattern; exhibit analog properties – that is, are approximately continuous; and reflect biomechanical constraints on the degrees of freedom of natural motions. In addition, mental transformations other than rotation have been reported; these include imagined transformations of size and color. Eye movements can be a possible artefact in some of these studies, but this is a problem only in those studies where the stimuli are presented simultaneously.

Some practical applications of mental rotation include identifying rotated characters, such as letters of the alphabet, detecting the symmetry of rotated patterns, distinguishing right and left turns, and judging relative directions from rotated perspectives.

REPRESENTATIONAL MOMENTUM

Imagined transformations, such as mental rotation, exhibit a property analogous to the momentum of physically moving objects. Freyd and Finke (1985) reported that memories for the final position of a pattern that had been depicted as rotating are forwardly shifted, in the same direction as the implied rotation. Like physical momentum, these memory shifts increase as the implied velocity of the pattern increases. The memory shifts appear to have a spontaneous onset, and represent continuous changes along the path of motion. This effect, called "representational momentum," suggests that mental transformations have a ballistic, inertial quality.

IMAGE REINTERPRETATION

Like actual visual patterns, mental images can sometimes be reinterpreted, yielding novel, unexpected discoveries. Pinker and Finke (1980) found that people could imagine rotating a configuration of objects and then "detect" familiar patterns "formed" by how the objects would look from different viewing perspectives. The recognized patterns could not be anticipated from the way the objects appeared from the initial viewing perspective (see FORM PERCEPTION).

However, there are limits on the extent to which mental images can be reinterpreted. Structurally "hidden" figures in patterns can rarely be detected using imagery, suggesting that images are constrained by structural descriptions initially given to the patterns. In addition, there is evidence that classic ambiguous figures cannot be perceptually "reversed" in imagery (see VISUAL ILLUSIONS). On the other hand, unexpected patterns can often be recognized following the imagined con-

struction and transformations of a familiar, starting pattern, or when people are given a randomly chosen set of parts to use during creative mental synthesis. Whether image reinterpretation is possible may therefore depend on the type or level of perceptual ambiguity depicted in the image.

CONCLUSIONS

Imagery appears to resemble perception in a number of important respects. Like actual objects and patterns, images can be scanned, rotated, inspected, and assembled. In addition, images exhibit other characteristics in common with perceived objects, such as spatial extent, limited resolution, and inertia. There are also important differences between imagery and perception. Imagery appears not to involve levels of the visual system where information about simple visual features is initially extracted. Nor can images be structurally reinterpreted to the same extent as perceived objects.

With regard to their practical implications, images can be used to improve perceptual performance, modify visual-motor coordination, verify spatial relations among objects, compare rotated objects, and discover patterns made up of novel combinations of features. Future studies in imagery research will most likely focus on these, and other practical uses of the perceptual properties of images.

See also COGNITIVE SCIENCE; DUAL-CODE THEORY OF IMAGERY.

BIBLIOGRAPHY

Brooks, L. R. (1968). Spatial and verbal components of the act of recall. *Canadian Journal of Psychology, 22*, 349–68.

Farah, M. J. (1985). Psychophysical evidence for a shared representational medium for mental images and percepts. *Journal of Experimental Psychology: General, 114*, 91–103.

Finke, R. A. (1979). The functional equivalence of mental images and errors of movement. *Cognitive Psychology, 11*, 235–64.

– –, & Schmidt, M. J. (1977). Orientation-specific color aftereffects following imagination. *Journal of Experimental Psychology: Human Perception and Performance, 3*, 599–606.

Freyd, J. J., & Finke, R. A. (1985). A velocity

effect for representational momentum. *Bulletin of the Psychonomic Society, 23*, 443–6.

Johnson, M. K., & Raye, C. L. (1981). Reality monitoring. *Psychological Review, 88*, 67–85.

Kosslyn, S. M. (1975). Information representation in visual images. *Cognitive Psychology, 7*, 341–70.

— —, Ball, T., & Reiser, B. J. (1978). Visual images preserve metric spatial information: Evidence from studies of image scanning. *Journal of Experimental Psychology: Human Perception and Performance, 4*, 47–60.

Pinker, S., & Finke, R. A. (1980). Emergent two-dimensional patterns in images rotated in depth. *Journal of Experimental Psychology: Human Perception and Performance, 6*, 244–64.

Podgorny, P., & Shepard, R. N. (1978). Functional representations common to visual perception and imagination. *Journal of Experimental Psychology: Human Perception and Performance, 4*, 21–35.

Segal, S. J., & Fusella, V. (1970). Influences of imaged pictures and sounds on detection of visual and auditory signals. *Journal of Experimental Psychology, 83*, 458–64.

Shepard, R. N., & Metzler, J. (1971). Mental rotation of three-dimensional objects. *Science, 171*, 701–3.

RONALD A. FINKE

implicit and explicit memory Implicit memory is defined as task performance which is enhanced by previous experiences, but with the enhancement occurring in the absence of conscious recollection (Schachter, 1987; *see* CONSCIOUSNESS); explicit memory is defined as task performance based on conscious recollection of previous experiences. Implicit memory is investigated by instructions which do not reveal the fact that memory is being assessed. In contrast, explicit memory is typically investigated by providing clear instructions that previously learned material is to be retrieved, and so traditional measures of memory such as free recall, cued recall, and recognition are all forms of explicit memory.

One of the ways of demonstrating that the distinction between implicit memory and explicit memory is of value is by showing that there are various manipulations which have very different effects on implicit and explicit memory performance. Jacoby and Dallas (1981) manipulated the processing of words so that they were processed either semantically or nonsemantically. Considerable previous research on LEVELS OF PROCESSING had shown that semantic processing is generally very beneficial for explicit memory, and this was replicated by Jacoby and Dallas with a test of recognition memory. However, the type of processing had no effect on implicit memory, which was assessed by means of a word-identification task.

The distinction between implicit and explicit memory has proved to be especially useful in research on AMNESIA. A crucial ingredient in amnesia is the presence of severely impaired long-term memory, but that impairment has historically nearly always been assessed by using tests of explicit memory. A quite different pattern of results is often found if tests of implicit memory are used. Graf, Squire, and Mandler (1984), for example, repeated the finding that amnesic patients perform extremely poorly on tests of explicit memory, using free recall, cued recall, and recognition memory. They also used a word-completion test as a measure of implicit memory. On this test, three-letter word fragments were presented, and the task was simply to write down the first word that was thought of which started with those letters. Implicit memory was measured by the extent to which the word completions corresponded to words on a list which had been presented previously. The amnesic patients were not impaired in their performance on the word-completion task.

Schachter (1987) argued that it is generally the case that amnesics will show reasonable or even normal memory performance when such performance does not require conscious awareness of remembering. Apart from the study by Graf et al. (1984), there are numerous studies on repetition priming and motor skills which are consistent with Schachter's (1987) point of view (*see* AMNESIA). It is important to note, however, that discovering that amnesic patients have almost normal implicit memory but severely impaired explicit memory does not provide an explanation for the amnesic condition. As Schachter (1987) noted, implicit and explicit memory are "*descriptive* concepts that are primarily concerned with a person's psychological experience at the time of retrieval" (p. 501).

There have been a number of recent attempts to make theoretical sense of the processes involved in implicit and explicit memory. According to activation theory (Graf et al., 1984), the presentation of a word produces automatic activation of its internal representation in memory. It is this activation which is responsible for enhancing performance on tests of implicit memory. On the other hand, explicit memory is facilitated by elaborative processing.

An alternative theoretical position was proposed by Roediger and Blaxton (1987). They proposed that data-driven processes are generally more important for performance on implicit memory tasks, whereas conceptually driven processes are of more importance on explicit memory tasks (*see* DATA-DRIVEN AND CONCEPTUALLY DRIVEN PROCESSES). According to this processing theory, it should be possible to obtain good implicit memory performance with novel information, because data-driven processes can be used with such information. In contrast, activation theorists such as Graf et al. (1984) claim that only words with pre-existing representations in memory can be activated. Therefore, novel information should not be activated, and this should prevent implicit memory for such information occurring. The evidence on this crucial theoretical point is rather inconsistent (Schachter, 1987).

A somewhat different explanation of the differences between implicit and explicit memory stems from the distinction between declarative and procedural memory, which has been proposed by Cohen (1984) and others (*see* DECLARATIVE AND PROCEDURAL KNOWLEDGE). According to this view, performance on explicit memory tasks depends largely on declarative knowledge, whereas performance on implicit memory tasks depends primarily on procedural knowledge. There is evidence that amnesic patients are generally much more impaired on tasks depending on newly acquired declarative knowledge than on newly acquired procedural knowledge, but the pre-cise relationships between declarative knowledge and explicit memory or between procedural knowledge and implicit memory remain unclear.

The terms "implicit memory" and "explicit memory" are both rather broad, and it is entirely possible that a number of different processes or structures can be involved. Therefore, all of the proposed theories may be partially correct. However, there is a particular problem for the theories proposed by Roediger and Blaxton (1987) and by Cohen (1984). According to the former theory, data-driven processes are not associated with conscious recollection, and according to the latter theory, procedural knowledge is not associated with conscious recollection. In neither case is there an adequate explanation of why this should be so.

BIBLIOGRAPHY

Cohen, N. J. (1984). Preserved learning capacity in amnesia: Evidence for multiple memory systems. In L. R. Squire & N. Butters (Eds), *Neuropsychology of memory*. New York: Guilford Press.

Graf, P., Squire, L. R., & Mandler, G. (1984). The information that amnesic patients do not forget. *Journal of Experimental Psychology: Learning, Memory, and Cognition*, *10*, 164–78.

Jacoby, L. L., & Dallas, M. (1981). On the relationship between autobiographical memory and perceptual learning. *Journal of Experimental Psychology; General*, *110*, 306–40.

Roediger, H. L., & Blaxton, T. A. (1987). Retrieval modes produce dissociations in memory for surface information. In D. S. Gorfein & R. R. Hoffman (Eds), *Memory and cognitive processes: The Ebbinghaus centennial conference*. Hillsdale, NJ: Lawrence Erlbaum Associates Ltd.

Schachter, D. L. (1987). Implicit memory: History and current status. *Journal of Experimental Psychology: Learning, Memory, and Cognition*, *13*, 501–18.

MICHAEL W. EYSENCK

inference An inference is made whenever a reasoner, either human or machine, goes beyond the evidence given. Inferences occur in all kinds of understanding and reasoning.

Sometimes the result of an act of inference may be valid, and sometimes not. Very often inferences may be made which are only likely to be the case, rather than necessarily the case. A number of aspects of inference are of interest to the psychologist. First, there is the question of how efficiently human beings draw conclusions which are licensed (or enabled) by the logic of a situation. Second, the same question can be asked of specified kinds of pragmatic reasoning, where the conclusion may be about the likelihood of something, rather than something necessarily being the case. But above all, inferences occur everywhere in perception, reasoning, understanding, and language comprehension. This raises the third and perhaps most important issue, that of what it is that controls and contains the inferences which one makes in a given situation, a particularly interesting issue, since in theory, most premisses will allow an indeterminately large set of inferences to be made.

LOGICAL (DEDUCTIVE) INFERENCE

A distinction is made between two types of inference: logical (or deductive), and inductive. With logical inference, the conclusion necessarily (always) follows from the premisses. For instance, if you know that "All men are mortal," and that "Fred Bloggs is a man," then you may infer that "Fred Bloggs is mortal," by set inclusion. The last statement is an inference, and it is a necessary inference, in that it can be proven logically that it must be the case. Other (inductive) inferences are not necessary in this sense, but are merely possible. For instance, if it is true that "Most men like dangerous sports," and "Fred Bloggs is a man" then it is only possible that "Fred Bloggs likes dangerous sports"; it is not necessarily the case, although we might deem it highly likely.

Psychologists have studied human efficiency at deductive inference with various tasks, including conditional reasoning problems. In a conditional reasoning task, subjects are invited to judge whether a conclusion follows from two premisses, one describing a rule, and one describing a state of affairs. For instance:

(1) If the ball rolls to the left, the green light comes on.
The green light comes on. Therefore the ball rolled to the left.
(2) If the ball rolls to the left, the green light comes on.
The green light does not come on. Therefore the ball did not roll to the left.

The correct answers to these are that (1) is undecidable, and that (2) is always true. Yet in a study carried out by Rips and Marcus (1977), 23 percent of responses to (1) were that the conclusion is always true, and to (2) 39 percent thought that the conclusion was "only sometimes" true. Such results confirm what philosophers have long suspected. People are very poor at doing tasks of logical reasoning, even when the inferences involved are very simple.

The classical syllogisms of Aristotle have also been extensively studied as cases of logical problem solving (see REASONING). Johnson-Laird (1983), for example, has studied the conclusions which subjects draw based on all of the possible combinations of classical premisses. For some arrangements, almost everyone draws the correct conclusion, for instance "All of the artists are beekeepers" and "All of the beekeepers are carpenters" results in everyone (validly) concluding that "All of the artists are carpenters." However, the following produces a very low rate of correct conclusions:
"Some boys are athletes"; "No cowards are athletes." The correct conclusion is that "Some of the boys are not cowards."
While some inferences may be valid deductions in a logical sense, the evidence thus shows that people do not find all inferences equally easy to make. Of course, some inferences require more computational operations than others to check, and Johnson-Laird (1983) has argued that the more alternative conceptions (see MENTAL MODELS) which have to be made in order to check a conclusion, the more likely people are to fail to complete all of the necessary processes. Johnson-Laird's mental model approach thus substitutes a process model of reasoning for the claim that humans either can or cannot reason logically.

CONTENT AND LOGICAL INFERENCE

Logical inferences stand independently of content. So, from a logical point of view, the following pieces of reasoning are equivalent:
(1) If "Some of the weightlifters are jockeys," and "All of the jockeys are weaklings," then "Some of the weightlifters are weaklings."
(2) If "Some of the healthy people are not vegetarians," and "All of the athletes are vegetarians," then "Some of the healthy people are not athletes."
(3) If "Some A are B," and "All B are C," then "Some A are C."
While the conclusion of (1) is valid, it is not believable. In contrast, the conclusion of (2) is valid, and believable. Example (3) is simply a generalized version. There is a long line of research showing that whether or not people make (or accept) a logically valid conclusion depends upon the believability of that conclusion. Recently, Oakhill and Johnson-Laird (1985) showed that conclusions which were false by definition exerted an even stronger influence over the deduction process than did pragmatically unlikely conclusions. That is, the truth of a conclusion seems to interfere with the assessment of its logical validity.

From a logical point of view, these effects should not occur. Their existence shows that human inference making is guided by what is believable about the world, and not merely by logic. This is not as bad an indictment as it may seem, since from a practical point of view, it is important that the conclusion we reach should correspond to states of affairs in the world. There are many other situations in which reasoning patterns have been shown to depend upon content, as discussed in Johnson-Laird (1983) and Sanford (1987).

PRAGMATIC INFERENCE

The second important class of inferences consists of those which are pragmatically licensed. For example, if you know that John ate seafood, and that later on he was sick, then you may infer that a likely cause of the sickness was the seafood. This inference is likely to be true because of the state of the world (what John did and how John is), and also because seafood is notorious as a potential cause of gastric problems. So while anything might have caused his sickness (so the conclusion is not logically deductive), we would assign a certain probability to it being due to the seafood. On the other hand, if John drank mineral water with his meal, we would be a lot less likely to attribute his sickness to that potential cause. With pragmatic inferences, we may never be absolutely sure that one thing follows from another, but we might be able to assign a likelihood, and rank order likelihoods relative to one another.

This kind of inference (inductive inference) plays a major role in thinking, understanding the world, and understanding language (*see* LANGUAGE COMPREHENSION). Our belief that the sun will rise in the east and set in the west tomorrow is a classic example of an inductive inference, since we cannot prove that something will not come along and change this state of affairs. But ordinary mortals are more concerned with situations of a more homely nature, such as believing that five minutes is long enough for John to get to the station by car, while leaving four minutes before will only result in a 75 percent chance of success. Such knowledge can be used to draw ready inferences:

John left for the station. He took the car because he had only two minutes before the train left.

On meeting this situation, we would infer that John was not likely to make it to the train in time.

Such inferences are extremely important, and their ubiquity can be illustrated by considering examples from narratives depicting simple situations. Suppose that one encounters the following pair of sentences:

John wanted to visit his aunt in India.

He reached for the airline timetable.

If we were to ask "Why did John reach for the airline timetable," the reply would surely be "To find out when there was a 'plane to get to his aunts." Of course there is nothing necessary about this inference. He could be doing it to decide where to go on holiday, for instance. Nevertheless, it would be unreasonable for us not to make that inference. This is because, in understanding discourse, we expect each contribution to be relevant to the aims of the discourse as a whole. Thus, having introduced John as having a goal (to visit his aunt), we would expect the next statement to be relevant to that goal. Note that there are still many ways in which this could happen. For example, the following different types of continuation are acceptable:

– He reached for the timetable.
(attempting to satisfy a subgoal)
– He cursed having to go to the conference next week.
(reaction to having the main goal blocked)
– He left first thing the next morning.
(implementation of part of the action sequence to satisfy the goal)
– He hadn't seen her for three years.
(reason for going)
– His uncle had just died.
(event putting aunt in a state where John's company would be desirable)

It is easy to create such lists, but in order to understand them, it is necessary to devise a taxonomy of states, goals, and actions, and to understand the relations between states, goals, and actions. An attempt to do this has been made by Schank and Abelson (1977), and Wilensky (1983). These people analyze how stories can be represented as goal- and plan-based structures, in which inferences serve to make the essential links between the structurally incomplete assertions that make up a story. But it is always easy to underestimate the amount of inference which goes on during understanding. For instance, in the last example of the list presented above, the reader will almost certainly have assumed that the uncle who died was married to the aunt in question. Again, this is by no means necessary, just highly plausible. It is these kinds of inference, which happen without being noticed, that provide the basis of understanding. At the same time as providing a foundation for understanding, because they rely upon what is plausible rather than what is necessary, they can lead to profound problems, as illustrated by the following puzzle:

"A man and his son were away for a trip. They were driving along the motorway when they had a terrible accident. The man was killed outright, but his son was alive although badly injured. The boy was rushed to hospital for emergency surgery. On entering the operating theatre, the surgeon said, in a shocked state: 'I can't do this operation. This boy is my son.'" How can this be explained?

People typically have great difficulty with this, since it does not occur to them that surgeons can be women (since in our culture, most of them are not). Thus, in the initial interpretation, people infer (unconsciously) that the surgeon must be a man, hence the boy's dead father. This kind of inference is quite different from the slow, deliberate problem solving found in syllogistic reasoning, for instance, and is almost certainly the result of a different underlying process. For a further discussion of this point, see Garrod (1985).

BAYESIAN INFERENCE

A particularly interesting case of probabilistic reasoning is Bayesian inference, after the Reverend Thomas Bayes, who first investigated its statistical underpinnings (see BAYES' LAW). This concerns the changing pattern of inference which people make as they get evidence about a situation. Suppose that you were interested in whether a particular science (S) or a particular arts student (A) would do better on a test of widget assembly. Data from the past might show that the odds in favor of arts students being superior were 10:1. In the absence of any other data, the odds favor A. Now suppose that you find that a test of thumb dexterity shows S to be superior over A; further, you know that superior thumb dexterity favors performance on widget assembly over poor thumb dexterity (2:1 in favor). Now, in the case of S and A, this bit of evidence favors S. So our opinion should shift a little towards S being good on widgets. Bayes' theorem would express the shift in the following terms:

Odds in favor of A = Prior odds × odds due to evidence

in the present case:

Odds in favor of A = $10/1 \times 1/2 = 5:1$

So the odds are 5:1 in the present case that, given the evidence, A will be the better person at widget assembly. Of course, if the evidence were stronger, it would exert a greater effect.

Human beings are notoriously poor at

approximating the correct values in these situations. In particular, they appear to be too ready to ignore base-rate (prior odds) information, paying attention more to information relevant to the particular case at hand (see especially Kahneman, Slovic, & Tversky, 1982). This can amount to a very strong effect on inference. For example, in one study, students were told that 70 engineers and 30 accountants attended an interview. They were then presented with a character sketch of one of the interviewees, which did not say anything to persuade the subjects that he might be an engineer or an accountant. Subjects were then asked what they thought the occupation of the interviewee to be. The average response was 50:50. This is wrong of course: the odds are 7:3 that he was an engineer. But subjects failed to utilize base-rate information properly. More subtle studies show that character sketch information unreasonably outweighs base-rate information. This means that if we know that 70 percent of Martians are dangerous, and we meet a Martian, if she appears to be a little trustworthy, this evidence should outweigh the baseline. We must all be familiar with our own examples.

This kind of inference is extremely important. In a practical situation, such as an interview of a schoolboy, a small piece of vivid evidence suggesting that the candidate will be good is hard to forget, while base-rate information, such as previous success rates on the job of people from the particular school, may be hard to remember (and may sound like prejudice). A rational decision must take into account base rate, of course.

THE SOCIAL FACE OF INFERENCES

In SOCIAL COGNITION, a great deal of work has been carried out on the question of inferential patterns, particularly in the explanation of events or states of affairs. This literature is generally known as "attribution theory" (*see* PERSON PERCEPTION) since it can be thought of as the study of how people assign blame (or credit) for situations to the people or things which happen in the world. First, we should note that explanations are normally required only for things which violate expectations. For instance, if we see someone buying things in a supermarket, then this requires no explanation; if someone goes around a supermarket without buying anything, then we might notice this and seek an explanation. This says a lot about inference: a large proportion of inferences arise from states of affairs in the world being tested against normative expectation: if expectation is substantially violated, then an explanation will be sought, leading to inferential behavior. From a computational point of view, this kind of inference generation is enormous, since it means testing all aspects of current input against all background normative information. Hilton and Slugoski (1986) further suggest that it is the detection of an abnormal condition which licenses the use of the term "The Cause." For example, suppose that you see a car run off the road and crash into a lamppost. There is an effectively infinite number of conditions which have to be met in order for this to come about, but they are not all dignified by the name "The Cause." Rather, an explanation in terms of the abnormal (or unacceptable) would be sought, such as:

The driver was driving abnormally quickly (relative to regulations).
The driver was abnormal because he was drunk.
The road was abnormal because there was a sheet of ice on it created by a shopkeeper throwing a bucket of water over it.

In the first two cases, it would be the driver's actions which were "the cause," while in the third, it is the shopkeeper's action. We might say in the third case that the shopkeeper caused the accident.

Note that this kind of inference is very selective, and is based on a notion of explanation at the level of human causality. This is not always appropriate. For example, Kahneman and Tversky (see Kahneman, Slovic, & Tversky, 1982) have studied the familiar "if only ...." explanation of disasters. In one sketch, they told a story of a man who decided to take a different route from usual home, and was killed in a crash at an intersection. The crash involved a truck driver who had been taking drugs. In a different version, the man's wife asked him to come home early, and the accident occurred. The most popular thing which people would have wanted to change was the route in the first case, and the time of departure in the other. Yet there were many other possibilities for conditions which, if changed, would have prevented the accident, such as arriving at the intersection a few seconds earlier in both cases. Subjects made explanatory inferences in terms of what was normal for the protagonist in the story, which is understandable, but not rational, or even useful.

Within the tradition of Attribution research, the importance of typicality information has been refined. Suppose that "Fred kicks a dog." If "almost everyone else kicks this dog" (high consensus), "John never kicks any other dog" (the dog is therefore highly distinctive), and "In the past, John has kicked this dog" (John is consistent), then we are forced to conclude that there is something enduringly special about the dog (e.g. it has a habit of attacking people). Kelley (1967) showed experimentally how people's attributions depend upon the manipulation of these three variables.

Attributional inferences are often made in the absence of all of the relevant information, of course, and show a number of fundamental patterns, or biases (see Nisbett & Ross, 1980). The first of these is the fundamental attribution error, which is to explain a person's behavior in terms of her dispositions, rather than in terms of environmental pressures on her. For instance, if the newsagent keeps running out of newspapers, we are going to assume he is inefficient (although there may be some good reason beyond his control). Closely related to this is the actor/observer bias. This bias is the tendency to make the fundamental error with others, but to explain our own behavior in terms of what the environment is doing to us! Many of these bias effects seem to result from what kind of information comes to mind in a particular situation (the "availability" bias). So we are very aware of the way the environment "causes" us to do things, but cannot so readily see another's point of view. Overcoming such a bias corresponds to the concept of empathy.

These social biases are complex, and depend upon a large number of factors, but they should not be underestimated. Once a person is type-cast, for example, it becomes easy to interpret her behavior in a way which is consistent with the type-casting.

Social inferences are but one type of inference, of course. They are important in their own right, and serve to illustrate the magnitude of the problem of classifying and understanding the kinds of inferences which people make. A proper understanding of thinking and comprehending requires a full study of inference making, and the design of computer systems which emulate human capacities demand a similar study (e.g. Gilhooly, 1989).

See also ANALOGIES; DECISION MAKING AND JUDGEMENT; PROBLEM SOLVING.

BIBLIOGRAPHY

Garrod, S. C. (1985). Incremental pragmatic interpretation versus occasional inferencing during fluent reading. In G. Rickheit & H. Strohner (Eds), *Inferences in text processing*. North-Holland: Elsevier.

Gilhooly, K. J. (1989). *Human and machine problem solving*. London: Plenum Press.

Hilton, D. J., & Slugoski, B. R. (1986). Knowledge-based causal attribution: The abnormal conditions focus model. *Psychological Review*, 93, 75–88.

Johnson-Laird, P. N. (1983). *Mental models*. Cambridge: Cambridge University Press.

Kahneman, D., Slovic, P., & Tversky, A. (1982). *Judgement under uncertainty: Heuristics and biases*. Cambridge: Cambridge University Press.

Kelley, H. H. (1967). Attribution in social psychology. *Nebraska Symposium on Motivation*, 15, 192–238.

Nisbett, R., & Ross, L. (1980). *Human inference: Strategies and shortcomings*. Englewood Cliffs, NJ: Prentice-Hall.

Oakhill, J. V., & Johnson-Laird, P. N. (1985). The effects of belief on the spontaneous production of syllogistic conclusions. *Quarterly Journal of Experimental Psychology*, 37A, 553–69.

Rips, L. J., & Marcus, S. L. (1977). Supposition and the analysis of conditional sentences. In M. A. Just & P. A. Carpenter (Eds), *Cognitive processes in comprehension*. Hillsdale, NJ: Lawrence Erlbaum Associates.

Sanford, A. J. (1987). *The mind of man*. Brighton: Harvester Press.

Schank, R., & Abelson, R. (1977). *Scripts, goals, plans, and understanding*. Hillsdale, NJ: Lawrence Erlbaum Associates.

Wilensky, R. (1983). *Planning and understanding*, Reading, Mass.: Addison-Wesley.

A. J. SANFORD

information processing *See* AUTOMATIC PROCESSING; CASCADE PROCESSING; DATA-DRIVEN AND CONCEPTUALLY DRIVEN PROCESSES.

intelligence There is general agreement that thinking, REASONING, and PROBLEM SOLVING are all of relevance to intelligence; there is less agreement about the extent to which other activities such as creativity and social "intelligence," or common sense form part of intelligence. Some theorists have argued against a unitary construct of intelligence and in favor of a more complex conceptualization in which there are two or more theoretical constructs related to intelligence.

Much research on intelligence during the first half of this century was based upon the factor-analytic approach. This approach (exemplified by the pioneering work of Spearman, 1923) achieved some success in describing the hierarchical structure of intelligence. Thus, for example, the evidence is consistent with the view that there is a general factor of intelligence (often referred to as "g"), together with a number of more specific factors.

One of the standard criticisms of the factor-analytic approach is that it was purely psychometric and failed to provide a cognitive theory of intelligence. However, it has been argued convincingly by Sternberg and Frensch (1990) that this criticism is misplaced. For example, Spearman (1923) proposed that intelligence depends on a number of qualitative principles of cognition (e.g. eduction of correlates: "the presenting of any character together with any relation tends to evoke immediately a knowing of the correlative character," p. 91). According to Spearman (1923), there are also five quantitative principles of cognition which are relevant to intelligence: conative control; fatigue; mental energy; primordial potencies; and retentivity.

While the factor theorists produced cognitive theories of intelligence, it was only in the early 1970s that the information-processing approach of cognitive psychology began to influence empirical research on intelligence. Hunt (e.g. 1978) was one of the first cognitive psychologists to investigate intelligence. He made use of pairs of letters (e.g. AA, aA) that could be the same or different physically or in name. Subjects either had to decide whether the letters were a physical match, or in another condition they had to decide whether they were a name match. It was argued on theoretical grounds that the difference between each subject's name-match time and physical-match time reflects the time taken to access lexical information in long-term memory. The typical finding is that this difference time correlates approximately $-.3$ with verbal intelligence as assessed psychometrically. This indicates that lexical access time is related to verbal intelligence, even if the strength of the relationship is not very impressive.

Sternberg (1977) investigated the relationship between psychometrically measured intelligence and performance on cognitive tasks that were more complex than those investigated by Hunt (1978). Several of his studies were concerned with analogical reasoning, and used componential analysis to assess the various cognitive processing stages involved (*see* ANALOGIES). The correlations between the speed with which individual component processes were performed and psychometric intelligence were somewhat variable, but were mostly higher than those obtained by Hunt (1978). It may be that performance on complex cognitive tasks generally correlates more highly with psychometric intelligence than does performance on simple tasks.

The cognitive approach to intelligence adopted by Hunt (1978), Sternberg (1977), and others served the valuable function of providing a relatively detailed analysis of some of the cognitive processes involved in intelligent functioning. However, the approach was limited in at least two important ways. First, while cognitive psychologists claimed that their approach was a considerable advance on that of the psychometricians, they nevertheless relied on psychometrically assessed intelligence as the criterion against which they judged the success of their cognitive measures. Second, it is becoming increasingly clear that intelligence can be understood only in part in terms of cognitive processing.

Gardner (1983) claimed that most previous conceptualizations of intelligence had been too narrowly based. He argued that evidence from several different sources (e.g. cross-cultural accounts of cognition, studies of exceptional groups, psychometric data, psychological training studies) pointed to the existence of several intelligences. In all, Gardner (1983) proposed that there are seven intelligences: linguistic; logical-mathematical; spatial; musical; bodily-kinesthetic; interpersonal; and intrapersonal.

One of the interesting characteristics of Gardner's theoretical approach is that several of the intelligences he identifies are not specifically cognitive in nature. However, there are grounds for doubting whether he has identified different intelligences rather than simply different abilities. As Sternberg and Frensch (1990) pointed out, it seems strange to describe someone who is tone deaf or physically uncoordinated as unintelligent.

Sternberg (1985) proposed a triarchic theory of intelligence. According to him, one needs to understand the mental mechanisms that underlie intelligent behavior, the use of these mental mechanisms in adapting to the environment, and "the mediating role of one's passage through life between the internal and external worlds of the individual." These three aspects of intelligence are dealt with by a componential subtheory, a contextual subtheory, and an experiential subtheory, respectively.

The componential subtheory is the most explicitly cognitive part of the triarchic theory. An important part of this subtheory is formed by various metacomponents (e.g. problem recognition, strategy selection, monitoring one's own problem solving (*see* METACOGNITION). There is substantial experimental support for most of these metacomponents. For example, MacLeod, Hunt, and Mathews (1978) found

that subjects having high spatial ability tended to use a pictorial-imagery strategy on a task involving comparisons between sentences and pictures, whereas those with high verbal ability tended to utilize a verbal-linguistic strategy.

In sum, it has proved fruitful to make use of the methods and theories of cognitive psychology in order to enhance our understanding of intelligence. No current theory adequately explains how the processes and structures of the cognitive system produce intelligent functioning, but considerable progress has been made in recent years.

BIBLIOGRAPHY

Gardner, H. (1983). *Frames of mind: The theory of multiple intelligences*. New York: Basic Books.

Hunt, E. B. (1978). Mechanics of verbal ability. *Psychological Review, 85*, 109–30.

MacLeod, C. M., Hunt, E. B., & Mathews, N. N. (1978). Individual differences in the verification of sentence–picture relationships. *Journal of Verbal Learning and Verbal Behavior, 17*, 493–507.

Spearman, C. (1923). *The nature of intelligence and the principles of cognition*. London: Macmillan.

Sternberg, R. J. (1977). *Intelligence, information processing, and analogical reasoning: The componential analysis of human abilities*. Hillsdale, NJ: Erlbaum.

——. (1985). *Beyond IQ: A triarchic theory of human intelligence*. New York: Cambridge University Press.

——, & Frensch, P. A. (1990). Intelligence and cognition. In M. W. Eysenck (Ed.), *International Review of Cognitive Psychology*. Chichester: Wiley.

MICHAEL W. EYSENCK

interference, proactive *See* PROACTIVE INTERFERENCE.

interference, retroactive *See* RETROACTIVE INTERFERENCE.

introspection The word "introspection" is derived from Latin and means "carefully looking within," in order to examine one's own mental processes and experiences. Since the beginning of modern civilization, philosophers have engaged in systematic introspection to uncover the origin and structure of mental experiences and thoughts (*see* CONSCIOUS-NESS). One of the first recorded introspections was Aristotle's reflection on the process of recall. Aristotle observed that desired information was often preceded by a sequence of related thoughts. In recalling "autumn" on one occasion, he first thought of "milk," then "white," then "air," then "fluid," which led him to "autumn." By reflecting on the relations between successive thoughts Aristotle identified several types of associative relations. Since then, numerous philosophers, such as Locke, Berkeley, and Hume, have introspected on their own experiences and thoughts and attempted to discover general principles underlying the origin and structure of thoughts and visual images. The preferred method of introspection was to let the mind wander and to examine the emerging thoughts and visual images.

Philosophers' introspections on spontaneously occurring experiences and thoughts could never be reproduced exactly even in the same individuals and obviously differed greatly between individuals. When psychology emerged as an empirical science during the nineteenth century, these introspections were rejected as unreliable. In the new psychological laboratories, equipment was developed for presentation of the same visual and auditory stimuli to many subjects. For example, by letting a metal ball fall from a prescribed height on to a surface, researchers could present the same sound to many individuals or observers; and by varying the height, they could produce systematic differences in intensity. The observers' task was to introspect repeatedly on their experiences and identify elementary sensations, which could then be related to basic neurophysiological processes. Through repeated analysis, complex experiences were decomposed into their corresponding basic sensations. For example, the experience of wetness was reduced to sensations of rapidly increased coldness, which could be produced without a liquid by sprinkling chilled talcum powder on the skin. Experienced observers agreed on the same sensory dimensions for the different senses such as pitch and loudness for auditory stimuli and their judgements of sensory experiences were found to be directly related to measurable physical characteristics of the presented stimuli. Similar methods for the analysis of sensory experiences are still being used in psychophysics and sensory perception.

Researchers used a similar introspective approach in the study of thought processes (see Danziger, 1980). To elicit thinking in the laboratory they gave observers tasks such as to report a word with a specified relation to a stimulus word. After a task was presented, the observers first generated their answers and then gave introspective reports on their thought processes during the trial. It was generally believed that introspection during thinking would interfere with and change the thought processes, and thus introspection had to be performed in retrospect from memory of the thought process.

The most controversial result reported in some introspective studies was that thoughts occurred without any observable neurological activity – that is, imageless thoughts. Other investigators were able to find kinesthetic images and muscular tension associated with those mental states. Still other investigators rejected the possibility of introspective analysis based on incomplete and unstable memory traces of thought processes. In heated arguments, investigators accused one another of being theoretically biased or insufficiently trained in introspection, and no acceptable empirical method to settle these disputes could be found. As a result, the method of gathering evidence through introspection was largely discredited in psychology and fell into disuse.

Historically, the most important criticism of introspection was offered by the Behaviorist John B. Watson, who argued that only directly observable behavior is acceptable psychological evidence (*see* COGNITIVE PSYCHOLOGY, HISTORY OF). Proposing alternative methods for studying thought processes, Watson was the first investigator to publish a study in which a subject was asked to "think aloud" while solving a problem. Although several early investigators, including Claparede and Duncker, independently used essentially the same method, it was not until A. Newell and SIMON (HERBERT) made extensive use of think-aloud reports in their study of human problem solving that the method gained general acceptance (*see* PROBLEM SOLVING).

Think-aloud verbalizations differ markedly from introspective reports (see Ericsson & Simon, 1984). When subjects think aloud while solving a problem such as a mental calculation of 36 × 24, subjects simply verbalize intermediate steps and products such as "4 times 6," "carry the 2," "144," "720." Direct verbalization of intermediate steps in the thought sequence has not been found to alter the sequence of thoughts and appears to differ from silent thinking only in that solution times are somewhat longer due to the additional time required for overt verbalization. Furthermore, brief instruction is sufficient to enable subjects to think aloud for the first time. This means that subjects can be kept naive with regard to the theoretical issues under investigation, a condition that was not possible for introspective observers, who required extensive training.

The analysis of data from think-aloud reports differs greatly from that of introspective reports, which had to be accepted essentially on trust. In contrast, verbalizations in think-aloud reports are viewed as behavior that the experimenter must account for. The first step in the data analysis is a task analysis, in which the experimenter specifies the various sequences of intermediate steps and thoughts that could hypothetically produce the correct answer. By comparing the verbalized steps to hypothesized intermediate steps the

experimenter can reject incorrect hypotheses about the thought processes. The verbal reports given in the previous example of a mental multiplication task would disconfirm hypotheses that the subject retrieved the answer directly from an extended multiplication table or generated it by relying on the short cut $(a+b)(a-b) = a_2-b_2$, or $36*24 = (30+6)(30-6) = 30**2-6**2 = 900-36 = 864$.

Think-aloud verbalizations only provide information about the sequence of reported thoughts mediating a cognitive activity. To gain more detailed information on the structure of thoughts and the processes generating or accessing them investigators have instructed subjects to go beyond thinking aloud and to provide explanations and descriptions of their thought processes. However explaining one's thinking disrupts and alters the thought processes and retrospectively given explanations often reflect speculations rather than direct knowledge of the underlying processes. More detailed knowledge of cognitive processes is best obtained by analyzing several additional indicators of the underlying processes such as solution times and pattern of eye fixations.

See also METACOGNITION; SELF-FOCUS AND SELF-ATTENTION.

BIBLIOGRAPHY

Danziger, K. (1980). The history of introspection reconsidered. *Journal of the History of the Behavioral Sciences, 16*, 241–64.

Ericsson, K. A., & Simon, H. A. (1984). *Protocol analysis: Verbal reports as data.* Cambridge, Mass.: MIT Press.

K. A. ERICSSON

J

James, William (*b.* New York, 11 January 1842; *d.* Chocura, New Hampshire, 26 August 1910). American psychologist and philosopher, the brother of the novelist Henry James. He entered Harvard Medical School in 1863 and graduated in 1869. He subsequently returned to Harvard, becoming in turn assistant professor of philosophy in 1880, professor of philosophy in 1885, professor of psychology in 1889, and then again professor of philosophy in 1897.

The contribution of William James to cognitive psychology rests very largely on his *Principles of psychology*, which was published in 1890. It is a difficult book to describe briefly. As Peters (1962) pointed out in his analysis,

> Already James had begun his opposition to systems and was determined to be systematically erratic. He announces that "the reader will in vain seek for any closed system in the book; it is mainly a mass of descriptive details, running out into queries which only a metaphysics alive to the weight of her task can hope successfully to deal with."

The unsystematic nature of the *Principles of psychology* occurred in part because of James's various interests: his medical training provided him with a good knowledge of physiology and biology, and his expertise in philosophy led him to a fascination with issues such as the stream of consciousness and free will.

It is impossible here to do more than identify a few of the contributions which James made directly to cognitive psychology. In the field of memory, he distinguished between primary memory or the psychological present, and secondary memory or the psychological past. This distinction has been very important over the past 30 years or so, although in modern terminology it is customary to distinguish between SHORT-TERM MEMORY and LONG-TERM MEMORY (*see also* MEMORY SYSTEMS). James emphasized the importance of ATTENTION, and particularly the necessity of selective attention. Indeed, according to James (1890), "Selection is the very keel on which our mental ship is built." Many of James's ideas about attention have had a strong influence on contemporary theories. While interest in attentional phenomena waned considerably during the Behaviorist era, it is now generally accepted that attention is of major significance. According to Keele and Neill (1978), the concept of attention has come to be regarded as lying "at the very core of cognitive psychology."

Another of the major contributions of William James was to the area of EMOTION. The so-called James–Lange theory of emotion argued in essence that the cognitive experience of emotion is heavily influenced by prior physiological changes. More specifically, there is first of all the perception of some external object or creature. This is followed by physiological changes and/or by movement. Finally, the observation of these changes produces the emotional experience. As James himself expressed it, "We are sad because we weep."

See also SELF-FOCUS AND SELF-ATTENTION.

BIBLIOGRAPHY

James, W. (1890). *Principles of psychology*. New York: Holt.

Keele, S. W., & Neill, W. T. (1978). Mechanisms of attention. In E. C. Carterette & M. P. Friedman (Eds), *Handbook of perception* (Vol. 9). London: Academic Press.

Peters, R. S. (1962). *Brett's history of psychology*. London: Allen & Unwin.

MICHAEL W. EYSENCK

judgement *See* DECISION MAKING AND JUDGEMENT.

L

language, pragmatics of In Charles Morris's (1938) scheme, pragmatics is the study of "the relation of signs to interpreters." It is distinguished from semantics, the study of "the relation of signs to the objects to which the signs are applicable," and syntax, the study of "the formal relation of signs to one another" (*see* GRAMMAR). So whereas semantics is the study of what words and sentences mean, pragmatics has come to be the study of what speakers mean in using them.

Most approaches to pragmatics have come out of the work of three Oxford philosophers, H. Paul Grice, Peter Strawson, and John Austin. It was Grice (1957) who noted that one must distinguish what words and sentences mean (word and sentence meaning) from what speakers mean in using them (speaker's meaning). The meaning of the sentence "I am now over here," for example, is built around the meanings of the words "I," "am," "now," "over," and "here." But that does not specify what a speaker is doing in uttering the sentence on a particular occasion. When Deirdre, say, utters it in London in 1945, she may use "I" to refer to herself, "now" to refer to that moment in 1945, and "over here" to refer to the side of Piccadilly opposite Dan, her addressee. She may be asserting to Dan that she is standing across the street from him. And, indirectly, she may also be requesting him to cross the street to meet her. Pragmatics, indeed, has focused on three issues illustrated in this example: (1) reference; (2) speech acts such as assertions and requests; and (3) implicatures, or what people imply in what they mean (Levinson, 1983).

A phrase like "the woman in the blue dress," Strawson (1950) argued, does not by itself refer to a particular woman. That comes only when a speaker uses it on a particular occasion. The problem is how addressees identify who or what the speaker is referring to. In many accounts, speakers and addressees presuppose a certain common ground – certain mutual knowledge, beliefs, and assumptions. Two people's common ground is based on their shared perceptual experiences, previous conversations (including the words just uttered), and shared culture. The way speakers succeed in referring is by designing their utterances to be interpreted against the common ground with their addressees. When Deirdre chooses the phrase "the woman in the blue dress," she assumes that Dan will be able to identify the woman being referred to as the most salient woman in a blue dress in their current common ground (*see* LANGUAGE COMPREHENSION).

Reference comes in many varieties. With demonstrative reference, the speaker performs an accompanying demonstration. Deirdre might say "That is Julius Marx" while pointing at a man, an empty chair, or a Rolls Royce; to understand the reference, Dan must find the most salient connection from the man, the chair, or the car to something that could be named Julius Marx. With anaphoric reference, the speaker refers to things mentioned earlier (*see* ANAPHORA). Deirdre might say "Sean let the dog off the leash and then put it in a drawer," using "it" anaphorically; Dan must recognize that she is referring to the leash and not the dog. With the proper noun Sean, Dan must determine which Sean she is referring to. And, finally, there are definite descriptions such as "the woman in the blue dress."

Language use, according to Austin (1962), is a form of action. When a speaker utters a sentence, he or she is indeed doing several things at once. Suppose Deirdre says to Dan, "Where is your car?" Among other things, she is performing the "utterance act" of issuing the utterance. She is also performing the "illocutionary act" of asking Dan where his car is. And she is performing the "perlocutionary act" of trying to get him to tell her where his car is. All of these acts are called speech acts. Most research has focused on illocutionary acts (*see* SPEECH PRODUCTION).

Illocutionary acts are of five main types (Searle, 1975). With assertives, speakers express a belief, as in saying "It's raining out." With directives, they try to get addressees to do things; commands, requests, and questions are types of directives. With commissives, speakers commit themselves to a future action; promises and offers are two types of commissives. With expressives, such as thanking, apologizing, congratulating, or greeting, speakers express certain feelings toward addressees. And finally, with declarations, speakers change some institutional state of affairs, as when judges sentence prisoners, referees call fouls, and ministers christen babies. Not all illocutionary acts fit neatly into these categories.

The issue is how speakers get addressees to recognize what acts they are performing. For illocutionary acts, the form of the sentence uttered is not enough. A request for the time, for example, can be made with a declarative sentence ("I'd like to know the time"), an imperative ("Please tell me the time"), or an interrogative ("What time is it?" or "Do you know the time?"). Which form is chosen depends on the speaker's purpose, status, and politeness.

What complicates the picture, Grice (1975) argued, is that speakers generally mean more than they say. When Deirdre asks Dan on the telephone, "Is Margaret there?" she may be asking him whether Margaret is there. She may also be *implicating* that he should call Margaret to the telephone if she is. Addressees derive such implicatures, according to Grice, by interpreting each utterance against the current purpose or direction of the talk exchange. They assume that the speaker is cooperative and, therefore, is trying to be informative, accurate, relevant, and clear. They compute what the speaker must mean based on this assumption. Implicatures too take many forms.

In the final analysis, what people do with language is accomplished within a discourse, and the primary form of discourse is face-to-face conversation. For a conversation to be coherent, the participants must make sure their common ground accumulates in a systematic way, and that takes collaboration. References, illocutionary acts, and implicatures in conversation are really collaborative efforts. It is not enough for Deirdre to utter to Dan the phrase "the woman in the blue dress" or the sentence "I am now over here." The two of them must do what it takes to reach the mutual belief that he has understood who she is referring to, or what she means. That may require several turns as Dan gives Deirdre evidence of understanding and they correct any misunderstandings that arise (Clark & Schaefer, 1989). The pragmatics of language cannot be divorced from the study of discourse, especially conversation (*see* LANGUAGE COMPREHENSION).

BIBLIOGRAPHY

Austin, J. L. (1962). *How to do things with words.* Oxford: Oxford University Press.

Clark, H. H., & Schaefer, E. F. (1989). Contributing to discourse. *Cognitive Science B,* 259–94.

Grice, H. P. (1957). Meaning. *Philosophical Review, 66,* 377–88.

——. (1975). Logic and conversation. In P. Cole & J. L. Morgan (Eds), *Syntax and semantics 3: Speech acts* (pp. 41–58). New York: Academic Press.

Levinson, S. C. (1983). *Pragmatics.* Cambridge: Cambridge University Press.

Morris, C. W. (1938). Foundations of the theory of signs. In O. Neurath, R. Carnap, & C. Morris (Eds), *International encyclopedia of unified science* (pp. 77–138). Chicago: University of Chicago Press.

Searle, J. (1975). A taxonomy of illocutionary acts. In K. Gunderson (Ed.), *Minnesota studies in the philosophy of language.* Minneapolis: University of Minnesota Press.

Strawson, P. F. (1950). On referring. *Mind, 59,* 320–44.

HERBERT H. CLARK

language acquisition Strictly speaking, there is a distinction between language acquisition and language development: language acquisition is the concern of theoretical linguists – notably Chomsky – whose aim is to describe linguistic knowledge rather than to investigate the relative linguistic abilities of children at different developmental stages. This latter task falls to psychologists and psycholinguists who are interested in language development. Within psychology, however, the two terms are often used interchangeably although many people prefer to use the term "development" since it is theoretically more neutral.

Children's language development forms a very important part of COGNITIVE DEVELOP-MENT and there has been much debate about the precise relationship between the two (*see* LANGUAGE AND THOUGHT). One of the major areas of debate has centered around the extent to which the processes involved in language development are similar to those involved in other aspects of cognitive development.

In one important sense language learning is unique. Many animals are capable of complex communication but only human beings are capable of acquiring language. What sets human language apart from ANIMAL COM-MUNICATION is that it is open-ended or "creative." Someone who has learned a language does not just know how to say a fixed number of words or phrases, or to understand only a fixed number of words or phrases. Knowing a language means that it is possible to produce and understand an infinitely large number of different messages, including completely novel ones.

Such linguistic creativity is possible because language has GRAMMAR: for any given language there are special syntactic rules that determine the way in which words are combined to make phrases and clauses. When children learn a particular language they not only have to learn what individual words mean, they also have to learn the grammar of that language. Experiments which have attempted to teach sign language to chimpanzees strongly suggest that what makes human beings unique is their capacity to master syntactic rules. Chimpanzees can be taught – and sometimes spontaneously learn – a large number of individual signs, but even the most successful animals have shown great difficulty in mastering grammar and seldom produce structured sequences of more than two or three signs. In this respect chimpanzees compare very poorly with deaf children who are

able to acquire sign language with the same facility that is evident in hearing children's acquisition of spoken language.

Although the ability to learn language appears to be restricted to human beings, it also appears to be an ability that all human beings possess. This has given rise to the view that children must be innately preprogramed to acquire language in the same way that they are preprogramed to develop in other ways. The strongest advocate of this position is Noam Chomsky, who has argued that children are endowed with specific linguistic skills that enable them to develop language. Chomsky originally put forward this view in 1959 in his now famous critique of Skinner's book, *Verbal behavior*, published in 1957. The greater part of *Verbal behavior* is devoted to an account of adult language but Chomsky's attack focused on Skinner's arguments about the nature of children's language development.

The essence of Skinner's claim was that language acquisition could be explained by extending the model of operant conditioning that he has used to account for the learning of simple tasks by laboratory animals. In operant conditioning the experimenter provides a reward – usually food or water – in order to train an aimal to produce a desired response in the presence of a particular stimulus. Through a process of "shaping," the animal is trained to produce more and more accurate responses. This is achieved by systematically tightening the criteria for rewarding responses. Skinner claimed that children learned language in an analogous way as a result of the reinforcement provided by their parents – in this case smiles and other signs of approval – which served to "shape" their initially incorrect utterances.

Chomsky's main objection to Skinner's view of language acquisition was that it in no way explained how a child could master the knowledge that was necessary to produce and understand completely novel utterances; it merely suggested how children could be taught a small repertoire of utterances. He also argued that Skinner placed far too much emphasis on the shaping role of the environment and too little emphasis on children's own active part in the process of language acquisition.

Chomsky's own view of language acquisition was radically different. He argued that language is only in the most marginal sense "taught" to children. Indeed, parents do not even talk to their children in a strictly grammatical way since speech is typically full of errors. Nevertheless almost all children do go on to learn their native language in spite of the incomplete and often inaccurate information they receive and, Chomsky argued, this would be possible only if they were born with specific linguistic skills and specific linguistic knowledge.

Describing the content and structure of such innate knowledge has proved to be remarkably difficult and highly controversial. The main problem is that any account of innate linguistic knowledge has to be sufficiently powerful to account for language development but, at the same time, sufficiently general to account for a child's ability to acquire *any* language. This is because the particular language – or languages – that children initially acquire is not determined by their genetic make-up but by the language that they are exposed to in the first years of life.

Since 1959 Chomsky has spelled out in great detail possible models for such a powerful but flexible system of innate linguistic knowledge. In the earliest formulation (Chomsky, 1965), he suggested that children develop hypotheses about the grammatical rules of the language to which they are exposed. These hypotheses are initially highly constrained by an innate endowment which sets tight limits on their possible form. The hypotheses are then tested to see if they are compatible with the language the child hears and revised if necessary. More recently, Chomsky (1986) has argued that the process of hypothesis selection – albeit a selection from among highly constrained hypotheses – would impose too high a cognitive demand on the child. Accordingly he now proposes that children are innately endowed with linguistic principles which have parameters. These can take one of several values according to the particular language concerned. In the principles and parameters model, language acquisition involves setting parameters to their correct values and this, Chomsky claims,

occurs automatically on the basis of minimal exposure to a particular language. The kind of language that children hear will have almost no influence on the rate at which they develop language.

To date there have been no experimental studies of Chomsky's proposals concerning parameter setting although they have received a great deal of interest from linguists. Recent psychological research has concentrated on the more basic question of whether language development is subject to environmental influences or whether, as Chomsky argues, the language that children hear exerts only a very minimal influence. Research in this area initially stemmed from a concern to determine what kind of language young children actually heard. The findings were remarkably consistent: parents – at least in Europe and North America – talked to children in short, grammatically correct, and highly repetitive utterances (for a summary see Harris & Coltheart, 1986). It is tempting to assume that syntactically simplified language of this kind might facilitate children's language development by providing them with language that they could easily analyze. However, an extensive longitudinal study carried out in Bristol by Wells and his co-workers (see, for example, Ellis & Wells, 1980) demonstrated that there were no clear links between the rate of children's language development and the length and complexity of their parents' speech. However, there was a relationship between the children's language development and the conversational style and topics of parental speech. The parents of the children showing the earliest and most rapid language development used more directives, asked more questions, and commented more on the child's own activity.

There are serious difficulties in interpreting the pattern of cause and effect in studies of parental speech and children's language development given that the way parents talk to children is strongly influenced by the children's response. However, there are good reasons why language development might be influenced by the conversational style and topic of parental speech. These stem from the proposal, originally put forward by Bruner

(1983), that children acquire language in a highly familiar social context which provides them with important clues about the meaning of the speech they hear.

Bruner argued that the early social games played by parent and child have an important role in assisting the early stages of language development. The idea is that the shared experience of social games presents the child with opportunities to relate sounds heard in parental speech to familiar actions and objects. Harris and co-workers (Harris, Jones, & Grant, 1983, 1984) have shown that this argument can be extended beyond social games to the nonverbal context of parental speech in general. This is because a very high proportion of all maternal speech to prelinguistic children refers to objects and activities on which the child is currently focusing attention.

Harris (1987) has suggested that, in the early stages of language development, the close relationship between parental speech and the child's own activity may facilitate vocabulary acquisition by allowing the child to observe the regular co-occurrence of particular words and particular nonverbal contexts. This is supported by research which shows that children's production of their earliest words is closely related to their mother's most frequent use of these words (Harris, Barrett, Jones, & Brookes, 1988); and also by a study showing that the language used to children with slow language development is different from that used to children with normal language development (Harris, Jones, Brookes, & Grant, 1986).

It appears, however, that children's language development is influenced by parental speech only in the very early stages. Barrett, Harris, & Chasin (in press) compared children's initial and subsequent uses of early words and found that, whereas there was a relationship between the child's initial use of a word and the mother's use of that same word in over 90 percent of cases, such a relationship was present for fewer than 50 percent of subsequent uses. Furthermore, syntactic development appears to be very little influenced by the language children hear, as Chomsky has always claimed (see Ellis & Wells, 1980; Gleitman, Newport, & Gleitman, 1984).

Children's developing ability to produce language does, however, appear to be closely related to their LANGUAGE COMPREHENSION. For most children there is a gap of several months between first being able to understand words and first starting to produce them. This means that children have a prior understanding of many of the words that they produce. However, this is not the case for all words, and there are individual differences in the proportion of words that the child can comprehend before producing them.

Bates, Bretherton, and Snyder (1988) present the most extensive data on the relationship between comprehension and production in the early stages. They studied 32 children from the ages of 10 months to 28 months, testing both comprehension and production at several points in development. Their main conclusion is that early lexical development has two separable strands. The first strand is what Bates et al. call "analyzed production" which is rooted in comprehension and consists of the child learning to produce words that he or she already understands. This strand is particularly evident in children who have large comprehension vocabularies and who go on to use nouns in a flexible way in production, that is, in a variety of situations. By contrast, the second strand – "unanalyzed production" – consists of words and phrases that the child has learned by rote or in fixed routines. Children do not appear to understand these latter words to the same extent that they understand words that form part of analyzed production.

Bates et al. go on to suggest that these two strands of language development have their counterparts in early multiword speech. They found that unanalyzed production was closely related to variation in MLU (mean length of utterance) at 20 months. Bates et al. explain this by arguing that variation in MLU stems mainly from the ability to use closed-class morphemes – that is, grammatical function words such as "and," "the," and "he" and morphological inflections such as the plural "s." By contrast, analyzed production was related to semantic-conceptual sophistication at 20 months – that is, the number of different semantic relationships the child expressed in both single words and multiword utterances.

This research highlights the fact that, even in the early stages of language development, several different processes appear to be operating; and that there are important differences between children.

See also PERCEPTUAL DEVELOPMENT.

BIBLIOGRAPHY

Barrett, M., Harris, M., & Chasin, J. (In press). Early lexical development and maternal speech: A comparison of children's initial and subsequent uses of words. *Journal of Child Language*.

Bates, E., Bretherton, I., & Snyder, L. (1988). *From first words to grammar: Individual differences and dissociable mechanisms*. Cambridge: Cambridge University Press.

Bruner, J. S. (1983). *Child's talk: Learning to use language*. Oxford: Oxford University Press.

Chomsky, N. (1959). Review of *Verbal behavior* by B. F. Skinner. *Language*, *35*, 26–58.

——. (1965). *Aspects of the theory of syntax*. Cambridge, Mass.: MIT Press.

——. (1986). *Knowledge of language: Its nature, origins and use*. New York: Praeger.

Ellis, R., & Wells, G. (1980). Enabling factors in adult–child discourse. *First Language*, *1*, 46–62.

Harris, M. (1987). The role of early interaction in language disorder. In *Proceedings of the first international symposium on specific speech and language disorders in children*. London: AFASIC.

——, & Coltheart, M. (1986). *Language processing in children and adults: An introduction to psycholinguistics*. London: Routledge & Kegan Paul.

Harris, M., Jones, D., & Grant, J. (1983). The nonverbal context of mothers' speech to infants. *First Language*, *4*, 21–30.

——. (1984). The social-interactional context of maternal speech to infants. *First Language*, *4*, 89–100.

Harris, M., Barrett, M. D., Jones, D., & Brookes, S. (1988). Linguistic input and early word meaning. *Journal of Child Language*, *15*, 77–94.

Harris, M., Jones, D., Brookes, S., & Grant, J. (1986). Relations between the non-verbal context of maternal speech and rate of language development. *British Journal of Developmental Psychology*, *4*, 261–8.

Skinner, B. F. (1957). *Verbal behavior*. New York: Appleton-Century-Crofts.

MARGARET HARRIS

language and thought One of the long-standing debates within psychology concerns the relationship between language and thought. The most extreme view of this relationship is set out in the Sapir–Whorf linguistic relativity hypothesis which states that people's perceptions of the world are strongly influenced by the language that they speak. Other influential views – concerning the development of language and thinking in children – have been put forward by PIAGET (JEAN) and Vygotsky (*see* COGNITIVE DEVELOPMENT; LANGUAGE ACQUISITION).

More recently the debate has been stimulated by Fodor in his seminal work, *The modularity of mind* (1983), which has had an important influence on research in philosophy and linguistics, as well as cognitive psychology and cognitive science. Fodor's thesis is that language is a "modular" process (*see* MODULARITY OF MIND). By this, Fodor means that there is an input system in the brain that is dedicated to the task of linguistic processing, just as there is a visual input system that is dedicated to the task of visual perception.

According to Fodor, the language module has certain crucial properties which it shares with other modules. The first is that modules are domain specific – that is, each one deals with only one kind of information. So the language module deals only with linguistic information – streams of speech sounds or sequences of letters – and the vision module deals only with visual information. The operation of modules is mandatory – that is, they operate automatically once a stimulus of the appropriate kind has been detected – fast, and largely unconscious (*see* AUTOMATIC PROCESSING). These claims about language modularity have not proved particularly controversial but Fodor's next claim, that modules are "informationally encapsulated," has led to enormous controversy.

The notion of information encapsulation lies at the heart of the debate about language and thought. Fodor's claim is that language

202

comprehension is carried out independently of any other cognitive processes. In other words, the process of interpreting a sentence is entirely "bottom-up" (*see* DATA-DRIVEN AND CONCEPTUALLY DRIVEN PROCESSES) and is not influenced by any extra-sentential – or nonlinguistic – information, that might be available to the listener or reader. According to the modularity hypothesis, LANGUAGE COMPREHENSION is physically as well as informationally separate from other cognitive processes in that those parts of the brain that analyze language have a pre-formed pattern of neural connections. Fodor argues that this "hard-wiring" of the language module means that language development in the child is largely innate (*see* LANGUAGE ACQUISITION) and also that brain damage will lead to characteristic and very specific language impairments (*see* APHASIA).

Much of the objection to Fodor's claim that language is informationally encapsulated has come from evidence that language comprehension can be subject to "top-down" influences. For example, Marslen-Wilson and Tyler (1980) showed that subjects' ability to identify words in continuous speech is affected by contextual cues. Subjects could recognize the word "lead" more quickly in sentence (1b) if it were preceded by sentence (1a):

(1a) The church was broken into last night.

(1b) Some thieves stole most of the *lead* off the roof.

The only way in which knowledge of sentence (1a) can influence processing of sentence (1b) is through a subject's knowledge of the material commonly used for church roofs. This knowledge is not specific linguistic knowledge but, rather, part of someone's general knowledge about the world. And, according to the modularity hypothesis, it should not be possible for general – non-linguistic – knowledge of this kind to have an influence on the process of word identification.

There are, however, cases where word recognition is modular and unaffected by top-down influences. Swinney (1979), for example, has shown that strong contextual cues do not prevent both possible meanings of a

homophonic word – like "bug" – being activated even though only one meaning – for example, "microphone" rather than "insect" – is consistent with the context.

Part of the inconsistency of the results obtained in this area may lie in the use of different modalities of presentation. Research by Marslen-Wilson and co-workers (see Marslen-Wilson, 1987) has concentrated on spoken word recognition whereas other experiments – for example, those of Swinney (1979) – have used visual presentation. However, in his most recent research, Marslen-Wilson (1987) has argued that, even in spoken word-recognition, bottom-up processes take priority over top-down information.

This conclusion focuses on one of the essential properties of linguistic communication. We cannot normally predict exactly what someone will say and, for this reason, language processing has to be largely independent of other cognitive activities. For, if it were not, we would hear only what we expected to hear and read only what we expected to read.

BIBLIOGRAPHY

Fodor, J. A. (1983). *The modularity of mind.* Cambridge, Mass.: MIT Press.

Green, J. (1987). *Memory, thinking and language: Topics in cognitive psychology.* London: Methuen.

Harris, M., & Coltheart, M. (1986). *Language processing in children and adults: An introduction to psycholinguistics.* London: Routledge & Kegan Paul.

Marslen-Wilson, W. D. (1987). Functional parallelism in spoken word-recognition. *Cognition, 25,* 71–102.

——, & Tyler, L. K. (1980). The temporal structure of spoken language understanding. *Cognition, 8,* 1–71.

Swinney, D. (1979). Lexical access during sentence comprehension: (Re)consideration of context effects. *Journal of Verbal Learning and Verbal Behaviour, 14,* 645–60.

MARGARET HARRIS

language comprehension Language comprehension refers to our ability to respond appropriately to messages in natural language, whether spoken or written. Sometimes the appropriate response is to take some action, sometimes it is to think about an issue, and sometimes it is simply to change our knowledge or beliefs about things. Through speech, people can learn of things of which they do not have personal experience, while the invention of writing systems enables people to learn of things created long ago and far away. Language comprehension is central to all human cultures, and occupies a significant portion of our waking experience.

For the psychologist, how we understand language is important in its own right, since it is a uniquely human activity, and is ubiquitous. But it is important for other reasons, too. Language is used to teach people things, to persuade people about things, and to make people think about issues. The study of rhetoric (how to bring about an effect optimally through the use of words) has its origins in classical times. Another important facet of language understanding concerns the development of natural-language interfaces between computers and human beings (see HUMAN–COMPUTER INTERACTION). The convenience of being able to communicate with a computer in natural language, whether typed or spoken, rather than through some seemingly unnatural set of commands, has long had appeal. However, in order to realize this end, it is necessary to understand how language is used (and hence understood) by human beings. Thus, the processes underlying language understanding have been a persistent and important topic in cognitive science and information technology as well as in cognitive psychology.

To understand an utterance, any language processor, human or machine, must relate the content of the utterance to its knowledge about the world. So any theory of language understanding has to address on one hand how the language itself is processed, and on the other how the processing of language interacts with other types of knowledge. While knowledge of a language and knowledge of the world may be largely independent, when language is in use, both are involved in complex ways.

For convenience, we may think of language understanding as requiring the recognition of characters or sounds which form meaningful groups (words). On the basis of this, it is possible to group the words into units (phrases), which in turn make up a sentence. Beyond that, interpretation involves recognizing the meaning of the sentence, and finally its significance in a communicative context. Although each one of these processes is a necessary part of the process of understanding, they are by no means independent sequential activities. Often the recognition of a word will depend upon its context, either syntactic or semantic. An extreme example of this is found in reading poor handwriting, where context is frequently used to identify a word or phrase (see INFERENCES). In much the same way, context may be important for deciding upon the syntactic interpretation of a sentence. The following example from Winograd (1972) is an illustration: "Put the pyramid on the block in the box." On one interpretation, the first noun phrase is the-pyramid-on-the-block, and the second is the-box. This interpretation makes sense if there is more than one pyramid, and one of them is on a block. On the other hand, if there is only one pyramid, and there is more than one block, then the first noun phrase becomes the-pyramid, and the second becomes the-block-in-the-box. Such ambiguities are commonplace in language, and illustrate how syntactic interpretation can be a function of states of affairs in the world.

The meanings of words in a sentence should compose to form the meaning of a sentence, but sometimes it is the interpretation of a sentence against general knowledge (in long-term memory) which tells the processor which sense of a word is intended. With the sentence "Mary dressed the baby," the sense of dressed selected is that of putting on clothes, whereas "Mary dressed the wound" leads to accessing the sense of bandaging the wound. Similar cases occur with noun phrases. Compare "The actress walked into the theatre" with "The surgeon entered the theatre." Just as syntactic interpretation can depend upon knowledge of the world, so semantics can depend upon general knowledge. In processing an utterance, an interpreter will use information from all sources to bring about recognition of the significance of the message.

NONLITERAL INTERPRETATION

Not all statements and utterances which we encounter are meant to be taken literally. If a writer asserts that "John kicked the bucket," the intention is to convey in a rather irreverent way that John died. In this case, the processor has to recognize that the expression is an idiom, and is not to be taken literally. All metaphors have this character. "John ran out of steam" is a commonplace metaphor, implying a lack of energy. For any process model of language comprehension, metaphor poses an interesting problem. Does a receiver first work out a literal interpretation, test it against the world, discover that it is false, and then discover that it is a metaphor? What evidence there is suggests that under many circumstances, it takes no longer to discover a metaphorical meaning than it does to discover a literal one, suggesting that the two-stage account is not correct.

The same sort of problem arises with indirect speech acts (Searle, 1975). If I want the salt at the table, I am more likely to say "Could you pass the salt, please" than "Pass the salt, please," although on the surface, the latter is a direct request, and the former is a query. Sometimes requests can be very indirect, as when a speaker says "It's freezing in here" (a statement), meaning "I would like you to close the window." To understand such statements, the listener must either know or infer the goals of the listener in order to make an appropriate interpretation. As with metaphor, there is evidence to suggest that it is not necessary to test for a literal interpretation before going on to recognize the speech act intended. Furthermore, indirect speech acts seem to serve an important social function in that they offer the listener an opportunity not to follow up the request being made, without overt denial (see Levinson, 1983).

The importance of the recognition of the goals of the listener when speaking is also of major importance. At the most general level, this amounts to a requirement that utterances be relevant to the communication, the main one of Grice's maxims (Grice, 1975). The

maxims for effective communication described by the philosopher Grice are (1) Quantity: be as informative as necessary, but not overinformative; (2) Quality: convey only true propositions; (3) Relation: contributions should be relevant; and (4) Manner: avoid ambiguity and obscurity. While these maxims are hardly detailed prescriptions, people do follow this sort of pattern in good dialog. Failure to do so can result in misunderstanding. Consider the question–answer pair:

Q: How many students failed formal logic in the 1856 philosophy class?
A: None.

This answer is fine, unless no formal logic was offered in 1856, in which case it is misleading. Similarly, if there was no philosophy class in 1856, it would also be misleading. But in neither case is it untrue! For an answer to be informative, it must not only be true, but it must also take into account at least a guess at what the presuppositions and goals of the person asking the questions might be (*see* LANGUAGE, PRAGMATICS OF). This problem is not only of theoretical interest, it is especially relevant to the design of natural language database enquiry systems.

TEXT AND INTERPRETATION

Psychologists have devoted much effort to the study of written text, since text understanding is an important part of the reading process. It is clear that texts convey ideas, and attempts have been made to show how texts can be broken down into idea units. The best known example is found in Kintsch and van Dijk (1978). The units are propositions, the smallest statement capable of independent verification. Thus, the statement "Snow is falling" corresponds to a single proposition, while "Snow is falling heavily" corresponds to two: that it is snowing, and that the snow is heavy. Propositions are written as predicates followed by a set of arguments: $(P, A_1, A_2, \ldots\ldots A_n)$. Thus "Snow is falling" is written as (FALL, SNOW), where the capitals show that the expressions stand for concepts.

It is possible to represent complete passages as connected networks of propositions. Thus, with the message "John stays home because the snow is falling heavily," the corresponding structure is:

(BECAUSE, ((FALL, SNOW)&(HEAVY, SNOW)), (STAY, JOHN, AT_HOME).

The sentence thus consists of four propositions, and can be represented as a simple tree structure corresponding to the bracket arrangement. For a more complete discussion, see Kintsch and van Dijk (1978) or Sanford (1985).

If the meaning of a discourse can be expressed in this way, then a major part of discourse understanding will be to identify the individual propositions, and produce a connected structure in long-term memory corresponding to the text. Kintsch and van Dijk suppose that when a text is read, a number of propositions are kept in a short-term memory store (buffer), where, if possible, they are connected to each other. Important propositions remain in the buffer, while unimportant ones are replaced by the next set being read in. If connections cannot be established in the buffer, then a search of long-term memory is required for a means of producing a connected structure. When such a search is executed, a time-consuming bridging inference is made.

This model emphasizes the connection of memory for discourse to text content itself. But there is evidence that what is remembered of a text often includes intrusions from general knowledge which was used in order to interpret the text. Thus, in recalling discourse, a reader may confuse what was meant or implied with what was actually said, a result which has been observed since the earliest days of studying memory for discourse. Furthermore, we have seen how knowledge of the situation influences sense selection of words. Considerations such as these have led researchers to consider in detail how knowledge combines with what is given in a discourse to produce an interpretation. The most general term for this class of theory is schema theories (*see* SCHEMATA). Essentially, when an utterance is interpreted, it is assumed that elements in the utterance activate information in memory of which those elements are a partial description. Theories of this type have been developed by Roger Schank, Marvin Minsky,

and Sanford and Garrod (see Schank & Abelson [1977] for a computational view, and Sanford & Garrod [1981] for a more psychological overview).

Imagine encountering the statements that "John was hungry, so he went into a restaurant." According to some versions of schema theory, this description matches a memory structure or script for activities at a restaurant, and this becomes active. One consequence of this activity is that representations of entities playing roles in the script will be active. For instance, "waiter" will be available. This can help explain why we can understand mentions of a waiter when we are talking about restaurants, even if the word has not been used before. Suppose the story above were continued with "The waiter showed John to a good table." Reading-time studies show that this sentence is easily processed in such a context. In contrast, if the context does not strongly predict a waiter, but merely allows it, then reading times are longer: "Max started arguing. The waiter changed his table." For controlled experiments on this problem, see Sanford and Garrod (1981).

THE CONTROL OF INFERENCES IN TEXT UNDERSTANDING

Because of the centrality of the problem, much attention has been paid to which INFERENCES are and are not made during reading. One taxonomy seeks to classify text-based inferences as either necessary or elaborative. Necessary inferences are those which have to be made in order for a coherent representation of the text to be constructed. It includes bridging inferences, the use of causal relations (see Keenan, Baillet, & Brown, 1984) and anaphoric references (*see* ANAPHORA). In contrast, elaborative inferences are those which are made merely to "fill out the picture." Consider the sentence pair "John dropped the porcelain vase. He always was clumsy." It is pragmatically likely that the vase broke, but to conclude this would be to make an elaborative inference, not a necessary one. On the other hand, to infer that "John" and "He" refer to the same person is a necessary inference, rather than merely elaborative. Such a distinction has been used to give investigators a theory of which inferences are made during reading: only necessary, or elaborative as well?

Unfortunately, such a simple distinction is problematic to maintain, and current research is aimed at a more detailed examination of just what is necessary for understanding. One important idea underlying the attempt to discover which inferences are and are not made is that it is not possible to make all possible inferences. There are a number of reasons for this. The number of inferences which might be made is effectively infinite, so if the processor is of limited capacity, then some selective principle must operate. Also, if an interpretation is to make sense, then one would expect the inferences which are made to be relevant to the intentions of the producer. It is a major research problem to produce a good theory of relevance on the one hand, and of how limited capacity influences the range of possible inferences (for different perspectives see Sperber & Wilson, 1986; Sanford, 1990).

Obviously, one important source of control over the inferences made by the reader is the writer's choice of wording, emphasis, and the rest of the armory of rhetoric. It might be said that part of the art of writing is to cause the reader to think about those things which the writer wants, and to pay little or no attention to those things which the writer wishes to be ignored. Part of this consists of making the reader access the desired background knowledge in order to make an interpretation. Normally, as readers we may be unaware that this is happening, but such selectivity can be revealed by certain types of jokes (see HUMOR) and other sorts of trick texts. Sanford and Garrod (1981) used the following example:

John was on his way to school. He was worried about the maths lesson.

Such a pair of statements seems to suggest that John is a schoolboy. So, if the following sentence is encountered, readers are a little thrown, and reading times are relatively long:

He was afraid that he would be unable to control the class.

The original representation, based on inappropriate inferences, produced a mental model (see INFERENCES) which had to be modified. In fact, if further sentences like the ones below are introduced, the way inferences are unwittingly made is even clearer:

– It was not fair of the teacher to leave him in charge.
– This was not a normal part of a janitor's duties.

Such phenomena as these simply demonstrate processes which are present all of the time in text understanding: going beyond what is said by using situation-specific knowledge to form a representation. A major challenge is to specify which inferences are made – for instance, what is it that caused John to be represented as a schoolboy in the mind of the reader? It seems likely that there are many subtle influences at work here, and any full theory of comprehension will have to answer such questions.

It is clear that access to knowledge of mundane things, events, and activities in the world plays a major role in the detail of language understanding, but there is much to be done to establish precisely how the system works. Part of the difficulty for the scientist arises from the effectively infinite variety of strings of words which can be used in communicating (a linguistic problem), and part arises from our as yet inadequate formulations of how knowledge and beliefs are structured and accessed. It is this very interplay which makes language understanding such a central topic in cognitive psychology, and more specifically in COGNITIVE SCIENCE.

See also DATA-DRIVEN AND CONCEPTUALLY DRIVEN PROCESSES; GRAMMAR; MENTAL MODELS; SPEECH PERCEPTION.

BIBLIOGRAPHY

Grice, H. P. (1975). Logic and conversation. In P. Cole and J. L. Morgan (Eds), *Syntax and semantics, 3.* New York: Academic Press.

Keenan, J. M., Baillet, S. D., & Brown, P. (1984). The effects of causal cohesion on comprehension and memory. *Journal of Verbal Learning and Verbal Behavior, 23,* 115–26.

Kintsch, W, & van Dijk, T. A. (1978). Toward a model of text comprehension and production. *Psychological Review, 85,* 363–94.

Levinson, S. (1983). *Pragmatics*. Cambridge: Cambridge University Press.

Rickheit, G., & Strohner, H. (1985). *Inferences in text processing*. Amsterdam: North-Holland.

Sanford, A. J. (1985). *Cognition and cognitive psychology*. London: Lawrence Erlbaum.

— —. (1990). On the nature of text-driven inference. In D. Balota, G. Flores d'Arcais, & K. Rayner (Eds), *Comprehension processes in reading*. Hillsdale, NJ: Lawrence Erlbaum.

— —, & Garrod, S. C. (1981). *Understanding written language*. Chichester: John Wiley.

Schank, R., & Abelson, R. (1977). *Scripts, goals, plans, and understanding*. Hillsdale, NJ: Erlbaum.

Searle, J. R. (1975). A taxonomy of illocutionary acts. In K. Gunderson (Ed.), *Minnesota studies in the philosophy of language*. Minneapolis: University of Minnesota Press.

Sperber, D., & Wilson, D. (1986). *Relevance, communication, and cognition*. Oxford: Basil Blackwell.

Winograd, T. (1972). *Understanding natural language*. New York: Academic Press.

A. J. SANFORD

language development *See* LANGUAGE ACQUISITION.

learning *See* COGNITIVE DEVELOPMENT; COGNITIVE SCIENCE; CONCEPT LEARNING; EXPERTISE; LEARNING STYLES; LEVELS OF PROCESSING; MOTOR CONTROL AND LEARNING, PIAGET, JEAN; READING DEVELOPMENT; STUDENT LEARNING; STUDY SKILLS.

learning styles The term "learning style" has been used in the literature in two distinct ways: (1) it has been used to indicate a broad description of relatively consistent behaviors related to ways of going about learning; it is treated as an individual difference of generality comparable to intelligence or personality, but describing consistency in the ways people tackle learning tasks; (2) the definition has been narrowed considerably to parallel the idea of cognitive style, with the use of bipolar traits, but described in relation to the learning tasks commonly found in educational contexts, as opposed to scores on psychological tests. Both uses of the term imply that learning style is related both to cognitive processes and to personality, but in the broader definition the emphasis is more cognitive, while the narrower definition is closer to personality. In both senses, the term has been used to cover a range of concepts which have emerged from attempts to describe aspects of student learning.

PROCESSES, SKILLS, TACTICS, STRATEGIES, AND STYLES

The next step in clarifying the meaning of the term learning style is to see it in relation to other terms describing cognitive activities arranged in ascending order of generality. "Cognitive processes" are basic cognitive activities taking place within the memory, involving coding or thinking processes, which are usually investigated within laboratory experiments. When these processes are described in terms of the ability of individuals consistently to carry out certain types of task, such as certain psychological tests, they are referred to as "cognitive skills." In everyday life, skills are brought into play in order to solve particular problems or to deal effectively with certain situations. Here a decision is required to select particular skills, or to apply processes in succession, within some overall plan. This can be seen as adopting "tactics." And if an organized series of tactics is required, perhaps depending also on a person's attitudes and motives, then these may be called "strategies." Finally, if a person tends to adopt a similar set of strategies consistently across different tasks and settings, this can be taken to indicate the existence of "learning styles." Schmeck (1988, pp. 3–20) provides valuable additional clarification of these and other related terms. Unfortunately, in the literature there is still considerable overlap in the use of this set of terms, not always consistent with the level of generality indicated here. For the purposes of clarity, however, these distinctions are useful in looking at the research into learning style.

COGNITIVE LEARNING STYLES

Research into cognitive learning styles has

developed from attempts to predict different levels and types of academic performance in students. Some of the earliest attempts at describing different learning styles came from the attention given to divergent thinking by J. P. Guilford. The tests of divergent thinking or "creativity," such as the Uses of Objects Test, which were subsequently developed encouraged comparisons between scores on conventional intelligence tests and those on the new open-ended tests (*see* CREATIVITY). As a result, Wallach and Kogan (1965) and Hudson (1966) drew attention to the existence of two distinct groups of children. Those with much higher scores on intelligence than creativity were labeled "convergers," while those with the reverse pattern of scores were called "divergers." Hudson reported that these two groups showed markedly different patterns of thinking, contrasting subject choices in school, and even varying personality configurations. The divergers were seen as being more impulsive, emotional, expressive, and humorous, while the convergers were more logical, rational, consistent, restrained, and conventional. Wallach and Kogan argued that the existing educational system appeared to favor the convergers and to penalize the divergers. Such arguments had a considerable impact on education at the time, encouraging the movement toward informal or open education, and also introduced researchers to the idea of individual differences in which cognitive differences were paralleled with personality differences. This pattern later became the hallmark of learning style.

Kolb (1983) also used the terms convergers and divergers, but with a rather different meaning. He has distinguished four learning styles based on two sets of distinctions – whether people prefer to deal with concrete or abstract information, and whether they process it reflectively or actively. Within this terminology, the convergers prefer abstract material and process it actively, while the divergers look for concrete information and process it reflectively. The remaining two styles are described as assimilators (abstractions processed reflectively) and accommodators (active, concrete). There are parallels here with C. G. Jung's "psychological types"

and with the distinctive thinking processes attributed to extraverts and introverts.

For as in the former case the purely empirical heaping together of facts paralyses thought and smothers their meaning, so in the latter case introverted thinking shows a dangerous tendency to coerce facts into the shape of its image, or by ignoring them altogether, to unfold its phantasy image in freedom.

(quoted by Entwistle, 1981, p. 186)

Again we see the connection between cognitive processes and personality (*see* PERSONALITY AND COGNITION).

A more recent set of distinctions can be found in the work of Biggs (1987), who has used ideas derived from information-processing theories to investigate the ways in which students learn and study. His three categories also describe characteristically different strategies for dealing with information, but these are related to the intentions and underlying motives of the learner. The styles here are actually referred to as "approaches to learning" due to the similarities which were demonstrated with the concept introduced by Marton (Marton, Hounsell, & Entwistle, 1984; *see also* STUDENT LEARNING) on the basis of interviews with students. Biggs's categories, however, were identified through factor analyses of inventories of study behavior and learning processes which showed the consistent and close link between strategy and motive. A "deep" approach brings together intrinsic and competence motivation with a learning strategy which involves the attempt to understand the meaning of what is being learned. An "achieving" approach is rooted in competition and ego enhancement and leads to a strategy which depends on well-organized study methods. Finally, a "surface" approach is driven by fear of failure and leads to a dependency on reproduction through rote learning.

Although all three of these descriptions of learning styles do contain both cognitive and non-cognitive components, or correlates, the descriptions put more emphasis on their cognitive origins. In contrast, the next set of concepts uses the narrower definition which emphasizes the bipolar nature of learning style.

BIPOLAR LEARNING STYLES

The research discussed in this section shows a more direct relationship to ideas in cognitive style. In distinguishing between abilities and cognitive styles Messick (1976, pp. 9–10) wrote that:

> Abilities are value directional: having more of an ability is better than having less. Cognitive styles are value differentiated: each pole has an adaptive value ... [which] depends upon the nature of the situation and upon the cognitive requirements of the task in hand.... Abilities are specific to a particular domain of content or function. Cognitive styles, in contrast, cut across domains. They appear to serve as high-level heuristics that organize lower-level strategies, operations, and propensities – often including abilities – in such complex sequential processes as problem-solving and learning.... In factor-analytic terms, if abilities and temperament traits are first or second-order factors, then cognitive styles are higher-order factors linking those domains.

Cognitive styles have most commonly been measured through perceptual tests such as the Embedded Figures Test or the Matching Familiar Figures Test (see Entwistle, 1981, pp. 202–7). In contrast, learning styles have been identified either by observing students working on learning tasks, or from inventory scores. In Biggs's categories, only students adopting a deep approach could be expected to reach a thorough understanding of what they were learning. Pask (in Schmeck, 1988) found that even when students were required to demonstrate understanding, they still showed differing strategies in the way they tackled the learning materials. Based on extended work in this area, he has concluded that some students have relatively strong and consistent *preferences* for adopting a particular type of strategy, which he takes to indicate their "learning style."

Some students adopt a "holist" style in which, right from the start, they try to see the task in the widest possible perspective, establishing an overview which goes well beyond the task itself. Their learning process involves the use of illustrations, examples, analogies, and anecdotes in building up an idiosyncratic form of understanding deeply rooted in personal experience and beliefs. Other students prefer a "serialist" style in which they begin with a narrow focus, concentrate on details and logical connections in a cautious manner, and look at the broader context only toward the end of the topic, if at all. Extreme holists are often impulsive, even cavalier, in their use of evidence, tending to generalize too readily and to jump to unjustified conclusions. Extreme serialists are often too cautious, failing to see important relationships or useful analogies, thus leaving their understanding impoverished.

These two main categories of description do, however, need qualification, as there are different ways of exhibiting stylistic preferences. Pask himself (in Schmeck, 1988, pp. 92–3) has described these differences as follows:

> Among all holists it is possible to recognize (a) those who depend upon the use of valid analogies or generalizations given within the material ...; and (b) those holists who depend upon the creation of (their own) valid analogies and generalizations between topics. This latter method incidentally seems to be one of the most productive methods of learning – by invention or discovery.... Among serialistic learners, it is possible to distinguish at least the following two types. One is the operation, or local rule, learner who progresses logically, step-by-step, moving to a different context only when he or she has assimilated one portion thoroughly and often asking for tutorial guidance on which topics to tackle next. The other is the rote learner, who follows the prescribed and narrow path. Unless the subject matter is trivial or the learner virtually has EIDETIC IMAGERY, rote learners have little chance of success in making use of the knowledge they have acquired, although they may perform quite competently in multiple choice or other types of

examination where special memorization skill places them at an advantage....

Pask follows Messick in arguing that learning styles are value differentiated. For some tasks a serialist strategy will be more effective, and for others a holist one. Students who have a strong preference for one or other style will find it difficult to shift strategy between different kinds of task. Pask showed that students learn more effectively from materials designed to match their particular learning style, while it seems likely that teachers adopt a teaching style which reflects their own learning style (Entwistle, 1981, pp. 231–9, 250). There thus seems to be a considerable advantage in being able to adapt readily to different presentational styles, adopting what Pask describes as a "versatile" style. It may be possible to help students to become more versatile by requiring them to practice their weaker style in some tasks, but stylistic preferences have been found to be unexpectedly strong (Pask, in Schmeck, 1988).

The strength of these preferences has been explained either in terms of underlying personality traits (Messick et al., 1976) or in terms of cerebral dominance of left (serialist) or right (holist) hemispheres of the brain, which differences Sperry (1983) has argued are inherited. This latter hypothesis underpinned the extensive work on learning styles conducted by Torrance (see Torrance & Rockenstein, in Schmeck, 1988), again with its origins in work on the measurement of CREATIVITY. Torrance has argued that creative thinking depends on the effective use of both sides of the brain, and sees learning styles as reflecting the predominant use of one or other side (see HEMISPHERIC LOCALIZATION).

Research on brain hemisphericity indicates that the left cerebral hemisphere is specialized primarily for verbal, analytic, abstract, temporal and digital operations.... [while] the right hemisphere [is] primarily specialized for non-verbal, holistic, concrete, spatial, analogic, creative, intuitive, and aesthetic functions.

(Torrance & Rockenstein, in Schmeck, 1988, p. 278)

Torrance's inventory identifies people in terms of whether they rely on right or left brain functions, or whether they integrate those functions by using both hemispheres equally. Torrance, like Pask, spells out the dangers of over-reliance on one style and suggests teaching methods designed to encourage "whole-brain creativity."

Elsewhere in the psychological literature there is a less enthusiastic endorsement of the link between hemisphericity and distinguishable thinking processes, with the current view being that there is no absolute specialization of function (Cohen, 1983). However, the parallels which emerge between the descriptions of Pask and Torrance suggest that whatever their physiological roots, there is good evidence that learners prefer to rely on distinctively different styles of learning, and that these styles have cognitive, motivational, and personality components. There have been some recent attempts to provide an integrated view of learning styles.

INTEGRATED DESCRIPTIONS OF LEARNING STYLES

In work paralleling that of Biggs (1987), Entwistle and Ramsden (1983) have described very similar factors derived from an inventory (see STUDENT LEARNING). They had, however, included scales of Pask's learning styles in their inventory and were able to show connections between approach, style, and motivation. The intrinsic deep approach was associated with a holist style while the anxious surface approach was linked with a serialist style. There was an additional fourth "non-academic" factor with low levels of motivation, negative attitudes, and with extreme learning styles linked to learning pathologies, as anticipated by both Pask and Torrance. Entwistle and Ramsden were also able to relate the two main approach/style factors to measures of cognitive style and personality to show that deep holists were likely to be impulsive "thinking introverts" with a theoretical outlook, esthetic interests, and complex conceptualization, who did well on tests of divergent thinking. The surface serialists had low scores of several of these dimensions, linked to a strong practical outlook.

Schmeck (in Weinstein, Goetz, & Alexander, 1988, p. 175) provides a tentative integrative model of learning style, which includes three distinctive learning styles, described by Schmeck as deep, elaborative, and shallow. This terminology had its roots in an inventory which contained items derived from the ideas on depth of processing in the memory, but subsequent research has persuaded Schmeck that there are important personality correlates as well. Essentially, the stable introvert is seen as adopting a *deep* style which develops effective schema and conceptions, through articulated or field-independent thinking processes involving predominantly analytic and synthetic reasoning. The stable extravert is more likely to use an *elaborative* style which involves an impulsive personalizing of knowledge through global or field-dependent thinking, making substantial use of examples and concrete instances, often drawn from real-world experiences. Finally, the anxious individual is likely to be categorized as having a *shallow* style which depends on memorizing, or repetitive rehearsal of information, leading to the literal reproduction of what was studied.

A similar but less developed model had been produced earlier by Entwistle (1981, p. 113). Now it seems worthwhile to try to combine the two models as a summary of the current state of thinking about learning styles. Table 1 presents that model. Again it has to be seen as tentative because the empirical findings are not sufficiently strong, or coherent, to allow it to be treated as more than a heuristic to guide thinking about learning styles, and future research. On the whole, this model fits quite well with that of Schmeck, with one important exception. Schmeck suggests that an elaborative style will be associated with stable extraversion. This style is, however, what Jung described as introverted thinking, and empirical findings show a positive correlation of introversion with holism, while there is a negative correlation with serialism (Entwistle & Ramsden, 1983, p. 235). The implicit association between inversion and inpulsivity, and caution and extraversion, contradicts previous research. Further research will be necessary to clarify this apparent contradiction.

There remains considerable debate about the nature, and even the existence, of learning styles, certainly in relation to their possible hemispheric origins. There is, however, sub-

Table 1 Categories of learning style: their components and correlates

Learning style	Versatile Strategic	Deep Holist Elaborative	Deep Serialist Analytic	Surface Shallow
Learning strategy	Organized	Personalizing	Conceptualizing	Memorizing
Cognitive style	Integrated	Field-dependent Divergent	Field-independent Convergent	Undeveloped
Motivation	Intrinsic Hope for Success	Intrinsic	Intrinsic	Extrinsic Fear of Failure
Personality	Stable Theoretical	Impulsive Introvert	Cautious Extravert	Neurotic
Learning processes	Alternating between overview and analysis	Building overview Reorganizing, relating	Attention to evidence and logical argument	Repetitive rehearsal for reproducing verbatim
Learning outcomes	Deep-level understanding	Over-readiness to generalize	Difficulty in seeing unusual connections	Superficial level of understanding

Adapted from Entwistle, 1981, p. 113 and Schmeck, 1988, p. 174.

stantial evidence that people do show strong and relatively consistent preferences for tackling learning tasks in distinctive ways. If that is what is taken to be learning styles, it seems important to take account of them in both research and educational practice.

BIBLIOGRAPHY

Biggs, J. B. (1987). *Student approaches to learning and studying.* Hawthorn, Victoria: Australian Council for Educational Research.

Cohen, G. (1983). *The psychology of cognition.* London: Academic Press.

Entwistle, N. J. (1981). *Styles of learning and teaching.* London: Wiley.

——, & Ramsden, P. (1983). *Understanding student learning.* London: Croom Helm.

Hudson, L. (1966). *Contrary imaginations.* London: Methuen.

Kolb, D. A. (1983). *Experiential learning: Experience as the source of learning and development.* Englewood Cliffs, NJ: Prentice-Hall.

Marton, F., Hounsell, D. J., & Entwistle, N. J. (Eds) (1984). *The experience of learning.* Edinburgh: Scottish Academic Press.

Messick, S., & Associates (1976). *Individuality in learning.* San Francisco: Jossey Bass.

Schmeck, R. R. (Ed.) (1988). *Learning styles and strategies.* New York: Plenum Press.

Sperry, R. (1983). *Science and moral priority.* Oxford: Blackwell.

Wallach, M. A., & Kogan, N. (1965). *Modes of thinking in young children.* New York: Holt, Rinehart & Winston.

Weinstein, C. E., Goetz, E. T., & Alexander, P. A. (1988). *Learning and study strategies.* New York: Academic Press.

NOEL ENTWISTLE

levels of processing Incoming stimuli can be processed at a number of different levels ranging from analysis of sensory features to semantic and conceptual processing. In the late 1960s and early 1970s theories of human memory were dominated by models involving memory stores. The "modal model" comprised three types of store: a peripheral set of sensory registers, each specific to a given input modality (*see* ECHOIC STORE; ICONIC STORE); a short-term or primary memory store whose salient characteristics included limited capa-

city, rapid forgetting, and "acoustic" encoding of linguistic material (*see* SHORT-TERM MEMORY); and third, long-term or secondary memory in which materials were encoded semantically, and which served as the relatively permanent repository of a person's experiences and knowledge (*see* LONG-TERM MEMORY). Such models were largely structural in nature, although control processes also played an important role in maintaining information within each store and in transferring information from one store to another. Such models (e.g. the version proposed by Atkinson and Shiffrin, 1968) were extremely useful and deservedly influential. However, they also embodied various limitations.

Craik and Lockhart (1972) pointed out that the central defining characteristics of stores – their capacity limitations, coding types, and forgetting functions – were not constant from one experimental paradigm to another. For example, visual stimuli are forgotten in times ranging from less than one second to minutes, hours, or days, depending on the particular stimuli used. Again, whereas linguistic material is often represented in short-term memory in acoustic or articulatory form, some experiments have shown clear indications of visual and semantic coding. As an alternative formulation, Craik and Lockhart suggested that memory should be thought of as the by-product of perceptual and conceptual analyses, and that such analyses were organized hierarchically. That is, incoming stimuli are first analyzed in terms of their sensory or surface features, and then at progressively deeper levels of processing, in terms of their phonemic, semantic, and conceptual properties. The early sensory analyses were considered to be relatively automatic and effortless, whereas deeper analyses required progressively more attentional effort. As an example, if a listener is only partially fluent in a foreign language, a radio broadcast in that language will be poorly understood. However, it is extremely easy for the listener to detect that a voice is present and that the speaker is female; the individual phonemes and syllables are also relatively easy to identify; individual words may be understood with greater effort; and finally, phrases, sentences, and the overall meaning of the communication may be understood with considerable effort.

Craik and Lockhart proposed that memory representations were the products of these various levels of analysis, and that deeper levels of processing were associated with longer-lasting memory traces (*see* ENCODING OPERATIONS IN MEMORY). This made sense from an adaptive biological viewpoint; surface features are usually less important for future actions than are the meaning and significance of experienced events. This formulation argues against thinking of memory in terms of discrete "stores" and suggests instead that memory be viewed as a continuum, going from the transient products of sensory analyses to the extremely durable products of semantic and conceptual processing. However, contrary to popular belief, the Craik and Lockhart article does *not* argue against the distinction between primary and secondary memory. Primary memory in their formulation is not a store, but is continued processing at some intermediate level of analysis – often involving phonemic information, but possibly involving visual or semantic analyses. Other ideas put forward included the distinction between two types of rehearsal: one type (later referred to as "maintenance rehearsal") serves to recirculate information in primary memory but does not lead to deeper analysis and therefore does not enhance later retention; the second type ("elaborative rehearsal") does involve further semantic analysis and therefore enhanced retention (*see* REHEARSAL). Finally, it is important to note that the *intention* to remember becomes much less salient in the levels-of-processing formulation; as long as deeper levels of analysis and elaborate types of processing are carried out, later memory for the information should be good.

This last idea formed the core principle for a series of empirical studies carried out by Craik and Tulving (1975) to illustrate the levels-of-processing framework. Subjects were induced to process words to shallow or deeper levels by asking them various questions about the word's characteristics – e.g. its type font (a shallow question), its rhyme qualities (an intermediate level of analysis), or its semantic qualities (a deep question). In a later un-expected memory test, subjects recalled or recognized words well or poorly depending on how deeply the word had been processed. Further experiments demonstrated that it was the qualitative type of processing that was critical for later retention, as opposed to the duration of processing or the motivation to learn a particular word.

The levels-of-processing framework has been criticized on a number of grounds by Baddeley (1978) and others. The criticisms include the difficulty of obtaining an index of "depth" independently from the memorial consequences of a specific processing task, and the ensuing circularity of the concept – if a particular task is associated with good retention, then processing must have been deep. A further objection is that processing associated with good retention in one situation may not be associated with good retention in another; for example, if rhyme retrieval cues are given, then rhyme encoding is typically superior to semantic encoding. This compatibility between the way an event is encoded and the most effective way to retrieve it is referred to as the ENCODING SPECIFICITY PRINCIPLE or as transfer-appropriate processing.

These criticisms may be countered by pointing out that there is excellent agreement among judges as to what types of processing are deeper than others, and that other concepts in psychology (such as "reinforcement") have proved valuable although they cannot be measured independently of their effects. Further, although transfer-appropriate processing is an important principle of memory, it does not negate the usefulness of a systematic taxonomy for encoding; a semantic encoding paired with an appropriate semantic retrieval cue typically yields higher performance than a rhyme encoding paired with a rhyme cue. The principles of depth of processing and transfer-appropriate processing are both necessary.

In conclusion, the levels-of-processing approach emphasizes various points about the nature of memory. First, memory should be seen as a set of processes or activities rather than as a structural entity. Second, memory is viewed as the by-product of encoding processes whose primary purpose is perception and comprehension. Third, retrieval processes are not separate from encoding processes, but represent attempts to recapitulate encoding operations. Finally, a well remembered event is typically one that has been encoded meaningfully – in terms of the person's organized body of expert knowledge.

See also MEMORY.

BIBLIOGRAPHY

Atkinson, R. C., & Shiffrin, R. M. (1968). Human memory: A proposed system and its control processes. In K. W. Spence & J. T. Spence (Eds), *The psychology of learning and motivation: Advances in research and theory* (Vol. 2) (pp. 89–195). New York: Academic Press.

Baddeley, A. D. (1978). The trouble with levels: A reexamination of Craik and Lockhart's framework for memory research. *Psychological Review, 85,* 139–52.

Craik, F. I. M., & Lockhart, R. S. (1972). Levels of processing: A framework for memory research. *Journal of Verbal Learning and Verbal Behavior, 11,* 671–84.

Craik, F. I. M., & Tulving, E. (1975). Depth of processing and the retention of words in episodic memory. *Journal of Experimental Psychology: General, 104,* 268–94.

F. I. M. CRAIK

long-term memory Long-term memory can be distinguished from SHORT-TERM MEMORY, which is concerned with the psychological present (James, 1890); in contrast, long-term memory is concerned with information which is not currently being processed which forms part of the psychological past.

There are various major issues relating to long-term memory. One such issue concerns the number of long-term memory systems that need to be postulated. One proposal is that there is a valid distinction between EPISODIC MEMORY and SEMANTIC MEMORY. Episodic memory is basically autobiographical memory, whereas semantic memory contains organized knowledge about the world. Episodic and semantic memory clearly differ in terms of content, but it remains a matter of controversy whether they are actually separate memory systems. A rather different proposal is that long-term memory should be divided into declarative memory and procedural memory

(*see* DECLARATIVE AND PROCEDURAL KNOWLEDGE). Declarative memory is concerned with knowing that, and includes knowledge to which we have conscious access. In contrast, procedural memory is concerned with knowing how, and includes motor skills such as bicycle riding and playing the piano. There is reasonably convincing evidence that some such theoretical distinction is useful.

Another issue, which is of particular relevance to semantic memory, concerns the kinds of units of information stored in long-term memory. There is general agreement that individual word concepts corresponding approximately to words in the language are stored in semantic memory, but there is increasing evidence that larger units of information are also stored in semantic memory. In particular, it is often assumed that SCHEMATA (i.e. large, organized packets of knowledge) are also to be found in semantic memory.

FORGETTING from long-term memory can probably occur for various different reasons. A major reason why information cannot be retrieved from long-term memory is because the information available at the time of retrieval does not provide a sufficiently good match with the information stored in long-term memory (*see* ENCODING SPECIFICITY PRINCIPLE). Other factors responsible for forgetting from long-term memory include PROACTIVE INTERFERENCE and RETROACTIVE INTERFERENCE. The above factors are relevant when the required information is still in long-term memory but is inaccessible, but it is also likely that some information is lost completely from the memory system for various physiological or other reasons.

Traditionally, long-term memory has been assessed by using memory tests where the rememberer is instructed explicitly that he or she is to attempt to remember certain information. Such tests are known as explicit memory tests. In contrast, it is possible to assess long-term memory by means of more indirect tests in which there is no awareness that memory is being tested. Such tests are known as implicit memory tests (*see* IMPLICIT AND EXPLICIT MEMORY). Studies of AMNESIA have revealed that the processes involved in implicit and explicit memory tests are very different. For example, amnesic patients generally have extremely poor long-term memory as assessed by conventional explicit memory tests, but often perform well on implicit memory tests of long-term memory.

See also LEVELS OF PROCESSING; PRODUCTION SYSTEMS.

BIBLIOGRAPHY

James, W. (1890). *Principles of psychology*. New York: Holt.

MICHAEL W. EYSENCK

M

memory The study of memory involves the demonstration that behavior has been altered as a consequence of the previous storage of information at some point in time ranging from a few seconds ago to several decades. There is an intimate relationship between learning and memory, since the existence of learning is typically revealed by the use of a memory test.

Probably the major issue in memory research concerns the number and type of MEMORY SYSTEMS that should be distinguished. Historically, a major distinction was proposed between SHORT-TERM MEMORY and LONG-TERM MEMORY. It was argued that information remaining in CONSCIOUSNESS between presentation and retrieval was in a short-term memory store, whereas information that left consciousness between presentation and its subsequent retrieval was in a long-term memory store. It was also argued by multi-store theorists (e.g. Atkinson & Shiffrin, 1968) that there are modality-specific stores. The visual modality-specific store is known as the ICONIC STORE, and the auditory store is called ECHOIC STORE.

The current view of short-term memory is that it should be regarded as a WORKING MEMORY. In the case of long-term memory, there have been various suggestions as to how it might be subdivided. Some have favored a distinction between EPISODIC MEMORY and SEMANTIC MEMORY, whereas others have argued in favor of a distinction between DECLARATIVE AND PROCEDURAL KNOWLEDGE. It is also important to consider how information is stored in long-term memory (*see* ENCODING OPERATIONS IN MEMORY; LEVELS OF PROCESSING), as well as how information is subsequently retrieved (*see* FORGETTING; RECALL; RECOGNITION MEMORY). Finally, it is of importance to analyse the relationship between the information that is stored in memory and the conditions obtaining at the time of retrieval (*see* ENCODING SPECIFICITY PRINCIPLE; STATE-DEPENDENT MEMORY).

Two approaches to the study of human memory have become very influential in recent years. The first approach is based on COGNITIVE NEUROPSYCHOLOGY, and involves the study of memory impairments in patients suffering from AMNESIA. This approach has proved useful in the task of developing a taxonomy of memory systems. The second approach is based on COGNITIVE SCIENCE and ARTIFICIAL INTELLIGENCE. It is based on the assumption that the human memory system can be regarded as a parallel distributed processing system (e.g. McClelland & Rumelhart, 1986). Computer programs based on that assumption have been devised, and have led to the development of CONNECTIONIST MODELS OF MEMORY.

See also AGING AND MEMORY; METACOGNITION; REALITY MONITORING.

BIBLIOGRAPHY

Atkinson, R. C., & Shiffrin, R. M. (1968). Human memory: A proposed system and its control processes. In K. W. Spence and J. T. Spence (Eds), *The psychology of learning and motivation* (Vol. 2). London: Academic Press.

McClelland, J. L., & Rumelhart, D. E. (1986). A distributed model of human learning and memory. In D. E. Rumelhart, J. L. McClelland, & the PDP Research Group (Eds), *Parallel distributed processing* (Vol. 2). *Psychological and biological models*. Cambridge, Mass.: MIT Press.

MICHAEL W. EYSENCK

memory, connectionist models of *See* CONNECTIONIST MODELS OF MEMORY.

memory, echoic *See* ECHOIC STORE.

memory, encoding operations in *See* EN-CODING OPERATIONS IN MEMORY.

memory, episodic *See* EPISODIC MEMORY.

memory, iconic *See* ICONIC STORE.

memory, long-term *See* LONG-TERM MEMORY.

memory, recognition *See* RECOGNITION MEMORY.

memory, semantic *See* SEMANTIC MEMORY.

memory, short-term *See* SHORT-TERM MEMORY.

memory, state-dependent *See* STATE-DE-PENDENT MEMORY.

memory, working *See* WORKING MEMORY.

memory and aging *See* AGING AND MEMORY.

memory development Memory development refers to the change of performance with age, in all kinds of memory tasks, such as recalling a sequence of digits, reconstructing experienced events such as a birthday party, or remembering to carry out a chore such as what to buy at a grocery store. For all these types of tasks, performance improves with age, in terms of both quantitative measures (the amount of RECALL) as well as qualitative measures (the way it is recalled). For instance, a very robust finding is how well children of different ages recall a sequence of digits in the exact order in which it was presented. The length of this sequence, referred to as the digit span, generally increases from around four digits at the age of 5, to around eight at college age. The qualitative aspect of this recall behavior is that older subjects tend to rehearse the digits prior to the actual recall (that is, repeat the digits over and over again), whereas younger children tend not to exhibit this kind of strategic behavior (see REHEARSAL). Different memory tasks use different quantitative and qualitative measures.

There are four possible explanations for such improvements with age. The two traditional explanations center on the capacity of SHORT-TERM MEMORY and the strategies that children and adults use to carry out such tasks (see, for example, the edited volumes by Kail & Hagen, 1977, and Chi, 1983). Two contemporary explanations center on either the domain-specific or general world knowledge that the child has gained with maturation (Chi & Ceci, 1987), and the metaknowledge that the child has about his or her own mental capacity and capabilities. Metaknowledge refers to what the child knows about his or her own memory (Flavell & Wellman, 1977), as well as his or her theory of mind (Wellman, 1985). Each of these four explanations will be presented below, along with challenges to some of these explanations.

That the capacity of children's memory improves with age seems to be a straightforward interpretation for the age-related improvement in memory performance. One can analogize the mind to a computer, with a given number of slots for the size of short-term memory. There are variants of this view, but this is the most concrete analogy. Suppose we assume that younger children have four hypothetical "slots" for temporarily storing information and that adults have eight slots: that would then easily explain results such as the digit span. The problem arises, however, if we assume that each slot can contain a chunk of information, so that the issue then becomes what constitutes a chunk of information for children versus adults (Chi, 1976) (see CHUNKING). For instance, a single digit may take up one slot of memory capacity for a 5 year old, whereas two digits (such as 9 and 6) can easily make up a double-digit number (96) for the older child and adult, so that 96 can be stored in a single slot. Using this logic, the adults' recall of eight digits may actually be a recall of four two-digit numbers, so that the actual number of slots is exactly equivalent. This line of reasoning makes it essential that we assess children's chunk size for each domain of knowledge. For example, Chi (1978) compared 10 year olds' recall of chess positions with that of adults. The twist in this study is that the 10 year olds are experienced chess players who have participated in chess tournaments, whereas the adults used to play chess when they were 10 years old, but have not pursued the game in adulthood. Thus, the children were actually more knowledgeable than the adults about the game of chess at the time that the study was done. The results showed that children could actually recall a greater number of chess pieces (9.3 pieces) than the adults (5.9 pieces). On the other hand, the same group of children could only recall 6.1 digits whereas the adults could recall 7.8 digits. These spans match exactly those obtained in the literature for these age groups. Hence, this study shows that the normally obtained digit span cannot be interpreted necessarily to reflect a smaller memory capacity per se. An alternative interpretation is that each slot of the capacity can hold a bigger chunk of information. Thus, the issue of the capacity increase becomes a moot point unless one is ready to assess the size of a chunk of information as well.

Closely related to the notion of capacity increase is the second interpretation, namely that young children do not adopt and use sophisticated processing strategies for remembering information, whereas older children and adults do. There is no question that young children do not use processing strategies, and that such use improves with age. Take rehearsal for a simple example. It is easy to demonstrate that children do not use such a strategy: you can look for the existence of labial movements (as measured by electromyographic recordings) during periods of retention, the existence of primacy effect in serial position curves, inter-item pause times during acquisition, or acoustic confusions during recall. It is trivial to point out that the non-use of such sophisticated strategies

obviously impairs the amount of recall. However, even when young children do adopt a rehearsal strategy, the characteristic of rehearsal varies with age. Very young children rehearse a string of digits by repeating each digit several times, followed by the next digit (Naus & Ornstein, 1983). So, for instance, in order to rehearse the string of digits 5 9 6 4 7 3, a young child might rehearse 5 5 5, 9 9 9, 6 6 6, and so on, whereas an older child would rehearse 596 473. It is clear that the first method will not facilitate sequential recall since no inter-digit associations have been formed.

But the real question is, why? One explanation which is intimately tied to the capacity notion is to postulate that because younger children have less capacity, most of it is taken up for processing, thus less is left for storage. Moreover, even if young children do know what to do in order to apply strategies, their application is so inefficient that such use would tax their capacity excessively. Presumably, older children and adults can use these processing strategies more efficiently, thus leaving more room for storage. Although somewhat circular, these explanations center on the logic that young children might not only have a smaller capacity, but even if they have the same size capacity as older children and adults, they need more capacity to process the complex strategies that adults use, thereby leaving fewer slots for storage. Such a hypothesis would be consistent with the digit span data. No definitive conclusion can be reached about the role of memory capacity, processing strategies, and the tradeoff between the capacity and the efficiency of applying them, in accounting for memory improvement with age. The reason is that it is extremely difficult to discriminate empirically between these differing hypotheses for explaining improving memory performance, both in the quantity of recall and in the use of strategies.

A third explanation for why memory performance improves with age is that knowledge (both general world knowledge as well as specific content domain knowledge) generally improves with age, both from daily experiences and from schooling. Although this hypothesis is intuitively obvious, it is curious that developmental psychologists did not actively explore the effect of this factor until the late 1970s. There are several reasons why the knowledge factor was ignored. First, many researchers implicitly assumed that the contribution of knowledge toward a task's performance is negligible. For a digit span task, for example, the usual assumption has been that having the capability to identify the digits is a sufficient criterion for performing maximally on that task, so that any deficiency in performance cannot be attributed to a knowledge factor. However, one could argue that measuring a child's ability to identify a digit (such as by name) is not a sufficiently sensitive measure of digit knowledge. A more sensitive measure might be how quickly a child can name a digit, so that the children's longer naming latencies (as compared to adults') may be indicative of greater search time, thereby suggesting that the associations surrounding that digit may be more sparse in the child's memory than in the adult's. For example, an adult may know many facts about a digit (i.e. 9 is the square of 3; 9 divides evenly into 18, 27, and 36; 9 is an odd number; and so on). These knowledge facts may be represented as a more intricate and densely related network in the adult's representation of the digit 9. The argument is that with a more densely represented network, the digit 9 may be named and recognized more readily, and their associations would thus be activated. Thus, for an adult, the digit 9 is encoded into a more richly interconnected representation, whereas for a child, 9 may be represented only as a digit with the label "nine" attached to it.

From the foregoing discussion, it is clear that in order to accept the hypothesis that knowledge is a critical factor in accounting for developmental differences, it is necessary to center our efforts on representing the knowledge. For instance, many researchers claim that the presence of knowledge itself is not an issue; rather, the problem is that children do not use or access the knowledge that they do have. They base this conclusion on the fact that they can probe children directly for knowledge relevant to the task, and show that children indeed do have the knowledge. Thus, failure to use that knowledge is attributed to a lack of skill or strategy for using that knowledge. However, consider an alternative hypothesis, that the knowledge that the child has is not represented in a way that is usable, rather than just merely having it or not having it. The following example should illustrate the point. A very robust finding in developmental psychology is the fact that children, when they free recall (irrespective of order) a list of 20 objects (such as dog, ice cream, skirt, paper, cat, gloves, plate, pencil, fur coat, etc.), typically will recall the "cat" and the "fur coat" consecutively, thus representing a kind of retrieval by association, whereas older children and adults recall by taxonomically clustering "cat" and "dog" together. This retrieval pattern is typically accounted for by the failure on the child's part to actively organize the input items into taxonomic categories during encoding, and then recalling them by their category structure. Taxonomic retrieval not only facilitates a more stable pattern of recall (resulting in a high clustering score, meaning that the same set of items is recalled consecutively together), but the taxonomic category will cue all the items that belong to that taxonomic class. The reason that such a result is not interpreted as a lack of knowledge is because when the younger children are probed directly for knowledge of the taxonomic categories, such as by asking them to pick out all the animals among the 20 items, it is shown that they indeed do know that "cat" and "dog" are kinds of animals.

The problem with such a conclusion is that no analyses have been made of the representation the child has of the knowledge probed. Directly probing for knowledge facts does not imply that the knowledge is organized in such a way as to make it usable in the task. The following example should illustrate the point. Suppose a 5-year-old child is asked to retrieve the names of his or her classmates (from an open-classroom type of environment which included first- and second-grade racially mixed boys and girls). Several retrieval patterns are possible, such as by age, gender, grade, race, or even alphabetical order. The child used none of these retrieval patterns. However, if one directly probed the child, he or she clearly knew the age, gender, grade, and race of each child, and even the letter of the alphabet with which the classmate's name began. If the study stopped at this point, then the conventional interpretation is that the child has the knowledge about each child's age, gender, grade, and race, but did not use such information to taxonomically organize the classmates so that retrieval could be more consistent, and perhaps also more complete. Thus, the interpretation is one of a deficiency in skill. Somehow the child is viewed as not actively noticing a taxonomic organization that is present, and thus not taking advantage of it. However, through various means of assessing the representation the child had of his or her classmates, it turned out that the child was using the spatial seating arrangement to organize his or her recall because this is how the child had represented his or her class-mates in memory. Using this organization to analyze the retrieval pattern showed complete consistency in that clusters of children's names were retrieved in a consistent order, depending on the seating locations (Chi, 1985). In conclusion, the point to be gained by this example is that direct probing for isolated factual knowledge in a piecemeal way does not mean that the child has that knowledge represented in an integrated and usable way. Thus, the inability to access that knowledge may not be due to a deficiency in an accessing skill, but rather, the knowledge is not represented in a way that it can be accessed for use in a specific task.

The foregoing discussion basically makes the point that what is often hypothesized as a processing or strategy deficiency in the younger children can really be attributed to the way that the younger children's knowledge is represented. Understanding how they organize and represent their knowledge would shed light on understanding why they perform the way they do in memory tasks. Viewed this way, the kind of research questions that should subsequently be asked should focus on the representation of children's knowledge, and how that representation changes with age. For instance, does it undergo gradual restructuring or radical restructuring (Chi & Ceci, 1987)? How do the changes affect all kinds of cognitive performance, memory and otherwise?

The fourth explanation for what produces memory improvements with age is that children develop more sophisticated knowledge about themselves as a memorizer, their own capabilities and limitations, and knowledge about how their mind works (Wellman, 1985) (see METACOGNITION). Early work along these lines failed to show a direct correlation between knowledge about memory and actual memory performance. However, a more interesting approach is to attempt to improve children's memory by making them more aware of their failure to use mnemonic strategies (Brown, 1978). At this point, it is too early to evaluate the outcome of this line of research, although the results are promising.

BIBLIOGRAPHY

Brown, A. L. (1978). Knowing when, where, and how to remember. In R. Glaser (Ed.), *Advances in instructional psychology* (Vol. 1) (pp.77–165). Hillsdale, NJ: Erlbaum.

Chi, M. T. H. (1976). Short-term memory limitations in children: Capacity or processing deficits. *Memory & Cognition*, 4, 559–72.

——. (1978). Knowledge structures and memory development. In R. Siegler (Ed.), *Children's thinking: What develops?* (pp.73–96). Hillsdale, NJ: Erlbaum.

——. (1983). *Trends in memory development research*. New York: Karger.

——. (1985). Interactive roles of knowledge and strategies in the development of organized sorting and recall. In S. Chipman, J. Segal, & R. Glaser (Eds), *Thinking and learning skills* (Vol. 2): *Research and open questions*. Hillsdale, NJ: Erlbaum.

——, & Ceci, S. J. (1987). Content knowledge: Its role, representation, and restructuring in memory development. *Advances in Child Development and Behavior*, 20, 91–141.

Flavell, J. H., & Wellman, H. M. (1977). Metamemory. In R. Kail & J. Hagen (Eds), *Perspectives on the development of memory and cognition*. Hillsdale, NJ: Erlbaum.

Kail, R. V., & Hagen, J. W. (1977). *Perspectives on the development of memory and cognition*. Hillsdale, NJ: Erlbaum.

Naus, M. J., & Ornstein, P. A. (1983). Development of memory strategies: Analysis, questions, and issues. In M.T.H. Chi (Ed.), *Trends in memory development research* (pp.1–30). Hillsdale, NJ: Erlbaum.

Wellman, H. M. (1985). The child's theory of mind: The development of conceptions of cognition. In S. R. Yussen (Ed.), *The growth of reflection* (pp.169–206). New York: Academic Press.

M. T. H. CHI

memory systems This term denotes putative brain/behavior and brain/cognition systems concerned with different forms of learning and memory. "Memory" is a general label for different forms of acquisition, retention, and utilization of information, skills, and knowledge. These different forms of learning and memory constitute a hierarchy in which forms that emerged early in evolution represent the lower levels, and forms evolving later represent the higher levels. Because evidence exists showing that the operations of different forms are related to different neuroanatomical substrates, the different forms of learning and memory have been increasingly thought of as constituting different memory *systems* (Weiskrantz, 1987). All systems have in common the ability to retain, and to make available for use in ongoing behavior and cognitive functioning, effects of earlier behavior and experiences. They differ in the kind of information they handle, and in the nature of their operations.

Separate neural systems are believed to underlie simple forms of learning, such as sensitization and habituation. Some evidence also exists for separable neural bases for SHORT-TERM MEMORY and LONG-TERM MEMORY. However, most of the research concerned with the classification of forms of learning and memory has revolved around three hypothetical systems: EPISODIC MEMORY, SEMANTIC MEMORY, and procedural memory (*see* DECLARATIVE AND PROCEDURAL KNOWLEDGE) (Tulving, 1985). These systems are considered here.

Episodic memory is the memory system that makes it possible for a person to remember concrete personal episodes or events dated in the subjective past – that is, to remember that he or she did or witnessed something on a particular occasion at a particular time. This ability to remember personal experiences is possessed by all normal individuals, but it is absent in very young children, and absent or less well developed in lower organisms. Episodic remembering is, in its essence, a *mental* phenomenon. It entails a conscious experience of a unique kind, one that every normal human can readily tell apart from other kinds of mental experiences, such as perceiving, imagining, dreaming, daydreaming, and hallucinating. The nature of the conscious experience of remembering a past event also differs qualitatively from the nature of the conscious experience resulting from the actualization of general knowledge about the world. The hallmark of episodic-memory capability is the rememberer's strong belief that the remembered event did in fact occur and that he or she was present when it occurred. JAMES (WILLIAM) (1890) described the difference between "remembering" one's own past states and experiences, and "conceiving" someone else's as follows: "Remembrance is like direct feeling; its object is suffused with a warmth and intimacy to which no object of mere conception ever attains."

At the next level of the classificatory scheme is semantic memory. It is concerned with what William James called "conception," or what today can be described as "general knowledge of the world." The term was introduced into the literature by Quillian in 1966, and the distinction between episodic and semantic memory, as "two parallel and partially overlapping information processing systems," was proposed by Tulving in 1972. Semantic memory was initially defined in close reference to knowledge expressible in language, but is now conceptualized much more broadly, consisting of a number of hypothetical subdivisions. The information that the semantic system handles need not have any personal relevance to the individual. Neither need it refer to the past, or any other particular time in the individual's existence. The semantic-memory system allows the individual to construct mental models of both concrete and abstract parts and aspects of the world. It makes possible the cognitive representation of stimuli, objects, situations, facts, and events, and the utilization of information thus represented in the absence of original stimuli and events.

Episodic and semantic memory have sometimes been grouped together as *declarative, or propositional*, or *factual* memory, since both entail acquisition, retention, and utilization (retrieval) of *factual knowledge* about objects, situations, and events, and about real or imaginable states of the world external to the individual. This knowledge can be introspectively contemplated by the individual in the absence of any overt behavior. The feasibility of such introspective contemplation is one of the important features that renders factual memory different from procedural memory (*see* DECLARATIVE AND PROCEDURAL KNOWLEDGE).

Procedural memory represents a lower, more general level of the classificatory hierarchy (Cohen, 1984). It is thought to be a large system that appeared early in evolution and that is shared in various forms by most living organisms. Procedural memory enables organisms to retain learned connections between stimuli and responses, including complex stimulus–response patterns and sequences. Learning in procedural memory is nonsymbolic; it can be expressed only in terms of specific *responses* or *behaviors*. This expression can occur "automatically," in the absence of directed attention (*see* AUTOMATIC PROCESSING). The stimuli controlling responding in the procedural system do not refer to, or represent, anything outside a given present situation. Thus, behavior mediated by procedural memory does not reflect any acquired "knowledge" about the world. This means that, unlike the information in episodic and semantic memory which may be true or false, what is learned procedurally has no truth value. Unlike episodic and semantic information that can be acquired very quickly, acquisition of most procedural-memory responses or skills occurs slowly.

The distinction between procedural and propositional (declarative) memory is now widely accepted not only in its psychological aspects but also with respect to the underlying neurophysiological mechanisms. The nature of the concepts of episodic and semantic memory, on the other hand, is still a subject of intense debate. Although most cognitive psychologists accept the distinction as a useful heuristic, many doubt that episodic memory is a distinct system. The issues are complex and involved, with the debate revolving around the interpretation of relevant evidence, the perceived usefulness and validity of neuropsychological findings, and even matters such as the proper appreciation of the principle of parsimony.

An open problem has to do with the relation between the various systems. Two different specific proposals have been made. One holds that procedural and declarative memory constitute two *parallel* subsystems of memory, with a further subdivision of declarative memory into the *parallel* classification of episodic and semantic memory. Another view is that episodic memory is embedded in and supported by semantic memory, and that semantic memory is embedded in and supported by procedural memory. It is not yet clear which of the two, or whether some other scheme altogether, describes Nature more adequately. The relevant empirical evidence includes the existence of single and double dissociations between, as well as the order of development of, memory functions reflecting the operations of different systems.

BIBLIOGRAPHY

Cohen, N. J. (1984). Preserved capacity in amnesia: Evidence for multiple memory systems. In L. Squire & N. Butters (Eds), *Neuropsychology of memory* (pp. 83–103). New York: Guilford Press.

James, W. (1890). *Principles of psychology.* New York: Holt.

Quillian, M. R. (1966). Semantic memory. Ph.D. dissertation, Carnegie Institute of Technology. Also in M. Minsky (Ed.), *Semantic information processing.* Cambridge, Mass.: MIT Press.

Tulving, E. (1972). Episodic and semantic memory. In E. Tulving & W. Donaldson (Eds), *Organization of memory* (pp. 381–403). New York: Academic Press.

— —. (1985). How many memory systems are there? *American Psychologist, 40,* 385–98.

Weiskrantz, L. L. (1987). Neuroanatomy of memory and amnesia: A case for multiple memory systems. *Human Neurobiology, 6,* 93–105.

ENDEL TULVING

223

mental maps *See* COGNITIVE MAPS.

mental models The contemporary idea of a mental model comes from Craik (1943), who argued that people translate an external situation into an internal model or simulation of the world. The concept of a mental model has been used to explain visual perception, discourse comprehension, knowledge representation, and reasoning. Human VISUAL PERCEPTION, according to Marr (1982), results in a three-dimensional model of the spatial relations among objects. Similarly, models of discourse make explicit the structure of states of affairs as we perceive them – that is, they represent the *reference* of a discourse, not the language in which the discourse is expressed (e.g. Johnson-Laird, 1983) (*see* LANGUAGE COMPREHENSION).

Discourse rarely provides us with a fully explicit description of a situation; instead we appear to make "bridging" INFERENCES whose conclusions have their source in a model of the situation (Garnham, 1987). An assertion can be true in an infinite number of models, e.g. the assertion: "All of the Dublin letters are in the same place as all of the Princeton letters" is true in many situations, referring to letters and places of different sizes, shapes, and so on. Because an infinite number of models cannot be held in mind, the initial representation of the assertion is *one* provisional model. If further discourse warrants it, the model can be altered. The procedures that construct and revise models capture the *meaning* of a discourse.

An opposing view of the nature of mental representations is that they are propositional – that is, composed of syntactically structured strings of symbols (e.g. Pylyshyn, 1973). PROPOSITIONAL REPRESENTATIONS are close to the structure of language. Theories based on such representations say nothing about how language relates to the world, and nothing about the truth or falsity of an assertion. In contrast, theories based on mental models propose that a discourse will be judged to be true if its mental model can be embedded in a model of the world (Johnson-Laird, 1988). A mental model can be constructed from an initial propositional representation; it need not give rise to an image, or to any conscious experience of the model.

Discourse can refer to abstract concepts such as possibility or causality (e.g. Miller & Johnson-Laird, 1976) and models can represent not only the physical world but also such abstract concepts (Johnson-Laird, 1983). For example, the model of the assertion, "There is no Cambridge letter" can be represented by the following:

$$\neg c$$

in which "c" denotes a Cambridge letter, and the conceptual tag "¬" denotes negation.

The representation of knowledge requires a mental representation that is like a working model of the known phenomenon (Gentner & Stevens, 1983). These models may differ in their content, but they are of the same structure as mental models in general, and they require the same processes to construct and manipulate them (Johnson-Laird, 1988). The development of a novice into an expert requires an enrichment of the content of their model, especially the level of abstraction of the content.

REASONING based on mental models relies on a semantic process, derived from the logical principle that an inference is valid only if the conclusion must be true whenever the premises are true. To make an inference, a model of the meaning of the premises must first be constructed. The following premises:

> None of the Princeton letters is in the same
> place as any of the Cambridge letters
> All of the Cambridge letters are in the same
> place as all of the Dublin letters

support the model:

$$| \,[p]\,[p]\,[p]\, | \,[c]\,[c]\,[c]\, | \,[d]\,[d]\,[d]\, |$$

where "p" represents "Princeton letters," "c" represents "Cambridge letters," "d" represents "Dublin letters," the vertical barriers "|" represent the boundaries of different places and the square brackets indicate that a set of individuals has been exhaustively represented. The model represents as much information as possible in an implicit way, because of the limitations on human WORKING

MEMORY, but it can be fleshed out to make the information explicit if necessary (Johnson-Laird & Byrne, 1990). The model supports the conclusion: "None of the Princeton letters is in the same place as any of the Dublin letters," which is valid because there is no other model of the premises that refutes it. Likewise, the following premises:

None of the Princeton letters is in the same place as any of the Cambridge letters
All of the Cambridge letters are in the same place as some of the Dublin letters

support the model:

| [p] [p] [p] | [c] [c] [c] d d |

where the Dublin letters are not exhaustively represented. The model supports the same conclusion as before, but in this case there is an alternative model of the premises that contradicts the conclusion:

| [p] [p] | [c] [c] [c] d d | [p] d |

The two models together support the conclusion: "Some of the Princeton letters are not in the same place as any of the Dublin letters," but again this conclusion is refuted by a third model of the premises:

| [p] [p] [p] d | [c] [c] [c] d d |

and the only conclusion that is valid over all of the models is: "None of the Princeton letters is in the same place as some of the Dublin letters." The procedures that construct models, formulate putative conclusions by describing the models, and test that there are no counterexamples to the putative conclusion, have been implemented in computer programs that simulate the theory (Johnson-Laird & Byrne, 1990). The theory predicts that inferences that depend on more than one model should lead to more errors than inferences that depend on just one model. This prediction has been pitted against propositional theories of reasoning (e.g. Braine, 1978; Rips, 1983), which propose that there are formal rules of inference in the mind, and that inferences are made by the construction of a mental derivation or proof of a conclusion. The predictions of the model theory have been corroborated for deductive reasoning

(e.g. see Byrne, 1989; Johnson-Laird & Byrne, 1989).

The idea of mental models has also been applied to understanding CONSCIOUSNESS and self-awareness (Johnson-Laird, 1983). The source of consciousness may lie in the recursive ability to embed a mental model within another mental model.

See also ANALOGIES.

BIBLIOGRAPHY

Braine, M. D. S. (1978). On the relation between the natural logic of reasoning and standard logic. *Psychological Review, 85*, 1–21.

Byrne, R. M. J. (1989). Suppressing valid inferences with conditionals. *Cognition, 31*, 61–83.

Craik, K. (1943). *The nature of explanation.* Cambridge: Cambridge University Press.

Garnham, A. (1987). *Mental models as representations of discourse and text.* Chichester: Ellis Horwood.

Gentner, D., & Stevens, A. L. (Eds.). (1983). *Mental models.* Hillsdale, N.J.: Erlbaum.

Johnson-Laird, P. N. (1983). *Mental models: Towards a cognitive science of language, inference and consciousness.* Cambridge: Cambridge University Press.

——. (1988). Mental models. In M. Posner (Ed.), *Foundations of cognitive science.* Cambridge, Mass.: MIT Press.

——, & Byrne, R. M. J. (1989). *Only* reasoning. *Journal of Memory and Language, 28*, 313–30.

——. (1990). *Deduction.* Hillsdale, NJ: Erlbaum. (forthcoming)

Marr, D. (1982). *Vision: A computational investigation in the human representation of visual information.* San Francisco: Freeman.

Miller, G. A., & Johnson-Laird, P. N. (1976). *Language and perception.* Cambridge, Mass.: Harvard University Press.

Pylyshyn, Z. W. (1973). What the mind's eye tells the mind's brain: a critique of mental imagery. *Psychological Bulletin, 80*, 1–24.

Rips, L. J. (1983). Cognitive processes in propositional reasoning. *Psychological Review, 90*, 38–71.

RUTH M. J. BYRNE

metacognition Metacognition may be defined as "knowledge or beliefs about one's own cognitive processes." This knowledge may also be used in the regulation of cognitive activities. If you know that you are usually late for appointments or are good at solving crosswords, these are examples of your own metacognitive knowledge. If you decide to enter a crossword competition on the basis of your knowledge of your crossword skill, you are making use of your metacognitive knowledge.

What a person knows about their own cognitive abilities is not often apparent, and psychologists have to elicit the knowledge from the individual. This may be done as simply as by asking the person involved, and many studies of, for example, memory have included questionnaires which ask the respondent to rate their memory ability. Thus, for example, Herrmann and Neisser (1978) required their respondents to rate on a seven-point scale the answers to questions such as "How often do you find that just when you want to introduce someone you know to someone else you cannot think of their name?" Another technique has been to ask the participants in the experiment to talk aloud as they work their way through the task. From an analysis of this protocol, the experimenter hopes to obtain a better understanding of the way in which the experiment is tackled by the participant than could be obtained by just observing his or her behavior.

An example of the use of this talk-aloud protocol is Newell's (1977) analysis of such protocols when subjects were asked to talk aloud the steps they used when solving the crypt-arithmetic problem

DONALD+GERALD=ROBERT

where each letter stands for one and only one digit and D=5. The protocols from the experimental subjects not only allowed the experimenter to understand the many stages in the particular route to the solution of the problem taken by each individual, but to develop a computational model of the methods by which such problems are tackled (see PROBLEM SOLVING).

An area in which metacognition has been widely studied is that of memory. The importance of knowledge about the strengths and limitations of the individual's memory abilities have been emphasized by several psychologists who have studied the development of memory. Flavell (1970), for example, showed that as children grow older they become more likely to adopt strategies that will improve their memory performance. The older children will rehearse items to be remembered, knowing that they will forget them during the interval between learning and recall. Adults often learn more sophisticated strategies, and are able to apply them when the situation demands. Thus, for example, psychology undergraduate students will normally apply the mnemonic techniques that they have heard about in their lectures on memory when they are presented with a memorizing task (see STUDENT LEARNING). In so doing they can often make a massive improvement in their performance. Campione, Brown, and Bryant (1985) conclude their review of individual differences in memory performance by asserting that such individual differences usually occur in strategy-intensive situations where there is opportunity for the individual learner to adopt a good, poor, or no specific memorizing strategy. Where such freedom to choose strategies is lacking, for example, when recognizing which of a set of faces has been shown before, there is much less variation between individuals (see FACE RECOGNITION). Thus, not only is the metacognitive knowledge of the individual important in determining his or her memory performance, it is important for the psychologist who wishes to explain and predict that performance to have as accurate a knowledge as possible of the metacognitive knowledge and skills employed by the individuals under study.

One commonly experienced element of metacognitive knowledge is the feeling of knowing. When, for example, presented with a definition such as "female spirit whose wail portends death" one may find oneself in a tip-of-the-tongue state, knowing that one knows the word but being unable to recall that it is "banshee" (see TIP-OF-THE-TONGUE PHENOMENON). A related and interesting state is the feeling of not knowing. If asked if you know the telephone number of Buckingham Palace you are likely to quickly feel it is unlikely, even though there has not been time for you to extensively search your memory for an answer. Such experiences can contribute useful information in the development of models of the memory and other cognitive processes.

So far this discussion has been concerned with the positive benefits of studying metacognition. However, researchers have encountered many problems as they have tried to use metacognitive knowledge in their study of psychology. A first, and central if obvious, point is that our metacognitive knowledge is extremely limited and liable to be erroneous. If the workings of our cognitive processes were known to everyone there would be no need for cognitive psychology – or at least, cognitive psychology would be a far easier subject. In reality, almost all of our cognitive processes take place without us being aware of what they involve or how they work. Even such a simple task as thinking of an example of an animal takes place with no obvious mechanism when we examine our own thought processes; the answer – "cat," "dog," or whatever we think of – seems to just pop into our consciousness without us being aware of how we retrieved it (*see* RECALL). Similarly, most of our cognitive processes are opaque to examination by introspecting upon the content of our CONSCIOUSNESS or by observing our behavior. We construct complex sentences to say or write, we drive cars, we perceive the world, without awareness of the very complex processes and mechanisms that must be employed to make this possible. There are, therefore, severe limitations to what is available to most individuals in developing their metacognitive knowledge. Furthermore, there is a major question as to the source of such metacognitive knowledge as individuals believe they possess. Where does it come from, and how is it acquired?

One possible source of knowledge about ones own cognitive processes would be through INTROSPECTION. However, as discussed earlier, much cognition is opaque to introspection. The result is that for the explanation of much of their behavior, people are likely to rely upon a mixture of folk and common-sense psychology, elaborated by their own memories of their thoughts and actions. Nisbett and Wilson (1977) provide a collection of demonstrations of the ignorance of subjects of the causal factors that influence changes in behavior and they conclude that "it may be quite misleading for social scientists to ask their subjects about the influences on their evaluations, choices or behaviour" (p. 247). They show, for example, that their subjects were unaware that the learning of the word pair "ocean–moon" increased their probability of naming "tide" when subsequently asked to name a detergent. Similarly, subjects showed a strong preference for the right-hand end of a display of four identical stockings when asked to choose a pair, but denied that position influenced their choice.

For most aspects of cognition, it is reasonable to agree with Nisbett and Wilson that the beliefs that most people hold about the causes and nature of the cognitive processes are likely to be incorrect and based on sources other than a direct knowledge of the processes themselves. Nevertheless, there are two good reasons for continuing to study metacognitions. One is that the ignorance that is associated with most cognition may not apply to the higher-level control processes. The second is that whether or not people's beliefs about their cognitive processes are accurate, they still form the basis of their decision making and their planning.

The limitation upon what one can observe of one's own cognitions highlighted by Nisbett and Wilson and others would be agreed by most people. If asked "Why (or how) did you choose to use the words in the last sentence you spoke?" most of us would accept that we were unaware of the processes underlying the construction of the sentence. However, if asked "Why (or how) did you choose your new house?" everyone would be able to give an account of their considerations of cost, location, convenience, appearance, and so on. Furthermore, this account would seem reasonable and it would be hard to doubt that it did reflect at least a part of the processing that led to the decision.

The difference between deciding the choice of words and the choice of house is matched by many others. In general, people seem to be consciously aware of at least some of the processes that determine the major choices in their lives, where they are exercising control over their behavior at a high level and where their actions are relatively complex and novel. On the other hand we have little awareness of cognitive processes that are more highly practiced, or at a lower level within the cognitive system. Morris and Hampson (1983) differentiate between a high-level control system responsible for controlling planning and novel actions which they call the "BOSS" system, and a multitude of lower, modular systems that they term "EMPLOYEES." They argue that our conscious awareness is associated with the information being made available to the BOSS system. We are, therefore, likely to be aware of the information upon which the high-level control decisions are made, but not of the actual workings of either the BOSS or the EMPLOYEE systems. The situations in which people are able to give helpful metacognitive reports are those in which they report upon the high-level activities. Thus, for example, it was noted earlier that reports of the stages taken in problem solving or the strategies adopted in memory experiments can provide useful and reliable information; they are drawing upon these high-level processes. Metacognitive reports of other processes need to be treated with more skepticism. For example, the answers given to questionnaires on metacognitive processes can be biased in many ways. Answers given to questions about the frequency of memory errors depend upon the respondent's ability to remember a suitable selection of such errors. However, the errors that are most likely to be recalled are not necessarily those that are most typical or frequent but those which have been most awkward or embarrassing to the individual (Morris, 1984). Such questionnaires are poor predictors of memory abilities when the latter are measured by more objective techniques (Herrmann, 1984).

Whatever the accuracy or otherwise of the metacognitive beliefs that people hold, the beliefs themselves will play a major part in shaping behavior. Where memory is suspect, for example, memory aids such as diaries and notes will be used. Where car drivers underestimate the likelihood of accidents, unnecessary risks will be taken. Many instances of behavior leading to major disasters, such as the Chernobyl nuclear power station explosion, incorporate in their causation overconfidence in their abilities by the operators (Reason, 1987). This false confidence is one form of incorrect metacognition, and one step toward safer control of complex systems involves making the operators aware of the common cognitive errors and the dangers of overconfidence.

Metacognition remains an area of cognitive psychology which more than most requires elaboration with richer theories and better data. Metacognitions can influence a wide range of behavior, but the nature, source, and accuracy of those cognitions deserve wider study.

See also AGING AND COGNITIVE CHANGE; REALITY MONITORING.

BIBLIOGRAPHY

Campione, J. C., Brown, A. L., & Bryant, N. R. (1985). Individual differences in learning and memory. In R. J. Sternberg (Ed.), *Human abilities: An information-processing approach* (pp. 103–26). New York: Freeman.

Flavell, J. H. (1970). Developmental studies of mediated memory. In H. W. Reese & L. P. Lipsitt (Eds), *Advances in child development and behavior* (Vol. 5). New York: Academic Press.

Herrmann, D. J. (1984). Questionnaires about memory. In J. E. Harris & P. E. Morris (Eds), *Everyday memory, actions and absentmindedness* (pp. 133–51). New York: Academic Press.

——, & Neisser, U. (1978). An inventory of everyday memory experiences. In M. M. Gruneberg, P. E. Morris, & R. N. Sykes (Eds), *Practical aspects of memory*. New York: Academic Press.

Morris, P. E. (1984). The validity of subjective reports on memory. In J. E. Harris & P. E. Morris (Eds), *Everyday memory, actions and absentmindedness* (pp. 153–72). New York: Academic Press.

——, & Hampson, P. J. (1983). *Imagery and consciousness*. London: Academic Press.

Newell, A. (1977). On the analysis of human problem solving protocols. In P. N. Johnson-Laird & P. C. Wason (Eds), *Thinking: Readings in cognitive science* (pp. 46–61). Cambridge: Cambridge University Press.

Nisbett, R., & Wilson, T. D. (1977). Telling

more than we can know: Verbal reports of mental processes. *Psychological Review, 84*, 231–59.

Reason, J. (1987). The Chernobyl errors. *Bulletin of the British Psychological Society, 40*, 201–6.

PETER E. MORRIS

mnemonics Mnemonics are methods for improving memory but the term is often reserved for techniques that appear unusual or artificial to the uninitiated. A mnemonic normally has little inherent connection with what is being learned but is adopted by the learner as a means of providing either meaning, memory cues, or some organization within what is otherwise disconnected and relatively meaningless material.

The word "mnemonic" derives from "Mnemosyne," the ancient Greek goddess of memory. Memory techniques date back to the days of the ancient Greeks when the poet Simonides is credited with the invention of the method of Loci or location or place. In the method of loci, the memorizer chooses a series of well known locations, such as the houses in his street or the rooms in her house. A visual, mental image is formed linking a representation of the item to be remembered with one of these locations so that, for example, a shopping list might be memorized by imagining each of the items to be purchased in a different room in one's house. Then, recall involves mentally recalling the image of each room and identifying the items imaged there. Greek and Roman orators used this technique to memorize the main points of their long speeches to avoid the use of notes.

The method of loci is very effective, surprisingly so for those who try it for the first time. A doubling of the amount recalled is commonly found (e.g. Groniger, 1971) or even better (Bower, 1973). The mnemonic works because it provides both easily accessible cues that the memorizer can systematically search when retrieval is required and a way of linking apparently unconnected information to those cues by the use of the mental images. The visual image allows a spatial relationship to be formed between each location and the item to be remembered. It is not the forming of the mental images themselves that improves recall but the use of the images to link items together (see Morris & Stevens, 1974) (*see* DUAL-CODE THEORY OF IMAGERY).

The method of loci has its limitations. For example, the learner is dependent upon having available in memory a well known set of locations and recall is easiest if the learner proceeds in her or his imagination through those locations in order (*see* RECALL). A more flexible adaptation of the method of loci is the Peg method. In the peg system, the loci systems locations are replaced by concrete words that the memorizer has previously learned for each number from, say, 1 to 100. For example, a common peg word for the number 25 is nail. Therefore, when using the mnemonic, one imagines the 25th item to be remembered, a library book for example, with a large nail driven through it. Most of the memory improvement systems that are offered in books and correspondence courses rely heavily upon the peg system. Memorizing pegs for numbers is made easier by learning a phonetic system in which each digit can be replaced by a consonant sound that, with the insertion of suitable vowels, can be composed into concrete words. So, for example, in the phonetic system, an "n" sound stands for the digit 2 and an "l" sound for the digit 5 – hence the peg word for nail used earlier. As with the method of loci, the peg method has been shown to lead to massive improvements in memory if lists of objects or other concrete things are to be remembered.

In recent years, other adaptations of the peg and loci systems have been developed. For example, a successful mnemonic for remembering people's names involves converting the name to some imageable representation and forming an image that links it with a distinctive part of the person's face (Morris, Jones, & Hampson, 1978). The keyword mnemonic applies a similar principle to learning foreign language words. For the foreign word, an English word that sounds similar is selected. An image is then formed that links together the similar sounding English word with the meaning of the foreign word (Atkinson & Raugh, 1975).

Not all mnemonics use mental imagery. Some involve linking items within a story while others use rhymes or the first letters of the words to be remembered. An example of a first letter mnemonic is CLOD to remember that Cambridge University colors are Light blue while Oxford University has Dark blue. First letter mnemonics have been shown to be effective in retaining information about order but not very good at helping the learning of new material (Morris & Cook, 1978).

Mnemonics can be very effective in situations where what must be learned is inherently unconnected and relatively meaningless. The mnemonics provide connection, meaning, and retrieval cues. However, they do so at the expense of requiring considerable mental effort from the memorizer. Consequently, the use of mnemonics, even where people are aware of the techniques, is usually restricted to situations where the benefits of successful recall outweigh the costs of the effort involved.

BIBLIOGRAPHY

Atkinson, R. C., & Raugh, M. R. (1975). An application of the mnemonic keyword method to the acquisition of a Russian vocabulary. *Journal of Experimental Psychology: Human Learning and Memory, 104,* 126–33.

Bower, G. H. (1973). How to ... uh ... remember! *Psychology Today, 7,* 63–70.

Groniger, L. D. (1971). Mnemonic imagery and forgetting. *Psychonomic Science, 23,* 161–3.

Morris, P. E., & Cook, N. (1978). When do first letter mnemonics aid recall? *British Journal of Educational Psychology, 48,* 22–8.

Morris, P. E., Jones, S., & Hampson, P. J. (1978). An imagery mnemonic for the learning of people's names. *British Journal of Psychology, 69,* 335–6.

Morris, P. E., & Stevens, R. (1974). Linking images and free recall. *Journal of Verbal Learning and Verbal Behavior, 13,* 310–15.

PETER E. MORRIS

modularity of mind Much theoretical description in cognitive science assumes that cognitive processes are composed of subsystems or modules which operate as distinct units and with a degree of independence. These modules are linked together in speci-fied parallel and serial fashion to produce information-processing models of cognitive abilities. This principle of cognitive organization is commonly referred to as "modularity of mind," and has been the source of much recent discussion following the publication of Fodor's (1983) book of this title.

The principle of modularity of mind has its roots in the work of Aristotle, who described a division of mental processes into such capacities as memory and estimation. Although Aristotle did not describe a modular system within these processes, he implied a modular organization between them. Much of the Cell Doctrine which developed subsequently and extended through to medieval times was concerned with trying in various ways to locate Aristotle's mental processes into the ventricles of the brain. A more detailed modularity of the mind was described by the phrenologists, in particular Franz Joseph Gall and Johann Spurzheim, in the nineteenth century. They were principly concerned with the modularity of personality, describing its numerous subcomponents as faculties which they located on different parts of the outer layer of the brain. However, included among the faculties were a number of cognitive capacities such as calculation. The phrenologists believed that the strength of these faculties was indicated by the area of brain tissue devoted to them and that this was reflected in the relative dimensions of the skull, which could be precisely measured. One of the first attempts to describe a modular organization within a cognitive domain was Lichteim's (1885) description of the components of language processing (*see* LANGUAGE COMPREHENSION). However, whereas such early models were concerned with specifying the anatomical location of their modular subcomponents, the current information-processing models, which have arisen following the computer era, are interested in the structure of the systems independent of their locations in the brain.

Nevertheless, current COGNITIVE NEURO-PSYCHOLOGY assumes that many modules have distinct, though unspecified, anatomical locations, which can therefore be differentially affected by focal brain damage. Certain modules may be impaired or destroyed while others are intact. Moreover, it is assumed that the operation of the system subsequent to its functional lesion provides evidence from which the structure and organization of the normal system can be inferred. Whereas traditional neuropsychologists looked for double dissociations in their patients' performances to infer distinct anatomical locations of processes, cognitive neuropsychologists look for functional double dissociations to infer distinct modules. Thus, for example, if one patient can recognize faces but cannot recognize colors while in another the reverse dissociation is observed, it is argued that distinct modular systems must be involved in object and color recognition. In similar fashion double dissociations delineate modules within systems. Thus, analyses of modularity apply at a number of levels.

Fodor (1983) described particular characteristics of modules. He stated that they operate in isolation from other modules with which they were not directly connected. Their independent processing was termed information encapsulation (*see* LANGUAGE AND THOUGHT). Fodor also stated that modules could process only one type of information input and were therefore domain specific.

It is argued (Marr, 1976) that a modular organization has biological advantage in that one subcomponent of a system may be adjusted and evolve without the necessity to reprogram the entire system. However, the relationship of biology to the structure of the system is debated. Fodor (1983) claimed that cognitive modules were of necessity innate. A more popular contemporary view is that modules can also be established through a process of learning. In particular, it is claimed that the organization of the reading system cannot be genetically endowed because of its comparatively late introduction into our cognitive repertoire. However, Marshall (1987) continues to argue that even reading modules are biologically given (*see* DUAL-ROUTE MODEL OF READING; READING DEVELOPMENT). The potential role of learning in the development of modules is relevant to the evolving field of developmental cognitive neuropsychology and the analogies which have been drawn between certain developmental disorders and acquired

disorders in neurological patients (Temple & Marshall, 1983; Temple, 1989). The selective cognitive disorders seen in these children indicate the relative independence of specific modules during development.

Fodor also claimed that the operation of modules was mandatory. The discussion of the role of voluntary control in the operation of modules has now extended to discussions of the extent of conscious awareness of the operation of modules. Studies of covert cognitive activity indicate influences upon performance of the activity of modules to which the patient has no conscious access. Thus, for example DeHaan, Young, and Newcombe (1987) have shown that a patient who fails to consciously recognize certain faces may still have his or her performance in classifying names of faces affected by the presence of the face (*see* FACE RECOGNITION).

Another current debate concerns the areas where modularity apples. Fodor claimed it did not extend to higher level reasoning. Reading, calculation, and face recognition have yielded better to fractionation into modules than have memory and attention. Motivation and creativity have yet to be addressed.

With the introduction of contemporary parallel distributed processing (PDP) systems (*see* CONNECTIONIST MODELS OF MEMORY), there is argument about the relationship of modules to the new structures (*see* COGNITIVE SCIENCE). Some claim that PDP eliminates the utility of modular models. Others argue that PDP merely describes methods of information processing and storage within modules.

See also IMAGERY, COMPUTATIONAL THEORY OF.

BIBLIOGRAPHY

DeHaan, E. D. F., Young, A., & Newcombe, F. (1987). Faces interfere with name classification in a prosopagnosic patient. *Cortex*, 23, 309–16.

Fodor, J. (1983). *The modularity of mind.* Cambridge, Mass.: MIT Press.

Lichteim, L. (1885). On aphasia. *Brain*, 7, 433–94.

Marr, D. (1976). Early processing of visual information. *Philosophical Transactions of the Royal Society, B, 375*, 483–524.

Marshall, J. C. (1987). The cultural and biological contexts of written languages: Their acquisition, deployment and breakdown. In J. R. Beech & A. Colley (Eds), *Cognitive approaches to reading*. Chichester: John Wiley.

Temple, C. M. (1989). Digit dyslexia: A category-specific disorder in developmental dyscalculia. *Cognitive Neuropsychology*, 6, 93–116.

——, & Marshall, J. C. (1983). Developmental phonological dyslexia. *British Journal of Psychology*, 74, 517–33.

CHRISTINE M. TEMPLE

mood disorders and cognition The major mood disorders are clinical anxiety and clinical depression. Of course, these are broad categories, and it is possible to subdivide them. Clinical anxiety has subcategories such as generalized anxiety disorder, social phobia, obsessive-compulsive disorder, panic disorder with agoraphobia, panic disorder without agoraphobia, agoraphobia without panic disorder, and post-traumatic stress disorder. Clinical depression has been subcategorized in various different ways. However, two of the most influential distinctions are between unipolar and bipolar depression and between endogenous and non-endogenous depression.

There are major differences in symptomatology among the various subcategories of clinical anxiety and depression. However, it is likely that there are important similarities among different types of clinical anxiety, with the same also being the case with respect to clinical depression. As a consequence, the broad categories of clinical anxiety and clinical depression will often be used in the subsequent discussion.

Patients with mood disorders have been found to differ from normal controls in several ways. These differences occur at the physiological, behavioral, and cognitive levels. Are there any persuasive reasons for assuming that there is particular value in focusing on the functioning of the cognitive system in mood-disordered patients? Lazarus (e.g. Lazarus, Kanner, & Folkman, 1980) has consistently claimed that cognitive appraisal is an essential ingredient in the experience of mood or affect. If that is correct, then that would appear potentially to give the cognitive system an extremely important role in describing and explaining mood disorders. However, Zajonc (1980) denied that affect or mood necessarily occurs only after cognitive operations such as recognition and classification, and he cited experimental evidence which appeared to support his position. Close examination of such evidence reveals that he considered only cognitive processes of which there is conscious awareness, and he failed entirely to consider the possibility that affect or mood depends to some extent on prior preconscious processing. In sum, the available evidence is entirely consistent with the notion that cognitive processes precede the experience of mood or affect (*see* EMOTION).

There is a somewhat puzzling state of affairs that exists when we consider cognitive factors in mood disorders. On the one hand, there are numerous cognitive therapists (e.g. Beck & Emery, 1985) who regularly treat mood disorders from the cognitive perspective. On the other hand, there was until recently remarkably little hard evidence available about the ways in which the cognitive functioning of mood-disordered patients differs from that of normals. In other words, COGNITIVE THERAPY for mood disorders has developed largely on the basis of clinical experience rather than being built on a solid foundation of research evidence. However, there is increasing interest in the possibility of studying cognitive functioning in anxious and depressed patients under laboratory conditions. The results of such studies, as we will shortly see, offer hope for enriching cognitive therapy in the future.

A further reason for considering cognitive functioning in depressed and anxious patients is to clarify the relationship between these two kinds of mood disorder. Anxiety and depression are often found to coexist in patients, but it is still usually claimed that they are conceptually distinct. As we will see, a comparison of the cognitive profiles of depressed and anxious patients provides substantial new evidence concerning the differences between depression and anxiety.

BASIC FINDINGS

Much of the research on cognitive factors in

depression has been influenced by the theoretical views of Beck (1976). He argued that depressed patients possess various cognitive schemas (schema = organized collection of knowledge stored in memory) (see SCHEMATA). These schemas primarily concern the self, and encompass themes such as personal worthlessness, self-blame, and guilt.

This schema theory has been investigated primarily by an experimental paradigm in which subjects make self-referent judgements (e.g. describes you?) about a series of adjectives, some of which are negative and others of which are positive. It is assumed that the existence of a relevant self-schema enhances recall, perhaps by providing a rich network of associations which can facilitate the retrieval process. Since depressed patients allegedly have several negative self-schemas, whereas normal controls do not, it is predicted that depressed patients should recall relatively more negative words relevant to their negative self-schemas than normal controls on this self-referent task. However, if the same words are judged in terms of how well they apply to someone else, then the depressed patients' self-schemas should not be activated, and a negative recall bias should not be found (see RECALL).

There have been numerous studies testing these predictions from Beck's (1976) schema theory (for a review, see Williams, Watts, MacLeod, & Mathews, 1988). While there are some exceptions, the general finding is that depressed patients have a negative recall bias on self-referent tasks but not on other-referent tasks. Sometimes depressed patients differ from normal controls more in terms of reduced recall of positive self-referent adjectives than enhanced recall of negative self-referent adjectives, but there is clear evidence that the balance between positive and negative is shifted in the negative direction in depressed patients.

Another expectation from Beck's (1976) schema theory is that the interpretation of ambiguous information would tend to be influenced by an individual's underlying schemas. This means that depressed patients would be more likely to provide a negative interpretation of ambiguous information than

would normals, especially if the information were of personal relevance. The results generally conform to expectation. There have been a number of studies using the Cognitive Bias Questionnaire, which provides a description of events together with four possible responses. The response which is selected may be considered to reflect the extent to which the event in question was interpreted in a negative fashion. Depressed patients consistently select more negative alternatives than normal controls. However, this self-report measure provides only a rather indirect assessment of the interpretative process, and it fails to exclude the possibility of response bias.

Some studies have considered the implications of Beck's schema theory for attentional and perceptual processes (see ATTENTION). The general expectations are that negative self-schemas in depressed patients would enhance attention to, and initial processing of, relevant negative stimuli. Despite the fact that there have been various experimental attempts to investigate these predictions, there is very little (if any) convincing evidence in their support.

In sum, the available evidence indicates that depressed patients differ in their memorial functioning from normal controls, and probably also in their interpretation of ambiguous information. However, they do not appear to show systematic differences from normals in their attentional and perceptual processing.

The evidence on cognitive functioning in anxious patients (primarily those with generalized anxiety disorder) and normal controls has been discussed at length by Eysenck (in press), and only a succinct account of the general trend of the research will be given here. An orienting assumption is that anxious patients are hypersensitive to threatening stimuli, and so differences in cognitive functioning between anxious patients and normals are more likely to be found with respect to the processing of threatening stimuli than with respect to neutral stimuli. Since physical health threats and social threats are the major areas of concern for generalized anxiety patients, most of the research has used threat-related words selected from these two domains. Anxious patients typically perform equivalently with physical health and social threat words, and so the findings will usually be described simply in terms of threat.

Anxious patients have fairly consistently been found to differ from normal controls in attentive and preattentive processes. For example, if a threatening and a neutral stimulus are presented concurrently, then anxious patients show a selective bias in favor of the threatening stimulus. There is additional evidence that anxious patients devote extra processing resources to threat-related stimuli even when these stimuli are presented below the level of conscious awareness.

Anxious patients also differ from normal controls in terms of distractibility. Patients with generalized anxiety disorder are more distractible than normals when a target stimulus must be detected as rapidly as possible in the presence or absence of distracting stimuli. The effect is there whether threatening or neutral distracting stimuli are used, but it is somewhat greater with threatening distractors.

Anxious patients differ considerably from normal controls in their interpretation of ambiguous stimuli. For example, one paradigm requires subjects to write down the spellings of auditorily presented homophones having a threatening and a neutral meaning (e.g. die; dye). Anxious patients consistently interpret such stimuli in a more threatening fashion than normals.

The major focus in studies of memorial functioning in anxious patients has been on the negative recall bias which has been shown so clearly in depressed patients. There have been numerous attempts to demonstrate a negative recall bias in patients with generalized anxiety disorder, but these attempts have been uniformly unsuccessful. The reason for this is not known, but it is possible that anxious patients adopt the strategy of inhibiting processing of negative personally relevant material.

In sum, anxious patients differ from normals in their preattentive and attentional processing of threatening stimuli, and in their interpretation of ambiguous information. However, they show no evidence of a negative recall bias along the lines of depressed patients. In general terms, non-normal cognitive functioning in anxious patients primarily relates to the early stages of information processing, whereas non-normal cognitive functioning in depressed patients relates more to later stages of processing. The findings for anxious patients are consistent with the view that the function of anxiety is to facilitate the early detection of potential threats.

THE CAUSALITY ISSUE

The fact that anxious and depressed patients differ from normal controls in several different aspects of cognitive functioning indicates that a cognitive approach to the mood disorders is viable. However, the findings which have been discussed so far fail to resolve an important theoretical issue. In essence, it is possible that non-normal cognitive functioning is found in anxious and depressed patients as a consequence of their current mood state. Alternatively, it may be that non-normal cognitive functioning plays some role in the development of mood disorders. In other words, there may be a cognitive vulnerability factor, in which non-normal cognitive functioning increases the probability that a given individual will subsequently develop a mood disorder. Realistically, of course, it may be the case that some aspects of non-normal functioning in mood-disordered patients reflect their current mood state, whereas others reflect a cognitive vulnerability factor.

It is very important theoretically and practically to attempt to solve the causality issue. The reason for this is that one must understand how and why mood disorders develop in order to improve attempts to prevent such disorders happening and to improve methods of treatment. The optimal way of investigating the causality issue would be by means of a prospective study. This will be discussed in relation to clinical anxiety, but precisely the same logic is applicable to clinical depression. Very large samples of normal individuals would be given a range of cognitive tasks. If those normal subjects who subsequently developed clinical anxiety resembled anxious patients in their cognitive functioning more than did those normals who did not subsequently develop clinical anxiety, then this would strengthen the argument that a cognitive vulnerability factor is involved in the development of clinical anxiety. In contrast, if those normal subjects who subsequently developed clinical anxiety were comparable to those normal subjects who did not subsequently develop clinical anxiety in their cognitive performance, this would be evidence against a cognitive vulnerability factor.

Since most prospective studies are extremely expensive and time-consuming, alternative approaches have generally been used. An approach which has been used extensively (discussed at length by Eysenck, in press) involves recovered patients. This will be described with reference to anxiety, but is equally applicable to depression. In essence, the approach requires thorough assessment of cognitive performance in three groups of subjects: currently anxious patients; recovered anxious patients; and normal controls. The major assumption which is made is that the cognitive functioning of the recovered anxious patients is comparable to their cognitive functioning before they became clinically anxious. This assumption may not be entirely warranted. If recovered patients are comparable to current patients in their cognitive performance, then it is possible to argue that this has occurred simply because they have not really recovered. Alternatively, it may be that suffering from clinical anxiety has a long-lasting effect on the cognitive system, so that it may never return to precisely the state it was in before the onset of the mood disorder. It is argued that those aspects of cognitive functioning reflecting a cognitive vulnerability factor should distinguish the normal controls from both of the other two groups, whereas those aspects reflecting anxious mood state should distinguish the current anxious patients from the recovered patients and the normal controls.

The evidence so far as clinical anxiety is concerned is somewhat equivocal (for details, see Eysenck, in press). Let us consider first studies of the interpretation of ambiguous stimuli having both a threatening and a non-threatening meaning. The proportion of homophones interpreted in a threatening fashion by recovered anxious patients is inter-mediate between that of current anxious patients and normal controls, suggesting that interpretation of ambiguity reflects a combination of cognitive vulnerability and anxious mood state. However, it was found in another study that current anxious patients recognized relatively more of the threatening interpretations of ambiguous sentences on a memory test than did normals, and that the recovered anxious patients closely resembled the normals in their performance. Those findings suggest that the tendency of anxious patients to perceive and to remember the threatening meanings of ambiguous material is primarily a reflection of anxious mood state.

Somewhat clearer findings have emerged from the study of attentional processes related to anxiety. It will be remembered that anxious patients have been found to be more distractible than normal controls, and that this enhanced distractibility is more in evidence with threatening distractors than with neutral ones. Recovered anxious patients have been found to resemble controls when neutral distractors are presented, but they are significantly more distractible than controls when threatening distractors are presented. An important theoretical implication of these findings is that the tendency for attention to be captured by emotionally threatening stimuli may constitute part of a cognitive vulnerability factor. It is entirely reasonable that those individuals who cannot avoid processing mildly threatening environmental stimuli should tend to be vulnerable to generalized anxiety disorder. More research is needed to see whether other aspects of cognitive functioning contribute to a cognitive vulnerability factor.

So far as depression is concerned, most of the available evidence indicates that non-normal cognitive functioning in depressed patients reflects their depressed mood state rather than a vulnerability factor. Consider, for example, a large prospective study that was carried out by Lewinsohn, Steinmetz, Larson, & Franklin (1981). They utilized questionnaires to assess a range of negative attitudes and cognitions. Their findings suggested that altered cognition in depressed individuals was due to being in a depressed state:

Prior to becoming depressed, ... future depressives did not subscribe to irrational beliefs, they did not have lower expectancies for positive outcomes or higher expectancies for negative outcomes, they did not attribute success experiences to external causes and failure experiences to internal causes, nor did they perceive themselves as having less control over the events of their lives.... People who are vulnerable to depression are not characterized by stable patterns of negative cognitions.

(Lewinsohn et al., 1981, p. 218)

There have been rather similar questionnaire studies of cognitive functioning in recovered depressed patients. It has usually been found in these studies that recovered depressed patients have fewer and less intense negative cognitions than current depressed patients, and they often appear to resemble normal controls.

One of the most consistent differences between depressed patients and normal controls in their cognitive functioning is that only the former group demonstrates a negative recall bias, i.e. depressed patients have a relative tendency to recall negative information encoded in relation to themselves. There have been attempts to decide whether or not recovered depressed patients have the same negative recall bias as current depressed patients. The findings are somewhat variable, but appear to indicate that recovered depressed patients either have no negative recall bias or a smaller one than current depressed patients. It is probably reasonable to conclude that there is as yet little support for the view that a vulnerability factor is involved.

The evidence which has been discussed appears to point to the conclusion that there is no cognitive vulnerability factor in depression. Such a conclusion would be premature. Most of the relevant research has made use of questionnaire assessment of cognition, and thus excludes any consideration of preconscious processes. Since controlled processes (or the products of such processes) have been investigated in most studies, rather little is as yet known about whether any automatic or preconscious processes might form part of a cognitive vulnerability factor for depression. In other words, no definite conclusions about the existence or otherwise of a cognitive vulnerability factor in depression can be reached until the cognitive system has been explored much more systematically.

In sum, most of the non-normal cognitive functioning in depressed and anxious patients which has been identified so far appears to reflect current mood state rather than a vulnerability factor. However, some indications of a cognitive vulnerability factor are present in the anxiety data, and studies of depression are too limited to justify any sweeping conclusions.

See also FORGETTING; PERSONALITY AND COGNITION; SELF-FOCUS AND SELF-ATTENTION; STATE-DEPENDENT MEMORY.

BIBLIOGRAPHY

Beck, A. T. (1976). *Cognitive theory and the emotional disorders*. New York: International Universities Press.

— —, & Emery, G. (1985). *Anxiety disorders and phobias: A cognitive perspective*. New York, Basic Books.

Eysenck, M. W. (in press). *Anxiety: The cognitive perspective*. London: Lawrence Erlbaum Associates Ltd.

Lazarus, R. S., Kanner, A. D., & Folkman, S. (1980). Emotions: A cognitive-phenomenological analysis. In R. Plutchik & H. Kellerman (Eds), *Emotion: Theory, research and experience* (Vol. 1). New York: Academic Press.

Lewinsohn, P. M., Steinmetz, J. L., Larson, D. W., & Franklin, J. (1981). Depression related cognitions: Antecedents or consequences? *Journal of Abnormal Psychology, 90,* 213–19.

Williams, J. M. G., Watts, F. N., MacLeod, C., & Mathews, A. (1988). *Cognitive psychology and the emotional disorders*. Chichester: Wiley.

Zajonc, R. B. (1980). Feeling and thinking: Preferences need no inferences. *American Psychologist, 35,* 151–75.

MICHAEL W. EYSENCK

motor control and learning Research on motor control considers *how*, as opposed to *why*, motor skills are performed. We know that people walk and run; eat; communicate by talking, writing, and typing; drive cars, dance, kick footballs, and so on. One way to view these motor activities is in terms of goals and outcomes: the person runs a mile, eats dessert, types an editorial, parks the car, scores a goal. However, the primary research focus is on the mechanisms and processes involved in specifying, producing, and correcting voluntary movements. Research on motor learning addresses the related questions of how motor skills are acquired and remembered.

What is the role for cognition in motor control and learning? Skill learning requires physical practice. One does not learn to drive a car, ski, or play the flute by reading a book of instructions and contemplating what must be done! It would be naive to view motor control strictly in terms of cognitive processes without an understanding of sensory processes, movement biomechanics, and the neuromuscular system. Likewise, frameworks that suggest that movements are linked directly to sensory events and frameworks that explain only neuromuscular hardware fail because they do not incorporate factors such as decision making and attention. Very basic motor processes can be influenced by cognitive factors such as expectations and goals. Most contemporary accounts of motor control acknowledge the interaction between the central information-processing components of movement and the more peripheral neuromuscular aspects of movement. Keele (1986), for example, suggested that motor skills can be viewed as series of central decisions and movements. Even accounts of motor control that eschew cognitive processes and instead place heavy emphasis on self-organizing systems (see Kugler & Turvey, 1987) recognize the importance of factors such as intention. The discussion below reflects the current trend for both the neurosciences and psychology to move beyond questions focused at a single level to emphasize the interaction of central and peripheral control processes in motor control and learning. The topics addressed to illustrate the roles of memory and cognition in motor control are (1) feedback and knowledge of results, and (2) central representations (motor programs) for motor skills. The inter-

ested reader could usefully refer to recent chapters by Pew and Rosenbaum (1988) and Keele (1986) and texts by Jeannerod (1988), Schmidt (1988), and Smyth and Wing (1984) for comprehensive reviews of the behavioral analysis of motor control and learning; and to Enoka (1988) for an introduction to the neuromechanical basis of movement.

FEEDBACK AND KNOWLEDGE OF RESULTS

Feedback refers to sensory information that the performer receives during and immediately after a movement, including information from muscle stretch receptors, golgi tendon organs, joint receptors, and cutaneous receptors and from the visual and auditory systems. Knowledge of results consists of extrinsic information about the success or consequences of an action: it may be a score or qualitative evaluation provided after a movement is completed. Consider the act of drinking a cup of coffee. Suppose that the cup starts to slip from the hand. Feedback includes information from muscle and cutaneous receptors as well as visual information about the movement of the hand and cup. Knowledge of results includes details such as the location of broken pieces and coffee from the spill.

There was early speculation that movement could not take place without feedback because feedback had to initiate each separate component in a sequence such as playing a series of notes on the piano; feedback from the first movement segment triggered the second, feedback from the second triggered the third, and so on. A prediction of this response-chaining hypothesis was that only the first segment would be possible if feedback were not available. In fact, movement can take place even though feedback systems are eliminated surgically (in animals) or impaired by injury or disease. Models assuming that feedback is required to trigger action are no longer tenable. However, open-loop systems that operate without benefit of feedback are very limited because they are unable to make fine adjustments, correct errors, or compensate for unexpected resistance. Even though feedback is not a trigger for voluntary action, it is an essential component of skill.

Feedback is necessary for fine tuning and on-line correction at the peripheral level of motor implementation. For example, cutaneous information that the coffee cup is slipping from the fingers will promote rapid adjustments of grip force and may prevent the spill. Likewise, when an action is perturbed by a change in resistance or an unanticipated obstacle, proprioceptive feedback leads to rapid correction in both the perturbed muscle group and other task-related muscle groups. For example, the upper as well as the lower lip compensates if the lower lip is perturbed during an utterance that requires lip closure; likewise, both the thumb and index finger compensate if the thumb meets unexpected resistance during a pinching movement. Feedback also contributes to postural maintenance. If the surface on which a person is standing moves forward or backward (as when standing in a bus), body sway "detected" by stretch at the ankles initiates correction patterns that involve sequenced muscle groups at the lower-legs/ankles and hips/upper-legs. This type of correction takes place so quickly that conscious cognitive intervention during the actual movement itself is not thought to be part of the correction process.

However, cognitive factors do affect correction processes. Factors such as the performer's intention prior to movement can affect the way proprioceptive feedback will be used during movement. Suppose that a subject holds the elbow at a 90-degree angle and is fitted with a small weight hanging from the hand. The experimenter can perturb arm position by adding weight to the hanging weight. The subject's instructions are either (1) to resist and try to maintain a stable position or (2) to "let go" and try to give with the perturbation. Responses that are triggered by feedback from muscle stretch caused by the added weight vary in magnitude for the "resist" and "let go' instruction. Stretch reflexes less than 30 msec. after the perturbation and long-loop reflexes that occur around 50 msec. after the perturbation may be attenuated in the "give" condition. These differences, which occur too quickly to reflect stimulus-driven cognitive intervention, suggest that prior instruction can change the influence of feedback and tailor the motor response to the situation at hand. Cognitive intervention based on experience can also affect standing-posture adjustments such as the response to stretch at the ankles caused by body sway. The magnitude of muscle responses to body sway caused by support-surface movement varies with the amplitude of surface movement if the displacement amplitude is expected but not if it is not.

Feedback includes major contributions from vision which provides particularly salient information about movement and its consequences (see PERCEPTUAL MOTOR COORDINATION). Vision is the major source of information about the relationship between the performer and the environment, including advanced information about the way the environment is changing. Like other sources of feedback, vision contributes to correction processes during movement. It is also a primary source of information needed to prepare the neuromuscular system for the impending consequences of action. If visual information is available it may reduce demands for active cognitive processing prior to and during movement. (See Jeannerod, 1988, for a discussion of roles for vision in motor control.)

Visual and proprioceptive feedback along with knowledge of results provides information that may be used following action. Most models of skill learning assume that performers pause and actively evaluate feedback in order to select the adjustments they will make when they try the action again. This process contributes to learning the central representation for the skill. A long-standing question now addressed from a cognitive framework is the extent to which beginners benefit from extrinsic information such as (1) augmented feedback (feedback beyond that inherent in the skill), and (2) knowledge of results. These aids often lead to improvements if they are used as a new skill is introduced. However, when stressed at the expense of other factors, they may promote rapid acquisition at the expense of retention. Augmented feedback and knowledge of results may slow or change the development of the central representation or influence the selection of the motor systems that are employed. (See Schmidt, 1988, and Magill, 1989, for a discussion of the role of feedback and knowledge of results in acquisition and retention).

Feedback has other roles including the traditionally emphasized functions of (a) triggering rapid protective responses and (b) providing the basis for kinesthesis, the perception of body position and motion. Finally, as noted below, feedback helps update and fine-tune motor programs and facilitates maintenance of accurate internal representations of ongoing motor skills.

MOTOR PROGRAMS

The term "motor program" has been used both to describe (1) the central memory for an action and (2) the specific motor commands used to execute a movement (see Keele, 1981, for a discussion of this second perspective). The more common first use, adopted here, defines the motor program as a central representation that exerts some type of superordinate control over motor performance. People are able to remember and repeat voluntary movements. The central motor program is the mechanism proposed to explain this ability. This abstract memory structure is assumed to include both rules for motor production and information about expected feedback. However, detailed motor commands may not be part of the program; specific final output commands may be consigned to lower levels in the system. It is also likely that the same central program can be used by different systems of muscles. For example, a single central program may govern writing with the right hand, the right arm, the left hand, the right foot, and so on; and a single program may govern playing the same piece of music on different musical instruments (see Keele, 1986).

An important, not-yet answered question is how detailed is a central program. One suggestion is that programs contain very detailed representations of movement parameters that unfold to produce movement. At the other extreme are suggestions that the central program contains only a bare outline of spatial coordinates, with all detail such as trajectory, joint positions, timing, and muscle activity specified at lower levels. A second and related question concerns the basis for grouping skills in the same program. Consider again the act of reaching for a cup of coffee. How would a single program specify the action needed to reach a cup that can rest in different positions on the table, vary in weight, and vary in height and diameter? One possibility is that a program centers around one invariant parameter and allows other parameters to vary. For example, reaching through different distances might be governed by a single program with one fixed muscle agonist burst duration and many possible agonist burst amplitudes, with larger amplitudes used for longer distances. Yet another possibility is that straight-line hand trajectories are the basis for programing efforts. A third proposal is that the program specifies relative timing for movement segments so that a single program governs fast to slow versions of the same movement. In this case the total duration of the movement varies but the duration of each segment of the movement remains a constant proportion of the total duration. Each of these guidelines is reasonable. When tested, each proves to hold in some but not all cases. (See Jeannerod, 1988, for a review of attempts to identify program parameters.) The notion that motor control depends on prescriptive central motor programs is widely accepted. However, the specific nature of the relationship between central and lower levels of operation and the interaction among levels remain to be determined. Just as verbal activity may depend on more than one memory system, motor control is apt to require modes of central representation that differ, depending on the nature of actions that are involved. Likewise there may be more than one representation for the same action and multiple ways of coordinating central and peripheral operations.

One hallmark of motor programs is that they are flexible. Expectations about the upcoming activity, such as the level of liquid in a to-be-lifted cup, influence motor planning. They may determine which program is selected for use or the parameters that will be used when the program is activated. The context in which an action is performed also influences movement kinematics; reaching for a cup is apt to differ at picnic tables and linen-covered dining tables and to depend on whether the intent is to drink from the cup or clear the cup from the table. A second aspect of flexibility is that the central memory representation can be changed to accommodate new demands. People adapt quickly to changing sensory information, changes in the relationship between sensory information and motor commands, changes in equipment, and so forth. For example, subjects asked to wear prisms that distort visual information adjust limb movements with relative ease. Likewise, reaching remains possible with the forearm in a plaster cast or extended by a tool held in the hand. Motor-program flexibility is also evident in situations with stable task demands. A program is not left to run "unattended." Suppose that a musician is trying to play an instrument in time with a metronome. Differences between the auditory feedback from the played note and the metronome beat are thought to affect central timing representation to provide a basis for slowing or speeding the playing of subsequent notes (see Smyth & Wing, 1984). Motor programs are not fixed permanent records, analogous to phonograph records or compact disks. Instead, programs can be changed on a temporary or permanent basis and, to permit this flexibility, rely on feedback to fine-tune and adjust the central representation.

SUMMARY AND CONCLUSIONS

Motor control and learning are best understood from an interdisciplinary perspective that recognizes and appreciates the contributions of cognitive processes, perception, and motor systems. This approach to motor control has lead to a growing conceptual understanding of the central representation of skill, the processes needed to specify, monitor, and correct skill, and the sophisticated interactions among cognitive states, motor production systems, and sensory information. Motor performance depends on an intricate interleaving of operations that occur at different levels. The boundaries between levels are not distinct and information can flow both from central toward more peripheral levels and from peripheral to central systems. Cognitive states influence how sensory feedback will be used during movement; sensory feedback influ-

ences the development and maintenance of motor programs; visual information contributes to ongoing skill production; feedback and knowledge of results from one attempt influence motor production for the next attempt; and so forth. Research perspectives that address the mechanisms and processes that operate at different levels – with an eye to the complex bi-directional interactions between central representations, sensory systems, and neuromuscular systems – are advancing the understanding of the ways we remember and produce voluntary movements.

BIBLIOGRAPHY

Enoka, R. M. (1988). *Neuromechanical basis of kinesiology*. Champaign, Ill.: Human Kinetics.

Jeannerod, M. (1988). *The neural and behavioural organization of goal-directed movement*. Oxford: Clarendon Press.

Keele, S. W. (1981). Behavioral analysis of movement. In V. B. Brooks (Ed.), *Handbook of physiology, Section 1: The nervous system. Volume II. Motor control, Part 2* (pp. 1391–414). Baltimore: Williams & Wilkins.

— —. (1986). Motor control. In K. R. Boff, L. Kaufman, & J. P. Thomas (Eds), *Handbook of perception and human performance*, Volume 1 (pp. 30-1 to 30-60). New York: Wiley.

Kugler, P. N., & Turvey, M. T. (1987). *Information, natural law, and the self-assembly of rhythmic movement*. Hillsdale, NJ: Erlbaum.

Magill, R. A. (1989). *Motor learning: Concepts and applicaitons* (3rd edn). Dubuque, Iowa: Wm. C. Brown.

Pew, R. W., & Rosenbaum, D. A. (1988). Human movement control: Computation, representation, and implementation. In R. C. Atkinson, R. J. Herrnstein, G. Lindzey, & R. D. Luce (Eds), *Stevens' handbook of experimental psychology*, 2nd edn, (Vol. 2) (pp. 473–509). New York: Wiley.

Schmidt, R. A. (1988). *Motor control and learning* (2nd edn). Champaign, Ill.: Human Kinetics.

Smyth, M. M., & Wing, A. M. (Eds). (1984). *The psychology of human movement*. Orlando, Fla: Academic Press.

BETH KERR

motor coordination *See* PERCEPTUAL MOTOR COORDINATION.

N

neuropsychology, cognitive *See* COGNITIVE NEUROPSYCHOLOGY.

nonverbal communication Much of the information we exchange during everyday social interaction is nonverbal: facial expressions, looks and glances, gestures, postural movements, changes in intonation, and so on. The signals and their functions can usefully be categorized as follows: emblems, illustrators, adaptors, regulators, and affect displays (Ekman & Friesen, 1969). Emblems are non-verbal acts which substitute for words and have a direct verbal equivalent: fingers-crossed, "wind up," obscene gestures. They are often used when conditions demand silence, and they are mostly culture specific. Illustrators are nonverbal acts which complement words and illustrate "pictorially" what is being said: flowing water, pounding heart, spiral staircase. Adaptors are habitual, idiosyncratic movements, especially self-grooming: scratching, rubbing eyes, tugging hair. Regulators are "turn-taking" signals which we use to offer and take over the floor so that the smooth to-and-fro of conversation is maintained: speed and tone of voice, hand and postural movements, gaze. Affect displays are expressions of emotion. Regulators and affect displays have attracted the most research attention.

The earliest research on regulators concentrated on the eyes (Kendon, 1967). When speakers approached the end of a long utterance, it was found, they generally looked up at the listener, to signal that they had finished. The listener then looked down, to acknowledge the signal and to begin to take over. The whole transition was accomplished smoothly, and apparently unselfconsciously. If the speaker did not look up, however, or the listener did not look down, there was an uncomfortable pause, sometimes followed by both people trying to speak. Other signals are

regulators too, of course – people manage perfectly smooth transitions over the telephone – but it is visual contact which gives face-to-face conversation its spontaneity (Beattie, 1983; Rutter, 1984).

Research on affect displays has concentrated on three main issues. The first is how accurately people recognize emotions in the face. The most common experimental technique has made use of photographs or videotape recordings of people posing emotions as actors or experiencing real emotions in experimental or natural settings (Ekman, 1983). Typically, seven "basic" emotions are recorded (happiness, sadness, anger, fear, surprise, disgust, interest) and the stimulus material is then shown to the experimenter's subjects, who are asked to say what emotion they think each photograph or recording portrays. Alternatively they may be told a story in which the character is faced with an emotional trigger (friends arrive unexpectedly, there is a death, a frightening animal appears) and the subjects are asked to choose the photograph they think fits best. Respondents are generally very accurate, unless a wider range than the standard seven is used or mixed emotions are portrayed, and there is normally good agreement. It has even been found that photographs taken in the USA are "decoded" accurately in remote countries like Borneo and New Guinea, and vice versa. Similarly, when emotions are provoked deliberately by the experimenter – by showing a stress-inducing film, for example – the facial expressions of the audience again show evidence of cross-cultural consistency, provided the culture's "display rules" are penetrated. According to Ekman, both encoding and decoding of affect displays may therefore suggest an inherited component.

The second question about affect displays concerns the way in which the various expressive signals combine. One important account is the intimacy model of Argyle (see Argyle, 1988). Imagine you are meeting someone for the first time, perhaps a new classmate or colleague. The emotions you both experience will be mixed, approach and avoidance, and you will have to negotiate how "intimate" the encounter is to be. The negotiation will be silent and you may even be unaware that it is happening, but intimacy will show in how much eye-contact there is, how close you sit, how personal a topic of conversation you choose, how much you smile, and so on. All the indices will combine in a state of equilibrium and, provided the equilibrium remains stable, the conversation will progress normally. However, if one of you upsets the balance – you move closer, perhaps – there will be compensation along one of the other dimensions, so that eye-contact will reduce, for example, or the conversation will move to a less threatening topic. A new level of intimacy will thus be negotiated and equilibrium will be restored. The intimacy model has received a great deal of empirical support, especially from the finding that eye-contact and distance are related inversely, and it continues to have a considerable influence on the literature.

The third question about affect displays concerns the relative weights of verbal and nonverbal cues. There have been two main types of experiment. First, imagine that someone said nice things to you but in a nasty manner. Which would you "believe," the verbal content or the nonverbal manner? In one of the early experiments (Argyle, Alkema, & Gilmour, 1971), subjects were shown clips of videotape in which an actor delivered a verbal message which was friendly, neutral, or hostile. At the same time, the facial expression and tone of voice were varied in the same way – friendly, neutral, and hostile – giving nine verbal–nonverbal combinations. The evidence showed that the nonverbal message "won" easily, so much so that people sometimes appeared to be unaware of the words altogether (see Argyle, 1988).

In the other type of experiment (e.g. Archer & Akert, 1977), people are shown recordings of everyday events, such as two men chatting after a basketball match, two women with a child, or someone talking on the telephone. After each one, they are asked a factual question – which of the two men won the match, which of the women is the child's mother, whether the listener at the other end of the telephone is male or female – and sometimes there is sound and vision but sometimes sound only. The results show that people do no better than chance when all they have is the sound track, but their accuracy increases markedly when the picture is present too. The evidence thus suggests once more that nonverbal signals carry considerable weight, sometimes more than words themselves. Much, though, will depend upon the people and the circumstances, and it would be wrong to forget that words matter too.

See also PERSON PERCEPTION.

BIBLIOGRAPHY

Archer, D., & Akert, R. M. (1977). Words and everything else: Verbal and nonverbal cues in social interpretation. *Journal of Personality and Social Psychology, 35,* 443–9.

Argyle, M. (1988). *Bodily communication* (2nd edn). London: Methuen.

——, Alkema, F., & Gilmour, R. (1971). The communication of friendly and hostile attitudes by verbal and non-verbal signals. *European Journal of Social Psychology, 1,* 385–402.

Beattie, G. W., (1983). *Talk: An analysis of speech and non-verbal behaviour in conversation.* Milton Keynes: Open University Press.

Ekman, P. (Ed.) (1983). *Emotion in the human face* (2nd edn). London: Methuen.

——, & Friesen, W. V. (1969). The repertoire of nonverbal behavior: Categories, origins, usage, and coding. *Semiotica, 1,* 49–97.

Kendon, A. (1967). Some functions of gaze direction in social interaction. *Acta Psychologica, 26,* 1–47.

Rutter, D. R. (1984). *Looking and seeing.* Chichester: Wiley.

D. R. RUTTER

P

parallel distributed processing *See* CON-
NECTIONIST MODELS OF MEMORY; PATTERN
PERCEPTION.

pattern perception This expression refers
to the process of detecting and discriminating
significant recurring combinations of spatially
or temporally distributed energy in the
environment in order to make appropriate
responses. This essay will examine the
mechanisms which may underly such discriminations, especially discriminations based
on combinations of environmental features.

Animal behavior provides many examples of
special pattern recognition systems, which
(usually) enable appropriate inbuilt responses
to occur to specific sensory inputs (McFarland, 1985). These inputs may be relatively
simple, characterized by one or very few
features. The male stickleback, for example,
responds with attack to any red stimulus,
including a red bus passing the window. A
single molecule of the pheromone bombykol
released by the female silkworm moth can
trigger approach by a male.

These simple dependencies are likely to be
controlled in the brain by a receptive cell, or
more likely a group of cells, which will fire
only to a particular external stimulus and
prime a set of possible responses, the precise
response emitted being determined by other
aspects of the environment. There is little
ability to discriminate appropriate from inappropriate stimuli because in the natural
environment this is largely unnecessary.

In more complex cases some combination
of stimulus characteristics is required. The
herring gull reacts to an egg outside the nest
by reaching beyond the egg with its bill and
retrieving it. Size, shape, background coloring,
and speckles all play an independent part in
eliciting the response, which also occurs
(though less strongly) to a range of variations

around the optimal egg pattern. The frog
responds to moving spots by orientation and
striking with the tongue. Neurons have been
located in the frog's optic nerve which fire
only to black moving dots. In order to respond
only to a moving dot of the right size within a
certain range, the detector cell in the frog's
optic nerve must receive a complex combination of inputs over time from the retina.

In species higher in the evolutionary scale,
inbuilt responses to particular stimuli are
relatively rare. More important is the ability to
learn to discriminate and identify complex
patterns – that is, combinations such as shape
and color or frequency and temporal duration,
and learn new responses to them. The average
human can immediately identify 50,000
words, if reasonably literate, or several
thousand faces, and in specialist areas like
chess an expert with extensive experience
(around 10,000 hours in the case of International Grandmasters) can achieve similar feats
for chess game positions. Apes have been
taught to identify signs of American Sign
Language and respond with signs of their own
and to recognize plastic colored shapes and
place them in combinations to make requests
for food and other requirements (McFarland,
1985). In the visual modality much pattern
perception involves the identification of
objects in a three-dimensional environment,
often referred to as FORM PERCEPTION.
However, there are other important aspects of
visual pattern perception in human beings,
such as FACE RECOGNITION, perception of
pictures, and reading (*see* READING DEVELOP-
MENT), while SPEECH PERCEPTION is the most
important human form of acoustic pattern
perception.

These pattern recognition abilities are
obviously much more complex and varied than
those discussed at the beginning of this essay.
They cannot depend on specialist innate
detectors for specific stimuli but rather on the

ability to discover critical differences and ignore irrelevant ones. A number of theories have attempted to explain how these feats might be possible and evidence has been drawn from neurophysiology, psychological experiments, and attempts to program computers to recognize patterns. As will emerge, most of the theories have been designed to cope with two-dimensional visual patterns varying in shape.

Some theories assume that a master copy or "template" exists in the brain for a pattern which is to be recognized and the input is compared as a whole to this template. This might be done (using a visual example) by a single neuron collecting evidence for the presence and absence of light over a certain area of the retina (as the unit in the frog's optic nerve collects evidence for the presence of a spot). Other theories assume intervening levels of analysis, whereby particular "feature detectors" first operate on the input, identifying straight lines and curves of different orientations, the presence of which is then signaled to a higher order unit which only fires when a particular combination of features is present. There are also theories which assume no structured analyzers operating on the input but simply an interconnected network of identical units, of which different subsets respond to different patterns. Recently there has been a revived interest in sophisticated versions of such parallel distributed processing (PDP) models.

Before discussing these theories in more detail, it should be noted that they assume that either the input is presented as an already isolated unit such as a letter or face on a uniform background, or that a preliminary process of segmenting the input and isolating a distinct unit has occurred (this is no less true for speech where the gaps we "hear" between words are not present in the physical input but are creations of our speech perception processes). The preprocessing required is far from simple, particularly in the case of natural scenes or pictures of such scenes. There are no ready-made boundaries between the significant elements; contours are blurred, hidden, or non-existent and false contours are present due to shadows and other "noise."

Marr (1982) has demonstrated how complex the processing is likely to be in visually segmenting natural scenes and implemented some possible algorithms in computer simulations (*see* PERCEPTION, COMPUTATIONAL THEORY OF). Some of the critical cues which induce segmentation in two-dimensional patterns have been identified, such as change in brightness or the orientation of texture (Pomerantz, 1985). The GESTALT PRINCIPLES OF PERCEPTUAL ORGANIZATION also embody principles of scene segmentation.

TEMPLATE THEORIES

Template theories are not taken very seriously by most theorists because it is unclear how they could cope with variations or imperfections in the input. You can recognize a picture of Winston Churchill, even a cartoon consisting of a few lines, when you have not seen it before, because it is similar to pictures you have seen before, but templates are usually taken to require exact matches. Yet even frogs and herring gulls can cope with variation in the stimulus. Elaborations of template theories have been suggested in which inputs are preprocessed to "normalize" position, size, and orientation, but it is unclear how the necessary normalization can be determined without already knowing the template to which the input is to be matched. At best these operations could only cope with stimuli of limited variability. Cells in the monkey's visual cortex which respond to visual presentation of a monkey's hand appear to offer some support for the notion of templates (Gross, Rocha-Miranda, & Bender, 1972). However, such cells can respond to a variety of hand patterns and the details of their make-up are unclear.

FEATURE ANALYSIS

Such problems encourage development of a feature analysis theory, whereby a complex pattern is decomposed into simpler elements which are detected by similar processes to those envisaged for templates (features are in fact miniature templates). Another modification is the assumption that the stored representation of each template or feature consists, not of an exact copy, but of a "prototype," or typical instance derived by averaging over instances which have been encountered (*see* CONCEPTS). A prototype can be defined more precisely as the sum of the averaged values of all the component features. This approach can in principle deal with examples like recognition of Churchill's face, but it should be noted that no precise account is offered as to how variability around the prototype is processed in the nervous system.

Hubel and Wiesel (1959) reported evidence for units in the cat's visual cortex responsive only to edges or bars of a particular orientation. Subsequently they also found units responsive to corners. Such units were originally thought to be basic feature detectors (though no units responsive to other important features such as curves have been found), but theorists such as Marr (1982) have argued more plausibly that these units are involved in the basic operation of locating contours at an early stage of input processing to create the "primal sketch" (*see* FORM PERCEPTION). Psychological evidence for use of features in identifying simple patterns comes from experiments such as those in which subjects search for a target letter consisting of curved lines in a background of straight letters. Search times increase markedly if the background letters are changed to a set consisting of curved lines but not if the new set also consists of straight lines (Rabbitt, 1967).

The best examples of reasonably plausible models of feature theories involve language processing (e.g. SPEECH PERCEPTION). Human speech is produced by forcing air through the vocal chords. Movement of different parts of the vocal tract reinforces distinct frequency bands in the resulting sound, which are known as "formants." Each vowel is typified by a particular combination of two main formants (though three or four are present). The formants are clearly apparent when the frequencies present at each instant are plotted on a graph over a period of time. Consonants appear as brief bursts of wide-frequency noise but have few invariant characteristics. Instead, their characteristics vary according to the succeeding vowel. However further cues are provided by the "transitions" – that is, the changes in the formants which occur between the consonant noise burst and the following vowel –

which show typical patterns for different consonants and can produce perception of a particular consonant even when the burst of wide frequency noise due to the consonant is removed. Removal of the transition, on the other hand, often eliminates consonant recognition. Thus, the important units seem to be consonants plus vowels (that is syllables) rather than single sounds or phonemes (*see* AUDITORY PERCEPTION).

The most elaborate feature model for word recognition is that of McClelland and Rumelhart (1981). Figure 1 shows the essentials. Input excites feature detectors which are connected to letter detectors with an excitatory connection where they form part of the letter and an inhibitory connection otherwise. Similar connections exist between letter detectors and word detectors and feedback also occurs in the reverse direction. The word units will respond correctly to partly obscured words because the correct solution receives some excitation from all the letters. Feedback from words to letters explains how letters can be more easily identified when presented in words than when presented on their own.

There are, however, many difficulties with feature analysis theories. While it may be possible to specify adequate features for restricted pattern sets, it is difficult or impossible to do this for many other patterns such as everyday three-dimensional objects and pictures of them (e.g. *see* FACE RECOGNITION). Second, the relevant features often depend on

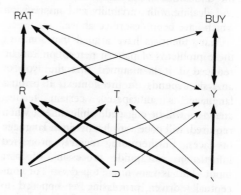

Figure 1 Part of a feature hierarchy for recognizing words. Thick lines indicate excitatory connections and thin lines inhibitory connections.

the current context and purpose. Deciding in the context of numbers whether a smudged item is a *3* or an *8* requires different information from deciding in the context of letters whether it is an *s* or a *g*. Third, the Gestalt psychologists argued that it was impossible to specify patterns adequately in terms of component parts, since complex patterns often produce an experience which is not predictable from the nature of their parts. VISUAL ILLUSIONS are the most striking examples. Later research has found other examples. Discrimination of the pattern ( ) from)) is much easier than discrimination of (from) even though the same element has been added to both, giving no extra discriminatory power on its own. The addition produces enclosed shapes which in effect provide a new feature (often called an "emergent feature"), so it is impossible to account for all pattern perception with a limited set of basic features (Pomerantz, 1985).

The most crucial objection to treating patterns as lists of features, however, is that *relations* between features are vital. L and T both have a vertical and a horizontal bar, K and Y both have a vertical bar and one left-inclined and one right-inclined bar; it is the spatial relations between these elements that differ. Hence, more elaborate theories are needed in which such relations are specified. Such theories are known as "structural description theories." These may appear more promising, but in practice they are still vulnerable to all the difficulties of specifying critical elements and dealing with variability and imprecision which have been described above.

Many theorists have argued that some of these problems of pattern perception can be reduced if it is assumed that the type of analysis depends on the context. If printed language is anticipated, certain feature analyzers will be engaged, while others, when required, will cope with handwritten language or faces. Furthermore, recently processed information can guide processing of later input. This is known as "top-down" or conceptually driven processing as opposed to "bottom-up" processing in which invariant and possibly inbuilt processes are applied to all inputs (*see* DATA-DRIVEN AND CONCEPTU-ALLY DRIVEN PROCESSES). Marr (1982) has argued that bottom-up processing is adequate in natural environments to produce a viewer-centered representation of objects in depth. Such a view is not, however, incompatible with a belief in the occurrence of top-down processing in other situations, especially where patterns created by humans are involved. For example, spoken words in sentences are identified more easily than those in isolation, though predicting ahead seems to play only a very restricted role in reading (Rayner & McConkie, 1977).

PARALLEL DISTRIBUTED PROCESSING THEORIES

None of the theories discussed so far offers an explanation of how features and feature combinations might be learned. It is clearly unlikely that preformed pattern detectors could exist for all the variations which can be processed and the great strength of pattern recognition in higher species is the ability to cope with new discriminations. The appeal of the newly developed connectionist theories of memory or PDP models is that they offer a viable approach to such learning as well as to the classic problems of variability and imperfection in the input (*see* CONNECTIONIST MODELS OF MEMORY). These theories do not envisage single specialist units which gather evidence for specific patterns. Instead, large numbers of identical units are connected up in specific ways. Each unit has a threshold and excitatory or inhibitory links, which vary in strength, with other units. A unit fires if it receives sufficient net excitation from others, and then it passes a signal to other units. Thus, Input A will excite one combination of receptor units which pass signals on through the system, and Input B excites another combination (which may include some of the same units). With some additional assumptions, which there is no space to describe here, it has been shown that such systems can be taught to discriminate different inputs by adjusting the strengths of the connections according to whether a desired output is achieved or not. When an error occurs, excitatory connections are weakened and inhibitory connections strengthened. Removal of some of the units or part of the input does not seriously impair performance. Hence, these systems offer impressive parallels for pattern discrimination in living organisms (for a readable account, see Johnson-Laird, 1988, chap. 10; and for detailed studies, see McClelland, Rumelhart et al., 1987). This is not to say that all pattern discrimination learning is of this gradual non-analytic nature. A child may learn the critical difference between *E* and *F* by explicitly attending to the relevant feature.

As stated earlier, feature theories have tended to concentrate on shape discrimination and PDP theories provide the best approach to shape discrimination by bypassing the problems of defining suitable features (though they are not limited to a specific form of input). However, many patterns have features other than shape, such as color, size, texture, and movement. Neurophysiological evidence suggests that separate specialist subsystems in the brain are responsible for processing different feature classes (Zeki, 1978). The processing of combinations of these feature classes has been investigated in psychological experiments by Treisman (1988) and her associates. Treisman has examined particularly the processing of color–shape combinations and has argued that color and shape are computed by independent processes and the results are combined in an "object file" which collects the information for a specific spatial position. A parallel scan can be carried out across the whole input field for a single feature value such as green, since a green item can be found just as quickly whether it is hidden among 10 or 20 blue items. The combining process, however, is sequential and requires direction of attention to a specific location (spatial or temporal), since time increases when searching for a green *T* among green *X*s and blue *T*s as the number of irrelevant items increases. Treisman argues that empirical criteria, such as whether parallel processing of the above kind is possible, can be established for identifying separate features. Clearly this work implies that the passive implicit learning embodied in PDP models could not provide a complete picture of the processes involved in pattern perception.

SUMMARY

Several different mechanisms responsible for processing input patterns have been suggested, including purpose-built innate systems for detecting specific stimuli, flexible PDP systems which learn discriminations in a non-analytic way, and synthesis of different feature classes present at a specific location or time to form a complete object. It is therefore unlikely that a single all-embracing theory of pattern perception is viable.

BIBLIOGRAPHY

Gross, C. G., Rocha-Miranda, C. E., & Bender, D. B. (1972). Visual properties of neurons in inferotemporal cortex of the macaque. *Journal of Neurophysiology*, *35*, 96–111.

Hubel, D. H., & Wiesel, T. N. (1959). Receptive fields of simple neurons in the cat's striate cortex. *Journal of Physiology*, *148*, 576–91.

Johnson-Laird, P. N. (1988). *The computer and the mind: An introduction to cognitive science.* Cambridge, Mass.: Harvard University Press.

Marr, D. (1982). *Vision.* San Francisco: Freeman.

McClelland, J. L., & Rumelhart, D. E. (1981). An interactive activation model of context effects in letter perception, Part 1: An account of basic findings. *Psychological Review*, *88*, 375–407.

McClelland, J., Rumelhart, D. E., & the PDP Research Group (1987). *Parallel distributed processing: Vol. 2: Psychological and biological models.* Cambridge, Mass.: MIT Press.

McFarland, D. (1985). *Animal behaviour.* London: Pitman.

Pomerantz, J. R. (1985). Perceptual organization in information processing. In A. M. Aitkenhead & J. M. Slack (Eds), *Issues in cognitive modelling* (pp. 127–58). London: Lawrence Erlbaum Associates.

Rabbitt, P. M. (1967). Learning to ignore irrelevant information. *American Journal of Psychology*, *80*, 1–13.

Rayner, K., & McConkie, G. W. (1977). Perceptual processes in reading: The perceptual spans. In A. S. Reber & D. L. Scarborough (Eds), *Toward a psychology of reading: The proceedings of the CUNY conference* (pp. 183–205). New York: Wiley.

Treisman, A. (1988). Features and objects: The

fourteenth Bartlett memorial lecture. *Quarterly Journal of Experimental Psychology*, *40a*, 201–37.

Zeki, S. M. (1978). Functional specialization in the visual cortex of the rhesus monkey. *Nature*, *274*, 423–8.

J. M. WILDING

pattern recognition *See* FORM PERCEPTION.

perception Perception has been increasingly thought of in cognitive terms, as is exemplified by the following definition from Roth (1986, p. 81): "The term perception refers to the means by which information acquired from the environment via the sense organs is transformed into experiences of objects, events, sounds, tastes, etc." In spite of the fact that perception can be studied in each of the sensory modalities, it is actually the case that most research and theory have focused on auditory and visual perception. It seems natural to assume that perception involves conscious awareness, but there is increasing evidence that extensive perceptual processing can occur in the absence of conscious awareness (*see* SUBLIMINAL PERCEPTION).

An important theoretical issue is the relative contribution to perception of bottom-up or data-driven processes and top-down or conceptually driven processes (*see* DATA-DRIVEN AND CONCEPTUALLY DRIVEN PROCESSES). Some theorists (e.g. Gibson, 1972) have argued that the stimulus is a very rich source of information, and typically provides the information required to produce veridical perception. In contrast to Gibson's (1972) emphasis on data-driven processes, constructive theorists have argued that conceptually driven processes play a major role in perception (*see* CONSTRUCTIVIST THEORIES OF PERCEPTION). Such theories provide an explanation of VISUAL ILLUSIONS, but appear to predict that perception should be more error prone than is actually the case.

While some perception theorists focus on general principles of perception, other theorists have concentrated on the perception of relatively specific categories of stimuli which are of major importance in everyday life. For example, speech is obviously a very significant form of auditory stimulus and human faces are important visual stimuli (*see* SPEECH PERCEPTION; FACE RECOGNITION).

Over the last 15 years or so, there has been increasing emphasis on considering perception from the perspectives of COGNITIVE NEUROPSYCHOLOGY and COGNITIVE SCIENCE. Among the conditions studied by cognitive neuropsychologists are AGNOSIA and BLINDSIGHT (Weiskrantz, 1986). The study of brain-damaged patients has provided a test bed for cognitive theories of perception. Cognitive scientists (e.g. Marr, 1982) have constructed numerous computer programs designed to reflect the ways in which human perceptual processing occurs (*see* PERCEPTION, COMPUTATIONAL THEORY OF). These programs have illustrated many of the lacunae in previous theories of perception put forward by cognitive psychologists.

See also AUDITORY PERCEPTION; DIRECT PERCEPTION; FORM PERCEPTION; GESTALT PRINCIPLES OF PERCEPTUAL ORGANIZATION; IMAGERY AND PERCEPTION; PATTERN PERCEPTION; PERCEPTUAL CONSTANCIES; PERCEPTUAL DEVELOPMENT; PERCEPTUAL MOTOR COORDINATION; PERSON PERCEPTION.

BIBLIOGRAPHY

Gibson, J. J. (1972). A theory of direct visual perception. In J. R. Royce and W. W. Rozeboom (Eds), *The psychology of knowing*. London: Gordon & Breach.

Marr, D. (1982). *Vision: A computational investigation into the human representation and processing of visual information*. San Francisco: W. H. Freeman.

Roth, I. (1986). An introduction to object perception. In I. Roth and J. P. Frisby, *Perception and representation: A cognitive approach*. Milton Keynes: Open University Press.

Weiskrantz, L. (1986). *Blindsight: A case study and implications*. Oxford: Oxford University Press.

MICHAEL W. EYSENCK

perception, auditory See AUDITORY PERCEPTION.

perception, computational theory of The logical foundations for claiming that a computational approach is appropriate in psychology rest on Turing's proof that "a language capable of defining 'effective procedures' suffices, in principle, to solve any computable problem ... [so that] ... If a psychological science is possible at all, it must be capable of being expressed in computational terms" (Boden, 1988, p. 259). At a practical level, computer simulations of cognitive processes have provided a brutally rigorous way of weeding out flawed ideas, or of refining valuable but rather vague notions into more precise formulations, and of directing attention to hitherto neglected theoretical problems. The end result has been working models of various cognitive processes. Taking vision as an example, visual systems capable of guiding sophisticated hand-like robot grippers in picking up and manipulating an object have now been demonstrated. To be sure, such systems are presently of limited scope compared with human vision in the range of objects and scenes they can deal with. But the fundamental change in outlook prompted by having at least some working models in the areas classically the concern of perceptual psychology is felt by many to have had a revolutionary impact on the subject. Computational ways of addressing problems have brought far greater clarity, precision, and detail into theories of perception than existed hitherto and the same is true of cognitive theories in general. Indeed, it seems fair to say that the point has now been reached where it is almost inconceivable for a cognitive psychologist intent on worthwhile theory development to have much chance of success without deep familiarity with the associated computational literature (often mathematical in nature in the case of perception).

The general character of the computational approach to perception will be outlined here by describing the conceptual framework advanced by David Marr. His work is chosen for illustrative purposes because he has had a larger impact on cognitive psychology than any other single figure engaged in developing computational models of perception. It should be realized, however, that he is far from being a lone voice: the computational literature on perception is an explosively increasing one with no signs of levelling-off at present, and Marr's own work is but a fragment of it. His work has been influential, partly because it was closely linked to studies of biological perceptual systems and partly because it offers a general framework for cognitive science. To ensure that its implications are brought out in sufficient detail in the limited space available, just one specific topic will be discussed – the stereo correspondence problem. That is fitting because it is a problem to which Marr gave considerable attention and which he used himself as a paradigmatic illustration of his approach.

The point has already been made that the power of the computational approach derives in large part from the discipline of creating a computer implementation of the theory of interest. This soon leads to the shortcomings of existing theory being revealed and, as adjustments are made to improve it, to an ever more thorough analysis of the nature of the task to be solved. At this level of analysis, called the "computational theory" level by Marr (1982; Marr & Poggio, 1976), the questions raised are twofold: first, what exactly is the goal of the computation?; and second, what method(s) can be devised for achieving the required goal? In applying the computational approach to perception, the answer to the first question is frequently an abstract specification of a desired mapping from one kind of information to another, and usually an ambiguity that must be resolved in order to make the mapping is identified. The answer to the second question is couched in terms of (a) *constraints* flowing from the nature of the viewed world and its projections into images, or sometimes arising from the logic of the task (Marr & Nishihara, 1978: see Marr, 1982); and (b) *demonstrations of methods* (preferably with a precise mathematical treatment) showing that these constraints are adequate in principle for achieving the desired mapping. Given this content, it is questionable whether Marr's choice of the term "computational" for this level of theoretical analysis is a helpful one but it has become established in the literature.

Exploiting the computational theory in a practical system requires attention to a second level of analysis, called by Marr the "algorithm level." Here the issues are to do with achieving a workable implementation of the abstractly defined method(s) specified in the computational theory. This forces choices about the particular input and output representations to be used and the detailed sequence of processing steps needed to achieve the required input-to-output transformation. Marr (1982, p. 20) defines a representation as a formal system for making explicit certain entities or types of information, together with a specification for how the system does this. He calls the result of using a representation a "description" of an entity in that representation. By an "explicit" description is meant one which makes the information required available for immediate use – that is, without any need for further work by subsequent processes using the description.

Marr's third level of analysis concerns the hardware: how can the algorithm be realized physically? Often the same algorithm can be implemented in quite different technologies. The choice will usually have much to do with practicalities such as availability and cost. For example, Marr (1982, p. 24) observes that

> wires are rather cheap in biological architecture, because they can grow individually and in three dimensions. In conventional [computer] technology, wire laying is more or less restricted to two dimensions, which severely restricts the scope for using parallel techniques and algorithms; the same operations are often better carried out serially.

This approach will now be illustrated by computational work on the stereo correspondence problem, for which the goal is to take two stereo images and map them into a single representation making explicit the binocular disparities of the various features in each image. The major difficulty, brought to the fore by Julesz's work using random-dot stereograms, is generally regarded as resolving ambiguities of matching: which point in the left eye's image should be matched to which point in the right eye's image? The kind of theory provided by the computational approach is the identification of constraints flowing from the nature of the viewed world

and its projections into stereo images. Numerous constraints have now been proposed (for reviews, see Mayhew, 1983; Frisby, 1990). Marr and Poggio (1976) suggested that it is generally reasonable to assume that the visual world is made up of matter that is separated into objects whose surfaces are smooth compared with their distance from the viewer. In other words, the visual world is *not* usually made up only of a cloud of identical dust particles: the matching problem would be intractable if it were. They called this the "cohesivity constraint" and they used it to justify their *continuity* binocular matching rule: *prefer possible matches that could have arisen from smooth surfaces.* Marr and Poggio also identified the "uniqueness constraint": a scene entity cannot be in two places at the same time, from which they derived the binocular matching rule: *each item from each image may be assigned at most one disparity value.* Marr (1982, p. 114) added to these two constraints a third called the "compatibility constraint" which leads to the binocular matching rule: only allow matches between descriptive elements derived from the two images which could have arisen from the same physical surface marking.

From these three constraints, Marr postulated the fundamental assumption of stereopsis: *If a correspondence is established between physically meaningful primitives extracted from the left and right images of a scene that contains a sufficient amount of detail, and if the correspondence satisfies the three matching constraints, then that correspondence is physically correct.* He stated that "... to isolate this fundamental assumption and to establish that it is valid is precisely what I mean by the computational theory of a process" (Marr, 1982, p. 115). What this amounts to is developing the assumption in more precise terms and then proving that the constraints do indeed force unique correspondences (Marr noted that phrases like "scene contains a sufficient amount of detail" and "physically meaningful primitives" are too imprecisely stated for mathematical proofs). He went on to show that, given the constraints, matches falling in same-disparity planes will be denser than on any others and hence preferred by the matching rules.

Marr and Poggio (1976) implemented their two matching rules in an algorithm that utilized a cooperative neural network (*see* CONNECTIONIST MODELS OF MEMORY). The nodes of the network represent potential matches and these nodes exchange excitation if they have the same disparity. This mutual facilitation implements the continuity constraint by giving preference to matches that could have arisen from smooth surfaces. The uniqueness constraint is implemented by inhibition exchanged between nodes lying along the same line of sight, the effect of which is to suppress more than one match for each primitive. This network could be realized in a variety of hardware architectures, varying from simulations on standard serial von Neumann machines through to specialized parallel processing devices – and, plausibly but speculatively, in biological neurones. For a tutorial introduction to the Marr and Poggio (1976) algorithm, as well as an introduction to the computational approach in general, see Frisby (1979).

As an illustration of what constitutes theory development using the computational approach, it is worth noting that it soon became evident that the form of facilitation used by the Marr and Poggio (1976) stereo algorithm is needlessly restrictive: insistence that only units with the *same* disparity exchange support limits the algorithm strictly to dealing with surfaces which lie locally in planes perpendicular to their viewing direction (e.g. frontoparallel planes near the fixation point). A broader interpretation of smoothness is implemented in the so-called PMF stereo algorithm which allows pairs of matches with different disparities to exchange support as long as the gradient of disparity between the pair is not too large. Pollard, Porrill, Mayhew, and Frisby (1986) prove that the use of this "disparity gradient limit" constraint imposes a form of scene-to-view and view-to-view continuity during stereo matching which can be informally described as allowing "jagged but not too jagged" surfaces to be dealt with. This proof admirably satisfies Marr's requirements for a computational theory, it extends and tightens up the mathematics expressing the nature of the smoothness constraint, and as a result it produces a more effective and more widely applicable stereo algorithm (Frisby, 1990). Such a development is an example of an advance in computational theorizing in perception.

Yet another use of the surface smoothness constraint is Mayhew and Frisby's (1980) "figural continuity" matching rule: because cohesive objects generate surface edges and surface markings that are spatially continuous, *prefer matches that preserve figural continuity*. This is mentioned here to bring out the point that diverse methods can often be derived from a broadly stated constraint. Indeed, the smoothness constraint is used more widely than just in stereo, playing a role as a so-called "regularizer" for what are technically known as "ill-posed problems" (i.e. mathematically over- or underdetermined problems) in algorithms capable of dealing with extracting surface shape from motion, shading, and other depth cues (Poggio, Torre, & Koch 1985; this paper provides a good entry point to the computational literature on low-level vision).

Marr and Poggio (1979) implemented the same two constraints, of smoothness and uniqueness, in a quite different *non*-cooperative stereo algorithm that used multiple spatial frequency tuned channels and a coarse-to-fine matching strategy. The key idea here was to exploit the fact that only a few edge points, and hence only modest ambiguity problems, arise in very coarse channels. Matches obtained in these can then be used to guide matching in more finely tuned channels. Ambiguities in all channels are reduced almost to zero by suitable coupling of spatial frequency tuning to the disparity range allowed for matching. This requires that the high spatial frequency channels have very narrow disparity ranges and that they therefore need to be "put in the right place to look" if they are to find the correct matches. The algorithm does this by generating appropriate vergence eye movements driven by the coarser channels. It is unlikely that human vision implements this algorithm in that disparities beyond the range allowed by the theory for high spatial frequencies can be fused without need of eye movements (Mayhew & Frisby, 1980). This experiment is an example of a psychophysical study being driven by computational theorizing.

The viability of their second algorithm depends, Marr and Poggio (1979) argued, on the same surface smoothness constraint used to underpin their first one. The details of this argument can be challenged (on the grounds that surface smoothness in three-space does not necessarily imply useful continuity across different spatial frequencies: Mayhew and Frisby, 1980; Prazdny, 1987). Nevertheless, Marr's claim that both algorithms depend on the same underlying constraints is a nice example of his belief that it is both useful and possible to distinguish different levels of analysis:

> These three levels of analysis [computational theory, algorithm, hardware] are coupled but only loosely: The choice of algorithm is influenced for example, by what it has to do and the hardware in which it must run. But there is a wide choice available at each level, and the explication of each level involves issues that are rather independent of the other two.
>
> (Marr, 1982, p. 25)

The need to distinguish different levels of discourse is accepted without question in computer science in the design and analysis of human-made complex information-processing systems. Many technical concerns at the level of digital hardware are quite irrelevant to the business of devising good algorithms to run on that hardware. This is reflected in the important notion of a "virtual machine" in computer science, defined as a set of information-processing operations:

> A physical mechanism (a calculator, a computer, or brain, perhaps) may instantiate a particular virtual machine which can be used as a basis for implementing other virtual machines (using programs which define operating systems, compilers, interpreters, and so on).
>
> (Sloman, 1980, p. 403)

Indeed, although Marr's particular prescription for the kind of analysis required at the computational theory level is distinctive, insistence on the general importance of this

separate explanatory level does not originate with him. The whole enterprise of artificial intelligence rests on Newell and Simon's assumption that "A physical symbol system has the necessary and sufficient means for general intelligent action" (see Boden, 1988), which itself can be traced to Turing's analysis on the notion of "computability" (for an introductory review, see Johnson-Laird, 1988). In other words, many different "physical symbol systems" can support intelligence, not just biological ones. This is also the central, though not unchallenged, claim of the functionalist approach to the philosophy of mind (see Churchland [1988] for a good introductory review). Also, Gregory's (1973) emphasis, by way of developing Helmholtz's dictum that "perception is unconscious inference" (*see* VISUAL ILLUSION), on the need to know the *strategies* embodied in a mechanism before one can be said to understand it, is yet another example of the widespread recognition that there is a need for at least one more level of discourse over and above that of hardware.

Marr's achievement was not therefore a new insight that different levels of analysis are required for understanding complex information-processing systems, but a specification for what those levels are and what each should be concerned with. It is of course too soon to tell whether his formulation will endure but Boden (1988), in reviewing the evolving body of computational and psychophysical studies deriving from his work, judged that

> We have here, then, the germ of what Lakatos called a "scientific research programme": a progressive body of hypothesis and experimentation, generated by a central theory that is amended as research proceeds.
>
> (Boden, 1988, p. 75)

Nevertheless, neuroscientists do not always find Marr's three-levels distinction a comfortable one. This may be because neural structures genuinely require a quite different form of analysis, one perhaps in which (at least) the algorithm and hardware levels are inextricably bound up together. Alternatively, it may simply be that a preoccupation with studying the neural mechanisms and phenomena of biological brains tends naturally (if regrettably) toward a neglect of the computational theory level of task analysis, whereas this level is manifestly important when faced with the task of trying to build an "artificial brain" using computers. For computational theorists, the simple demonstration of a "grandmother cell," the classic *reduction ad absurdum* in debates about stimulus encoding by highly specifically tuned neurones, is irrelevant to their principal concern, which is "an answer to how you, or a cell, or anything at all, does it" (Mayhew, 1983, p. 214), not just knowledge of how the concept of grandmother is finally encoded in the brain. Yet another additional factor may be that the training and skills of biologists often render the computational literature rather inaccessible to them because of its mathematical leanings. However, the bridge between the computational and biological literatures is now being traversed more and more often. Indeed, the term "computational neuroscience" has been coined for the difficult but potentially richly rewarding enterprise of placing psychophysical and physiological knowledge about neural systems within a computational framework that provides a detailed analysis of the nature of the task(s) being solved by those systems.

In an entertaining and provocative epilogue with an imaginary interlocutor, Marr (1982) expresses in trenchant terms his view that analysis at the computational theory level has been neglected in much cognitive psychology and also in much artificial intelligence. For example:

As a computing mechanism, a production system [*see* PRODUCTION SYSTEMS] exhibits several interesting ideas – the absence of explicit subroutine calls, a blackboard-like communication channel, and some notion of a short-term memory. However, just because production systems display these side effects does not mean that they have anything to do with what is really going on [in human cognition]. For example, I would guess that the fact that short-term memory can act as a storage register is probably the least important of its functions. I expect that

there are several "intellectual reflexes" that operate on items held there about which nothing is yet known and which will eventually be held to be the crucial things about short-term memory. Studying our performance in close relation to production systems seems to me a waste of time, because it amounts to studying a mechanism, not a problem. Once again, the mechanisms that such research is trying to penetrate will be unravelled by studying the problems that need solving, just as vision research is progressing because it is the problem of vision that is being attacked, not neural visual mechanisms.

(Marr, 1982, p. 348)

As might be expected, such criticisms have not gone unchallenged. For example, Sloman (1980) believes Marr's three-levels assumption is "confused" because it rests on the mistaken belief that the topmost computational level of theorizing can in general be separated from the level of algorithms and the study of representations (see also Morgan, 1984; Boden, 1988). The point at issue here may prove to be a deep one or it may be no more than a matter of terminology. Marr (1982, p. 23) uses the term representation in the context of (level two) discussions of practical design questions about how to devise an effective set of procedures for implementing a set of constraints. An example of such a question is: should a node in the Marr–Poggio neural net stereo algorithm "represent" a dot, or an edge point, or whatever? Others might wish to use the term "representation" in different (more abstract?) senses in (level one) debates about what constraints are available and what mathematical proofs can be demonstrated regarding the implications of those constraints.

This raises a further complaint from Sloman (1980): pursuing Marr's set of levels is likely to divert attention from difficult and messy problems in psychology to relatively simple mathematical problems:

Many of the most important issues in AI have been concerned with the study of trade-offs between ... space and time, efficiency and flexibility, completeness and speed, clarity and robustness. It is possible that such trade-offs are the key to much of the complexity of human and animal psychology, and ultimately neurophysiology. If so, it may be a serious impediment to scientific progress to advocate an over-simple methodological stance.... The rigidity of function of a typical calculator makes it unnecessary for our understanding of it to involve consideration of many layers of implementation or the kinds of trade-offs and mixtures of levels found in human psychology. By contrast, when we study *human* arithmetical expertise (acquired after many years of individual learning), most of the mathematical theory of numbers is an irrelevant digression. Instead we have to consider issues of storing many "partial results", indexing them, linking them to methods of recognising situations where they are applicable, associating them with monitoring processes for detecting slips and mistakes, and so on.

(Sloman, 1980, p. 403)

Marr's answer to this would probably be Yes and No! (One can say only probably, because Marr died from leukemia at the age of 35.) Sloman's list of trade-offs is important and they are exactly the kinds of things that need to be understood at the algorithm and hardware levels. But it is premature to consider their significance via tasks such as mental arithmetic (or chess) which are:

... problems for which human skills are of doubtful quality and in which good performance seems to rest on a huge base of knowledge and expertise. I would argue that these are exceptionally good grounds for *not* yet studying how we carry out such tasks. I have no doubt that when we do mental arithmetic we are doing something well, but it is not arithmetic, and we seem far from understanding even one component of what that something is. I therefore feel we should concentrate on the simpler problems first, for here we have some hope of genuine advancement.

(Marr, 1982, p. 348)

The controversy continues. Marr's book is an excellent and largely nontechnical introduction to his approach over a wide range of vision problems: he and his colleagues did much more than tackle the stereo correspondence problem used as illustration here. Boden (1988) provides an impressively detailed and illuminating discussion of the usefulness both of Marr's strictures and of the computational approach in general to the whole field of cognition. Her book brings out with exceptional force how the language of computation has provided a new way of speaking about cognition, and a conceptual framework which offers the promise of unified treatment of diverse cognitive phenomena (*see* IMAGERY, COMPUTATIONAL THEORY OF). For a more introductory account of cognitive science and the way it has been stimulated by the advent of the digital computer, consult Johnson-Laird's (1988) excellent review.

See also ANALOGIES.

BIBLIOGRAPHY

Boden, M. (1988). *Computer models of mind.* New York: Cambridge University Press.
Churchland, P. M. (1988). *Matter and consciousness* (rev. edn). Cambridge, Mass.: MIT Press.
Frisby, J. P. (1979). *Seeing: Illusion, brain and mind.* Oxford: Oxford University Press.
——. (1990). Computational issues in solving the stereo correspondence problem. In M. Landy & J. A. Movshon (Eds), *Computational models of visual processing* (in press). Cambridge, Mass.: MIT Press.
Johnson-Laird, P. N. (1988). *The computer and the mind: An introduction to cognitive science.* Glasgow: Fontana.
Marr, D. (1982). *Vision.* San Francisco: W. H. Freeman & Co.
——, & Poggio, T. A. (1976). A cooperative computation of stereo disparity. *Science, 194,* 283–7.
——. (1979). A theory of human stereopsis. *Proceedings of the Royal Society of London, B, 204,* 301–28.
Mayhew, J. E. W. (1983). Stereopsis. In O. J. Braddick & A. C. Sleigh (Eds), *Physiological and biological processing of images* (pp. 204–16). Berlin: Springer Verlag.
——, & Frisby, J. P. (1980). Psychophysical and computational studies towards a theory of

human stereopsis. *Artificial Intelligence*, *17*, 349–85.

Morgan, M. J. (1984). Computational theories of vision. (A critical notice of *Vision*, by D. Marr.). *Quarterly Journal of Experimental Psychology*, *36A*, 157–65.

Poggio, G. F., & Poggio, T. (1984). The analysis of stereopsis. *Annual Review of Neuroscience*, *7*, 379–412.

Poggio, T., Torre, V., & Koch, C. (1985). Computational vision and regularisation theory. *Nature*, *317*, 314–19.

Pollard, S. B., Porrill, J., Mayhew, J. E. W., & Frisby, J. P. (1986). Disparity gradient, Lipschitz continuity and computing stereo correspondences. In *Proceedings of the Third International Symposium of Robotics Research*. Gouvieux, France (pp. 19–26). Cambridge, Mass.: MIT Press.

Prazdny, K. (1987). On the coarse-to-fine strategy in stereomatching. *Bulletin of the Psychonomic Society*, *25*, 92–4.

Sloman, A. (1980). What kind of indirect process is visual perception? *The Behavioural & Brain Sciences*, *3*(3), 401–4.

JOHN P. FRISBY

perception, constructivist theories of *See* CONSTRUCTIVIST THEORIES OF PERCEPTION.

perception, direct *See* DIRECT PERCEPTION.

perception, form *See* FORM PERCEPTION.

perception, pattern *See* PATTERN PERCEPTION.

perception, person *See* PERSON PERCEPTION.

perception, speech *See* SPEECH PERCEPTION.

perception, subliminal *See* SUBLIMINAL PERCEPTION.

perception and imagery *See* IMAGERY AND PERCEPTION.

perceptual constancies Perceptual constancies are to be found in various sense modalities; they refer to the fact that our perception of objects, sounds, and so on remains relatively constant in spite of substantial variations in sensory input. If our perception of the properties of objects were completely based upon the information that our sensory receptors receive at any moment, then our world would seem as chaotic as the Wonderland that Alice found at the bottom of the rabbit hole. Consider our visual impressions, for instance (*see* FORM PERCEPTION; PATTERN PERCEPTION). A piece of white paper ought to appear black when viewed in the moonlight, since the amount of light in the image on the retina of your eye is no brighter, under these conditions, than that from a piece of coal viewed in normal room light. Since the retinal image is larger when objects are closer, as we move the piece of paper nearer to us it should appear to increase in size. This same piece of paper would appear to change shape continually as we tilt it, since the retinal image would vary from rectangular to trapezoidal depending upon the inclination. The color of the white paper should also appear to fluctuate, appearing yellow under incandescent lighting, blue in fluorescent light, and white in sunlight. Fortunately, our visual perception of objects is much more *constant* than it would be if the only information available to consciousness was the retinal image itself. Thus, the piece of paper appears to be a white rectangular object with a fixed size, even though you might sense the fact that the light falling on it has changed in intensity or color, or that its distance from you or angle of tilt have changed. These examples illustrate a basic principle of perception, namely that *the properties of objects tend to remain constant in consciousness even though our perception of the viewing conditions may change*.

There are many different types of perceptual constancies. One set includes specific object properties, such as an object's size, shape, color, or the whiteness of its surface;

another set pertains to the location of the object relative to the observer's body. Each is named on the basis of the aspect of the object that remains unchanged. Thus, "size constancy" refers to the fact that the size of the object remains unchanged in perception despite the fact that the retinal image size changes, "color constancy" refers to the fact that object color remains unchanged despite changes in the color of the illumination, and so forth.

To understand how constancies come about it is important to recognize that each constancy may be analyzed into two major stages of operation. In the first stage we have "registration," a function in which changes in the sensory input are encoded for further processing. The individual is not necessarily consciously aware of this registration process. The second stage of processing involves "apprehension," or the actual subjective experience. Apprehension refers to the conscious component of your perceptual experience that is available for you to describe. Under normal conditions, registration is oriented toward a "focal stimulus," which simply refers to the object that you are paying attention to. While you are registering the focal stimulus you will also be registering many of the stimuli that are nearby, or stimuli that reach your sensory receptors around the same time. These additional stimuli form the "stimulus context." During apprehension you become aware of two different classes of properties. The first involves the "object properties" of the focal stimulus. These include the size, shape, and color of the object, which are the properties that tend to remain constant in consciousness. The second set involves "situation properties," which include the more changeable aspects of the environment, such as your distance from the object or the amount or color of the available light. Situation properties are derived from cues found in the context.

All of this may sound a bit complicated in theory, but in practice it is really quite straightforward. To see how the various categories of stimuli interact, refer to Table 1. It describes the various sets of stimuli for several different constancies and is based upon Coren

and Ward's (1989) treatment of this problem. To understand how to use this table let us consider "size constancy" as an example. Notice that the focal stimulus (what you pay attention to) is the size of the retinal image of the object. The context stimuli are all of the surrounding cues that indicate the distance of the object. Although you process these stimuli during the registration phase, you are generally not consciously aware of them. During the apprehension stage, you become aware of two aspects of the object, one that changes and one that does not. In size constancy it is the object's size that remains invariant while its distance changes.

The context is very important for each of the constancies. Thus, for size constancy, if we remove the cues that indicate the distance of the object, constancy breaks down. Now changes in distance result in the perception of the size of the object changing as the retinal image size increases or decreases (e.g. Harvey & Leibowitz, 1967; Chevrier & Delorme, 1983). Furthermore, if the viewing conditions are strange, and the context is unfamiliar or unusual, constancy fails (Day, Stuart, & Dickinson, 1980). To see your size constancy break down you need only climb to the top of a tall building and you will see that people below appear to be tiny dolls and automobiles appear to be toy cars. This is because the far distance, and unusual viewing angle (from the top) make the context less interpretable, and size constancy can not be maintained.

The perceptual constancies, then, are a complex set of "corrections" based upon the availability of context stimuli. They take into account the ongoing conditions and allow us to extract a stable set of object properties from the continuous flow of changing sensory inputs at our receptors. Were it not for the perceptual constancy corrections, objects would have no permanent properties in consciousness at all, but would change in size, shape, lightness, and color, with every move that we make or with every change in environmental conditions.

BIBLIOGRAPHY

Chevrier, J., & Delorme, A. (1983). Depth

Table 1 Various perceptual constancies depend upon the registration of focal and context stimuli, which in turn results in apprehension of a constant and a change aspect in conscious perception (adapted from Coren & Ward, 1989).

	REGISTRATION (the encoding of the information at the sensory receptors)		APPREHENSION (our conscious impression of the object's properties)	
Constancy Name	*Focal Stimulus*	*Stimulus Context*	*Constant (object properties)*	*Changes (situation properties)*
Size constancy	Retinal image size	Distance cues	Object size	Object distance
Shape constancy	Retinal image shape	Orientation cues	Object shape	Object orientation
Lightness constancy	Intensity of light on the retina	Illumination cues	Surface whiteness intensity	Apparent illumination
Color constancy	Color of retinal image	Illumination cues	Surface color	Apparent illumination color
Position constancy	Retinal location of image	Sensed head or eye position	Object position in space	Head or eye position
Loudness constancy	Intensity of sound at the ear	Distance cues	Loudness of sound	Distance from sound

perception in Pandora's box and size illusion: Evolution with age. *Perception, 12,* 177–85.

Coren, S., & Ward, L. M. (1989). *Sensation and perception* (3rd edn). San Diego: Harcourt Brace Jovanovich.

Day, R. H., Stuart, G. W., & Dickinson, R. G. (1980). Size constancy does not fail below half a degree. *Perception & Psychophysics, 28,* 263–5.

Harvey, L. O. Jr., & Leibowitz, H. (1967). Effects of exposure duration, cue reduction, and temporary monocularity on size matching at short distances. *Journal of the Optical Society of America, 57,* 249–53.

STANLEY COREN

perceptual development This term is concerned with the systematic changes in perceptual abilities and processes manifested by children as they develop. "Perception" and "cognition" are often distinguished in that the former refers to the basic detection and processing of sensory information, while cognition refers to the ability to extract sense, order, and meaning from this information – i.e. what sense does the infant make of what is seen or heard? While this distinction, in practice, is often difficult to make, the theme "from sensation to cognition" is a focus of this entry, which concentrates particularly on visual perception. This bias is justified on the grounds that vision is the modality whose development has been most explored, and it can be argued that it is the most important of the senses. Coordination between the senses, and the senses of taste, olfaction, and audition, are discussed later.

BASIC VISUAL CAPACITIES

As we might expect, the visual information detected by the newborn is very impoverished when compared with that detected by the adult. Sensitivity to contrast differences is poor. A black and white pattern gives a contrast approaching 100 percent, and under good viewing conditions adults can discriminate between shades of gray giving contrast values of less than 1 percent; a contrast value of 30–40 percent is close to the newborn's threshold of detectability. Visual acuity, the ability to detect fine detail, is also poor. The most commonly used procedure to measure visual acuity is the visual preference method, where black and white stripes (gratings) are shown to the infant paired with an equal luminance gray patch: the width of the stripes is progressively reduced and when the infant no longer looks at the stripes in preference to the gray patch it is assumed that the acuity threshold has been reached. Acuity estimates for newborns measured in this way are about 1 cycle per degree, equivalent to the ability to detect stripes 2 mm wide shown at a distance of 30 cm from the eyes. This level of acuity is, curiously, not too different from that for the adult cat (about 3 cycles per degree), and acuity improves quickly in the postnatal months so that adult levels (30–40 cycles per degree) are reached sometime after six months of age.

Other basic visual capacities are present at, or develop shortly after, birth. Accommodation, the ability to focus on objects at different distances, improves along with changes in acuity, so that from two months, or earlier, all normal infants alter their accommodation in the appropriate direction as the distance of a visual target changes.

Newborn infants have some degree of color vision. Adams, Maurer, and Davis (1986) reported that newborns differentiated gray from green, from yellow, and from red: for each of these colors they preferred color and gray checkerboards to gray squares matched for overall luminance. However, the newborns showed no evidence of discriminating between gray and blue. While we do not yet have a detailed account of its development, it seems likely that adult-like color vision is present by about three months of age.

By being physically separated in space the two eyes provide slightly different images of the perceived world. Detection of these differences, or disparities, provides the basis for an important binocular cue to depth, known as stereopsis, and several studies suggest that stereoscopic depth perception emerges around three months of age (see Braddick &

Atkinson, 1983). However, the ability to detect disparity differences does not necessarily mean that they specify different depths to the infant, although, of course, they may do so. Other studies, described later, have given more definite evidence of depth perception in infants.

EARLY VISUAL PERCEPTION

From birth, infants make eye movements which regularly shift fixation from one part of the visual world to another, and the patterning and direction of these eye movements suggest that at all ages infants must be considered to be active seekers of stimulation. Newborn infants, when shown pairs of stimuli, will display consistent preferences between them, in the sense of looking more at one member of the pair: for example, they will prefer moving to stationary, large to small, three-dimensional to two-dimensional, high contrast to low contrast stimuli (Slater, 1989). One procedure that has proven to be particularly useful in uncovering infants' discriminatory abilities is "habituation": if one stimulus is presented repeatedly over a period of time infants will spend progressively less time looking at it, and they will often subsequently "dishabituate" (show recovery of attention) when a different, novel stimulus is shown. This procedure works with infants from birth. For example, after newborns had been habituated to one of four simple geometric shapes (a square, cross, circle, or triangle), they gave novelty preferences when the familiar shape was paired with one they had not seen before. While this is evidence of early shape discrimination, the basis of the discrimination is unclear since any two shapes will differ in features such as orientation of lines and angles, overall size, density of contour, enclosed versus open, and so on. These sorts of "low order" variables are discriminated by newborns and it is likely that they are discriminating between configurations on the basis of these features rather than on the basis of "true" form perception. An experiment by Cohen and Younger (1984) illustrates this. Six- and fourteen-week-old infants were habituated to a simple stimulus consisting of two connected lines which made either an acute (45°) or obtuse (135°) angle. On subsequent test trials the six-week-olds dishabituated to a change in the orientation of the lines (where the angle remained unchanged), but *not* to a change in angle alone, while the fourteen-week-olds did the opposite in that they recovered attention to a change in angle, but not to a change in orientation. This suggests that shape perception in infants six weeks and younger may be dominated by attention to lower order variables such as orientation. However, from two months of age infants are able to perceive angular relationships, which may be the basic elements or building blocks of perception. Beyond about two months of age infants begin to demonstrate the ability to perceive wholes, rather than parts of visual stimuli and to classify and categorize stimuli on the basis of perceiving similarities and differences between different examples – for example, recognizing that several different rectangles are members of a class separate from a square or a circle.

We have seen earlier that sensitivity to binocular disparity, stereopsis, as a cue to depth, appears around three months of age. Motion-carried, or "kinetic" depth cues are responded to even earlier. Newborn infants will selectively fixate a three-dimensional stimulus in preference to a photograph of the same stimulus, even when they are restricted to monocular viewing and the major depth cue is motion parallax. Appreciation of pictorial depth cues – those cues to depth that are found in static scenes such as might be found in photographs – has been found from about five months. One such cue is relative size, the larger of two otherwise identical figures usually being perceived as the closer. Yonas, Cleaves, and Pettersen (1978) used the "Ames window," a trapezoidal window rotated around its vertical axis. When adults view the two-dimensional Ames window monocularly a powerful illusion is perceived of a slanted window with one side (the larger) closer than the other. Yonas et al. reported that six-month-old infants wearing an eye patch (to remove binocular information) are twice as likely to reach for the larger side of the distorted window than for the smaller side, suggesting that this depth cue is detected by this age.

Important organizational features of visual perception are the visual constancies, such as brightness, size, and shape constancy, and these are probably present at birth (*see* PERCEPTUAL CONSTANCIES). Evidence of shape constancy at birth was reported by Slater and Morison (1985). They familiarized newborns (mean age 1 day, 23 hours) to a shape, either a square or a trapezium, which changed in slant during the familiarization trials. On subsequent test trials the newborns gave a strong novelty preference for a different shape when this was paired with the familiarized shape, the latter in a different orientation from any seen earlier. This experiment gives clear evidence of infants' response to distal cues from birth.

Finally in this section we will consider perception of the human face. The face is three-dimensional and contains regions of high contrast and when seen by the infant the face is usually animated or moving. These aspects of stimulation are highly salient to newborn and older infants, which ensures that the face will be attention getting and holding, but the interesting question is whether there is a predisposition to respond to the face other than as a collection of stimuli. The question becomes, "Do infants have an innate perceptual knowledge of the face?" There is no easy answer to this question, but certain lines of evidence suggest that we can offer a tentative "yes." Newborns quickly learn some of the characteristics of faces and, 49 hours from birth, they show a reliable preference for their mother's face when paired with that of an adult female stranger. Such evidence of early learning may be only a specific example of a more general learning ability, and we need to look elsewhere for convincing evidence of a special response to the face. Perhaps the most compelling evidence is the suggestion that newborns will imitate adult facial gestures. An early report of neonatal imitation of mouth opening, tongue protrusion, and lip pursing was that of Meltzoff and Moore (1977). Similar reports of newborn facial imitation have also appeared, which implies that infants have an inborn representation of the face on to which they can map their own facial movements.

OBJECTS, EVENTS, AND ENCOUNTERS

From the 1970s there has been a growing increase in the number of studies which have shown moving and changing "dynamic" stimuli to their infant subjects. Much of this research is inspired by Gibson's theory of DIRECT PERCEPTION. According to Gibson, perception of basic stimulus invariants is direct in that it does not need enhancing as a result of particular experiences. In line with this approach many researchers have argued that visual perception is most meaningful, and is most meaningfully studied, under conditions of change. A few illustrative experiments are described here.

Kellman, Spelke, and Short (1986) described a series of experiments investigating young infants' perception of partly occluded objects. Four-month-old infants were habituated to a stimulus, usually a rod, which moved back and forth behind a block which occluded its center portion. Following habituation, the babies were shown two test displays without the occluder, one being the complete rod, the other being the top and bottom parts of the rod, with a central gap where the occluder had been. On these test trials the infants looked more at the *discontinuous* stimulus (the two rod pieces), suggesting that they had seen the object as being connected or complete behind the occluder in the habituation trials – i.e. they were "filling in" the unseen portions of the rod. Baillargeon, Spelke, and Wasserman (1985) reported that five-month-old infants appreciated the continued existence of a *completely* invisible object. Their babies were shown a solid block, which was then hidden by a screen, but which should have prevented or blocked a moving drawbridge from traveling through a full 180° rotation. They spent more time looking at the "impossible" complete 180° rotation than at a "possible" 120° rotation, suggesting that they were aware not only of the block's continued existence behind the screen, but that they "knew" that its presence constituted an obstacle to the drawbridge's movement.

These experiments investigated infants' understanding of occluded objects by using what have been called "events," defined as dynamic changes to the optic array which do not require activities of the infant observers. An "encounter" is where the observer is actively involved, and an example of infants' responses to encounters is in the "moving room" procedure, in which the whole of the visual environment moves relative to the infant. Butterworth and Cicchetti (1978) tested infants who were seated or held inside a small room in which the floor (and the baby) was stationary, but the three walls and the ceiling were made to move toward and away from the baby. In these studies the babies (like adults) lose balance, and the loss of balance is always appropriate to the direction of movement (i.e. if the room moves toward them they sway, or lurch forward). Under normal circumstances the flow patterns of visual information that occur in the "moving room" correspond to those that occur when the baby moves, or sways backward and forward: their presence in the absence of the baby's movement disrupts the infant's normal, visually guided, postural control.

In summary, babies enter the world with an immature visual system, but the basic visual capacities develop quickly in early infancy. The immediate visual input is that which impinges upon the flat, two-dimensional retinae, but at no age do infants perceive a two-dimensional world, and from birth infants perceive *distal* cues in the sense of perceiving the world "out there" rather than responding only to proximal retinal cues. Visual perception is active and organized at birth, and babies soon learn to perceive shapes as wholes, and to classify and categorize visual stimuli. Studies of "dynamic" perception tell us that from birth infants use visual information to guide their own movements in the world, and that by four or five months they perceive a world of coherent, spatially connected, unified, whole, and permanent objects.

COORDINATION BETWEEN THE SENSES

There is evidence that the senses are coordinated from birth. We can distinguish at least two types of sensory coordination. One is where information from one modality specifies or has consequences for information from another. Examples are visually guided reaching, or turning in the direction of a sound source. With respect to the latter, Butterworth (1983) has argued that when newborn babies turn their eyes in the direction of a sound stimulus they *expect* the sound to have a visual consequence – i.e. they expect to see the thing that produced the sound. This suggests that, from birth, infants can differentiate the sensory information given by the different modalities. A second type of sensory coordination is where different modalities provide equivalent information. Meltzoff and Borton (1979) gave evidence for the detection of intersensory equivalence in a habituation experiment. One-month-olds were familiarized to one of two dummies (pacifiers), the dummy being placed in the babies' mouths. One dummy had a smooth nipple while the other, nubby nipple, had protuberances on it. Following familiarization the babies were shown visual replicas of the two dummies and they showed a reliable visual preference for the one they had previously perceived orally. This experiment gives evidence of early intermodal matching, supporting the view that there is an innate unity of the senses.

TASTE, OLFACTION, AND AUDITION

Research on taste and olfaction has concentrated on newborn infants, with a paucity of research in the later months of infancy. The newborn infant is as well equipped with taste buds as at any later time in life, and distinguishes between the four basic taste sensations – sweet, salty, sour, and bitter – as shown by differential sucking and ingestion of solutions, and by facial gestures. While taste has a number of "primary" sensations this does not appear to be the case for olfaction, and perhaps because of this infants' responses to a great variety of chemical olfactory stimuli have been studied. Space does not permit a detailed description of these studies: suffice it to say that the sense of smell is clearly active from birth. There is also evidence that newborns will learn about and orient toward preferred odours: Macfarlane (1975) found that six-day-old infants would orient toward their mother's breast pad in preference to one from another lactating mother. The chemical senses are probably important in the early control of feeding and serve to enhance the intake of nutritious foods and to inhibit ingestion of non-nutritive, harmful, or toxic substances.

After vision, hearing is the modality which has received the greatest attention, and much of the research has focused on SPEECH PERCEPTION. While the foetus experiences an auditory environment that is quite different from that of the adult, there is good evidence both for auditory perception, and for learning about auditory stimuli, before birth. DeCasper and Spence (1986) had pregnant women recite a passage of speech aloud, in a quiet room, every day during the last six weeks of pregnancy. Shortly after birth (an average of 2 days 8 hours) the infants preferred the mother's previously recited passage to one spoken by a female stranger: in this experiment "preference" was indexed by the baby being more prepared to change sucking patterns to hear the mother's voice. While auditory thresholds at birth are much higher than for adults, it is known that thresholds reduce during infancy, and that infants display good discrimination between stimuli that differ in intensity and/or pitch during the first year.

Infants also make discriminations between speech sounds which may suggest that they are innately attuned to the phonetic characteristics of human speech. For example, there is an auditory continuum known as voice-onset time (VOT) which separates pairs of phonetic units – i.e. /ba/ and /pa/, /ga/ and /ka/, /ta/ and /da/ – and infants as young as one month discriminate these sounds across the boundaries of the continuum, but not within categories. More recently it has been discovered that other species, including chinchillas, rhesus monkeys, and Japanese monkeys (Macaques), give the same discrimination performance, perhaps suggesting that as language evolved it capitalized on general auditory perceptual mechanisms for sound discrimination, rather than developing specific mechanisms for processing speech (Kuhl & Padden, 1982).

The fine distinctions between general auditory, and speech-specific, mechanisms will exercise researchers in the years to come.

It cannot be doubted, however, that human infants are uniquely predisposed to acquire speech (*see* LANGUAGE ACQUISITION). Since research on young infants has focused on their discrimination between isolated speech sounds, we do not know when they discriminate words as separate auditory segments. However, comprehension of speech sounds is clearly present in the second half of the first year, and the baby's first words are uttered toward the end of the first year, indicating responsivity to word meanings from an early age.

CONCLUSION: FROM SENSATION TO PERCEPTION TO COGNITION

The senses are functioning from birth and, where opportunity allows, are functioning *in utero*. No modality operates at adult-like levels at birth, but such levels are achieved surprisingly early in infancy, leading to recent conceptualizations of the "competent infant." Infants' COGNITIVE DEVELOPMENT begins before birth, and the senses provide information for the gradual organization and construction of a coherent world. It is never easy to draw a distinction between perception and cognition, but a reasonable view is that early perceptual competence is matched by cognitive incompetence, and that much of the reorganization of perceptual representation is dependent upon the development and construction of cognitive structures that give access to a world of objects, people, language, and events.

See also PERCEPTUAL MOTOR COORDINATION; PIAGET, JEAN.

BIBLIOGRAPHY

Adams, R. J., Maurer, D., & Davis, M. (1986). Newborns' discrimination of chromatic from achromatic stimuli. *Journal of Experimental Child Psychology, 41*, 267–81.

Baillargeon, R., Spelke, E. S., & Wasserman, S. (1985). Object permanence in five-month-old infants. *Cognition, 20*, 191–208.

Braddick, O. J., & Atkinson, J. (1983). Some recent findings on the development of human binocularity: A review. *Behavioural Brain Research, 10*, 71–80.

Butterworth, G. E. (1983). Structure of the mind in human infancy. In L. P. Lipsitt & C. K. Rovee-Collier (Eds), *Advances in infancy research* (Vol. 2). Norwood, NJ: Ablex Publishing Corp.

— —, & Cicchetti, D. (1978). Visual calibration of posture in normal and motor retarded Down's Syndrome infants. *Perception, 7*, 513–25.

Cohen, L. B., & Younger, B. A. (1984). Infant perception of angular relations. *Infant Behavior and Development, 7*, 37–47.

DeCasper, A. J., & Spence, M. J. (1986). Prenatal maternal speech influences newborns' perception of speech sounds. *Infant Behavior and Development, 9*, 133–50.

Kellman, P. J., Spelke, E. S., & Short, K. R. (1986). Infant perception of object unity from translatory motion in depth and vertical translation. *Child Development, 57*, 72–86.

Kuhl, P. K., & Padden, D. M. (1982). Enhanced discriminability at the phonetic boundaries for the voicing feature in macaques. *Perception and Psychophysics, 32*, 542–50.

Macfarlane, A. (1975). Olfaction in the development of social preferences in the human neonate. In *Parent–infant interaction* (CIBA Foundation Symposium 33). Amsterdam: Elsevier.

Meltzoff, A. N., & Borton, R. W. (1979). Intermodal matching by human neonates. *Nature, 282*, 403–4.

Meltzoff, A. N., & Moore, M. K. (1977). Imitation of facial and manual gestures by human neonates. *Science, 198*, 75–8.

Slater, A. (1989). Visual memory and perception in early infancy. In A. Slater & G. Bremner (Eds), *Infant development*. Sussex: Erlbaum.

— —, & Morison, V. (1985). Shape constancy and slant perception at birth. *Perception, 14*, 337–44.

Yonas, A., Cleaves, N., & Pettersen, L. (1978). Development of sensitivity to pictorial depth. *Science, 200*, 77–9.

A. M. SLATER

perceptual motor coordination This expression refers to our ability to generate appropriate muscular commands so that our limbs reach positions in space specified by our perceptual systems. We demonstrate this ability effortlessly all the time, but analyzing an apparently simple action like reaching out and picking up a glass allows us to appreciate the difficulties involved in perceptual motor coordination.

First, we must represent the position of the glass and the hand that is going to grasp it in terms of a common set of coordinates. The primary source of perceptual information about the position of the glass is the image on the retina. But the position of the image does not specify the position of the object in space because the eye can move in its orbit and the head can rotate about the trunk. To know where the glass is relative to the major body axes we must combine information about the retinal position of the image with proprioceptive information about the rotation of the eye relative to the head, and the rotation of the head relative to the body. Further, proprioceptive information is then required to identify where the various segments of the arm are, relative to the same body axes.

Second, we need to have learnt mapping rules which will specify what muscular commands will take the limb from its current position to the target. By combining the inputs about the position of the glass and the various limb segments with these mapping rules it is possible to generate a motor program which will move the different segments in such a way that the hand arrives at the glass. The program must also contain precise instructions to open and close the fingers at the right time, and in the right orientation, to ensure that the glass is grasped rather than knocked over. During the movement visual feedback about the position of the arm may indicate that an adjustment is required to some program parameter. The program must be structured in such a way these modifications can be incorporated into the program during execution.

This complex sequence of events has been investigated with a wide range of the techniques available to experimental psychology. I will review a number of these approaches.

PRISM ADAPTATION EXPERIMENTS

One component of perceptual motor coordination is the mapping rules which specify the relation between positions in space generated by the perceptual system and motor commands which will move a limb to that position. These have to be learnt initially, and as limbs grow and change size, they have to be modified. One way of investigating this process has been prism adaptation experiments. In these an adult with fully developed perceptual motor coordination views the world through prisms which distort the sensory input. The process of learning to adapt to the new relation between visual input and the appropriate motor output (i.e. learning to modify the mapping rules) can then be studied.

If you view the world through a prism the apparent position of an object is displaced from its real position. In the earliest and most famous of these adaptation studies, Stratton wore prisms which inverted his view of the world. He found that he learnt to adapt to this distortion in the course of a few days and could carry out normal actions successfully. Modern studies tend to use a more controlled version of this task with a wedge prism which produces a simple lateral displacement of the viewed world. If one points at an object viewed through such a prism without being able to see the hand, it will point at the apparent position rather than the real position. With feedback about the error people quickly adapt (i.e. adjust the mapping between sensory input and motor output) and point in the correct direction. If the prisms are then removed, initial movements show a compensatory error in the opposite direction, the result of learning to adjust for the distortion produced by the prism. The correct mapping is quickly relearnt if feedback is available about the error. It appears that adaptation takes place by adjustment of both the sensory and motor components of the mapping process. Following a well known series of experiments by Held in the 1960s it was believed that adaptation only took place if the subject actively moved his or her arm. It now seems that although active movement is the most effective way to produce adaptation, it can still occur if the limbs are moved passively. (For a review of prism adaptation experiments, see Howard, 1982.)

The results of prism adaptation experiments suggest that sensory signals specifying target position, the instructions to muscles, and the consequences of the movements are all stored in such a way that they allow mapping rules to emerge as an average consensus of past experience. It is clear that the rules are expressed in such a way that they can be used to generate plausible movements by extrapolation from similar situations experienced previously in novel situations. This form of storage demonstrates a general functional property of the nervous system for which Bartlett coined the term "schema" (*see* BARTLETT, SIR FREDERIC; SCHEMATA). We store our past experience in such a way that we can benefit from any general regularities which it exhibits, not just from the exact repetition of past situations. Bartlett pointed out the advantage of such a system by analyzing tennis strokes. Each one is played in a circumstance which is similar but not identical to past examples. The ideal memory system must allow us to benefit from the similar experiences in the past, without being affected by the fact that the circumstances are not an exact match. The design of physical systems which demonstrate this property (i.e. the ability to generalize from similar but not identical instances) is a major topic of current investigation (*see* CONNECTIONIST MODELS OF MEMORY).

DEVELOPMENTAL STUDIES

Prism adaptation experiments emphasize the fact that the mechanism which maps sensory space on to motor action is one which learns and adapts easily. It is not hardwired in humans as it is in some simpler organisms which never learn to adapt to distorted sensory input. However, experiments with neonates show that it has some wired-in structure even in humans. Newborns will follow moving targets with appropriate eye and head movements (*see* PERCEPTUAL DEVELOPMENT). Remarkably, they also have the ability to imitate certain facial gestures such as protrusion of the tongue. This requires a specific sensory to motor mapping as well as a complex level of visual analysis.

Visual experience quickly allows complex mappings between visual information and motor action to develop. Hofsten (1983) has shown that by the age of five months infants make appropriate preparatory orientation of

the hand when about to grasp objects of different shapes; they can time the moment of hand closing to coincide with the moment when they will touch an object they are trying to grasp; and they can launch a successful anticipatory movement to intercept an object coming past them at 30 cm/sec.

USE OF VISUAL FEEDBACK

Prism adaptation experiments study the mapping between position specified by our sensory system and the motor actions used to program reaching movements toward those positions. Such movements can be modified by visual feedback once they have been launched. Two points have received much attention. The first is that there is a speed–error trade-off – faster movements are less accurate. The second is that a certain minimum time is required for feedback to be processed and modify the movement.

The most influential modern study of these effects was by Paul Fitts in 1954. His subjects had to move a stylus as quickly as they could from a start button to a target. Fitts varied the width of the target and the amplitude of the movement from the start to the center of the target. For a given degree of accuracy, movement time was greater for larger movements or smaller targets. He found that the following relation between movement time (*MT*), target width (*W*), and movement amplitude (*A*) fitted the data:

$$MT = a + b\log_2(2A/W)$$

where *a* and *b* are constants.

This relation is called Fitts' law. True to the spirit of his time Fitts assumed that the significant fact here was the logarithmic relationship between movement time and task difficulty and interpreted his result in terms of information theory. More recently various authors have found that the somewhat implausible application of information theory to movement control is not necessary because the data can be modeled by assuming that the movement is controlled by visual feedback. The relation between speed and accuracy is predicted by models which assume continuous correction to the movement, or intermittent corrections, or an initial ballistic movement and a single terminal correction. If the experimenter requires the movement to be made in a precise time, rather than ending in a precise place, then a linear trade-off between speed and accuracy is found in place of Fitts' logarithmic one. In this case the origin of the speed–accuracy trade-off appears to be the increased variability of the impulse required to drive faster movements.

Corrections take time to make. In many experiments it has been found that about 200 milliseconds elapse between an unpredictable visual signal appearing and the production of an appropriate response. This lag in the human information-processing system can be readily seen in many games; a ball which swings late is very hard to hit in cricket, it is difficult to adjust a shot to a net-cord in tennis, an unpredictable jab by a boxer cannot be dodged. A review of explanations of Fitts' law, and of the time to react to unpredictable stimuli, can be found in Chapter 3 of Jeannerod (1988).

TRACKING AND MANUAL CONTROL

The lag in responding to unpredictable visual events also sets a limit on the performance of the human operator in any control system where rapid response is required to visual signals. With inputs which vary at more than about 1 Hz, human response lags so far behind the input that the controller would often do better if he or she put no input into the system at all. Studies of the human in the control loop have revealed a number of ways in which people can overcome this intrinsic limitation. Given either a statistically predictable stimulus, or preview of upcoming stimuli, people can prepare a response in advance and fire it off at the appropriate time, thereby overcoming their reaction time lag completely. Thus, for example, when approaching a corner a skillful driver prepares his or her movement of the steering wheel beforehand and executes it to coincide with arrival at the bend.

The picture which emerges from studies of the human operator as a system controller is of a hierarchy of levels of visual motor control. Given preview of the input to come, or memory of previous similar situations, plausible outputs can be generated in open-loop mode, i.e. without using the error signal present at the time. If this response is not quite correct any residual error will be removed by a closed-loop servo mechanism. A review of the visual motor performance of the human operator in manual control systems which does not rely on complex mathematical or engineering concepts is Pew (1974).

THE GIBSONIAN PERSPECTIVE

A different approach to studying the relation between vision and action was pioneered by J. J. Gibson (see DIRECT PERCEPTION). He emphasized the importance of the optic flow field at the eye as an individual moved through the environment. Gibson maintained that the information required for many actions is specified by some property of the optic flow field. Thus, for example, if the optic flow field in peripheral vision streams forward one is probably falling over backward and should make an appropriate postural adjustment. (It has been shown experimentally that manipulating optic flow fields by moving walls of rooms does indeed make people stagger, i.e. it induces them to make inappropriate postural adjustments.)

One of the goals of Gibson's followers has been to discover situations in which there are invariant properties of the optic flow field which are always sufficient to specify appropriate action. An interesting discovery of this sort is that as an object approaches an observer, its time of arrival is given by the ratio of the size of the retinal image to the rate of expansion of the image. The key point is that it is not necessary to know the object's distance or speed or size. Time of arrival is specified by the optic flow field on the retina irrespective of any property of the object. Thus, for example, all objects arriving in 1 sec. will give the same ratio of retinal size to retinal velocity whether they are near and slow, or far and fast. For many acts relative to approaching objects the time of arrival is sufficient for controlling action. We either wish to move before it arrives (e.g. avoid it) or we wish to act at its moment of arrival (e.g. grasp it or hit it). Lee has suggested that the optically specified time-of-arrival variable controls a wide range of behavior from hitting approaching balls and controlling gait to deciding when to brake while driving a car. He has also suggested that it is used by diving sea-birds to ensure that they fold their wings before they hit the sea. These ideas are explored in more detail in Lee (1980).

Gibson and his followers have made some important and interesting observations about the relation between perception and action. However, the views of Gibson himself frequently seem somewhat obscure to readers who are not already convinced that he is right. And the framework in which Gibsonians operate deliberately avoids many of the concepts used by others studying perceptual motor coordination, so it is often difficult to relate work in orthodox and Gibsonian traditions. An introduction (by a non-Gibsonian) can be found in Bruce and Green (1985). Some of Gibson's own ideas can be found in Gibson (1979).

PATIENT STUDIES

It appears from studies of brain damaged patients that one region, the posterior part of the parietal lobe, plays a particularly important part in visual motor coordination (see COG-NITIVE NEUROPSYCHOLOGY). Patients with damage to this area often show difficulty in tasks such as pointing to an object, although they have no serious visual or motor deficits. The problem appears to be in *mapping* visual information on to motor commands rather than in the visual system or the motor system themselves.

Patients with unilateral parietal lesions show normal pointing with the arm under control of the undamaged hemisphere. With the arm controlled by the damaged hemisphere, pointing without visual feedback is systematically distorted away from the target. But with visual feedback, pointing will often be accurate, although slow and with an abnormal pattern of acceleration and deceleration. This observation supports the separation suggested for normal movement control between a mechanism which generates a program by mapping perceptual space on to motor space, and a separate mechanism which can use feedback to correct a movement already underway. A further dissociation, between the

mechanism required to point accurately and that required to grasp the object correctly once the hand has reached the target, is suggested by patients who have one skill but lack the other. It seems that these two parts of the reaching motor program are specified independently. A review of results found in patients with visuo-motor coordination problems, and animal work relating to them, can be found in Jeannerod (1988).

EYE MOVEMENTS

In terms of the underlying neurology the best understood perceptual motor system is that which controls eye movements. One of the roles of this system is to keep an object of interest centered on the fovea, the part of the retina which can perform detailed discrimination, as either the observer or the object moves. The neural circuits which compute retinal slip as the image moves off the fovea are known, as are those which produce corrective signals for the muscles which move the eye. This system is discussed in detail in Miles and Evarts (1979) and Gouras (1985).

See also MOTOR CONTROL AND LEARNING.

BIBLIOGRAPHY

Bruce, V., & Green, P. (1985). *Visual perception: Physiology, psychology and ecology.* London: Lawrence Erlbaum.

Gibson, J. J. (1979). *The ecological approach to visual perception.* Boston: Houghton Mifflin. (Republished in 1986: Hillsdale, NJ: Lawrence Erlbaum.)

Gouras, P. (1985). Oculomotor system. In E. Kandel & J. Schwartz (Eds), *Principles of neural science* (2nd edn) (pp. 571–83). New York: Elsevier.

Hofsten, C. von (1983). Catching skills in infancy. *Journal of Experimental Psychology: Human Perception and Performance, 9,* 75–85.

Howard, I. (1982). *Human visual orientation.* Chichester: Wiley.

Jeannerod, M. (1988). *The neural and behavioural organisation of goal-directed movements.* Oxford: Oxford University Press.

Lee, D. (1980). The optic flow field: The foundation of vision. *Philosophical Transactions of the Royal Society of London, B, 290,* 169–79.

Miles, F., & Evarts, E. (1979). Concepts of

motor organization. *Annual Review of Psychology*, 30, 327–62.

Pew, R. (1974). Human perceptual motor performance. In B. Kantowitz (Ed.), *Human information processing*, pp. 1–39. Hillsdale, NJ: Lawrence Erlbaum.

PETER MCLEOD

perceptual organization, Gestalt principles of *See* GESTALT PRINCIPLES OF PERCEPTUAL ORGANIZATION.

personality and cognition Because substantial individual differences exist in cognitive functioning, any complete theory of cognition must account for these differences; among the numerous relevant dimensions of individual differences are those relating to personality. Although personality theorists have diverse views about which personality dimensions or traits are most important, they generally agree that personality traits not only are semi-permanent dispositions to feel and to behave in certain ways, but also relate to individual differences in the emotional, motivational, and intellectual spheres (*see* INTELLIGENCE).

There are various valuable reasons for studying the relationship between personality and cognition. First, the study helps to account for and to understand individual differences in cognitive performance. If personality is not considered, then individual differences in cognitive performance are usually relegated to the error term in analyses of variance. The introduction of personality variables offers the possibility of accounting for at least some of the error variance.

Second, the study of personality and cognition can clarify theoretical controversies in cognitive psychology. Suppose, for example, that two separate tasks allegedly measure the same underlying theoretical construct. If a given personality dimension or trait is consistently related to performance on one of those tasks but not on the other, then the implication is that the two tasks are not equivalent measures of the same construct.

Third, it is often theoretically fruitful to consider personality dimensions or traits from the cognitive perspective. For instance, individuals differ in their characteristic level of anxiety or trait anxiety (Spielberger, Gorsuch, & Lushene, 1970). Analysis of the differences in cognitive functioning between individuals high and low in trait anxiety is useful not only because it is relevant to a description of what is meant by having high or low trait anxiety, but also because it may contribute to an understanding of the development of the anxious or the non-anxious personality. If these differences do play a part, then they may be pertinent to explaining individual differences in trait anxiety.

DIMENSIONS OF PERSONALITY

While it is not true that as many dimensions of personality exist as do personality traits, it sometimes appears to be nearly true. Despite the myriad of personality dimensions that have been postulated, many of them overlap substantially with one another (H. J. Eysenck & M. W. Eysenck, 1985). The three independent "superfactors" of introversion–extraversion, stability–neuroticism, and psychoticism define a central three-dimensional personality space. The great majority of other personality dimensions or traits that other theorists have proposed can be related to this three-dimensional framework. Thus, for example, trait anxiety not only correlates highly with neuroticism, but also shows a modest negative correlation with extraversion.

Introversion–extraversion, neuroticism–stability, and psychoticism can be regarded as the major personality factors, at least so far as individual differences in emotional and motivational terms are concerned. However, other theoretical approaches are based on a broader definition of personality and attempt to identify so-called cognitive styles that distinguish one person from another. One of the best known of these cognitive styles is field dependence–independence (Witkin et al., 1954). In essence, field-dependent individuals are said to be less "psychologically differentiated" from others and from the external environment than field-independent individuals. Field-dependent individuals rely heavily on external cues from the environment, whereas field-independent individuals are more responsive to self-generated cues and are less dependent on external stimuli.

Pask (1976) proposed another kind of "cognitive style" that has been influential, one based on a distinction between serialism and holism. Serialists allegedly learn and remember a body of information simply as strings of items, whereas holists store and retrieve the information as a whole.

In light of the foregoing discussion of some major dimensions of personality, consideration must now be given to their relevance to cognition. (Psychoticism will not be discussed, because there has been insufficient research relating this personality dimension to cognitive functioning.)

TRAIT ANXIETY

The relationship between trait anxiety and cognition has been studied extensively (for a review, see M. W. Eysenck & Mathews, 1987). Several differences in cognitive functioning between individuals high and low in trait anxiety have been identified, especially when the testing conditions involve an element of stress (e.g. failure feedback or ego-involving instructions). Generally, those high in trait anxiety show increased attentional selectivity combined with decreased attentional control and high susceptibility to distraction. If attention can be likened to a beam of light, then those high in trait anxiety have a beam not only narrower but also more mobile than those low in trait anxiety (see ATTENTION).

Trait anxiety affects both attentional processes and memorial functioning. At least when stressed, individuals high in trait anxiety have reduced short-term and long-term storage of information, and evidence suggests that retrieval efficiency is reduced.

Some of these cognitive differences can be understood by reference to a hypothesis about WORKING MEMORY. Specifically, when individuals high in trait anxiety are stressed, they have reduced available working-memory capacity, especially the central executive component of the working-memory system. A possible explanation for this reduced capacity in high anxiety is that "task-irrelevant processing relating to concerns about performance

and negative self-evaluations may be pre-empting some of the resources of the central executive" (M. W. Eysenck & Mathews, 1987, p. 202).

This approach is limited in that it demonstrates little or nothing about the factors involved in the development of the anxious personality. The relationship between high anxiety and reduced available working-memory capacity presumably occurs because high anxiety reduces available capacity, rather than because reduced available capacity increases anxiety, although the causality possibly operates in both directions. By adopting a rather different approach based on assessing individual differences in the processing of threatening stimuli, more is likely to be discovered about cognitive factors involved in the etiology of the anxious personality. The fundamental assumption is that individuals high in trait anxiety will be more sensitive to threat-related stimuli (e.g. words referring to social or physical health threats) and will devote more processing resources to such stimuli than will individuals low in trait anxiety.

When only one stimulus is presented at a time, individuals high and low in trait anxiety do not differ greatly in their processing of threatening stimuli. However, substantial individual differences occur when threatening and neutral stimuli are presented concurrently: those high in trait anxiety allocate more processing resources to the threatening stimulus than to the neutral stimulus, whereas those low in trait anxiety exhibit the opposite tendency. In other words, individuals high and low in trait anxiety differ in terms of selective bias.

A related line of research interprets ambiguous stimuli in either a threatening or a neutral fashion. As might be expected, individuals high in trait anxiety tend to interpret such stimuli in threatening ways, whereas those low in trait anxiety generally interpret them in neutral ways (see LANGUAGE COMPREHENSION).

That high-anxiety and low-anxiety individuals differ in their processing of threatening and ambiguous stimuli is potentially relevant to the etiology of the anxious personality. An individual who typically engages in excessive processing of threatening stimuli at the expense of neutral stimuli and who focuses on the threatening interpretations of ambiguous stimuli is likely to find the environment much more subjectively threatening than do other individuals. Since the amount of anxiety experienced is presumably determined in part by how threatening the environment appears, it can be seen that individual differences in cognitive processing of threatening stimuli may partially determine individual differences in trait anxiety. However, to date no definitive evidence indicates that the causality operates in this direction.

INTROVERSION–EXTRAVERSION

Most of the research on cognitive functioning in introverts and extraverts has taken as its starting point H. J. Eysenck's theoretical assumption that introverts are more cortically aroused than extraverts (see H. J. Eysenck & M. W. Eysenck, 1985). The findings reinforce the viability of this view of the major difference between introverts and extraverts; they also suggest the value of a hierarchical conceptualization of the information-processing system.

The basic strategy of research in this area has been to compare the effects of introversion–extraversion on cognitive performance with those of other manipulations said to affect the level of arousal (e.g. white noise, and incentive). The term "arousal" is rather amorphous, but there allegedly exists a continuum of arousal ranging from deep sleep or coma at one extreme, to panic-stricken terror or great excitement at the other extreme.

In summary, introverts generally differ from extraverts in that they have greater attentional selectivity, superior long-term memory, reduced speed but increased accuracy of performance, greater distractibility, and impaired retrieval efficiency. On the assumption that introverts are more cortically aroused than extraverts, it is difficult to determine the pattern of the effects of introversion–extraversion, since no two so-called arousing agents have precisely the same effects on cognitive functioning. However, the modal pattern associated with high arousal consists of increased attentional selectivity, reduced short-term storage capacity, improved long-term memory, increased speed but decreased accuracy of performance, and greater distractibility.

Although the above findings indicate that some similarities exist between the effects of introversion–extraversion and those of arousing agents on cognitive performance, there are a number of differences. Introverts fail to show impaired short-term storage capacity, are slow and accurate rather than fast and inaccurate, and show impaired retrieval efficiency. These differences pose problems for an arousal theory of introversion–extraversion.

Revelle, Humphreys, Simon, and Gilliland (1980) identified further problems. First, the impulsivity component of extraversion, rather than extraversion per se, is related to cognitive performance. Second, and more damaging, the relationship between impulsivity and arousal in the evening is the opposite of that in the morning: high impulsives are less aroused than low impulsives in the morning, but more aroused in the evening. Thus, it cannot be argued that some individuals are characteristically more aroused than others, since an individual's relative level of arousal is dependent on time of day.

Arousal theory cannot account for the differences in cognitive performance between introverts and extraverts. However, a different and altogether more cognitive theory would probably have greater success. In several studies, introverts and extraverts have performed cognitive tasks either under arousing conditions (e.g. after ingestion of caffeine, or while exposed to intense white noise) or under normal conditions. Typically, such manipulations affect the performance of introverts much less than extraverts, a finding that can be accounted for by assuming that introverts and extraverts differ in terms of an executive control system. Introverts are more likely than extraverts to use their executive control system to maintain performance in the face of varying levels of arousal, whereas extraverts are more affected by the prevailing level of arousal. Greater understanding of the executive control system may be achieved by comparing the performance of introverts and extraverts in different situations.

FIELD DEPENDENCE

There have been numerous studies concerned with field dependence and cognitive functioning (for a review, see M. W. Eysenck, 1977). Most of the studies have dealt with either perception or memory. From their work on individual differences in perception, Witkin, Dyk, Faterson, Goodenough, and Karp (1962) concluded that field-independent individuals are less likely than field-dependent individuals to show distortions and inaccuracies in perception under difficult perceptual conditions.

The findings from memory experiments have been more complex. Commonly, field-independent individuals show higher levels of intentional learning than field-dependent ones; however, the results for incidental learning are less consistent. When social stimuli are presented (e.g. human faces or words having clear relevance to social interaction), field-dependent subjects tend to exhibit more incidental learning than do field-independent subjects. This last finding may occur because field-dependent individuals need support and guidance from others and are therefore particularly attentive to social stimuli (Witkin et al., 1962).

Investigations of the relationship between field dependence and cognition are rather disappointing theoretically, in that they have taken little account of developments within cognitive psychology. For example, researchers have not seriously attempted to decide whether differences in memory performance as a function of field dependence result from individual differences in attention, short-term storage capacity, rehearsal strategies, efficiency of retrieval, or cautiousness in responding.

Moreover, some controversy exists about precisely what is being measured by tests of field dependence such as the Rod-and-Frame Test or the Embedded Figures Test. In particular, evidence increasingly indicates that field dependence correlates negatively with intelligence as assessed by standard intelligence tests; that is, field-independent individuals tend to be more intelligent than field-dependent individuals. To conclude that field-independent subjects generally outper-

form field-dependent subjects on perceptual and memorial tasks because of their higher level of intelligence rather than because of their cognitive style per se is therefore tempting.

HOLISM VS. SERIALISM

Pask's (1976) theoretical distinction between holism and serialism, introduced previously, defines the precise nature of the distinction as follows:

> Some students are disposed to act "like holists" (*comprehension* learners) and others "like serialists" (*operation* learners), with more or less success. There are also students able to act in either way, depending on the subject matter, and if they excel in both pursuits, we refer to those students as *versatile*. It is these distinctions which can, more appropriately, be referred to as learning style.
> (Pask, 1976, p. 133) (*see* LEARNING STYLES)

The essence of this theoretical approach lies in the notion that important qualitative differences exist in learning strategies. The preferred learning strategy or style of a given individual can be assessed by using introspective reports (*see* INTROSPECTION). Although the holistic strategy is generally more effective than the serialist one, both approaches have clear-cut limitations under severe time pressure. Serialists tend to present facts without an overview (which Pask terms "improvidence"), whereas holists tend to produce a personal conclusion without any supporting evidence ("globetrotting").

Reasonable evidence supports the holism–serialism distinction. However, being able to characterize correctly most individuals as either holists or serialists is a hazier distinction. The learning strategy adopted depends not only on the learner's initial preferences, but also on features of the learning situation (e.g. the nature of the task, or the time available for learning).

CONCLUSIONS

Investigations of the relationships between personality and cognition serve to increase the understanding of both personality and cognition. Studying how individuals of different personality types vary in their cognitive functioning can enrich personality theory, especially if some of those cognitive differences contribute to the development of personality. Taking account of the ways in which individual differences influence cognitive functioning can advance theories within cognitive psychology. Individuals differ emotionally, motivationally, and in their cognitive styles. Cognitive psychologists ignore these major aspects of individual differences at their peril.

See also MOOD DISORDERS AND COGNITION.

BIBLIOGRAPHY

Eysenck, H. J., & Eysenck, M. W. (1985). *Personality and individual differences*. New York: Plenum.

Eysenck, M. W. (1977). *Human memory: Theory, research and individual differences*. Oxford: Pergamon.

— —, & Mathews, A. (1987). Trait anxiety and cognition. In H. J. Eysenck & I. Martin (Eds), *Theoretical foundations of behavior therapy* (pp. 197–213). New York: Plenum.

Pask, G. (1976). Styles and strategies of learning. *British Journal of Educational Psychology, 46*, 128–48.

Revelle, W., Humphreys, M. S., Simon, L., & Gilliland, K. (1980). The interactive effect of personality, time of day and caffeine: A test of the arousal model. *Journal of Experimental Psychology: General, 109*, 1–31.

Spielberger, C. D., Gorsuch, R., & Lushene, R. (1970). *The State–Trait Anxiety Inventory (STAI) test manual form X*. Palo Alto, Calif.: Consulting Psychologists Press.

Witkin, H. A., Dyk, R. B., Faterson, H. F., Goodenough, D. R., & Karp, S. A. (1962). *Psychological differentiation: Studies of development*. New York: Wiley.

Witkin, H. A., Lewis, H. B., Hertzman, M., Machover, K., Meissner, P. B., & Wapner, S. (1954). *Personality through perception*. New York: Harper & Row.

MICHAEL W. EYSENCK

person perception Person perception refers to a cognitively oriented subfield of social psychology concerned with the ways that human beings use information about other people to form impressions, make judgements, predict behavior, and interact. The primary focus has been on the implications of various kinds of stimuli (especially personal appearance and behavior) for various kinds of judgements (especially trait attributions).

Person perception research is closely related to SOCIAL COGNITION, a field directly concerned with the role that cognitive processes play in people's interpersonal involvements. However, person perception tends to focus less on memory organization or other basic cognitive processes than does social cognition. Moreover, whereas social cognition tends to adopt the fundamental concepts, theories, and methods of experimental cognitive psychology, person perception work frequently relies on somewhat autonomous approaches, as described below. Nonetheless, the issues of concern are similar in each realm, as well as in other cognitively oriented subfields of social psychology, such as ATTITUDES. It is therefore not surprising that these areas are becoming increasingly integrated in the published literature.

ACCURACY OF IMPRESSIONS

An important issue in early person perception research was the accuracy of people's perceptions of each other. It seemed reasonable that some people might be especially skilled in judging others' personalities from various kinds of cues, and that such people might be more socially adept and more successful as leaders, personnel managers, or psychological counselors. Empirical efforts to identify such individuals were largely disappointing, and Cronbach's influential 1955 critique of the area brought a halt to most such work. Cronbach noted that the apparent accuracy of a person perception is affected by many factors that are unrelated to perceptiveness about individuals' traits. For example, if a perceiver tends to project his or her own attributes on to others, the apparent accuracy of those impressions will fortuitously improve with increases in actual similarity between the perceiver and those being judged.

Another difficulty with studies of impression accuracy is the need for an objective criterion. A researcher who wishes to examine the accuracy of trait judgements, for example, must be able to determine the traits that objectively characterize the individual being judged. Yet the personality traits of common interest in such research are judgemental ones (e.g. kindness and honesty) for which objective measures would be difficult to create. Despite these difficulties, a resurgence of interest has occurred in the accuracy issue. Recent research generally takes care to differentiate various components of accuracy, focuses on situational determinants of accuracy rather than on individual differences, and defines accuracy in terms of verifiable criteria such as behavior (see Kenney & Albright, 1987).

IMPRESSION FORMATION

The preponderance of research on person perception simply identifies the nature of impressions formed from different kinds of information about people, without addressing the accuracy or inaccuracy of those impressions. The following overview is presented with the caveat that many findings are qualified by such factors as the other kinds of information simultaneously available, and the characteristics and goals of the individual forming the impression.

Facial appearance appears to influence impressions primarily through perceivers' reactions to configurations of features, rather than through the implications of individual features. A few exceptions include scars or deformities (derogation is common), hair color ("blonds have more fun"), and spectacles (which lead to inferences of intelligence). Configurations of features may convey age, gender, and ethnicity (all of which can imply a variety of stereotypical attributes), physical attractiveness (which generally leads to a wide range of positive inferences), and facial "type" (e.g. "baby-facedness" implies childlike qualities such as submissiveness and naivety; Berry & McArthur, 1986). As long as the overall reaction to a face is not negative, merely being exposed to it repeatedly can increase positive feelings about the person (see Zajonc, 1968).

Facial expressions communicate people's emotional states and their truthfulness or sincerity. The kinds of expressions indicative of many emotions (including happiness, surprise, anger, disgust, and sadness) are essentially the same across most cultures. As a rule, positive expressions (e.g. happiness) produce more favorable impressions in observers. Facial expressions can also "leak" indications that a person is being deceptive or insincere, though even better indications are provided by body movements, voice tone and rhythm, and incongruencies between these several sources of information (Zuckerman, DePaulo, & Rosenthal, 1981).

Style of dress, body type, and posture reliably elicit an assortment of inferences. Dress can imply attributes such as self-confidence or non-conformity, and can also prime stereotypes of various occupations or subcultures. In many cultures, height is associated with status, and girth with good-naturedness. Body posture and physical gestures (sometimes jointly referred to as "body language") can convey approachability or deceptiveness (see NONVERBAL COMMUNICATION). For example, crossed arms are often viewed as a defensive posture, suggesting wariness, hostility, or tension.

Other subtle or minimal behaviors also have implications for impression formation. A person (especially a female) who makes eye contact and touching gestures will often be viewed positively, unless these behaviors are extreme (e.g. staring), inappropriately intimate, or seemingly manipulative. Similarly, an individual's perceived likeability is increased by closer physical proximity, within narrow limits prescribed by different cultures and different kinds of relationships.

Various nonsemantic aspects of spoken language (often termed "paralanguage") contribute to impressions: lower-pitched voices are often viewed as indicative of strength and composure, while higher-pitched voices and irregular or halting speech rhythms are viewed as indicative of nervousness; faster speech sometimes implies self-confidence and expertise, though it can also suggest nervousness or insincerity; and dialects or accents can evoke ethnic and national stereotypes.

Naturally, the contents of verbalizations

also affect impressions. A person who compliments a perceiver will be more positively evaluated, perhaps even when the compliment is known to be insincere. A person who boasts can sometimes influence perceptions related to the boasted attribute, though frequently at the expense of perceived modesty. "Self-disclosures" of personal secrets often enhance others' evaluations, unless such disclosures seem too personal to be appropriate for a given relationship, or unless they create an uncomfortable demand on the perceiver to make similar disclosures.

More substantive behaviors also influence perceiver's impressions of the actor. However, reactions to such behaviors may reflect complex reasoning processes. Investigators examining such influences have therefore constructed special approaches, called "attribution theories," to explain the impact of observed behavior on person perceptions.

ATTRIBUTION THEORIES

The two major attribution theories – Jones and Davis's (1965) correspondent inference theory and Kelley's (1967) ANOVA model – imply that perceivers do not, and should not, always perceive an actor's behavior as indicative of underlying personality characteristics (*see* INFERENCES). The theories suggest that an occasional reluctance to draw inferences from people's behavior follows from the multiplicity of potential determinants for any specific act. In correspondent inference theory, perceivers discount socially desirable acts (sometimes characterized as role consistent or expected acts), and acts that produce numerous outcomes that would not otherwise have occurred ("noncommon effects"). The former might reflect social norms or pressure, and the latter create too much uncertainty regarding the actual intentions or motivations of the actor. "Correspondent inferences" regarding an actor's traits are predicted to follow most readily from socially undesirable behaviors that cause relatively few noncommon effects.

In Kelley's ANOVA model, perceivers discount "high consensus" behaviors, which are typical of how most people would act in a situation, and "high distinctiveness" or "low con-

sistency" behaviors, which are atypical of how the actor him- or herself would act in other situations or at other times. The "ANOVA" label reflects the premiss that perceivers evaluate the causes of behavior by attending to patterns of behavior across actors, situations, and time – a process analogous to the statistical technique of analysis of variance (ANOVA).

Although different in approach, these theories both derive from work by Fritz Heider (1958) – especially his discounting and covariance principles. Writers have criticized these theories for ostensibly implying that people make attributions logically and after considerable cognitive effort. Whether or not such criticisms are entirely justified, they did lead the critics to identify logical "errors" in people's attributions, and eventually to develop more "automatic" conceptions of the attributional process.

A wide variety of attributional errors and biases was identified, demonstrated, and labeled with special terms. (These "errors" might be more properly understood simply as deviations from the logic of the major attribution theories.) Researchers showed that people often make the "fundamental attributional error" of inferring actors' traits even from coerced behaviors. Research on "actor–observer differences" demonstrated people's willingness to make trait inferences from others' behaviors that they would not make from their own. Perhaps some "ego-defensive" biases are introduced into self-attributions by people's motivation to think and communicate positive things about themselves. "False-consensus biases" occur because people tend to think that most others will act as they themselves would. This may explain why the kind of "consensus information" to which Kelley referred often seems not to affect attributions as his theory predicted. Finally, some "errors" may occur because people are prone to fixate on information that is especially salient in the environment, accessible in memory, or consistent with expected patterns (*see* SCHEMATA).

Reference to causal schemata, or sometimes to CONNECTIONIST MODELS OF MEMORY, is characteristic of recent arguments that trait inferences are made with less deliberation than classic attribution theories seem to imply. Instead, some theorists argue, people may derive trait impressions from perceived behaviors through relatively effortless and non-conscious AUTOMATIC PROCESSING. For example, features of a behavior or situation may simply be associated in memory with causes of the events and characteristics of the participants. (The associative structures relating behaviors to traits and traits to other traits are sometimes called "implicit personality theories.") Alternatively, certain patterns of events and circumstances may instantiate schemata which have implications about event causes and participant characteristics. These newer approaches to attribution have their own critics, but the issues they raise illustrate the complexities involved in trying to understand attributions based on behavioral information.

COMBINATORIAL PROCESSES

Additional issues arise from the multiplicity of cues that can contribute to person perception – cues including appearance, body language, tone of voice, and overt behavior, to remention just a few. One such issue concerns the way in which so many sources of information are combined into a unitary impression. Information integration models (see, for example, Anderson, 1974) suggest that the evaluative implications of individual pieces of information are added or averaged together. People's actual impressions often seem to be more influenced by extreme or negative information than simple integration models would predict. These widespread "extremity and negativity biases" have been explained in terms of several different models, including attribution theory and categorization processes (for a review, see Skowronski & Carlston, 1989).

Other approaches to combinatorial processes view various pieces of information as interacting, the implications of each piece changed by the others in a manner consistent with GESTALT PRINCIPLES OF PERCEPTUAL ORGANIZATION. (One example of such interactions is the "halo effect" – the common tendency for a person known to have one positive attribute to be evaluated more positively on other attributes as well.) Research generally confirms that people attend to larger configurations of cues, rather than to isolated pieces of information, in making impression judgements.

Another issue concerns the way that impressions are affected by the sequencing of cues about a person. Early research suggested a "primacy effect" such that the first information encountered has the most profound influence on people's impressions (even though recent information is often remembered best). An explanation consistent with the Gestalt viewpoint is that early information creates a general impression that then affects people's interpretation of subsequently encountered cues. Subsequent research confirmed the importance of first impressions, but also suggested that recency effects can occur if informational cues imply that the person being perceived may have changed.

As the Gestalt explanation for primacy effects implies, the processes involved in perceiving information about people can be selective and interpretative. In other words, it is the subjective encoding of cues, rather than their objective implications, that influences impressions. For example, research suggests that ambiguous information is often misperceived as more consistent with other things known about a person, and that consistent information often contributes most to an evolving impression. (However, under certain circumstances, it is inconsistent information that is best remembered.) Situational demands and interaction goals also affect the way that information about people is perceived: for example, we tend to think more highly of people we know we will have to interact with.

People are clearly capable of forming impressions from diverse sources of information, and of using these impressions to respond to a variety of different kinds of judgement questions. However, it is unclear exactly what kinds of impressions, and what kinds of judgements, people ordinarily make on their own. Some theorists argue that people spontaneously form trait impressions ("She's kind and smart"), whereas others believe that people normally assign others to categories

("He's an absent-minded professor"). Recent theories of person perception hold that impressions comprise multiple implications and representations at the same time (cf. various chapters in Srull & Wyer, 1988). The implication is that many different kinds of integration and judgement processes may be involved in forming and reporting our impressions of others.

PERSON VS. OBJECT PERCEPTION

A recurrent debate in person perception concerns the similarity or dissimilarity between the processes involved in person perception and those involved in the perception of inanimate objects. Some theorists argue that person perception is not fundamentally different from object perception, whereas others view person perception as a special instance of object perception – one that brings more complex and specialized perceptual processes into play.

Although one may question the extent to which fundamentally different processes are involved, there do seem to be some characteristic differences between person and object perception. First, in person perception that which is being observed has important animate properties that are frequently absent in object perception: people tend to be active, complex, difficult to fully understand, aware that they are being observed, and capable of misrepresentation. Second, the observer may have different characteristics when engaged in person perception than when engaged in object perception: the observer may be emotionally involved or actively interacting with the person, may need to be circumspect in examining that person, and may be aware that the person is looking back, simultaneously forming impressions of the observer. As a consequence, then, person perception may often require more cognitive analysis, produce more emotional involvement, and involve more self-reference than does object perception.

In any case, the area of person perception has much in common with object perception and with other areas of cognitive psychology. At the same time, it has made independent contributions to the study of cognitive processes because of the unique issues that arise in studying how people perceive each other.

BIBLIOGRAPHY

Anderson, N. H. (1974). Cognitive algebra: Integration theory applied to social attribution. In L. Berkowitz (Ed.), *Advances in experimental social psychology* (Vol. 7), pp. 1–101. New York: Academic Press.

Berry, D. S., & McArthur, L. Z. (1986). Perceiving character in faces: The impact of age-related craniofacial changes in social perception. *Psychological Bulletin, 100*, 3–18.

Cronbach, L. J. (1955). Processes affecting scores on "understanding of others" and "assumed similarity." *Psychological Bulletin, 52*, 177–93.

Heider, F. (1958). *The psychology of interpersonal relations.* New York: Wiley.

Jones, E. E., & Davis, K. E. (1965). From acts to dispositions: The attribution process in person perception. In L. Berkowitz (Ed.), *Advances in experimental social psychology* (Vol. 2). New York: Academic Press.

Kelley, H. H. (1967). Attribution theory in social psychology. *Nebraska Symposium on Motivation, 15*, 192–241.

Kenney, D. A., & Albright, L. (1987). Accuracy in interpersonal perception: A social relations analysis. *Psychological Bulletin, 102*, 390–402.

Schneider, D. J., Hastorf, A. H., & Ellsworth, P. C. (1979). *Person perception* (2nd edn). Reading, Mass.: Addison-Wesley.

Skowronski, J. J., & Carlston, D. E. (1989). Negativity and extremity biases in impression formation: A review of explanations. *Psychological Bulletin, 105*, 131–42.

Srull, T. K., & Wyer, R. S. Jr (Eds) (1988). *Advances in social cognition* (Vol. 1): *A dual process model of impression formation.* Hillsdale, NJ: Erlbaum.

Zajonc, R. B. (1968). Attitudinal effects of mere exposure. *Journal of Personality and Social Psychology, 9*, 1–27.

Zuckerman, M., Depaulo, B. M., & Rosenthal, R. (1981). Verbal and nonverbal communication of deception. In L. Berkowitz (Ed.), *Advances in experimental social psychology* (Vol. 14) (pp. 1–59). New York: Academic Press.

DONAL E. CARLSTON

Piaget, Jean (1896–1980). Jean Piaget, a Swiss biologist and psychologist, originated by far the most influential theory in developmental psychology. He produced a reasonably simple theory of development which could explain an astonishingly broad range of behavior in children. He was a gifted observer of the oddities of children's behavior and realized that these might provide the key to understanding children's intellectual and social development (*see* COGNITIVE DEVELOPMENT). A third reason for his pervasive influence is that he possessed, and used to good effect, a wide knowledge of many different subjects, being a biologist, and an expert in philosophy and in some aspects of mathematics.

The central idea in Piaget's theory is that logic develops. He thought that there are three major periods in this development of logic. The first, called "the sensori-motor period," covers the first two years of life. During this period the child acquires a basic understanding of space and time (Piaget, 1954): he or she learns for example that objects exist even when not perceived, that one object can only be in one place at a time, and that particular events and actions have particular consequences. Piaget's best known observations during this period concern the understanding of "object permanence." He reported (a report amply confirmed by others) that the six month baby loses interest in an attractive toy as soon as it is put, for example, under a cover even though the baby could in principle easily lift the cover off and retrieve the object. Piaget's explanation was that the baby does not realize at first that objects go on existing when he or she can no longer perceive them and thus lives in an apparently impermanent and capricious world. Older babies (nine to twelve months) solve this problem but make a curious mistake with another task. If at first they see the object hidden in one place (A) and retrieve it but then see it hidden in a second place (B), they often continue (quite wrongly) to look for the object in the first place (A): this is called the AB̄ error, which Piaget attributed to babies thinking that the action of going to the first location (A) creates the object. This phenomenon led Piaget to the idea that children

remember spatial position in terms of their own actions or movements: their idea of space, he argued, was at first egocentric and much of the development during this period consists in shedding this egocentrism. Although the developmental changes during these first two years are very striking, Piaget insisted that the children were acquiring only a "practical intelligence."

The second major stage, "the concrete operations period," begins during the preschool years and ends roughly speaking at the beginning of adolescence. Its two most important features are (1) that the child begins to be able to solve logical problems, and (2) that this logical development happens because of an underlying change in the child's ability to "manipulate" perceptual information. At the beginning of the concrete operations period the child is dominated by his or her immediate perceptual input. By its end he or she is able to imagine what something in his or her environment would look like under changed conditions. Piaget called this new ability "reversibility" and he linked it to a wide variety of logical moves. An example is a task with three sticks (A,B,C) in which children are shown first that A>B then separately that B>C, without seeing A and C together, and are then asked how A and C compare. Young children, Piaget claimed, cannot make this "transitive" inference because they cannot combine the separate premises: older children succeed because they can manipulate their memories of the separate premises and can imagine the three sticks in an A>B>C series.

Another instance where the development of reversibility is said to lead to the solution of a cognitive problem is Piaget's well known conservation task (Piaget, 1952; Piaget & Inhelder, 1974). Children are given two perceptually identical quantities (A and B), say two identical glasses holding the same amount of water, and then see the liquid in one glass (B) poured into a much narrower container (B1). They are then asked whether there is the same amount of liquid in A as in B1. Younger children tend to give the wrong answer. Piaget concluded that they think that the change in the appearance of the transformed quantity signifies that its actual quantity had changed too. Older children answer the question correctly, and Piaget claimed that they do so because, as the liquid is tipped from one container into the other, they can imagine what it would look like if it were tipped back into the first one: this ability to cancel out a perceived change (reversibility) leads to the proper understanding of the principle of invariance.

Piaget also claimed (Piaget & Inhelder, 1963) that during this period the child begins to be able to work out what a scene seems like to other people looking at it from a different point of view than his or her own. This is described as a change from "egocentrism" to "allocentrism." Piaget extended the idea of egocentrism to social and moral problems and argued that young children, being egocentric, are unable to work out the intentions of another person and therefore judge what that person does in terms of the consequences of his actions rather than of his intentions.

The final period, "the formal operations period," roughly covers the time of adolescence. It is the period of "operations on operations": adolescents begin to be able to think about thinking. This leads them to be able to work out how to test hypotheses, and allows them to see, for example, the value of testing one variable at a time while holding all the others constant. Piaget did establish that there were striking changes in children's success in testing their hypotheses during this period, but he admitted later on that "operations on operations" are not universal. A sizeable number of reasonably intelligent adults may never achieve formal operations.

This account has dealt only with Piaget's description of developmental changes. Another part of his theory concerns the causes of these changes. Piaget (1975) argued that children learn mainly through their own informal experiences. He claimed that children seek intellectual "equilibrium" which depends on their being able to explain events to themselves satisfactorily. However, they find, from time to time, that they have two mutually incompatible ways of explaining the same events. Such internal conflicts lead to internal "disequilibrium" and stimulate children to find a new internally consistent way of understanding the events in question. In order

to do so the child must employ more sophisticated intellectual strategies, and thus the resolution of the conflict and the return to cognitive equilibrium sparks off intellectual changes.

Piaget's ideas have had their critics. Three kinds of doubt have been expressed. The first is that the numbers or mean ages of the children concerned are rarely given, and some of his most influential work was only carried out on his own children. However, most objections of this sort can be ruled out because his work has been replicated with striking success in systematic research in other universities. Second, it has been suggested, most notably by Donaldson (1978), that Piaget ignored the effects of the social context in which his experiments took place. In the conservation experiment, for example, the child may be misled by the apparent importance which the experimenter attaches to the change in the object's appearance into thinking that it must be right to say that its quantity has changed too.

Finally, Piaget's work has been criticized for faulty experimental design. Most of his experiments have little or nothing in the way of controls. Children's failures in transitive inference tasks may be due to their forgetting the premises rather than to an inability to combine these premises inferentially. The design of the conservation task can also be criticized on the grounds that it tests a great deal more than just the understanding of invariance, which means that children may fail in the task for several different reasons. The task involves memory, and one also needs to make an inference to reach the correct answer, as well as to have grasped the invariance principle. Much of the work on infants can be interpreted in more than one way: the baby's failure to retrieve a hidden object may simply signify that he or she does not know how to do so rather than that he or she thinks that the object no longer exists (Bremner, 1988).

Boden (1979) pointed out that Piaget was ahead of his time in that all his work was done before ARTIFICIAL INTELLIGENCE (AI) made any noticeable impact on psychological theory. Piaget would certainly have given AI models his enthusiastic attention, and it is a reasonable assumption that he would have used them to strengthen the least convincing part of his theory – his causal hypothesis. Nevertheless, the inventiveness and the power of Piaget's theory and of the considerable empirical evidence that he amassed for it demand our respect. He remains the most significant developmental psychologist.

BIBLIOGRAPHY

Boden, M. A. (1979). *Piaget*. London: Fontana.

Bremner, J. G. (1988). *Infancy*. Oxford: Basil Blackwell.

Donaldson, M. (1978). *Children's minds*. London: Fontana.

Elkind, D. (1967). Piaget's conservation problems. *Child Development, 38*, 15–27.

Piaget, J. (1952). *The child's conception of number*. London: Routledge & Kegan Paul.

——. (1954). *The construction of reality in the child*. London: Routledge & Kegan Paul.

——. (1975). *The development of thought: Equilibration of cognitive structures*. Oxford: Basil Blackwell.

——, & Inhelder, B. (1963). *The child's conception of space*. London: Routledge & Kegan Paul.

——. (1974). *The child's construction of quantities*. London: Routledge & Kegan Paul.

PETER BRYANT

positron emission tomography and cognition Positron emission tomography (PET) is a technology which is based on the use of positron emitting radiotracers (typically Fluorine 18 and Oxygen 15) to label brain function. Elegant cognitive models can now be tested with direct, regional brain functioning assessments made with the powerful technology of PET. Questions concerning localization of function are particularly amenable to PET analyses.

The emitted positrons used with the PET technology produce gamma rays which travel in opposite directions 180° apart. When the head is placed in a ring of gamma ray detectors (i.e. the PET scanner), every simultaneous detection at two points in the ring 180° apart is counted. A large number of such detections from all points around the ring results in a mathematical reconstruction showing a slice view of brain metabolic activity. Cognitive activity requires energy from glucose delivered in the blood. Greater neural activity requires more glucose and greater regional blood flow to deliver oxygen and remove carbon dioxide. The tracer uptake period can vary from 40 seconds (using O_{15}, as a blood flow tracer with a half-life of 123 sec.) to 35 minutes (using 18-flurodeoxyglucose, FDG, as a metabolic tracer with a half-life of 110 minutes).

The first use of PET to study lexical processing was reported by Petersen et al. (1988). Normal volunteers (11 females, 6 males) were scanned in four conditions.

In the first condition, subjects were instructed only for visual fixation with no lexical task. In the second condition, words were presented passively, in either a visual or auditory way. In condition 3, the subject spoke each word presented and in condition 4, the subject said a use for each word presented. Data analyses were based on subtracting scans of each subject in two conditions to see the added brain activity as the conditions required more operations. Three sets of subtractions were reported. Condition 2 minus condition 1 highlighted brain areas used in sensory input and word-form processing. Condition 3 minus condition 2 highlighted output coding and motor control. Condition 4 minus condition 3 highlighted areas of semantic processing.

Group results indicated a small number of highly localized areas of brain activity for each cognitive component addressed in the subtraction sequences. Visual and auditory sensory input activated different areas (condition 2−1) in occipital and temporal cortex, respectively (*see* AUDITORY PERCEPTION). Output and semantic conditions overlapped between visual and auditory presentations. Output tasks (conditions 3–2) activated rolandic, sylvian, and premotor cortex areas. Semantic tasks (conditions 4–3) activated prefrontal and cingulate areas. The results support multiple, parallel routes for sensory specific components of lexical processing, at least for this combined sample of right-handed males and females of normal language ability.

LaBerge and Buchsbaum (1989) used PET to test a specific model of attentional filtering which predicts involvement of the pulvinar nucleus of the dorsal thalamus (*see* ATTENTION). Seven normal, right-handed women performed a visual identification task with a filtering display in either the right or left visual field. Each subject was scanned twice, on different days, alternating the side of the filtering display. FDG with an uptake period of 35 minutes was used to label brain glucose metabolic activity. As predicted, when the filtering display was in the right visual field, the left pulvinar showed more activity than the right pulvinar and this reversed when the filtering display was in the left visual field. A control area for the thalamus, the mediodorsal nucleus, showed no such reversal. No general hemispheric effect using frontal white matter for contrast was found with analysis of variance, nor was there a hemispheric effect in 20 areas of the occipital lobe.

A different attention paradigm using the degraded Continuous Performance Test (CPT) has been used to study normal/psychiatric group differences (Buchsbaum et al., 1982, 1989). In general, areas in the right frontal and parietal cortex are elevated in normals doing the CPT compared to schizophrenics and compared to other normals doing a control task (CPT stimuli only with no task).

Complex reasoning was studied with PET by Haier et al. (1988) using the Raven's Advanced Progressive Matrices (RAPM). Eight normal right-handed males were compared to matched groups doing the degraded CPT and the CPT control task (stimuli only). Left posterior cortical areas were more active during the RAPM than the other two conditions, consistent with neuropsychological models. Since the RAPM was designed to highlight individual differences in performance, scores on the RAPM were correlated with glucose metabolic rate in all cortical areas. Significant inverse correlations (i.e. the better the cognitive performance, the less glucose used) were interpreted as consistent with brain efficiency models of INTELLIGENCE. Individual differences in CPT performance showed much smaller, non-significant, positive correlations with cortical glucose.

In a similar study, Parks et al. (1988) con-firmed inverse correlations between glucose use in frontal, temporal, and parietal cortex and verbal fluency scores (see also Berent et al., 1988). However, Chase et al. (1984) reported positive correlations between Weschler Adult Intelligence Scale scores and cortical glucose use in a group of mostly Alzheimers patients.

Additional PET studies of memory, aphasia, brain organization, and other neuropsychological tasks have been reported. As the PET technology becomes more readily available, more elegant research designs with new radiotracers and with larger sample sizes can be expected. The spatial resolution of PET scanners will improve to about 2mm so smaller brain areas can be studied.

BIBLIOGRAPHY

Berent, S., Giordani, B., Lehtinen, S., Markel, D., Penney, J. B., Buchtel, H. A., Starosta-Rubinstein, S., Hichwa, R., & Young, A. B. (1988). Positron emission tomographic scan investigations of Huntington's disease: Cerebral metabolic correlates of cognitive function. *Annals of Neurology*, *23*(6), 541–6.

Buchsbaum, M. S., Nuechterlein, K. H., Haier, R. J., Wu, J., Sicotte, N., Hazlett, E., Asarnow, R., Potkin, S., & Guich, S. (1990). Glucose metabolic rate in normals and schizophrenics during the continuous performance test assessed by positron emission tomography. *British Journal of Psychiatry*, *15*, 216–27.

Buchsbaum, M. S., DeLisi, L. E., Holcomb, H. H., Cappelletti, J., King, A. C., Johnson, J., Hazlett, E., Dowling-Zimmerman, S., Post, R. M., Morihisa, J., Carpenter, W., Cohen, R., Pickar, D., Weinberger, D. R., Margolin, R., & Kessler, R. M. (1984). Anteroposterior gradients in cerebral glucose use in schizophrenia and affective disorders. *Archives of General Psychiatry*, *41*, 1159–66.

Chase, T. N., Fedio, P., Foster, N. L., Brooks, R., Di Chiro, G., & Mansi, L. (1984). Weschler adult intelligence scale performance: Cortical localization by flurodeoxyglucose F18-positron emission tomography. *Archives of Neurology*, *41*, 1244–7.

Haier, R. J., Siegel, B. Jr., Nuechterlein, K. H., Hazlett, E., Wu, J. C., Paek, J., Browning, H. L., & Buchsbaum, M. S. (1988). Cortical glucose metabolic rate correlates of reasoning and attention studied with positron emission tomography. *Intelligence*, *12*, 199–217.

LaBerge, D., & Buchsbaum, M. S. (1990). PET measurements of pulvinar activity during an attention task. *Journal of Neuroscience*, *10*, 613–19.

Parks, R. W., Loewenstein, D. A., Dodrill, K. L., Barker, W. W., Yoshii, F., Chang, J. Y., Emran, A., Apicella, A., Sheramata, W. A., & Duara, R. (1988). Cerebral metabolic effects of a verbal fluency test: A PET scan study. *Journal of Clinical and Experimental Neuropsychology*, *10*(5), 565–75.

Petersen, S. E., Fox, P. T., Posner, M. I., Mintun, M., & Raichle, M. E. (1988). Positron emission tomographic studies of the cortical anatomy of single-word processing. *Nature*, *331*, 585–9.

RICHARD J. HAIER

Posner, Michael (*b.* 1936). Several core ideas and methods in cognitive psychology have originated with Michael Posner, who has been affiliated with the University of Oregon since 1965. His work has focused on elementary cognitive processes involved in perception, action, and attention. Two of the most important concepts from his work are mental codes and the distinction between controlled and automatic processing. The methods Posner has used have been as important as the principles he has uncovered.

Information can be used for different purposes. Its visual appearance can be admired, its sound can be enjoyed, and so forth. This suggests that the brain may be able to represent information in terms of distinct cognitive "codes." Much of what we know about such codes has been revealed through a task developed by Posner and Mitchell (1967). People indicate whether two linguistic stimuli match on some dimension – for example, whether two letters are both vowels. Posner and Mitchell found that when the two letters have the same name (e.g. "A" and "a") the decision is made more quickly than when they have different names (e.g. "A" and "e"). The decision is made still more quickly when the two letters are physically identical (e.g. "A" and "A"). Based on these and related results,

obtained both in Posner's laboratory and elsewhere, it has been established that the same stimulus can be transformed into visual codes, name codes, and semantic codes, and that these codes are available at different times (for a review see Posner, 1978).

By presenting a prime stimulus prior to the two items to be compared, Posner and Snyder (1975) obtained evidence for a distinction between controlled and automatic processing. If the prime does not match one of the test items, the time to compare the test items increases, but this is true only when the prime reliably predicts one of the test items. The result suggests that people can deliberately ignore the prime when it is unreliable – an instance of *controlled* processing. If the prime *matches* one of the test items, performance is enhanced no matter how reliable the prime is. Thus the prime can also facilitate processing of the test item *automatically*. A great deal of research on the distinction between automatic and controlled processing has followed up this elegant experimental demonstration (for a review see Posner, 1978) (*see* AUTOMATIC PROCESSING).

Another domain in which Posner has studied automatic and controlled processing is the shift of attention from one spatial location to another. By cuing different locations with stimuli of varying reliability and by measuring the speed with which people can detect stimuli at those locations or make eye movements to them, Posner and his colleagues (e.g. Posner, Inhoff, Friedrich, & Cohen, 1987) have identified several processes involved in the control of spatial attention. These include general alerting, disengaging attention from the currently attended site, moving attention to the new target site, and engaging attention at the new target site. Posner, Cohen, and Rafal (1982), Posner, Walker, Friedrich, and Rafal (1984), and Rafal and Posner (1987) found that patients with lesions in specific brain regions show impairments in one or more of these processes, suggesting that each of the processes is controlled by a particular part of the brain (*see* ATTENTION; HEMISPHERIC LOCALIZATION).

Posner, Petersen, Fox, and Raichle (1988) introduced another technique for investigating the localization of cognitive functions in the brain. They obtained positron emission tomography (PET) scans from the brains of volunteers engaged in tasks differing with respect to one or more processes, such as repeating a word or saying aloud a use for the object named by the word (e.g. "pound" in response to "hammer"). Semantic information is required only for the second task, which means that if a part of the brain "lights up" during the second task but not the first, that part of the brain can be identified as a locus of semantic information processing. Through this method, Posner et al. (1988) identified brain locations subserving different cognitive operations. The success of the technique points to close correspondences between mental operations and their biological substrates, and encourages cooperation between cognitive and neural scientists (see COGNITIVE NEUROPSYCHOLOGY; POSITRON EMISSION TOMOGRAPHY AND COGNITION).

BIBLIOGRAPHY

Posner, M. I. (1978). *Chronometric explorations of mind.* Hillsdale, NJ: Lawrence Erlbaum Associates.
Posner, M. I., & Mitchell, R. F. (1967). Chronometric analysis of classification. *Psychological Review, 74,* 392–409.
Posner, M. I., & Snyder, C. R. (1975). Facilitation and inhibition in the processing of signals. In P. M. A. Rabbitt & S. Dornic (Eds), *Attention and performance V* (pp. 669–81). London: Academic Press.
Posner, M. I., Cohen, Y., & Rafal, R. D. (1982). Neural systems control of spatial orienting. *Proceedings of the Royal Society of London, B298,* 187–98.
Posner, M. I., Inhoff, A., Friedrich, F. J., & Cohen, A. (1987). Isolating attentional systems: A cognitive-anatomical analysis. *Psychobiology, 15,* 107–21.
Posner, M. I., Petersen, S. E., Fox, P. T., & Raichle, M. E. (1988). Localization of cognitive operations in the human brain. *Science, 240,* 1627–31.
Posner, M. I., Walker, J. A., Friedrich, F. J., & Rafal, R. D. (1984). Effects of parietal lobe injury on covert orienting of visual attention. *Journal of Neuroscience, 4,* 1863–74.
Rafal, R. D., & Posner, M. I. (1987). Deficits in human spatial attention following thalamic lesions. *Proceedings of the National Academy of Sciences, 84,* 7349–53.

D. A. ROSENBAUM

pragmatics of language See LANGUAGE, PRAGMATICS OF.

priming The term "priming" refers to a technique developed to study how context influences performance; the technique involves the measurement of responses to a second (target) stimulus as a function of its relation to a first stimulus (the prime). The prime thus serves as a context for the target. By varying the relations between the two stimuli, and the temporal interval separating the prime from the target, an experimenter can effect close control over the nature of the context effect due to the prime.

Priming has been widely adopted in studies of word and picture recognition. Different forms of priming can be distinguished, by varying the time interval between the stimuli and the probability that the prime and target are related. When there is a low probability that the prime and target are related (i.e. when primes are uninformative) subjects are not able to predict the target from the prime on any particular trial in an experiment. Under these circumstances, any effect of priming can be said to be "automatic." In contrast, when there is a high probability that primes and targets are related (i.e. when primes are informative), subjects can generate expectancies of targets from primes. Priming can then be said to be strategic or expectation dependent. Automatic priming can occur even when there are short intervals between primes and targets (i.e. with short prime-target intervals, there are few effects of the informativeness of the prime). Expectation-dependent priming tends to be most pronounced with longer prime-target intervals (when the effects of the informativeness of the prime emerge). This difference in the "time-course" of the different effects suggests that subjects take some non-negligible time to generate expectancies of targets from contexts (see Posner & Snyder, 1975).

Primes can be informative both about the identity of targets and about their time of occurring (if the prime-target interval is constant across a block of trials). To distinguish temporal from identity priming, a *neutral* prime condition can be included, where the prime only serves as a warning signal for the occurrence of the target (e.g. the neutral prime might be a row of *X*s while all the other stimuli in the experiment are words). The effects of identity priming can then be assessed relative to the neutral prime baseline. When this is done, both positive (facilitatory) and negative (inhibitory) priming effects can be identified. When the subjects generate expectations of targets from primes, and the expectation on a particular trial turns out to be incorrect (e.g. the prime and target are unrelated and not related as expected), responses are inhibited relative to the neutral baseline. When the expectations are confirmed (e.g. the prime and target on a given trial are related), responses are facilitated. However, under conditions of automatic priming, only facilitatory priming tends to occur (when the stimuli are related). Relative to the neutral baseline, there are no costs when primes and targets are unrelated (Neely, 1977).

Thus, automatic and expectation-dependent priming can be distinguished using a number of operational criteria. Automatic priming is fast acting, unaffected by the informativeness of the prime, and produces benefits (when the stimuli are related) without costs (when the stimuli are unrelated). Expectation-dependent priming is relatively slow acting, affected by the informativeness of the prime, and produces both benefits and costs (depending upon whether primes and targets are related or unrelated). By studying the relations between primes and targets that give rise to automatic priming effects, we can learn about the properties of stimuli that are processed automatically, and are not dependent on particular strategies adopted by subjects (*see* AUTOMATIC PROCESSING).

When automatic priming has been examined, various forms of relationship between the prime and the target have been found to be important. For instance, priming effects occur when the stimuli have the same identity (i.e. the target is a repeat of the prime, e.g. Jacoby & Dallas, 1981), when they are associates of one another (e.g. Fischler & Goodman, 1978), when the target is a word following a highly predictive sentence (Stanovich & West, 1983), and so forth. Such effects are often attributed to the prime "pre-activating" an internal representation that mediates target processing. When the target's representation is pre-activated, less information is required from the target for a response to occur.

Interestingly, associative and repetition priming differ considerably in their time course. Associative priming tends to occur only when there are short intervals between primes and targets (e.g. 5 seconds or less; Meyer, Schvaneveldt, & Ruddy, 1975). Repetition priming can last considerably longer, and can be measured when stimuli are re-presented a day or even a year later. Also, the effects of associative priming are additive with those of repetition priming, so that the benefits due to each alone sum to produce the overall benefit when the associates are re-presented in an experiment (Wilding, 1986). These results suggest that associative and repetition priming reflect different processes. Associative priming may reflect temporary activation within an associative or contextual recognition system. Repetition priming may reflect longer term persistence within a perceptual recognition system or a specific and relatively long-lasting memory of the perceptual aspects of the prime. Also, repetition priming tends to be much larger if stimuli are re-presented within the same modality (words as words, pictures as pictures), relative to when they are re-presented in different modalities (words as their pictorial equivalent, or vice versa). This last finding can be taken to indicate that perceptual recognition systems are modality specific, with there being separate perceptual recognition systems for pictures, words, and so on.

Priming techniques thus provide a general procedure for examining the kinds of internal representation mediating information processing. Recent work also suggests that priming can occur even when subjects are unaware that they have processed the primes (e.g. if primes are presented too briefly for conscious identification; Cheesman & Merikle, 1985), and it has similarly been adopted to study the effects of brain damage on human performance – since patients may sometimes be primed by stimuli they fail to identify explicitly. In such cases priming provides an important technique for studying the kinds of information to which we gain access implicitly, or even without conscious awareness.

See also ATTENTION, INHIBITORY PROCESSES IN.

BIBLIOGRAPHY

Cheesman, J., & Merikle, P. M. (1985). Word recognition and consciousness. In D. Besner, G. E. MacKinnon, & T. G. Waller (Eds), *Reading research: Advances in theory and in practice.* New York: Academic Press.

Fischler, I., & Goodman, G. O. (1978). Latency of facilitation in memory. *Journal of Experimental Psychology: Human Perception and Performance, 4,* 455–70.

Jacoby, L. L., & Dallas, M. (1981). On the relationship between autobiographical memory and perceptual learning. *Journal of Experimental Psychology: General, 3,* 306–40.

Meyer, D. E., Schvaneveldt, R. W., & Ruddy, M. G. (1975). Loci of contextual effects on visual word recognition. In P. M. A. Rabbutt & S. Dornic (Eds), *Attention and performance V.* New York: Academic Press.

Neely, J. H. (1977). Semantic priming and retrieval from lexical memory: The roles of inhibitionless spreading activation and limited-capacity attention. *Journal of Experimental Psychology: General, 106,* 226–54.

Posner, M. I., & Snyder, C. R. R. (1975). Attention and cognitive control. In R. L. Solso (Ed.), *Information processing and cognition: The Loyola symposium.* Hillsdale, NJ: Erlbaum.

Stanovich, K. E., & West, R. F. (1983). On priming a sentence context. *Journal of Experimental Psychology: General, 112,* 1–36.

Wilding, J. (1986). Joint effects of semantic priming and repetition in a lexical decision task: Implications for a model of lexical access. *Quarterly Journal of Experimental Psychology, 38A,* 213–28.

G. W. HUMPHREYS

proactive interference (PI) A term derived from interference theory which describes the tendency for prior learning to interfere with subsequent learning – sometimes known as proactive inhibition. In general PI will be a function of the similarity between information learned on different occasions: the more similar the material the greater the PI.

PI can be noted in everyday life when, for example, we mistakenly give our old address rather than the new address to which we have just moved. However, investigations of PI have centered on controlled studies of verbal learning. Underwood (1957), one of the principal proponents of interference theory (*see* FORGETTING), attempted to explain why students who had learnt a list of nonsense syllables showed so much forgetting over a 24-hour period. Because his subjects had done many other similar experiments, he reasoned that their forgtting might be due to PI caused by the number of previous lists they had learnt. His analysis supported this view but it was not the entire explanation of forgetting. Students who had not learnt any previous lists also showed substantial forgetting. Attempts to attribute this to other sources of PI were unsuccessful.

An alternative approach to the phenomenon of PI comes from studies that have used the Brown–Peterson technique. This examines the ability of subjects to remember small amounts of information over short periods of time. During these periods the subject performs a distracting activity to prevent rehearsal. If a subject is tested repeatedly there will be a build up of PI in that performance becomes increasingly worse as the number of trials increases. Such effects are more marked if the to-be-remembered information shares a common dimension (e.g. semantic category), but these effects can be ameliorated by increasing the interval between successive trials.

Studies of PI in the Brown–Peterson paradigm led to the view that PI is caused by the development of cue overload. As more and more similar information is presented, the cues for retrieving information from any particular trial become associated with information from other trials. This theory was supported by a phenomenon known as release from PI. Again using the Brown–Peterson task, this manipulation showed that the gradual build up of PI caused by presenting similar information across trials could be destroyed by presenting information that was dissimilar (Wickens, 1973). According to cue overload theory, release from PI arises because subjects are able to encode the information in terms of a different cue to that used in retrieving information on other trials. However, an experiment by Gardiner, Craik, and Birtwhistle (1972) suggests that release from PI is due to factors that happen at retrieval rather than initial encoding. They showed that a change in the nature of information presented on different trials could still cause release from PI, even when the change was only indicated to the subjects at the point of recall.

PI is therefore a useful descriptive term when discussing the causes of impaired memory performance but, as yet, the mechanism or mechanisms underlying it are unclear (*see* FORGETTING; RETROACTIVE INTERFERENCE).

BIBLIOGRAPHY

Gardiner, J. M., Craik, F. I. M., & Birtwhistle, J. (1972). Retrieval cues and release from proactive inhibition. *Journal of Experimental Psychology*, *103*, 71–8.
Underwood, B. J. (1957). Interference and forgetting. *Psychological Review*, *64*, 49–60.
Wickens, D. D. (1973). Characteristics of word encoding. In A. W. Melton & E. Martin (Eds), *Coding processes in human memory*. Washington, DC: Winston.

A. J. PARKIN

problem solving

DEFINITION

"Problem solving" is cognitive processing directed at transforming a given situation into a goal situation when no obvious method of solution is available to the problem solver. This definition involves four basic ideas. First, problem solving is cognitive – that is, it occurs inside the mind or cognitive system of the

problem solver so that its existence can only be inferred indirectly from the behavior of the problem solver. Second, problem solving is a process – that is, it involves manipulating knowledge in the problem solver's mind or cognitive system (i.e. performing cognitive operations upon internal symbolic representations). Third, problem solving is directed – that is, it is intended to produce a solution to a problem. Fourth, problem solving is personal – that is, the difficulty of transforming a given state of a problem into a goal state depends on the existing knowledge of the problem solver.

A "problem" exists when a situation is in a given state, the problem solver wants the situation to be a goal state, and there is no obvious way of transforming the given state into the goal state. Hayes (1978, p. 177) summarized this definition as follows: "If you want to do something but do not know how, then you have a problem"; and Duncker (1945, p. 1) wrote that a problem arises when a problem solver "has a goal but does not know how this goal is to be reached." It follows that problem solving is what happens when a problem solver tries to reduce the difference between the given and goal states of a problem. Polya (1968, p. ix) characterized problem solving as "finding a way out of a difficulty, a way around an obstacle, attaining an aim that was not immediately attainable"; and Duncker (1945, p. 1) noted that "such thinking has the task of devising some action which may mediate between the existing and the desired situations."

For example, the left side of Figure 1 shows the "nine dot problem" in which the problem solver is asked to draw four straight lines that pass through all nine dots, without raising the pencil from the paper (Adams, 1974). In this case, the given state is the nine dots, the goal state is having four straight connected lines through the dots, and the allowable operators are to draw four straight lines without raising the pencil from the paper. A solution to the problem appears in the right side of the figure below, and requires realizing that the drawn lines may go outside the area bounded by the dots.

Problems may differ in how specifically the given state, goal state, and allowable operators

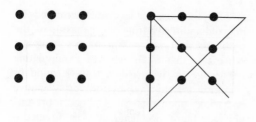

Figure 1

are presented. In *well defined problems*, such as playing a game of chess, each of these components is clearly presented; in *ill-defined problems*, such as finding a solution to the energy crisis, one or more of these components is not clearly presented. *Routine problems* occur when a problem solver possesses a pre-existing strategy for solving the problem, whereas *non-routine problems* occur when a problem solver does not. For example, for normal adults, a long-division problem such as $7891 \div 13 = $ ———, is a routine problem; whereas establishing a budget for household finances is a non-routine problem. The distinction between routine and non-routine problems may be best viewed as a continuum in which the degree of required creativity is varied; creativity in problem solving involves generating and evaluating novel alternatives about how to represent the problem or how to design a solution plan (*see* CREATIVITY). An extremely routine problem, in which the solution method is obvious to the problem solver, would not be classified as a problem at all because there would be no obstacles.

To place problem solving within the context of cognitive psychology, it should be noted that the former is a type of thinking (namely, directed thinking rather than undirected thinking – Gilhooly, 1982) and that thinking is a type of cognition (namely, a cognitive process involving manipulation of existing knowledge). Further, problem solving subsumes reasoning, including both inductive and deductive reasoning (*see* REASONING).

TYPES OF PROBLEMS

Greeno (1978) has described three types of problems. *Problems of inducing structure* occur when a problem solver is given a series of instances and must discover a pattern or rule, such as series completion and analogy problems (*see* ANALOGIES) (Sternberg, 1977). *Problems of transformation* occur when a problem solver is given a problem in an initial state and must determine a sequence of operations that produces the goal state of the problem, such as water jar problems (Luchins, 1942) and Tower of Hanoi problems. *Problems of arrangement* occur when the problem solver receives all the parts of the problem and must arrange them in a way that solves the problem, such as anagram problems and cryptarithmetic problems.

Gilhooly (1982) has distinguished between *adversary problems* such as the games of chess, GO, and poker, and *non-adversary problems* in which a single problem solver or group attempts to solve a problem. Further, reasoning problems include inductive reasoning problems, in which a problem solver must extrapolate a rule based on limited information, and deductive reasoning problems in which a problem solver must apply logically correct procedures to given information in order to derive a proven conclusion. Inductive and deductive reasoning problems can be categorized as problems of inducing structure and problems of transformation, respectively.

PROCESSES IN PROBLEM SOLVING

The process of problem solving can be analyzed into four interrelated processes: representing, planning, executing, and monitoring. The representing process occurs when a problem solver translates the given problem into an internal mental representation of the givens, goals, and available operators in the problem (Mayer, 1983). Polya (1945) refers to this process as "understanding the problem" and Hayes (1978) calls it the "understanding process." The planning process involves establishing a hierarchy of subgoals for solving the problems, a process that Polya calls "devising a plan." The executing process occurs when the problem solver implements the plan by carrying out a series of actions, a process that Polya calls "carrying out the plan." Finally, the monitoring process occurs when the problem solver analyzes his or her progress in solving the problem and determines how each executed action fits into the solution plan.

For example, consider the following problem (Riley, Greeno, & Heller, 1983):

Joe has 8 marbles.
He has 5 more marbles than Tom.
How many marbles does Tom have?

To represent the problem, one might mentally construct three sets of marbles, arrange the sets in part–whole relation to one another, and assign values to each set. Figure 2 summarizes one possible correct representation of the marble problem.

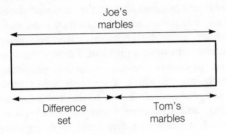

Figure 2

To devise a plan, one might mentally construct the following plan based on the equation, (Tom's marbles) = (Joe's marbles) − (Difference set):

1 To get the value of Tom's marbles, subtract the value of Joe's marbles and the value of the difference set.
2 To carry out goal 1, find the value of Joe's marbles and the value of the difference set.

To execute the plan, one might carry out the computation, $8 - 5 =$ ____, yielding an answer of 3. To monitor, one might ask, "Does this answer make sense?" For example, some problem solvers incorrectly represent the marble problem as indicated in Figure 3. In this case, the problem solver might devise a plan to add the two numbers in the problem and then carry out the computation $8 + 5 = 13$. In monitoring one's problem solving, a problem solver might ask "Is it possible that Joe has more than Tom, if Joe has 8 and Tom has 13?"

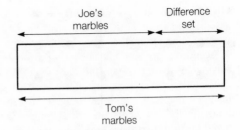

Figure 3

The problem solving process depends on the knowledge that the problem solver brings to the problem solving task (Mayer, 1985). For example, representing the problem depends on linguistic knowledge such as knowledge of the English language and factual knowledge such as knowing Tom and Joe are boy's names. Planning depends on schematic knowledge such as knowing problem types similar to the marble problem and strategic knowledge such as knowing how to establish subgoals. Execution depends on algorithmic knowledge such as knowing how to add and subtract whole numbers. Monitoring depends on the problem solver's evaluation skills such as determining whether two facts are consistent with one another. Finally, the problem solver's beliefs about problem solving may affect the amount of effort put into solving the problem.

THEORETICAL APPROACHES TO PROBLEM SOLVING

Historically, there have been three major theoretical approaches to the scientific study of problem solving: associationism, Gestalt psychology, and computer simulation.

According to the associationist view, problem solving can be described as the exercise of a chain of pre-existing links in the problem solver's associative network. The major activity in problem solving is to apply actions determined by the strengths of existing connections until by trial and error the problem is solved (Thorndike, 1898). For example, anagrams that make common words such as UGARS (SUGAR) are easier to solve than anagrams that make less common words

OBRAC (COBRA), presumably because the associative links are stronger to common words (Mayzner & Tresselt, 1966).

According to the Gestalt view, problem solving involves reorganizing a problem and can be described as a search for structural insight – that is, a search for understanding of how all the elements in the problem fit together to satisfy the requirements of the goal. The major creative act in problem solving is to mentally represent the elements of the problem within the context of the goal. For example, in the six stick problem, problem solvers are asked to construct four equilateral triangles from six identical matchsticks, as shown in the left side of Figure 4. A solution is to build a pyramid with a triangle as the base, as shown in the side of the figure.

Figure 4

The major insights in this problem are recognizing that the functional requirements of the goal are such that each stick must be part of two triangles and that to accomplish this, three-dimensional space rather than two dimensional space must be used.

The Gestalt psychologists produced several lasting contributions to our understanding of problem solving. First, Gestalt psychologists distinguished between *reproductive thinking* – applying pre-existing solution procedures based on past experience to a new problem – and *productive thinking* – generating a novel solution to a new problem (Wertheimer, 1959). Second, Gestalt psychologists introduced the idea that stages of problem solving involve successive reformulations of the problem, including increasingly more specific representations of the given state and goal state of the problem (Duncker, 1945). Third, Gestalt psychologists provided evidence that past experience can create rigidity in problem solving, including the inability to use an object

in a novel way to solve a problem (Luchins, 1942; Duncker, 1945).

According to the computer simulation view, problem solving involves applying a set of strategy rules to guide the search of a problem space. The problem space is a representation of the given state, goal state, and all possible intervening states produced by applying the operators to each state. A widely used search strategy, "means–ends analysis" (Newell & Simon, 1972), works like this: if there is an obvious action to solve the problem, it is carried out; if not, the problem solver establishes a subgoal of reducing the difference between the current state and goal state; if the problem solver finds an action that can be directly applied, it is carried out; otherwise, the problem solver establishes a subgoal of removing any constraints on applying the action, and so on. In Newell and Simon's (1972) computer simulation of means–ends analysis, the search rules serve to establish each of three major types of subgoals: (1) "transform state A into state B," in which the problem solver compares the current state of the problem to the desired state in order to determine the differences between the two states; (2) "reduce difference D between state A and state B," in which the problem solver identifies an operator that can be applied to one of the states in order to reduce the difference between the states; and (3) "apply operator Q to state A," in which either a new state is created or the problem solver determines a new constraint that precludes applying the operator.

More recent advances in COGNITIVE SCIENCE – particularly theories in the field of ARTIFICIAL INTELLIGENCE that build upon or are stimulated by the pioneering work of Newell and Simon (1972) – have added new perspectives on how to characterize problem solving in both humans and machines. In particular, the advances most relevant for problem solving are techniques for representing knowledge and planning processes in novice and expert problem solvers (*see* MENTAL MODELS; SCHEMATA).

See also COGNITIVE DEVELOPMENT; DECISION MAKING AND JUDGEMENT; INFERENCES; INTROSPECTION; METACOGNITION; SIMON, HERBERT; STRESS, ADAPTATION TO.

BIBLIOGRAPHY

Adams, J. L. (1974). *Conceptual blockbusting.* San Francisco: Freeman.

Duncker, K. (1945). On problem solving. *Psychological Monographs, 58*(5) (Whole No. 270).

Gilhooly, K. J. (1982). *Thinking: Directed, undirected, and creative.* London: Academic Press.

Greeno, J. G. (1978). Natures of problem solving abilities. In W. K. Estes (Ed.), *Handbook of learning and cognitive processes* (Vol. 5). Hillsdale, NJ: Erlbaum.

Hayes, J. R. (1978). *Cognitive psychology: Thinking and creating.* Homewood, Ill.: Dorsey Press.

Luchins, A. S. (1942). Mechanization in problem solving. *Psychological Monographs, 54*(6) (Whole No. 248).

Mayer, R. E. (1983). *Thinking, problem solving, cognition.* New York: Freeman.

——. (1985). Mathematical ability. In R. J. Sternberg (Ed.), *Human abilities: An information-processing approach.* New York: Freeman.

Mayzner, M. S., & Tresselt, M. E. (1966). Anagram solution times: A function of multiple-solution anagrams. *Journal of Experimental Psychology, 71*, 66–73.

Newell, A., & Simon, H. A. (1972). *Human problem solving.* Englewood Cliffs, NJ: Prentice-Hall.

Polya, G. (1945). *How to solve it.* Princeton, NJ: Princeton University Press.

——. (1968). *Mathematical discovery : On understanding, learning, and teaching problem solving* Vol 2. New York: Wiley.

Riley, M. S., Greeno, J. G., & Heller, J. (1983). Development of children's problem-solving ability in arithmetic. In H. P. Ginsburg (Ed.), *The development of mathematical thinking.* New York: Academic Press.

Sternberg, R. J. (1977). *Intelligence, information processing, and analogical reasoning.* Hillsdale, NJ: Erlbaum.

Thorndike, E. L. (1898). Animal intelligence: An experimental study of the associative processes in animals. *Psychological Monographs, 2*(8).

Wertheimer, M. (1959). *Productive thinking.* New York: Harper & Row.

RICHARD E. MAYER

procedural knowledge *See* DECLARATIVE AND PROCEDURAL KNOWLEDGE.

processing, automatic *See* AUTOMATIC PROCESSING.

processing, bottom-up *See* DATA-DRIVEN AND CONCEPTUALLY DRIVEN PROCESSES.

processing, cascade *See* CASCADE PROCESSING.

processing, conceptually driven *See* DATA-DRIVEN AND CONCEPTUALLY DRIVEN PROCESSES.

processing, data-driven *See* DATA-DRIVEN AND CONCEPTUALLY DRIVEN PROCESSES.

processing, levels of *See* LEVELS OF PROCESSING.

processing, sentence *See* SENTENCE PROCESSING.

processing, top-down *See* DATA-DRIVEN AND CONCEPTUALLY DRIVEN PROCESSES.

production systems These are computer programs that make use of IF…THEN rules or productions to model cognitive phenomena computationally. Computational models of cognition based on production systems have been applied in a wide variety of topic areas in cognitive psychology; from problem solving and reasoning to learning and language understanding. Before reviewing some of these production system models, let us first examine the basic components of what can loosely be called "the standard production system."

Standard production systems have a WORKING MEMORY and a permanent or LONG-TERM MEMORY of productions (i.e. IF…THEN rules). A production rule consists of a "condition" and an "action": the condition specifies one or more conditions that must be met for the action to be carried out. For example, one could have a production for identifying a dog consisting of "IF something has four legs and is furry THEN it is a dog." This production has the following condition and action:

Production for Identifying a Dog
condition:
>   x has four legs
>   x is furry

action:
>   x is a dog

In most production systems, information input from the environment is added to working memory. On a given cycle of the system, the contents of working memory are matched against the conditions of all the productions in long-term memory. If a match is found to one of these productions, then it is fired and the effect of its action is added to working memory. So, if an object in the environment is encoded in working memory as having four legs and being furry, then the information that it is a dog will be added to working memory, when the dog-identifier production rule fires.

In this way, the contents of working memory are modified on successive cycles through the repeated application of the productions in long-term memory. Typically, over a number of successive cycles "rule chaining" occurs; that is, one rule adds something to working memory, that then calls a new rule on the next cycle. If we also allow working memory to contain goals, this rule chaining can easily model problem solving behavior. For example, assume that working memory has the following contents:

>   Goal: keep safe
>   x is furry
>   x has four legs
>   x is growling

and apart from the dog-identifier rule, there is also an "escape rule":

Production for Escaping
condition:
>   Goal: keep safe
>   x is a dog
>   x is growling

action:
>   run like hell

These rules can be chained to propose an action that will keep us safe. Initially, the dog-identifier rule will add the information that "x is a dog" to working memory after matching on "x is furry" and "x has four legs." Then the escape rule will fire on the next cycle since the information that matches its condition is present, suggesting the action of running away.

Finally, standard production systems also have special production rules called "conflict resolution rules." On any given cycle, several productions may have conditions that match the contents of working memory. However, most systems will only allow one rule to fire on any cycle. Therefore, conflict resolution rules must be applied to decide which one of several rules should be fired. For example, assume we have a third rule for identifying cats:

Production for Identifying a Cat
condition:
>   x has four legs
>   x is furry
>   x miaows

action:
>   x is a cat

and the contents of working memory are as follows:

>   x has four legs
>   x is furry
>   x miaows

Both the dog- and cat-identifier rules match these contents, so a conflict resolution rule must decide between them. Intuitively, we would want the cat-identifier rule to fire since it is more accurate. This intuition could be realized by a conflict resolution rule that prefers the production with more matching conditions. Typically, this conflict resolution principle is termed "specificity," as it favors rules that have a more detailed fit to the contents of working memory.

Apart from specificity, there are three other main conflict resolution principles used in standard production systems: refractoriness, recency, and production ordering. "Refractoriness" prevents a rule matching the same elements in working memory over and over again; hence, it is designed to stop looping. For instance, in the above escape example, without refractoriness the dog-identifier rule might match on the furry and four-legged elements again and again, adding to working memory the information that a dog is present repeatedly. "Recency" is a very powerful principle that prefers a rule with conditions that match those elements most recently added to working memory. Thus, in the escape example, on the second cycle the dog-identifier rule and the escape rule would have come into conflict. If recency were the only conflict resolution rule available then the escape rule would be preferred because one of its conditions would match the most recently added "x is a dog" element in working memory. Finally, one can also decide between competing rules by simply ordering the set of production rules according to some criterion (e.g. order them in terms of importance). Then, when a conflict arises, that rule which is higher up the list is preferred to one lower down.

Although the basic ideas are very simple, production system models can become very complicated. As the number of productions increases, the number of possible interactions between the rules becomes very difficult to control and predict. In this sense, the conflict resolution principles are critical to the successful operation of the system. In artificial intelligence, where production systems are used in expert systems technology, it has been found repeatedly that large production systems will sometimes grind to a halt because of such unforeseen interactions.

PRODUCTION SYSTEM MODELS IN COGNITIVE PSYCHOLOGY

The relationship between production systems and information-processing psychology is a bit of a chicken and egg situation. It is not wholly clear whether information-processing ideas were formed in the image of production systems or production systems were a particularly good method for realizing information-processing ideas.

The close relationship between production systems and information processing psy-chology can, to a great extent, be attributed to Allen Newell and Herb Simon (see SIMON, HERBERT). These two founders of information-processing psychology were among the first to model cognitive behavior using production systems (see Simon, 1969; Newell & Simon, 1972). The first and most well known of these production systems was the General Problem Solver (GPS; see Newell, Shaw, & Simon, 1958). GPS was applied to a variety of puzzle-like problems and was a vehicle for the development of Newell and Simon's ideas about the general-purpose heuristics (like means–ends analysis) that underlie human PROBLEM SOLVING. Production systems, like GPS, instantiate several psychological features that have remained central to many subsequent psychological theories. First, the standard production system has a limited working memory that parallels the limitations of human working memory. Thus, by limiting the number of items working memory can hold, the effects of information loss in a cognitive task can be simulated (e.g. see Atwood & Polson, 1976). Second, knowledge is instantiated as rules that manipulate symbols in working memory, so differences in knowledge between human information processors can be simulated by varying the number and/or the content of the rules brought to a cognitive task (e.g. see Anderson, 1983).

Several further developments of production systems have been made since the initial work on GPS. Anderson's "Adaptive Control of Thought" theory (1976, 1983, 1987) (see DECLARATIVE AND PROCEDURAL KNOWLEDGE) has been realized in a series of production systems, the most well known of which is the ACT* system (pronounced ACT-star). ACT*, which has been used to model skill learning and other psychological phenomena (see COGNITIVE SCIENCE), makes several changes to the standard production system architecture.

The first main modification to standard production systems is the addition of a second long-term memory. In ACT* there are two distinct long-term memories; a declarative memory and a production memory. The "declarative memory," modeled by a semantic network of interconnected concepts (see SE-

MANTIC MEMORY), contains "declarative knowledge" whereas the production memory contains a set of productions that make up the system's "procedural knowledge" (*see* DECLARATIVE AND PROCEDURAL KNOWLEDGE). The second main modification is that working memory is not a distinct entity with a number of slots for holding elements but is simply that part of declarative memory which is currently active.

Third, ACT* uses two main conflict resolution principles. In the first conflict resolution method, preference is given to rules that match the goals currently in working memory over those that do not. The second way in which conflicts between rules are resolved makes use of the differential strengths of rules. In ACT*, whenever a rule is fired successfully its strength is increased by one unit. Thus, when a number of rules match the contents of working memory, that rule which is the strongest, or that rule which has been most successful in the past, is fired. These ideas about rule strengthening are used to model the ubiquitous effects of practice in cognitive skills.

Finally, unlike standard production systems, the ACT* system can also learn by applying rules to the contents of declarative and production memory. "Proceduralization" results in the formation of new productions from the contents of declarative memory and the trace of applying more general-purpose heuristic rules (e.g. learning by analogy) to a problem situation. "Composition" collapses a long sequence of productions into a shorter sequence or a single production rule. In the process of "production tuning," existing productions can be modified by the generalization or discrimination of their conditions.

While ACT* is an impressive cognitive architecture, in the range of phenomena to which it has been applied, several other competing schemes have been proposed to challenge it. Recently, Holland, Holyoak, Nisbett, & Thagard (1986) have modeled a variety of cognitive processes using a different type of production system. They argue that the most important difference in their system is that it allows many rules rather than a single rule to be fired on a given cycle.

Holland et al. point out that the restriction of firing only one rule on each cycle means that it is necessary to have a single rule for every step in a problem. This seems reasonable, accepting that one can specify all the necessary rules, but it also means that difficulties arise when the system has to deal with novel situations that do not match any useful rule. Recall the cat-identifier rule which states that "If something has four legs, is furry and miaows, then it is a cat." Suppose we have heard the animal miaow and seen that it is furry but we can only see its front two legs. In a single-rule-firing production system with this information present in working memory, the cat-identifier rule would fail to fire. However, clearly we would want the system to be able to "assume" that the entity had two other legs and make the conjecture that it might be a cat. The only way this can be done in a standard production system is to allow partial matching on the conditions of a rule, but this is not a very adequate solution to the problem. As Holland et al. point out, if a system has the following rule:

Production for Crossing a Lake
condition:
> Goal: cross a body of water
> body of water is about a mile wide
> you are a strong swimmer

action:
> swim across

and it wants to cross a large body of water, but is a weak swimmer, partial matching on the conditions of the rule will result in a dramatic decrease in the system's life expectancy. As a solution to this problem, Holland et al. allow multiple rules to fire on a given cycle. By having this "limited parallelism" in rule firing, several different rules can summate converging evidence and can use multiple sources of weak support to arrive at a confident conclusion. Thus, there may be converging evidence for the cat-identifier rule from other rules fired simultaneously on other aspects of the situation. Like the ACT* system, Holland et al.'s system is concerned with learning and problem solving; the framework has been applied to several psychological phenomena – including analogy, reasoning, statistical judgements and scientific discovery – although implemented programs in each of these areas have not been carried out.

The final production system that deserves mention is, fittingly, the latest model to emerge from the work of Newell and his associates (see Rosenbloom & Newell, 1986; Laird, Newell, & Rosenbloom, 1987; Newell, in press). This system, called SOAR (standing for State, Operator And Result), is also designed to be a cognitive architecture or a unified theory of cognition. Like more recent production systems, one of its central features is two learning mechanisms. The first of these is called "universal subgoaling," which can be viewed as another method for conflict resolution. In SOAR, whenever an impass is reached (e.g. when several rules can be applied to the contents of working memory), a new subgoal is established to resolve this impasse. In deciding between conflicting rules, therefore, SOAR will set up a subgoal to choose one from the set. This subgoal might be achieved by extrapolating the various consequences of applying the alternative productions and then choosing one on the basis of considering the pros and cons of these consequences. The second learning mechanism used by SOAR, that is reminiscent of Anderson's compilation, is called "chunking" (for a related idea see CHUNKING). This mechanism replaces long sequences of rules with a single production that does the same task. SOAR has been tested more computationally than psychologically, in the sense that its proponents have used it to model established psychological phenomena rather than to generate new predictions for psychological experiments.

Whenever we find production system models in cognitive psychology we also invariably find a large-scale attempt to model psychological phenomena in a cognitive architecture. Thus, production systems have played a central role in many parts of cognitive psychology. The fate of them as computational modeling techniques for cognitive psychologists rests, therefore, to a large degree on the future of the research program to create cognitive architectures. Two negative outcomes suggest themselves. First, accepting

that unified theories of cognition are possible, production systems may not turn out to be the best vehicle for such an enterprise. Some other modeling scheme may be more appropriate. As Newell himself pointed out in the William James lectures (see Newell, in press), the great wave of connectionism may drown research efforts using production systems. Touretzky and Hinton (1988), for example, have recently shown that many production system features can be replicated in a connectionist scheme (see CONNECTIONIST MODELS OF MEMORY). Second, the current quest for a unified theory of cognition may be radically premature, in which case production systems may be tainted by the failure.

If the current production system architectures succeed, then they will remain a central part of cognitive psychology; if they fail then they will be the dinosaurs of the future. It remains to be seen which of these two rules will fire.

See also PERCEPTION, COMPUTATIONAL THEORY OF.

BIBLIOGRAPHY

Anderson, J. R. (1976). *Language, memory and thought*. Hillsdale, NJ: Erlbaum.
——. (1983). *The architecture of cognition*. Cambridge, Mass.: Harvard University Press.
——. (1987). Skill acquisition: Compilation of weak-method problem solutions. *Psychological Review*, *94*, 192–210.
Atwood, M. E., & Polson, P. G. (1976). A process model for water jug problems. *Cognitive Psychology*, *8*, 191–216.
Holland, J. H., Holyoak, K. J., Nisbett, R. E., & Thagard, P. (1986). *Induction: Processes in inference, learning and discovery*. Cambridge, Mass.: MIT Press.
Laird, J. E., Newell, A., & Rosenbloom, P. (1987). SOAR: An architecture for general intelligence. *Artificial Intelligence*, *33*, 1–64.
Newell, A. (In press) *Unified theories of cognition*. Cambridge, Mass.: Harvard University Press.
——, & Simon, H. A. (1972). *Human problem solving*. Englewood Cliffs, NJ: Prentice-Hall.
Newell, A., Shaw, J. C., & Simon, H. A. (1958). Elements of a theory of human problem solving. *Psychological Review*, *65*, 151–66.
Rosenbloom, P., & Newell, A. (1986). The

chunking of goal hierarchies: A generalised model of practice. In R. S. Michalski, J. G. Carbonell, & J. M. Mitchell (Eds), *Machine learning II: An artificial intelligence approach.* Los Altos, Calif.: Kaufmann.

Simon, H. A. (1969). *The sciences of the artificial.* Cambridge, Mass.: MIT Press.

Touretzky, D. S., & Hinton, G. E. (1988). A distributed connectionist production system. *Cognitive Science, 12,* 423–66.

MARK T. KEANE

propositional representations These are abstract, amodal, language-like symbols that constitute the language of the mind; as mental representations they are a universal *mentalese*, the basic code in which all cognitive activities are proposed to be carried out.

One of the hallmarks of information-processing psychology is the attempt to specify the mental representations and processes that are involved in a particular cognitive task. A large part of this enterprise is, therefore, concerned with specifying the mental representations that are manipulated by cognitive processes. Given that people the world over, irrespective of the native language they speak, can understand one another and manifest broadly similar patterns of mental abilities, it has been proposed that there must be a universal code in which cognitive activities are carried out. Furthermore, given that each of us can know the world via a variety of modalities (e.g. sight, smell, and sound) and yet use that acquired knowledge in a modality-independent manner, it has been argued that there must be a central code for representing information that is independent of its original source. Many have proposed that these representations are propositional in their format and that they are the medium in which all cognition is carried out (e.g. see Pylyshyn, 1984).

However, this propositionalist view raises several important issues about mental representations. First, there is the practical problem of specifying the nature of these representations; how can something which is universal to all languages and independent of the senses be specified? As we shall see, propositional representations are usually specified in terms of the predicate calculus. Second, while it may be admitted that propositional representations exist, it is reasonable to suppose that they are only one among a number of different codes used by the mind; that other modality-specific codes also play a role in cognition. We shall examine briefly both of these issues in the present essay.

SPECIFYING PROPOSITIONAL REPRESENTATIONS

Propositional representations characterize concepts in a format that is not specific to any language (whether it be Russian, Irish, or Sanskrit) or to any modality (whether it be vision, audition, olfaction, or touch). How, then, are we to talk about them? When theorists want to be explicit about propositional representations they usually specify them in terms of a logical system called the "predicate calculus." In logics like the propositional and predicate calculi, a proposition is defined as *an entity which represents a single idea.*

In the predicate calculus, propositions are detailed in terms of "predicates" and their "arguments." A predicate is anything which takes one or a number of arguments. Thus, the proposal that "Ronan hit Conor with the pole and the pole was hard" can be represented using the predicates HIT and HARD (note that the capitals denote that it is not the word that is represented but its conceptual content) and the arguments RONAN, CONOR, and STICK. These can be combined together in a bracketed notation, as follows:

HIT(RONAN, CONOR, POLE) & HARD(POLE)

Whenever one has a predicate and a number of arguments combined in this fashion the whole form is called a "proposition"; furthermore, any combination of several such forms is also considered to be a proposition (i.e. the whole of the above expression is also a proposition). It should be noted that predicates can take any number of arguments; they can take one argument, in which case they are called one-place predicates [like HARD-

(POLE)], or multi-placed [like HIT (RONAN, CONOR, POLE)]. The predicate calculus comes in different versions called orders: first-order predicate calculus, second-order predicate calculus. First-order predicates are predicates which take object constants as their arguments (like RONAN, CONOR, and POLE), whereas second-order predicates can take propositions as their arguments. Thus, in characterizing the sentence "When Ronan hit Conor with the pole, Conor was hurt" we can use the second-order predicate CAUSE to predicate the two other propositions:

CAUSE [
    HIT (RONAN, CONOR, POLE)
    HURT (RONAN, CONOR)
  ]

In conclusion, cognitive psychologists have used the predicate calculus to express *mental, propositional representations*. However, psychologists do not use all the strictures employed by logicians. The detailed axioms of the calculus are not often used and other aspects may be changed. For example, strict adherence to formal definitions of truth, falsity, and formal validity are often ignored or passed over. In short, typically, theorists merely use the notion that ideational content can be stated in terms of predicates taking one or more arguments. It is a moot point whether this is the best way to employ the predicate calculus.

However, one of the main benefits of using the predicate calculus is that any theory that assumes propositional representations can be modeled easily in a computer program. This is because many of the modern artificial intelligence computing languages like LISP (Hasemer & Domingue, 1989) and PROLOG (Clocksin & Mellish, 1981) have a close relationship to the predicate calculus (*see* ARTIFICIAL INTELLIGENCE). In fact, PROLOG essentially *is* the predicate calculus with some computational additions. Thus, the use of propositional representations has allowed researchers to be very precise about their theoretical proposals, by permitting them to construct and run computer models of cognitive processes.

ONE MENTAL CODE OR MANY?

There are actually two separate issues when we come to consider the question of whether there is one or more mental codes. First, there is the definitional issue of whether it is possible to categorically distinguish between different representational formats. Second, even if one assumes that different codes can be discerned, there is the remaining question about the role these different representations should play in psychological theories. We will consider each of these issues in turn.

Traditionally, propositional representations have been contrasted with "analogical representations." Analogical representations are images which may be either visual, auditory, olfactory, tactile, or kinetic (*see* ANALOGIES); in short, they are modality specific. The prime example of an analog representation is a visual image, although several distinct types can be identified (e.g. auditory images). Propositional representations are, as we have seen, amodal.

However, beyond this distinction it has often been difficult to specify the exact sense in which the two types of representation differ. It has been proposed that analogical representations parallel the things they represent in a way that propositional representations do not; that analogical representations are *analogous* to what they represent, in the sense that they retain the same structure. For example, a visual image could be argued to retain the spatial structure of a set of objects in the world, in a way that a propositional representation of the same state of affairs would not. However, this distinction is not as cut and dried as it seems because the exact relationship between any mental representation and things in the world is very difficult to specify.

It has also been suggested that analogical representations are continuous and nondiscrete whereas propositional representations can be partitioned into discrete entities. That is, one can take an image and circumscribe any arbitrary part of it and it will still refer to something. A portion of an image of a cigarette will still represent a portion of the cigarette. Propositional representations cannot be divided arbitrarily and continue to represent entities in a similar manner. Rather, they consist of discrete conceptual entities that can only be divided up in ways that are determined by strict rules of combination (for a useful discussion of such issues, see Boden, 1988). However, it is clear that both types of representations must have some rules of combination; perhaps the rules of combination for analogical representations are just more flexible.

Setting aside the difficulties of finding definite distinctions between the two types of representations, the assumption that they *do* differ has formed the basis for one of the most controversial debates in cognitive psychology. This so-called, imagery–propositional debate has been prompted by assertions about the singularity of propositional representations in human cognition. In this debate the strong propositionalist view has argued that (a) conceptions of analogical representations are ill-specified to the point of vacuity; (b) even if they were well specified, analogical representations are epiphenomenal in the sense that, even though they may accompany cognition, they do not play a central causal role in it; and (c) if a significant role can be attributed to analogical representations in cognitive behavior, that role can also be accounted for in propositional terms because analogical representations are reducible to propositional representations (e.g. see Pylyshyn, 1984).

Several theorists from the analogical or imagery camp have argued against this view (e.g. see Kosslyn, 1983; Paivio, 1986). They have made three main counter-claims: (a) that imagery is not a vacuous construct but can be well specified; in particular, it can be stated with sufficient precision to be modeled computationally (see Kosslyn, 1983); (b) that it is necessary to posit a separate, image-based processing and representational system in order to account for the results of numerous experiments on a wide spectrum of cognitive behavior (see Paivio, 1986); and (c) that visual images are represented in a spatial medium which has special emergent properties that are not manifested by propositional representations (Kosslyn, 1983) (*see* DUAL-CODE THEORY OF IMAGERY; IMAGERY, COMPUTATIONAL THEORY OF).

Several empirical and theoretical attempts have been made to resolve this imagery–propositional controversy, usually by attempting to muster support for one view over the other. However, for several reasons, the issue has remained unresolved and has been abandoned by most researchers as an active topic of debate. This state of affairs can be largely attributed to the empirical intractability of the issue. That is, it is probably impossible to decide empirically between the two views because any cognitive task that is asserted to be the result of one type of mental representation acted upon by a given set of processes can be mimicked by another set of processes acting on a different form of mental representation. Furthermore, part of the controversy may proceed from fundamentally different philosophical stances on the nature of scientific knowledge and the means by which truth is to be achieved (see Eysenck & Keane, 1990, chap. 7). Imagery researchers like Paivio take a strong empiricist stand on scientific knowledge whereas propositional theorists are more rationalist in their leanings.

A final twist to the controversy is that it is possible to admit a propositional view and yet uphold the need for an analysis of cognitive behavior in terms of analogical representations. Johnson-Laird (1983), for example, has made the point that an analysis of cognition solely in terms of propositional representations would be too detailed. It would be like attempting to write programs solely in machine code rather than in some high-level programing language. People, he maintains, have higher-level analogical representations, just as programers have high-level programing languages, to reduce the complexity of tasks and their information-processing loads. Psychological theories must, therefore, be pitched at a level that captures the use of these analogical representations, even though ultimately they may rely on detailed propositional representations (*see* MENTAL MODELS).

CONCLUSION

Propositional representations are one of the most centrally used theoretical constructs in all of cognitive psychology. They are either implicitly or explicitly assumed in a wide range of cognitive theories. In language comprehension, they are used to characterize the underlying conceptual representations of verbs and nouns (e.g. Norman & Rumelhart, 1975). In memory organization, they are assumed to underlie the representation of semantic memory, schemata, scripts, and other knowledge structures (e.g. Norman & Rumelhart, 1975; Schank & Abelson, 1977; Anderson, 1983). They are assumed to be central to problem solving and reasoning skills (e.g. see Newell & Simon, 1972; Anderson, 1983) (*see* PROBLEM SOLVING). The irony of this situation is that the extensiveness of their use is paralleled by a paucity of direct tests of their properties. The properties of propositional representations that are only tested indirectly; they are tested as they emerge when propositions are combined into more complex structures (like schemata). In contrast, analogical representations, on to which the burden of proof has often fallen, have had to show that their specific properties are revealed in a wide variety of experimental situations.

BIBLIOGRAPHY

Anderson, J. R. (1983). *The architecture of cognition.* Cambridge, Mass.: Harvard University Press.

Boden, M. (1988). *Computer models of mind.* Cambridge: Cambridge University Press.

Clocksin, W., & Mellish, C. (1981). Programming in PROLOG. New York: Springer-Verlag.

Eysenck, M. W., & Keane, M. T. (1990). *Cognitive psychology: A student's handbook.* London: Lawrence Erlbaum.

Hasemer, T., & Domingue, J. D. (1989). *Common lisp programming for artificial intelligence.* Wokingham: Addison Wesley.

Johnson-Laird, P. N. (1983). *Mental models.* Cambridge: Cambridge University Press.

Kosslyn, S. M. (1983). *Ghosts in the mind's machine: Creating and using images in the brain.* New York: Norton.

Newell, A., & Simon, H. A. (1972). *Human problem solving.* Englewood Cliffs, NJ: Prentice-Hall.

Norman, D. A., & Rumelhart, D. E. (1975). *Explorations in cognition.* San Francisco: Freeman.

Paivio, A. (1986). *Mental representations: A dual coding approach.* Oxford: Oxford University Press.

Pylyshyn, Z. (1984). *Computation and cognition.* Cambridge, Mass.: MIT Press.

Schank, R. C., & Abelson, R. P. (1977). *Scripts, plans, goals and understanding.* Hillsdale, NJ: Erlbaum.

MARK T. KEANE

R

reaction time *See* DISCRIMINATION REACTION TIME.

reading, dual-route model of *See* DUAL-ROUTE MODEL OF READING.

reading development To some extent the way a child learns to read (i.e. its reading development) will be influenced by the particular language and writing system that is involved. Written English presents particular problems because it is orthographically irregular – that is, there is a very inconsistent relationship between spelling and sound. For example, the letters *ough* can be pronounced in several different ways. Such irregularity means that adult readers have to use a lexical procedure for reading many words rather than being able to rely solely on the use of rules for converting letters to sounds (*see* DUAL-ROUTE MODEL OF READING).

There are several different theories about how children learn to read English – and other orthographically irregular languages – but there is general agreement that several different stages or phases are involved. One of the best known models is that of Frith (1985) who proposes a three-phase theory of reading development in which the child uses a different strategy at each phase.

In the first phase, the child uses a "logographic strategy" in which words are recognized as wholes. During this first phase, the child builds up a sight vocabulary of familiar words but is unable to make any attempt at reading unfamiliar words. By the second, "alphabetic phase," the child is able to convert graphemes into phonemes and relies on this ability when attempting to pronounce unfamiliar words. However, such attempts will only be successful with orthographically regular words and unfamiliar irregular words will be mispronounced.

Passing through the alphabetic phase is seen by Frith as a necessary precursor for attainment of the third phase of reading development, the "orthographic phase." In this phase, the child develops an orthographic strategy in which words are broken down into orthographic units – strings of letters. Unlike the alphabetic stage, these units are not converted to phonemes. The development of an orthographic strategy allows the child to attempt the pronunciation of irregular words.

One problem with Frith's theory is that she does not clearly explain exactly how reading occurs in the orthographic phase, or how this phase differs from the logographic phase (see Stuart & Coltheart, 1988). However, there is evidence for a phase in reading development where phonological decoding is paramount, and a later phase where children rely less on phonological coding. The evidence comes from an experiment by Doctor and Coltheart (1980) in which young normal readers at five age levels (six to ten years) were asked to read short sequences of words and decide whether or not they made sense. The meaningless sentences were of two kinds. Half were sentences like (1a) which, if read by a grapheme–phoneme conversion procedure, would sound meaningful. The other half were like (1b) and did not sound meaningful:

(1a)   Tell me wear he went.
(1b)   Tell me knew he went.

The purpose of presenting these two different kinds of meaningless sentence was to see whether children were using a grapheme–phoneme conversion procedure in reading. For children who were using such a procedure, sentences like (1a) and (1b) should seem very different whereas, for children who were reading using a more visual strategy which did not involve phonological recoding, both types of sentence should be equally meaningless.

Doctor and Coltheart found that six-year-old children frequently thought that sentences like (1a) were meaningful although they correctly decided that sentences like (1b) were not meaningful. This suggests that they were relying on a grapheme–phoneme conversion procedure in reading (see DUAL-ROUTE MODEL OF READING). However, the older children in the experiment treated the two types of sentence as equally meaningless, suggesting that, by the age of seven years, most children are using a reading procedure that does not involve phonological recoding.

An alternative to Frith's model has been put forward by Seymour (Seymour & MacGregor, 1984), who argues for the existence of three broad and partially overlapping stages in reading development. Seymour uses the same names for these stages as Frith but there are important differences between the models in the two latter stages.

The initial, "logographic," stage is essentially the same as that proposed by Frith. The child builds up a limited sight vocabulary on the basis of purely visual differences between words. This is followed by the learning of simple grapheme–phoneme correspondences (and analogous phoneme–grapheme correspondences for spelling) in an "alphabetic" stage. These correspondences operate at the level of single letter–sound (and sound–single letter) and so are different from the correspondences occurring in Frith's alphabetic stage which involve larger units. In the final, "orthographic," stage, the child develops a sophisticated model of orthography which includes knowledge of morphology and the use of lexical analogies in reading new words (see GRAMMAR). This latter ability allows the child to read unfamiliar words on the basis of their visual similarity to known words.

Seymour's main interest is in how these different stages of reading interrelate. Models of adult reading often make use of the notion of dual or triple routes (see DUAL-ROUTE MODEL OF READING): Seymour's model is of a dual lexicon. In this model, the child who is reading by use of a logographic strategy is setting up a logographic lexicon in which words are discriminated one from another on the basis of visual characteristics.

There has been considerable debate about the precise nature of these visual characteristics. One suggestion has been that, in this initial – sight-vocabulary – stage of reading, children recognize words in terms of their overall shape. However, Harris and Coltheart (1986) report data on the reading ability of a four-year-old child, Alice, who was at this early stage of reading. Alice could read about 30 words and most of these had been "picked up," rather than being taught. One such word was the name "Harrods" which Alice had seen on the side of buses and on shopping bags from the Harrods store. This word was particularly interesting because Alice had almost certainly only ever seen this word written in one typescript – that used in the store logo.

Alice was presented with this word in an entirely different format, using a different typeface and alternating upper and lower case letters: 'hArRoDs." If Alice were reading using information about visual shape, she should have had great difficulty in reading this visually unfamiliar version of the familiar word. However, this was not the case, and she immediately read the word as "Harrods."

If Alice's performance is typical of other children at the initial stage of reading development, it is clear that the basis of the visual recognition of words in a sight vocabulary is not overall word shape. This conclusion is supported by data from Seymour and Elder (1986) who suggest another possibility, namely that words are discriminated on the basis of some – or perhaps only one – of their letters. However, Alice demonstrated that she was able to pick out the word "Max" from the following items: mAx, rAx, mOx, mAv. This would only have been possible if she were taking account of all the letters in this word.

Whatever the precise nature of the discrimination involved in the first stage of reading, it does seem clear that it involves visual characteristics of words rather than their sounds; and hence gives rise to a visually organized – logographic – lexicon. In Seymour's model, the child also develops another lexicon. This is initially an alphabetic lexicon – arising from the alphabetic stage of reading – which is a rudimentary grapheme–phoneme convertor based on single letter–sound translations. This lexicon is later superseded by an orthographic lexicon which contains the more sophisticated orthographic knowledge developed during the third stage of reading development. Once established, both the orthographic and the logographic lexicons remain through life.

Both Frith's model and that of Seymour have been used to explain why some children have difficulties in learning to read (*see* DYSLEXIA: DEVELOPMENTAL); and evidence concerning disordered patterns of reading development has been used to question the assumption that all children learn to read in the manner described by theories of normal reading development (see Stuart & Coltheart, 1988). One particular controversy concerns the role of phonological awareness in reading development.

For normally developing children, learning to read occurs some time after learning to speak. This means that, when children first encounter written words, they already know a great deal about how words sound when they are spoken. Since one part of learning to read involves the development of grapheme–phoneme conversion skills, some researchers have suggested that children's ability to segment words into phonemes will affect the rate at which they learn to read. This possibility was explored in a study by Bradley and Bryant (1983), who investigated the ability of pre-reading children to analyze words into their constituent sounds. In one test they presented children with sets of three one-syllable words (such as "hill," "pig," and "pin") and asked them to say which was the odd one out. (The correct answer is "hill" because the other two words both begin with the sound "pi.")

Bradley and Bryant found that, when the children's subsequent reading performance was measured after three years of schooling, those children who had initially been good at analyzing words into their constituent sounds were better readers than those children who had not been good at this task.

In another study, Bradley and Bryant gave various forms of training to prereading children who were poor at the sound analyzing task (*see* DYSLEXIA: DEVELOPMENTAL). One group of children was trained to analyze words in terms of their sounds; another was trained to analyze words in terms of their meaning, not their sounds. A third group of children was given the sound training and also taught that individual sounds could be represented by letters. Three years later the children's reading progress was assessed and it was found that the group who had received sound training had learned to read more successfully than the group who had been trained to classify words by meaning. The group who had received both sound and letter training had the highest reading scores.

The results of the Bryant and Bradley study suggest that the ability to divide words into their constituent sounds does facilitate reading development. However, there is also good evidence that learning to read increases phonological awareness (Stuart & Coltheart, 1988) so it would appear that reading development both facilitates and is facilitated by children's knowledge of the phonological structure of spoken language.

BIBLIOGRAPHY

Bradley, P., & Bryant, L. (1983). Categorizing sounds and learning to read: A causal connection. *Nature*, *301*, 419–21.

Doctor, E., & Coltheart, M. (1980). Children's use of phonological encoding when reading for meaning. *Memory & Cognition*, 8, 195–209.

Frith, U. (1985). Beneath the surface of developmental dyslexia. In K. E. Patterson, J. C. Marshall, & M. Coltheart (Eds), *Surface dyslexia*. London: Erlbaum.

Harris, M., & Coltheart, M. (1986). *Language processing in children and adults: An introduction to psycholinguistics*. London: Routledge & Kegan Paul.

Seymour, P. H. K., & Elder, L. (1986). Beginning reading without phonology. *Cognitive Neuropsychology*, *3*, 1–37.

Seymour, P. H. K., & MacGregor, C. J. (1984). Developmental dyslexia: A cognitive experimental analysis of phonological, morphemic and visual impairments. *Cognitive Neuropsychology*, *1*, 43–83.

Snowling, M. E. (1987). *Dyslexia: A cognitive developmental perspective*. Oxford: Blackwell.

Stuart, M., & Coltheart, M. (1988). Does reading develop in a sequence of stages? *Cognition*, *30*, 139–81.

MARGARET HARRIS

reality monitoring The ability to discriminate between externally derived memories that originate from perceptions and internally derived memories that originate from imagination has been called reality monitoring. External memories are based directly on sensory information, and represent events that really occurred, objects that were really perceived, actions that were performed, words that were heard or spoken, read or written. Internal memories are mental constructions, and represent events that have only been imagined or dreamed of, actions that were planned or considered, words that were thought but never uttered. The ability to distinguish between these two kinds of memory is to know the difference between facts and fantasies, and reality monitoring is obviously essential for competence in everyday life. However, the importance of this aspect of memory was largely unrecognized until Johnson and Raye (1981) coined the term "reality monitoring" and began an intensive study of it.

Traditional studies of memory have concentrated on the ability to retain information, but the recent trend toward studying memory in naturalistic real world situations has highlighted the fact that it is often important to remember the source of that information (Schachter, Harbluk, & McLachlan, 1984). For example, in social interactions or at work we may need to remember not only what was said, but who said it, and where and when. Source memory is the ability to remember the origin of information and usually involves distinguishing between a number of possible external sources. Reality monitoring is a special form of source memory involving the distinction between internal and external sources.

Although at first sight the distinction may seem to be obvious, it is, in fact, often a difficult one. This is because many memories are neither purely external, nor purely internal, but involve components from both sources. According to the constructivist view of memory, widely accepted today, an external memory is not a direct copy of the physical information received through the senses. Constructivist theories emphasize the role of elaboration, interpretation, and reconstruction based on prior knowledge in the form of stored SCHEMATA, such that a memory is composed of externally derived sensory information integrated with internally derived knowledge. It follows that the distinction between internal and external memories is relative rather than absolute, and may sometimes be difficult to make. Childhood memories, or anecdotes that have been retold many times, often comprise this sort of mixture of perceived and self-generated material, with the original experience being imaginatively embellished or transformed until fact and fiction can no longer be distinguished.

Reality monitoring characteristically breaks down in schizophrenia, in dementias such as Alzheimer's, and other mental disorders involving hallucinations or obsessions, and it is temporarily disrupted by delirium or intoxication. In these cases, people may be unable to distinguish between the real and the imaginary in current experience as well as in memory. It has also been suggested that reality monitoring is imperfect in the very young and the very old. And, although normal adults are generally able to distinguish competently between fact and fantasy, failures of reality monitoring in everyday life are not uncommon.

It is sometimes difficult to distinguish between the memory of performing an action and the memory of planning that action, or forming the intention to perform it. People may be uncertain, for example, whether they have actually locked the door, turned off the light, added salt to the soup, taken a dose of medicine, or only thought about doing these things. Similar confusions arise with respect to utterances. People may be mistaken about whether they have actually said something or only intended to say it. Uncertainties or confusions of this kind produce errors of performance, and the direction of confusion affects the kind of error that is made. When a planned or imagined act is mistaken for the memory of a real act, an omission error occurs because the actor concludes wrongly that the act has already been performed. Conversely, if the memory of a performed action is mistaken for an imagined one, the result is a repetition error. In this case, people are liable to take a second dose of medicine or to put salt in the soup twice over. Failures of reality monitoring may also underlie losing objects if the memory of putting objects, such as keys or spectacles, in a particular place is in fact the memory of an intention rather than a memory of an action. The quality of social interactions can also be adversely affected if errors of reality monitoring cause repetition errors such that the speaker tells the same person the same thing more than once.

Johnson and Raye (1981) have put forward a model to explain how reality monitoring decisions are made. They suggested that there are two ways in which internal and external memories can be distinguished. The first method consists of evaluating the features of the memory trace. According to the model, external memories are characterized by being richer in sensory attributes such as sound, color, and texture. They also are accompanied by more contextual information linking them to a specific time and place of occurrence, and to preceding and succeeding events (see EPISODIC MEMORY). Internally generated memories, by contrast, are more schematic and lacking in contextual details. They are also more likely to contain traces of the cognitive operations, such as reasoning, inferring, or imaging, that produced them. Thus, according to the model, the origin of a memory can generally be determined by evaluating the extent to which it possesses these characteristics. However, rules of this kind may not always yield a clear-cut decision. Internal memories can sometimes be unusually clear and detailed, or external memories may be blurred and vague. The failures of reality monitoring observed in everyday life confirm that the two kinds of memory representation are qualitatively confusable, and cannot always be differentiated. A second method for making the distinction is to employ the criteria of coherence and plausibility. If a memory is externally derived it ought to make sense and

conform to our knowledge of the world. Internally derived memories can sometimes be recognized because they fail to fit this criterion. Dreams and fantasies, for example, may conflict with natural laws or violate common sense.

These strategies may be successful in distinguishing between internal and external memories, but a different strategy may be needed for determining the particular source of an external memory. It is sometimes necessary to remember whether an action was performed by oneself or by someone else, or whether an utterance was made by oneself or by someone else. These decisions involve what is known as the "generation effect" whereby self-generated actions and utterances are remembered much better than other-generated ones. Relying on the fact that self-generated memory traces are reliably stronger, people assume that they would be able to recognize the origin of a memory if it were something they had done or said themselves (I'd know if I'd done it). If they are not confident that the memory trace was self-generated, they attribute the action or utterance, by default, to another person. The attribution of the memory is based on the degree of confidence.

This model of reality monitoring has been tested by experimentally manipulating the characteristics of internal and external memories and observing the effects on reality monitoring judgements. Johnson, Raye, Wang, and Taylor (1979) tested the prediction that people who are unusually good at forming vivid and detailed visual images should be poor at reality monitoring because the vividness of their self-generated images would make them qualitatively similar to externally derived memories (see IMAGERY AND PERCEPTION). As predicted, when asked to view objects and to image the same objects for a varying number of times, good imagers overestimated the frequency with which they had really seen the objects. The judged frequency was inflated by the number of times they had imagined the object.

Other experiments have been designed to manipulate the amount of cognitive operations in the memory trace. For example, subjects were asked to generate words under conditions which made it either easy or difficult to retrieve the required words. Later, when they had to identify which words they had spoken themselves and which words had been spoken by somebody else, they were more accurate at identifying the words that had been difficult to generate. According to the model, these words were easier to recognize because the memory representation contained traces of more cognitive operations. The model predicts a gradient of confusability such that it is harder to distinguish between memories with more similar origins, and this prediction was confirmed in a study by Anderson (1984). She found that subjects were more likely to confuse two different kinds of self-generated memories, those for performed actions and those for imagined actions, than to confuse a self-generated memory with an other-generated memory of an action performed by someone else.

Experimental studies examining age effects have confirmed anecdotal reports that both young and old have more difficulty in reality monitoring. Young children have been found to make more errors in distinguishing between what they said and what they only thought, although they were successful at distinguishing between self-generated and other-generated utterances and between different external sources (Foley, Johnson, & Raye, 1983). A similar pattern emerged in children's memory for actions. Elderly people are also liable to confuse imagined and performed actions, and have shown a consistent bias in the direction of this confusion such that they tend to misidentify imagined events as real (Cohen & Faulkner, 1989). One possible explanation for these age effects is that children and elderly people are failing to encode enough of the sensory and contextual features that should characterize an external memory. Another possibility is that the elderly adopt a strategy of "if in doubt decide it is real." That is, they may operate on the assumption that it is better to make the false positive error of deciding an event occurred when it was only imagined than to make the false negative error of denying that it happened when it really did (*see* AGING AND MEMORY).

Another method for investigating reality monitoring relies on what Johnson (1988) has called the experimental phenomenological approach. This approach involves asking people to complete a questionnaire giving ratings for the sensory, contextual, and cognitive characteristics of each memory. It is then possible to compare these ratings for memories of different origins, or to manipulate factors such as the retention interval or the amount of rehearsal and observe the effects on phenomenological aspects of the memory. The results have been consistent with the model, showing that memories of perceived events received higher ratings for sensory and contextual information and for the presence of supporting memories than memories of imagined events. Furthermore, it appears that the distinction is maintained as memories degrade over time by a differential loss rate. Imagined memories lose sensory details faster than external perceived memories so that they can still be distinguished after a lapse of time. Some kinds of REHEARSAL, especially rehearsing the thoughts and feelings associated with an event, appear to reduce the phenomenological difference between the two kinds of memory.

This kind of approach to the study of reality monitoring has also been applied to naturally occurring memories as well as to experimentally induced memories. For instance, ratings of autobiographical memories have shown that recent autobiographical memories can be readily distinguished from imagined events, whereas for childhood memories the differences were weaker. It has also been found that when people are asked how they know whether a particular remembered event is real or imagined, they justify a reality decision by reference to several kinds of evidence including perceptual detail, context, emotions, consequences of the event and inferences about plausibility based on general knowledge. Diary studies recording everyday slips of action (Reason, 1979) (*see* ABSENT-MINDED-NESS) have indicated that failures of reality monitoring occur most commonly with routine, frequently performed actions. The distinction between performed and planned actions appears to grow weaker when the action is often repeated. This might occur because routine actions are performed automatically and would therefore lack traces of cognitive operations (*see* AUTOMATIC PROCESSING). This might then make it impossible to distinguish between the memory of locking the door and the memory of planning to lock the door. Thus the general principles of the model proposed by Johnson and Raye are supported by the objective evidence of error rates and by phenomenological evidence in both experimental and natural situations.

The principles of reality monitoring have real-world applications and are particularly relevant to EYEWITNESS TESTIMONY, where it has been shown that the testimony of a witness may contain a mixture of veridical recall and "memories," based on post-event suggestions, of nonexistent objects and happenings. Schooler, Gerhard, and Loftus (1986) found that, when the verbal descriptions supplied by witnesses were analyzed, judges could be trained to discriminate between real memories, and those based on suggestions, by employing the appropriate criteria. The same kind of methods that people use to evaluate their own memories can be applied to other people's memories. Another application of reality monitoring principles can be found in medical history-taking. It is recognized that patients' estimates of the frequency and intensity of symptoms or episodes of illness may be inaccurate. It is likely that patients, especially those who are depressed or solitary, who spend a lot of time mentally rehearsing these events may later be unable to distinguish between real and imagined episodes and so inflate their estimates of frequency of occurrence.

Reality monitoring should be considered as a form of METACOGNITION since reality monitoring decisions depend on the exercise of metamemory – that is, on knowledge about how memory works. As well as affecting speech and actions, reality monitoring also affects knowledge and beliefs. This is because our judgements about the source of our own knowledge, and the source of other people's knowledge and beliefs, influences the weight we attach to them. Knowledge based on our own real experiences or on information that is judged to come from a reliable external source will be more influential. We are less likely to be convinced by internally generated beliefs or when an informant is judged to be speculating, exaggerating, or romancing. The ability to make these judgements therefore determines, to a considerable extent, what we believe. Current research suggests that self-reports of the phenomenal qualities of memories can yield potentially useful data and help us to understand more about mechanisms of memory and metamemory and their functional significance. Another goal of this research is to gain more understanding of what is happening in cases of memory disorder when reality monitoring breaks down. Reality monitoring is an aspect of metacognition which is theoretically important and which is an essential component in the control of action, speech, and thought.

BIBLIOGRAPHY

Anderson, R. E. (1984). Did I do it or did I only imagine doing it? *Journal of Experimental Psychology: General, 113*, 594–613.

Cohen, G., & Faulkner, D. (1989). Age differences in source forgetting: Effects on reality monitoring and on eyewitness testimony. *Psychology and Aging, 4*, 1–8.

Foley, M. A., Johnson, M. K., & Raye, C. L. (1983). Age-related changes in confusion between memories for thought and memories for speech. *Child Development, 56*, 1145–55.

Johnson, M. K. (1988). Reality monitoring: A phenomenological approach. *Journal of Experimental Psychology: General, 117*, 390–4.

——, & Raye, C. L. (1981). Reality monitoring. *Psychological Review, 88*, 67–85.

Johnson, M. K., Raye, C. I., Wang, A., & Taylor, T. (1979). Facts and fantasy: The role of accuracy and variability in confusing imaginations with perceptual experience. *Journal of Experimental Psychology: Human Learning and Memory, 5*, 229–46.

Reason, J. T. (1979). Actions not as planned: The price of automatization. In G. Underwood & R. Stevens (Eds), *Aspects of consciousness* (Vol. 1). London: Academic Press.

Schachter, D. L., Harbluk, J. L., & McLachlan, D. R. (1984). Retrieval without recollection: An experimental analysis of source amnesia.

Journal of Verbal Learning and Verbal Behavior, 23, 593–611.

Schooler, J. W., Gerhard, D., & Loftus, E. F. (1986). Qualities of the unreal. *Journal of Experimental Psychology: Learning, Memory and Cognition*, 12, 171–81.

GILLIAN COHEN

reasoning The rule-based process of logically deciding what to believe is known as reasoning. When people reason, they use information that is known or assumed to be true or probably true to support a belief. A distinction is often made between deductive and inductive reasoning. In deductive reasoning, the process begins with a set of statements, called premisses, that are used to infer if another statement, called the conclusion, is valid (*see* INFERENCES). Deductive reasoning is sometimes described as reasoning "down" from beliefs about the nature of the world to particular instances. For example, if we believe that winters are cold in Canada, we would use this information to decide that Vancouver, a city in Canada, is cold in the winter. In inductive reasoning, on the other hand, observations and experiences are used to support generalizations. Sometimes inductive reasoning is described as reasoning "up" from observations and experiences to create new beliefs about the nature of the world. For example, if we know that winters are cold in Toronto, Calgary, Saskatchewan, Ottawa, and Halifax, which are cities in Canada, we would generalize from this information to decide that all of Canada is cold in the winter.

Although deductive and inductive reasoning are theoretically distinct processes, this distinction is not particularly useful in understanding how people reason in most everyday contexts. The usual process of reasoning involves repeated alternations between deductive to inductive processes. Our hypotheses and beliefs about the world guide the observations we make, while our observations, in turn, modify our hypotheses and beliefs. Thus, most informal reasoning involves a continuous interplay of deductive and inductive processes.

DEDUCTIVE REASONING

When people reason deductively, they use their knowledge of two or more premisses to infer if a conclusion is valid. There are several models of deductive reasoning, each with its own set of rules: categorical syllogisms; linear reasoning; and conditional reasoning.

Categorical syllogisms There are four types of assertions or moods that are used to describe category membership in reasoning tasks. These four different moods are formed by combinations of positive and negative statements with the terms "all" or "some." They are listed in the left hand column of Figure 1. As you can see from Figure 1, a statement is universal if it contains the terms "all" or "no"; it is particular if it contains the term "some"; it is negative if it contains "no" or "not"; and it is affirmative if it is not negative. Thus, it is easy to classify the mood of any statement by searching out the key terms.

Consider the following syllogism which has two premisses and a conclusion:

All cognitive psychologists are intelligent.
Some intelligent people are professors.
Therefore, some cognitive psychologists are professors.

In syllogistic reasoning, the usual task is to determine if the conclusion is valid. A conclusion is valid if it must be true when the premisses are true. One way of determining if a conclusion is valid is with the use of circle diagrams which are spatial arrays that represent category membership. Venn diagrams, Euler diagrams, and ballantines are three different types of circle diagrams that are used in syllogistic reasoning tasks. Each of these types of circle diagrams has its own set of rules for combining circle representations of the premisses to determine if the conclusion is valid. Circle diagrams that correspond to each of the four moods are shown in the right-hand portion of the figure. When circle diagrams are used to determine the validity of a syllogism, the circle diagrams corresponding to each of the two premisses are combined. A conclusion is valid if the combined diagrams contain the information in the conclusion.

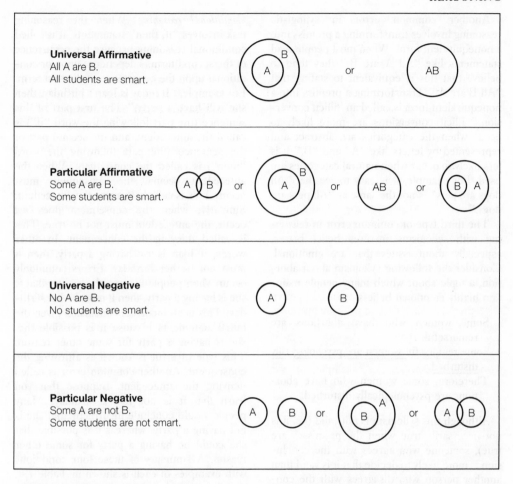

Figure 1 Circle diagrams depicting correct interpretations of the premisses used in syllogisms. Note that "all" can have two correct interpretations, "no" has one correct interpretation, and "some – not" can have three correct interpretations.

Syllogistic reasoning is common in everyday conversations. Of course, the statements are embedded in discourse and not labeled as premiss and conclusion. In natural language, terms like "only" and "each" signal a universal mood, terms like "many" and "few" signal a particular mood, and "none" and "no one" signal a negative mood.

Research on the way people solve syllogisms in real-world contexts has shown that there are three types of errors that are common. The most prevalent type of error is the confusion between a conclusion that is valid and one that is true. A conclusion may be both valid and false. Consider the following example:

All Americans maintain an allegiance to the Queen.

<u>All New Yorkers are Americans.</u>

Therefore, all New Yorkers maintain an allegiance to the Queen.

This is an example of a conclusion that is both valid (i.e. it must be true if the premisses are true) and false. It is false because the premisses are false. By contrast, a conclusion must be true when it is valid and the premisses are true.

Another common error in syllogistic reasoning involves transforming a premiss into a nonequivalent form. When most people read statements like "All A are B," they tend to believe that this is equivalent to stating that "All B are A." Transforming a premiss into a nonequivalent form is called an "illicit conversion." Illicit conversions are more likely to occur when the categories are abstract and represented by letters like "A" and "B." It is less likely to occur when natural categories are used. For example, it is easy to see that "All dogs are pets" is not the same as "All pets are dogs."

The third type of common error in reasoning with syllogisms involves belief biases, especially about issues that are emotional. Consider the following syllogism about abortion, a topic about which many people maintain highly emotional beliefs:

Some women who have abortions are remorseful.
Some remorseful women are psychologically disturbed.
Therefore, some women who have abortions are psychologically disturbed.

Although this syllogism is not valid (i.e. it is not necessarily true when the premisses are true), someone who agrees with the conclusion is more likely to decide that it is valid than another person who disagrees with the conclusion. This is an example of the way in which personal beliefs can alter the reasoning process.

Linear reasoning When a reasoning problem involves an ordered array of terms, it is called a linear reasoning problem. Consider the following simple example:

Nigel is taller than Roberto.
Henri is shorter than Roberto.
Who is tallest?

In this example, the three boys form a linear array with regard to height so that it is easy to determine that Nigel must be tallest. It is usually helpful to draw a line and mark the relative size of each term for more complex linear reasoning tasks.

Conditional reasoning When the reasoning task involves "if, then" statements, it is called conditional reasoning because the occurrence of the second term is dependent upon or conditional upon the occurrence of the first term. For example, "If today is Joan's birthday, then she will have a party." The first part of this sentence (the part following the word "if") is called the antecedent, and the second part of the sentence (the part following the word "then") is called the consequent. When the antecedent occurs, the consequent must occur. This is called affirming the antecedent. Similarly, when the consequent does *not* occur, the antecedent must not be true. This is called denying the consequent. In other words, if Joan is *not* having a party, then it must not be her birthday. Errors commonly occur when people incorrectly assume that if she is having a party, then it must be her birthday. This is an incorrect conclusion given the initial statements because it is possible that she is having a party for some other reason. This type of error is known as affirming the consequent. Another common error is called denying the antecedent. Suppose that you learn that it is not Joan's birthday. Many people would conclude incorrectly that she is not having a party, whereas it is possible that she could be having a party for some other reason. A summary of these four conditions with examples of each is shown in Table 1.

INDUCTIVE REASONING

When we reason deductively, we can be certain about the validity of a conclusion. By contrast, when people reason inductively, they are making judgements about the probable certainty of a conclusion. Much of our knowledge about the world was learned through the process of inductive reasoning. Consider the following example:

Evan gets a rash on the days he eats strawberries.
Evan does not get a rash on the days he doesn't eat strawberries.
Therefore, Evan is allergic to strawberries.

While there may be other explanations for Evan's rash (perhaps he eats strawberries on the same days he eats watermelon or perhaps

Table 1   Examples of valid and invalid reasoning with "if, then" statements.

	Antecedent	Consequent
Affirming:	*Affirming the Antecedent* (Valid reasoning) If this is Tuesday, then we are in France. This is Tuesday. Therefore, we are in France.	*Affirming the Consequent* (Invalid reasoning) If this is Hamlet, then it is written by Shakespeare. This is written by Shakespeare. Therefore, this is Hamlet.
Denying:	*Denying the Antecedent* (Invalid reasoning) If they are men, then they are wearing pants. They are not men. Therefore, they are not wearing pants.	*Denying the Consequent* (Valid reasoning) If she is rich, then she wears diamonds. She does not wear diamonds. Therefore, she is not rich.

he wears a wool sweater on those days), the premises make it likely that Evan is allergic to strawberries. Evan could test this conclusion by carefully eliminating other variables and verifying the observation that he gets a rash from strawberries.

In everyday contexts, we need to be able to figure out the causes for a host of events in order to reduce uncertainty (Holland, Holyoak, Nisbett, & Thagard, 1986). People usually have to generate their own list of possible premises and then evaluate how well the premises explain the conclusion. These are the same processes that scientists use to generate and test hypotheses about the physical world.

Of the two processes involved, hypothesis generation and evaluation, the generation phase is probably the more difficult. Consider the problem of Evan's allergy. In order to consider strawberries as a likely cause for the rash, he has to detect events that vary in regular manner along with the rash. (In statistics, this is called detecting covariation.) In arriving at the possibility that strawberries are responsible, he may have considered and eliminated many other variables such as a type of soap or the insulation used in the building at his school. This is a high-level cognitive task that requires consideration of many factors that might cause the appearance of a rash. When children learn that their parents will appear when they cry or that they will succeed if they work hard, they are engaging in an inductive reasoning task.

Just as there are errors that commonly occur in deductive reasoning tasks, there are common errors in inductive reasoning. Perhaps the most prevalent error is an insensitivity to sample size when deciding if the conclusion is supported by the premises. Consider once again the example given above about strawberries as the cause of a rash. If Evan broke out in a rash after he ate strawberries one time, this would be weaker support for identifying strawberries as the cause of the rash than if he had eaten strawberries ten times and got a rash each time.

Another common error in inductive reasoning tasks is the ubiquitous tendency to seek confirming rather than disconfirming evidence (*see* CONCEPT LEARNING). In order to test the hypothesized relationship between a food and an allergy, for example, most people would look for evidence that the two are related. It is even more critical to look for instances when the two events are unrelated. Are there rashes at other times or with other foods and are there times when strawberries were eaten and there was no rash?

A third common error is an insensitivity to variability. All people and all events are unique. Consider the relationship between smoking and lung cancer. Although there is a strong relationship between these two variables, some people are heavy smokers and will not develop lung cancer. Newspapers and magazines like to feature stories about old people who claim to have smoked two packs of cigarettes a day since a young age and are now approaching 100 years of age in good health. It would be wrong to conclude that there is no relationship because it is not found in every instance.

EVERYDAY REASONING

We are constantly bombarded with statements that provide support for conclusions. Informally, the premisses or statements that provide support are called reasons. Reasons are provided to persuade a reader or listener that the conclusion is true. The reasons are the "why" part of an argument; the conclusion is the "what" part of an argument. Most of our conversations and virtually all advertising follows this simple principle:

Buy Bif's Beer because it has fewer calories than the other brands.

In this example, the conclusion is presented first: "Buy Bif's Beer." The reason that is offered to support this conclusion is: "because it has fewer calories than the other brands."

All arguments or attempts to persuade a listener or reader to do something or believe something will contain at least one conclusion and at least one premiss or reason to support the conclusion. Sometimes the premisses or the conclusion is implied, and the listener has to supply the missing part of the argument. Real-world arguments may also contain counterarguments or reasons that suggest that the conclusion is not true and assumptions that modify the meaning of the premisses. When people reason (i.e. use reasons to determine the truth or probable truth of a conclusion), they need to consider three criteria for sound arguments:

1 The premisses have to be consistent and acceptable. A premiss is acceptable if it is probably true or if it is reasonable to believe that it is true. Premisses are consistent if they do not contradict each other.

2 The premisses must support the conclusion. If you read that dogs make good pets because oil has been discovered in Mexico, you would surely wonder about the connection between the premiss and the conclusion. This is an example of a poor argument because the premiss does not provide any reasons for believing that the conclusion is true.

3 Premisses have to be strong enough to support the conclusion. This criterion is sometimes called adequate grounds. Suppose you read that two rock stars are getting divorced. The reason for this conclusion is an observation that they did not have dinner together one night last week. When considered alone, the premiss or evidence for the conclusion is too weak to support the notion that they are getting a divorce.

Thus, in everyday reasoning, the quality of the reasons and the nature of the support they provide for a conclusion are considered in assessing the acceptability of a conclusion. Reasoning is the cognitive process that underlies all rational decision making (*see* PROBLEM SOLVING).

See also MENTAL MODELS.

BIBLIOGRAPHY

Govier, T. (1988). *A practical study of argument* (2nd edn). Belmont, Calif.: Wadsworth.

Halpern, D. F. (1989). *Thought and knowledge: An introduction to critical thinking* (2nd edn). Hillsdale, NJ: Erlbaum.

Holland, J. H., Holyoak, K. J., Nisbett, R. E., & Thagard, P. R. (1986). *Induction: Processes of inference, learning, and discovery.* Cambridge, Mass.: MIT Press.

Johnson-Laird, P. N. (1985). Deductive reasoning ability. In R. J. Sternberg (Ed.), *Human abilities: An information processing approach* (pp. 173–94).

Nickerson, R. S. (1986). *Reflections on reasoning.* Hillsdale, NJ: Erlbaum.

DIANE F. HALPERN

recall A characteristic of recall is that it involves the reproduction of information from

memory. It is often contrasted with RECOG-
NITION MEMORY, which involves not reproduction but instead the identification of a
match between information in memory and
information that is newly available.

The importance of reproduction in recall
poses a problem in studying the recall of
material (e.g. pictures) for which reproduction
may be poor even in the absence of a memory
burden. This factor has probably tended to
propel the study of recall toward using readily
reproducible linguistic symbols as material to
be recalled: letters, numbers, words, sentences, stories. Certainly, verbal materials
have predominated in studies of recall.

Two principal methods of experimenting on
recall can be distinguished: cued recall and
free recall. In cued recall, the person is provided at recall with a cue (or cues) – information that is related in some way to the
information to be reproduced. In free recall,
no such cue is provided. For example, a person in a cued recall experiment might be
shown ten pairs of words, with one member of
each pair subsequently being provided as a
cue for the other. A person in a free recall
experiment, on the other hand, might be
shown ten single words and subsequently
simply attempt to reproduce all ten.

By varying the number and the nature of the
cues that are present in a cued-recall procedure, it is readily shown that the probability
of successful recall depends upon the outcome
of the various retrieval processes that they set
in train. With a free-recall procedure, the role
of retrieval processes is not made explicit in
this way (one can of course point nevertheless
to implicit cues specifying, say, the most
recently presented set of words). As a consequence, the use of free-recall procedures has
often been associated with a focus upon processes in memory hypothesized to occur prior
to retrieval. Chief among these processes have
been those concerned with FORGETTING
owing to limitations of storage.

A number of proposals have been made as
to how forgetting occurs owing to limitations
of storage. Information stored in memory may
in general decay over time. Information in a
particular memory store may be lost by displacement when the demands on that store

exceed its capacity. Or the preservation of
stored information may depend upon the way
in which it is initially processed. These three
possibilities – the decay approach, the
memory-stores approach, and the LEVELS OF
PROCESSING approach – have generally been
regarded as exclusive alternatives, although it
is not clear that they are in fact necessarily
exclusive. Of the three proposals, the
memory-stores approach has over the last
30 years proved the most influential. The
limited-capacity memory stores that have been
proposed include ECHOIC STORE, ICONIC
STORE (see SHORT-TERM MEMORY, RETRIEVAL
FROM), and components of WORKING MEMORY
such as the articulatory loop.

Before turning to cued recall, we may note a
particular variety of free recall. This is serial
recall, in which a person attempts to reproduce a set of events in the same order as
that in which they occurred previously (rather
than reproducing them in an unspecified
order, as is usually the case in free recall).
Serial recall is the procedure adopted in
measuring memory span. A person's memory
span is usually defined as the size of a list of
items which that person can serially recall
without error on 50 percent of occasions. A
figure of around seven items indicates the
usual order of magnitude of memory span
although, as might be expected, the size of a
person's span depends not only upon the person but also upon the nature of the material
being recalled (see SHORT-TERM MEMORY).

As implied earlier in this essay, studies
using cued recall make it clear that forgetting
occurs not only as a consequence of limitations upon storage but also as a consequence
of the absence of appropriate retrieval cues (it
may be noted incidentally that this kind of
forgetting, unlike forgetting due to limitations
of storage, may be overcome when the right
cue becomes available). Indeed, it has been
suggested that in principle all forgetting could
be the consequence of retrieval problems.
This view can be related to two other
approaches to understanding the origins of
errors in recall. The first of these is the idea
that forgetting may be the consequence of a
process of repression (e.g. Freud, 1901/
1960). The second is interference theory,

which holds that forgetting results from contamination by other information stored either earlier in time (PROACTIVE INTERFERENCE) or later in time (RETROACTIVE INTERFERENCE).

When target information is successfully reproduced in cued recall, two possibilities may be distinguished concerning the way in which it is retrieved from memory. The first possibility, which has been termed the ENCODING SPECIFICITY PRINCIPLE, asserts that reproduction is successful only if the cue directly matches the original stored information. The second possibility, which has been termed the generation–recognition hypothesis (Bahrick, 1970), asserts that for reproduction to be successful the cue need not directly match the original stored information, but rather need only be related to it in some way. In this latter case, two separate stages of recall can be distinguished. The first stage is one of generation, in which information in memory that is related to the cue is activated. The second stage is one of recognition, in which it is assessed whether segments of this activated information do in fact comprise the target information. The different retrieval possibilities identified by the encoding specificity principle and the generation–recognition hypothesis have generally been regarded as exclusive alternatives, in a manner similar to that described earlier in the case of forgetting due to limitations of storage. But again it is not clear that exclusivity is appropriate, and in this case evidence has in fact been provided (see Jones, 1987) that retrieval can proceed along both the direct-access route envisaged by the encoding specificity principle and the indirect route envisaged by the generation–recognition hypothesis.

See also ENCODING OPERATIONS IN MEMORY; MNEMONICS; RECENCY EFFECT; REHEARSAL; STATE-DEPENDENT MEMORY; STUDY SKILLS.

BIBLIOGRAPHY

Bahrick, H. P. (1970). Two-phase model for prompted recall. Psychological Review, 77, 215–22.

Freud, S. (1960). The standard edition of the complete psychological works of Sigmund Freud (Vol. 6): The psychopathology of everyday life (A. Tyson, Trans., & J. Strachey, Ed.). London: Hogarth Press. (Original work published 1901).

Jones, G. V. (1987). Independence and exclusivity among psychological processes: Implications for the structure of recall. Psychological Review, 94, 229–35.

G. V. JONES

recency effect The term denotes enhanced memory for the last items in a series. When people attempt to remember a series of events, the chance of their correctly remembering a particular event is usually a function of its position within the series. In its commonest form, the shape of this function (usually termed a serial position curve) resembles a letter U: the level of performance declines over the first handful of items (the primacy effect), stays roughly flat over the central part of the list, and then climbs again over the last handful of items (the recency effect).

From the preceding description, it is apparent that the recency effect may alternatively be described by saying that the items in the list which occurred most recently are remembered particularly well. Given that few are likely to find this result surprising, why has the recency effect been for some decades the focus of much theoretical interest in the study of human memory? The answer is that under different experimental conditions the recency effect has been found to wax and wane, to disappear altogether, or even to become negative in value. As more and more is discovered about it, the recency effect bids fair to become the drosophila of human memory.

Since the 1960s, the most commonly used tool for investigating the recency effect has been the method of free RECALL. A person is presented with a list which contains, say, 20 words and subsequently attempts to recall these in any order. The level of recall of the last half dozen or so items increases steadily above the level of earlier items, corresponding in all to about three extra items recalled at these last positions. This recency effect may be abolished by interposing a short period of distracting activity (say, half a minute of mental arithmetic) between presentation and recall. A very influential interpretation of the recency effect has therefore been that it represents the recall of a small number of items held in a SHORT-TERM MEMORY store from which they are readily displaced by distractor activity (e.g. Atkinson & Shiffrin, 1971). In contrast, remaining items are assumed to be held not in short-term (or primary) memory but rather in long-term (or secondary) memory (*see* LONG-TERM MEMORY). Consistent with this, it is found that some other factors, such as rate of presentation, appear to differentially affect pre-recency but not recency items.

The short-term memory explanation of the recency effect has been extended in a number of directions. As one example, it is found that the effect is somewhat greater over the last one or two items when presentation is auditory than when it is visual, and this has been attributed to auditory items having available to them a further small modality-specific memory store. As another example, the explanation is consistent with the observation of negative recency. If people are given a final free recall test for all the items from a series of lists, then under these circumstances the level of recall of the last few items of a list may dip below the level for prerecency items. This is what would be expected if those items had earlier had less opportunity to be transferred from short-term to long-term memory, owing to the end of their presentation periods being abruptly reached.

The main problem for the short-term memory account of the recency effect comes from the fact that rather similar effects are observed in a number of other situations that appear to exclude short-term memory involvement, for example when items are learnt slowly over repeated presentations or when a distractor task is performed after the presentation of each item (see Greene, 1986). In these cases it has been suggested that it is the greater distinctiveness of items close to the extremities of a list which leads to their advantage in recall. But if this is so, then a distinctiveness type of explanation could presumably apply also to the results described earlier.

BIBLIOGRAPHY

Atkinson, R. C., & Shiffrin, R. M. (1971). The control of short-term memory. *Scientific American*, 225(2), 82–90.
Greene, R. L. (1986). Sources of recency effects in free recall. *Psychological Bulletin*, 99, 221–8.

M. MARTIN

recognition memory The identification of a match between newly available information and previously acquired information held in memory is referred to as recognition memory. It may be contrasted with RECALL, in which the previously acquired information is reproduced from memory. Recognition is a more flexible method of interrogating memory than is recall, in that it is readily used even in cases when information (such as that concerning faces) is difficult to reproduce (*see* FACE RECOGNITION). Recognition differs also from recall in that it is often considered from the standpoint of perception rather than that of memory. Thus, in the study of word recognition, for example, interest often resides primarily in the classificatory processes whereby a written or spoken item comes to be identified as corresponding to an entry of the mental lexicon, rather than interest focusing on the memorized lexicon itself (*see* READING DEVELOPMENT; SPEECH PERCEPTION).

Any act of recognition presumably involves adopting a particular degree of confidence to be satisfied concerning the degree of match between new and old information. Thus, in considering the determinants of recognition performance we may make a distinction between those that relate to the match with memory and those that relate to the translation from match to action. The latter kind of factor is exemplified by the consequences of manipulating recognition procedures in experiments. For example, the fewer the number of alternatives from among which a target item is to be recognized, the higher is generally the level of recognition. In principle, this relation could arise because guesses are more likely to be correct when there are fewer alternatives. Suppose a person has an underlying probability of matching new and old information, *m*, but achieves a higher apparent probability of recognition, *r*, by guessing randomly among *n* alternatives (one of which is the correct one) when a match has not been detected. Then *r* is of course an inverse function of *n* and indeed *m* could be estimated following a simple correction for guessing as

$$[r-(1/n)]/[1-(1/n)].$$

The preceding classical analysis can be viewed as a form of threshold model, in that a discontinuity between matched and non-matched states is assumed. An attractive alternative is to replace this assumption in a manner similar to that which occurred with the advent of signal-detection theory within psychophysics. This type of analysis can be used not only for the *n*-alternative forced-choice procedure described earlier but also when the candidates for recognition are considered one by one, and the match/nonmatch decision is conveyed either by a confidence judgement or else by a simple yes/no (see Murdock, 1974). There have been some attempts to choose between different theoretical models within the signal-detection theory framework, but empirical discrimination between models has proven quite difficult to achieve. Instead, signal-detection theory analysis of recognition is generally pursued not as an end in itself but only as a means to an end. A particularly tractable model (the equal-variance normal-distribution model) is employed in what is hoped to be a theoretically neutral role to transform raw recognition data into two types of parameter value. One of these, d' ("d-prime"), relates to the quality of memory evidence and the other, β ("beta"), relates to the evaluation of that evidence.

In addition to studying the accuracy of recognition, we may also study the speed with which it proceeds. For this, the simple yes/no method of assessing recognition is generally used. For a given recognition test, latency is likely to be a function of accuracy – the greater the accuracy, the greater the latency – and thus a complete specification of recognition performance would involve mapping an extensive speed–error trade-off function. In actuality, this formidable undertaking is rarely attempted and instead mapping only of one of its boundaries is attempted (more accurately, a second boundary, if we count as first boundary the level of accuracy observed when recognition performance is not speeded at all). In this latency mapping, the aim is to measure speeds when they are kept at as high a level as is consistent with the maintenance of error-free performance (in practice, the error rate that is observed is usually low, rather than zero).

Some of the most extensive work on recognition latencies has been carried out using a method in which a person is presented with a short list of up to about six items (see Sternberg, 1975). This is followed by a further item, and the person makes a speeded judgement as to whether or not that item was in the preceding list. Mean latency is generally found to be a linear function of list length, consistent with recognition involving the attempted matching of the target item with each item of the memorized list in turn. However, it has been shown that these results are consistent not only with serial scanning but also with a number of alternatives, including the possibility that attempted matching of all memorized items proceeds in parallel, but that the greater their number the longer it takes for them all to be completed (*see* SHORT-TERM MEMORY, RETRIEVAL FROM).

Finally, one empirical phenomenon that promises to throw light on the underlying relation between recognition and recall is that of recognition failure – or, more fully, recognition failure of recallable information (see Tulving, 1983). When the same memories are probed, recognition performance is usually better than recall performance. However, recognition superiority may on occasion be reversed, and is in any case generally incomplete. A proportion of items is recalled but not recognized and, further, the size of this proportion appears to be a parabolic function of the overall level of recognition. A number of explanations of this result have been suggested. It has, for example, been shown that a function of this type would arise if RECALL could occur in two different ways, one route (namely, generation–recognition) being dependent upon recognition and the other (namely, direct-access) being independent of recognition.

See also SENTENCE PROCESSING.

BIBLIOGRAPHY

Murdock, B. B. (1974). *Human memory: Theory and data.* Potomac, Md.: Erlbaum.

Sternberg, S. (1975). Memory scanning: New findings and current controversies. *Quarterly Journal of Experimental Psychology, 27,* 1–32.

Tulving, E. (1983). *Elements of episodic memory.* Oxford: Clarendon Press.

G. V. JONES

reductionism Reductionism is the process of trying to explain events occurring at one level in terms of events at a more basic level. Explaining a car accident in terms of the laws of physics is an example of reductionism. In cognitive psychology, the search for causal explanations and attempts to specify the mechanisms that underlie cognition tend to generate reductionist explanations. However, reductionist explanations are not always causal. They may take the form of ANALOGIES whereby our understanding of cognitive processes is illuminated by the fact that they are analogous to simpler, more basic mechanisms.

In physiological reductionism cognitive processes or aspects of behavior are explained in terms of physiological structures and functions, including both biochemistry and neurophysiology. Thus, for example, biochemical reductionism provides a biochemical explanation of depression, whereby the overt behavioral symptoms are caused by a noradrenaline deficiency. Similarly, biochemical abnormalities are offered as explanations for alcoholism and other forms of addiction. Critics object that biochemical reductionism ignores other causal factors, such as social and environmental ones, that are implicated in those conditions, so the reductionist explanation is incomplete. However, a same-level explanation, couched solely in terms of social factors, is equally incomplete. It is generally agreed that a complete account of depression or alcoholism must include causes at several different levels.

Neurophysiological reductionism allows cognitive processes of perception, memory, and language to be modeled as neural networks. Malfunctions are explained in terms of underlying neural pathology, and many cognitive processes such as PRIMING, interference, or reaction latencies are explained in terms of neural properties such as thresholds, levels of activation, and inhibition. One objection to this kind of reduction is that the mapping of the cognitive event to the neural event lacks precision.

Information-processing reductionism provides an analogy rather than a causal explanation. Cognitive processes such as selective attention, recoding, storage, and retrieval are represented as a sequence of stages in the familiar box and arrow models. Clarification is achieved at the expense of drastic simplification. Some salient aspects of the cognitive processes are abstracted out and represented, but others, such as individual strategies, intentions, and emotions, are neglected.

Machine reductionism, whereby cognition is explained in terms of computational processes operating on symbolic representations, achieves a precise and detailed mapping of cognitive processes on to computational ones, but is also open to the objection that many features of human performance are missed out of the equation (*see* COGNITIVE SCIENCE).

Animal reductionism has been applied to human social behavior with ethological observations of the simpler social interactions of animals supplying interpretations for analogous behavior in humans. The advantage of this approach is that experimental manipulation is less ethically constrained, but species differences may make extrapolation invalid.

Non-reductionist, same-level explanations may be phenomenological, or humanist, explaining behavior in terms of feelings, beliefs, or desires. However, this approach is also incomplete. It may identify correlations between same-level events but fails to specify causal mechanisms.

BIBLIOGRAPHY

Searle, J. R. (1980). Minds, brains and programs. *The Behavioural and Brain Sciences, 3,* 417–67.

GILLIAN COHEN

rehearsal When attempting to remember verbal information, people show a natural tendency to repeat the information either aloud or silently to themselves; psychologists call this kind of behavior "rehearsal" and there have been many experiments investigating its importance in memory function. Rundus (1971) examined the relationship between rehearsal and free recall of a word list (*see* RECALL). He found that, overall, the extent to which people recalled words correlated with how often they were heard to rehearse those words during the learning process. However, rehearsal rate bore no relation to how well the last few words in the list were recalled, thus indicating that rehearsal is an unimportant factor in determining recall of very recent information (*see* RECENCY EFFECT).

There are occasions when an experimenter may wish to prevent a subject from rehearsing during a memory experiment. One example is experiments which attempt to measure the rate at which people forget information. Clearly, if rehearsal is allowed, there can be no clear time point from which forgetting can be measured. This problem can be overcome with the use of a distractor task in which, following presentation of the information, the subject is required to engage in some irrelevant verbal activity such as counting backwards in 3s prior to recall. This appears to be an effective means of preventing rehearsal but one must note that the degree of distractor task difficulty does influence the extent to which memory is affected. In addition, distractor task performance must be monitored so as to prevent concurrent rehearsal.

Rehearsal is thought to improve memory by increasing the likelihood of forming associations between the information being learned. This form of rehearsal is often termed elaborative and it can be distinguished from maintenance rehearsal where repeating items is not thought to promote retention but merely retain information in consciousness. There are doubts, however, about whether this form of rehearsal can occur (Nelson, 1977).

Many theorists have identified rehearsal as a crucial process in the transfer of new information from temporary to permanent storage. Unfortunately there are difficulties with this view. One problem is that much of what we remember cannot be easily rehearsed, either because it is too complex, such as the content of a speech, or because the information cannot be described verbally, as is the case with smells. Furthermore, the concept of rehearsal suggests that learning is an intentional process in that what we remember is determined by what we decide to rehearse. Intentionality does play some role in learning but evidence from incidental learning studies indicates that much of what we learn occurs without any intention on our part to do so.

Rehearsal is best regarded as a specific learning strategy that can promote the retention of verbal information but it does not constitute a general principle of memory function. *See also* LEVELS OF PROCESSING.

BIBLIOGRAPHY

Nelson, T. O. (1977). Repetition and depth of processing. *Journal of Verbal Learning and Verbal Behavior*, 16, 151–72.
Rundus, D. (1971). Analysis of rehearsal processes in free recall. *Journal of Verbal Learning and Verbal Behaviour*, 89, 63–77.

A. J. PARKIN

representations, propositional *See* PROPOSITIONAL REPRESENTATIONS.

retrieval from short-term memory *See* SHORT-TERM MEMORY, RETRIEVAL FROM.

retroactive interference (RI) A term derived from interference theory (*see* FORGETTING), describing the tendency for new learning to interfere with memory for information learned earlier. RI is sometimes known as retroactive inhibition. The amount of RI observed will increase as the number of learning trials interpolated between learning and test increases. The amount of RI observed will also be influenced by the degree of similarity between the information being tested and the information presented during the interpolated learning sequence: the greater the similarity, the greater the amount of RI.

The mechanism or mechanisms responsible for RI have not as yet been discovered. However, it remains a useful descriptive term when examining the various factors that can contribute to forgetting (*see* PROACTIVE INTER-FERENCE).

BIBLIOGRAPHY

Underwood, B. J. (1957). Interference and forgetting. *Psychological Review, 64,* 49–60.

A. J. PARKIN

S

schemata Schemata consist of structured groups of concepts which constitute the generic knowledge about events, scenarios, actions, or objects that has been acquired from past experience.

Bartlett (1932) (*see* BARTLETT, SIR FREDERIC) made use of schemata to explain why it is that, in understanding and remembering stories, people tend to reconstruct the story to fit in with expectations based on their prior knowledge and past experience. The original story undergoes processes of rationalization, deletion, elaboration, and distortion which, according to Bartlett's view, are shaped and guided by pre-existing schemata. Bartlett's ideas were ahead of his time. In the prevailing behaviorist ethos of that period, such mentalistic notions were rejected as being too vague, subjective, and unobservable. However, in the cognitive psychology of the 1970s, with the growing interest in mental representations, schemata have been reinstated and modern versions play a central role in current theories of memory (*see* COGNITIVE PSYCHOLOGY, HISTORY OF).

A schema can represent any kind of knowledge, from simple knowledge about, for example, the shape of the letter A, to more complex knowledge about topics like political history or physics. Schemata can be linked together into related sets, so that the schema for "table" would be linked to other schemata for "furniture," "rooms," and "houses." These groups of schemata may be organized hierarchically with high-level general schemata (like "shopping") subsuming more specific, lower order schemata (like "buying new shoes"). A schema consists of relations together with slots, or variables, which can be filled with optional values. So the "buying shoes" schema would include the relation "buy" and variable slots which could be filled with values like "walking shoes" or "trainers." Schemata also supply default values which

are the most probable or typical values and these are assumed if a slot is unfilled. In a schema for "table," for example, the slot for "material" would take the default value "wood." In this case, if somebody tells you about a table you will tend to assume it is made of wood unless you are specifically told it is made of plastic.

According to schema theory, schemata influence the way that new information is processed in a number of ways. The schema that is currently activated guides the selection of what is encoded and stored in memory, so that information relevant to that schema is more likely to be remembered than irrelevant information. The schema provides a framework within which the information can be stored and which can be used at retrieval to guide search processes. The effects of schema-driven processes are that information becomes more abstract and general: specific details drop out and the features that are common to other similar experiences are retained. Memories are normalized to fit the expectations derived from pre-existing schemata, so bizarre or unexpected features are omitted or transformed. Missing information is added to the memory representation as the schema supplies default values.

Schank and Abelson (1977) extended the idea of schemata to explain how knowledge of complex event sequences is represented. These knowledge structures, called "scripts," represent the elements common to repeated experiences of events like eating in restaurants. A script consists of a sequence of goal-directed actions which are causally and temporally ordered and includes the actors, objects, and locations that are typically involved. Like schemata, scripts can be broken up into hierarchically organized scenes and subscripts. Script elements function as default values and allow us to supply missing elements and to infer what is not explicitly stated. A narrative about a restaurant experience need not state that the diners sit down or that they pay for their dinner, since these actions are already present in the pre-existing script.

Experimental evidence for the psychological reality of schemata and scripts (*see* SEMANTIC MEMORY) has accumulated. Bower, Black, and Turner (1979) asked subjects to generate scripts for events like visiting the dentist or attending a lecture, and found good agreement about the component actions and sequencing. In tests of memory for scenes or events, people often falsely remember having experienced stereotypical elements that are part of the script or schema, but which were not part of the actual experience. The strongest evidence comes from findings that memories can be dramatically manipulated by supplying inappropriate schemata or no schemata at all (Bransford & Johnson, 1973) or by changing schemata (Anderson & Pichert, 1978) (*see* LANGUAGE COMPREHENSION).

In spite of this supporting evidence there are some problems with schema theory. The theory does not explain how schemata are acquired in the first place or how any sense can be made of unique or novel events for which no schema exists. A poorly specified process of abstraction or induction is assumed to underly schema acquisition. Another difficulty is that whereas schema theory predicts that schema-consistent, script-relevant information should be remembered best, it is often the unexpected, unusual, or deviant aspects of experiences that seem to be particularly memorable. To accommodate this finding the so-called schema-plus-tag model (Graesser & Nakamura, 1982) proposes that a specific memory trace consists of a pointer to the relevant generic schema plus a tag, or tags, encoding any deviant or novel aspects of the experience. In this way the specific details of a particular experience can be recovered. A number of current models of memory conform more or less closely to this pattern, incorporating a generic memory representation (the schema) linked with a specific memory representation.

See also CONCEPT LEARNING; MOOD DISORDERS AND COGNITION; SOCIAL COGNITION.

BIBLIOGRAPHY

Anderson, R. C., & Pichert, J. W. (1978). Recall of previously unrecallable information following a shift in perspective. *Journal of Verbal Learning and Verbal Behavior*, *17*, 1–12.

Bartlett, F. C. (1932). *Remembering*. Cambridge: Cambridge University Press.

Bransford, J. D., & Johnson, M. K. (1973). Consideration of some problems of comprehension. In W. G. Chase (Ed.), *Visual information processing*. New York: Academic Press.

Bower, G. H., Black, J. B., & Turner, T. J. (1979). Scripts in text comprehension and memory. *Cognitive Psychology*, *11*, 177–220.

Graesser, A. C., & Nakamura, G. V. (1982). The impact of a schema on comprehension and memory. In G. Bower (Ed.), *The psychology of learning and motivation: Advances in research and theory* (Vol. 16). New York: Academic Press.

Schank, R. C., & Abelson, R. P. (1977). *Scripts, plans, goals and understanding*. Hillsdale, NJ: Lawrence Erlbaum Associates.

GILLIAN COHEN

scripts *See* BARTLETT, SIR FREDERIC; SCHEMATA.

self-focus and self-attention The concept of self is one of the oldest and most basic in all of psychology. The word pertains simultaneously to the sense of personal continuity that characterizes every individual's personality; to the organized body of knowledge that everyone has about who one is, what one feels and believes, and who one wishes to be; and to the subjective sense of being at the center of the experiences in which one is involved. The self also exhibits a curious and unique property that has been termed reflexivity. That is, the self has the capability of somehow turning backward on itself, of taking aspects of its own content and its own functioning as the object of its awareness. When a person is making use of this reflexive capability, that person is in a state of self-focused attention.

BACKGROUND

The self's reflexive capability has captured interest at least since the time of William

James. Though many eminent theorists made reference over the years to the potential importance of self-directed attention, the idea led to virtually no empirical work until, in 1971, Wicklund and Duval first published experimental research on the possibility that self-directed attention might exert an influence on people's behavior and judgements. The success of these studies led to an expanded program of research and theoretical work on their part (Duval & Wicklund, 1972). These efforts sparked the interest of others, and a good deal of further work ensued (for a review see Carver & Scheier, 1981; Scheier & Carver, 1988).

Relationship to cognitive psychology The work described here was done by social and personality psychologists rather than cognitive psychologists. Unlike most researchers in "social cognition," those studying self-focus have only rarely adopted the research techniques of cognitive psychology and have examined aspects of behavior that are relatively molar rather than molecular. With few exceptions, the work has tended to focus on regulation of people's overt actions and on subjective judgements such as emotional states, attributions, and the like.

The theorists working in this area have also been less precise in their treatment of the concepts that underlie the construct of self-focus than most cognitive psychologists might prefer. That is, they have not fully articulated either theories of the self or theories of attentional processes. What is of interest is the consequence of directing more versus less attention to the self. No stand is usually taken on the question of whether attentional resources are divided or are instead time-shared. Indeed, even the usual assumption of a relatively fixed attentional capacity often seems pro forma.

Operationalizations The typical procedure for increasing self-focus is simply to place subjects before a stimulus that serves to remind them of themselves: e.g. mirrors, TV cameras, or audiences. The introduction of the manipulation usually is timed so as to coincide with the point in the experiment at which a brief state of self-focus should in theory be most relevant to the behavior of interest. Although unorthodox, these manipulations do produce the psychological state they are intended to produce.

Another technique was also developed to vary self-focus in research. In 1975, Fenigstein, Scheier, and Buss published the Self-Consciousness Scale, a measure that captures individual differences in the tendency to spend time thinking about the self. The individual differences measured by this scale are indicative of differences in the ease or the frequency with which people slip naturally into states of self-focus.

Researchers who use both experimental and personality techniques have adopted a terminological shorthand to distinguish between the two operationalizations. In general, the term "self-awareness" is used to reflect experimental manipulations; the term "self-consciousness" is used to reflect individual differences. Terms such as self-focus and self-attention are used more indiscriminately. We have adopted this convention throughout our discussion here.

COGNITIVE CONSEQUENCES OF SELF-FOCUS

What are the consequences of attending inward to the self? Because the informational content that defines the self has many aspects, the phenomenology of self-directed attention can take several forms, and the consequences of self-focus can vary considerably. The effects of self-focus range, in fact, from very simple to very elaborate. We begin our discussion by addressing relatively simple effects, which we have characterized here as "cognitive" consequences of self-focus.

Salience and weighing effects A very simple consequence of self-attention is to cause a self-aspect that is salient to seem phenomenologically more prominent. This tendency toward greater phenomenological prominence is reflected in several different ways, depending on what aspect of self is situationally salient.

In some circumstances, the most salient aspect of self is some transitory internal state.

For example, when people have been exposed to an affect-inducing stimulus, affect tends to be salient as an aspect of the self's experience. When attention is self-focused after a feeling state has been created, the feeling is subjectively more intense. On the other hand, there are also occasions when people are led to expect internal states that fail to occur. In these situations, self-focus appears to lead to greater awareness of the *absence* of the expected condition. Thus, self-focused people are less likely to be misled about what is happening inside them (see Carver & Scheier, 1981).

Sometimes what is salient is not so much an internal state as a more global sense of the self as an entity that plays a role in events in the day to day world. In some instances, this awareness means that the self becomes more salient as a potential causal force. Thus, when people make causal attributions for hypothetically experienced events, greater self-focus seems to produce a greater weighting of the self as a causal agent, and causes greater attribution of causality to the self (e.g. Duval & Wicklund, 1972).

If self-focus enhances the salience of the self's involvement in events, self-focus should also increase the extent to which people view themselves as being the target of others' actions. There is substantial evidence that this is so (Fenigstein, 1984).

Self-focus, self-knowledge, and articulation of self-knowledge Does the scrutiny of self-focus provide a clearer or more accurate reading of stored information about the self? The implicit assumption underlying this possibility is that enhanced self-attention prompts a more thorough search of relevant memories. The result would be a more accurate self-report of one's prior actions, or of one's more general action tendencies. This hypothesis has been supported in a number of studies, using self-reports of such qualities as hostility, dominance, and sociability to predict actual behavior in subsequent sessions (reviewed in Carver & Scheier, 1981).

An additional derivation from this line of thought is that attending to the self over a long period should promote greater articulation of self-knowledge (Nasby, 1985). Indeed, it is

arguable that this is why self-reports of very self-conscious people are more valid than those of less self-conscious people. That is, having spent so much time thinking themselves, people high in self-consciousness have well developed and highly articulated schematic representations of themselves.

The idea that self-consciousness leads to better developed representations of the self leads to several predictions, two of which have been tested in research paradigms adopted from cognitive psychology. In one paradigm, subjects in an initial phase rate the self-descriptiveness of a large number of adjectives. In phase two, they view a subset of the adjectives, and indicate (yes or no) whether each is self-descriptive. After a distractor task, another set of adjectives is presented in phase three, some of which had been presented in phase two (old) and some of which had not (new). The task in phase three is to identify which items are old and which are new.

The tendency to misjudge new words as being old is termed the "false alarm" effect. It is most common among words rated initially as highly self-descriptive. This tendency is strongest among subjects high in self-consciousness. Among words previously rated as *not* self-descriptive, in contrast, highly self-conscious subjects were more likely to correctly judge new words as new. Taken together, these findings are consistent with the idea that highly self-conscious persons have a more articulated representation of themselves than do less self-conscious persons (Nasby, 1985).

A similar conclusion emerges from an incidental learning (depth of processing) paradigm, in which subjects make a decision about each of a series of words, decisions ranging from superficial (involving only shallow processing of the word) to more complex (involving deeper processing). After a distractor task, subjects are given a surprise recall test for the words in the first task. Incidental recall (reflecting deeper processing) is particularly high for words applied to the self in the first task (via the question "Does this word describe you?"), a finding that is commonly termed the "self-reference" effect. Hull and Levy (1979) found that the self-reference effect is stronger among subjects high in self-consciousness than among those lower in self-consciousness. Again, this finding is consistent with the idea that highly self-conscious people have highly articulated self-schemas.

SELF-REGULATORY CONSEQUENCES OF SELF-FOCUS

A more complex set of consequences follows from self-focus when self-attention is invoked under other circumstances. Because these effects appear to have an impact on the guidance of behavior, we will characterize them here as self-regulatory in nature.

Attention to standards and adjustments in self-regulation A person who is engaged in goal directed activity has adopted some value, standard, or point of reference as a guideline for his or her action. In these circumstances, self-focus appears to have two interrelated effects: it enhances the tendency to compare one's present state or action with the salient point of reference, and it promotes an adjustment in one's behavior so that the former comes into closer conformity with the latter.

Evidence that self-focus causes an increased tendency to compare one's current behavior with salient reference values is difficult to obtain. The difficulty stems from the fact that the postulated comparison is an internal mental check, a process of monitoring that takes place at an abstract level and is not directly observable. Indirect access to this event can be obtained, however, in situations where the abstract comparison requires concrete information that is available to the subject but must be sought out. A series of studies based on this reasoning has yielded evidence that seeking of comparison-relevant information is increased by self-focus – before starting a task, while engaged in a task, and even after the task is finished (Scheier & Carver, 1983).

The comparison between behavior and standard is presumed to lead to behavioral adjustments (when possible) that reduce discrepancies between the two values. This discrepancy reduction effect was one of the first consequences of self-directed attention to be. shown experimentally (Wicklund & Duval, 1971) and it has since been obtained in

numerous conceptual replications. Subjects follow instructions more closely, adhere more closely to salient norms, and adjust their actions more in response to systematic situational pressures, when they are more self-focused at the time than when they are less so.

Why does self-focus lead to discrepancy reduction? Two explanations have been offered, which differ substantially in their metatheoretical underpinnings. According to Duval and Wicklund's (1972) view, any discrepancy between one's current state and a salient standard creates an aversive drive state. The larger the discrepancy, the more aversive is self-focus and the stronger is the drive state. One option for reducing that aversive state is to reduce the discrepancy.

Carver and Scheier (1981) have proposed a different view (a view more compatible with the thrust of contemporary cognitive psychology): that the discrepancy reduction effect is a straightforward illustration of the process of feedback control. In a feedback loop, a sensor perceives a current quality. The perception is compared against a reference value. If a discrepancy between the two is discerned, an adjustment is made in a behavioral output. If the adjustment is appropriate, the subsequent perception of present state either will be closer to the reference value or will not deviate from it at all.

This, according to Carver and Scheier, is what happens when attention is self-focused in a setting where a reference value for behavior has previously become salient. People monitor the fit between what they see themselves doing and what they intend to be doing, and make adjustments as needed to diminish discrepancies between the two. In this view, the discrepancy reduction effect is a natural aspect of the feedback-based self-regulation of action (see Carver & Scheier, 1981, 1986; Scheier & Carver, 1988).

Self-focus and disengagement Though self-directed attention promotes behavioral conformity to salient standards in many circumstances, sometimes the opposite effect occurs. This is most likely to occur when movement toward the goal seems beyond one's capabilities or is precluded by some aspect of the situation one is in. When a giving-up response is evoked, self-focus enhances the extent to which it is carried out. As a result, self-focus sometimes results in diminished persistence or even in withdrawal from the behavioral situation entirely (Carver & Scheier, 1981, 1986).

Carver and Scheier's interpretation of this sort of effect is that it involves a second critical element besides self-attention. In this view people continue to exert effort (and thus are facilitated by self-focus) until they become convinced that they are unable to attain the goal they are pursuing. Only when they pass this psychological watershed of loss of confidence does the impetus to disengage begin to emerge and self-focus yield a decrement in behavior (see Figure 1 overleaf). Thus, the important co-determinant of this effect of self-focus is an unfavorable outcome expectancy (Carver & Scheier, 1986).

Sometimes the disengagement impulse that follows from these unfavorable expectancies is expressed indirectly, rather than overtly. In some behavioral settings, overt withdrawal is prevented by implicit social sanctions. In other settings physical constraints prevent behavioral disengagement. The Carver and Scheier position is that in these settings the disengagement impulse is often expressed covertly, via activities such as daydreaming or off-task thinking (Figure 1). If the person is supposed to be engaged in a task during this period, the off-task mentation can result in performance impairment.

The model displayed in Figure 1 appears to be consistent with the results of research that examined the consequences of self-focus under circumstances of difficulty or adversity (Carver & Scheier, 1981, 1986, review issues in this literature; see Duval & Wicklund, 1972, for an alternative view). That is, even under conditions of adversity, if subjects have confidence of being able to overcome the adversity, self-focus enhances efforts and outcomes. If subjects are doubtful enough about attaining their goals, however, self-focus is associated with reduced efforts and impaired outcomes.

We should make one further point here, which deviates slightly from the theme of self-focus per se, but which also has implications for that theme. Disengagement (behavioral or mental) often is a viable response to impediments. Life would be impossible if people did not give up some of the goals they took up. On the other hand, it is difficult to disengage from a goal which is proving difficult or impossible to attain but to which one is very committed. In this situation, when attention is self-directed a cycle occurs. The person focuses on the comparison with the desired goal, assesses expectancies, finds them unfavorable, experiences the impulse to disengage, cannot execute it fully because of the importance of the goal, and is precluded from moving toward the goal by the disengagement impulse. Because the goal is important, it is repeatedly reconfronted and focused on. This cycling produces a phenomenology of self-deprecatory rumination and enhanced distress.

As a concrete example, consider the situation of a test-anxious student taking an exam, whose most fervent wish is to escape from the test room. Though he or she does not do that, the student lapses into off-task thinking as a way of disengaging mentally. This withdrawal of mental resources makes failure more likely. Moreover, even this mental disengagement cannot be sustained for long, as attention repeatedly returns to the test and thence to the unfavorable expectancies that induced the disengagement impulse in the first place.

It has long been recognized that test-anxious persons experience the resulting phenomenology of self-deprecatory rumination while in test settings (Wine, 1971). Though this phenomenology is often termed self-focus, we believe that such a label for that phenomenon is too simple and is potentially misleading (Carver & Scheier, 1986), because it implies that self-focus is antithetical to task focus. The fact is that self-focus impairs performance under some circumstances, but *enhances* performance under other circumstances – and does so even among the test anxious.

One final point, which stems from considering disengagement and discrepancy reduction effects together. We have characterized the difference between these two classes of phenomena here in terms of dif-

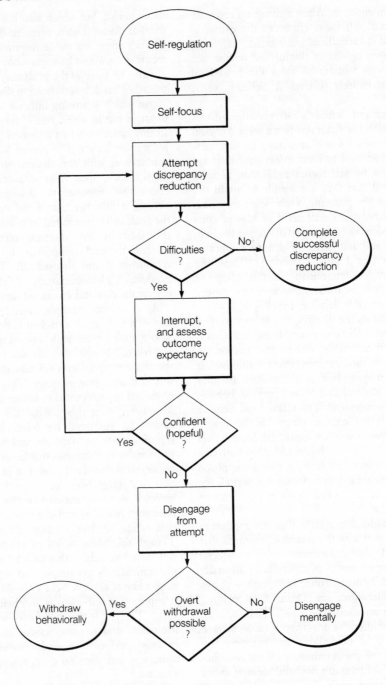

Figure 1 Consequences of self-focus as a function of degree of confidence of goal attainment and situational constraints preventing overt withdrawal.

ferences in people's expectancies for the outcomes of their goal directed efforts. It is important to recognize that this characterization places these effects of self-attention squarely in the tradition of expectancy-based analyses of motivation. From this viewpoint, self-focus effects are not a curious and somewhat esoteric side topic. Rather, they are embedded in a major perspective on behavior.

Public and private aspects of self There is one more important issue to address before closing our discussion of self-directed attention. This issue stems from the multifaceted nature of the self. That the self is multifaceted should already be apparent, given the range of topics we have touched on thus far. However, the issue has also been treated in a more systematic manner than is apparent from our discussion to this point. More specifically, a distinction has been made between public self-aspects and private self-aspects (Fenigstein et al., 1975).

Private aspects of the self are self qualities that are covert, hidden, and bear on personal desires and preferences. Public aspects of self are self qualities that are overt, more explicitly open to others' scrutiny, and bear on self-presentational desires or communal values. This simple dichotomy appears to capture a fundamental and important division within the self, although it will be obvious that each of these self-facets can also be further subdivided.

Given this dichotomy among self-aspects, a dichotomy can also be imposed among instances of self-focus. At any given moment, it is possible to direct attention selectively to one or the other of these facets of the self. The consequences of self-attention can be expected to depend on which aspect of self is taken as the object of one's inward focus. This statement is simple, and the processes to which it refers are also simple, but the idea has far-reaching implications.

To go further, we must first consider how the distinction has been operationalized in research. The individual difference measure of self-consciousness incorporates the distinction in its design. Separate scales of the Self-Consciousness Scale measure tendencies to attend to public and private aspects of the self, respectively. The existence of separate scales implies that the two tendencies are not assumed to oppose each other. Indeed, the scales correlate positively, implying that people who tend to think about one aspect of self also tend to think about the other aspect of self. On the other hand, the correlation is usually not so high as to make it difficult to study the effects of each tendency separately.

Many researchers have now concluded (based partly on convergence between effects of manipulations and effects of dispositions) that experimental manipulations of self-focus also embody the public–private distinction. Small mirrors, placed in such a manner as to make it clear that there is no hidden observer behind them, appear to make people selectively attentive to private aspects of the self. TV cameras, the sound of the subject's own voice, and the presence of observers (particularly evaluative observers) make people selectively attentive to public aspects of the self.

Behavioral consequences of the public–private distinction have been examined in a substantial number of studies (for a review, see Carver & Scheier, 1985). Of greatest interest is a set of studies that focused on situations in which the private self and the public self can be expected to exert *opposite* influences on behavior. Due to the juxtaposition of competing values in these situations, it is very important which self-aspect the person takes as focal. The results of these studies are strikingly uniform. When placed in situations that engender this sort of conflict, people act in accord with their private beliefs and perceptions to the extent that they are focused on their private selves. They act in accord with consensual preferences and self-presentational considerations to the extent that they are focused on their public selves (see Carver & Scheier, 1985).

APPLICATIONS TO THE
CONCEPTUALIZATION OF PATHOLOGY

An outline of principles relating to self-attention should include at least some mention of two additional literatures. One of them deals with the effects of alcohol, the other with depression. Neither case is a simple application of the ideas already outlined – in each case the theorists have developed statements of their own – but both cases fit reasonably well with the ideas already outlined.

Alcohol and the reduction of self-awareness The first of these literatures grows from the hypothesis that an important consequence of alcohol ingestion is a reduction in self-awareness. This hypothesis, developed by Hull (1987), accounts for a variety of observed effects of drinking. For example, if self-focus promotes self-regulation (as we argued earlier), a reduction in self-focus via alcohol should cause behavior to become more poorly regulated. Consistent with this, it is well known that people's behavior when intoxicated is more responsive to cues of the moment, and less responsive to personal values and principles, than is the behavior of the same people when sober.

More important, Hull and his colleagues have gone on to investigate directly the effects of alcohol consumption on various manifestations of self-awareness in a series of studies (for a review, see Hull, 1987). In our view, the most interesting of the findings concerns the idea that people use alcohol as a vehicle for what Hull calls "the strategic avoidance of self-awareness." We said earlier that if people feel unable to attain desired goals, they feel an impulse to disengage from those goals. Diminishing self-focus via alcohol would produce an effect similar to successful disengagement. Moreover, this tactic can be used even when actual disengagement is precluded. This strategic use of alcohol tends to put certain people (those who have a strong motive to disengage) at an elevated risk for sustained drinking problems. The considerable support that Hull (1987) has obtained for his predictions make this theory an important candidate for further exploration.

Depression and self-focus The second literature to be addressed here bears on depression (*see* MOOD DISORDERS AND COGNITION). It has frequently been noted that depression is correlated with self-consciousness. Pyszczynski and Greenberg (1987) have proposed a mechanism by which that

association comes to exist. In their view, depression develops when a person loses some important source of self-worth (thus having a large discrepancy between perceived self and desired self) and is unable to move toward regaining it (see also Carver & Scheier, 1986). The person becomes immersed in self-deprecatory rumination (and concomitant distress) in the manner we outlined earlier.

As this pattern of negative self-focused thought begins to solidify and stabilize, the person's self-image becomes more negative, and the person tends to focus selectively on negative self-attributes. The result is a "depressive self-focusing style," in which the person is more likely to seek out self-awareness after failure than after success (Pyszczynski & Greenberg, 1987), a pattern that is opposite to that found among non-depressed persons. This selective focusing on the negative helps to maintain and even exacerbate the depression. Though the precise reason for this selective focus on the negative remains to be determined, this approach to understanding aspects of the phenomenology of depression seems a promising one.

See also CONSCIOUSNESS; INTROSPECTION.

BIBLIOGRAPHY

Carver, C. S., & Scheier, M. F. (1981). *Attention and self-regulation: A control-theory approach to human behavior.* New York: Springer-Verlag.

——. (1985). Aspects of self, and the control of behavior. In B. R. Schlenker (Ed.), *The self and social life* (pp. 146–74). New York: McGraw-Hill.

——. (1986). Functional and dysfunctional responses to anxiety: The interaction between expectancies and self-focused attention. In R. Schwarzer (Ed.), *Self-related cognitions in anxiety and motivation* (pp. 111–41). Hillsdale, NJ: Erlbaum.

Duval, S., & Wicklund, R. A. (1972). *A theory of objective self-awareness.* New York: Academic Press.

Fenigstein, A. (1984). Self-consciousness and the overperception of self as a target. *Journal of Personality and Social Psychology*, 47, 860–70.

——, Scheier, M. F., & Buss, A. H. (1975). Public and private self consciousness: Assessment and theory. *Journal of Consulting and Clinical Psychology, 43,* 522–7.

Hull, J. G. (1987). Self-awareness model. In H. T. Blane & K. E. Leonard (Eds), *Psychological theories of drinking and alcoholism* (pp. 272–304). New York: Guilford Press.

— —, & Levy, A. S. (1979). The organizational functions of the self: An alternative to the Duval and Wicklund model of self-awareness. *Journal of Personality and Social Psychology, 37,* 756–68.

Nasby, W. (1985). Private self-consciousness, articulation of the self-schema, and recognition memory of trait adjectives. *Journal of Personality and Social Psychology, 49,* 704–9.

Pyszczynski, T., & Greenberg, J. (1987). Self-regulatory perseveration and the depressive self-focusing style: A self-awareness theory of reactive depression. *Psychological Bulletin, 102,* 122–38.

Scheier, M. F., & Carver, C. S. (1983). Self-directed attention and the comparison of self with standards. *Journal of Experimental Social Psychology, 19,* 205–22.

— —. (1988). A model of behavioral self-regulation: Translating intention into action. In L. Berkowitz (Ed.), *Advances in experimental social psychology* (Vol. 21) (pp. 303–46). New York: Academic Press.

Wicklund, R. A., & Duval, S. (1971). Opinion change and performance facilitation as a result of objective self-awareness. *Journal of Experimental Social Psychology, 7,* 319–42.

Wine, J. D. (1971). Test anxiety and direction of attention. *Psychological Bulletin, 76,* 92–104.

CHARLES S. CARVER AND MICHAEL F. SCHEIER

semantic memory Perhaps the first formal definition of semantic memory was provided by Tulving (1972, p. 386) who described it as

the memory necessary for the use of language. It is a mental thesaurus, organized knowledge a person possesses about words and other verbal symbols, their meaning and referents, about relations among them, and about rules, formulas, and algorithms for the manipulation of these symbols, concepts, and relations.... Semantic memory does not register perceptible properties of inputs, but rather cognitive referents of input signals.

The term semantic memory has been used very broadly in modern memory research. At a descriptive level the term has much in common with other attempts to distinguish between the representation of knowledge about the world, and the events that gave rise to that knowledge (cf. the philosopher A. J. Ayer's distinction between habit and event memory).

Semantic memory is one dimension of Tulving's (1985) tripartite division of long-term store into episodic, semantic, and procedural memory (*see* DECLARATIVE AND PROCEDURAL KNOWLEDGE; EPISODIC MEMORY; MEMORY SYSTEMS).

At an experiential level Tulving has attempted to distinguish each of the forms of memory in terms of the nature of conscious experience that accompanies retrieval. Episodic memory is autonöetic in that recollection of an event reflects some awareness of a contiguity between the event and other features of the temporal record. Semantic memory is nöetic – conscious awareness is involved but retrieval of information is not associated with any temporal contingencies. Retrieval from semantic memory does not therefore require access to the learning episodes that provided the original basis for that knowledge. In contrast, episodic memory requires, ipso facto, access to the individual's record of personal experience. Finally, procedural memory is anöetic because access to this store of knowledge proceeds without conscious involvement (for a fuller account of procedural memory *see* DECLARATIVE AND PROCEDURAL KNOWLEDGE).

At the experimental level it seems relatively easy to think of tasks which unambiguously tap semantic memory. Defining the meaning of words, answering quiz questions, and solving mathematical problems are all acts of memory which do not appear to require the retrieval of specific personal experiences before we can come up with an answer. However, when experimenters have attempted to distinguish semantic memory from episodic memory in normal human subjects difficulties have arisen. The primary problem is that episodic and semantic memory, as conceived by Tulving, are likely to be highly interactive. Consider the simple semantic memory task of lexical decision which requires the subject to decide whether a string of letters is an English word or not. Experiments have shown, for example, that repeats of the same letter string produce faster responses – a finding that can, in part at least, be attributed to subjects remembering their previous (episodic) encounter with that stimulus. For reasons such as this the separable existence of semantic and episodic memory has been difficult to establish through experiments on normal people.

These difficulties have led proponents of semantic memory to emphasize clinical data in support of their arguments. The human amnesic syndrome (*see* AMNESIA) can be characterized by a gross impairment in the ability to remember both new information and loss of memories acquired before the illness or accident that gave rise to the memory impairment. However, finer analysis of the deficit reveals that some abilities that would be classified as semantic memory, namely language and general intelligence, are largely unaffected. In contrast, memories that appear episodic in nature are grossly impaired. These findings have led a number of researchers, notably Tulving (e.g. 1985) to propose that semantic memory is selectively spared in amnesia.

Unfortunately there are a number of flaws in this argument. First, the demonstration of normal language and intelligence is usually based on performance levels attained on the Wechsler Adult Intelligence Scale (WAIS). However, WAIS primarily tests information that has been acquired early in life. Thus, rather than suggest intact semantic memory, normal WAIS scores may simply represent the sparing of early overlearned information.

The separable existence of semantic memory, at least in Tulving's terms, is further undermined by more detailed analysis of amnesia. If semantic memory is spared in amnesics, one would expect retrograde amnesia (loss of memories acquired before the brain trauma causing amnesia) to be restricted to event-based knowledge. There are several lines of evidence that show that this is not the case. Amnesics do, for example, have difficulty

defining vocabulary that has come into use in the decade or so preceding the brain injury that caused their memory loss. Also they have great difficulty recognizing once-familiar people – a response that could not have conceivably depended on episodic memory when the patient's memory was intact. Finally, attempts to show that semantic memory can continue to function in the absence of episodic memory have been completely unsuccessful. The famous patient HM became amnesic in 1953 and is still alive at the time of writing. Despite constant exposure to the evolving English Language HM has learned only three new words and attempts to teach him new vocabulary have met with complete failure (Parkin, 1987).

Despite difficulties in asserting the independent existence of semantic memory, the term is still accepted, relatively unambiguously, as referring to that aspect of long-term store concerned with the representation of language and other aspects of knowledge. It also provides a useful umbrella term for a wide range of research enterprises concerned with understanding the representation and organization of knowledge.

Semantic memory was an important research topic in the 1970s and may prove so again with the advent of neural network models. The principal aim of semantic memory research was to examine how knowledge about the meaning of concepts was organized and how this knowledge was utilized. Ideas about the nature of semantic memory have been heavily influenced by developments in the parallel field of ARTIFICIAL INTELLIGENCE. A primary feature of a computer is that it can store and retrieve information. Given that this is something that humans also do it seemed reasonable to suppose that the representational system used by a computer might provide insights into the system used by the brain itself.

Collins and Quillian (1969) developed a computer-based hierarchical network model of semantic memory called the Teachable Language Comprehender (TLC). In TLC, information is represented as various combinations of three types of structure – units, properties, and pointers. A unit corresponds to anything that would be represented by a noun or noun phrase (e.g. a concept, an object). A property is something which can qualify the nature of a unit (e.g. "is blue" can qualify "sea"). Pointers provide the links between units and properties (e.g. "sea" → "is blue'). Within TLC the meaning of a unit is therefore expressed in terms of the properties associated with that unit.

It is not difficult to imagine how vast this network would have to be in order to represent the typical semantic memory of an individual (although, to be fair, this is a problem for all theories of knowledge representation). To simplify matters Collins and Quillian considered how their hierarchical network might represent knowledge about one category – animals. They proposed that networks would be organized hierarchically. Thus, the units "bird" and "fish" would point to the common node "animal." In order to be economical it was assumed that properties common to all animals would only be associated with the animal node. At subordinate units only those properties unique to that unit would be represented – a principle which was termed cognitive economy. Thus, in order to establish that a fish has skin it would be necessary to move from the "fish" unit to the "animal" unit – this follows because "has skin" is a property found in all animals. In contrast, knowing that a fish has fins would be accessible directly from the "fish" node because, barring a few prehistoric monsters, "has fins" is a unique feature of fish.

TLC made clear predictions about the time required to retrieve different items of knowledge. It asserted that verification time for a sentence such as "X has Y?" would be a positive function of the distance between the unit X and the unit at which property Y was stored. Taking our above example, "A fish has fins?" would be verified more quickly than "A fish has skin?" because, in the former case, the property is stored at the same level as the unit.

Initial experiments measuring verification times suggested that TLC might be a valid model of semantic memory. It was found that subjects did take longer to confirm more "distant" relationships (e.g. "does a fish have skin?") than closer ones (e.g. "does a fish have fins?"). However various pieces of evidence failed to support TLC. First, subjects did not always respond as if their semantic memory was organized hierarchically. Consider the two sentences "a bear is a mammal?", "a bear is an animal?" TLC predicts that the former should be verified more quickly because the distance between bear and mammal is shorter than that between bear and animal. In fact the reverse was found. However, one might argue that people are not natural zoologists and that the concept "mammal" may not be represented very clearly. Many people, for example, think of birds as separate entities from other animals.

There were a number of objections to the approach of Collins and Quillian. At a theoretical level it was pointed out that many concepts do not have a clear set of defining features and could not be fitted easily into a hierarchical structure. Another problem was the "typicality effect" in which people took longer to confirm that atypical exemplars belong to a category than typical exemplars, e.g. "ostrich" is more difficult to define as a bird than "robin." Results such as this forced Collins and Loftus (1975) to abandon the TLC model and substitute it with the "spreading activation" theory of semantic memory. They rejected the hierarchical structure and instead proposed that semantic relatedness was the primary basis of organization. Within the model the meaning of a given unit or "node" is expressed by the nature and strength of its relationships with other units and properties. Thus, a typical instance of category (robin) is confirmed as such more rapidly because it shares many of the defining features (e.g. "flies") of a bird. Atypical exemplars (ostrich) have less in common and therefore result in a slower decision process.

The notion of spreading activation refers to the process by which activation of a given node also activates other nodes to which it is linked. The extent of spreading activation of other nodes was assumed to be directly proportional to the strength of the links between those nodes and the initially activated nodes and, furthermore, the weaker the link the longer the time required for activation. Unfortunately, only evidence supporting the second prediction has been found.

Despite its limitations, the spreading activation model does provide a reasonable account of subjects' performance on sentence verification tasks. However, the theory is rather complicated and this, along with other considerations, has resulted in an alternative "feature" theory of semantic memory. Smith, Shoben, and Rips (1974) suggest that the meaning of a word (e.g. a bird) is represented by a set of features that define its various attributes (e.g. has wings, flies, lays eggs). The feature theory provides a good account of typicality effects by arguing that typical exemplars are identified more quickly because they possess more overlapping attributes than atypical exemplars. However, the theory is somewhat constrained in that it has evolved principally to explain how subjects verify that items are or are not members of a given category. Clearly, semantic memory allows us to achieve much more than that but feature theory offers little account of this. It cannot, for example, explain how we verify a sentence such as "the woman has a watch," in which the subject and the object do not have any overlapping features. Furthermore, the theory suffers because defining features for a given concept cannot always be specified.

An alternative view of representation in semantic memory is provided by prototype theory. Within this framework a concept is represented not by defining features, but by a set of characteristics which are considered, in differing degrees of importance, to be representative of that concept. In the case of "bird," for example, "feathers" and "wings" are highly representative features whereas "seven feet tall" and "flightless" are not. As a result "parrot" is close to the prototype of bird whereas "ostrich" is not.

The prototype theory accounts nicely for typicality effects in sentence verification (see above) as well as a number of other findings. When asked to generate items from a category people are far more likely to produce exemplars that are close to the prototype than exemplars that are not. Research on color categories (e.g. Rosch, 1975) has shown that, despite immense variation in the number and nature of color boundaries in different cultures, people are reasonably consistent in what they consider to be the best example of a focal color (e.g. red). Prototype theory is also supported by various linguistic conventions. People say, for example, that "technically speaking" a tomato is a fruit but that most people think of it as a vegetable. This suggests that people have some awareness of prototypical knowledge. The existence of prototypes can also be demonstrated in the learning of novel material. One study, for example, has shown that people falsely identify previously unexposed schematic faces that are prototypes of faces that were in the learning sequence.

However, like other theories of semantic memory, prototype theory also has its inadequacies. Although the notion of a prototype is easily understood with simple categories such as "bird", prototypes cannot be so easily identified when other sorts of concept (e.g. a belief) are considered. Prototype theory has also some difficulty explaining why people attach greater salience to some features than to others when forming a new concept. Despite these and other objections the available evidence indicates that prototypical information is a salient aspect of representation in semantic memory.

Psychologists have also attempted to understand how knowledge more complex than simple concepts is represented in semantic memory. Relational concepts (e.g. hit) have received some investigation and the evidence suggests that, like simple object concepts, their representation is prototypical rather than one based on defining features. However, most research into more complex knowledge has concentrated on the role of schemata (singular schema) and the derivative ideas of frames (see COGNITIVE SCIENCE) and scripts (see SCHEMATA).

The existence of schemata was first proposed by the neurophysiologist Head but introduced to psychology by BARTLETT (SIR FREDERIC). Bartlett argued that, through experience, people build up a set of expectancies about what should and should not happen in any particular circumstances and it was this that he termed a schema. Thus, when remembering or interpreting information people use schema as a means of filling in missing facts in a way that is consistent with their view of the world.

The idea of internal schema was revived by a number of psychologists. Schank and Abelson (1977) proposed that people have scripts which we use in our comprehension of everyday events such as going to a restaurant. Studies have given plausibility to the idea of scripts. When describing the typical events in a restaurant, for example, people show a high degree of consistency in the component acts they describe. Script theory is also supported by experiments showing that information consistent with the script for a sequence of events is remembered differently to events that are not normally associated with that script (Mandler, 1984).

It has also been argued that people impose sets of expectancies during perceptual processing and it is these that are most often called frames (Yekovich & Thorndyke, 1981). The basic idea is that, by expecting certain features to be present in a particular scene, the amount of processing effort for this information can be reduced and thus more applied to the unexpected and more difficult aspects of the percept. The existence of frames has been supported by several lines of evidence, including the finding that people are far more likely to notice changes in components of a visual scene that are unexpected compared with components which are consistent with the frame.

Schema theory has a lot of intuitive plausibility but there are a number of problems. First, there seems to be no experimentally proven theory as to how schemata arise. Also, if much of perceptual analysis involves the use of frames derived from expectancies we ought to experience more difficulty than we do in comprehending wholly unexpected events. If, without warning, an elephant were to crash through the ceiling during a seminar we would have no difficulty realizing what had happened. This rather extreme example illustrates that although scripts and frames may facilitate our mental activity, we must have other more fundamental mechanisms which enable us to deal with experiences independently of our expectancies. For this reason the explanatory power of scripts and frames may be far less than some have claimed.

See also CONCEPT LEARNING; DYSLEXIAS: ACQUIRED.

BIBLIOGRAPHY

Collins, A. M., & Loftus, E. F. (1975). A spreading activation theory of semantic processing. *Psychological Review, 82*, 407–28.

Collins, A. M., & Quillian, M. R. (1969). Retrieval time from semantic memory. *Journal of Verbal Learning and Verbal Behavior, 8*, 240–8.

Mandler, J. M. (1984). *Stories, scripts, and scenes.* Hillsdale, NJ: Lawrence Erlbaum Associates.

Parkin, A. J. (1987). *Memory and amnesia: An introduction.* Oxford: Basil Blackwell.

Rosch, E. (1975). The nature of mental codes for colour categories. *Journal of Experimental Psychology: General, 104*, 192–223.

Schank, R. C., & Abelson, R. P. (1977). *Scripts, plans, goals, and understanding.* Hillsdale, NJ: Lawrence Erlbaum Associates.

Smith, E. E., Shoben, E. J., & Rips, L. J. (1974). Structure and process in semantic memory: A featural model for semantic decisions. *Psychological Review, 81*, 214–41.

Tulving, E. (1972). Episodic and semantic memory. In E. Tulving & W. Donaldson (Eds), *Organisation of memory.* London: Academic Press.

——. (1985). How many memory systems are there? *American Psychologist, 40*, 385–98.

Yekovich, F. R., & Thorndyke, P. W. (1981). An evaluation of alternative functional models of narrative schemata. *Journal of Verbal Learning and Verbal Behavior, 20*, 454–69.

A. J. PARKIN

sentence processing A great deal of research in psycholinguistics has been devoted to uncovering the very complex processes that are involved when we understand and produce sentences. One area of particular study has been the unit of analysis involved in sentence comprehension and production. The question at issue is this: do we process language in sentential units or is the unit of analysis smaller than a sentence?

There are good reasons for supposing that,

for spoken language, the sentence is a rather artificial unit. Indeed, it has been argued that sentences only exist in written text where their boundaries are delineated by capital letters and full stops. Spoken language typically consists of incomplete sentences as any attempt to provide a written transcription of spontaneous speech will readily show (see Brown & Yule, 1983, chap. 3). For this reason, it is probably more appropriate to think of something more like a clause as the main unit in both language production and comprehension.

Research on language production has shown that there are many differences between written and spoken forms. Most notably, spoken language usually contains frequent pauses and fillers (like "ah" and "um") as well as various kinds of error. The pattern of pauses produced by speakers provides important insights into the processes that are involved in language production. Beattie (1983) analyzed pauses occurring in spontaneous speech and found that over half appeared immediately before the start of a clause. This finding may be taken as evidence that the clause is an important unit in spontaneous speech. However, Beatties's data also suggest that when people are talking, they do not plan one clause at a time but instead plan several clauses together.

Beattie argues that spontaneous speech has a cyclical character in which hesitant and fluent phases follow one after the other. During a hesitant phase – which is characterized by a great deal of pausing and the use of short clauses – the speaker is planning ahead, not only to the next clause, but also to the next sequence of clauses. Once this forward planning has been completed, the speaker then enters a fluent phase during which there is significantly less hesitation and the speaker tends to use longer clauses. Once the limits of forward planning have been reached, the speaker then enters another hesitant phase. In Beattie's data, a complete cycle – a hesitant phase followed by a fluent phase – lasted for about nine clauses.

Planning what to say involves several different activities including the choice of topic, the organization of ideas within that topic, and the selection of appropriate words and syntactic structures to convey those ideas (see SPEECH PRODUCTION). The listener's task is, in some sense, the reverse of the speaker's because the listener has to derive intended meaning from what a speaker says. An important part of this task is concerned with integrating information contained in successive phrases and clauses (see LANGUAGE COMPREHENSION) and making necessary inferences (see LANGUAGE, PRAGMATICS OF). But before such higher level processes of comprehension can come into operation, essential processes of syntactic and semantic analysis are necessary.

It has been proposed – in the "clausal hypothesis" (Fodor, Bever, & Garrat, 1974) – that the clause is the main unit of analysis for the earlier processes of comprehension. In its strongest form, the clausal hypothesis makes two claims. The first is that syntactic and semantic processing does not begin until a whole clause has been heard or read. The second is that, immediately a clause has been processed, it is expunged from working memory and only its meaning is retained in long-term memory; details of syntactic structure and the particular words used by the speaker are lost.

Several experiments have shown that, in general, people do rapidly forget information about linguistic form. For example, subjects in a study by Sachs (1967) listened to a passage and were then presented with a single sentence (the test sentence) and asked whether it had occurred in the passage. Sometimes the test sentence was identical to one that had occurred in the passage (the target sentence), but on other trials, the test sentence was slightly different, either in meaning or in form, from a sentence that subjects had actually heard.

Sachs systematically varied the position of the target sentence in the passage and she found that when the target sentence was the most recent one that subjects had heard, they could accurately recognize changes in either meaning or form. However, when several sentences had intervened between the target sentence and the test sentence, subjects could reliably recognize only changes in meaning.

Sachs's experiment strongly suggests that, with the exception of the most recently heard sentence, only the meaning – and not the form – of sentences is retained in memory (*see* LEVELS OF PROCESSING). However, while the general conclusion of Sachs's experiment is undoubtedly correct, it is by no means clear that forgetting occurs on a simple sentence-by-sentence or, even, on a simple clause-by-clause basis. Indeed, an elegant experiment by Jarvella (1971) shows that the extent to which lexical and syntactic details of a clause are lost depends on its structural relationship to other clauses.

Subjects in Jarvella's experiment listened to prose passages. At various points, their listening was interrupted and they were asked to recall what they had just heard. There were two versions of each passage and the main focus of interest was subjects' ability to recall the three clauses that were presented immediately before recall. In one condition the most recently heard clause was structurally independent of the immediately preceding clause. In the other condition the same clause was structurally related to the immediately preceding clause. An example of Jarvella's materials is shown below (clause 3 was the one heard immediately before recall):

Structurally independent target clause	**Structurally dependent target clause**
1 The document also blamed him	1 The tone of the document was threatening.
2 for having failed to disprove the charges.	2 Having failed to disprove the charges
3 *Taylor was later fired by the president.*	3 *Taylor was later fired by the president.*

Jarvella found that, as expected, subjects in both conditions were very accurate at recalling the clause they had just heard. However, recall of the immediately preceding clause (clause 2) was significantly different in the two conditions. Where clause 2 was structurally dependent on the most recently heard clause, subjects could recall about 80 percent of clause 2, whereas when clause 2 was structurally independent of the last heard clause, recall dropped to 50 percent.

These data suggest that, in the case where a preceding clause is structurally related to the clause that follows it, the preceding clause is remembered almost verbatim until the following clause has been fully analyzed. It is easy to see why this is the case. Imagine that you came across the clauses that Jarvella used. If you heard "Having failed to disprove the charges," you would realize that there was more information to come even though you could carry out the majority of the syntactic analysis of that clause. In particular, you would know that "someone" had failed to disprove some charges but you would not know that person's identity. It would only be on hearing the next clause that this information would become available, and it would only be on determining this that you could fully complete the analysis of the earlier clause. Once the analysis of clause 2 was complete – and only then – would it be appropriate to expunge verbatim information about it from WORKING MEMORY.

There is another way in which some modification is required of the claim that verbatim information about clauses is immediately lost once they have been processed. This arises from findings of Kintsch and Bates about long-term recall of speech in real life (Kintsch & Bates, 1977, Bates, Kintsch, Fletcher, & Giuliani, 1980). Kintsch and Bates tested students on their memory for lectures. The students had not been warned in advance that they were to be tested but, somewhat surprisingly, 48 hours after the lecture students were able to remember quite a lot of information about the form, as well as the meaning, of what they had heard. On a recognition memory test, they were able to make reliable distinctions between sentences that had been in the lecture and paraphrases that meant the same.

One reason why the performance of the students in the Kintsch and Bates study was so much better than that of other experiments that have tested memory for language form – such as Sachs (1967) and Garrod and Trabasso (1973) – lies in the complex relationship between the form and meaning of language. The way in which we choose to say something is usually not arbitrary. Important pragmatic factors influence the selection of a particular linguistic form to convey a particular piece of information. For example, the choice of a passive rather than an active form – that is, the choice of "Several candidates were chosen by the committee" rather than "The committee chose several candidates" – is strongly influenced, among other things, by the viewpoint of a particular discourse (see Harris & Coltheart, 1986).

Such pragmatic factors were undoubtedly at work in the natural discourse that Kintsch and Bates studied, and these may explain why the form of some parts of the lectures that the students heard was particularly memorable. However, pragmatic factors influencing the choice of linguistic forms are usually ignored in the construction of stimuli for experiments that look at memory for language and hence there is no reason why the form of sentences in such experiments should be remembered.

Another aspect of the clausal hypothesis has also proved to be open to doubt. This concerns its first claim, that speech processing does not begin until a listener has heard an entire clause. A series of experiments by Marslen-Wilson and his co-workers (Marslen-Wilson & Tyler, 1980; Marslen-Wilson, 1987) has demonstrated that processing of syntactic, semantic, and pragmatic information is carried out as soon as the first word in a clause has been heard. Subjects in Marslen-Wilson's experiments performed a variety of tasks in which they had to identify a particular word in a sentence to which they were listening. Target words occurred in different serial positions across the test sentences, varying from the second to the tenth position. The syntactic, semantic, and pragmatic plausibility of target words was also varied by using three different types of prose. The first of these, normal prose, consisted of sentences such as "Some thieves stole most of the lead off the roof," which were pragmatically, schematically, and syntactically appropriate, whereas the second condition, anomalous prose, consisted of sentences such as "No buns puzzle some in the lead off the text," which obeyed the rules of English syntax but were meaningless. The third condition, scrambled prose, consisted of strings of randomly ordered words that obeyed neither the rules of syntax nor semantic-pragmatic constraints.

If processing of the syntax, semantics, and pragmatics of language does not begin until an entire clause has been heard, then the plausibility of a word should not have any influence on the speed with which that word can be recognized unless that word occurs right at the end of a clause. That is, the time taken to identify a word should not be affected either by its position in a sentence or by the prose condition in which it occurs. (The argument here is that syntactic, semantic, and pragmatic plausibility within a sentence can only operate once information about these various linguistics aspects has been processed.)

Marslen-Wilson's data clearly demonstrate that, in the normal and anomalous prose conditions, the time taken to recognize a word decreased with its position in the sentence – that is, the later in a sentence a target word appeared, the faster subjects were to identify it. Words occurring right at the end of a sentence were identified faster than words occurring at an earlier position, but there was a steady decrease in recognition time *throughout the entire sentence*. However, for the scrambled prose condition – where words occurred in random order – recognition time was the same for all word positions.

This result is only explicable if we assume that subjects were processing the sentence as they heard each word and were thus able to exploit syntactic, semantic, and pragmatic constraints that built up throughout the sentence. Subjects did not delay processing until they had heard an entire clause.

Recognition time for words in the normal prose condition was also influenced by whether there was a context sentence preceding the one containing the target word. Words occurring early in a sentence were recognized faster if there was a preceding context sentence. This is because information from a previous sentence can also influence the plausibility of a word and so make it easier to recognize.

The fact that recognition of a word is influenced by information from previous sentences, as well as that contained in earlier parts of the same sentence, suggests that processing is not only carried out as we hear each new word, but also that information from new sentences is rapidly integrated with information that has been extracted from earlier ones.

BIBLIOGRAPHY

Bates, E., Kintsch, W., Fletcher, C. R., & Giuliani, V. (1980). Recognition memory for surface forms in dialogue: Explicit vs. anaphoric reference. In *Papers from the parasession on pronouns and anaphora*. Chicago: Chicago Linguistics Society.

Beattie, G. (1983). *Talk: An analysis of speech and non-verbal behaviour in conversation*. Milton Keynes: Open University Press.

Brown, G., & Yule, G. (1983). *Discourse analysis*. Cambridge: Cambridge University Press.

Fodor, J. A., Bever, T. G., & Garrat, M. F. (1974). *The psychology of language: An introduction to psycholinguistics and generative grammar*. New York: McGraw-Hill.

Garrod, S., & Trabasso, T. (1973). A dual-memory information processing interpretation of sentence comprehension. *Journal of Verbal Learning and Verbal Behavior, 12*, 155–67.

Harris, M., & Coltheart, M. (1986). *Language processing in children and adults: An introduction to psycholinguistics*. London: Routledge & Kegan Paul.

Jarvella, R. J. (1971). Syntactic processing of connected speech. *Journal of Verbal Learning and Verbal Behavior, 10*, 409–16.

Kintsch, W., & Bates, E. (1977). Recognition memory for statements from a classroom lecture. *Journal of Experimental Psychology: Human Learning and Memory, 3*, 150–9.

Marslen-Wilson, W. D. (1987). Functional parallelism in spoken word-recognition. *Cognition, 25*, 71–102.

— —, & Tyler, L. K. (1980). The temporal structure of spoken language understanding. *Cognition, 8*, 1–71.

Sachs, J. S. (1967). Recognition memory for syntactic and semantic aspects of connected discourse. *Perception and Psychophysics, 2*, 437–42.

MARGARET HARRIS

short-term memory Short-term memory refers to memory for events which occurred within the last few seconds; theoretically, it has been argued that there is an important distinction between short-term memory on the one hand and LONG-TERM MEMORY on the other. The essence of the theoretical distinction was embodied in James's terms "primary memory" and "secondary memory" (*see* JAMES, WILLIAM). According to James (1890), primary memory is concerned with information that remains in consciousness after it has been processed, and thus forms part of the psychological present. In contrast, secondary memory is concerned with information about events that have left consciousness, and as a consequence form part of the psychological past.

One of the major differences between the short-term memory store (or primary memory) and the long-term memory store (or secondary memory) is in terms of their capacity. There are no known limits on the capacity of long-term memory, but it was argued by Miller (1956) in a very influential article that no more than approximately seven chunks (i.e. familiar units of information) can be stored in short-term memory at any given time.

The notion that there are separate short-term and long-term memory stores was incorporated into a number of major theories of memory (e.g. Atkinson & Shiffrin, 1968). Some of the strongest support for this notion came from research into amnesic patients (*see* AMNESIA). In essence, it was discovered that most amnesic patients have severely impaired long-term memory but largely intact short-term memory. However, there are a few amnesic patients who exhibit the opposite pattern of deficient short-term memory but essentially intact long-term memory. It is difficult to account for these findings without assuming that there is a valid distinction between short-term and long-term memory systems.

In spite of the empirical support for the distinction between short-term and long-term memory stores, it has increasingly been realized that neither the short-term store nor the long-term store is unitary. For example, Baddeley and Hitch (1974) and Baddeley (1986) argued that the concept of a unitary short-term store postulated by Atkinson and Shiffrin (1986) should be replaced by that of a working memory system consisting of three components (*see* WORKING MEMORY). This conceptualization has the advantage of providing a more adequate account of the complexities of short-term memory. It also has the advantage that the working-memory system, combining as it does active processing and transient storage of information, provides an explanation of performance on a wide range of cognitive tasks which are not explicitly concerned with short-term memory.

BIBLIOGRAPHY

Atkinson, R. C., & Shiffrin, R. M. (1968). Human memory: A proposed system and its control processes. In K. W. Spence & J. T. Spence (Eds), *The psychology of learning and motivation* (Vol. 2). London: Academic Press.

Baddeley, A. D. (1986). *Working memory.* Oxford: Oxford University Press.

— —, & Hitch, G. (1974). Working memory. In G. H. Bower (Ed.), *The psychology of learning and motivation* (Vol. 8). London: Academic Press.

James, W. (1890). *Principles of psychology.* New York: Holt.

Miller, G. A. (1956). The magic number seven, plus or minus two: Some limits on our capacity for processing information. *Psychological Review, 63,* 81–93.

MICHAEL W. EYSENCK

short-term memory, retrieval from Information in SHORT-TERM MEMORY or WORKING MEMORY is information which is currently being processed. As JAMES (WILLIAM) (1890) pointed out, information in short-term memory forms part of the psychological present, whereas information in long-term memory forms part of the psychological past. In light of these considerations, there has been little interest in assessing the probability of retrieval from some short-term memory store, since it has been assumed that all information actually in that store can be retrieved. As a consequence, research and theory on retrieval from short-term memory have focused on the speed with which information can be retrieved from short-term memory rather than on the accuracy of retrieval.

It is a matter of some theoretical importance to establish as precisely as possible the characteristics of short-term memory. The short-term memory or working memory system is obviously involved in many memory tasks, but its significance extends far beyond that. It appears to be the case that this system is used in the performance of most cognitively demanding tasks, so that understanding the detailed functioning of the short-term memory system may increase our knowledge of the processes involved in comprehension, PROBLEM SOLVING, mental arithmetic, and so on.

The basic paradigm for studying speed of retrieval from short-term memory was introduced into psychology by Sternberg (1969). In this paradigm, between one and six items are presented to the subject, and these items are generally referred to as the "memory set." A probe item is presented very shortly after the memory set, and the subject's task is to decide as rapidly as possible whether or not it matches one of the items in the memory set.

Since relatively few errors are usually made on this task, interest centers on the speed of positive and negative responses as a function of the number of items in the memory set. While the pattern of results is affected by various factors, the most common finding is that the positive and negative functions are both linear and parallel. According to Sternberg (1969), the results are consistent with a serial exhaustive model in which the probe is compared against each of the items in the memory set at a rate of 25–30 items per second. It might seem more likely that there would be a self-terminating scan, in which the search would stop as soon as a match for the probe was located. With a self-terminating scan, half of the memory-set items would be searched on positive trials, whereas all of the items would be searched on negative trials. The natural prediction on a self-terminating scan view is that increasing the number of items in the memory set would increase the response time to the probe at approximately twice the rate on negative trials as on positive trials, but this does not happen.

Sternberg's (1969) complete theory consists of four separate processing stages, which together account for the time taken to respond to the probe. We have so far considered the serial comparison stage, which is the second of these four stages. The first stage is that of probe encoding, the third stage is that of decision (i.e. whether to respond "yes" or "no'), and the fourth stage is that of translation and response organization. According to Sternberg, manipulations of memory-set size affect only the serial comparison stage and have no effects on the remaining stages.

Although Sternberg's model provided an accurate and elegant account of the basic findings from his paradigm, it became clear that there were various findings which it could not readily accommodate. For example, since the search through the memory set is allegedly exhaustive, it should not make any difference to the response speed whether the probe matches with the first item, the last item, or one of the middle items of the memory set. In practice, however, there is frequently a recency effect, in which the probe is responded to fastest if it matches with the last item or two in the memory set.

An alternative view of performance on the Sternberg paradigm is that the speed of performance is determined almost entirely by the strength or familiarity of the probe. According to a strength theory, the reason why subjects take longer to respond when there are more items in the memory set is that under such circumstances the average familiarity of the memory-set items declines. The recency effect has been accounted for by assuming that the last item in the memory set is in some sense stronger than the other items.

Atkinson and Juola (1974) proposed an interesting theory which combined elements of the Sternberg and strength theory approaches. According to them, subjects respond rapidly to the probe on the basis of its strength or familiarity if its strength is very high or very low. If its strength is intermediate, then there is a slower search through the memory-set items. This search may or may not be the serial exhaustive scan proposed by Sternberg.

One of the advantages of the Atkinson and Juola model is that it provides a reasonable explanation of speed–accuracy trade-off (i.e.

subjects can choose to respond rapidly but at the expense of making many errors, or slowly but accurately). If subjects attempt to respond rapidly, then this can be done by basing nearly all of their decisions on familiarity or strength alone. If they want to be accurate, then they can nearly always make use of the search process. More detailed predictions from the model have been confirmed in various studies (e.g. Banks & Atkinson, 1974).

BIBLIOGRAPHY

Atkinson, R. C., & Juola, J. F. (1974). Search and decision processes in recognition memory. In D. H. Krantz, R. C. Atkinson, and P. Suppes (Eds), *Contemporary developments in mathematical psychology*. London: W. H. Freeman.

Banks, W. P., & Atkinson, R. C. (1974). Accuracy and speed strategies in scanning active memory. *Memory & Cognition*, 2, 629–36.

James, W. (1890). *Principles of psychology*. New York: Holt.

Sternberg, S. (1969). The discovery of processing stages: Extensions of Donders' method. *Acta Psychologica*, 30, 276–315.

MICHAEL W. EYSENCK

Simon, Herbert Alexander (*b.* Milwaukee, 15 June 1916). Herbert Simon has been Professor of Computer Science & Psychology at Carnegie-Mellon University since 1967. Even when we set aside his work in economics (for which he received the Nobel prize in 1978) and his fundamental contribution to ARTIFICIAL INTELLIGENCE (for which he received the Turing Award of the ACM in 1975), Herbert Simon can be credited with being one of the founders of modern, information-processing psychology.

His seminal work with Allen Newell (see Newell & Simon, 1972) on the development of problem-space theory of human PROBLEM SOLVING had an important influence on the methodology and theoretical style of modern, cognitive psychology. This research involved a mixture of computer simulation, psychological experimentation, and the detailed analysis of single subject protocols. One of the first computational models of psychological phenomena emerged from it in the form of the General Problem Solver (Newell, Shaw, & Simon, 1958). The General Problem Solver was the foundation for the production system models that are used commonly today to model many cognitive processes (*see* PRODUCTION SYSTEMS).

Early experimental work by Simon on what have come to be called well defined, puzzle problems (like the Tower of Hanoi problem) expanded into the consideration of aspects of induction (with Lea), transfer between isomorphic problems (with Hayes), processes of understanding problem instructions (with Hayes), the nature of CHUNKING in WORKING MEMORY, the development of problem-solving strategies (with Reed and, later, Anzai), the sources of difficulty in problem solving (with Kotovsky and Hayes), and eventually dealt with more ill-defined problems involving considerable amounts of knowledge, in the form of studies of chess (with Chase) and physics expertise (with Larkin and others). Many of these studies have been milestones in the advances that cognitive psychology has made in the last three decades.

The methodological practice of testing theories against the protocol evidence of a single subject, supported by computer models, has become one of the important techniques used currently by cognitive psychologists. And, in the 1980s, Simon (with Ericsson) specified the conditions under which one might expect to receive reasonable introspective evidence from subjects in experiments (*see* INTROSPECTION). More recently, he has worked (with Larkin) on the role of diagrammatic representations in problem solving and (with Langley, Bradshaw, Zytkow, and Kulkarni) on the mechanisms involved in scientific discovery.

Much of this research has concentrated on human thought and represents a formidable contribution to cognitive psychology. It takes us from the artificial strictures of simple puzzles to the natural complexity of scientific thinking. On the way the discoveries made by Simon and his co-workers have propagated outward into other fields of cognitive psychology, in ways that are too numerous to elaborate. Without Herbert Simon's contribution, our knowledge of human cognition would be a lot more ill-defined.

See also DECISION MAKING AND JUDGEMENT.

BIBLIOGRAPHY

Ericsson, K. A., & Simon, H. A. (1984). *Protocol analysis*. Cambridge, Mass.: MIT Press.

Klahr, D., & Kotovsky, K. (1989). *Complex information processing: The impact of Herbert A. Simon*. Hillsdale, NJ: Erlbaum.

Langley, P., Simon, H. A., Bradshaw, G. L., & Zytkow, J. (1987). *Scientific discovery: Computational explorations of the creative process*. Cambridge, Mass.: MIT Press.

Newell, A., & Simon, H. A. (1972). *Human problem solving*. Englewood Cliffs, NJ: Prentice-Hall.

Newell, A., Shaw, J. C., & Simon, H. A. (1958). Elements of a theory of human problem solving. *Psychological Review*, 65, 151–66.

Simon, H. A. (1969). *The sciences of the artificial*. Cambridge, Mass.: MIT Press.

——. (1979, 1989). *Models of thought*, vols 1 & 2. New Haven, Conn.: Yale University Press.

MARK T. KEANE

skills acquisition *See* AUTOMATIC PROCESSING; DECLARATIVE AND PROCEDURAL KNOWLEDGE; EXPERTISE; STUDY SKILLS.

social cognition The study of social knowledge (its structure and content) and cognitive processes (including acquisition, representation, and retrieval of information) provides a key to understanding social behavior and its mediating factors (see Wyer & Srull, 1983; Fiske & Taylor, 1984). Social cognition leans heavily on the theory and methodology of cognitive psychology to provide precise and detailed models of social information processing. In particular, memory processes (encoding, storage, and retrieval) are seen to play a significant role in mediating a range of social judgements.

Although the popularity of the cognitive approach to social psychology has grown in the last ten years, it is not new. Indeed, it owes a great deal to the input of Gestalt ideas into American social psychology from Europeans such as Kurt Lewin and Fritz Heider. The vast majority of social-psychological data are about thoughts – as judgements, opinions, attitudes, or attributions. Furthermore, cognition pervades social psychology at three levels – the level at which the problem is formulated, the level of methodology, and the level of theorizing (see Markus & Zajonc, 1985). Arguably, social cognition is more complex than cognition in general, as evidenced by several general features. First, social perceivers typically go beyond the information given. Second, the objects of social cognition can be changed by being its focus, because it has consequences for them (thus, social psychologists talk of self-monitoring, objective self-awareness, and evaluation apprehension). Third, nearly all perception and cognition is evaluative; a consequence of this affective involvement is increased encoding idiosyncrasy, the between-subjects variance that social psychologists seek to explain.

Three fundamental questions underlie the study of social cognition: first, what type of social information is stored and how is it organized in memory?; second, how does social information stored in memory affect subsequent information processing, decision making, and behavior?; and third, how and when is stored information changed, both by new information and by cognitive processes? (Sherman, Judd, & Park, 1989).

Conceptually, the metatheory driving the social cognition approach is that of the "cognitive miser." Its central idea is that people are seen as capacity-limited information processors, who can deal with only a small amount of information at any time. Given these limitations, people use short cuts and strategies (heuristics) to simplify complex problems of judgement, decision, and attribution (see DECISION MAKING AND JUDGEMENT). These heuristics produce fast and quite adequate, rather than slow, normatively correct, solutions, as illustrated by three heuristics governing intuitive prediction and judgement (see Wyer & Srull, 1983; Fiske & Taylor, 1984). According to *the representativeness heuristic*, an object is assigned to a conceptual category by virtue of the extent to which its main features represent or resemble

one category more than another. *The anchoring/adjustment heuristic* refers to people's general failure to adjust their initial judgements in the light of subsequent evidence. *The availability heuristic* refers to the general tendency to judge events as frequent, probable, or causally efficacious to the extent that they are readily available in memory. This approach provides a general understanding of human judgement, although it remains difficult to evaluate the different heuristics competitively and rigorously.

SOCIAL CATEGORIZATION

The process of social categorization is another example of an information-processing shortcut. It involves matching a target person to an existing social category, and it is suggested that the process is set in motion as soon as information sufficient to activate a relevant social category has been encountered. The information necessary to cue an appropriate category can take several forms. For example, it may take the form of an observable feature (e.g. skin color or clothing). Alternatively, and more common in psychological research, it may take the form of a written category label or a cluster of category-consistent attributes. Rather than try to process all the stimulus information available, the social perceiver simplifies matters by assigning individuals to social categories on the basis of their perceived similarities (*see* CONCEPTS).

To the extent that social categories capture and reflect real differences and similarities between people, then social categorization can be considered a valuable cognitive tool. A growing number of studies have, however, demonstrated biases which stem from the very process of social categorization itself. For example, once a person has been classified into a particular social group, it is assumed that he or she possesses all the characteristics that define the group as a whole, and shares these characteristics with the other group members (*see* INFERENCES; PERSON PERCEPTION). That is, the person is deemed to possess a range of category-relevant attributes, despite the fact that none of these attributes may have served as the basis for the initial categorization. Furthermore, once we have classified two people into different categories, we tend to ignore their similarities and exaggerate their differences. Conversely, once we have assigned two people to the same category, we exaggerate their similarities and ignore their differences. These effects are accentuated if the social perceiver belongs to one of the groups in question (i.e. ingroup or outgroup). In general, the perceiver shows greater differentiation between ingroup members, with representations of ingroup members generally more complex than those of outgroup members. Consequently, ingroups and outgroups reflect an asymmetrical relationship, with perceived ingroup heterogeneity being contrasted with outgroup homogeneity (Tajfel, 1981; Fiske & Taylor, 1984).

SCHEMATA

The process of social categorization is central to both theorizing and experimentation within social cognition. This is because once a social category has been activated it plays an important part in subsequent information processing. The activated category affects the encoding, representation, and retrieval of social information. A central tenet of social cognition is that people assimilate what they observe to pre-existing cognitive structures or SCHEMATA. These abstract knowledge structures, stored in memory, specify the defining features and relevant attributes of a stimulus domain, and the interrelations among those attributes. Five main types of schemata have been identified (person, self, role, event, and procedural), each of which can influence three main types of social information processing: perception of new information; memory for old information; and, especially, inferences that go beyond both (see Fiske & Taylor, 1984).

The impact of schemata on social information processing can be interpreted in terms of both functions and liabilities. They tend to aid memory for schema-consistent information, increase confidence in schema-consistent recognition, enhance memory for schema-consistent information that was, in fact, never presented, and guide inferences and predictions. Further, it appears that under certain conditions people will tend to remember different types of information. For example,

when forming an impression of someone subjects tend to show preferential recall of schema-inconsistent information. This is consistent with a range of studies that suggest that the presentation of relatively infrequent, novel, or salient behaviors will result in increased attention during impression formation and, as a consequence, be more accessible in memory. Schema-inconsistent information also tends to be preferentially recalled when stimulus targets are perceived as being members of groups. In contrast, consistent information is more readily recalled when targets are perceived as individuals, and when established beliefs or impressions are being tested.

The social cognition perspective has been usefully applied to the study of stereotypes, attitudes, and the self, via the concept of schemata. Stereotypes, as social categories, may be formed and represented in memory much like any other object categories. Thus, they may be organized around a prototypical representation, with exemplar or specific instance information stored as well. Social cognition research is currently evaluating prototypic and exemplar-based representational models in this domain (see Sherman et al., 1989). Stereotypes have been equated with schemata and, as such, have been shown to influence all stages of social information processing. This approach has been particularly useful in clarifying how stereotypes are formed, how they are maintained, and also how they might be changed.

A range of cognitive biases are implicated in the formation of stereotypical conceptions. These include differential attention to salient stimuli, and illusory correlation. The causes of social salience all depend upon contextual factors. Fiske and Taylor (1984) state that a person can be salient relative to the perceiver's: (a) immediate context; (b) prior knowledge or expectations; and (c) attentional tasks. Regardless of the cause of social salience, its effects are robust. Salience or prominence accentuates a range of stimulus-based judgements. Essentially, evaluations and judgements are exaggerated in whichever direction they initially tend. For example, if a person is viewed negatively, being socially salient will increase this negative evaluation. Similarly, an initially positive evaluation will be accentuated if the person becomes salient. Illusory correlation concerns the imposition of a relationship between two variables when none actually exists. The main factor claimed to be responsible for the phenomenon is paired distinctiveness. This basis of illusory correlation has been used to account for the negative stereotyping of minority group members. Majority group members rarely interact with minority group members, and in comparison with positive behaviors, negative behaviors are relatively infrequent. It is therefore suggested that majority group members perceive an illusory correlation between the two and overestimate the frequency of occurrence of negative behaviors by minority group members.

At the stereotype-maintenance stage, researchers have demonstrated persistent biases in patterns of causal attribution and in memory retrieval which allow the perceiver's erroneous stereotypical beliefs to persevere in the face of potentially disconfirming information. Specifically, perceivers tend to attribute stereotype-confirming behavior to internal, stable causes, and to attribute disconfirming behavior to external, unstable causes. Such an attributional tendency allows the perceiver to explain away stereotype-discrepant behavior. Similarly, the preferential recall of stereotype-confirming information, together with the tendency to select only confirming information when testing stereotypical beliefs, further perpetuates social stereotypes. Finally, schematic models of how stereotypes might change in response to the amount and distribution of disconfirming information have been tested. Research has shown that it is better to disperse disconfirming information across several outgroup members (each of whom displays some goodness of fit with the category prototype), rather than to concentrate disconfirming information in a few, highly atypical members. Interest here centers on when subcategories may be formed as a result of encountering new group exemplars that are divergent from the category prototype or central tendency. Thus, a social cognition approach to "intergroup contact" emphasizes that successful contact (i.e. positive contact that generalizes to other outgroup members) depends upon the prototypicality of the outgroup member (category exemplar) with whom contact takes place.

ATTITUDES also appear to function like schemata, as illustrated by selective attention to, and encoding, retention, and retrieval of, attitude-relevant information. For example, attitudes facilitate recall of attitude statements that were strongly agreed or disagreed with, compared with statements that elicit more moderate responses on the agreement scale. Thus, the social cognition perspective has led to a major shift in the way attitudes are defined and assessed. In many situations evaluations seem to be formed spontaneously and stored in long-term memory for future retrieval and use. Other information stored with the evaluation may include information about the attributes of an attitude object, affective responses elicited by the object, past behavior toward the object, and the evaluations of significant others. The cognitive approach has also stimulated interest in the manipulation and measurement of cognitive responses to persuasive communications (Petty & Cacioppo, 1986). Persuasion via a central route requires active processing of the message, which itself requires cognitive effort (as when we are highly involved in an issue). Persuasion via a peripheral route involves minimal cognitive elaboration of the message, and is due to non-message factors (e.g. high credibility of the source). The amount and quality of cognitive responding can be measured by a written thought-listing technique, which has also been used to specify more precisely the cognitive processes involved in social influence by majorities and minorities.

There is now theoretical and empirical support for a multifaceted and complex concept of the self as a cognitive structure (see Markus & Zajonc, 1985) (see SELF-FOCUS AND SELF-ATTENTION). The self is conceived as a special kind of schema, or a system of schemata, owing to its size, complexity, and affect. Each schema is a generalization about what the self is like and contains trait information, behavioral information, and inferences. The self is involved in attention to, and encoding and interpretation of, new information, but a person may be "schematic" or "aschematic" with respect to certain roles or traits. There is a general finding, however, that material is better recalled when encoded with reference to the self (the self-reference effect).

METHODOLOGY

As social psychologists have studied the metaphor of information processing, so they have used a wider array of cognitive measures: visual attention, subject self-reports, requests for information, recall (quantity, errors, sequence, clustering), recognition, and chronometric analyses (looking time, decision time; see Taylor & Fiske, 1981). These measures all attempt to sidestep a major methodological problem – the fact that we can never tap directly what is going on in the heads of our research subjects. Examples of problems studied include encoding vs. retrieval biases in memory for stereotypical information about group members, and negative mood-priming in relation to antisocial behavior.

More ambitious still are attempts to use these different measures to build process models. A process model is, simply, the description of everything that goes on in the subject's head, from start to finish of an experimental task (cf. think-aloud verbalizations – INTROSPECTION). It is a statement of the presumed stages through which information is processed, such as encoding, storage, retrieval, recall, and attribution. The aim of process analysis is to provide methodological precision, to specify the stages in social information processing and at what stage a given effect occurs. In the area of causal attribution, process models have been constructed to investigate several issues. Salience-based attribution, for example, was examined by using structural modeling techniques to relate measures of visual salience, attention, recall, and attribution. Process models have also been used to explore whether causal attribution involves AUTOMATIC PROCESSING. Different response times for measures of causal judgement, trait judgements about an actor, and the actor's intent indicated that causal judgement was not an automatic process, and indeed that, under certain circumstances, it was mediated by more basic trait judgements and intention judgements.

Theories about process are potentially more general than theories about content, because the same procedure may operate over a wide range of stimuli, and they can provide methodological precision. By definition, however, the attempt to measure cognitive processes interferes with normal thinking and may not be informative about normal, extra-laboratory social information processing.

AFFECT AND MOTIVATION

Because social cognition is rarely dispassionate, or emotionally neutral, it is important to integrate social cognition with affect and motivation. Feeling states, negative and positive, influence what people think about and the judgements they make, and thus have important effects on social behavior. Social cognition is still central, however, because the impact of feeling states can be best understood as a function of cognitive processes such as perception, memory, and inference. Thus, people in a positive feeling state are more likely to retrieve positive material from memory than people who are not (Isen, 1987). The affective state seems to function as a cue to prime and organize related cognitive material, via both automatic and controlled processes.

It has also been suggested that extremity in mood and evaluation is tied to the complexity of knowledge structures. More simple thinking about a domain (e.g. an outgroup about whom one has little knowledge) is associated with more extreme affective reactions within that domain (e.g. liking or disliking); greater complexity is associated with more moderate reactions. Research has also suggested that affect is stored with schemata, and is available immediately upon categorization (fitting an instance to a schema) (see STATE-DEPENDENT MEMORY).

Social interaction and information processing about other people is often motivated by factors such as current concerns, values, and beliefs. In particular, social cognition is often goal directed, whether in terms of personality analysis, self-presentation, or information seeking. This motivational side of social cognition has been rather overlooked (but see Sorrentino & Higgins, 1986). The goals individuals bring to social situations may influence their perception of and memory for others' behavior; thus, subjects are more likely to organize information around individuals in memory, if they anticipate future interaction.

CONCLUSIONS

Social cognition represents an approach or set of assumptions guiding research in social psychology, rather than a separate theory or domain of enquiry within the discipline. The fruits of this approach to a variety of traditional substantive domains can be seen in relation to causal attribution, attitudes, and attitude change, intergroup relations (especially stereotyping), judgement and decision making, and the self.

BIBLIOGRAPHY

Fiske, S. T., & Taylor, S. E. (1984). *Social cognition*. New York: Random House.
Hewstone, M. (1989). *Causal attribution: From cognitive processes to collective beliefs*. Oxford: Basil Blackwell.
Isen, A. M. (1987). Positive affect, cognitive processes, and social behavior. In L. Berkowitz (Ed.), *Advances in experimental social psychology* (Vol. 20). San Diego, Calif.: Academic Press.
Markus, H., & Zajonc, R. B. (1985). The cognitive perspective in social psychology. In G. Lindzey & E. Aronson (Eds), *The handbook of social psychology* (Vol. 1) (3rd edn). New York: Random House.
Petty, R. E., & Cacioppo, J. T. (1986). *Communication and persuasion: Central and peripheral routes to attitude change*. New York: Springer.
Sherman, S. J., Judd, C. M., & Park, B. (1989). Social cognition. *Annual Review of Psychology*, 40, 281–326.
Sorrentino, R. M., & Higgins, E. T. (Eds) (1986). *Handbook of motivation and cognition: Foundations of social behavior*. New York: Wiley.
Tajfel, H. (1981). *Human groups and social categories: Studies in social psychology*. Cambridge: Cambridge University Press.
Taylor, S. E., & Fiske, S. T. (1981). Getting inside the head: Methodologies for process analysis in attribution and social cognition. In J. H. Harvey, W. J. Ickes, & R. F. Kidd (Eds), *New directions in attribution research* (Vol. 3). Hillsdale, NJ: Erlbaum.
Wyer, R. S., & Srull, T. K. (Eds) (1983). *Handbook of social cognition* (3 vols). Hillsdale, NJ: Erlbaum.

MILES HEWSTONE AND C. NEIL MACRAE

social psychology *See* ATTITUDES; COGNITIVE DISSONANCE; PERSON PERCEPTION; SOCIAL COGNITION.

speech perception Research on speech perception attempts to understand how the brain can recognize in speech discrete linguistic units, such as words or phonemes. Traditionally the field has concentrated on the sound of speech, but recent research has indicated the contribution of vision. The classical work in the field pointed out the complex relationship between acoustic cues and phonetic categories. Current work compares the contributions of auditory and specialized phonetic mechanisms to phonetic perception, explores the development of speech perception in infants, and tackles the problem of extracting words from the speech stream.

THE NATURE OF THE SPEECH SIGNAL

The unusually complex nature of speech sounds was revealed in the 1940s by the recently invented spectrograph. The spectrograph revealed two basic properties of the speech signal: first, that speech was a continuously changing pattern of sound, rather than a sequence of discrete elements; and second, that the pattern in the region of a particular linguistic element (such as a phoneme) varied with context. These two properties reflect two aspects of the way in which even careful speech is produced. First, the articulators must move from one target position to another, so the sound that emerges also makes transitions. Second, the specification of consonants generally involves only a subset of the articulators (e.g. closing the lips for a bilabial stop), leaving the other articulators free to anticipate subsequent segments (e.g. the tongue body is free in the bilabial stop to take up the position appropriate for the following vowel). This phenomenon is known as co-articulation.

Normal, rapid, casual speech introduces

further complications since the target positions of segments may be undershot or the segments themselves may disappear as a result of the problems of moving the articulators rapidly enough (e.g. "What do you want?" becomes "Wotchawan?") Speakers adjust the clarity of their speech depending on the listening conditions and the context available to help the listener (Lieberman, 1963).

Yet more variability in the relationship between the linguistic segments and the sound wave is introduced by the fact that different speakers have different-sized heads and speak different dialects and idiolects (Ladefoged & Broadbent, 1957). Finally, the environment through which sound passes from speaker to listener adulterates sound, and adds in sound from other speakers and sound sources.

As an antidote to this emphasis on variability, Stevens (1972) has pointed out that the articulation of some consonants uses places of articulation that give a stable acoustic output despite small perturbations in the place of articulation. His emphasis on invariant acoustic cues to phonetic categories has been taken up by Blumstein and her colleagues (e.g. Blumstein, Isaacs, & Mertus, 1982).

Fundamental research on the acoustic cues to phonetic categories has been conducted (mainly at Haskins Laboratories) since the early 1950s. It has emphasized the complex relationship between acoustic cues and phonetic categories (for a review, see Liberman, Cooper, Shankweiler, & Studdert-Kennedy, 1967) and pointed out a number of perceptual phenomena (categorical perception, left-hemisphere advantage) which appear to be confined to speech perception. Mattingly and Liberman (1988) later proposed that speech is perceived by a specialized module that is responsible for phonetic, "speech-mode" percepts. Perceiving sound as speech requires knowledge of the particular constraints that apply to sounds produced by the human vocal tract. These relationships do not apply to the general sounds of the environment. Although few workers would disagree that speech perception must require some separate mechanisms from general auditory perception, the need for a module, and the particular perceptual phenomena which

demonstrate special processes are both contentious.

Our ability rapidly to label the continuous flow of speech sound with discrete linguistic categories lies at the heart of speech perception. Research has concentrated on two aspects of this labeling: where listeners put the boundary between one phoneme category and another, and our apparent inability to distinguish sounds within a particular category (categorical perception).

PHONEME BOUNDARIES AND TRADING RELATIONS

There has been considerable debate over the question of whether the position of phoneme boundaries is determined by general auditory constraints, or by the operation of special speech perceptual mechanisms. For the voice-onset time (VOT) continuum which cues the voicing distinction between, say, "ba" and "pa," there is clear evidence that chinchillas trained to respond differently to the two ends of the continuum show a behavioral boundary at the same point as do human listeners (Kuhl & Miller, 1978). The boundary occurs at around 30 millisec VOT. There is a good reason why the boundary cannot occur at a shorter value than this, namely that the (chinchilla) auditory system is unable to represent accurately the difference between VOTs from this continuum shorter than 30 millisec. Such purely auditory limitations obviously constrain the position of phonetic boundaries: different phonetic categories must be both easily articulated and easily heard. But other phenomena concerning the position of phoneme boundaries cannot be attributed to general auditory mechanisms. One such class of phenomena involves "trading relations" between the acoustic cues to phonetic categories.

In general phonetic categories can be cued by a variety of different acoustic events. Thus, for instance, "say" can be turned into "stay" by introducing silence after the /s/ and lowering the subsequent starting frequency of the first formant transition (both of these cues are consequences of closing the vocal tract for the /t/). Listeners show both a sharp and consistent boundary between "say" and "stay."

They are also sensitive to changes in both of these cues, trading off a change in one cue against a change in the other. Such trading relations can be used to demonstrate perception in the speech mode. The demonstration uses an intriguing stimulus called "sine-wave" speech, in which sine waves track the formant frequencies. Naive listeners can hear these sounds as either nonspeech whistles or as distorted speech, depending on their perceptual set. Listeners who hear sine-wave analogs of "say" and "stay" which differ both in silence duration and first formant onset frequency treat the two cues quite differently than listeners who hear the same sounds as speech. The particular trading relation between the two cues found for more natural sounds is only apparent for listeners that hear the sounds as speech. It is impossible to attribute this difference to an underlying psychoacoustic or physiological cause.

CATEGORICAL PERCEPTION

For sounds along simple physical continua (frequency, intensity, etc.), we are better at discriminating pairs of sounds than we are at labeling them as distinct categories. This principle appeared to be dramatically violated by the "categorical perception" of certain speech sounds. Here, for some complex auditory continua that cue simple phonetic distinctions (e.g. voicing – between "ba" and "pa," or place of articulation – between "ba," "da," and "ga"), listeners can discriminate much better between pairs of sounds that fall into different phonetic categories than they can between pairs that do not. In extreme cases, the ability to discriminate along the continuum is predictable from the ability to assign different phonetic labels, hence perception is "categorical." This striking phenomenon provided much of the impetus for special theories of speech perception, and continues to attract considerable attention (for a review, see Repp, 1984).

For some continua (e.g. VOT) the peak in discrimination at the phoneme boundary does appear to be due to auditory limitations. Kuhl's (1981) chinchillas show peaks in similar places to human listeners. Moreover,

the peaks persist when discrimination is tested using a fixed rather than a roving standard, which is a technique that reduces the contribution that perceptual categories make to discrimination performance. Discrimination measured with a roving standard (the normal ABX method) can show peaks near category boundaries which disappear when the more stringent fixed standard method is used. So some of the peaks in discrimination functions reported in the literature are attributable to basic auditory mechanisms; others are a consequence of phonetic labeling.

The traditional ABX method of testing speech sound discrimination nevertheless remains a useful indication of a native listener's perceptual categories. Adult listeners of a language that does not make a particular distinction (e.g. between [l] and [r] in Japanese) show very poor ability to discriminate sounds along the appropriate continuum when tested with the conventional ABX procedure. The contrast between this poor ability of adults for making within-category discriminations, and the infant's remarkable abilities to discriminate speech, has led to some of the most interesting recent work on speech perception.

INFANT SPEECH PERCEPTION

Eimas, Siqueland, and Jusczyk (1971) introduced the first viable technique for detecting an infant's ability to discriminate sounds (see PERCEPTUAL DEVELOPMENT). Infants will suck a pacifier to hear a sound but soon habituate if the same sound is repeated. Sucking increases again if the sound is changed and gives an index of the perceptibility of the change to the infant. Eimas's experiment showed that one- and four-month-old infants more readily discriminated sounds which straddled the /ba/–/pa/ boundary along the VOT continuum than those that did not, a result which with hindsight probably reflects general auditory mechanisms rather than a special speech perception one. Subsequent work has shown that young infants are able to distinguish not only the phonemic contrasts used in the language to which they are exposed, but also many that are not (see Kuhl, 1987). We know that adult listeners can be insensitive to contrasts that their language does not use (at

343

least when tested by some discrimination procedures), so does the infant gradually lose the ability to hear within category distinctions? Careful and imaginative work by Janet Werker and her colleagues has shown that around 10 to 12 months infants lose the ability to hear differences between sounds that are not distinguished by their native language. But the same distinctions are preserved in infants and adults exposed to the appropriate languages (Hindi or Nthlakapmx). Werker emphasizes that the loss of the ability to make these discriminations is not a basic psycho-acoustic loss, since adults who study the language can learn to (re-)hear the foreign distinctions and because more sensitive discrimination paradigms also reveal some appropriate ability. Mann (1986), for instance, has shown that although Japanese listeners are not able explicitly to distinguish [l] from [r], they are nevertheless sensitive to the consequences of their different articulations. Mann showed that Japanese listeners, like English-speaking listeners, required different cues after [r] than after [l] to hear /d/ (versus /g/). The Japanese listeners were thus sensitive to the co-articulatory consequences of [l] or [r], even though they could not explicitly hear the difference between the two sounds.

VISION IN SPEECH PERCEPTION

Most people are not aware how much speech perception is helped by visual information about articulation, despite the common observation that "I can hear you better with my glasses on." The McGurk effect (McGurk & MacDonald, 1976) encapsulates the bimodal nature of speech perception with a striking illusion. A dubbed video that shows a face executing the movements of /ga/ together with the sound of /ba/ is "heard" as /da/. The listener (be he or she a trained phonetician or naive) is not aware of any conflict between sight and sound. The visual information about articulation is smoothly incorporated into the auditory percept by the brain.

Even very young infants appear to be sensitive to the relationship between seen and heard speech articulation since they will look selectively at the face that is articulating a heard vowel rather than a visually different one. Blind infants are slower than sighted ones at developing phonological categories that have visual features.

The importance of seen as well as heard articulation for speech perception has emphasized the links between perception and the dynamics of action (see, e.g., Summerfield, 1987).

AUDITORY WORD RECOGNITION

The last 15 years have seen an increasing interest by psycholinguists in the perception of spoken (rather than the technically more tractable written) language (*see* LANGUAGE COMPREHENSION). Marslen-Wilson's work (e.g. Marslen-Wilson & Welsh, 1978) stimulated research on the temporal course of lexical access from the speech wave, drawing attention both to the interaction with higher constraints and to the fact that under appropriate conditions lexical decisions could be made before the physical end of the relevant word. The role of different processing units in lexical access remains contentious with spectral templates, phonemes, and syllables all having their advocates; equally the mechanism whereby context influences the perception of words continues to be debated. These issues are reviewed by Frauenfelder and Tyler (1987; see also other papers in the same special journal issue).

Under good listening conditions, a word becomes perceptible at its uniqueness point – the point in the word at which the word first becomes distinct from other words in the language. However, speech is still intelligible under conditions where word onsets may be indistinct, so it is likely that listeners are forced to use subsequent as well as preceding context and to rely on the most acoustically distinct parts of words for their identification. Stressed syllables are generally the most intense and the most carefully articulated, and for English at least may play an important role in the difficult problem of segmenting the speech stream into words.

See also AUDITORY PERCEPTION; CASCADE PROCESSING; PATTERN PERCEPTION; SPEECH PRODUCTION.

BIBLIOGRAPHY

Blumstein, S. E., Isaacs, E., & Mertus, J. (1982). The role of the gross spectral shape as a perceptual cue to place of articulation in initial stop consonants. *Journal of the Acoustical Society of America*, *72*, 43–50.

Eimas, P. D., Siqueland, E. R., & Jusczyk, P. W. (1971). Speech perception in infants, *Science*, *171*, 303–6.

Frauenfelder, U. H., and Tyler, L. K. (1987). The process of spoken word recognition: An introduction. *Cognition*, *25*, 1–20.

Kuhl, P. K. (1981). Discrimination of speech by nonhuman animals: Basic auditory sensitivities conducive to the perception of speech-sound categories. *Journal of the Acoustical Society of America*, *70*, 340–9.

— —. (1987). Perception of speech and sound in early infancy. In P. Salapatek & L. Cohen (Eds), *Handbook of infant perception* (Vol. 2). New York: Academic.

— —, & Miller, J. D. (1978). Speech perception by the chinchilla: Identification functions for VOT stimuli. *Journal of the Acoustical Society of America*, *63*, 905–17.

Ladefoged, P., & Broadbent, D. E. (1957). Information conveyed by vowels. *Journal of the Acoustical Society of America*, *29*, 98–104.

Liberman, A. M., Cooper, F. S., Shankweiler, D. P., & Studdert-Kennedy, M. (1967). Perception of the speech code. *Psychological Review*, *74*, 431–61.

Lieberman, P. (1963). Some effects of semantic and grammatical context on the production and perception of speech. *Language and Speech*, *6*, 172–87.

McGurk, H., & MacDonald, J. W. (1976). Hearing lips and seeing voices. *Nature*, *254*, 746–8.

Mann, V. A. (1986). Distinguishing universal and language-dependent levels of speech perception: Evidence from Japanese listeners' perception of English "l" and "r." *Cognition*, *24*, 169–96.

Marslen-Wilson, W. D., & Welsh, A. (1978). Processing interactions during word-recognition in continuous speech. *Cognitive Psychology*, *10*, 29–63.

Mattingly, I. G., & Liberman, A. M. (1988). Specialized perceiving systems for speech and other biologically significant sounds. In G. W. Edelman, W. E. Gall, & W. M. Cowan (Eds), *Functions of the auditory system*. New York: Wiley.

Repp, B. H. (1984). Categorical perception: Issues, methods and findings. In N. J. Lass (Ed.), *Speech and language: Advances in basic research and practice* (Vol. 10). New York: Academic.

Stevens, K. N. (1972). The quantal nature of speech: Evidence from articulatory-acoustic data. In E. E. David & P. B. Denes (Eds), *Human communication: A unified view*. New York: McGraw-Hill.

Summerfield, A. Q. (1987). Some preliminaries to a comprehensive account of audio-visual speech perception. In B. Dodd & R. Campbell (Eds), *Hearing by eye: The psychology of lip-reading*. London: Erlbaum.

C. J. DARWIN

speech production Approaches to speech production should explain speech planning and execution, and the explanation for planning should account for novelty in speech. Speech exhibits novelty ("generativity") in two fundamental ways: speakers produce novel, yet informative sentences, and they coin words. They can utter novel, understandable sentences, because sentences are composed of familiar parts – words – ordered and marked according to also-familiar syntactic rules. Speakers coin words by combining familiar morphemes (stems or stems and affixes) or phonemes (consonants and vowels) in new, ruleful ways.

A comprehensive theory of speech production should explain both kinds of novelty, and it should also explain other aspects of planning and execution. Such a theory has yet to be developed, but there are theories of each part (for a review, see Fowler, 1985).

PLANNING

Speech utterances must be planned, in part because the sequential order of words in a sentence is linguistic; it is not inherent in aspects of an idea or event being described. Also, the syntax allows creation of nonlocal dependencies (e.g. between underlined subject and predicate in *"the pen* I bought yesterday *has run out of ink"*); production of the first dependent part anticipates production of the second, however separate the parts.

Spontaneous speech errors ("slips of the tongue") provide important evidence concerning speech planning. Dell (1986), Garrett (1980), and Shattuck-Hufnagel (1987) offer theories based on slips. Slips of the tongue are fluently produced departures from an intended utterance. Table 1 provides some examples.

Table 1 (Target → Error)[1]

Word substitution:	pass the pepper → pass the salt
Word anticipation:	sun in the sky → sky in the sky
Morpheme exchange:	thinly sliced → slicely thinned
Phoneme exchange:	York library → lork yibrary
Phoneme perseveration:	beef noodle → beef needle

[1]Errors from Dell, 1986.

The errors are not, literally, slips of the tongue, but, rather, planning mistakes. A very unlikely series of motor slips would cause "salt" to substitute for "pepper," for example.

Components of utterances that move individually in errors are just those that recombine generatively in language: words, morphemes, and phonemes. Apparently, the freedom to create new orderings of familiar elements also enables serial ordering errors.

Errors reveal that planning takes place in stages, each one sensitive to different linguistic attributes. When words exchange over long distances (e.g. "I don't know that I'd hear one if I knew it" for "I don't know that I'd know one if I heard it"), they are almost always the same parts of speech. When affixes are stranded in the exchange, a word moving next to an affix integrates with it, resulting, almost always, in a real word. But when words or stems exchange over short distances (within a phrase), they are generally different parts of speech, and, integrations of stems and affixes may create nonwords (e.g. "slicely thinned").

Phonemes slip over short distances, between words of different grammatical classes, and the errors often create nonwords. Constraints on phoneme slips are phonological. Apparently, successive planning stages focus on progressively narrower sentential domains and on progressively lower-level linguistic elements and attributes.

Finally, errors reveal that the different levels of planning are largely analogous; all involve inserting elements into frames. Exchange errors show this most clearly. In exchanges at all planning levels, element B replaces A in A's intended location, and A replaces B in B's. By implication, when B replaces A, it leaves an empty slot for the left-over A to occupy. Thus, planning involves successively selecting elements at three linguistic levels and inserting them into planning-frame slots.

EXECUTION

Speakers control the respiratory system, larynx, nasal cavity, and articulators of the oral cavity. During speech, they approximate the vocal folds of the larynx (for all but unvoiced sounds, such as /p/ or /s/) so that exhaled air causes the folds to cycle open and closed. We hear the cycling rate as voice pitch. Consonants are produced by constrictions in the oral cavity, for example at the lips (/p/, /b/), or the hard palate using the tongue tip (/s/, /d/). In addition, during some consonantal constrictions (e.g. /m/), the soft palate lowers allowing air to pass through the nose. For vowels, the oral cavity is unobstructed, and the tongue body creates different cavity shapes. The acoustic speech signal reflects sound frequencies of the laryngeal source filtered by the changing oral cavity shape.

In contrast to the neat correspondence between units of language and of speech planning as revealed by speech errors, the correspondence between those units and vocal-tract movements is complex and poorly understood. Whereas planned elements are discrete and sequentially ordered, movements of the articulators are continuous and overlapped. Planned phonemes "coarticulate"; that is, movements of different articulators for different phonemes overlap temporally, and influences of different phonemes converge on common articulators.

Coarticulation is necessary. For example, anticipatory production of vowels during consonantal constrictions prevents production of unintended vocalic sounds as consonantal occlusions are released. However, its effects are to obscure articulatory evidence of the discrete, ordered, context-free phonemes of the speech plan.

Listeners can recover phonemes from speech, however, and so phonemes must be present in some as yet unknown guise (*see* SPEECH PERCEPTION). Appreciation of the role of "synergies" in speech production (e.g. Kelso, Tuller, Vatikiotis-Bateson, & Fowler, 1984) provides a promising lead. Synergies are organized relationships among articulators that achieve a goal. A synergy between the jaw and lips allows closure at the lips for /p/, /b/, and /m/ despite variable contributions to closure by the jaw caused by co-articulating vowels. More generally, synergies allow phonemic goals to be achieved invariantly despite the context-conditioned variability of movements contributing to goal achievement. Successive, partially overlapping implementation of consonantal and vocalic synergies may allow ordered, sufficiently context-free realization of phonemes in vocal tract activity.

BIBLIOGRAPHY

Dell, G. (1986). A spreading activation theory of retrieval in sentence production. *Psychological Review, 93*, 283–321.

Fowler, C. (1985). Current perspectives on language and speech production: A critical review. In R. Daniloff (Ed.), *Speech science* (pp. 193–278). San Diego: College-Hill.

Garrett, M. (1980). The limits of accommodation: Arguments for independent levels in sentence production. In V. Fromkin (Ed.), *Errors in linguistic performance: Slips of the tongue, ear, pen and hand* (pp. 263–71). London: Academic Press.

Kelso, J. A. S., Tuller, B., Vatikiotis-Bateson, E., & Fowler, C. (1984). Functionally-specific articulatory cooperation following jaw perturbation during speech: Evidence for coordinative structures. *Journal of Experimental Psychology: Human Perception and Performance, 10*, 812–32.

Shattuck-Hufnagel, S. (1987). The role of word-onset consonants in speech production planning: New evidence from speech error patterns. In E. Keller & M. Gopnik (Eds), *Motor and sensory processes of language* (pp. 17–52). Hillsdale, NJ: Lawrence Erlbaum Associates.

CAROL A. FOWLER

spelling Writing is only 5000 or so years old, and until recently the skill of writing was possessed by only a small minority of individuals, even in literate societies. Only within the last hundred years has the expectation arisen that all members of an advanced society will be able to both read and write. When considering the problems children now experience in learning to spell, we should bear in mind the fact that the English spelling system was not designed with ease of learning for the general population in mind. Given that we spend perhaps a dozen years learning to write, then 60 practicing the skill, it could be argued that the design features of writing systems should still be biased toward the expert rather than the novice writer.

WRITING shares with speech production the property of not being easy to study experimentally. Much of what we know about spelling and writing comes from one of two sources. The first is the analysis of the involuntary slips of the pen that even skilled writers make from time to time; the second is investigations of the various patterns of spelling and writing impairment that may occur in previously literate individuals as a consequence of brain injury.

The latter approach, based in COGNITIVE NEUROPSYCHOLOGY, provides the bulk of the evidence to support the idea of there being two cognitive "procedures" for spelling available to the skilled speller that are at least semi-independent one from the other. These may be termed the "lexical" and "sublexical" procedures, and may be likened to the two procedures that are being invoked to account for aspects of skilled word recognition in reading (*see* DUAL-ROUTE MODEL OF READING).

The "sublexical" procedure is the one that would be invoked by a skilled speller who was asked to construct a plausible spelling for an unfamiliar word or invented nonword. It requires that the sound pattern of a word be broken down into its constituent syllables and phonemes (distinctive speech sounds) and that a string of letters be assembled on the basis of the speller's knowledge of English sound-spelling correspondences.

The use of this procedure is highly error prone in English because of the number of "irregular" words whose spelling does not match their pronunciation (words like women, yacht, and biscuit). Attempts to spell such words using the sublexical procedure result in "phonetic" misspellings such as wimmen, yott, and biskitt. The spellings of irregular words *must* be stored in memory and retrieved as whole units. In fact, the evidence suggests that skilled writers store and retrieve the spellings of *all* familiar words in this way, even the spellings of highly regular words which they could, in principle, assemble *de novo* on each occasion using the sublexical procedure. One line of evidence pointing to this conclusion comes from studies of patients with acquired "phonological dysgraphia" whose brain injury has deprived them of the capacity to spell using the sublexical procedure but who remain able to spell a high proportion of familiar words, both regular and irregular.

Phonetic misspellings look childish, the reason for that being that children, whose store of memorized spellings is still limited, use this procedure regularly, especially in spontaneous writing where a child may not want to break off to seek the correct spelling of a word. A similar pattern can be seen in patients with acquired "surface" dysgraphia. These patients are in many ways the converse of the patients with phonological dysgraphia. Surface dysgraphics can no longer remember the conventional spellings of many once-familiar words but retain a capacity for spelling by the sublexical procedure. Because that procedure will often generate the correct spelling of a regular word, surface dysgraphics show a regularity effect (spelling regular words more accurately than irregular words), and the errors they make are predominantly phonetic.

The processes by which the conventional spellings of familiar words are stored and

retrieved may be termed the "lexical" procedure). Little is known about the storage and retrieval mechanisms involved, though they are generally thought to involve a distinct long-term memory system. Skilled writers will occasionally make involuntary slips of the pen in which they produce a real word different from the one intended. The error word in such circumstances is often either a homophone of the intended word (e.g. writing their for there, or seen for scene) or a word similar in sound (e.g. writing surge for search). Sometimes, though, the error is similar in meaning to the target word (e.g. writing speaking for reading, or last for next). It has been suggested that such errors arise because spellings are retrieved from memory in response to specifications of both the meaning and the sound-form of the intended word. If only the meaning were used to retrieve spellings, then it could be impossible to differentiate between words of similar meanings, and if only the sound-form were used it would be impossible to differentiate between homophones with the same pronunciations. The combination of a meaning and a sound-form specifies each word in a speller's vocabulary uniquely and may be the most efficient combination of cues to use for the retrieval of spellings. The price of this combination is occasional similar-sound and similar-meaning slips of the pen.

The lexical and sublexical procedures, though partially separable in neuropsychological patients, may not be totally insulated one from another in the cognitive systems of normal writers. The fact that the spellings of words that a subject has recently written in a dictation task can influence the way that subject then spells an invented nonword shows that there is some interaction between the lexical and sublexical procedures. Both the lexical and sublexical procedures must result in the creation of a representation of a string of letters that is relatively abstract, and has been termed a "graphemic" representation. The abstractness of this representation is shown by the fact that it can be used to "drive" output in a range of different forms, including cursive handwriting, print, typing, and oral spelling. Patients have been reported who can still spell aloud but are no longer able to write, suggesting a locus of impairment between the abstract graphemes and the execution of pen movements. Certain slips of the pen (e.g. the tripling of double letters as when a writer produces "buttter" for "butter") may have a similarly peripheral locus of origin.

See also DYSLEXIA: DEVELOPMENTAL; DYS-LEXIAS: ACQUIRED.

BIBLIOGRAPHY

Ellis, A. W. (1984). *Reading, writing and dyslexia: A cognitive analysis*. London: Lawrence Erlbaum Associates.
Frith, U. (1980). *Cognitive processes in spelling*. London: Academic Press.

ANDREW W. ELLIS

state-dependent memory Though it has long been known that events experienced in a certain physical or psychological state are best remembered in that state – Winslow (1860), for example, related the story of an Irish porter who, having lost a package while drunk, got drunk again and remembered where he had left it – only within the last 25 years has state-dependent memory become a subject of sustained scientific enquiry. In this essay, we chronicle the principal research developments of this period, beginning with mid 1960s demonstrations of drug-dependent memory in animals, and progressing through to late 1980s studies of mood-dependent memory in humans.

The first contemporary researcher to study state dependence in a systematic manner was Donald Overton (see Overton, 1984). In a series of experiments published in 1964, Overton trained undrugged rats to turn right in a T-maze, in order to avoid an electric shock to their paws. All of the rats learned to make the correct directional response within six training trials. On trials 7 through 15, the rats were drugged with a high dose of the barbiturate pentobarbital, and trained to turn left in the maze, again to escape shock. Next, a set of 28 test trials was given, alternately with and without drug. On these trials the rats could escape shock by turning either to the right or to the left. Overton observed that the rats consistently turned right when undrugged and left when drugged, indicating that the animals' memory for a particular directional response could be evoked simply by reinstating the particular drug condition under which the response had been learned.

Today, 25 years after Overton's seminal studies were reported, a large literature exists on the state-dependent effects of drugs in animals, from which several replicable findings have emerged. Chief among these are that drug-dependent memory is (a) associated with several classes of centrally acting agents, including anesthetics, anxiolytics, and anti-muscarinics (and to a lesser extent with hallucinogenics, narcotic analgesics, and tricyclic antidepressants); (b) positively correlated with drug dosage (i.e. performance deficits produced by a shift from, say, drug-present training to drug-absent testing are magnified as the dosage is raised); (c) negatively correlated with response training (i.e. shifts in drug state typically do not impair the performance of well-practiced, overlearned responses); (d) demonstrable in the performance of either aversively or appetitively motivated responses by a variety of infrahuman species (e.g. goldfish, mice, monkeys, and, as already mentioned, rats); and (e) often, though not always, asymmetric in form (i.e. a shift from drug-present training to drug-absent testing results in poorer performance than does a shift in the reverse direction). Later in this essay we will discuss asymmetric drug-dependent memory in more detail.

Though drugs are the most common means of eliciting state dependent effects in animals, a number of nonpharmacological methods are also available. As an example, responses learned by rats within minutes after the administration of electroconvulsive shock (ECS) are more apt to be performed if ECS is delivered rather than withheld prior to retention testing. This pattern of results has been obtained in studies involving whole-brain ECS, as well as in those employing either kindled convulsions of the amygdala or sub-seizure stimulation of the caudate. Other effective nonpharmacological manipulations include movitational drives such as hunger or thirst, changes in body temperature, and even changes in time of day (see Overton, 1984).

Like their animal-learning counterparts, students of human memory initially sought to secure evidence of state dependence through research involving drugs. Representative of this type of research is a study by Goodwin, Powell, Bremer, Hoine, and Stern (1969). Their study entailed two sessions, which we will refer to as "encoding" and "retrieval." During the encoding session, medical students completed a collection of cognitive tasks, such as generating associations to words and memorizing a series of pictures. The students completed these tasks after they had consumed either a soft drink or a potent cocktail containing an average of 10 ounces of 80-proof vodka. During the retrieval session, held one day later, the students performed a new battery of tasks, which included recall of the previously generated associations and recognition of the previously memorized pictures. Subjects performed this second set of tasks either in the same drug state – sobriety or intoxication – that they had experienced the day before or in the contrasting pharmacological context.

Results of the test of association recall revealed reliable evidence of state-dependent memory: on average, subjects committed 45 percent fewer errors of recall when their encoding and retrieval states matched than when they mismatched. There was, however, no significant sign of state dependence in recognition memory for the pictures: only 9 percent fewer errors were made under matched as opposed to mismatched conditions.

In the decade following publication of Goodwin et al.'s (1969) research, many other studies of human drug-dependent memory were conducted. Most of these studies employed moderate doses of commonly used – and frequently abused – drugs such as alcohol, amphetamine, and marijuana, and most – like Goodwin et al.'s – produced mixed results, with drug-dependent effects materializing in some situations but not in others. Indeed, by the late 1970s, roughly half of the published studies could be counted as successful demonstrations, and half as failures. Consequently, human drug-dependent memory came to be commonly regarded as a capricious phenomenon of little practical or theoretical significance.

The unpredictability of human drug-dependent memory proved to be more apparent than real. Reviewing the results of 27 studies comprising 57 separately identifiable experimental conditions or cases, Eich (1980) observed that when retrieval of the to-be-remembered or target events occurred in the presence of specific, experimenter-provided reminders or cues (as in tests of cued recall or recognition), evidence of drug-dependent memory rarely emerged (3 of 31 cases, or 10 percent). Conversely, when retrieval occurred in the absence of such cues (as in free recall), the odds of demonstrating a reliable drug dependent effects improved sharply (23 of 26 cases, or 88 percent).

Why was this the case? According to one account (Eich, 1980), if what is stored in memory about a target event includes information about the state – drugged or undrugged – in which the event was encoded, then that state can act as a cue for the event's retrieval. Hence, restoration of the state in which the event was encoded may be seen to provide the remember with an "invisible" cue for its retrieval. However, if other powerful "observable" cues are available, then the rememberer will rely on them, which will overshadow the more subtle state cues. When observable cues are not provided, then the invisible state cues come into play. Consequently, drug-dependent effects are more apt to obtain when memory is assessed in the absence of potent observable cues than in their presence.

It is of interest to note that the presence or absence of observable cues is a critical factor not only in the occurrence of *drug*-dependent memory, but of *mood*-dependent memory as well. That is, a shift in affective state from, say, elation at encoding to depression at retrieval has sometimes been shown to impair the free recall of target events, but to have no appreciable influence on cued recall or recognition performance (Eich, 1980; Bower, 1981; *see* EMOTION; FORGETTING).

Still, even under conditions of free recall, mood dependence seems to be a "now-you-see-it, now-you-don't" effect. Bower (1981), for instance, described a study that used post-hypnotic suggestions to induce happy and sad moods in highly susceptible subjects. Every participant learned one list of words while happy and a second list while sad. Later, the subjects were tested for recall of both lists in either a happy or a sad mood. Recall averaged 70 percent when learning and testing moods matched and 46 percent when they mismatched, signaling a strong mood-dependent effect. Nevertheless, a direct replication attempt by Bower and Mayer (1985) failed to find this pattern of results. Conflicting outcomes – some positive (e.g. Mecklenbrauker & Hager, 1984), some negative (e.g. Johnson & Klinger, 1988) – have also been obtained in studies in which moods were modified by non-hypnotic means. It is no surprise, then, that the status of mood dependence as a bona fide phenomenon of human memory is currently a matter of controversy and concern (Bower & Mayer, 1989).

Ultimately, the matter will only be resolved through programatic research aimed at understanding which factors play pivotal roles in the expression of mood-dependent effects. One such factor may be the nature of the moods in which the encoding and retrieval of target events take place. Just as drug-dependent effects in animals are correlated with the amount of drug administered, so too might mood-dependent effects in humans be correlated with the intensity of the moods induced. Thus, for example, it is possible that a shift from an extremely happy to an extremely sad state would impair memory more than would a shift from extreme happiness to a neutral mood, or from moderate happiness to moderate sadness. Data directly relevant to this possibility have not yet been collected, but it merits mentioning that some of the most robust mood-dependent effects ever reported were obtained in studies involving patients with either manic-depressive illness or multiple-personality disorder (see Eich, 1989) – conditions characterized by profound alterations in affect or mood.

A second potentially important factor has to do with how people perceive the relation between their present mood and the events that transpire within it. Recently, Bower (1987) has hypothesized that in order to establish effective associations between ongoing events and the mood in which they occur, contiguity alone between the events and the mood is not sufficient. Rather, people must perceive the events as causing their current mood, for only then will a change in mood cause the events to be forgotten. Though initial tests of Bower's hypothesis have yielded variable results (Bower & Mayer, 1989), additional research is clearly called for. As an aside, it should be noted that a similar idea has been advanced by Fernandez and Glenberg (1985) in connection with environmental context or place-dependent memory. On their account, events experienced in a particular physical environment (a classroom, a courtyard, or the like) may not become associated with that place unless subjects conceive of the environment as causing or enabling the events to happen. This too is an attractive idea that warrants further investigation.

Yet a third factor of potential importance is the source of the target events. Intuitively, it seems reasonable to suppose that events that are generated through internal mental operations such as reasoning, imagination, and thought may be more colored by or connected to one's current mood than are those that emanate from external sources. If so, then a shift in mood state, between the occasions of event encoding and event retrieval, should have a greater adverse impact on memory for internal than for external events.

To investigate this inference, Eich and Metcalfe (1989) performed four experiments that relied on a lengthy regimen of music plus guided imagery to induce rather intense and enduring levels of happiness or sadness. During the encoding session of each experiment, subjects either read a target item that was paired with a category name and a related exemplar (e.g. *milkshake flavors:* chocolate – VANILLA), or they generated (with a very high probability) the same item when primed with its initial letter, in combination with the category name and exemplar cues (e.g. *milkshake flavors:* chocolate – V). In this manner, memory for one and the same target item could be assessed in relation to its source:

either internal (the generated condition) or external (the read condition). Assessment of memory ensued two days later, during the retrieval session, and entailed tests of both free recall and old/new recognition.

Pooling the results from the four experiments, two key findings emerged. First, relative to subjects whose encoding and retrieval moods matched, those who experienced a shift in state recalled 32 percent fewer generated items but only 18 percent fewer read items. Thus, as anticipated, mood-dependent effects were more pronounced for internal than for external events. Second, there was no reliable difference between matched and mismatched moods in the recognition of either generated or read items, which is consistent with the claim, made earlier, that mood dependence is seldom seen when retrieval is tested in the presence of specific, observable cues. Taken together, these two findings imply that the more one must rely on internal resources, rather than on external aids, to generate both the target events at encoding and the cues required for their retrieval, the more likely is one's memory for these events to be mood dependent.

These, then, are three of the factors that may figure prominently in the manifestation of mood-dependent effects. Doubtless there are more, and there is also no doubt that their identification represents a difficult and demanding task. Yet there are other, broader, perhaps even tougher challenges in store. One is to determine whether drug-, mood-, and place-dependent memory are fundamentally different phenomena, or whether retrieval impairments produced by shifts in pharmacological state or physical environment are mediated by alterations in affect (see Bower, 1981; Eich, 1989). Another is to explore the practical and clinical implications of state-dependent memory, especially as they may apply to drug abuse, dissociative amnesias, and negative thinking in depression (Bower, 1981; Overton, 1984; *see* MOOD DISORDERS AND COGNITION).

A third challenge pertains to the observation, alluded to earlier, that animals who shift from drug-present training to drug-absent testing perform more poorly than do those who experience the opposite shift in state. This asymmetric pattern has also been found in several studies of drug-dependent memory in humans. For instance, in a study of the state-dependent effects of marijuana on the free recall of conceptually categorized words (see Eich, 1980), the difference in mean percentage recall between the encode intoxicated/retrieve intoxicated and encode intoxicated/retrieve sober conditions (8 percent) was more than twice the difference between the sober/sober and sober/intoxicated conditions (3 percent). Similar results have been realized using other centrally acting depressants, such as alcohol, and also with the psychomotor stimulant, nicotine (see Eich, 1989). What is more, asymmetry appears to be an attribute of mood-dependent as well as drug-dependent memory. To illustrate, one study (Bartlett & Santrock, 1979) showed that although reinduction of a happy mood was crucial for the recall of words which children had learned while they were happy, a neutral mood at recall conferred little, if any, advantage on the recall of words memorized during a prior neutral state. Generally speaking, then, it seems that information transfers more poorly in the direction of an abnormal or special state of consciousness (such as drug intoxication or extreme happiness) to a normal or standard state (such as sobriety or a neutral mood) than it does in the reverse direction. How and why this happens is currently unclear; several plausible proposals have been offered, but none has yet been thoroughly articulated (see Overton, 1984; Eich, 1989). Granted that asymmetric state dependence runs counter both to most people's intuitions and to most established theories of the phenomenon (especially those that incorporate the venerable concept of stimulus generalization), and given that asymmetry is demonstrated by humans as well as animals, its explanation would seem to be an essential step in understanding the mechanisms that subserve state-dependent memory.

BIBLIOGRAPHY

Bartlett, J. C., & Santrock, J. W. (1979). Affect-dependent episodic memory in young children. *Child Development*, 50, 513–18.

Bower, G. H. (1981). Mood and memory. *American Psychologist, 36*, 129–48.

——. (1987). Commentary on mood and memory. *Behavioral Research and Therapy, 25*, 443–55.

——, & Mayer, J. D. (1985). Failure to replicate mood-dependent retrieval. *Bulletin of the Psychonomic Society, 23*, 39–42.

——. (1989). In search of mood-dependent retrieval. *Journal of Social Behavior and Personality, 4*, 121–56.

Eich, E. (1980). The cue-dependent nature of state-dependent retrieval. *Memory & Cognition, 8*, 157–73.

——. (1989). Theoretical issues in state dependent memory. In H. L. Roediger & F. I. M. Craik (Eds), *Varieties of memory and consciousness* (pp. 331–54). Hillsdale, NJ: Erlbaum.

——, & Metcalfe, J. (1989). Mood dependent memory for internal versus external events. *Journal of Experimental Psychology: Learning, Memory, and Cognition, 15*, 443–55.

Fernandez, A., & Glenberg, A. M. (1985). Changing environmental context does not reliably affect memory. *Memory & Cognition, 13*, 333–45.

Goodwin, D. W., Powell, B., Bremer, D., Hoine, H., & Stern, J. (1969). Alcohol and recall: State dependent effects in man. *Science, 163*, 1358–60.

Johnson, T. L., & Klinger, E. (1988). A non-hypnotic failure to replicate mood-dependent recall. *Bulletin of the Psychonomic Society, 26*, 191–4.

Mecklenbrauker, S., & Hager, W. (1984). Effects of mood on memory: Experimental tests of a mood-state-retrieval hypothesis and mood-congruity hypothesis. *Psychological Research, 46*, 355–76.

Overton, D. A. (1984). State dependent learning and drug discriminations. In L. L. Iverson, S. D. Iverson, & S. H. Snyder (Eds), *Handbook of psychopharmacology* (Vol. 18) (pp. 59–127). New York: Plenum.

Winslow, F. (1860). *On obscure diseases of the brain, and disorders of the mind.* Philadelphia: Blanchard & Lea.

ERIC EICH AND LEE RYAN

statistical inference Psychological interest in statistical inference lies in the study of judgements and inferences that people make about probability and uncertain events – not necessarily involving data normally described as "statistics." Such *intuitive* statistical inferences and judgements arise in many situations when, for example, we forecast the likelihood of a future event (e.g. the chance of rain on a summer weekend) or when we draw general conclusions from our experiences (as when we form our opinion of the quality of a restaurant by our experience of eating a few meals).

Psychological interest in intuitive statistical inferences stems from the study of decision making. It is generally assumed that choice between alternative actions is made by considering the likely consequence of each decision and trying to assess which will lead to the most beneficial result in the long term. Thus, decision making involves forecasting possible states of the world that are conditional upon the decision made (*see* BAYES' LAW). However, the world is full of uncertainties and the great majority of decisions will require us to estimate probabilities of different outcomes of our choices. *Decision theory* has been developed to deal with the problem of how to make optimal choices under uncertainty, and a number of psychologists have been involved in helping decision makers to apply the theory to their real-world problems, a practice known as "decision analysis" (see von Winterfeldt & Edwards, 1986). However, such analysis depends upon the ability of people to generate useful estimates of probability.

Much research has, then, focused upon the notion of whether or not humans are good intuitive statisticians. Research in the 1960s initially led to an optimistic conclusion (Peterson & Beach, 1967). However, subsequent research has led many, if not most, psychologists in this area to the view that probability judgements are biased by a large variety of factors, and that real decision making is not based upon the principles of formal decision theory (see Slovic, Fischhoff, & Lichtenstein, 1977; Kahneman, Slovic, & Tversky, 1982). This view is, however, disputed by some contemporary psychologists, who insist on a more rational picture of human judgement (e.g. Beach, Christensen-Szalanski, & Barnes, 1987).

The major theoretical influence in recent years has arisen from the publications of Daniel Kahneman and Amos Tversky, who have advocated what is known as the "heuristics and biases" approach. The theory proposes that intuitive inferences and judgements are based not upon the laws of probability or decision theory, but on simple "rule of thumb" heuristics. One proposal, for example, is that people judge the likelihood of events by the ease with which they can draw examples to mind (Tversky & Kahneman, 1973). While often useful, this "availability" heuristic can lead to systematic errors and biases due to ways in which human memory and retrieval is organized. For example, a clinician might maintain a false theory of the diagnostic value of a procedure, by selective encoding and retention of case-studies in which the expected association between test result and diagnosis was observed.

BIBLIOGRAPHY

Beach, L. R., Christensen-Szalanski, J., & Barnes, V. (1987). Assessing human judgement: Has it been done, can it be done, should it be done? In G. Wright & P. Ayton (Eds), *Judgemental forecasting*. Chichester: Wiley.

Kahneman, D., Slovic, P., & Tversky, A. (1982). *Judgment under uncertainty: Heuristics and biases*. Cambridge: Cambridge University Press.

Peterson, C. R., & Beach, L. R. (1967). Man as an intuitive statistician. *Psychological Bulletin*, 68, 29–46.

Slovic, P., Fischhoff, B., & Lichtenstein, S. (1977). Behavioral decision theory. *Annual Review of Psychology*, 228, 1–39.

Tversky, A., & Kahneman, D. (1973). Availability: A heuristic for judging frequency and probability. *Cognitive Psychology*, 5, 207–32.

von Winterfeldt, D., & Edwards, W. (1986). *Decision analysis and behavioural research*. Cambridge: Cambridge University Press.

J. ST. B. T. EVANS

stress, adaptation to There have been three different approaches to the study of stress and to the way people cope with stress: the stimulus based or engineering approach, the response based or medico-physiological approach, and the interactional approach exemplified by "appraisal" theories of stress (see Cox, 1978, 1990; or Cox & Mackay, 1981). This essay briefly considers the nature of stress in the framework of appraisal theory, then explores how people attempt to cope with such experiences, and the role of individual differences in coping. This discussion of coping and adaptation to stress is necessarily limited to individual processes, and makes no sustained reference to social processes, such as social support and group coping, although they are important elements in the complete picture.

The engineering approach treats stress as a stimulus characteristic of the person's environment, usually cast in terms of the load or level of demand placed on the person or some aversive or noxious element of that environment. Stress, so defined, produces a strain reaction. In contrast, the medico-physiological approach considers stress as a "generalized and non-specific" response to aversive or noxious environmental stimuli. Stressors give rise, among other things, to a stress response. These approaches have been judged to be inadequate both in terms of their ability to account for the available data and in terms of their theoretical sophistication. Essentially, they fail to take account of individual differences and the perceptual cognitive processes which underpin such differences and which drive the experience of stress. The interactional approach to the study of stress treats it as a psychological state: the internalization of a particular transaction between the person and his or her environment. Such theories owe much to the work of Lazarus (1966) and his notion of "cognitive appraisal." It is interesting to note that not all avowedly *cognitive* theories of stress adopt this interactional perspective. Those that are rooted in the assumptions of information theory, and usually wedded to laboratory experimentation, tend to have more in common with the engineering approach in their treatment of the processes involved and in their essentially "local" nature. In contrast, those concerned with "appraisal" offer more of a "framework" for understanding and draw on a variety of methods for developing and testing such a framework. Framework theories place an emphasis on "synthesis" and "consensus" between different models and include natural observation as well as experimentation as legitimate data sources.

APPRAISAL THEORIES OF STRESS

Appraisal models of stress make explicit its psychological definition. They treat stress as a psychological state which is the internal representation of a particular and problematic transaction between the person and his or her environment. Appraisal is the evaluative process that imbues such situational transactions with meaning. Numerous authors have offered appraisal theories of stress and there is a high degree of consensus between them.

In many ways, Lazarus's ideas formed the initial platform on which most other appraisal theories have been constructed. According to Lazarus's approach the outcome of a stressful transaction is mediated by two components, appraisal and coping (see Lazarus, 1966).

Appraisal is composed of primary and secondary processes. With regard of the former, individuals ask themselves the question: "Is this particular encounter relevant to well-being and in what way?" If the encounter is relevant and is defined as stressful, rather than as benign, three more specific appraisals are then made, those of loss, threat (of harm), and challenge. Primary appraisal is associated with the emotional content of stressful transactions. Secondary appraisal is concerned with the question: "What, if anything, can be done to overcome or prevent harm?"

Influenced by the work of Lazarus and his colleagues, and also by that of McGrath (1970), the theoretical contribution of Cox, and of Cox and Mackay, has been developed over the last 12 years. Originally their "transactional" model of occupational stress was described in terms of five stages (Cox, 1978). The first stage, it was argued, represents the sources of demand faced by the person and is part of his or her environment. The person's perception of these demands in relation to ability to cope represents the second stage: effectively primary appraisal. Stress was des-

cribed as the psychological state which arose when there was a personally significant imbalance or mismatch between the person's perceptions of the demands on him or her and his or her ability to cope with those demands. The psychological and physiological changes which are associated with the recognition of such a stress state, and which include coping, represent the third stage of the model, which leads into the fourth stage, which is concerned with the consequences of coping. The fifth stage is the general feedback (and feed forward) which occurs in relation to all other stages of the model.

This model has been further developed in three respects. First, the authors have attempted to describe the process of primary appraisal in more detail (Cox, 1985; Cox & Mackay, 1981). According to the authors cognitive appraisal appears to take into account:

1. the external and internal demands that people experience, *matched* against;
2. their personal coping resources and behavioural style;
3. the constraints under which they have to cope; and
4. the support that they receive from others in coping.

Second, the stress process (including coping) has been set in the context of "problem solving" and a clear distinction has been made between primary appraisal (is there a problem?) and secondary appraisal (how and how well can I cope with it?) (Cox, 1987) (*see* PROBLEM SOLVING). Primary appraisal is seen as a continual process of monitoring while secondary appraisal is seen as a more discrete activity contingent on the outcome of primary appraisal. Third, there has been some discussion of the problem of measuring stress based on this approach (Cox, 1985, 1990) with the development of possible subjective measures of the experiential (mood) correlates of the stress state (see Cox & Mackay, 1985).

There is a conceptual overlap between the work at Nottingham of Cox and his colleagues, and that of French, Caplan, and van Harrison at Michigan. Those authors and their colleagues have been responsible for the development and popularity of the Person–

Environment Fit (P–EF) model of occupational stress (see French, Caplan, & van Harrison, 1982). This model distinguishes between objective and subjective variables, both of which can refer to either the environment (E) or the person (P). Furthermore, the authors refer to both *demands* on the person's abilities and *supplies* for the person's motives (such as income). Mental health is then defined in terms of four dimensions: (a) objective person–environment fit (P–EF); (b) subjective P–EF; (c) accessibility of self (fit between objective and subjective P variables); and (d) contact with reality (fit between objective and subjective E variables). This model, and the hypotheses that it has been used to generate, have been tested by the authors through a series of survey-based field studies.

Useful additions to "appraisal" theory have been made by Pearlin and Schooler (e.g. Pearlin & Schooler, 1978). They distinguish between acute and chronic stress, and suggest that together eventful experiences (acute events) and chronic strains (hassles) drive the perception of stress: possibly through the experience of life events causing people to be more aware of daily hassles. They also make a distinction between, on the one hand, coping resources (both personal and social) and, on the other, coping responses – the former being what is available to the individual and the latter what they actually do.

Appraisal theories generally offer "frameworks" for understanding, and sadly have not always been used to generate the detailed hypotheses necessary for experimental validation. Having said this, there has been a proliferation of quasi-experimental and survey-based field studies which have contributed to the development of such theories.

COPING

There have been two approaches to the study of coping: that which considers coping as a problem solving *process*, and that which attempts to classify the different types of coping which exist and produce a comprehensive *taxonomy* of such strategies.

Coping as problem solving Coping is increasingly being viewed as a problem solving strategy (e.g. Cox, 1987). Cox (1987), for example, has described a cycle of activities, beginning with recognition and diagnosis (analysis) following through actions and evaluation to re-analysis, which possibly represents the ideal problem-solving process. However, all this implies only the positive side of a double-edged sword and Schonpflug and Battmann (1988) have emphasized a more negative "problem generation" side: that is, by adopting the wrong actions, or by failing in coping, a person may create further problems and stress. At the same time, Meichenbaum (1983) argues that "catastrophizing" or overreacting to such failure serves no adaptive purpose. It is often said that one of the few positive aspects to coping with stress is that the person learns from such experience. However, Einhorn and Hogarth (1981) suggest that there are, at least, three problems with this proposition: first, one does not necessarily know that there is something to be learned; second, what is to be learned is not clear; and third, there is ambiguity in judging whether one has learned. Furthermore, the problem solver may be fully occupied and not have any spare cognitive capacity for learning, and the emotion associated with stress may interfere with the learning process.

Notwithstanding, detailed models of coping based on rational problem solving and decision making have been offered (see Cox, 1987).

Coping taxonomies In an attempt to develop a parsimonious understanding of the coping process, various authors have tried to identify and categorize the different coping strategies which exist.

Lazarus (1966) sees coping as having three main features. First, it is a process: it is what the person actually thinks and does in a stressful encounter. Second, it is context dependent: coping is influenced by the particular appraisal that initiates it and by the resources available to manage that encounter. Finally, coping is defined "independent of outcome" (see, for example, Lazarus & Folkman, 1984).

In dealing with a stressful situation, Lazarus (1966) argues, the person usually combines task- and emotion-focused coping strategies.

The former attempt some form of action directly targeted on dealing with the source of stress: adaptation *of* the environment, while the latter attempt to attenuate the emotional experience associated with that stress: adaptation *to* the environment. The perceived success, or otherwise, of such strategies feeds back into the appraisal process to alter the person's perception of the situation. Lazarus and his colleagues also emphasize that the importance of the situation to the individual is critical in determining the intensity of his or her response.

Pearlin and associates (e.g. Pearlin & Schooler, 1978) further develop this view and distinguish between responses concerned with changing the situation, those concerned with changing its meaning, and those relating to the management of the symptoms of stress. In a different vein, Miller (1979) has distinguished between two informational styles which she terms "blunters" and "monitors": the former tend to use denial strategies and the latter information-seeking strategies in relation to stressful situations. However, these various coping strategies are not meant to be mutually exclusive and most authors emphasize that no one type is necessarily better than any other in solving a problem. Most people use a mixture of strategies in most situations, although certain situations may tend to be associated with particular types of strategy.

Dewe (1987), for example, examined sources of stress and strategies used to cope with them in New Zealand ministers of religion. Using factor-analytical techniques, he identified five clusters of strategies: seeking social support, postponing action by relaxation and distracting attention, developing greater ability to deal with the problem, rationalizing the problem, and drawing on support through spiritual commitment. It was possible to classify 33 percent of the strategies which made up these clusters as task focused and 67 percent as emotion focused. The most frequent source of stress experienced by the ministers related to the emotional and time difficulties associated with crisis work, and the experience of such problems appeared to be associated with coping by seeking social support and rationalizing the problem.

Individual differences and coping Coping does not occur in a vacuum, but is context dependent and partly reflects an interaction between personal and social resources, and situational demands and constraints (*see* PERSONALITY AND COGNITION). Attribution of control, hardiness (Kobasa, 1979) and type A behavior, informational styles, and several other factors, have been implicated in the coping process and in determining the effects of stress. For example, increases in perceived control have been shown to be important in reducing the effects of stress on performance and on health. Control is one of the defining traits in Kobasa's (1979) concept of hardiness: control, commitment, and challenge. Hardy individuals report less illness than non hardy individuals when exposed to high levels of stress. Hardiness appears to affect the person's appraisal of events: hardy individuals, for example, experience events in a quantitatively similar but qualitatively different way to type A individuals. Kobasa, Maddi, and Zola (1983) suggest a further difference between the two groups: hardy individuals may be intrinsically motivated while type A individuals appear extrinsically motivated.

Coping may be seen as functional in its attempts to manage demands, by either changing them, redefining them, or adapting to them. The styles and strategies used need to be relevant and applicable to the situation at hand. The choice and successful use of these responses will be determined by the nature of the situation, by the personal and social resources available, and also by the type of causal reasoning adopted (appraisal).

BIBLIOGRAPHY

Cox, T. (1978). *Stress*. London: Macmillan.
——. (1985). The nature and measurement of stress. *Ergonomics, 28*, 1155–63.
——. (1987). Stress, coping and problem solving. *Work & Stress, 1*, 5–14.
——. (1990). The recognition and measurement of stress: Conceptual and methodological issues. In J. Wilson & N. Corlett (Eds), *Methods in ergonomics*. London: Taylor & Francis.
——, & Mackay, C. J. (1981). A transactional approach to occupational stress. In N. Corlett

& P. Richardson (Eds), *Stress, work design and productivity*. Chichester: Wiley & Son.

——. (1985). The measurement of self reported stress and arousal. *British Journal of Psychology, 76,* 183–6.

Dewe, P. J. (1987). New Zealand ministers of religion: Identifying sources of stress and coping strategies. *Work & Stress, 1,* 351–63.

Einhorn, H. J., & Hogarth, R. M. (1981). Behavioural decision theory: Processes of judgement and choice. *Annual Review of Psychology, 32,* 53–88.

French, J. R. P., Caplan, R. D., & van Harrison, R. (1982). *The mechanisms of job stress and strain*. New York: Wiley & Sons.

Kobasa, S. (1979). Stressful life events, personality, and health: An inquiry into hardiness. *Journal of Personality and Social Psychology, 37,* 1–13.

Kobasa, S., Maddi, S., & Zola, M. (1983). Type A and hardiness. *Journal of Behavioural Medicine, 6,* 41–51.

Lazarus, R. S. (1966). *Psychological stress and the coping process*. New York: McGraw-Hill.

——, & Folkman, S. (1984). *Stress, appraisal and coping*. New York: Springer Publications.

McGrath, J. E. (1970). *Social and psychological factors in stress*. New York: Holt.

Meichenbaum, D. (1983). *Coping with stress*. London: Century Publications.

Miller, S. (1979). Controllability and human stress: Method, evidence and theory. *Behavioural Research and Therapy, 17,* 287–304.

Pearlin, L., & Schooler, C. (1978). The structure of coping. *Journal of Health and Social Behaviour, 19,* 2–21.

Schonpflug, F., & Battmann, A. (1988). The costs and benefits of coping. In S. Fisher & J. Reason (Eds), *Handbook of life stress, cognition and health*. Chichester: Wiley & Son.

TOM COX

Stroop effect Asked to name the ink color of a stimulus, people are much slower to say "green" for the incongruent word RED in green ink than for the control stimulus XXX in green ink. This is the Stroop effect, first reported by J. Ridley Stroop (1935) in his dissertation. Of particular interest is the fact that interference is asymmetrical: asked instead to read the word aloud, people are no slower to say "red" for the incongruent stimulus than for the control word RED in normal black ink. Later studies also demonstrated a small facilitation effect: ink color naming time is faster for congruent stimuli such as the word RED in red ink than for the XXX control.

There are several hundred Stroop-related studies in the literature (for reviews, see Dyer, 1973; MacLeod, in press). Numerous analogs now exist, such as the picture–word task, where a word is embedded in a line drawing of an object (e.g. a picture of a cat containing the word DOG). Here, interference and facilitation occur when naming the picture but not when reading the word. Because of its magnitude and reliability, the Stroop effect has long been treated as a benchmark measure of attention (*see* ATTENTION, INHIBITORY PROCESSES IN).

Two related explanations of the Stroop effect have dominated theoretical efforts: relative speed of processing and automaticity. The "relative speed of processing" account starts from the longstanding observation (Cattell, 1886) that people read a word faster than they name an ink color (or other perceptual quality of a stimulus). The idea is that word reading and ink color naming occur in parallel, but a response is produced faster by word reading. Assuming a limited capacity response buffer, if the response requested is the ink color name, the wrong response reaches the buffer first, causing interference.

The automaticity account, also due to Cattell, emphasizes the much greater practice accrued by word reading relative to ink color naming. This extensive practice has made reading automatic: it is beyond volitional control and does not require attention. In contrast, ink color naming is a controlled process requiring attention. An automatic process will interfere with a nonautomatic one, but not vice versa, producing asymmetrical interference (*see* AUTOMATIC PROCESSING).

These two theories differ in that automaticity does not hinge on a direct mapping from processing speed to interference outcome. Thus, a slower but more automatic process could interfere with a faster but less automatic one. Recent studies suggest that the "relative speed of processing" view cannot accommodate all of the data, most notably when the

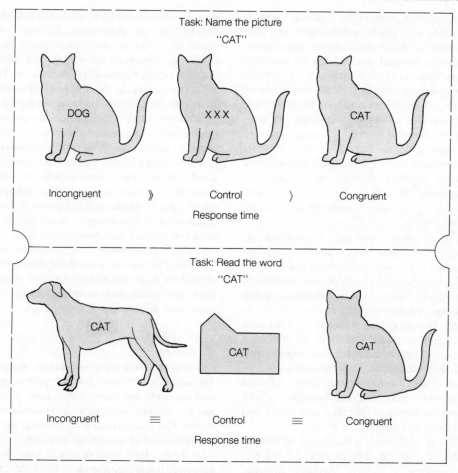

Figure 1 Interference and facilitation occur when naming the picture but not when reading the word in the picture–word analog of the Stroop task.

onset asynchrony between the word and the ink color is systematically varied. Instead, a continuum of automaticity has been suggested as a better explanation. Direction and magnitude of interference are determined by the relative automaticity of the two stimulus dimensions (assuming a reasonable index of automaticity, such as extent of practice). This explanation directly links attention to learning and memory.

BIBLIOGRAPHY

Cattell, J. M. (1886). The time it takes to see and name objects. *Mind, 11,* 63–5.

Dyer, F. N. (1973). The Stroop phenomenon and its use in the study of perceptual, cognitive, and response processes. *Memory and Cognition, 1,* 106–20.

MacLeod, C. M. (in press). Half a century of research on the Stroop effect: An integrative review. *Psychological Bulletin.*

Stroop, J. R. (1935). Studies of interference in serial verbal reactions. *Journal of Experimental Psychology, 18,* 643–62.

COLIN M. MACLEOD

student learning Although students in universities and colleges have been the subjects of experimental studies in cognitive psychology for many years, it is only recently that the ways they tackle their everyday academic learning tasks have been systematically examined and related to cognitive theory (*see* LEARNING STYLES). A rapidly developing area of research has made use of existing theories from cognitive psychology, but it has also led to the identification of quite different concepts rooted in the experiences of the students themselves. This essay presents brief summaries of the research derived from existing cognitive theories which are well represented in other entries, with greater detail being provided here of the less familiar experiential concepts.

The dominant approach to research on student learning in North America has taken concepts and theories of learning and memory and investigated their application to student learning. In Europe, a quite different tradition has been developed over the last ten years, largely by educational researchers. They have used both qualitative analyses of interviews and questionnaire surveys to develop concepts and theories derived from students' descriptions of their own learning. These different approaches make different assumptions both about the nature of learning and about data collection and analysis.

The first approach is familiar. The data are collected from carefully controlled laboratory experiments in which specially designed learning materials avoid the effects of previous knowledge. Knowledge is generally viewed quantitatively and measured in terms of, say, the percentage accuracy of verbatim RECALL. Concepts and theories then emerge from the statistical analysis of the data. These are used either to generate inventories in which students report their processes of learning and study activities within that predetermined theoretical framework, or to design interventions intended to improve students' learning strategies.

The second approach is a more recent development. It starts from the experience of the students themselves. Learning is generally seen as a process by which students alter their conceptions of the topic being studied. The outcomes of learning have, therefore, to be assessed qualitatively in terms of different levels of understanding or conceptions. Beside investigating the qualitatively different outcomes of learning, this research has also looked at the contrasting ways in which students tackle common academic tasks. The initial work was based on semi-structured interviews with transcripts being subjected to rigorous qualitative analysis. This process involves the repeated reading of the transcripts to identify the most distinctive similarities and differences among the students, which are refined iteratively until the most powerful descriptive concepts and categories are identified. These concepts, rooted in the students' own descriptions, have then been used to construct self-report inventories.

In exploring these two approaches we shall be looking for convergence in the descriptions of student learning, which may also suggest more appropriate ways of helping students to learn more effectively.

CONCEPTS FROM COGNITIVE PSYCHOLOGY

Perhaps the two most important lines of development deriving from cognitive psychology itself are those which have investigated learning strategies in experimental studies and those which have investigated the dimensionality of study strategies using inventory surveys. Both areas of research have subsequently led to training procedures designed to improve the efficiency of student learning.

Experiments on learning strategies Although there is a long history of attempts to assist students with their learning strategies, until recently the evidence of their success was not strong. There was little transfer from the training situation to everyday studying. There is now a set of related studies which show much greater benefits, and this is believed to be attributable to their firmer roots in cognitive psychology. Probably the best known system of strategy training is that developed by Dansereau and his colleagues using the acronym MURDER (see Weinstein, Goetz, & Alexander, 1988). Students were encouraged to set a positive Mood for studying, concentrate while reading on Understanding, actively Recall what had been read, try to

Detect errors in that recall, use mental imagery and previous knowledge to Elaborate what was being learned, and finally to Review what was to be remembered. This method has only rather indirect linkages to cognitive theory, and yet more recent methods, emerging more directly from work on metacognition, have pointed up similar components as being valuable and effective in strategy training, even in the earlier stages of education. In particular, training in elaboration and monitoring seems to lead to improvements in academic performance (see articles in Weinstein et al., 1988).

Surveys of study strategies The idea of differing levels of processing in the memory has provided a productive theoretical framework for thinking about student learning (*see* LEVELS OF PROCESSING). The idea that recall will be stronger where a deep level of processing, including elaborative processing, has been utilized has led to the development of inventories and related intervention strategies. The most direct application of these ideas can be seen in the work of Schmeck who developed a so-called Inventory of Learning Processes. This inventory contains four scales: deep processing, elaborative processing, fact retention, and methodical study. The first three of these scales contain items guided by cognitive psychology theory, while the final scale described study activities. Beside being rooted in this body of theory, these four dimensions have also repeatedly emerged from the factor analyses of the items (see articles in Schmeck, 1988).

Weinstein has developed the so-called Learning and Study Strategies Inventory, which contains scales derived from both cognitive psychology and the study skills literature. Its theoretical base includes ideas about both memory and metacognitive processes, while from the literature on study skills came, not just descriptions of organized studying, but also motivation and anxiety. A scale of information processing has been found to correlate fairly closely with Schmeck's elaborated processing (Schmeck, 1988). In parallel with the construction of the inventory, Weinstein has also developed a course on individual learning skills designed

to help students form a more systematic and reflective approach to studying. The inventory is used to monitor progress and to adapt the course to student needs. Evaluations show substantial improvements both in the quality of work and grade-point average (Weinstein et al., 1988).

EDUCATIONAL RESEARCH

The work on student learning carried out by educational researchers has led to the definition of a series of concepts and categories derived from the qualitative analysis of interview transcripts and the parallel development of inventories to measure those concepts. The qualitative studies have been concerned with the learning of subject matter as well as the processes of learning and studying.

Recalling information and developing concepts Effective learning of academic subject matter depends not only on the storage and recall of information, but also the formation and appropriate use of abstract concepts. The contrast between rote learning and meaningful learning is well established in the psychological literature, but a substantial amount of student learning in higher education and in schools is of an intermediate kind. It is of the form that Ausubel has described as meaningful reception learning in which information is conveyed in a lecture or a book and "directly" absorbed by incorporation into cognitive structure with little, if any, conscious effort. Of course, subsequent reorganization and systemization occurs, particularly during revision, but the initial process has neither the rehearsal properties of rote learning nor the active establishment of linkages which is the characteristic of more active forms of meaningful learning. This type of learning, although prevalent, has been rather ignored by researchers.

A good deal of effort has, however, been put into describing the differing conceptions held by students, particularly of scientific concepts. The starting point was in schools, where many pupils were found to have naive concepts of physics which interfered with their understanding of the scientific concepts they were supposed to be acquiring. Marton has since developed a research methodology – phenomenography – which describes in terms of a few distinctive categories the range of conceptions held by students. In this research, knowledge and understanding are seen as being reconstructed and adapted as new information is acquired or problems solved (Marton & Entwistle, 1989), and it is interesting to see how recent ideas in cognitive psychology have suggested a similar, more holistic, view of knowledge and the way it is stored.

Intellectual development Perry (1970) was one of the first researchers to use interviews to create a set of categories describing differences between students in their ways of studying. Analysis of the transcripts suggested that there was a distinct series of "positions" through which students progressed, representing a dimension of intellectual development from "dualistic" to "relativistic" thinking. Dualism indicates a belief in the existence of "right" and "wrong" answers, with successful students being those who are able to acquire a large number of "right" answers, and effective teachers being those who know those answers and can convey them in the clearest possible form.

The dualist position does not last long and thereafter students begin to see both the nature and the implications of relativism – that many answers are incomplete, have to be qualified, or are provisional. The degree of uncertainty perceived in relativism creates anxiety in some students and leads them to resist further progression. Those who persist, however, begin to recognize how evidence is used in the construction of sound argument, then begin to make a "commitment" to their own theoretical stance and to defend it effectively.

The implications of these ideas on the intellectual and ethical development of students have been explored in relation to the level at which first-year courses should be pitched, the need to emphasize skills as well as content in curriculum planning, and the counseling of students who find relativism threatening.

Approaches to learning Perhaps the most influential concept describing aspects of student learning was introduced by Marton and his colleagues. They asked students to read an academic text and to be ready to answer questions afterwards. The questions explored not just what was understood, but also how the students went about reading the article. Using rigorous qualitative analysis, they found that the concept which most clearly distinguished between the ways students tackled the article and their levels of understanding was their *approach to learning*. Students adopted either a deep approach or a surface approach to the task.

The crucial difference lies in the contrasting *intentions* shown by students. A *deep approach* draws on a sophisticated conception of learning with an intention to reach a personal understanding of the material presented. To do this, the student has to interact critically with the content, relating it to previous knowledge and experience, as well as examining evidence and evaluating the logical steps by which conclusions have been reached. In contrast, a *surface approach* involves a simple conception of learning as memorization and an intention merely to satisfy task or course requirements, seen as external impositions largely remote from personal interests. The surface approach can still be active, but it relies on identifying the elements within the task most likely to be assessed, and then memorizing those details (in Marton, Hounsell, & Entwistle, 1984).

Marton's study was carried out as a naturalistic experiment, but in everyday studying the influence of assessment on approach has to be taken into account. Ramsden asked students about their ways of tackling their academic work. Again the deep and surface approaches represented important distinctions, but it was also necessary to add a third category – *strategic approach* – which related to studying as well as to learning. In this approach, the student adopts deep and surface approaches in a combination designed to achieve the highest possible grades. The approach involves using well organized study methods and careful time management, but above all there is an alertness to any cues given by tutors about what they are looking for in deciding grades or marks, or what questions they are going to set in the examinations (Entwistle & Ramsden, 1983). Students appear to have two distinct foci of attention – the content and the teacher's reward system. While lecturers expect the students to focus on the former, assessment demands shift attention to the latter.

Although the idea of approach to learning had its origins in a single naturalistic experiment, it has since been extended or modified to describe most tasks found in everyday studying (Marton et al., 1984), and has been introduced into many staff training workshops to help faculty understand the different ways students go about their academic work.

Study orientations Attempts to operationalize the concepts derived from the interviews led to the Approaches to Studying Inventory (Entwistle & Ramsden, 1983), which also contained scales describing motivation and study attitudes and methods. Factor analyses of the items showed that each approach was associated with a different form of motivation – deep approach correlated closely with intrinsic motivation, surface was linked with fear of failure and instrumental motivation, while strategic was associated with need for achievement. These combinations of scales held together so consistently that they have been referred to as "study orientations" – meaning, reproducing, and achieving. A final "non-academic" orientation is characterized by low levels of motivation, negative attitudes to studying, and disorganized study methods.

A similar pattern linking motive to strategy has been reported independently by Biggs (1987) using his own theoretical framework and a different inventory. He has used this inventory, in ways similar to Weinstein, to suggest how students can be weaned from reliance on mechanical study skills to meta-cognitive awareness of their own goals and strategies.

The approaches to learning and studying are, however, not simply to be seen as reflecting consistent individual differences. They also reflect reactions to the students' perceptions of their learning environment. Approach is influenced not just by assessment procedures, but also by the perceived quality of

the teaching, freedom in learning, and workload (Entwistle & Ramsden, 1983).

One of the important growth points in this area of research seems to be the investigation of the parallelism, and the interactions, between study strategies and perceptions of the learning environment. It is becoming clear that approaches to learning have correlations not only with distinctive motivations, but also with contrasting perceptions of their learning environment (Entwistle in Richardson, Eysenck, & Warren-Piper, 1987; Ramsden in Schmeck, 1988; Janssen in Entwistle & Marton, 1990; Entwistle & Tait, 1990).

RECONCILING THE CONTRASTING METHODOLOGIES

There are rather few opportunities for cognitive psychologists and educational researchers to discuss their different approaches to describing student learning. When they do attend the same conferences, the differences in methodology and theoretical perspective are marked (Richardson et al., 1987) and mutual criticism strong. Cognitive psychologists attack both the methodology and the concepts used by educational researchers. For example, the qualitative analyses have been described as unconvincing, with the "approach to learning" being seen as a diffuse concept with too many component parts. In their turn, educational researchers have criticized the ecological invalidity of applying concepts derived from artificial experiments to the very different context of student learning, and also point out the limitations imposed by what they see as a mechanistic conception of learning and a reductionist research strategy (Entwistle & Marton, 1990) (*see* ECOLOGICAL VALIDITY).

It is clear that cognitive psychologists seek a different level of explanation from educational researchers. They focus on the common cognitive processes within the individual, paying little or no attention to individual differences or contextual variability. For the educational researcher, the internal cognitive processes are of only peripheral interest. What concerns them is how to explain, and influence, the study behavior of the student. The terminology used by the cognitive psychologist also creates a barrier of communication with their colleagues – hence the need for concepts which, while broad and somewhat diffuse, are essentially communicable and carry with them metaphorical meanings which encourage reflection on teaching and learning.

The research by cognitive psychologists has, however, led to interventions which have been shown to support student learning. The value of continuing to investigate common cognitive processes, and of exploring their applications, has thus been demonstrated. There is nevertheless a remaining area of concern about this approach. The focus on cognitive processes in these interventions leads to an overemphasis on the importance of strategy training. This has two disadvantages. First, much cognitive strategy training puts control of the learning in the hands of the instructor who decides what treatment to apply. Yet it has been found more beneficial to encourage students to take charge of their own learning and develop metacognitive awareness (*see* METACOGNITION). Second the strong influence of assessment procedures and teaching indicates that the quality of student learning can only be improved by a re-evaluation of the whole learning environment (Newble & Clark in Richardson et al., 1987; and Eizenberg in Ramsden, 1988), and a recognition of how the various aspects of the environment are likely to interact with the strengths and weaknesses of individual students (Entwistle in Richardson et al., 1987).

See also STUDY SKILLS.

BIBLIOGRAPHY

Biggs, J. B. (1987). *Student approaches to learning and studying.* Hawthorn, Vic.: Australian Council for Educational Research.

Entwistle, N. J., & Ramsden, P. (1983). *Understanding student learning.* London: Croom Helm.

Entwistle, N. J., & Tait, H. (1990). Approaches to learning, evaluations of teaching, and perceptions of the learning environment. *Higher Education, 19,* 169–94.

Entwistle, N. J., & Marton, F. (Eds) (1989). The psychology of student learning. *European Journal of the Psychology of Education* (Vol. IV: Whole issue).

Marton, F., Hounsell, D. J., & Entwistle, N. J. (Eds) (1984). *The experience of learning.* Edinburgh: Scottish Academic Press.

Perry, W. G. (1970). *Forms of intellectual and ethical development in the college years: A scheme.* New York: Holt, Rinehart and Winston.

Ramsden, P. (1988). *Improving learning: New perspectives.* London: Kogan Page.

Richardson, J. T. E., Eysenck, M. W., & Warren-Piper, D. (Eds) (1987). *Student learning: Research in education and cognitive psychology.* London: SRHE/Open University Press.

Schmeck, R. R. (Ed.) (1988). *Learning styles and strategies.* New York: Plenum Press.

Weinstein, C. E., Goetz, E. T., & Alexander, P. A. (Eds) (1988). *Learning and study strategies.* New York: Academic Press.

NOEL ENTWISTLE

study skills Skills which lead to effective studying are those that make use of the processes that normally lead to good comprehension of what is being studied and, subsequently, to good recall. It is usually the case that the material being studied has a logical and meaningful content and structure, although identifying this may at first present a challenge to the student. Comprehension and memory are usually closely related (*see* LANGUAGE COMPREHENSION). If the full sense of the text is not properly comprehended then it will be difficult to remember. Bransford and Johnson (1972), for example, showed that when subjects were given, in advance, the title "washing clothes" that clarified the theme of an otherwise obscure passage which they were given to read, subsequent recall of the passage was more than doubled.

Both comprehension and memory depend upon the use of the existing knowledge that the person possesses in the active construction of a new mental representation of the information that is being conveyed in the material under study. It is, therefore, not surprising that study techniques usually emphasize an active approach to the material to be learned, along with methods to ensure that the learner's existing knowledge of the area has been fully activated (*see* SCHEMATA).

There are many further opportunities to improve upon the memorization of information beyond its initial comprehension. However, many students expect to be able to remember the details of a textbook after passively reading it through. They rarely check shortly after reading the passage to see how much they can remember. Such testing of one's memory is a very valuable component in effective study. Not only does it provide awareness of what has and has not been learned but it also makes the future recall of the information that can be remembered far easier (see Cooper & Monk, 1976) (see RECALL).

Several other central factors in determining memory also need to be incorporated into effective study skills. One is that the more salient and interesting the material appears to the learner, the better it will be acquired. If the information falls within an area in which the person is already knowledgeable then the new information will be acquired more quickly (e.g. Morris, Tweedy, & Gruneberg, 1985). This is in addition to the need to use existing knowledge to comprehend the material being memorized. Recall depends heavily upon the availability of cues at the time of remembering that will activate the memories. Where the information being learned has a framework or structure that can be used to organize both the learning and the retrieval, then memory is often considerably improved (e.g. Bower, Clark, Lesgold, & Winzenz, 1969). Study techniques need to reveal such organization in the material under study and, if necessary, impose a framework if one is not clearly discernible. Memory is much influenced by the similarities between items that have been encoded. Any activities by the learner which improve the distinctiveness of the information being memorized will increase its probability of later retrieval.

In the light of these general principles about comprehension and memory, various study systems have been developed. The oldest and most widely recommended of such schemes is the SQ3R system (Robinson, 1946; Higbee, 1988). The technique involves the three stages: Survey, Question, Read, Recite, Review. This technique is principally intended to improve learning from textbooks. In the first, Survey, stage the student reads the chap-

ter summary, skips through looking at headings, pictures and graphs, and so on and attempts to obtain an overview of the topics covered. In so doing they begin to identify the structure of the material and to cue from their memory knowledge that is related to the chapter or book under study. In the Question stage the learner again skims through the material, this time asking questions based upon the headings of the sections. These questions should relate both to the learner's own interests and to what they expect to find within the learning material. By so doing, they maximize their interest in the material and develop an active approach to their subsequent reading. In the next stage they read through the chapter. Then, in the Recite stage they reread the chapter, but do so by first attempting to anticipate what will come in each section and to answer the questions they set earlier. In the final, Review, stage the student surveys his or her success in the Recite stage and examines the extent to which the original questions have been answered and locates such weaknesses and the need for further learning as will be required.

Study skills such as SQ3R can improve the efficiency of study. However, students to whom the system is taught often complain that it involves too much mental effort and tend to fall back on more passive approaches to learning, despite the dangers for their future performance (see STUDENT LEARNING).

In addition to study systems, there are other important aspects of memory that students should consider. One is the normal finding that spaced or distributed practice leads to better learning than does massed practice. The benefits of distributed practice have been demonstrated in language learning by Bloom and Shuell (1981) and in Learning to Type by Baddeley and Longman (1978). Thus, for example, more will be learned from three one-hour sessions on some given material than from one three-hour session.

When studying to remember information later, overlearning is beneficial. That is, rather than practicing upon and studying the material for just so long as one can report it from memory, the student should continue studying and recalling the material so that recall becomes progressively easier. Studies of overlearning have shown that it increases long-term retention. Material that is very considerably overlearned is particularly resistant to forgetting and may be retained for a lifetime while information that has been crammed for an examination will be rapidly forgotten (Bahrick, 1984).

BIBLIOGRAPHY

Baddeley, A. D., & Longman, D. J. A. (1978). The influence of length and frequency of training sessions on rate of learning to type. *Ergonomics*, *21*, 627–35.

Bahrick, H. P. (1984). Semantic memory content in permastore: Fifty years of memory for Spanish learned at school. *Journal of Experimental Psychology: General*, *113*, 1–29.

Bloom, K. C., & Shuell, T. J. (1981). Effects of massed and distributed practice in the learning and retention of second-language vocabulary. *Journal of Educational Research*, *74*, 245–8.

Bower, G. H., Clark, M. C., Lesgold, A. M., & Winzenz, D. (1969). Hierarchical retrieval schemes in recall of categorized word lists. *Journal of Verbal Learning and Verbal Behavior*, *8*, 323–43.

Bransford, J. D., & Johnson, M. K. (1972). Contextual prerequisites for understanding: Some investigations of comprehension and recall. *Journal of Verbal Learning and Verbal Behavior*, *11*, 717–26.

Cooper, A. J. R., & Monk, A. (1976). Learning for recall and learning for recognition. In J. Brown (Ed.), *Recall and recognition* (pp. 131–56). London: Wiley.

Higbee, K. L. (1988). *Your memory: How it works and how to improve it* (2nd edn). New York: Prentice-Hall.

Morris, P. E., Tweedy, M., & Gruneberg, M. M. (1985). Interest, knowledge, and the memorizing of soccer scores. *British Journal of Psychology*, *76*, 365–71.

Robinson, F. (1946). *Effective study*. New York: Harper & Row.

PETER E. MORRIS

subliminal perception Subliminal perception is the phenomenon of responding to stimuli below the awareness threshold. It has been shown to occur (see Dixon, 1981) for all sense modalities and in the context of several different research paradigms. The latter include presenting stimuli of low intensity or short duration, or at frequencies beyond the normal range for conscious perception. Signal to noise ratios for achieving "perception without awareness" may also be brought about by masking or by presenting stimuli in sensory channels that are not currently mediating conscious perception.

Subliminal perception implies that the processes responsible for conscious perceptual experience are not identical with those which mediate the transmission of information through the brain from receptors to effectors. Whereas the latter depends upon the classical sensory pathways linking peripheral receptors with their cortical projections, CONSCIOUSNESS of sensory inflow necessitates a coincident contribution of cortical excitation from the ascending fibres of the reticular system.

The theory that subliminal perception occurs when external stimulation is too weak or too brief to produce sufficient activation of the reticular system is supported by the research findings of Libet and his co-workers (1967). Recording from the somato-sensory cortex of fully conscious human subjects, they were able to detect electrical potentials initiated by tactile stimuli presented at subliminal intensities. When stimulation was increased to supraliminal intensities, subjects reported awareness of the stimulus at the same time as the wave form of the evoked potential manifested a contribution from the reticular activating system.

Yet other researches (see Dixon, 1981) have shown that visual evoked responses, galvanic skin responses, verbal behavior, conscious perception of supraliminal stimulus arrays, and even dreams, may be significantly influenced by the meaning of verbal and/or pictorial stimuli presented below the awareness threshold. The data from such studies imply that subliminal stimuli may be subjected to extensive preconscious processing involving unconscious long-term memory and emotional classification of sensory inflow (*see also* BLINDSIGHT).

By far the most extensively researched

manifestations of subliminal perception are those of perceptual defense and vigilance. The data from a variety of experimental paradigms suggest that prior to awareness of a visually presented word or picture, which is gradually increasing in brightness or duration of exposure, a preconscious semantic analysis of the latter's meaning may result in the raising or lowering of the threshold for conscious perception of the material in question.

The fact that stimulation below the awareness threshold is not subject to conscious appraisal has led to several clinical applications of subliminal perception (*see* MOOD DISORDERS AND COGNITION). These include the investigation of unconscious psychopathology (Silverman, 1975), the treatment of various neurotic disorders, and the identification of accident prone candidates among applicants for flying duties in military airforces. In the Defense Mechanism Test (Kragh, 1962; see also Dixon, 1981) the candidate for a flying career has to describe what he sees when flashed a complete picture in which the central figure is flanked by a "subliminal" threatening male face.

Prolonged validation studies have confirmed that those candidates whose perception of the central figure is distorted by the unconsciously perceived "threat" will be particularly accident prone during military training. By using such a test in the selection of military fliers many countries have shown a considerable saving in lives and aircraft.

Subliminal stimulation has also been used in a therapeutic context. For example, the reduction of anxiety by subliminal presentation of reassuring messages has proved helpful in reducing compensatory overeating (Silverman et al., 1978) and improving performance at mathematics (Ariam, 1979).

Presumably because of the threat it poses to notions of free will there has been considerable resistance to accepting the reality of subliminal perception. A favorite criticism has been that so-called subliminal effects are only responses to consciously perceived fragments of the stimulus array. A recent study by Groeger (1984) which showed that semantic influences were *greater* for a subliminal stimulus than for one presented at the awareness threshold suggests that subliminal perception cannot be explained away by this "partial cue" hypothesis.

BIBLIOGRAPHY

Ariam, S. (1979). The effects of subliminal symbiotic stimuli in Hebrew on academic performance of Israeli High School Students. Unpublished Ph.D. dissertation: New York University.

Dixon, N. F. (1981). *Preconscious processing.* Wiley: Chichester.

Groeger, J. A. (1984). Preconscious influences on language production. Unpublished Ph.D. thesis: University of Belfast.

Kragh, U. (1962). Precognitive defense organisation with threatening and non-threatening peripheral stimuli. *Scandinavian Journal of Psychology, 3,* 65–8.

Libet, B., Alberts, W. W., Wright, E. W., & Feinstein, B. (1967). Responses to human somato-sensory cortex to stimuli below the threshold for conscious sensation. *Science, 158* (3808), 1, 597–1600.

Silverman, L. H. (1975). An experimental method for the study of unconscious conflict – a progress report. *British Journal of Medical Psychology, 48,* 291–8.

Silverman, L. H., Martin, A., Ungaro, R., & Mendelsohn, E. (1978). Effect of subliminal stimulation of symbiotic fantasies on behaviour modification treatment of obesity. *Journal of Consultative Clinical Psychology, 46*(3), 432–41.

NORMAN F. DIXON

T

therapy, cognitive *See* COGNITIVE THERAPY.

tip-of-the-tongue phenomenon There are many times when people try to recall an answer, are unable to at that time, but still know something about the answer, i.e. the tip-of-the-tongue phenomenon. For instance, suppose someone is asked, "What is the capital of Denmark?" Just because the person does not immediately recall the answer, that does not necessarily mean the person does not know anything about the answer. Sometimes, a person who cannot recall the answer may nevertheless be able to recall something about the *attributes of the word* that is the correct answer. For instance, in response to the aforementioned question a person who cannot recall the answer "Copenhagen" may still recall that the answer begins with "C" or even "Cop" or that it contains four syllables. Other times, a person who cannot recall the answer may nevertheless be able to recall information about the *attributes of the referent* of the answer. For instance, in response to the aforementioned question a person who cannot recall the answer may still recall that the referent of the question is a city near the sea or that it is the city in which the Tivoli Gardens are located. Recall of either of these two kinds of attributes, in the absence of recall of the answer itself, is called the "tip-of-the-tongue phenomenon" (first investigated by Brown & MacNeill, 1966).

The phenomenon is conceptually different from (and is easily confused with) a related phenomenon called the "feeling of knowing." The latter refers to people's predictions about their subsequent performance on a nonrecalled item. The most common kind of prediction is about the person's subsequent likelihood of recognizing an answer that currently cannot be recalled (first investigated by Hart, 1965). For instance, for the question above, a person might not be able to recall the answer but might be quite certain that he or she could recognize it (e.g. pick it out of a list of Scandinavian cities).

Sometimes the attributes that are recalled during the tip-of-the-tongue phenomenon may serve as a basis for the feeling of knowing (Koriat & Lieblich, 1974). For instance, if someone who could not recall the answer "Copenhagen" was nevertheless able to recall that the answer began with *C* and contained four syllables, then on that basis the person might predict that he or she could correctly recognize the answer if confronted with a list of Scandinavian cities (this and other related bases that might underlie the feeling of knowing are discussed by Nelson, Gerler, & Narens, 1984). Although the tip-of-the-tongue phenomenon and the feeling of knowing are not identical, both of them are indicants of underlying knowledge about an answer that cannot be recalled.

BIBLIOGRAPHY

Brown, R., & MacNeill, D. (1966). The "tip of the tongue" phenomenon. *Journal of Verbal Learning and Verbal Behavior, 5*, 325–37.

Hart, J. T. (1965). Memory and the feeling-of-knowing experience. *Journal of Educational Psychology, 56*, 208–16.

Koriat, A., & Lieblich, I. (1974). What does a person in a "TOT" state know that a person in a "don't know" state doesn't know? *Memory & Cognition, 2*, 647–55.

Nelson, T. O., Gerler, D., & Narens, L. (1984). Accuracy of feeling-of-knowing judgments for predicting perceptual identification and relearning. *Journal of Experimental Psychology: General, 113*, 282–300.

T. O. NELSON

top-down processing *See* DATA-DRIVEN AND CONCEPTUALLY DRIVEN PROCESSES.

V

visual dominance The term visual dominance refers to the fact that, under conditions of conflicting input from different sensory modalities, visual input tends to dominate. For instance, Gibson (1933) had subjects wear distorting prisms that made straight lines appear curved. Subjects then maintained that a straight edge felt curved to their touch when they saw and felt the edge at the same time. Similar effects occur in studies of prism adaptation, where subjects wear distorting lenses for a prolonged period until they adapt to behaving appropriately to the distorted visual input (Kohler, 1972). Thus, walking up stairs is initially very difficult, even though proprioceptive and kinesthetic input from our joints should be sufficient to enable the behavior to occur (since we can walk up stairs with our eyes closed).

Different accounts can be offered as to why visual dominance occurs. Posner, Nissen, and Klein (1976) proposed that it occurs because visual signals tend to be less alerting than other signals. An auditory tone works as a warning signal to visual and auditory stimuli even when the signal is unexpected and cannot be predicted. In contrast, a visual warning signal may sometimes be effective only when its occurrence is expected (Posner et al., 1976). Because visual signals need not alert us automatically we may need to pay them greater attention than other stimuli – so producing visual dominance.

However, visual dominance could occur for other reasons too. Some visual signals, particularly those produced by movement of observers or objects in the environment, may link directly to motor responses (such as balance reactions). Vision dominates some aspects of motor behavior because these direct links do not exist for other senses (such as audition). If an object looms toward an observer, the observer tends to sway backward (and there can be forward sway if an object

looms away) – suggesting a direct link between balance reactions and visual cues for movement (Lee & Aaronson, 1974). The extent of visual dominance then depends on the relative strength of other signals to the motor system – with vision dominating when proprioceptive cues are reduced (as in young children).

BIBLIOGRAPHY

Gibson, J. J. (1933). Adaptation, after-effect and contrast in the perception of curved lines. *Journal of Experimental Psychology, 16*, 1–31.
Kohler, I. (1972). Experiments with goggles. In R. Held & W. Richards (Eds), *Perception: Mechanisms and models. Readings from* Scientific American. San Francisco: W. H. Freeman.
Lee, D. N., & Aaronson, E. (1974). Visual proprioceptive control of standing in human infants. *Perception & Psychophysics, 15*, 529–32.
Posner, M. I., Nissen, M. J., & Klein, R. (1976). Visual dominance: An information-processing account of its origins and significance. *Psychological Review, 83*, 157–71.

G. W. HUMPHREYS

visual illusion An illusion is a perception which deviates systematically from physical fact. This definition is due to Gregory (1973) who nevertheless notes deep philosophical problems lurking in the notion of "physical fact." In practice, however, most psychological studies of illusions ignore these difficulties by taking as the question of interest: why should the perception of a given entity differ from measurements of that entity using instruments such as rulers, protractors, light meters, and so on? The latter measurements thus serve as operational definitions of "physical reality." The requirement in the definition of illusions for *systematic* deviations is to exclude the random fluctuations around some average response that are characteristic of all observations, whether by the senses or by human-made instruments. Numerous visual illusions exist: a useful reference work which reviews most of them and the classic psychological theories proposed to account for them is Robinson (1972).

Sharply differing views are held about the value of illusions for furthering understanding of perceptual mechanisms. At one extreme, J. J. Gibson held that illusions arise from impoverished stimulation that is quite uncharacteristic of the richly structured ambient optic array which normally confronts the observer. Gibson used this controversial assertion to conclude, equally controversially, that illusions provide a misleading basis on which to erect theories of perception (*see* DIRECT PERCEPTION).

Gregory (1970, 1973) has championed the opposite view. He holds that illusions can provide valuable clues about how perceptual processes work both when they produce correct outputs and when they produce illusions. He suggests that illusions might be generated in two basic ways: (a) malfunction of physiological mechanisms, and (b) inappropriateness of the strategies built into those mechanisms. He suggests these two types of illusions might be called, in biological terms, "physiological" and "cognitive" illusions respectively; or in engineering terms, "mechanism" and "strategy" illusions.

Gregory believes that the "after-images" experienced following exposure to bright lights following a period of dark adaptation are clear examples of physiological/mechanism illusions. This is because their origins can be traced to physiological processes in the retina which are "over loaded" by bright lights following dark adaptation. He calls this state of affairs a "loss of calibration" (Gregory, 1973, pp. 58, 73).

Gregory offers the size–weight illusion as "probably the clearest and simplest case of a purely cognitive illusion" (1973, p. 60): if an observer lifts up two objects of differing sizes but with the same scale weight, then the smaller of the two objects is perceived to be heavier than the larger. Here the conclusion seems inescapable that the misperception is due to normal assumptions about the size/weight relations of objects being inappropriate for the atypical densities of the two objects generating

the illusion. The illusion is a compelling one despite there being nothing unusually impoverished about the stimuli. If Gregory is right, an explanation of the effect must include an account of the strategies incorporated into the mechanisms subserving weight perception. Here the strategies are ones that use visual information to access stored information about the typical weights of objects in order to set the muscle effort likely to be necessary to lift things.

Gregory's view of cognitive illusions falls within the empiricist and constructivist traditions of perceptual theorizing. The famous dictum summarizing this approach is that of Helmholtz: "perception is unconscious inference." This is explicated by Gregory (1973, p. 51) as follows:

> Perceptions [are] "conclusions" [or "hypotheses"], more or less likely to be true, depending on the sensory data available and the difficulty of the perceptual problem to be solved ... [they] are given by inference, from data given by the senses and [from data] stored in memory. On this view, any perception may be false, just as any argument may be false. It may be false because its assumptions are incorrect, or because the form of the argument is fallacious. On this view of perception, illusions take on the same importance that paradoxes and ambiguities have for philosophers concerned with the nature of argument; or how data can be used to discover a truth, or a fact.

Anyone who has programed a computer will find Gregory's basic distinction between mechanism and strategy an easy one to grasp in principle. Computer users frequently have to ponder whether some unwanted aspect of their machine's operation is a hardware fault or limitation, or some failing in the software. That question is not always an easy one to answer, and the same is true of visual illusions. Indeed, Gregory observes that the "Physiology or Cognition?" question is a particularly tricky one for geometric distortion visual illusions. These are phenomena to which he has devoted considerable attention because he thinks that at least some of them might be caused by the inappropriate triggering of size-constancy mechanisms that work for images of normal scenes but which produce "errors" when applied to two-dimensional line drawings for which they were not designed (*see* PERCEPTUAL CONSTANCIES).

But even if it is granted that the question "Physiology or Cognition?" is a useful one to bear in mind when considering these and other visual illusions, it needs to be remembered that when an illusion is judged to have its roots in a misapplied processing strategy, that does not render uninteresting the mechanisms that carry out that strategy. In other words, to fully understand visual systems requires understanding those systems at both the mechanism *and* strategy levels (and perhaps also other levels besides).

One can be in sympathy with Gregory's view that many illusions reflect the application of inappropriate assumptions and yet still doubt whether studying illusions is, in itself, an entirely satisfactory way of studying perception. The inconclusive nature of the controversy, after more than two decades of experiments, surrounding Gregory's interpretation of geometric distortion illusions as caused by inappropriately triggered size constancy scaling mechanisms is not an encouraging sign. The missing required ingredient seems to be computational experiments aimed at testing the putative value of processing strategies suggested by an illusion. Such experiments force attention to many important details which are otherwise all too easily neglected in psychological theories, and they thereby provide much needed clarification of the issues involved.

In computational theories of vision, a major requirement is identifying *constraints* which serve as assumptions (usually about the nature of the viewed world) upon which can be built useful methods for interpreting visual input data to satisfy some clearly stated goal (*see* PERCEPTION, COMPUTATIONAL THEORY OF). The mention of assumptions here clearly finds an echo in Gregory's views on perception: if the assumptions embedded in a computational theory are inappropriate for a given set of inputs then incorrect outputs ("illusions") will be generated. Numerous examples of this kind of reasoning can be found in the computational vision literature (Frisby, 1979).

Sometimes the constraints used in computational theories derive from knowledge of human vision, sometimes a computational study itself leads to the identification of a useful constraint. In the latter instance, this may in turn lead to experimental studies of biological vision systems aimed at testing whether they implement the constraint by seeing if they suffer from an illusion predicted by the computational theory when fed with certain sorts of inputs. Here the study of illusions plays a valuable role, but a secondary one, that of providing evidence as to whether a given computational theory is implemented in the visual system of interest. That is, the interpretation of illusions is much the same as in Gregory's cognitive account, but the research program has a different starting point: first, the computational problem and the identification of constraints, second, the search for an illusion to see if the constraints are used in a biological vision system. But whichever way around the process of enquiry proceeds, a key element for success seems to be computational experiments providing rigorous tests of whether the right questions are being asked. A recent collection of review papers on computational work relating to biological visual systems is provided by Landy and Movshon (1990).

See also CONSTRUCTIVIST THEORIES OF PERCEPTION.

BIBLIOGRAPHY

Frisby, J. P. (1979). *Seeing: Illusion, brain and mind*. Oxford: Oxford University Press.
Gregory, R. L. (1970). *The intelligent eye*. London: Weidenfeld & Nicolson.
——. (1973). The confounded eye. In R. L. Gregory & E. H. Gombrich (Eds), *Illusion in nature and art* (pp. 49–96). London: Duckworth.
Landy, M., & Movshon, T. A. (1990). *Computational Models of Visual Processing*. Cambridge, Mass.: MIT Press.
Robinson, J. O. (1972). *The psychology of visual illusion*. London: Hutchison.

JOHN P. FRISBY

visual perception *See* PERCEPTION.

W

working memory The term generally refers to a system which is involved in both cognitive processing and in the transient storage of information that is being processed during the performance of a wide range of cognitive tasks. Cognitive tasks of any degree of complexity (e.g. problem solving; comprehension of text) involve a number of different processing stages, and working memory allows the updated "state of play" on the task to be stored and readily available. There is clearly some overlap between the notion of a "working memory" and that of a "short-term memory store" (*see* SHORT-TERM MEMORY), but the concepts actually differ in a number of important ways. The short-term memory store was typically regarded as unitary, i.e. it was assumed that it operated in a single, uniform fashion (e.g. Atkinson & Shiffrin, 1968). In contrast, the most developed theory of a working-memory system (Baddeley, 1986; Baddeley & Hitch, 1974) is based on the assumption that working memory consists of a number of different components.

The short-term memory store was used almost exclusively to account for data from cognitive tasks in which the subject's sole task was to remember various items of information. In contrast, working memory is, at least in principle, involved in numerous tasks where the primary focus is not on memory at all. For example, the focus in mental arithmetic is on the performance of accurate arithmetical calculations, but there is good evidence that working memory plays an important role on mental arithmetic tasks (Hitch, 1978).

The notion of working memory, or of something rather similar, is to be found in various theories in cognitive psychology. However, the only systematic theory which is centered squarely on working memory is that originally proposed by Baddeley and Hitch (1974), and subsequently modified by Baddeley (1986). In its original version, Baddeley and Hitch (1974) put forward a working-memory system consisting of the following three components: a modality-free central executive closely resembling ATTENTION; an articulatory loop which can hold a limited amount of phonological or speech-based information; and a visuo-spatial scratch pad, which is devoted to spatial and/or visual coding. This working-memory system is hierarchical. The central executive is at the apex of the hierarchy, and beneath it are its two "slave" systems, namely the articulatory loop and the visuo-spatial scratch or sketch-pad.

The three components of working memory will now be considered in more detail. One of the major characteristics of attention is that it possesses limited capacity. Baddeley and Hitch (1974) assumed that the same was also true of the central executive, but they did not investigate its functioning systematically. Baddeley (1986) subsequently argued that the central executive may be rather similar to the supervisory attentional system described by Shallice (1982). Among the purposes for which the supervisory attentional system is used are to perform tasks requiring planning or decision making, to handle situations where poorly mastered response sequences are involved, and generally to fulfill a troubleshooting function when lower levels of the processing system are inadequate to the task in hand.

Baddeley (1986) also speculatively suggested that damage to the frontal lobes may impair the functioning of the central executive component of working memory. According to Rylander (1939, p. 20), the typical pattern following damage to the frontal lobes involves "disturbed attention, a difficulty in grasping the whole of a complicated state of affairs, well able to work along routine lines ... cannot learn to master new types of task, in new situations." As this description makes clear, those suffering from frontal lobe damage behave as if they no longer have a control system which permits the flexible and appropriate deployment of processing resources. This is exactly what one would expect if the central executive were located in the frontal lobes.

The articulatory loop has strictly limited capacity. The evidence suggests that its capacity is determined by temporal duration in similar fashion to a tape loop. Baddeley, Thomson, and Buchanan (1975) proposed that the articulatory loop can hold approximately as much verbal information as can be spoken out loud in two seconds. They discovered that subjects could provide accurate immediate serial recall of more words that could be pronounced rapidly than of words that had a long pronunciation time, and they argued that the apparent time-based limitation on immediate serial recall reflected the limitations of the articulatory loop.

Subsequent neuropsychological evidence (*see* COGNITIVE NEUROPSYCHOLOGY) indicated that the original view of the articulatory loop was an oversimplified one. Several patients appear to have patterns of impairment which could not be accounted for by the theory proposed by Baddeley and Hitch (1974). For example, there was a patient, P.V., who was studied in some detail by Basso, Spinnler, Vallar, and Zanobio (1982). She seemed to have reasonably intact articulatory processes as revealed by her ability to recite the alphabet. In spite of this, she did not use this ability when asked to provide immediate serial recall of a series of visually or auditorily presented letters. This was demonstrated by using an articulatory suppression task, in which the subject has to repeat something simple over and over again, at the same time as the letters for recall were being presented. Despite the fact that articulatory suppression largely prevents use of the articulatory loop for other purposes, it was found that P.V.'s performance on immediate serial recall was unaffected by the presence of the articulatory suppression task. The crucial additional finding was that her memory for auditorily presented letters was worse when these letters were phonologically similar (i.e. when they sounded alike) than when they were phonologically dissimilar. In other words, P.V. appeared to be processing phonologically (i.e. in a speech-based manner), but she was doing this without making any use of articulation.

In the revised version of the working-memory model (Baddeley, 1986), a distinction is drawn between an active articulatory process that is linked to speech production and a passive phonological store that is concerned with SPEECH PERCEPTION. Phonological information can enter the phonological store in a direct fashion through auditory presentation of verbal material, or it can enter indirectly either through subvocal articulation or via phonological information stored in long-term memory. Within the framework of this theoretical framework, the impairments shown by the patient P.V. (and by other patients) can be accounted for by assuming that she has a deficient phonological store. Since auditory presentation of words always involves the phonological store, whereas visual presentation does not, it follows that P.V. should experience greater problems with auditory presentation than with visual presentation, and that is, indeed, the case.

An interesting issue relevant to this revised theory concerns the precise mechanisms involved in the subvocal articulation component of the articulatory loop. One obvious possibility is that the speech musculature is involved, but is also entirely possible that these articulatory processes occur at a rather more central level. It is relevant here to consider patients suffering from anarthria. This is a condition in which impairments to the system controlling the speech musculature mean that they are unable to speak, but in spite of this they possess essentially normal language abilities in other respects. It has been found that patients with anarthria can make use of subvocal articulation in spite of the inability to use their speech musculature (Baddeley & Wilson, 1985). As Baddeley (1986, p. 107) concluded,

The loop and its rehearsal processes are operating at a much deeper level than might at first seem likely, apparently relying on central speech control codes which appear to be able to function in the absence of peripheral feedback.

The visuo-spatial scratch-pad (or sketch-pad) was defined by Baddeley (1986, p. 109) as "a system especially well adapted to the temporary storage of spatial information, much as a pad of paper might be used by someone trying for example to work out a geometric puzzle." In their investigation of the sketch-pad, Baddeley and Lieberman (1980) started from the assumption that there is an important difference between spatial and visual processing. For example, someone who is blind is by definition largely or entirely unable to use visual processes. However, a blind person may still possess rather accurate information about the spatial layout of objects in a room in spite of his or her visual impairment.

The experimental approach adopted by Baddeley and Lieberman (1980) made use of a task in which the location of digits within a matrix was described in an auditory message, with the subject being required to reproduce the matrix afterwards. The message was constructed so as to be either easy or difficult to visualize. In an earlier study by Baddeley, Grant, Wight, and Thomson (1975), it was found that concurrent performance of the pursuit rotor (i.e. tracking a light along a circular track) produced a severe impairment in memory for easily visualized messages, but had no effect on memory for messages that were difficult to visualize.

Since the pursuit rotor involves both visual and spatial processing, it is not clear from these findings precisely why there was an interference effect on easily visualized messages. Baddeley and Lieberman (1980) devised a task which involved spatial but not visual processing. The subject, who was blindfolded, tried to point at a moving pendulum. When he or she was successful, there was an auditory signal. When this task was performed at the same time as memorizing an auditory message, it impaired recall of visualizable messages but not nonvisualizable ones. In contrast, a concurrent task that involves visual but not spatial processing impaired performance more on the nonvisualizable message than on the visualizable one. The implication of these findings is that the processing of visualizable messages depends primarily on spatial processing, and it is for this reason that a concurrent spatial task has such a disruptive effect.

In sum, there is reasonable evidence to support the notion of a three-component working memory system. However, far more is known about some components than others. The detailed functioning of the articulatory loop is reasonably clear, whereas it has proved very difficult to examine the central executive. The modular nature of the working-memory system is generally in line with current thinking (*see* MODULARITY OF MIND). However, several cognitive neuropsychologists (*see* COGNITIVE NEUROPSYCHOLOGY) have postulated the existence of several modules, and it may well be that the working-memory model will need to be expanded beyond its current three components.

See also COGNITIVE DEVELOPMENT; PERSONALITY AND COGNITION.

BIBLIOGRAPHY

Atkinson, R. C., & Shiffrin, R. M. (1968). Human memory: A proposed system and its control processes. In K. W. Spence (Ed.), *The psychology of learning and motivation: Advances in research and theory* (Vol. 2). New York: Academic Press.

Baddeley, A. D. (1986). *Working memory*. Oxford: Oxford University Press.

— —, & Hitch, G. J. (1974). Working memory. In G. Bower (Ed.), *Recent advances in learning and motivation* (Vol. VIII). New York: Academic Press.

Baddeley, A. D., & Lieberman, K. (1980). Spatial working memory. In R. S. Nickerson (Ed.), *Attention and performance* (Vol. VIII). Hillsdale, NJ: Lawrence Erlbaum Associates Ltd.

Baddeley, A. D., & Wilson, B. (1985). Phonological coding and short-term memory in patients without speech. *Journal of Memory and Language*, 24, 490–502.

Baddeley, A. D., Thomson, N., & Buchanan, M. (1975). Word length and the structure of short-term memory. *Journal of Verbal Learning and Verbal Behavior*, 14, 575–89.

Baddeley, A. D., Grant, S., Wight, E., & Thomson, N. (1975). Imagery and visual working memory. In P. M. A. Rabbit & S. Dornic (Eds), *Attention and performance* (Vol. V). London: Academic Press.

WRITING

Basso, A., Spinnler, H., Vallar, G., & Zanobio, E. (1982). Left hemisphere damage and selective impairment of auditory short-term memory: A case study. *Neuropsychologia*, 20, 263–74.

Hitch, G. J. (1978). The role of short-term working memory in mental arithmetic. *Cognitive Psychology*, 10, 302–23.

Rylander, G. (1939). Personality changes after operations on the frontal lobes. *Acta Psychiatrica Neurologica*, Supplement No. 30.

Shallice, T. (1982). Specific impairments of planning. *Philosophical Transactions of the Royal Society London, B*, 199–209.

MICHAEL W. EYSENCK

writing The first rendering of spoken language in pictograms and subsequent developments of the phonetic alphabet, the printing press, and possibly the word processor are landmarks in intellectual and technological history. For centuries the study of writing has been central to rhetoric and education. Curiously, writing was virtually ignored by psychologists until the 1970s, but then drew the attention it deserves alongside other complex forms of thinking. Cognitive psychology diverged from the earlier literary approaches to writing by focusing on the process of composing rather than on the resulting text.

Flower and Hayes (1980) presented an influential model of writing processes. Planning included generating ideas, organizing ideas, and setting goals to be achieved in the structure of the text. Translating or sentence generation included the subprocesses of language production, such as lexical selection, that are also involved in speech. Reviewing included reading the evolving text and editing it for errors. These processes are controlled by an executive monitor that allocates limited attentional capacity (*see* ATTENTION). They occur within the context of a task environment, consisting of the writing assignment and the text produced thus far, and the writer's long-term memory.

Memory holds vast realms of diverse knowledge, methods of composing, and personality characteristics. The writer possesses extensive knowledge of language, topic, and audience.

Strategies for retrieving relevant knowledge and for creating new concepts are an important aspect of the writer's method, as are the tools selected for composing and editing. Finally, personality characteristics such as anxiety and achievement motivation are needed to account for writer's block, on the one hand, and prolific productivity, on the other (*see* PERSONALITY AND COGNITION).

Empirical work by Flower and Hayes and others suggests that writers recursively attend to planning, translating, and reviewing processes throughout prewriting, first draft, and subsequent draft phases of text development. For example, even when working on a final draft the writer interweaves planning, translating, and reviewing. This constant juggling of processes is highly effortful and frequently overloads the writer's limited attentional capacity.

Research on planning indicates important developmental differences. For example, in generating ideas immature writers rely heavily on an associative search of memory that Bereiter and Scardamalia (1987, pp. 7–8) have termed "a knowledge telling strategy." Identifiers of the topic, genre, and discourse type serve as cues that automatically retrieve related material from memory. As writers develop in skill, they continue to use knowledge telling, but add a strategy called knowledge transforming. This is a directed search of memory that arises from the writer interactively reflecting on both content problems (e.g. How do I define this concept?) and rhetorical problems (e.g. How do I express this thought clearly?). The writer consciously searches for solutions to the difficulties at hand. Because of reflective planning, the writer's thoughts emerge through the act of composing itself; composing causes a transformation of knowledge, not merely a telling of it.

As another example, immature writers fail to organize information effectively, often presenting it in the order in which it was generated. More experienced writers attempt to order the text in a manner that is appropriate to communicating the subject matter to a particular audience using a particular type of discourse structure (Flower, 1979). For adult

375

writers, creating an outline during prewriting results in superior quality texts. Kellogg (1988) found that outlining improved the quality of composition by alleviating attentional overload during the drafting of an essay; writers who outlined had less need to juggle planning, translating, and reviewing simultaneously.

Some research on translation overlaps with studies of SPEECH PERCEPTION and SPEECH PRODUCTION. For example, whether an autonomous syntactic component operates during sentence generation, as predicted by generative grammar models, is open to debate in both speech and writing. Other research focuses on the differences between speaking and writing (Faigley, Cherry, Jolliffe, & Skinner, 1985, p. 45). For example, oral discourse achieves cohesion in part through nonverbal means, such as posture and gestures, whereas written discourse relies exclusively on explicit lexical and syntactic ties (see LANGUAGE, PRAGMATICS OF).

Finally, investigations of reviewing indicate a progression of editing strategies as young writers mature (Graves, 1979). Initially, only changes in the forms of letters occur. Then spelling changes followed by word substitutions are noted. Later still comes rearrangement of sentences and paragraphs. Young writers review relatively little, whereas mature writers generally review extensively for long, difficult writing assignments. It should be noted, however, that highly skilled writers who are thoroughly comfortable with their writing assignments are capable of planning a document in such detail that revising is largely unnecessary (Faigley et al., 1985, p. 60).

Although the Flower and Hayes (1980) model has been influential, major disagreements with it abound (e.g. Nystrand, 1982). One argument against it is that sentence generation and planning cannot be neatly separated. Another is that writing is inherently a social act, a point underemphasized by their model. Instead of focusing on the cognitive processes of an individual, the social approach studies the writer as an agent in a literate community of discourse.

BIBLIOGRAPHY

Bereiter, C., & Scardamalia, M. (1987). *The psychology of written composition*. Hillsdale, NJ: Erlbaum.

Faigley, L., Cherry, R. D., Jolliffe, D. A., & Skinner, A. M. (1985). *Assessing writers' knowledge and processes of composing*. Norwood, NJ: Ablex.

Flower, L. (1979). Writer-based prose: A cognitive basis for problems in writing. *College English, 41*, 19–37.

——, & Hayes, J. R. (1980). The dynamics of composing: Making plans and juggling constraints. In W. Gregg & R. Steinberg (Eds), *Cognitive processes in writing* (pp. 31–50). Hillsdale, NJ: Erlbaum.

Graves, D. H. (1979). What children show us about revision. *Language Arts, 56*, 312–19.

Kellogg, R. T. (1988). Attentional overload and writing performance: Effects of rough draft and outline strategies. *Journal of Experimental Psychology: Learning, Memory, and Cognition, 14*, 355–65.

Nystrand, M. (1982). Rhetoric's "Audience" and linguistics' "speech community": Implications for understanding writing, reading, and text. In M. Nystrand (Ed.), *What writers know: The language, process, and structure of written discourse* (pp. 1–30). New York: Academic Press.

RONALD T. KELLOGG

Y

Yerkes–Dodson law The Yerkes–Dodson law (YDL) summarizes a complex relationship between performance, motivation, and task difficulty. As currently understood, it asserts that (a) performance efficiency is a single-peaked function of arousal, and (b) the level of arousal associated with optimal performance is a negative monotonic function of task difficulty. That is, for easy tasks, arousal generally facilitates performance while for more difficult tasks, performance is an inverted-U function of arousal; the more difficult the task, the lower the level of arousal associated with optimal performance.

In their eponymic study, Yerkes and Dodson (1908) had dancing mice learn one of three visual discriminations that differed in difficulty; the amount of shock used to punish the incorrect choice was varied across animals. As degree of shock increased, the average number of trials required to learn the easy discrimination decreased. On the more difficult tasks, the number first decreased but then increased; the level of shock associated with fewest trials for the most difficult task was lower than that for the intermediate difficulty task. Originally presented as an interactive effect of the difficulty of habit formation and stimulus intensity on speed of learning, the YDL has since been interpreted more broadly in terms of a generalized nondirectional energizer (first drive; later arousal) rather than stimulus intensity, and performance efficiency rather than learning.

Substantial evidence is consistent with the YDL but there are exceptions. Clear evaluation of the data is made complicated by several obstacles to investigation of the effect: First, there are problems with the concept of a generalized nondirectional energizer; moreover, there are methodological and interpretative difficulties associated with research on a hypothetical abstraction such as arousal. That many activation states involve changes in

effort or affect in addition to arousal is of particular concern, as recent research suggests that both effort and affect have effects on performance that are independent of the effects of arousal. Second, performance efficiency is a multifaceted construct, representing a complex combination of subcomponents which may be traded for one another (*see* MODULARITY OF MIND). Moreover, cognitive performance measures are often a nonlinear function of the latent performance variable, making interpretation of ordinal interactions difficult. A third obstacle is that because monotonically increasing, inverted-U, and monotonically decreasing functions are each single peaked, compelling evidence for the inverted-U hypothesis requires complicated experimental designs. Finally, aggregating across subjects may lead to erroneous conclusions because group means do not provide an adequate basis for inferences regarding intraindividual effects.

Despite these difficulties, the available research suggests that the YDL is valid. The hypothesis that performance is a single-peaked function of arousal has received particularly strong support, with evidence coming from studies that have provided a probabilistic bias against a single-peaked function while also employing multiple operationalizations of arousal. The hypothesis of a negative relationship between optimal arousal and task difficulty has received less consistent support, although the weight of evidence favors the YDL. Reports of arousal-related performance decrements on very easy tasks are rare, whereas more complex tasks are susceptible to arousal-related disruption. It is also important to note that generalizations of the YDL seem legitimate: the effect is not limited to (a) manipulations involving shock, threat, or anxiety, (b) learning, or (c) visual discrimination tasks. Instead, the YDL has been supported in research using a broad range of arousal-related variables (e.g. stimulant drugs, introversion–extraversion, and muscle tension), a broad range of tasks (e.g. verbal ability and intelligence questions, proofreading, and letter transformation tasks), a broad range of performance measures (e.g. indexes of rate of learning, sensitivity in the signal-detection sense, and overall efficiency), and a broad range of species (e.g. humans, rats, and chimpanzees) (*see* PERSONALITY AND COGNITION).

Several fundamental questions regarding the YDL remain unanswered. Most centrally, it is not yet clear why the YDL occurs. A related question involves task difficulty, as the pertinent dimension or dimensions of cognitive demand are as yet unknown. Transmarginal inhibition (protective deactivation in response to intense stimulation) cannot explain the majority of the evidence. Further, the mediation of the arousal–performance relationship by task difficulty is not likely to be solely attributable to arousal induced by task difficulty itself. Few response-competition models can predict the inverted-U relationship; those that can lead to predictions for either a task-difficulty effect opposite to the YDL or for differences in the types of errors made with under- and overarousal that are difficult to reconcile with the available data.

Currently, the most plausible explanations of the YDL are those of Easterbrook (1959) and Humphreys and Revelle (1984). Easterbrook argued that (a) arousal reduces the range of cue utilization, (b) irrelevant cues are eliminated before relevant ones as capacity diminishes, and (c) task difficulty is a direct function of the required range of cue utilization. Underarousal deficits would thus result from simultaneous use of relevant and irrelevant information, and overarousal deficits from incomplete utilization of relevant information. Humphreys and Revelle argued that

(a) arousal facilitates sustained information transfer (somewhat similar to attention), and (b) arousal hinders short-term or WORKING MEMORY (*see* ATTENTION). Performance at low arousal would thus be limited by the attentional component, and at high arousal by the memory component. Further research is needed to clarify the bases for the YDL and hence to allow prediction of when performance will be helped or hindered by arousal.

BIBLIOGRAPHY

Anderson, K. J. (1990). Arousal and the inverted-U hypothesis: A critique of Neiss's "Reconceptualizing arousal." *Psychological Bulletin, 107,* 96–100.

Broadbent, D. E. (1971). *Decision and stress.* London: Academic Press.

Broadhurst, P. L. (1959). The interaction of task difficulty and motivation: The Yerkes–Dodson Law revived. *Acta Psychologica, 16,* 321–38.

Brody, N. (1983). *Human motivation: Commentary on goal-directed action.* New York: Academic Press.

Easterbrook, J. A. (1959). The effect of emotion on cue utilization and the organization of behavior. *Psychological Review, 66,* 183–201.

Eysenck, M. W. (1982). *Attention and arousal: Cognition and performance.* Berlin: Springer.

Hebb, D. O. (1955). Drives and the C.N.S. (conceptual nervous system). *Psychological Review, 62,* 243–54.

Humphreys, M. S., & Revelle, W. (1984). Personality, motivation, and performance: A theory of the relationship between individual differences and information processing. *Psychological Review, 91,* 153–84.

Yerkes, R. M., & Dodson, J. D. (1908). The relation of strength of stimuli to rapidity of habit-formation. *Journal of Comparative Neurology and Psychology, 18,* 459–82.

KRISTEN JOAN ANDERSON

INDEX

BY RICHARD HOUSE

Page references to the major entries in the dictionary are in **bold** type. Columns (designated "a" and "b") are only differentiated when the subject is restricted to one column on any page. Further information can be obtained by following up the cross-references in the text, and by referring to the article bibliographies.